THE
FOOTSTEPS
OF THE
MESSIAH

A Study of the Sequence of Prophetic Events

Arnold G. Fruchtenbaum, Th.M., Ph.D.

POST OFFICE BOX 3723
TUSTIN, CALIFORNIA 92681

MINISTRIES PRESS

II

To Rev. Burl Haynie
    Who discipled me in my early Christian life
    Who taught me how to study the Word
    Who gave me a love for the prophetic Word
this volume is affectionately dedicated.

**OTHER BOOKS BY
DR. ARNOLD G. FRUCHTENBAUM**

Jesus Was A Jew

*Hebrew Christianity:
Its Theology, History and Philosophy*

A Passover Haggadah for Jewish Believers

Biblical Lovemaking: A Study of The Song of Solomon

Israelology: The Missing Link in Systematic Theology

If you shall see kingdoms rising against
each other in turn, then give heed and
note *the footsteps of the Messiah.*

Bereshit Rabbah XLII:4

VI

FOREWORD

Charles C. Ryrie

Eschatology seems to suffer at the hands both of its friends and foes. Those who play it down usually avoid assigning specific meaning to prophetic texts. Those who play it up often assign too much.

But the prophetic portions of the Bible won't go away. The biblical interpreter must interact with them and in the detail and specificity in which they were written. Mr. Fruchtenbaum has done that, seeking always to try to understand the full meaning of the biblical revelation. His frame of reference is dispensational, pretribulational premillennialism—the only one that can provide a consistently harmonious interpretation of prophecy.

The author's consideration of the biblical material is thorough and thought-provoking. His conclusions will not always meet with full agreement even by those who share his approach, but those who read this book cannot help but be instructed and stimulated by his work.

VIII

PREFACE

The main burden of this book is a study of prophecy in relationship to the sequence of events. It is written from the viewpoint of the dispensational pretribulational and premillennial viewpoint. Because it is primarily concerned with the study of the sequence of events, the author chose not to deal with the various other viewpoints such as mid- and posttribulationalism or a- or postmillennialism. This has been ably done through the writings of J. Dwight Pentecost (*Things to Come*), John F. Walvoord (*The Rapture Question, The Blessed Hope and the Tribulation, The Return of the Lord, The Millennium*), Charles C. Ryrie (*The Basis of the Premillennial Faith, Dispensationalism Today*), among many others. Whatever variations are discussed in this volume are only those within the dispensational, pretribulational, and premillennial position.

It is hoped that this volume will make a contribution within the dispensational school of thought in relationship to eschatology, especially concerning the sequence of events.

All Scriptures quoted, unless otherwise noted, are from the American Standard Version of 1901.

My special appreciation goes to Kim Bachman who painstakingly worked over the four charts and the map contained in this work.

My most grateful thanks goes to Mrs. Mark (Charmaine) O'Neill for the many hours she spent typing and retyping this manuscript. She worked on the manuscript while holding down a full time job and her faithfulness has been much appreciated.

Special thanks also goes to my wife Mary Ann who painstakingly read the manuscript and proofs and made many helpful suggestions which were incorporated into the final product.

It has taken over six years to complete this work and I am thankful to the Lord for the grace and the privilege to put it together. It represents work done during many travels in many states and two nations, one of which (Israel) plays the major role in this book.

Arnold G. Fruchtenbaum
San Antonio, Texas
December 15, 1977

TABLE OF CONTENTS

CHARTS AND MAP

PART I

INTRODUCTION

CHART #1

CHRONOLOGY OF ESCHATOLOGY

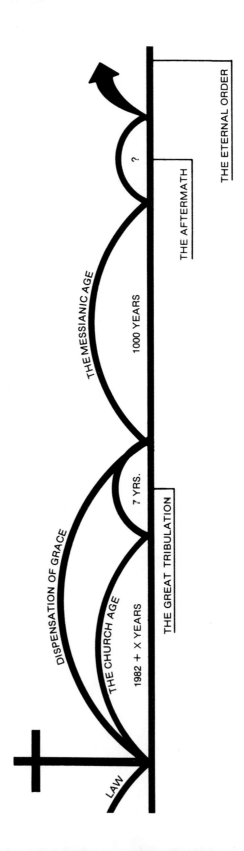

CHAPTER I

INTRODUCTION

This book is a study of prophecy. More specifically, it is a study of *eschatology,* the study of the last days.

This work will examine prophecy chronologically; it will deal with the sequence of events as they are revealed in Scripture. It will deal with the prophecies which are being fulfilled at the present time and with the sequence of events as they unfold in the Tribulation and the Millennium culminating in the Eternal Order.

But before the specifics can be dealt with, it is first necessary to take up some matters of introduction.

A. THE RULES OF INTERPRETATION

The first matter of introduction concerns the rules of interpretation, especially those which the author was guided by in formulating this study. All too often Bible expositors have had one set of rules for the interpretation of non-prophetic passages, but have been unable, or refuse to apply that same set of rules to prophetic passages. In this way prophecy has often suffered in the hands of its enemies. But prophecy has also suffered at the hands of its friends. Even when the same set of rules is applied to prophecy as to other passages, there has often been an inconsistency in the application of the rules giving way to a tendency to spiritualize and/or sensationalize parts of a passage. This has been done even by those who insist on literal interpretation. Prophecy has thus suffered from the hands of its friends, which in turn has often given prophecy a bad name.

Since this is a book on eschatology and not on hermeneutics, it is impossible to deal with all the rules of interpretation found in a textbook of hermeneutics. Hence it will be necessary to limit this study to those rules which are especially relevant to prophecy.

There are four basic rules of interpretation which are keys to understanding the prophetic word.* The first is called *The Golden Rule of Interpretation:*

> When the plain sense of Scripture makes common sense, seek no other sense; therefore, take every word at its primary, ordinary, usual, literal meaning, unless the facts of the immediate context, studied in the light of related passages and axiomatic and fundamental truths, indicate clearly otherwise.

Simply put, this law states that all biblical passages are to be

---

* These four rules were formulated by Dr. David L. Cooper, the late director of the Biblical Research Society.

taken exactly as they read unless there is something in the text indicating that it should be taken some other way than literally. If this rule is applied consistently, much of the present day tangents and "newspaper exegesis" can be avoided as well as other errors, such as amillennialism. So when the plain sense of Scripture makes sense, no other sense needs to be sought. The Bible should not be approached on the assumption that it is loaded with symbols and hence hard to understand. It is not. The Bible should be approached with the assumption that this book can be understood just like any other book that is taken literally. The Bible does use symbols. But the symbols are usually explained, and they are explained by the usage of literal words. But unless the text indicates clearly that it should be taken symbolically, the passage should be understood literally. This golden rule of interpretation is the first of four basic rules of interpretation and by far the most important. It lays the foundation for the other three.

The second law is called *The Law of Double Reference*. This law observes the fact that often a passage or a block of Scripture is speaking of two different persons or two different events that are separated by a long period of time. But in the passage itself they are blended into one picture, and the time gap between the two persons or two events is not presented by the text itself. The fact that a gap of time exists is known because of other Scriptures, though in the particular text itself the gap of time is not seen.

A good example of this law is some of the Old Testament prophecies regarding the first and second comings of Christ. Often these two events are blended into one picture with no indication that there is a gap of time between the first and second coming of Christ. Zechariah 9:9-10 is a good example of the law of double reference. Verse nine is speaking of the first coming of Christ. But verse ten is speaking of the second coming of Christ. But these two comings are blended into one picture with no indication that there is a separation of time between the two. Another example is Isaiah 11:1-5. Verses 1-2 speak of the first coming, while verses 3-5 speak of the second coming. But again the two are blended into one picture with no indication of a gap of time between the two. Since a number of prophetic passages follow the principle of the law of double reference, this is an important rule to know.

This rule should not be confused with another rule often called *Double Fulfillment*. This author does not accept the validity of the principle of double fulfillment. This law states that one passage may have a near and far view; hence, in a way, it may be fulfilled twice. Isaiah 7:14 is often used as an example of this view. The near view would be a reference to a child being born in Ahaz's day; but the far view is that of a virgin-born child, which is the birth of Christ. This author, however, does not believe that there is such a thing as double fulfillment. A single passage can refer to one thing only, and if it is prophecy, it can have only one fulfillment unless the text itself states that it can have many fulfillments. The law of double reference differs from the law of double fulfillment in that the former states that while two events are blended into one picture, one part of the passage refers to one event and the other part of the passage to the second event. This is the case in Zechariah 9:9-10. Verse nine refers only to the first coming, while verse ten refers only to the second coming. But there is no double fulfillment of both verses. There are not two fulfillments of verse nine and two fulfillments of verse ten. Isaiah 7:14 must either refer to a child in Ahaz's day or to the birth of Christ. It cannot refer to both. Isaiah 7:13-17 could be better explained if it is taken as following the law of double reference rather than the principle of double fulfillment. Verses 13-14 refer to the virgin birth of Christ only. These verses are addressed to the house of David in general, as can be seen by the usage of plural pronouns in these two verses in the Hebrew text. Then verses 15-17 refer to a child in Ahaz's day. For the address is to Ahaz alone, as can be seen in the shift to singular pronouns in the Hebrew text. This child is probably Shear-Yashuv of verse three. Hence the double reference speaks of two persons separated by a period of time. It avoids the pitfalls of double fulfillment. For if the verse could refer to a non-virgin birth, then there is no real evidence for a real virgin birth in the Old Testament.

The third law is *The Law of Recurrence.* This law describes the fact that in some passages of Scripture there exists the recording of an event followed by a second recording of the same event giving more details to the first. Hence, it often involves two blocks of Scripture. The first block presents a description of an event as it transpires in chronological sequence. This is followed by a second block of Scripture dealing with the same event and the same period of time, but giving further details as to what transpires in the course of the event.

An example of the law of recurrence is Ezekiel 38:1-39:16. Ezekiel 38:1-23 gives a complete account of the invasion of Israel from the north and the subsequent destruction of the invading army. This is followed by the second block of Scripture, Ezekiel 39:1-16, which repeats some of the account given in the first block and gives some added details regarding the destruction of the invading army. Another example is in Isaiah 30-31. Isaiah 30 gives a complete account of the fall of Judah's alliance with Egypt. Chapter 31 simply repeats the prophecy adding more detail. An example found in a non-prophetic passage is Genesis 1:1-2:25. Genesis 1:1-2:3 records the seven days of creation in strict chronological sequence. The passage ends on the seventh day. But then the second block of Scripture, Genesis 2:4-25, in

keeping with the law of recurrence, goes back to the sixth day to provide added details as to the manner by which Adam and Eve were
created.

The fourth law is: *A text apart from its context is a pretext.* A verse
can only mean what it means in its context and must not be pulled out
of its context. When it is pulled out of its context, it is often presented
as meaning something that it cannot mean within the context. A good
example of this is Zechariah 13:6. This verse is often used as a
prophecy of Christ. Pulled out of its context, it does indeed sound like
it refers to Christ. But the context (Zechariah 13:2-6) is speaking of
false prophets. So verse six cannot refer to Christ unless Christ is
taken to be a false prophet. This is the danger of studying a verse by
itself rather than in its context. The common saying, "You can prove
anything by the Bible" is only true when this rule is violated.

These are the four basic rules which, if followed, will help in the
study of the Scriptures in general and in prophecy in particular. In
these four principles lie the understanding of the prophetic word as
well as the whole Bible. While most expositors apply these rules to
non-prophetic passages of the Bible, they often fail to apply them to
prophetic portions. This has led to some gross errors. The principles
of interpretation should be applied consistently to the whole Bible.

B. THE OUTLINE OF ESCHATOLOGY

The second thing by way of introduction involves the basic out-
line of eschatology (see chart #1). Eschatology proper begins with the
sixth dispensation. The cross, which ended the fifth Dispensation of
Law, also began the sixth Dispensation of Grace. The Dispensation of
Grace is divided into two ages. The first is the Church Age (see chart
#2). Viewed from the standpoint of the visible church, it began at
Pentecost and will continue until the beginning of the Tribulation
period. Viewed from the standpoint of the invisible church, it began at
Pentecost and will continue until the Rapture.

The second age is the Great Tribulation which will last for seven
years, and will be the last seven years of the Dispensation of Grace
(see chart #3).

After a short interval following the Tribulation and the Dispensation of Grace will be the seventh dispensation of the Messianic
Kingdom for 1,000 years (see chart #4). Following the Kingdom there
will be an aftermath period during which several things occur. Finally,
there will be the Eternal Order: Eternity. This is eschatology in its
basic outline. The particulars, along with detailed charts, will be taken
up in this study.

C. THE BOOK OF THE REVELATION

A third matter by way of introduction concerns the book of the Revelation itself. The purpose of this work is to study the whole scope of Bible prophecy which involves much more than just the book of the Revelation. But Revelation will serve as a base. Other portions of Scripture will be brought in at appropriate times as needed to develop the areas chronologically. Hence, as far as this study is concerned, the book of Revelation will serve as a foundation, and other parts of the Bible will be studied in their appropriate place and order.

1. THE OUTLINE OF THE BOOK OF REVELATION

The outline of the book of Revelation is given by the book itself in 1:19: *Write therefore the things which thou sawest, and the things which are, and the things which shall come to pass hereafter.*

This verse divides the book of Revelation into three sections: the things that John saw; the things which are; and, the things which must come to pass hereafter. Using this three-fold outline, we can outline the book of Revelation as follows:

Introduction   1:1-3

Salutation   1:4-8

I.   The Things That John Saw — 1:9-20
  A.   The Glorified Son of Man — 1:9-11
  B.   The Revelation — 1:12-16
  C.   The Interpretation — 1:17-20

II.   The Things Which Are — 2:1-3:22
  A.   Ephesus — 2:1-7
  B.   Smyrna — 2:8-11
  C.   Pergamum — 2:12-17
  D.   Thyatira — 2:18-29
  E.   Sardis — 3:1-6
  F.   Philadelphia — 3:7-13
  G.   Laodicea — 3:14-22

III.   The Things Which Must Come to Pass Hereafter — 4:1-22:21
  A.   Events in Heaven Preceeding the Great Tribulation — 4:1-5:14
    1.   The Throne of God — 4:1-11
    2.   The Lamb and the Seven Sealed Scroll — 5:1-14
  B.   The Great Tribulation — 6:1-18:24
    1.   The First Half — 6:1-9:21
      a.   The Seal Judgments — 6:1-17
      b.   The 144,000 Jews and the World Wide Revival — 7:1-17
      c.   The Trumpet Judgments — 8:1-9:21

This is the outline of the book of Revelation that will be followed in this study.

The author of the book of Revelation is the Apostle John who also authored the Gospel of John and the three epistles of I, II, and III John.

2. OLD AND NEW THINGS IN THE REVELATION

What is really new in the Revelation? And how much of it is really old, that is, already found in the Old Testament?

The book of the Revelation has no direct quotations from the Old Testament, but it has 550 references back to the Old Testament. The majority of the things found in the first twenty chapters of Revelation are found elsewhere in the Old Testament. Only the last two chapters are dealing with anything new.

If this is true, what is the importance of the book of Revelation? The Old Testament prophecies are scattered throughout the books of Moses and the various prophets and writings. It would have been impossible to develop these prophecies into any chronological sequence of events. The value of the book of Revelation is not that it provides new information, but rather that it takes the scattered Old Testament prophecies and puts them in chronological order so that the sequence of events can be determined. This book provides a framework for the understanding of the order and the sequence of events found in the Old Testament prophecies. This is the reason for so many references to the Old Testament.

But the material found in the last two chapters is totally new material which describes the Eternal Order. The Old Testament prophets never foresaw anything beyond the Messianic Kingdom. Indeed, the Kingdom was the high point of Old Testament prophecy and no prophet ever saw anything beyond that. But the Eternal Order is the high point of New Testament prophecy, and Revelation 21 and 22 provide new information, as they describe the Eternal Order.

3. THE USAGE OF SYMBOLS IN THE REVELATION

Another important preliminary area is the matter of symbols. The book of Revelation uses many symbols. The existence of these symbols has led to two extremes. One extreme states that the existence of these symbols shows that this book cannot be understood and must simply be interpreted in terms of a general conflict between good and evil; the good winning out in the end. Beyond this, they say the book is not to be understood in any great detail. This is how the book has suffered from its enemies.

In the second extreme, the symbols are used for unchecked speculation, sensationalism, and all kinds of guess-work trying to interpret these symbols in terms of current events. Such speculation has resulted in far-fetched interpretations, and changes are made as current events change. It has also led to date setting. In this area the book of Revelation has suffered from its friends.

There is a balance between the two extremes.

For this study, the symbols will be examined in accordance with the golden rule of interpretation. While recognizing the existence of the symbols, there will be no resorting to guess-work. Rather, this study will proceed on the premise that all the symbols in the book of Revelation are explained elsewhere: either in a different part of the book of Revelation or in some other part of the Bible. So there are symbols. But the Bible itself will explain what these symbols mean either by direct statement or through a comparison of the usage of the symbol elsewhere in the Scriptures. The meaning of the symbols will not be determined by speculation.

While the Bible does use many symbols, it is consistent in its usage of symbols. A specific symbol will mean the same thing throughout the Old and New Testaments in the vast majority (though not all) of cases.

4. THE INTRODUCTION TO THE REVELATION 1:1-3

Finally, in the area of introductory material, it is necessary to look at the first chapter of the book of Revelation. This is the first major division of the book according to 1:19, and it belongs to the realm of "the things that John saw." In verses 1-3 John's introduction is given to his book:

> The Revelation of Jesus Christ, which God gave him to show unto his servants, even the things which must shortly come to pass: and he sent and signified it by his angel unto his servant John; who bare witness of the word of God, and of the testimony of Jesus Christ, even of all things that he saw. Blessed is he that readeth, and they that hear the words of the prophecy, and keep the things which are written therein: for the time is at hand.

It has been customary to call this book "The Revelation of John" although the very first verse states that this is "the Revelation of Jesus Christ," and only after a process did it reach John. The revelation given to John originated with God the Father and culminates with the believer in Christ. The source of the revelation is God the Father who gave it to God the Son, Jesus the Messiah. From Christ it was conveyed to the third person in the progressive transmission, an unnamed angel. Angels were often used in biblical revelation, especially in the revelation of prophecy. Angels were used for the revelation of the Law of Moses (Galatians 3:19; Acts 7:53; Hebrews 2:2). They were active in the presenting of prophetic truth to Daniel (7:16-27, 8:16-26, 9:20-27, 10:1-12:13) and to Zechariah (1:9, 2:3, 4:1,5,

5:5, 6:4,5). Angels were used to announce the birth of John to Zacharias (Luke 1:11-20) and the birth of Jesus to Mary (Luke 1:26-38) and to Joseph (Matthew 1:20-21). Since angels were frequently used in the revelation of prophecy, it is not unusual to find angels involved in revealing the events and the contents of the book of Revelation, the crowning book of prophecy. Angels will play a prominent role in this book not only in revealing prophecy to John, but also in carrying the prophecies out.

From the angel it was given to the fourth person in the progression, the Apostle John, who was commanded to write down the revelation in a book. John was a recipient of divine inspiration and through the Holy Spirit recorded the words exactly as God desired and free from error as far as the original manuscript is concerned (verse 2). The revelation has been put into writing in order for it to be conveyed to the fifth person, the believer.

Verse one further states that the things that are being revealed "must shortly come to pass." This is often misunderstood to mean that all the prophecies of the book were to be fulfilled soon after they were given. Others use this phrase to teach that since these prophecies were not fulfilled soon after they were given, it isn't necessary to take these prophecies too seriously. However, the word "shortly" simply means that once the day for fulfillment comes, there will be no delay in its execution.

Verse three puts an obligation on the fifth person of the progression, the believer, while at the same time giving a promise. The obligation is for the believer to study this book. The promise is one of blessing. This is the only book in the Bible that promises a blessing to those who study it. There are many blessings of God which are unconditional, and the believer is entitled to them simply by virtue of the fact that he is a believer. But other blessings of God are conditional, and the blessing of God available to the believer who studies this book is one of them. Studying prophecy gives one a love and longing for the return of Christ. Those believers who love and look for His return are promised a special crown, one which will be discussed later. But believers often rob themselves of certain blessings available to them because they fail to take God's conditional aspects seriously. The promise attached to the study of Revelation is one of these conditional ones. So while blessings are available for the study of God's word in general, a unique blessing is available through the study of this particular book.

Not only is the blessing to those who *read* and *hear* the words of the book, but also to those who *keep* the things which are written. The word for *keep* also means *watch*, which is the sense in which it should be taken here. The believer, after reading and listening to what the Revelation is teaching, should also be watching for these things to

come to pass and be on the alert for the fulfillment of these things.
The same admonition to watch is given in Christ's Olivet Discourse in
Matthew 24:42-44 and 25:13.

5. THE SALUTATION — REVELATION 1:4-8

The introduction to the book of Revelation is followed by the
salutation in verses 4-8:

> John to the seven churches that are in Asia: Grace to you and peace, from
> him who is and who was and who is to come; and from the seven Spirits
> that are before his throne; and from Jesus Christ, who is the faithful
> witness, the firstborn of the dead, and the ruler of the kings of the earth.
> Unto him that loveth us, and loosed us from our sins by his blood; and he
> made us to be a kingdom, to be priests unto his God and Father; to him
> be the glory and the dominion for ever and ever. Amen. Behold, he
> cometh with the clouds; and every eye shall see him, and they that
> pierced him; and all the tribes of the earth shall mourn over him. Even so,
> Amen. I am the Alpha and the Omega, saith the Lord God, who is and who
> was and who is to come, the Almighty.

Verse 4a states to whom this book is being written, especially
chapters 2 and 3 of the book: *the seven churches that are in Asia.* John
uses the Greek definite article *the* indicating totality. However, history
shows that there were more than just these seven churches in Asia
that are mentioned in the context. One church in Asia that was not
mentioned was the church at Colossae. Yet, though it was in Asia, it is
not listed among the seven. So how are these seven churches with the
definite article to be understood? The number seven throughout Scripture signifies completeness. Even in this chapter the number seven
will be used again in this way with a different subject. The point here,
then, is that this is a message to the whole church. So when John
addresses himself to *the seven* churches of Asia, he is signifying that
he is writing to the whole church. All believers are to learn from what
will be written to the seven churches of Asia.

Verses 4b-5a indicates again that John was a secondary author.
The primary author is the triune God. The originator was God the
Father in verse one and is here described as the one *who is and who
was and who is to come.* Mentioned next is the Holy Spirit, who is the
source of revelation and inspiration (II Peter 1:20-21). The Holy Spirit is
described as *the seven Spirits that are before his throne.* Again the
definite article *the* is used with the number seven to signify totality
and completeness. It is a reference to Isaiah 11:2 where the seven
attributes of the Holy Spirit are described. Finally, the Second Person
in the progression found in verse one is mentioned, *and from Jesus
Christ, who is the faithful witness, the firstborn of the dead, and the
ruler of the kings of the earth.*

Then in verse 5b-6 John turns to glorify the Son with praise and thanksgiving to Him because: (1) He loved us; (2) loosed us from our sins by His blood; (3) made us to be a kingdom; (4) to be priests unto God the Father; and (5) to Him be the glory and dominion for ever and ever.

While verse 19 gives the outline of the book, verse seven gives the *theme* of the book which is the second coming of Christ.

> Behold, he cometh with the clouds; and every eye shall see him, and they that pierced him; and all the tribes of the earth shall mourn over him. Even so, Amen.

The return of Christ to this earth is the central theme of this book. It will deal with events leading up to the second coming, events accompanying the second coming, and events following the second coming.

Finally, in verse eight Christ describes Himself as the eternal one encompassing the beginning and the end. He is the over-all sovereign God who is in control of history and will bring to pass the events described in the Revelation.

6. THE THINGS THAT JOHN SAW — REVELATION 1:9-20

Verses 9-20 is the first major section of the Revelation, *the things that John saw*. What John saw was *The Glorified Son of Man*. This passage can be subdivided into three sections. *First,* in verses 9-11 there is the introduction given to John:

> I John, your brother and partaker with you in the tribulation and kingdom and patience which are in Jesus, was in the isle that is called Patmos, for the word of God and the testimony of Jesus. I was in the Spirit on the Lord's day, and I heard behind me a great voice, as of a trumpet saying, What thou seest, write in a book and send it to the seven churches: unto Ephesus, and unto Symrna, and unto Pergamum, and unto Thyatira, and unto Sardis, and unto Philadelphia, and unto Laodicea.

In verse nine John states that he was on the island of Patmos at the time of the receiving of the Revelation. Patmos is an island off the west coast of present-day Turkey, and it was an island for exiles banished there by the Roman government. This was true in the case of John. Therefore, he identifies himself as *a partaker with you in the tribulation*. This was the period of the persecution of the church by the emperor Domitian, and during this persecution John was banished to Patmos. That this was the cause of the banishment is clearly stated: *for the word of God and the testimony of Jesus.*

In verse ten he describes that one Lord's day, or perhaps better translated "lordy day," being under the control of the Holy Spirit, he heard a magnificent voice so great that he compared it to a trumpet. In the Greek the term translated "Lord" is not a noun but an adjective. It does not refer to a specific day of the week such as the Sabbath (Saturday) or Sunday. Rather, it was a day in which John was enraptured by prophetic and divine ecstasy and received divine revelation. It was a day in which he fell under the control of the Holy Spirit and was given prophetic inspiration.

In verse eleven he is commissioned to write what he sees to the seven churches, followed by a list of where these churches were to be found.

Then *secondly,* in verses 12-16, there is the revelation to John which included the actual things that John saw:

> And I turned to see the voice that spake with me. And having turned I saw seven golden candlesticks; and in the midst of the candlesticks one like unto a son of man, clothed with a garment down to the foot, and girt about at the breasts with a golden girdle. And his head and his hair were white as white wool, white as snow; and his eyes were as a flame of fire; and his feet like unto burnished brass, as if it had been refined in a furnace; and his voice as the voice of many waters. And he had in his right hand seven stars: and out of his mouth proceeded a sharp two-edged sword: and his countenance was as the sun shineth in his strength.

When John turned around to see the owner of the voice, he saw a vision of Christ that he had never seen before. He saw the Christ as the Glorified Son of Man. The different figures used in describing the Glorified Son of Man all come from the Old Testament. In essence they describe Christ in His third office, that of King. Christ holds three offices: Prophet, Priest, and King. However, Christ does not function in all three offices contemporaneously, but rather chronologically. His first office was that of Prophet. He functioned in that office during His first coming. The second office is that of a Priest. He is functioning in that role now in His present position at the right hand of God the Father as the High Priest of the believer. When Christ returns, He will begin to function in His third role, that of a King. Christ has all three offices, but He does not function in all three roles contemporaneously. He has functioned as a Prophet in the past. He is now functioning as a Priest. In the future He will function in His office as a King. So John's vision of Jesus is that of a King. But a king has many roles, one of which is to serve as a judge. The various figures used here describe Christ as a King in His role as a Judge, for He is seen as about to come and judge the world at His second coming. A subtheme of this book is judgment; the whole book deals with one judgment after another.

Furthermore, Christ is seen to be among the seven candlesticks. Here we find one of the many symbols used in the book. As has been stated earlier, every symbol in this book will be explained either in the book itself or elsewhere in the Scriptures. In this case, the meaning is explained in verse 20 where it states that the seven candlesticks represent the seven churches. The picture then is of Christ in the midst of the churches ready to move out in judgment.

Thirdly, in verses 17-20, John received the *interpretation* of what he had seen. In verses 17-18 there is the *identification* of who he saw:

> And when I saw him, I fell at his feet as one dead. And he laid his right hand upon me, saying, Fear not; I am the first and the last, and the Living one; and I was dead, and behold, I am alive forevermore, and I have the keys of death and of Hades.

In the identification, Christ identifies Himself as the eternal one (*I am the first and the last*) and the resurrected one (*I was dead, and behold, I am alive*), and also the conqueror of death and hell.

In verse 19 John received the *instruction*:

> Write therefore the things which thou sawest, and the things which are, and the things which shall come to pass hereafter;

In this directive he received the outline of the book that he was about to write. It is a three-fold division: *the things which thou sawest* (1:9-20); and, *the things which are* (2:1-3:22); and, *the things which must come to pass hereafter* (4:1-22:21). The latter are the things which follow "the things which are."

Then in verse 20 is an *explanation* of the things which are:

> The mystery of the seven stars which thou sawest in my right hand, and the seven golden candlesticks. The seven stars are the angels of the seven churches: and the seven candlesticks are seven churches.

This verse explains two of the figures used earlier. The seven candlesticks represent the seven churches. The seven stars of verse 16 are the seven angels appointed to these churches. While the figure of the candlestick is not used elsewhere in the Scriptures, the stars as symbols of angels are. Wherever the word star is used symbolically, it will always be a symbol of an angel. This is true in the Old Testament. This is also true in the New Testament including the various parts of the book of Revelation.

With this verse the first major section of the book of Revelation is completed: *the things that John saw.*

CHAPTER II

THE TIMES OF THE GENTILES

Another area of introductory material needed for the understanding of prophecy involves the understanding of the nature and the course of The Times of the Gentiles. A definition of the times of the Gentiles can be gleaned from Luke 21:24:

> And they shall fall by the edge of the sword, and shall be led captive into all the nations: and Jerusalem shall be trodden down of the Gentiles, until the times of the Gentiles be fulfilled.

The times of the Gentiles can best be defined as that long period of time from the Babylonian Empire to the second coming of Christ during which time the Gentiles have dominance over the city of Jerusalem. This does not rule out temporary Jewish control of the city, but all such Jewish control will be temporary until the second coming of Christ. Such temporary control was exercised during the Maccabbean period (164-63 B.C.), the first Jewish revolt against Rome (66-70 A.D.), the second Jewish revolt against Rome (132-135 A.D.), and since 1967 as a result of the Six Day War. This, too, is temporary as Gentiles will yet trod Jerusalem down for at least another 3½ years (Revelation 11:1-2). Any Jewish take-over of the city of Jerusalem before the second coming of Christ must, therefore, be viewed as a temporary one and does not mean that the times of the Gentiles have ended. The times of the Gentiles can only end when the Gentiles can no longer trod down the city of Jerusalem.

To understand the course of the times of the Gentiles, four passages will need to be studied and then combined.

A.   DANIEL 2:31-45

The basic content of Nebuchadnezzar's dream is in verses 31-35:

> Thou, O king, sawest, and, behold, a great image. This image, which was mighty, and whose brightness was excellent, stood before thee; and the aspect thereof was terrible. As for this image, its head was of fine gold, its breast and its arms of silver, its belly and its thighs of brass, its legs of iron, its feet part of iron, and part of clay. Thou sawest till that a stone was cut out without hands, which smote the image upon its feet that were of iron and clay, and brake them in pieces. Then was the iron, the clay, the brass, the silver, and the gold, broken in pieces together, and became like the chaff of the summer threshing-floors; and the wind carried them away, so that no place was found for them; and the stone that smote the image became a great mountain, and filled the whole earth.

After a general description of the awesomeness of the image (verse 31), Daniel describes the composition of the image (verses 32-33). The image is described as having a head of gold, the breast and arms composed of silver, the belly and thighs of brass, legs of iron, culminating with the feet and toes of part iron and part clay. Two things should be noted concerning these metals: first, they increase in strength; but secondly, they decrease in value. The fulfillment will be in the decrease of the character of authority and rule. Yet there will be an increase in strength. Then the image is destroyed by a stone, and the stone smites the image on its feet (verses 34-35a). Then, with the image destroyed, the stone becomes a great mountain that fills the entire earth (verse 35b).

Having thus described the awesome image that Nebuchadnezzar dreamed, Daniel proceeded to give the interpretation in verses 36-45:

> This is the dream; and we will tell the interpretation thereof before the king. Thou, O king, art king of kings, unto whom the God of heaven hath given the kingdom, the power, and the strength, and the glory; and wheresoever the children of men dwell, the beasts of the field and the birds of the heavens hath he given into thy hand, and hath made thee to rule over them all: thou art the head of gold. And after thee shall arise another kingdom inferior to thee; and another third kingdom of brass, which shall bear rule over all the earth. And the fourth kingdom shall be strong as iron, forasmuch as iron breaketh in pieces and subdueth all things; and as iron that crusheth all these, shall it break in pieces and crush. And whereas thou sawest the feet and toes, part of potters' clay, and part of iron, it shall be a divided kingdom; but there shall be in it of the strength of the iron, forasmuch as thou sawest the iron mixed with miry clay. And as the toes of the feet were part of iron, and part of clay, so the kingdom shall be partly strong, and partly broken. And whereas thou sawest the iron mixed with miry clay, they shall mingle themselves with the seed of men; but they shall not cleave one to another, even as iron doth not mingle with clay. And in the days of those kings shall the God of heaven set up a kingdom which shall never be destroyed, nor shall the sovereignty thereof be left to another people; but it shall break in pieces and consume all these kingdoms, and it shall stand for ever. Forasmuch as thou sawest that a stone was cut out of the mountain without hands, and that it brake in pieces the iron, the brass, the clay, the silver, and the gold; the great God hath made known to the king what shall come to pass hereafter: and the dream is certain, and the interpretation thereof sure.

After the declaration of the interpretation (verse 36), Daniel interprets the meaning of the head of gold (verses 37-38) as being Nebuchadnezzar, the head of the Babylonian Empire. It was with this empire that the times of the Gentiles began, when Nebuchadnezzar destroyed Jerusalem and the Solomonic Temple in 586 B.C. Thus Babylon was the first of the four Gentile empires to dominate Jerusalem.

The two arms of silver united into the breast of silver represents the two nations of the Medes and the Persians who established the Medo-Persian Empire (verse 39a).

The Medo-Persian Empire was followed by the Greek or Hellenistic Empire symbolized by the belly and two thighs of brass (verse 39b) for the third territorily embraced both east and west. The two thighs may also represent Syria and Egypt which arose out of the Hellenistic Empire and controlled Jewish territory.

The rest of the image represents the fourth Gentile empire (verses 40-43). This fourth empire goes through several stages, three of which are presented in this text. First there is the united stage (verse 40). But this united stage gives way to the two division stage (verse 41) which still has the strength of iron. Eventually, however, the fourth Gentile empire gives way to a ten division stage as is seen in the ten toes (verses 42-43) being composed of iron and clay. Part of this ten division stage will be strong and part will be brittle and weak. The fourth Gentile empire is unique from all the previous ones. It totally subdues and crushes all that precedes it. It is the fourth Gentile empire that is particularly emphasized by the text dealing with the times of the Gentiles.

However, the fifth empire, that will follow it, will not be Gentile but Jewish (verses 44-45). Two prominent symbols are used here, but they are consistent with their usage elsewhere. Whenever the word *stone* is used symbolically, it is always a symbol of the Second Person of the Trinity, God the Son, the Lord Jesus Christ, the Messiah of Israel. Whenever the word *mountain* is used symbolically, it is always a symbol of a king, kingdom, or throne. Thus, following the fourth Gentile empire, God will set up His own kingdom. The kingdom is set up during the ten division stage (verse 44a), and this brings to an end the domination of the other kingdoms (verse 44b). In the end the image of Gentile domination will be smashed at the second coming. Once Gentile domination is thus smashed by the stone, Christ, the kingdom of God is set up, and it is set up by this stone.

To summarize the first passage dealing with the times of the Gentiles, this is a period of time when four Gentile empires will follow one another in sequence with the fourth empire going through several different stages. But eventually this will give way to God setting up His own kingdom. In chart form it may be seen as follows:

1. The Babylonian Empire
2. The Medo-Persian Empire
3. The Greek-Hellenistic Empire
4. The Fourth Empire
   a. The United Stage
   b. The Two Division Stage

      c.   The Ten Division Stage
    5.   The Messianic Kingdom

B. DANIEL 7:1-28

The second passage is found in Daniel 7:1-28. Verses 1-14 describe four visions that Daniel saw:

> In the first year of Belshazzar king of Babylon Daniel had a dream and visions of his head upon his bed: then he wrote the dream and told the sum of the matters. Daniel spake and said, I saw in my vision by night, and, behold, the four winds of heaven brake forth upon the great sea. And four great beasts came up from the sea, diverse one from another. The first was like a lion, and had eagle's wings: I beheld till the wings thereof were plucked, and it was lifted up from the earth, and made to stand upon two feet as a man; and a man's heart was given to it. And behold, another beast, a second, like to a bear; and it was raised up on one side, and three ribs were in its mouth between its teeth: and they said thus unto it, Arise, devour much flesh. After this I beheld, and lo, another, like a leopard, which had upon its back four wings of a bird; the beast had also four heads; and dominion was given to it. After this I saw in the night-visions, and behold, a fourth beast, terrible and powerful, and strong exceedingly; and it had great iron teeth; it devoured and brake in pieces, and stamped the residue with its feet: and it was diverse from all the beasts that were before it; and it had ten horns. I considered the horns, and, behold, there came up among them another horn, a little one, before which three of the first horns were plucked up by the roots: and behold, in this horn were eyes like the eyes of a man, and a mouth speaking great things. I beheld till thrones were placed, and one that was ancient of days did sit; his raiment was white as snow, and the hair of his head like pure wool; his throne was fiery flames, and the wheels thereof burning fire. A fiery stream issued and came forth from before him: thousands of thousands ministered unto him, and ten thousand times ten thousand stood before him: the judgment was set, and the books were opened. I beheld at that time because of the voice of the great words which the horn spake; I beheld, even till the beast was slain, and its body destroyed, and it was given to be burned with fire. And as for the rest of the beasts, their dominion was taken away: yet their lives were prolonged for a season and a time. I saw in the night-visions, and, behold, there came with the clouds of heaven one like unto a son of man, and he came even to the ancient of days, and they brought him near before him. And there was given him dominion, and glory, and a kingdom, that all the peoples, nations, and languages should serve him: his dominion is an everlasting dominion, which shall not pass away, and his kingdom that which shall not be destroyed.

After giving the time and location of the four visions (verse 1), in verses 2-6 the first vision is described. It begins with a vision of the sea (the Mediterranean), representing the Gentile world (Isaiah 17:12-13, Matthew 13:47-50, Revelation 13:1, 17:1,15), troubled by the four winds (verse 2). Suddenly four beasts arise from this sea, each one being different from the other (verse 3). All four then arise out of the Mediterranean area. The first beast is lion-like (verse 4), representing the Babylonian Empire (Jeremiah 4:7, 48:40, 49:19,22, 50:17,44, Ezekiel 17:3). The latter part of verse four is probably a reference to Nebuchadnezzar's experience recorded in Daniel 4:1-37.

The second beast is bear-like and represents the Medo-Persian Empire (verse 5). The bear is lop-sided, being raised up on one side; for although the Medes and the Persians were confederate, the Persians were by far the dominant power and it was a lop-sided alliance. Furthermore, the bear is found to have three ribs in its mouth, having devoured the flesh. Historically, these three ribs represent the three kingdoms conquered by the Medo-Persian forces giving them their empire status: Lydia, Babylonia, and Egypt. The bear is less majestic than the lion and is bulky and weighty. Medo-Persia conquered by shear force of numbers.

The third beast is leopard-like, representing the Hellenistic Empire (verse 6). The leopard is also less majestic than the lion and less grand than the bear but is swifter than both. With leopard-like speed Alexander the Great conquered the Medo-Persian Empire and greatly extended the Hellenistic Empire. At his death, however, the empire split into four kingdoms. The four wings represent the four kingdoms rising out of Alexander's empire, and the four heads represent the four generals who took control of the four kingdoms: Ptolemy over Egypt, Palestine and Arabia Petrea; Seleucus over Syria, Babylonia, and as far east as India; Cassander over Macedonia and Greece; and Lysimachus over Thrace and Bithynia.

The second vision found in verses 7-8 describes the fourth beast. Unlike the others it is non-descript. While the others are given animal-like descriptions, none is given for this one. This fourth beast is described as being diverse, emphatically different, from all the others. It completely subdues and breaks in pieces all that **precedes** it. It appears as far more ferocious than the previous three empires.

The fourth beast has ten horns. But while it began with ten horns, an eleventh horn arises, *the little horn*, who uproots three of the ten others. Having uprooted the other three, it begins to speak great things. With the uprooting of three horns, seven of the original remain and the little horn is now an eighth.

Once again, as in Daniel two, the uniqueness of the fourth empire is emphasized stating that it goes through several stages. The interpretation will be discussed later. But for now it is enough to note that the fourth beast does represent a fourth Gentile empire.

The third vision is found in verses 9-12. This third vision takes place in heaven. In verses 9-10 the vision is of the throne of God the Father who is described under the title of the Ancient of Days. He is viewed as a judge and the book of judgment is opened. He is surrounded by myriads of angels who will be responsible to carry these judgments out. What is being judged is the fourth Gentile empire (verses 11-12). In verse 11 it is the fourth beast, particularly the little horn, that is judged and destroyed. As for the other three (verse 12), two things are stated: first, their dominion was taken away; and secondly, their lives were prolonged for a season and a time. The exact meaning of this will be discussed under the third passage relating to the times of the Gentiles. The third vision is of God the Father, ready to move out in judgment against the fourth empire.

Verses 13-14 contain the fourth vision. It begins with the setting of the kingdom of God following the destruction of the fourth Gentile empire. In verse 13 the second coming of Christ is viewed and this is followed by the setting up of the messianic kingdom in verse 14.

Having described the four visions which he saw, which present essentially the same overview of the four Gentile empires as was found in Daniel two, he now gives the interpretation in verses 15-27. The major emphasis will be upon the fourth empire:

> As for me, Daniel, my spirit was grieved in the midst of my body, and the visions of my head troubled me. I came near unto one of them that stood by, and asked him the truth concerning all this. So he told me, and made me know the interpretation of the things. These great beasts, which are four, are four kings, that shall arise out of the earth. But the saints of the Most High shall receive the kingdom, and possess the kingdom for ever, even for ever and ever. Then I desired to know the truth concerning the fourth beast, which was diverse from all of them, exceeding terrible, whose teeth were of iron, and its nails of brass; which devoured, brake in pieces, and stamped the residue with its feet; and concerning the ten horns that were on its head, and the other horn which came up, and before which three fell, even that horn that had eyes, and a mouth that spake great things, whose look was more stout than its fellows. I beheld, and the same horn made war with the saints, and prevailed against them; until the ancient of days came, and judgment was given to the saints of the Most High, and the time came that the saints possessed the kingdom. Thus he said, The fourth beast shall be a fourth kingdom upon earth, which shall be diverse from all the kingdoms, and shall devour the whole earth, and shall tread it down, and break it in pieces. And as for the ten horns, out of this kingdom shall ten kings arise: and another shall arise after them; and he shall be diverse from the former, and he shall put down three kings. And he shall speak words against the Most High, and shall wear out the saints of the Most High; and he shall think to change the times and the law; and they shall be given into his hand until a time and times and half a time. But the judgment shall be set, and they shall take away his dominion, to consume and to destroy it unto the end. And the kingdom and the dominion, and the greatness of the kingdoms under the whole heaven, shall be given to the people of the saints of the Most High: his kingdom is an everlasting kingdom, and all dominions shall serve and obey him.

After Daniel requests the interpretation in verses 15-16, he is given a summary interpretation in verses 17-18. In verse 17 Daniel is told that these four beasts represent four kingdoms. Nevertheless, it is the servants of the Most High who will possess the kingdom; for whatever will be possessed by the four Gentile empires will be only temporary (verse 18).

Having received this summary interpretation, in verses 19-22 Daniel requests further interpretation regarding the fourth beast. In making this request Daniel further describes what he saw regarding the fourth beast. In verse 19 its diverseness is pointed out. It is important to note how the diverseness of the fourth empire is continually emphasized. For this diverseness Daniel seeks a meaning. He further wishes to know the meaning of the ten horns (verse 20a) and finally the little horn (verses 20b-22). In requesting this Daniel gives further information regarding the activity of the little horn: he causes three of the ten horns to fall (verse 20b); he speaks great things (verse 20c); he wars against the saints and is allowed to prevail over them (verse 21). But finally he is personally defeated by the coming of the Ancient of Days. Once the judgment is passed on the little horn by the Ancient of Days, he will be done away with, and the kingdom will pass over to the saints.

Having made his request, in verses 23-26 Daniel is given the interpretation of the fourth beast. As in Daniel two, the fourth empire is seen as going through several stages, though not always the same stages as found in chapter two. In verse 23a, the fourth empire is seen in its united stage, and it is in this first stage that its diverseness from the other previous three empires is seen. This is followed by the second stage, that of a one-world government; for in verse 23b it states that the fourth empire will devour the *whole* earth. This will be followed by the ten kingdom stage (verse 24a) which, in turn, will be followed by the little horn, or the Antichrist stage (verses 24b-26). These verses state that he arises after the ten division stage (verse 24b). While the fourth empire is diverse from the previous three, the little horn is diverse from the other ten (verse 24c). He eventually puts down three of these kings (verse 24d). Verse 25 again points out his speaking great things as seen here in his speaking against God and against the saints. He seeks to change the times and the seasons, and he will be allowed to rule for only *a time, times, and a half a time*, which, from other passages (Daniel 9:27, 12:7, Revelation 11:2,3, 12:6,14, 13:5) means 3½ years. But finally his domination is destroyed (verse 26).

With the destruction of the little horn, the messianic kingdom is set up for the saints (verse 27). The "saints" in Daniel refer to righteous Israel, or the remnant of Israel, and not to the church. The chapter ends with Daniel's conclusion regarding his reaction to what he has just seen (verse 28).

Daniel seven, then, further develops with greater detail what was given in chapter two, especially in relationship to the fourth empire. In outline form the information found in chapter seven could be viewed as follows:

    1. The Babylonian Empire
    2. The Medo-Persian Empire
    3. The Hellenistic Empire
    4. The Fourth Empire
       a. The United Stage
       b. The One World Government Stage
       c. The Ten Division Stage
       d. The Antichrist Stage
    5. The Messianic Kingdom

C. SUMMARY AND COMBINATION OF DANIEL CHAPTERS TWO AND SEVEN

In order to clearly understand the times of the Gentiles, the two chapters of Daniel two and seven must be compared before looking at the two other passages involved. Daniel two and seven describe the four Gentile empires with an emphasis on the last which goes through several stages. Outlined side by side the comparison would be as follows:

Daniel Two	Daniel Seven
1. The Babylonian Empire	1. The Babylonian Empire
2. The Medo-Persian Empire	2. The Medo-Persian Empire
3. The Hellenistic Empire	3. The Hellenistic Empire
4. The Fourth Empire	4. The Fourth Empire
a. The United Stage	a. The United Stage
b. The Two Division Stage	b. The One World
c. The Ten Division Stage	Government Stage
5. The Messianic Kingdom	c. The Ten Division Stage
	d. The Antichrist Stage
	5. The Messianic Kingdom

In most of the features the two passages present the same thing. Both agree that there are to be four Gentile empires, one following the other, culminating with the destruction of the fourth empire by Christ and the setting up of the messianic kingdom. Both passages point out the diverseness of the fourth kingdom and the fact that it goes through several stages. It is in these stages that there is a slight difference between the two texts.

Daniel two shows three stages of the fourth empire, two of which are mentioned by Daniel seven. Daniel seven mentions four stages of the fourth empire, two of which are mentioned by Daniel two. Combining the two outlines together, they would be viewed as follows:

1. The Babylonian Empire
2. The Medo-Persian Empire
3. The Hellenistic Empire
4. The Fourth Empire
    a. The United Stage
    b. The Two Division Stage
    c. The One World Government Stage
    d. The Ten Division Stage
    e. The Antichrist Stage
5. The Messianic Kingdom

1. THE SUMMARY OF THE FIRST THREE EMPIRES

The *first* empire is the Babylonian Empire which included the head of gold and the lion-like beast. Different aspects of this empire are depicted by Daniel 1:1-5:30 and 7:4. The *second* empire is the Medo-Persian Empire represented by the arms and breasts of silver and the bear-like beast. Different aspects of this empire are described in Daniel 2:39a, 5:31-6:28, 7:5, 8:1-7, and 10:1-11:2. This is followed by the *third* empire, the Hellenistic Empire represented by the belly of brass and the leopard-like beast. It started out as a unit under Alexander the Great but split into four divisions at his death. This empire is subject to considerable revelation in Daniel 2:39b, 7:6, 8:7-27, and 11:3-35.

2. THE FOURTH AND IMPERIALISTIC EMPIRE

This is followed by the fourth empire which is emphasized as being diverse from all the others. Daniel describes this empire in 2:40-43, 7:7-12, 19-27, 9:27, and 11:36-45. It goes through five different stages with Rome being merely the first of these five stages, for Rome cannot be viewed as the entire fourth empire. What made the fourth empire, beginning with Rome, different from all the previous empires? The key difference was in the type of government initiated by Rome, which was a government of *imperialism*. When the Babylonians conquered an area, they did not set up Babylonian rulers, but set up nationals to rule. In its conquest of Judah, Babylon first set up Zedekiah, and later Gedaliah was appointed to rule. Under Medo-Persia the same thing was done, and Jewish governors such as Zerrubbabel and Nehemiah ruled. The Hellenists worked in the same way. Instead of sending in Greeks to rule, they allowed the Jewish high priests to rule throughout the period of Greek domination.

But Rome began a new system called *imperialism*. This is what made the fourth empire *diverse* from all the others. When Rome conquered, Romans were sent in to rule (e.g. Pontius Pilate). This was the policy of imperialism. The name for the fourth empire should be "Imperialism," not Rome. For Rome was merely the first of five stages of the fourth empire of Imperialism. Hence, the fourth empire will be referred to as the Imperialistic Empire.

Both Daniel passages make it clear that the fourth Gentile empire begins with the end of the third and continues until Christ comes to set up his kingdom. The long continuous existence of the Imperialistic Empire is to go through five successive stages, and it is now necessary to study the five stages individually in order to see where history fits in this development.

a.   THE UNITED STAGE: ROME

The first stage was the United Stage which was the Roman Empire. While it has been common to call the fourth Gentile empire by that name, it is only true of the first stage of the Gentile Empire of Imperialism. It has become customary to think in terms of a revival of the Old Roman Empire, but no such concept is really warranted. It is more consistent to simply follow through the five stages with the Roman Empire being the first stage, or the United Stage, which lasted from 63 B.C. to 285 A.D. Neither of the Daniel passages allows for gaps or for a revival of the Old Roman Empire.

b.   THE TWO DIVISION STAGE

The second stage of the Empire of Imperialism was the Two Division Stage. This stage was foreseen by Daniel two but not by Daniel seven. It is a stage that began in 364 A.D. when Emperor Valentinian divided the Roman Empire into an East and West division. From that point on the Empire of Imperialism was divided into an East-West balance of power. Since then, history continued to develop essentially in an East-West balance of power axis. It began in 364 A.D. with the Western Roman Empire headquartered in Rome and the Eastern Roman Empire in Constantinople. In the original division of the East-West axis, these two cities controlled the balance of power. Since then the centers of the balance of power have shifted, but it has remained an East-West division.

The Eastern division of power remained in Constantinople until 1453 when it collapsed in the Turkish invasion. When Constantinople collapsed, the political rulers, scribes, and scholars fled northward into Russia and infiltrated the government there, setting up a Roman type of government (imperialism). The rulers called themselves *Czars*, which is Russian for Caesar. After a while, Russia gave herself the official title of the Third Roman Empire. Up to the present time the eastern balance of power has been centered in the Soviet Union and includes the communist block of nations.

The western division of power remained in Rome from 364 to 476 when Rome fell. From there it shifted to France, especially with the power gained by Charlemagne in 800 A.D. He called his domain the Holy Roman Empire of the Frankish Nation. In 962 Otto I of Germany defeated the Franks and set up the Holy Roman Empire of the German Nation. The leaders named themselves *Kaisers*, which is German for Caesar. Since then, especially after World War I, the western balance of power has been centered in the democratic nations of the west.

So then, in 364 the Two Division Stage began and continues to the present day. The centers of the balance of power may shift again, but it will remain essentially an East-West balance until it gives way to the third stage.

c.   THE ONE WORLD GOVERNMENT STAGE

The next three stages of the Empire of Imperialism are all future. At some point the East-West balance of power will break down leading to a one world government. This stage is seen by Daniel seven but not by Daniel two. Daniel 7:23 clearly states that at some point the fourth empire *devours the whole earth*. This is something that Rome never did. Some attempt to make this expression mean the "then known world" but it cannot be said that Rome even conquered the then-known world. As soon as one empire conquers up to a certain point of territory, it is very obvious that there is more to follow beyond that. So it is foolish to say that Rome conquered the then-known world. Rome did not even extend as far east as the empire of Alexander the Great. The Greeks went as far as the Indus River in India, and Alexander would have gone further except for the refusal of his generals who wished to go no further. But even the area beyond the Indus River was part of the then-known world. Rome did not even extend that far. Furthermore, Rome never fully conquered the Parthian Empire, and that, too, was part of the known world. The area of Scotland was also part of the known world that Rome did not conquer. Rome had to build the Hadrian Wall in order to keep the nomads of northern Scotland from overrunning that part of Britain controlled by Rome. So by no means did Rome conquer the whole known world. Furthermore, other usages of the word in the Old Testament clearly teach universality (Genesis 8:9, 9:19, 11:1, Isaiah 6:3, 14:26, 28:22, 54:5, Jeremiah 15:10, Zechariah 4:10, 14). Although in Daniel 2:39 the word is used of the Hellenistic Empire, it only states that such authority was given to it as it was to Babylon in Daniel 2:37-38, but neither of these two empires chose to exercise this authority. In the case of the fourth empire, the wording states that it will *devour* the whole earth. The text demands that the fourth empire will at some time control the whole world and will devour it. So if literal interpretation is maintained, then the fourth Empire of Imperialism is yet to control the whole world in the formation of a one world government, which is something that has not yet been accomplished.

For this reason Rome must not be seen as the total fourth empire, but only as the first stage of the Empire of Imperialism. The third stage, which will be a one world government stage, will happen at some point when the East-West division stage collapses. The timing of the third stage will be discussed in Chapter IV.

d. THE TEN DIVISION STAGE

This stage was seen by both Daniel two in the ten toes and in Daniel seven in the ten horns. The ten division stage is clearly stated to come out of the one world government stage. For some reason, not given by the text, the one world government will divide into ten kingdoms that will cover the whole world—and not merely Europe. It has become common today to refer to the ten kingdoms as being of Europe only, especially the Common Market. But the text does not allow for this kind of interpretation. At the very best, the European Common Market might become one of the ten, but it could hardly become all of the ten. A careful reading of the Daniel passage states that once the fourth empire rules the whole world, then this one world government will split into ten kingdoms. This requires the ten kingdoms to cover the entire world, not just the territory known as Europe. It would be a mistake to make too much of the European Common Market as being the Ten Division Stage. It would be far more consistent with the text to view it as possibly one of the ten, but not the entire ten. More consistent with Daniel's prophecy is the suggestion of the Club of Rome that recommended that the world be divided into ten administrative districts to avoid a world economic collapse.

The timing of this stage will also be discussed in Chapter IV.

e.   THE ANTICHRIST STAGE

It is during the ten kingdom stage that the Antichrist will begin his rise to power. Eventually, he will be strong enough to uproot three of the ten kings, and the other seven will simply submit to his authority. Once the other seven submit their authority to the Antichrist, this will begin the fifth and final stage of the Fourth Gentile Empire, the Antichrist Stage, which is the stage of *absolute* imperialism. In this sense he is *diverse* from the other ten.

The timing of this stage will be discussed in Chapter XI.

The combined chart seen earlier on the two chapters in Daniel can now be redone with the added information as follows:

1. The Babylonian Empire
2. The Medo-Persian Empire
3. The Hellenistic Empire
4. The Fourth Empire — The Empire of Imperialism
   a. The United Stage — The Roman Empire
   b. The Two Division Stage — The East-West
      Balance of Power
   c. The One World Government Stage
   d. The Ten Division Stage — The Ten Kingdoms
   e. The Antichrist Stage — Absolute Imperialism
5. The Messianic Kingdom

With this information in hand, it is now necessary to consider the other two passages dealing with the times of the Gentiles.

D. REVELATION 13:1-10

The third passage is found in Revelation 13:1-10:

. . . . And I saw a beast coming up out of the sea, having ten horns and seven heads, and on his horns ten diadems, and upon his heads names of blasphemy. And the beast which I saw was like unto a leopard, and his feet were as the feet of a bear, and his mouth as the mouth of a lion; and the dragon gave him his power, and his throne, and great authority. And I saw one of his heads as though it had been smitten unto death; and his death-stroke was healed: and the whole earth wondered after the beast; and they worshipped the dragon, because he gave his authority unto the beast; and they worshipped the beast, saying, Who is like unto the beast? and who is able to war with him? and there was given to him a mouth speaking great things and blasphemies; and there was given to him authority to continue forty and two months. And he opened his mouth for blasphemies against God, to blaspheme his name, and his tabernacle, even them that dwell in the heaven. And it was given unto him to make war with the saints, and to overcome them: and there was given to him authority over every tribe and people and tongue and nation. And all that dwell on the earth shall worship him, every one whose name hath not been written from the foundation of the world in the book of life of the Lamb that hath been slain. If any man hath an ear, let him hear. If any man is for captivity, into captivity he goeth: if any man shall kill with the sword, with the sword must he be killed. Here is the patience and the faith of the saints.

Most of this passage will be discussed at a more appropriate time. At this point it is only necessary to deal with it as it relates to the times of the Gentiles. In verses 1-2 John describes the beast that comes out of the sea. The sea in Revelation 13 is the same as the one in Daniel seven, which represents the Gentile world. Daniel two surveyed all the four empires. Daniel seven summarized the four empires, and then focused its attention on the fourth Empire of Imperialism in its various stages. But Revelation 13 is completely focused on the fourth empire, emphasizing a particular stage of the fourth empire, namely the fifth stage of the Antichrist.

The beast that John saw is the same beast that Daniel saw in chapter seven where it was nondescript. But here the beast is given a description. In verse one the beast has ten horns and seven heads. The ten horns are found in Daniel seven, and they represent the ten kingdoms which is the fourth stage of the Empire of Imperialism. While the Ten Division stage gives way to the fifth stage, the ten kingdoms continue to exist to the end. The difference between the two stages is that in the fourth stage the world is divided into ten kingdoms ruled co-equally by ten men, while in the fifth stage the world in all ten divisions is ruled by the Antichrist, and the other kings are subject to the Antichrist.

A new element is introduced by Revelation 13: the beast has seven heads. The meaning of these seven heads will be explained in the fourth major passage to be discussed later in this chapter.

In verse two the beast has a leopard-like body, bear-like feet, and lion-like mouth. This, then, is the interpretation and explanation of the verse found in Daniel 7:12:

> And as for the rest of the beasts, their dominion was taken away: yet their lives were prolonged for a season and a time.

The dominion of the first three empires was over, but their lives were prolonged. Their lives were prolonged in that the previous empires left their influence on the fourth empire. From the Daniel seven passage it is clear that the leopard-like body represents the Hellenistic influence; the bear-like feet represents the Medo-Persian influences; and the lion-like mouth represents the Babylonian influences. Thus, while their dominion ended, their lives were prolonged.

In verses 3-10 the text concentrates on the fifth stage of the fourth empire, the Antichrist Stage. The details will be discussed later in a more appropriate place, so a concise summary is all that will be needed here.

In verse three the death and resurrection of the Antichrist is viewed. One of the heads is smitten unto death and the death-stroke was healed. It is the seventh head that is smitten, and the full meaning of the head and heads will be discussed with the fourth major passage dealing with the times of the Gentiles.

In verse four the worship of the Antichrist is described. In verses 5-7 the activities of the Antichrist are described, and they are similar to those recorded in Daniel seven: he speaks great things (verse 5a); he reigns with absolute control for 3½ years (verse 5b); he blasphemes against all heaven (verse 6); he wars against the saints (verse 7a) and the nations (verse 7b).

In verse eight the worship of the Antichrist is described again. The passage concludes in verses 9-10 with a warning to those that do so.

This passage will be discussed in detail in the chapter dealing with the events of the middle of the tribulation. What is seen in Revelation 13 is the fourth Gentile Empire of Imperialism viewed in its fifth and final stage, the Antichrist Stage, and his activities in the second half of the tribulation are described.

The ten horns represent the ten kingdoms of the fourth stage which precede the fifth stage of the Antichrist. But chapter 13 adds the fact that this beast has seven heads which is not mentioned in any of the previous passages dealing with the times of the Gentiles. The fourth and final passage will focus on the seven heads.

E.   REVELATION 17:7-14

The fourth passage which deals with the times of the Gentiles is Revelation 17:7-14:

> And the angel said unto me, Wherefore didst thou wonder? I will tell thee the mystery of the woman, and of the beast that carrieth her, which hath the seven heads and the ten horns. The beast that thou sawest was, and is not; and is about to come up out of the abyss, and to go into perdition. And they that dwell on the earth shall wonder, they whose name hath not been written in the book of life from the foundation of the world, when they behold the beast, how that he was, and is not, and shall come. Here is the mind that hath wisdom. The seven heads are seven mountains, on which the woman sitteth: and they are seven kings; the five are fallen, the one is, the other is not yet come; and when he cometh, he must continue a little while. And the beast that was, and is not, is himself also an eighth, and is of the seven; and he goeth into perdition. And the ten horns that thou sawest are ten kings, who have received no kingdom as yet; but they receive authority as kings, with the beast, for one hour. These have one mind, and they give their power and authority unto the beast. These shall war against the Lamb, and the Lamb shall overcome them, for he is Lord of lords, and King of kings; and they also shall overcome that are with him, called and chosen and faithful.

From verse seven it is clear that the beast is the same as the one found in Revelation 13 and is the same as the fourth beast of Daniel seven. This beast has ten horns and seven heads. What the ten horns represent was explained earlier: the fourth stage of the fourth empire—the ten kingdoms. What is about to be explained is what the seven heads represent. In verse eight, as in Revelation 13, the death and resurrection of the Antichrist is seen along with the subsequent worship of him. Details of this will be discussed in Chapter XI.

Then verses 9-10 explain the meaning of the seven heads. Verse nine states that the seven heads are seven mountains. Unfortunately, too many Bible teachers have stopped here, ignored the following verse, and consequently concluded that the seven mountains represent Rome, for Rome is a city sitting upon seven hills. However, a number of cities in the Middle East claim to sit upon seven hills or mountains. So this is not enough to pinpoint Rome as the place to which this passage refers. But the identification with Rome becomes totally unwarranted if the verse is seen in its complete context. The fact that the seven heads are said to be seven mountains shows that these mountains are to be taken symbolically. Whenever the word "mountain" is used symbolically, it is always a symbol of a king, kingdom, or throne. This is the case here. In fact, the very next verse, verse ten, actually interprets the meaning of the seven mountains. Verse nine does not end the sentence, since the sentence continues into verse ten. Having stated that the seven heads are seven mountains in verse nine, he clearly states in verse ten that these seven mountains represent something other than real mountains: *And they are seven kings.* The meaning of mountains here is quite consistent with its symbolic usage everywhere else in the Scriptures. In verse nine the seven heads are seven mountains, and in verse ten the pronoun *they* clearly states that these seven mountains are to be viewed as seven kings. It is not Rome the city that is meant, but seven kings that are meant. Verse ten further states that of these seven heads-mountains-kings, five were fallen by John's day, one was present at that time, and one more was yet to come. If this refers to Rome the city, then five hills should no longer be in existence, only one should be there now with another to arise in the future! Contextually then, this is an impossible interpretation. So while both the ten horns and seven heads are representative of kings, there is a difference between them. The ten horns are kings that are *contemporary* with each other. They all rise and reign at the same time. But the seven heads are *chronological* or *sequential.* One follows the other in chronological sequence, and no two are ever contemporary. At the time of the writing of the Revelation, five had already gone into history and were no more. The sixth head-mountain-king was present and in control, and there was one more to go.

With this information in hand, what these seven heads represent can be deduced from a study of history. As has already been said, the fourth empire is the Empire of Imperialism. This is what was present in John's day, and hence, Imperialism represents the sixth head. It was

also the time of the first stage of the Empire of Imperialism, the United
Stage or the Roman Empire Stage. Looking at Roman history, it is
known that Rome went through five types of governments before it
developed into the first stage of the Empire of Imperialism. They are
as follows:

The Tarquin Kings	753-510 B.C.	(The First Head)
The Counsulors	510-494 B.C.	(The Second Head)
The Plebians or Dictators	494-390 B.C.	(The Third Head)
The Republicans or Decimvers	390-59 B.C.	(The Fourth Head)
(Oligarchy of Ten)		
The Triumvirate	59-27 B.C.	(The Fifth Head)

These represent the five heads which are fallen and were a part of
history by the time that John wrote his book. Before the fourth Gentile
Empire of Imperialism developed, these five types of governments
preceded it. The sixth head was the one that was then present, which
began in the year 27 B.C. and will continue into the middle of the
Tribulation period. So the sixth head is the first four stages of the
fourth Gentile Empire of Imperialism.

There is one head still to come, that is, the seventh head, which is
the Antichrist stage and the stage of absolute Imperialism. Once the
seventh head is established, *he must continue for a little while*,
namely 3½ years.

Thus, the seven heads represent a chronological development
from the Tarquin kings to absolute Imperialism. Five heads are fallen,
the sixth head of Imperialism now exists, and one is yet to come, the
Antichrist.

After the reference to his death and resurrection, John describes
in verse 11 the position of the Antichrist as being an eighth, but of the
seven. He is of the seven in that there are seven heads, and the Antichrist is the seventh head. The heads are chronological and sequential, coming one after the other with the Antichrist being the last to
appear in the final period of the history of the seven heads.

But he is also an eighth. In what way is he an eighth? This is seen
in his relationship to the ten horns. The ten horns represent the ten
kingdoms that come out of the one world government. It is the fourth
stage of the fourth Gentile Empire of Imperialism. These ten kings are
contemporary and rule together. But as was seen from Daniel seven,
when the Antichrist begins to take control, he uproots three of the ten
horns. He kills three of the ten kings, leaving seven for the remainder
of the tribulation period. The Antichrist is contemporary with these
seven, making him an eighth. He is an eighth contemporary king ruling over the other seven kings who have submitted to his authority.
Yet he is "of the seven," for he is the seventh head of the

chronological ruling governments. The term "seven" refers to the heads, while the term "eight" refers to the horns.

The word *beast* in the book of Revelation, then, is a reference to the Empire of Imperialism in its final and fifth stage, the Antichrist Stage. Hence, it is proper to view the beast both as the fourth Gentile empire in its final stage as well as personally of the Antichrist himself. In the book of the Revelation the word will be used in both senses: sometimes it will be used to describe the fourth Gentile empire as a whole in its fifth final form, while at other times it will be used to describe the Antichrist personally.

In verses 12-13 the ten horns are discussed. In verse 12 the ten horns are stated to be ten kings and to exist in the future beyond John's time. In verse 13 they surrender their authority to the Antichrist. The details will be studied later. Finally, in verse 14 the fourth empire is destroyed by Christ Himself.

F. SUMMARY OF THE FOUR CHAPTERS

To summarize the four chapters of Scripture dealing with the times of the Gentiles three points should be noted.

First, the entire period of the times of the Gentiles is to be composed of four Gentile empires: Babylonian, Medo-Persian, Hellenistic, and Imperialistic. *Second,* the fourth Empire of Imperialism developed from five previous forms of Roman governments: the Tarquin Kings (The First Head), the Counsulors (The Second Head), the Plebians (The Third Head), the Republicans (The Fourth Head), and the Triumvirate (The Fifth Head). *Third*, the fourth Gentile Empire of Imperialism was to undergo five stages. The first four being the United Stage (Rome), the Two Division Stage (East-West Balance of Power), the One World Government Stage, and the Ten Kingdom Stage. These first four stages are all the Sixth Head. This will be followed by the fifth stage, the Antichrist Stage, the stage of absolute Imperialism, which is also the Seventh Head.

The details will be discussed more fully in Chapters IV and XI.

The understanding of the course of the times of the Gentiles is invaluable to the understanding of the course of eschatology itself.

Combining all these chapters into outline form, it can be viewed as follows:

1. The Babylonian Empire
2. The Medo-Persian Empire
3. The Hellenistic Empire
(Developmental Prelude to the Fourth Gentile Empire)
    a. Tarquin Kings — The First Head
    b. Counsulors — The Second Head

    c. Plebians — The Third Head
    d. Republicans — The Fourth Head
    e. Triumvirate — The Fifth Head

4. The Fourth Gentile Empire — Imperialism

    a. The United Stage — The Roman Empire ⎤
    b. The Two Division Stage — The   ⎮
       East-West Balance of Power   ⎮ The
    c. The One World Government Stage   ⎮ Sixth
    d. The Ten Kingdom Stage — The   ⎮ Head
       Ten Horns (Ten Kings)   ⎦
    e. The Anti-Christ Stage — The Seventh
       Head (The Eleventh Horn and the
       Eighth Horn)

5. The Messianic Kingdom

PART II

THE COURSE OF
THIS AGE

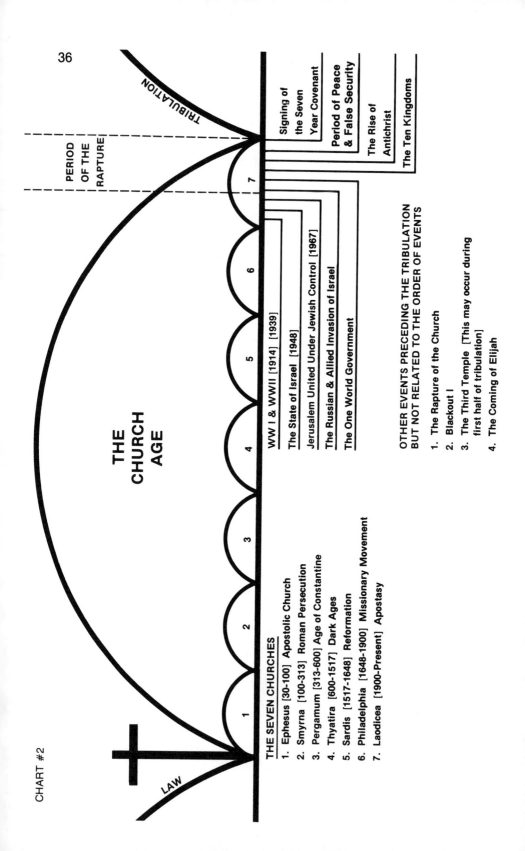

CHART #2

36

THE CHURCH AGE

LAW

TRIBULATION

PERIOD OF THE RAPTURE

THE SEVEN CHURCHES

1. Ephesus [30-100] Apostolic Church
2. Smyrna [100-313] Roman Persecution
3. Pergamum [313-600] Age of Constantine
4. Thyatira [600-1517] Dark Ages
5. Sardis [1517-1648] Reformation
6. Philadelphia [1648-1900] Missionary Movement
7. Laodicea [1900-Present] Apostasy

WW I & WWII [1914] [1939]

The State of Israel [1948]

Jerusalem United Under Jewish Control [1967]

The Russian & Allied Invasion of Israel

The One World Government

Signing of the Seven Year Covenant

Period of Peace & False Security

The Rise of Antichrist

The Ten Kingdoms

OTHER EVENTS PRECEDING THE TRIBULATION BUT NOT RELATED TO THE ORDER OF EVENTS

1. The Rapture of the Church
2. Blackout I
3. The Third Temple [This may occur during first half of tribulation]
4. The Coming of Elijah

CHAPTER III

THE ESCHATOLOGY OF THE VISIBLE CHURCH
THE THINGS WHICH ARE — THE SEVEN CHURCHES

Revelation chapters two and three comprise the second major division of the book. This division is *the things which are*: the seven churches. It is a description of the church age contained in seven short letters to the seven churches.

A. CHARACTERISTICS

There are several characteristics found in these seven churches that should be noted. First, these are all messages of Christ to the churches, and they are the last audible statements of Christ given in the Scriptures. Previous to this the last audible statements were to Paul on the Damascus road.

Secondly, they involve the visible rather than the invisible church. The latter is the body of Christ, composed of all true believers since Pentecost. It is sometimes referred to as the universal church. But the visible church is the local body or local church which may have both believers and unbelievers. It includes all professing believers whether they really are or not. While the invisible church has only believers, the visible church can have both. As it shall be seen, the seven churches contain some of both.

A third characteristic is that Christ has something against five of these churches and nothing against two. Furthermore, Christ finds something good in six of these churches but nothing good in the seventh church; the seventh church is entirely outside of His favor.

A fourth characteristic is that there are four common things in all seven letters. The first thing in common is that every letter has a description of Christ taken from the description of the glorified Son of Man found in chapter one. Then each description is somehow related to what follows in that particular letter. Chapter one gave a complete description of the glorified Son of Man. Each one of these letters then takes a part of that description and relates it to the content of the individual letter.

The second thing in common is that all seven letters contain the words, *I know*. Five times it is, "I know thy works"; once, "I know thy tribulation"; and once, "I know where thou dwellest". The point being made is that Christ is intimately aware of the state of each individual local church.

The third statement common to all seven letters is, *he that overcometh*, followed by a promise which is somehow related to the particular nature of that church.

The fourth and final common statement in all seven letters is the phrase, *he that hath an ear let him hear what the Spirit saith to the churches.* It is an admonition to obedience. The churches are responsible to conform to the demands of the letters.

B.   INTERPRETATION

The key question is how these letters are to be interpreted. For one thing, there are statements made in these letters which can be true only of the individual church. On the other hand, there are statements that can hardly be limited to that particular church and that particular local situation and sometimes cannot be true of it at all. The best way of interpreting these letters is to use the historical-prophetic method of interpretation. This method of interpretation states three things concerning these letters.

First, it recognizes that these seven churches were seven real churches to whom John was writing. They are seven churches existing in John's day, and they represent seven types of churches that existed at that time.

The second factor in the historical-prophetic interpretation is the recognition that all seven church types exist throughout the Church Age. No matter what part of church history one may turn to, he will find all seven types of churches. All seven types will continue to exist until the Rapture.

The third factor in the historical-prophetic viewpoint is the recognition that while all seven types of churches always exist, one type dominates a particular era of church history. Throughout church history all seven types of churches will be present, but one type will tend to dominate a particular period of church history. Thus, these letters present a prophetic picture of the seven historical periods in which the visible church will develop. These letters are being written to *the seven* churches, representative of the whole. These seven were chosen, first, because of the particular meaning of their names, and second, because the situation of that particular local church will also be characteristic of a future period of church history. Certain statements made to individual churches cannot be true of the strictly local situation, and they must have a far wider meaning. To fully understand *the things which are*, it will be important to keep all three factors in mind as they are studied.

C.   BASIC OUTLINE

The seven letters all follow a basic outline containing six items:

Destination
Description of Christ

Commendation
Condemnation
Exhortation
Promise

Not all seven letters have all six points of the outline, nor are they necessarily in that order. But this is the basic structure of each letter.

D.   THE SEVEN LETTERS

1.   EPHESUS: THE APOSTOLIC CHURCH — 30-100 A.D.

The first letter is in Revelation 2:1-7:

> To the angel of the church in Ephesus write: These things saith he that holdeth the seven stars in his right hand, he that walketh in the midst of the seven golden candlesticks: I know thy works, and thy toil and patience, and that thou canst not bear evil men, and didst try them that call themselves apostles, and they are not, and didst find them false; and thou hast patience and didst bear for my name's sake, and hast not grown weary. But I have this against thee, that thou didst leave thy first love. Remember therefore whence thou art fallen, and repent and do the first works; or else I come to thee, and will move thy candlestick out of its place, except thou repent. But this thou hast, that thou hatest the works of the Nicolaitans, which I also hate. He that hath an ear, let him hear what the Spirit saith to the churches. To him that overcometh, to him will I give to eat of the tree of life, which is in the Paradise of God.

The *destination* of the letter is Ephesus which means "desired." It represents the period of the Apostolic Church which began in 30 A.D. and continued to about 100 A.D., the time of the death of the last apostle, John, the author of the book of Revelation. Ephesus was the type of church that typified the Apostolic Church.

This is followed by a *description of Christ* taken from Revelation 1:13, 16, 20. It points to the control Christ has over the destiny of the churches.

The *commendation* is found in verses 2, 3 and 6. First, they are commended for condemning false teachers (verses 2-3). In Acts 20:29-31 Paul warned the elders at Ephesus that false teachers would come and despoil the church. By the time Paul wrote the books of I and II Timothy, the false teachers had arrived and were causing corruption in the church (I Timothy 1:3-4, 18-20, 6:3-10, 20-21; II Timothy 2:14-18, 4:1-4). These false teachers created havoc, and Timothy was somewhat discouraged when Paul gave him some advice as to how to handle the situation. By the time this first letter is written, the church at Ephesus had overcome the problem and resisted the false teachers, and they are commended for it.

Secondly, they are commended for hating the work of the Nicolaitans (verse 6). In church history there is no record or mention of this group, so clues as to its identity need to be sought elsewhere. The meaning of the word in Greek is "rulers of the people." This meaning may imply that this was an attempt to divide and make a distinction between the clergy and the laity, creating a division in which the clergy exercised rulership over the laity. The Ephesians hated this kind of thing and are commended by Christ for it.

The *condemnation* is found in verse 4. They have lost their first love, referring to love of Christ and love of the Word. The second generation of believers have grown lax and have become cold. They did not have the fervor of the first generation, hence there is condemnation. A similar problem is seen in the recipients of the letter to the Hebrews: a group of second generation Jewish believers who, due to persecution, had grown lax and hence had lost their first love.

The *exhortation* is found in verse 5. They are urged to remember their first love, repent, and return to it. Failure will result in the removal of their candlestick; the removal of their witness.

The *promise* is found in verse 7. While the letters are addressed to the churches as a whole, the promises are all to individuals in the church who overcome the problem of the church as a whole. So to the one who does overcome and returns to his first love, there is promised the privilege of eating of the fruit of the tree of life in the Eternal Order. Eating with someone implies fellowship: so the one who overcomes will fellowship with Christ. Since this also involves the Tree of Life, this is a promise of a share in the Eternal Order. Further comment will be reserved until the last chapter of Revelation where these symbols are found again.

This is the letter to the church of Ephesus. Certain things true of the local church are also true of the Apostolic Church in the second generation stage. This is the type of church that dominated the first period of church history.

2. SMYRNA: THE CHURCH OF THE ROMAN PERSECUTION — 100-313 A.D.

The second letter is in Revelation 2:8-11:

And to the angel of the church in Smyrna write: These things saith the first and the last, who was dead, and lived again: I know thy tribulation, and thy poverty (but thou art rich), and the blasphemy of them that say they are Jews, and they are not, but are a synagogue of Satan. Fear not the things which thou art about to suffer: behold, the devil is about to cast some of you into prison, that ye may be tried; and ye shall have tribulation ten days. Be thou faithful unto death, and I will give thee the crown of life. He that hath an ear, let him hear what the Spirit saith to the churches. He that overcometh shall not be hurt of the second death.

The *destination* is in verse 8a, and it is to the church in the city of Smyrna. Smyrna means "myrrh", which is associated with death and embalming (John 19:39-40). Thus this church becomes the fitting symbol to represent the second period of church history, that of the Roman persecution from about 100 to 313 A.D.

The *description of Christ* is in verse 8b, and it is taken from Revelation 1:18. He tells the church that He is the first and the last and that He Himself died and lived again. Although He died violently, He nevertheless did live again because of the resurrection. Since many of these people will also die violent deaths, this description is given as one of comfort for them, for they, too, will live again by way of resurrection.

The *commendation* is found in verse 9. First, they are commended for having patience in sufferings. They are good examples of what the writer of the book of Hebrews tells its recipients that they need: patient endurance. They have suffered fiercely, but they endured it patiently.

Secondly, they are commended for enduring the blasphemy of those who claim to be Jews, but they are not and are of the synagogue of Satan. In the local situation this may refer to a particular incident for which we lack historical confirmation. In church history this may refer to the Romans who considered themselves to be the people of God with the emperor being a god himself. The Christians were thus being persecuted by those claiming to be the people of God, but were not. Christians were often killed on the very grounds that they refused to sacrifice to the emperor.

Smyrna is one of the two churches that Christ had nothing against, and so there is no condemnation. The passage proceeds to the *exhortation* found in verse 10. The exhortation concerns three things. First, they are urged not to fear the things that they are about to suffer. Secondly, he warns them that they are about to suffer persecution for a period of ten days. Ten literal days of persecution may apply to the local situation, and perhaps there was a ten day period in which many suffered and died. But there may be a wider meaning, for it is interesting to note that between the years 96-313 A.D., while there were more than ten Roman emperors, only ten of them actually and officially persecuted the church. They were Domitian (96), Trajan (98-117), Hadrian (117-138), Antonius Pius (138-161), Marcus Aurelius (161-180), Septimus Severus (193-211), Maximin (235-238), Decius (249-251), Valarian (251-260), and Diocletian (284-305). These ten Roman emperors might be represented in the ten days of persecution. Thirdly, they are exhorted not to fear death, for if they die as martyrs, then they shall secure the crown of life.

The *promise* is found in verse 11. Although they may die violently once, they will not die the second time, which is the Second Death.

The nature of the Second Death will be discussed in detail at a more appropriate time in the course of this study. But their killers who are persecuting them will die the first time and will die a second time as well.

3. PERGAMUM: THE CHURCH OF THE AGE OF CONSTANTINE— 313-600 A.D.

The third letter is in Revelation 2:12-17:

And to the angel of the church in Pergamum write: These things saith he that hath the sharp two-edged sword: I know where thou dwellest, even where Satan's throne is; and thou holdest fast my name, and didst not deny my faith, even in the days of Antipas my witness, my faithful one, who was killed among you, where Satan dwelleth. But I have a few things against thee, because thou hast there some that hold the teaching of Balaam, who taught Balak to cast a stumblingblock before the children of Israel, to eat things sacrificed to idols, and to commit fornication. So hast thou also some that hold the teaching of the Nicolaitans in like manner. Repent therefore; or else I come to thee quickly, and I will make war against them with the sword of my mouth. He that hath an ear, let him hear what the Spirit saith to the churches. To him that overcometh, to him will I give of the hidden manna, and I will give him a white stone, and upon the stone a new name written, which no one knoweth but he that receiveth it.

The *destination* of the letter is in verse 12a and is said to be to Pergamum which means "thoroughly married." It was a major city of idolatry with many temples, one of which was the Temple of Esculapius, containing an idol in the form of a serpent. This may be what "Satan's throne" has reference to. It is the church of the age of Constantine which saw the church married to the state. In 313, Emperor Constantine made Christianity the official state religion of the Roman Empire, and thus the church was married to the state.

The *description of Christ* in verse 12b is taken from Revelation 1:16. This description is one of judgment, especially of that exercised by the Word of God.

In verse 13 is the *commendation*. They are commended for not denying the faith, singling out one of their faithful members, Antipas, who suffered martyrdom for his witness. Nothing more is known of Antipas, yet this gives us a small hint of what occurred in the local church at Pergamum. His name means "against all" and may indicate that he stood against all satanic worship. The war against their faith was being inspired by satanic opposition. The Pergamum church is said to be dwelling where Satan himself dwells; where Esculapius, the serpent-son, was worshipped.

The *condemnation* is found in verses 14-15. They are condemned for two things. First, in verse 14 they are condemned for allowing some to hold the teachings of Balaam. Balaam, in Numbers 22-24, was a seer of Mesopotamia. He was hired by Balak, the king of Moab, in league with the Midianites, to pronounce a prophetic curse on Israel. Although on four different occasions he tried to curse the Jews, God took control of the seer so that on all four occasions he pronounced a blessing on the Jews instead. With the failure of pronouncing a prophetic curse on Israel, Balaam used a different tactic to have Israel cursed by God. At his recommendation, the females of Moab and Midian were sent out to entice the Jewish men sexually. Part of the enticement included the worship of the gods of Moab and Midian. The plot worked, Israel was cursed, and many died in a plague. However, this scheme later caused the destruction of the Midianites and the death of Balaam himself (Numbers 25:1-16, 31:1-20, Deuteronomy 23:3-6). The teaching of Balaam was encouragement of corruption by intermarriage resulting in fornication and idolatry. No doubt in the city of Pergamum, intermarriage with the pagan world was a real problem. Because civil and religious life were so intertwined, for Christians to accept social engagements probably meant some involvement with paganism. Apparently many believers compromised anyway.

In the age of Constantine the church became married to the state which eventually resulted in spiritual fornication and idolatry. Now that the church was made a state religion, people all over the Roman Empire were baptized into the church without any real regard to personal faith. By simply being baptized, they were able to join the new establishment. As a result a massive amount of pagans entered the church bringing many of their pagan practices with them. Idolatry entered the church as these people added Jesus to the many other gods that they already had. This led to spiritual fornication and idolatry. It planted the seeds for what later developed into the Roman Catholic Church. Thus, they were rightly condemned for holding to the teachings of Balaam.

Secondly, in verse 15 they are condemned for permitting the teachings of the Nicolaitans. The very group that Ephesus was commended for not tolerating, Pergamum was condemned for tolerating. It was during this period of church history that a distinction began to emerge between the clergy and the laity with different sets of laws and regulations for each group. A priestly order was set up in the church which further corrupted and laid the foundation for what was to follow in the next phase of the church age.

The *exhortation* is found in verse 16. They are exhorted to repent (change their minds) and to clean up the church or it will be judged.

The *promise* is in verse 17 and it is three-fold. First, the one who overcomes is promised hidden manna. Manna in the Old Testament provided food for the children of Israel when they departed from the land of Egypt. The person leaving the state church might be deprived of his job and welfare. But in spite of what he may be deprived of, God will provide his sustenance.

Secondly, they are promised a white stone. In the ancient world there were two ways that one received a white stone. One way was when a person was found innocent in a trial, he was given a white stone as a symbol of acquittal. Another way was when a person was to be received into the membership of a private club, he would be given a white stone which was a symbol of his acceptance. Both elements might be included in this second promise. He will be acquitted of the guilt of that particular church, and it will be a mark of his acceptance with Christ.

The third promise is that he will be given a new name written on the stone which only he will know. Often in Scripture a new name was given to a person after he had overcome certain spiritual problems. One example is that of Jacob who was given the name Israel (Genesis 32:22-32). Another is Abram whose name was changed to Abraham (Genesis 17:1-8).

4. THYATIRA: THE CHURCH OF THE DARK AGES — 600-1517 A.D.

The fourth letter is in Revelation 2:18-29:

> And to the angel of the church in Thyatira write: These things saith the Son of God, who hath his eyes like a flame of fire, and his feet are like unto burnished brass: I know thy works, and thy love and faith and ministry and patience, and that thy last works are more than the first. But I have this against thee, that thou sufferest the woman Jezebel, who calleth herself a prophetess; and she teacheth and seduceth my servants to commit fornication, and to eat things sacrificed to idols. And I gave her time that she should repent; and she willeth not to repent of her fornication. Behold, I cast her into a bed, and them that commit adultery with her into great tribulation, except they repent of her works. And I will kill her children with death; and all the churches shall know that I am he that searcheth the reins and hearts: and I will give unto each one of you according to your works. But to you I say, to the rest that are in Thyatira, as many as have not this teaching, who know not the deep things of Satan, as they are wont to say; I cast upon you none other burden. Nevertheless that which ye have, hold fast till I come. And he that overcometh, and he that keepeth my works unto the end, to him will I give authority over the nations: and he shall rule them with a rod of iron, as the vessels of the potter are broken to shivers; as I also have received of my Father: and I will give him the morning star. He that hath an ear, let him hear what the Spirit saith to the churches.

The *destination* in verse 18a is the church of Thyatira which means "continual or perpetual sacrifice." It becomes a fitting description of the church of the Dark Ages as embodied in the Roman Catholic doctrine of the continual sacrifice in the Mass. In Roman Catholic theology, when the priest blesses the wafer and the cup, they are said to become the real body and the real blood of Christ (Transubstantiation), and so Christ is resacrificed. The laity were given only the wafer and were refused the cup because of the belief that the real blood might be accidentally spilled. The cup was for the clergy alone. Thus, the distinction between the clergy and the laity begun by the Nicolaitans had been brought to fruition.

The *description of Christ* is found in verse 18b and is taken from Revelation 1:14-15. They are symbols of judgment. It is Christ who is the Son of God, and He alone is to be worshipped. There is to be no addition whatsoever.

In verse 19 is the *commendation*. They are commended for their works of love, faith, ministry, and patience and that these works were increasing.

This is followed by a lengthy *condemnation* in verses 20-23. In verses 20-21, the condemnation involves the toleration of a woman named Jezebel. Conceivably there may have been a woman by that name in the local church at Thyatira. But this is most likely a reference to the Old Testament Jezebel to describe the state in Thyatira just as Balaam was used in describing the state of the church in Pergamum.

Jezebel was a Sidonian princess who became the wife of Ahab, the king of Israel (I Kings 16:29-33). She was responsible for introducing a pagan religion into Israel that surpassed all the previous sins of idolatry in the northern kingdom. Idolatry in the northern kingdom began with Jereboam I, the first king. But there was a difference between the sins of Jereboam and the sins of Baal worship introduced by Jezebel. The sins of Jereboam were a corruption of the true religion. Jereboam set up a golden calf in Dan and Bethel, but these golden calves represented the God that brought them out of the land of Egypt. This was idolatry, but it was a corruption of the true Jehovah worship (I Kings 12:25-33). Furthermore, Jereboam could cite a precedent in the worship of the golden calf built by Aaron. His words concerning the golden calf in I Kings 12:28 are a quotation of Aaron's words in Exodus 32:4.

But with Jezebel, it was not merely a corruption of the true religion, but a whole new god and system of worship were introduced in Israel (I Kings 16:29-33). Through Jezebel Baal worship came into the land resulting in more idolatry than ever before. Involved in the worship of Baal was sexual immorality. In the corruption of Jehovah worship, morality was still present but in the worship of Baal there was total immorality.

Jezebel thus became a very real picture of what the Roman Catholic Church evolved into during the period of the Dark Ages. It introduced a paganism that resulted in idolatry and spiritual fornication, and it became a new religious system bearing little resemblance to the New Testament church. It was during this period that ten false doctrines were introduced into the church:

1. Justification by works—not simply by faith;
2. Baptismal regeneration—that a person is saved by baptism;
3. Worship of images;
4. Celibacy—forbidding priests to marry, a further distinction between clergy and laity;
5. Confessionalism—where sins are confessed to a priest who then declares absolution of those sins;
6. Purgatory—a place of confinement which is neither heaven nor hell, but a place where one has to be refined before going into heaven; hence sanctification was not complete at death;
7. Transubstantiation—the concept of the continual and perpetual sacrifice of Christ;
8. Indulgences—where through the giving of money, a person's time in purgatory could be reduced;
9. Penance—involving the torment of one's body in order to reduce time in purgatory; and,
10. Mariolotry—the worship of the virgin Mary, her elevation as the mother of God and the declaration of her deity.

All this led to idolatry and spiritual fornication. Jezebel in Thyatira is the Roman Catholic Church within Christendom of the Dark Ages.

In verses 22-23 there is a description of the judgment on Jezebel. In verse 22 the woman is to be cast into the Great Tribulation. This means that unlike the true church, the Roman Catholic Church will go into the Great Tribulation and will play a role during that time. The nature of that role and the nature of the judgment will be discussed in Chapter X. For now it is enough to note that as part of her judgment, the Roman Catholic Church will be cast into the tribulation period.

In verse 23 the children of Jezebel, that is, the adherents of the Roman Catholic Church, will suffer physical violence and death as part of God's judgment on Jezebel.

The *exhortation* is found in verses 24-25. The exhortation involves those who are not part of the Jezebel system and do not know the deep things of Satan. The Roman Catholic Church must be viewed as Satan's counterfeit. In the exhortation to those who are not involved in Satan's counterfeit, they are told to hold fast to that which is pure. They are told to hold fast to the New Testament truth as over against the Roman Catholic Church system.

Finally, in verses 26-29 there is the *promise* which is two-fold. First, the one overcoming will have a part in the messianic kingdom. In contrast to the false authority of the Roman Catholic Church, they will have true authority over the nations during the messianic kingdom. Secondly, they will have the morning star. Here another figure is being used in the book of Revelation, but no speculation is needed. In Revelation 22:16 Christ Himself is declared to be the Morning Star. Thus, they will possess Christ. The possession of the true faith presupposes a possession of the person of Christ.

5. SARDIS: THE CHURCH OF THE REFORMATION — 1517-1648 A.D.

The fifth letter is in Revelation 3:1-6:

And to the angel of the church in Sardis write: These things saith he that hath the seven Spirits of God, and the seven stars: I know thy works, that thou hast a name that thou livest, and thou art dead. Be thou watchful, and establish the things that remain, which were ready to die: for I have found no works of thine perfected before my God. Remember therefore how thou hast received and didst hear; and keep it, and repent. If therefore thou shalt not watch, I will come as a thief, and thou shalt not know what hour I will come upon thee. But thou hast a few names in Sardis that did not defile their garments: and they shall walk with me in white; for they are worthy. He that overcometh shall thus be arrayed in white garments; and I will in no wise blot his name out of the book of life, and I will confess his name before my Father, and before his angels. He that hath an ear, let him hear what the Spirit saith to the churches.

The *destination* of the fifth letter in verse 1a is Sardis which means "those escaping." It represents the church of the Reformation which began in 1517 with Martin Luther's posting of his Ninety-Five Theses and ended in 1648 with the signing of the Peace of Westphalia. It could also be approximated as ending in 1700.

In verse 1b there is the *description of Christ* taken from Revelation 1:4, 16, and 20. It is a reference to the seven Spirits of God as over against a church without spirit.

Then in verse 1c is the *condemnation*. They have a name that lives, but actually they are dead. This is a valid description of the church of the Reformation as it developed in its later stages. They had a name that lived: the Reformation resulted in much doctrinal correction and good creeds. Much of the wrong done and the doctrines promulgated by the Roman Catholic Church were corrected by the Reformation. The different churches developing in the Reformation had good creeds and solid biblical doctrine. Nevertheless, they were dead: there was no spiritual vitality. They became dead, because they failed to rectify the basic problem which was the unity of church and state. After they broke away from the Roman Catholic Church, they too became state churches. In Germany and Scandinavia the Lutheran church became the state church. In England it was the Anglican church or Church of England; in Scotland the Presbyterian church; in one part of Switzerland the Calvinists or Reformed church; in another part of Switzerland the Zwinglian church. The Reformation failed to correct the problem of church and state unity. Therefore, it eventually became a dead church.

What corrupted Pergamum also corrupted Sardis. Because of the existence of state churches, children who were born in a given locality were simply baptized and by this means became members of the church. Personal faith had little or nothing to do with becoming a member of the church. So in a matter of time the greater part of the church was composed of unbelievers.

The churches all had good solid creeds, and so it appeared that they were living churches. But they were dead. There was no spiritual life because of the lack of personal faith, and a great part of each church was composed of unbelievers. Even to this day there are state churches in Europe which have good doctrinal creeds, but they are composed of people who are spiritually dead.

The *exhortation* is found in verses 2-3. In verse two they are exhorted to resurrect that which is about to die; that is, to go back to spiritual life as well as good doctrinal creeds. Spiritual life is impossible without good doctrine. But good doctrine without spiritual life is dead. Both are therefore necessary. In verse three the point is made that deadness will result in Christ coming unexpectedly. A church with spiritual life will not be surprised when Christ returns for the church. But a dead church will be caught unawares, because they will not be expecting Him.

In verse four there is the *commendation* to "those escaping." Their garments are undefiled and white. Hence, these are the ones who have exercised faith and do have spiritual life and have overcome the deadness of the church.

The *promise* in verses 5-6 is three-fold. First, they will have white garments. The symbol used here is explained in a different part of the Revelation. Revelation 7:14 states ". . . and they washed their robes, and made them white in the blood of the Lamb." Thus, the white garments are a symbol of salvation. The first promise to those escaping is salvation, because for them the good doctrine is not dead, but alive in Christ. A second promise is that their names will not be blotted out of the Book of Life. The Book of Life will be discussed at a more appropriate place. But this promise also involves their salvation which will be eternally secure, because their names will not be blotted out. It is a promise of eternal security. Then thirdly, the name of the believer will be confessed by Christ before the angels.

6. PHILADELPHIA: THE CHURCH OF THE
GREAT MISSIONARY MOVEMENT — 1648-1900 A.D.

The sixth letter is in Revelation 3:7-13:

And to the angel of the church in Phliadelphia write: These things saith he that is holy, he that is true, he that hath the key of David, he that openeth and none shall shut, and that shutteth and none openeth: I know thy works (behold, I have set before thee a door opened, which none can shut), that thou hast a little power, and didst keep my word, and didst not deny my name. Behold, I give of the synagogue of Satan, of them that say they are Jews, and they are not, but do lie; behold, I will make them to come and worship before thy feet, and to know that I have loved thee. Because thou didst keep the word of my patience, I also will keep thee from the hour of trial, that hour which is to come upon the whole world, to try them that dwell upon the earth. I come quickly: hold fast that which thou hast, that no one take thy crown. He that overcometh, I will make him a pillar in the temple of my God, and he shall go out thence no more: and I will write upon him the name of my God, and the name of the city of my God, the new Jerusalem, which cometh down out of heaven from my God, and mine own new name. He that hath an ear, let him hear what the Spirit saith to the churches.

The *destination* is the church in the city of Philadelphia which means "brotherly love." It is a fitting symbol of the church during the great missionary movement from 1700 through 1900. It was a period of great missionary names like Hudson Taylor, Adoraim Judson, and others.

The *description of Christ* in verse 7b is taken from Revelation 1:18, picturing Christ as the one with authority to open and close doors.

This is the second church for which there is no condemnation. So, like Smyrna, Christ finds nothing against this church and is satisfied with it.

The *commendation* is found in verse 8. They are commended for making use of the open door. It is Christ Himself who opened the door, and the Philadelphians were faithful in making use of the open door. During the period of 1700-1900 there was virtually no place where a missionary could not go. Every place was open to them. Today, more and more countries are closing their doors to missionaries. But during those two centuries there were virtually no limitations, and this church took advantage of it. They had a little power; it was a minority supporting these missionaries. Yet the little power was used to accomplish great things. They are commended for it.

The *promise* found in verses 9-10 and 12-13 is four-fold. First, in verse nine they are promised fruit from those who claim to be Jews or the people of God and are not. It is still the period described by Hosea (1:8-9, 2:23) when Israel is on the sideline of God's program and considered to be *not my people*. But in the future they will again become *my people* (Hosea 1:10-2:1, 3:5). It is interesting to note that it is during this time that Jewish missions came into its own, and by 1900 some 250,000 Jews came to Christ. Jewish missions first began in Germany, took root in England, and finally came to fruition in the United States.

It was a time when many of the natural branches were regrafted into their own olive tree. It is also possible that this verse deals more literally with those who claim to be Jews but they are not. This is also the period that saw the rise of cults such as Mormonism, Jehovah's Witnesses, Christian Science and others. One common element among them is to claim to be the "real" Jews by claims to be the 144,000 Jews or the ten lost tribes of Israel. Nevertheless the Philadelphia church will win converts among these as well.

The second promise is in verse ten: they will not go into the Great Tribulation period. This verse will be discussed in more detail in the chapter dealing with the Rapture (Chapter VI). But for now, suffice it to say that this church is promised deliverance from the Great Tribulation period. The Jezebel element in the Thyatira church will go through the tribulation, but the church of Philadelphia will not.

The third promise in verse twelve is that they will serve as a pillar in the temple of God. On one hand, this may be a reference to being a part in the temple of God as is seen in the invisible church. On the other hand, it may also refer to the millennial temple; the promise then would be that they will have a share in the millennial temple during the messianic age.

The fourth promise (verse 13) is that they will have on them three new names: the name of God; the name of Jerusalem; and the new name of Christ.

The *exhortation* is in verse eleven. It is merely for them to continue to do as they are doing, for they are doing well.

7. LAODICEA: THE CHURCH OF THE APOSTASY —
1900-PRESENT DAY

The seventh and final letter is in Revelation 3:14-22:

And to the angel of the church in Laodicea write: These things saith the Amen, the faithful and true witness, the beginning of the creation of God: I know thy works, that thou art neither cold nor hot: I would thou wert cold or hot. So because thou art lukewarm, and neither hot nor cold, I will spew thee out of my mouth. Because thou sayest, I am rich, and have gotten riches, and have need of nothing; and knowest not that thou art the wretched one and miserable and poor and blind and naked: I counsel thee to buy of me gold refined by fire, that thou mayest become rich; and white garments, that thou mayest clothe thyself, and that the shame of thy nakedness be not made manifest; and eyesalve to anoint thine eyes, that thou mayest see. As many as I love, I reprove and chasten: be zealous therefore, and repent. Behold, I stand at the door and knock: if any man hear my voice and open the door, I will come in to him, and will sup with him, and he with me. He that overcometh, I will give to him to sit down with me in my throne, as I also overcame, and sat down with my Father in his throne. He that hath an ear, let him hear what the Spirit saith to the churches.

The *destination* of the letter in verse 14a is to Laodicea which means "people ruling." This is set in contrast to God ruling in the church. It is a church entirely ruled by men, for the Holy Spirit is not present and doing His ministry of guiding. This becomes an avid description of the church of the Apostasy which began in the early 1900's and continues to the present day.

The *description of Christ* is in verse 14b and is taken from Revelation 1:4, 6, and 7. Christ is described as the faithful and the true witness, whereas this church is neither faithful nor true to the Word.

All six of the previous churches had at least one word of commendation, but this church has none. There is nothing commendable in this church as it is entirely an unsaved church.

Hence, the text continues to the *condemnation* in verses 15-17. In verses 15-16 they are characterized by lukewarmness. In verse 17 they are characterized by richness in worldly goods, but are self-deceived for they are spiritually poor, blind and naked. This is a very good description of the Apostate church. For all these traits, they are condemned.

Apostasy can be defined as *the departure from the truth that one professed to have*. It does not mean that they actually possessed the truth. Seldom do apostates actually possess the truth. Rather, it is a departure from a truth they professed to have because of an affiliation with a particular church. For example, a minister of a Baptist, Presbyterian, or Methodist church is professing by virtue of his very position to believe the doctrines of the Baptist, Presbyterian or Methodist churches respectively. But actually the apostate denies these doctrines and has departed from the truth that he professes to have. This has indeed been the characteristic of the visible church in these decades of the twentieth century.

That there would be an apostasy of the church in the latter days was clearly predicted in two New Testament passages. First, in II Thessalonians 2:1-3, Paul wrote:

> Now we beseech you, brethren, touching the coming of our Lord Jesus Christ, and our gathering together unto him; to the end that ye be not quickly shaken from your mind, nor yet be troubled, either by spirit, or by word, or by epistle as from us, as that the day of the Lord is just at hand; let no man beguile you in any wise: for it will not be, except the falling away come first, and the man of sin be revealed, the son of perdition.

This text will be dealt with in Appendix II. For now it is only necessary to show its connection with the problem of apostasy. As will be shown in Chapter VIII, the term *Day of the Lord* is always a reference to the tribulation period. In this passage two things are to occur before the tribulation can begin, one of which is the *falling away.* The Greek word here is *apostosia* which can be translated as the apostasy. Before the tribulation is to begin, the apostasy must come first. Thus, it was inevitable that the church would become apostate in the closing days of its history.

The second passage is I Timothy 4:1:

> But the Spirit saith expressly, that in later times some shall fall away from the faith, giving heed to seducing spirits and doctrines of demons.

Again, the prophetic word declares that there would be a falling away or an apostasy from the faith. The Laodicean church is a description of the apostasy of the last days.

In three New Testament passages there is a description of the *character* of the apostasy. The first is found in I Timothy 4:1-3:

> But the Spirit saith expressly, that in later times some shall fall away from the faith, giving heed to seducing spirits and doctrines of demons, through the hypocrisy of men that speak lies, branded in their own conscience as with a hot iron; forbidding to marry, and commanding to abstain from meats, which God created to be received with thanksgiving by them that believe and know the truth.

This passage declares that the source of apostasy is demons, for apostates have essentially given in to seducing spirits and are preaching a system of doctrine which is a doctrine of demons. Furthermore, they speak lies through hypocrisy, and their conscience has become insensitive. Part of this demonic doctrine involves an attack on Christian liberty characterized by the forbidding to marry and the instructing to refrain from eating meats. This example makes it clear that the Roman Catholic Church fell into apostasy a long time ago. But such apostasy will increase as church history unfolds throughout the last days. These elements will become more prevalent in the visible church.

The second passage relating to the character of the apostasy is found in II Timothy 3:5:

> Holding a form of godliness, but having denied the power thereof: from these also turn away.

In verses 1-4 there is a description of the general character of the world during the last days, and it can hardly be denied that these elements are true in this present day. But verse five centers on the religious front where the characteristic of the last days will be men having a form of godliness but denying the power thereof. Apostate ministers, retaining the clerical garb and church titles, have a form of godliness. But they have denied the power thereof for they have denied the true power of godliness.

The third passage is found in II Peter 2:1-22:

> But there arose false prophets also among the people, as among you also there shall be false teachers, who shall privily bring in destructive heresies, denying even the Master that bought them, bringing upon themselves swift destruction. And many shall follow their lascivious doings; by reason of whom the way of the truth shall be evil spoken of. And in covetousness shall they with feigned words make merchandise of you: whose sentence now from of old lingereth not, and their destruction slumbereth not. For if God spared not angels when they sinned, but cast them down to hell, and committed them to pits of darkness, to be reserved unto judgment; and spared not the ancient world, but preserved Noah with seven others, a preacher of righteousness, when he brought a flood upon the world of the ungodly; and turning the cities of Sodom and Gomorrah into ashes condemned them with an overthrow, having made them an example unto those that should live ungodly; and delivered righteous Lot, sore distressed by the lascivious life of the wicked (for that righteous man dwelling among them, in seeing and hearing, vexed his righteous soul from day to day with their lawless deeds): the Lord knoweth how to deliver the godly out of temptation, and to keep the unrighteous under punishment unto the day of judgment; but chiefly them that walk after the flesh in the lust of defilement, and despise dominion. Daring, selfwilled, they tremble not to rail at dignities: whereas angels, though greater in might and power, bring not a railing judgment against them before the Lord. But these, as creatures without reason, born mere animals to be taken and destroyed, railing in matters whereof they are ignorant, shall in their destroying surely be destroyed, suffering wrong as the hire of wrong-doing; men that count it pleasure to revel in the day-time, spots and blemishes, revelling in their deceivings while they feast with you; having eyes full of adultery, and that cannot cease from sin; enticing unstedfast souls; having a heart exercised in covetousness; children of cursing; forsaking the right way, they went astray, having followed the way of Balaam the son of Beor, who loved the hire of wrongdoing; but he was rebuked for his own transgression: a dumb ass spake with man's voice and stayed the madness of the prophet. These are springs without water, and mists driven by a storm; for whom the blackness of darkness hath been reserved. For, uttering great swelling words of vanity, they entice in the lusts of the flesh, by lasciviousness, those who are just escaping from them that live in error; promising them liberty, while they themselves are bondservants of corruption; for of whom a man is overcome, of the same is he also brought into bondage. For if, after they have escaped the defilements of the world through the knowledge of the Lord and Savior Jesus Christ, they are again entangled therein and overcome, the last state is become worse with them than the first. For it were better for them not to have known the way of righteousness, than, after knowing it, to turn back from the holy commandment delivered unto them. It has happened unto them according to the true proverb, The dog turning to his own vomit again, and the sow that had washed to wallowing in the mire.

As one reads through the passage, he does not see Peter displaying any attitude of love or tolerance towards the apostates. The

Bible is not tolerant toward apostasy and it castigates it very severely, as these verses clearly show.

Having described the character of apostasy, another question involves their teachings. What, after all, is *the mark of the apostate?* In II Peter 2:1 their teachings are portrayed as destructive denials:

> But there arose false prophets also among the people, as among you also there shall be false teachers, who shall privily bring in destructive heresies, denying even the Master that bought them, bringing upon themselves swift destruction.

The teachings of the apostates are called *destructive heresies.* The content entails "denying even the Master that bought them." In other words, the content of apostate teaching involves the denial of the person and work of Jesus Christ. Other New Testament passages give us more specific aspects of this denial. First, a denial of the Trinity is dealt with in I John 2:22-23:

> Who is the liar but he that denieth that Jesus is the Christ? This is the antichrist, even he that denieth the Father and the Son. Whosoever denieth the Son, the same hath not the Father: he that confesseth the Son hath the Father also.

Second, I John 4:2-3 comments on a denial of the incarnation:

> Hereby know ye the Spirit of God: every spirit that confesseth that Jesus Christ is come in the flesh is of God: and every spirit that confesseth not Jesus is not of God: and this is the spirit of the antichrist, whereof ye have heard that it cometh; and now it is in the world already.

The same is true in II John 7:

> For many deceivers are gone forth into the world, even they that confess not that Jesus Christ cometh in the flesh. This is the deceiver and the antichrist.

Third, the denial of the second coming of Christ is the concern of II Peter 3:3-4:

> Knowing this first, that in the last days mockers shall come with mockery, walking after their own lusts, and saying, Where is the promise of his coming? for, from the day that the fathers fell asleep, all things continue as they were from the beginning of the creation.

Thus, the teachings of apostasy involve the destructive denials of the person and work of Jesus Christ, especially with regard to His place in the Trinity, His deity, His incarnation as the God-Man by means of the virgin birth, and the fact that He is coming back physically. Basic to all these denials, of course, is the denial of the inspiration of the Scriptures themselves. Once a person moves away from the acceptance of the authority of Scripture, there is no longer any safeguard for other crucial doctrines.

In Jude 17-19 the *deeds* or *types of actions* preferred by apostates is given:

> But ye, beloved, remember ye the words which have been spoken before by the apostles of our Lord Jesus Christ; that they said to you, In the last time there shall be mockers, walking after their own ungodly lusts. These are they who make separations, sensual, having not the Spirit.

One type of deed that will be performed by apostates is mockery (verses 17-18). They will mock the fundamentals of the faith such as the verbal inspiration of the Scriptures, the virgin birth, the substitutionary death of Christ, and His physical resurrection from the dead. II Peter 3:3 states that they will also mock the doctrine of the second coming of Christ.

A second deed is that of creating schisms or separations (verse 19). Because they begin denying some of the fundamentals of the faith, they convince some but not others. In the course of time the two factions develop into a split within the church. The process begun by mockery results in a division of the church. Throughout this age of apostasy there has been schism after schism. Church after church and denomination after denomination have split over the destructive denials of the Trinity, the incarnation, and the second coming of Christ.

These characteristics, heretical teachings, and deeds of separations have become more prevalent as church history has progressed from about 1900 to the present day. This is the age of the church of the apostasy.

If the present age of the apostasy had a definite beginning (and this is impossible to determine), it might well have been January 20, 1891. On that day a man named Charles Augustus Briggs gave his inaugural address at the Union Theological Seminary in New York City. At that time, Union was a Presbyterian seminary training ministers for Presbyterian pulpits. In this inaugural address Briggs made six points, some of which involved destructive heresies: 1) there are three great fountains of truth: the Bible, the church, and reason. Thus, reason and the church became equal in authority with the Scriptures; 2) not only were some of the Old Testament prophecies not fulfilled, but they were also reversed; 3) he questioned the Mosaic authorship of the five books of Moses; 4) he questioned the unity of Isaiah; 5) he stated that those who died unsaved would have a second chance; 6) sanctification is not complete at death.

Briggs was not the first modernist. But this address was the first public affirmation of modernism in a theological seminary in the United States. Charges were brought against Briggs by the New York Presbytery on two occasions (1891 and 1893). But the charges were dropped, mainly to preserve the unity of the church rather than to deal with what was actually said. When the General Assembly of the Presbyterian church put Briggs on trial in 1893, he was suspended from the Presbyterian church. As a result, Briggs became an Episcopalian, and the Union Theological Seminary withdrew from the Presbyterian church and became independent. But although the Union Theological Seminary became independent, they still continued to train ministers for the Presbyterian church and for their pulpits. This set the stage for the way that apostasy would develop in the course of the twentieth century. Apostasy would first begin in a denominational school and thus affect the training of ministers who were to fill the pulpits of the churches for those denominations. Eventually, more and more liberals took over the pulpits, and more and more churches became liberal themselves.

So throughout the first two decades of the twentieth century, apostasy took over the schools and trained ministers for the denominational churches. In an effort to stem the tide, in 1910 the General Assembly of the Presbyterian church issued the Five Fundamentals of the Faith which included: 1) the inspiration of Scriptures; 2) the virgin birth; 3) the substitutionary atonement; 4) the resurrection of Christ; and, 5) the miracles of Christ. Those who subscribed to these five points were labeled Fundamentalists, and so a new word was coined. Those who denied these fundamentals were called Modernists or Liberals. The General Assembly issued these in 1910 and reaffirmed them in 1916 and 1923.

The decade of the 1920's was characterized by the great Modernist-Fundamentalist battles. There were many attempts to fight Modernism from within the church. But towards the end of the decade, it became apparent that the Modernists were firmly in control of both the denominational church positions (this included all the major denominations except the Southern Baptist Convention) and their schools.

This led to the separatist movements of the 1930's as the Fundamentalists pulled out of denominations either by starting new denominations or by forming independent churches. Emerging from the United Presbyterian Church of the United States of America was a group led by J. Greshem Machen, which unfortunately split into three separate denominations (Orthodox Presbyterians, Bible Presbyterians, and the Evangelical Presbyterians) due to internal struggles. Out of the American Baptist Convention came the General Association of Regular Baptists (GARB). Out of the United Methodist Church came the Evangelical Methodists. The schisms that the Bible predicted would occur as a result of the apostasy began to occur in the separatist movements of the 1930's.

The 1940's to the present day has been characterized by ecumenical movements. In 1948 the World Council of Churches was organized on two principles: 1) the unity of all churches on the basis of liberal tenets; and 2) the unity of all religions. In 1950 the old Federal Council of Churches was reorganized into the National Council of Churches, again attempting to unify all the churches in the United States along liberal tenets. The Council on Church Unity (COCU) is an attempt by several denominations to form a super church comprised of these denominations.

Consequently, the visible church is primarily apostate today. Even among conservative denominations some can already see the threat of apostasy in the taking over of the schools and the supplying of liberal ministers for the pulpits. Even the once strong Southern Baptist Convention has not escaped this trend.

The *exhortation* in Revelation 3:18-20 is a call to salvation. First, they are urged to seek spiritual wealth in Christ. Secondly, because they are spiritually naked, they are urged to receive the white garments of salvation from Christ. Throughout the book of the Revelation the white garments represent and symbolize salvation. In Revelation 3:4 these garments are on people considered worthy; in 3:5 they are coupled with not being blotted out of the Book of Life; in 6:11 they are seen as the garments of the saints in heaven; in Revelation 7:9, 13, and 14, the garments are white because they have been washed in the blood of the Lamb. The key problem in the Laodicean church is that they are spiritually naked and lack salvation. Therefore, they are urged to appropriate it from Christ. Thirdly, because they are spiritually blinded, they are urged to seek Christ's eyesalve so that they can begin to see spiritually. There is no indication that this is a saved church. While all the other churches have had at least a small saved element in it, this church has none whatsoever. Hence, there is a complete absence of commendation for it.

Verse 20 emphasizes that Christ is outside the church, knocking. Christ is not in any way within the church, for it is a totally unsaved church. The exhortation is to any individual in the apostate church to hear Christ's voice and open his heart to Him, and then Christ will enter and they will have fellowship. It is another exhortation to salvation.

The *promise* is in verses 21-22. The one who overcomes the problem of apostasy and accepts Christ is promised a share in the messianic kingdom.

The greater part of this church will find itself in the tribulation period. However, the overcomer will receive a portion in the millennium, while the others receive a portion in the tribulation.

In concluding this discussion of the apostasy, a question should be asked: What is the believer's responsibility in the face of apostasy? The Scriptures outline this responsibility in three areas.

First, believers are not to fellowship with apostates. On this point there has been too much extremism. It must be kept in mind that an apostate is not merely an unbeliever, nor is he merely a member of an apostate church. The apostate is one who is actively propagating within the local church the destructive denials of the Trinity, the virgin birth, the deity of Christ, and the second coming. The apostates the Bible talks about are not mere unbelievers, but are teachers of apostate doctrines, who propagate their destructive denials.

That the believer is not to fellowship with such an individual is spelled out in II John 7-11:

> For many deceivers are gone forth into the world, even they that confess not that Jesus Christ cometh in the flesh. This is the deceiver and the antichrist. Look to yourselves, that ye lose not the things which we have wrought, but that ye receive a full reward. Whosoever goeth onward and abideth not in the teaching of Christ, hath not God: he that abideth in the teaching, the same hath both the Father and the Son. If any one cometh unto you, and bringeth not this teaching, receive him not into your house, and give him no greeting: for he that giveth him greeting partaketh in his evil works.

So if someone does fit the description portrayed here, fellowship is forbidden, even to the point of not allowing him into one's home.

The second obligation concerns the apostate that is in the local church. If a member is found proclaiming a destructive denial, he is to be ousted from the church. As Paul stated in Galatians 1:8-9:

> But though we, or an angel from heaven, should preach unto you any gospel other than that which we preached unto you, let him be anathema. As we have said before, so say I now again, If any man preacheth unto you any gospel other than that which ye received, let him be anathema.

If anyone in the local church is found to be apostate, he is to be declared *anathema*. Anathema means untouchable. So in relationship to apostates outside the church, the believer is not to fellowship with them. In relationship to apostates inside the church, they are to be ousted from the church.

But the third area of responsibility concerns the situation where apostates are in control of the leadership of the church and cannot be ousted. What should a believer do in this case? The obligation here is separation from the church, for he is to be separated from apostasy. In II Timothy 3:5, after characterizing apostasy as having "a form of godliness but denying the power thereof," Timothy is admonished *from these also turn away.* Timothy was urged to separate himself from such apostasy.

A more extended treatment of this problem is found in II Corinthians 6:14-7:1:

> Be not unequally yoked with unbelievers: for what fellowship have righteousness and iniquity? or what communion hath light with darkness? And what concord hath Christ with Belial? or what portion hath a believer with an unbeliever? And what agreement hath a temple of God with idols? For we are a temple of the living God; even as God said, I will dwell in them, and walk in them, and I will be their God, and they shall be my people. Wherefore Come ye out from among them, and be ye separate, saith the Lord, and touch no unclean thing; And I will receive you, And will be to you a Father, And ye shall be to me sons and daughters, saith the Lord Almighty. Having therefore these promises, beloved, let us cleanse ourselves from all defilement of flesh and spirit, perfecting holiness in the fear of God.

This is an important passage for it admonishes the believer to separate himself from the apostates and not to continue to worship with them in the assembly. Verse 14a has usually been used to refer to marriage between believers and unbelievers, but the context is dealing with a worship situation and not marriage. So worshipping with unbelievers is considered an unequal yoke.

Verses 14b-16a provide the reasons why this is an unequal yoke. Again, it must be kept in mind that this is in a context of worship. Five questions are asked which, in the Greek, demand negative answers. Five terms are given around which the reasons revolve: fellowship, communion, concord, portion, and agreement. There can be no *fellowship* between unrighteousness and righteousness. Believers are a part of righteousness, whereas unbelievers are part of iniquity, and there can be no fellowship between the two in the same church. Furthermore, there is no *communion* between light and darkness. Believers are of the light, but unbelievers are of the darkness. There is no common ground between the two. There can be no *concord* between Christ and Satan. They have two separate areas of operation. They have two distinct programs. The believer is part of Christ's program while the unbeliever is part of Satan's program. The believer has no *portion* with unbelievers. One is destined for heaven and the other is destined for hell. Their two destinies are very different and in worship mutually exclusive. Finally, there is no *agreement* between the temple of God and the temple of an idol. The believer is indwelt by the Holy Spirit, but the unbeliever is not. Because there is no fellowship, communion, concord, portion, or agreement in the area of worship, worshipping with an unbeliever is an unequal yoke.

In verse 16b Paul gives the basis for separation, that is, that we are the temple of God. Since we are the temple of God, we are not to place ourselves in a worship situation with unbelievers.

In 17a the command of separation involves three phases: 1) Come out from among them; 2) Be ye separate; and 3) Touch not the unclean thing.

In verses 17b-18 a promise is given to those who comply and separate themselves. Just as there are three phases of separation, there are three statements of promises for those who obey: 1) I will receive you; 2) I will be to you a Father; and 3) You will be to me sons and daughters.

In 7:1 the passage concludes urging the believer, on the basis of these promises, to follow through on his separation from apostasy where necessary.

Thus, when faced with apostasy, we are to 1) have no fellowship with them; 2) oust apostates from the church; or 3) separate from them if apostasy is in control of the church.

CONCLUSION

This concludes the discussion of the seven churches. As has been stated earlier, all seven churches can be found in every period of church history. The author travels widely among churches all over the country as a conference speaker and can testify to the existence of all seven churches today. The Ephesus-type church can be found in the young church with a second generation that has lost the fervor of the first. Often it is found in those churches which had pulled out of the apostasy in the 1930's, but the second generation has grown lax. The Smyrna-type church can be seen in those behind the Iron Curtain and out on mission fields where they are being persecuted for their faith. The Pergamum-type church still exists in countries of Europe which continue to have a state church. The Thyatira-type church is very evident in the Roman Catholic Church. The Sardis-type church is often found in high churches with good sound creeds, yet they are spiritually dead. It can also be seen in Bible churches where sound doctrine is preached from the pulpit, but the deadness is there because of a lack of spiritual vitality. The sound doctrine has not been allowed to seep deep into a person's life and stays as knowledge in his mind only. The Philadelphia-type church can be seen in both denominational and independent churches with large missionary budgets, with a strong evangelistic fervor, and also where many of their members are found on the mission field.

Nevertheless, the dominant church today is obviously the Laodicean or apostate church. It can hardly be denied that the majority of churches today have given in to and become a part of the apostasy.

CHAPTER IV

THE SEQUENCE OF PRE-TRIBULATIONAL EVENTS

The Great Tribulation is not imminent. The world stage has to be set in a certain way before the tribulation can actually begin. A number of events are clearly stated to precede the tribulation period. Some of these pre-tribulational events are simply prophesied as occurring some time before the tribulation and are not related to any sequence of events. These will be discussed in the next two chapters. But this chapter is concerned with the sequence of those events which can be traced and lead up to the tribulation. The tribulation will not begin until this sequence of events is completely worked out. Altogether nine such events can be deduced from the Scriptures. On one hand, these events come before the tribulation; but on the other, they consecutively lead up to the tribulation.

A. WORLD WARS I AND II

A question that is raised so many times in prophetic conferences is: *Are we living in the last days*? Invariably the answer is: Yes! But when asked, *How do we know*?, the answers tend to be rather general and usually rest on crises of these present days, and what these crises are change with the times. Often they are determined on the basis of how these crises affect the United States, as if that is the determining factor of what constitutes the last days. In this area many "newspaper exegetes" have had a field day seeing almost every major world event as a partial fulfillment of prophecy and another proof that these are indeed the last days. However, it is very dangerous to spend so much time and so much effort trying to fit so many events into areas of fulfilled prophecy. Prophecy must first be determined from the Scriptures, then applied to current events; rather than current events being taken and forced into some kind of scriptural passage. Only after one's eschatology has been developed exegetically from the Scriptures should current events be taken into account to see if there are any that are fulfilling prophecy. Only if the current events fit the demands of Scripture *perfectly* are these events to be identified as a fulfillment of prophecy. But to go to current events first and then, because of *possible similarities*, begin to identify these as partial fulfillments or as indications of future fulfillments is to engage in "newspaper exegesis" rather than biblical exegesis.

Nevertheless, these are the last days because certain pre-tribulational events have been fulfilled. The first is that of World War I followed by World War II. This is found in Matthew 24:1-8:

And Jesus went out from the temple, and was going on his way; and his disciples came to him to show him the buildings of the temple. But he answered and said unto them, See ye not all these things? verily I say unto you, There shall not be left here one stone upon another, that shall not be thrown down. And as he sat on the mount of Olives, the disciples came unto him privately, saying, Tell us, when shall these things be? and what shall be the sign of thy coming, and of the end of the world? And Jesus answered and said unto them, Take heed that no man lead you astray. For many shall come in my name, saying, I am the Christ; and shall lead many astray. And ye shall hear of wars and rumors of wars; see that ye be not troubled: for these things must needs come to pass; but the end is not yet. For nation shall rise against nation, and kingdom against kingdom; and there shall be famines and earthquakes in divers places. But all these things are the beginning of travail.

The background to this passage is found in verses 1-2. Following the denunciation of the Jewish religious leadership in chapter 23, and as a followup of His statements in 23:37-39, in 24:1-2 Christ pronounced doom on the temple, a prophecy fulfilled in 70 A.D.

This statement aroused questions in the minds of the disciples, and they approached Christ with these three questions: 1) When shall these things be?, i.e., the destruction of the temple spoken of in verses 1-2; 2) What shall be the sign of Thy coming?, and 3) What shall be the sign of the end of the age? The first question is not answered in the Matthew account of the Olivet Discourse, but is found in the parallel passage of Luke 21:20-24. The second question is answered in Matthew 24:29-31.

It is the third question that is of concern here: What shall be the sign of the end of the age? What is the sign that marks that the end days have indeed begun? What is the one single event that will determine that the last days have begun and that we are indeed living in the last days?

This question is answered by Christ, first negatively and then positively. Negatively, he first told them what will not be the sign that the end of the age has begun. This was followed positively by what the sign will indeed be.

Verses 4-6 contain the negative answer. Christ simply described what will be characteristic of this age, and none of these things mean that the end of the age has begun. First, in verses 4-5, the age will be characterized by false messiahs. But the rise of false messiahs in no way proves that the end has begun. Furthermore, in verse 6, local wars in various parts of the world will also characterize this age. But this, too, does not mean that the end of the age has begun. So neither the rise of false messiahs, nor local wars in any part of the world indicate that the end of the age has begun. These are just general characteristics of this age. *For these things must needs come to pass, but the end is not yet.*

The positive side of the answer is in verses 7-8 where Christ revealed the single event that will indicate that the end of the age has begun. This sign is said to be when "nation shall rise against nation, and kingdom against kingdom." This is to be coupled by famines and earthquakes. It is clearly stated that these things are *the beginning of travail.* Throughout the prophetic portions of Scripture, the end days are pictured by the word *travail* which means "birth pang," the pain a woman goes through before giving birth to a baby. Just as a woman goes through a series of birth pangs before giving birth to a child, even so the closing days of this age will go through a series of birth pangs before giving birth to the new age of the kingdom. The use of the word "travail" will be noted a number of times as the prophetic Scriptures are studied in this work.

The key factor then is to find out the meaning of the idiom, "nation shall rise against nation, and kingdom against kingdom." This idiom, taken in the Jewish context of the day when it was spoken, points to a total conflict of the area in view. This idiom is found in two Old Testament passages.

First, it is found in Isaiah 19:1-4:

> The burden of Egypt. Behold, Jehovah rideth upon a swift cloud, and cometh unto Egypt: and the idols of Egypt shall tremble at his presence; and the heart of Egypt shall melt in the midst of it. And I will stir up the Egyptians against the Egyptians: and they shall fight every one against his brother, and every one against his neighbor; city against city, and kingdom against kingdom. And the spirit of Egypt shall fail in the midst of it; and I will destroy the counsel thereof: and they shall seek unto the idols, and to the charmers, and to them that have familiar spirits, and to the wizards. And I will give over the Egyptians into the hand of a cruel lord; and a fierce king shall rule over them, saith the Lord, Jehovah of hosts.

In this passage the land of Egypt is in view and the idiom points to a conflict all over the land of Egypt as the nation is engrossed in civil war.

The second place is in II Chronicles 15:1-7:

> And the Spirit of God came upon Azariah the son of Obed: and he went out to meet Asa, and said unto him, Hear ye me, Asa, and all Judah and Benjamin: Jehovah is with you, while ye are with him; and if ye seek him, he will be found of you; but if ye forsake him, he will forsake you. Now for a long season Israel was without the true God, and without a teaching priest, and without law: but when in their distress they turned unto Jehovah, the God of Israel, and sought him, he was found of them. And in those times there was no peace to him that went out, nor to him that came in; but great vexations were upon all the inhabitants of the lands. And they were broken in pieces, nation against nation, and city against city; for God did vex them with all adversity. But be ye strong, and let not your hands be slack; for your work shall be rewarded.

In this passage it is the Middle East that is in view, and the idiom points to conflict all over the Middle East.

In the Olivet Discourse it is the whole world that is in view, as is clear from verses 14, 21, 30, and 31. Hence, the idiom refers to a world-wide conflict, and this world-wide conflict is the first birth pang signifying that the last days have begun.

In Christ's day the expression of "nation against nation, kingdom against kingdom" was a Jewish idiom of a world war preceding the coming of the Messiah. The *Bereshit Rabbah* states:

> If you shall see kingdoms rising against each other in turn, then give heed and note the footsteps of the Messiah.

The *Zohar Chadash* states:

> At that time wars shall be stirred up in the world. Nation shall be against nation and city against city; much distress shall be renewed against the enemies of the Israelites.

The first time that such a world-wide conflict occurred was in the years 1914-1918 with World War I. Most historians agree that World War II was really a continuation of World War I.

This world-wide conflict that signaled the beginning of the last days was to be coupled with famines and earthquakes. As far as famines are concerned, during the war years of 1918-1919 a pestilence killed 23 million people. In 1920 the great Chinese famine occurred followed by the great Russian famine in 1921.

The earthquake factor is even more interesting. According to the *Encyclopedia Americana*, between the years 63-1896 there were only 26 recorded earthquakes. Most of the world's earthquakes began to occur since 1900. In conjunction with World War I, there were several significant earthquakes: 1905 India—20,000 killed; 1908 Italy—75,000 killed; 1915 Italy—30,000 killed; 1920 China—180,000 killed; 1923 Japan—143,000 killed.

More recent and devastating earthquakes include one in China in 1932 killing 70,000 people; 1935 Italy—60,000 killed; 1939 Chile—30,000 killed. That same year one in Turkey killed 23,000 people. 1960 Morocco—12,000 killed; 1968 Iran—12,000 killed; 1970 Peru—50,000 killed.

There has been a tremendous increase in earthquake activity in conjunction with World War I. The ones listed here are only the major ones with a death rate of 12,000 or more. Added to this are a greater number with smaller death rates.

The first sign or the first birth pang signifying that the last days of the age have begun was to be a world-wide conflict coupled with famines and earthquakes. This was fulfilled in 1914-1918. This also marks the first of the events leading up to the tribulation period.

B. THE RE-ESTABLISHMENT OF ISRAEL

The re-establishment of the Jewish state in 1948 has not only thrown a wrench in amillennial thinking, but it has also thrown a chink in much of premillennial thinking. Amazingly, some premillennialists have concluded that the present state of Israel has nothing to do with the fulfillment of prophecy. For some reason the present state somehow does not fit their scheme of things, and so the present state becomes merely an accident of history. On what grounds is the present state of Israel so dismissed? The issue that bothers so many premillennialists is the fact that not only have the Jews returned in unbelief with regard to the person of Jesus, but the majority of the ones who have returned are not even Orthodox Jews. In fact, the majority are atheists or agnostics. Certainly, then, Israel does not fit in with all those biblical passages dealing with the return. For it is a regenerated nation that the Bible speaks of, and the present state of Israel hardly fits that picture. So on these grounds, the present state is dismissed as not being a fulfillment of prophecy.

However, the real problem is the failure to see that the prophets spoke of two international returns. First, there was to be a regathering in unbelief in preparation for judgment, namely the judgment of the tribulation. This was to be followed by a second world-wide regathering in faith in preparation for blessing, namely the blessings of the messianic age. Once it is recognized that the Bible speaks of two such regatherings, it is easy to see how the present state of Israel fits into prophecy.

One passage clearly dealing with a return in unbelief in preparation for judgment is found in Ezekiel 20:33-38:

> As I live, saith the Lord Jehovah, surely with a mighty hand, and with an outstretched arm, and with wrath poured out, will I be king over you: and I will bring you out from the peoples, and will gather you out of the countries wherein ye are scattered, with a mighty hand, and with an outstretched arm, and with wrath poured out; and I will bring you into the wilderness of the peoples, and there will I enter into judgment with you face to face. Like as I entered into judgment with your fathers in the wilderness of the land of Egypt, so will I enter into judgment with you, saith the Lord Jehovah. And I will cause you to pass under the rod, and I will bring you into the bond of the covenant; and I will purge out from among you the rebels, and them that transgress against me; I will bring them forth out of the land where they sojourn, but they shall not enter into the land of Israel: and ye shall know that I am Jehovah.

In this passage Ezekiel draws a simile between the Exodus and the future return. At the Exodus the entire nation of Israel was brought out of the land of Egypt into the Sinai Peninsula. While in the wilderness of Sinai, God's plan was to give them the law and for them to build the tabernacle. After accomplishing these two things, they were to enter into the promised land. But because of a series of murmurings and rebellions, God finally entered into judgment with His people at a place called Kadesh Barnea. The judgment condemned them to forty years of wandering until the entire generation from the age twenty upward, except for two men, died out in the wilderness. Forty years later a whole new nation, a nation born as free men in the wilderness and not as slaves in Egypt, was able to enter the land under Joshua. Now, according to Ezekiel, a similar thing is to occur in the future. God will first of all regather His people from all over the world where they have been scattered. That this gathering is not in faith, but in unbelief, is seen from the fact that this gathering is "with a mighty hand, and with an outstretched arm, with wrath poured out." This phrase is repeated twice and is found in verses 33 and 34. This regathering in unbelief occurs after wrath has been poured out on the people. It is no accident that out of the fires of the Nazi Holocaust, the State of Israel was born. Once this gathering has taken place, God will enter into judgment with His people, namely the tribulation judgments. By means of these judgments the rebels will be purged out. Then there will be a whole new nation, a regenerated nation, that will be able to enter the messianic land of Israel under King Messiah. But this passage clearly speaks of a regathering in unbelief in preparation for judgment.

Another passage making the same point is found in Ezekiel 22:17-22:

> And the word of Jehovah came unto me, saying, Son of man, the house of Israel is become dross unto me: all of them are brass and tin and iron and lead, in the midst of the furnace; they are the dross of silver. Therefore thus saith the Lord Jehovah: Because ye are all become dross, therefore, behold, I will gather you into the midst of Jerusalem. As they gather silver and brass and iron and lead and tin into the midst of the furnace, to blow the fire upon it, to melt it; so will I gather you in mine anger and in my wrath, and I will lay you there, and melt you. Yea, I will gather you, and blow upon you with the fire of my wrath, and ye shall be melted in the midst thereof. As silver is melted in the midst of the furnace, so shall ye be melted in the midst thereof; and ye shall know that I, Jehovah, have poured out my wrath upon you.

This passage also speaks of a regathering in preparation for judgment. Furthermore, this passage clearly states that this is a regathering in unbelief relating it particularly to Jerusalem.

While primarily dealing with the regeneration of Israel, Ezekiel 36:22-24 nevertheless makes it clear that a regathering takes place before the regeneration:

> Therefore say unto the house of Israel, Thus saith the Lord Jehovah: I do not this for your sake, O house of Israel, but for my holy name, which ye have profaned among the nations, whither ye went. And I will sanctify my great name, which hath been profaned among the nations, which ye have profaned in the midst of them; and the nations shall know that I am Jehovah, saith the Lord Jehovah, when I shall be sanctified in you before their eyes. For I will take you from among the nations, and gather you out of all the countries, and will bring you into your own land.

Another passage dealing with the same question is found in Isaiah 11:11-12:

> And it shall come to pass in that day, that the Lord will set his hand again the second time to recover the remnant of his people, that shall remain, from Assyria, and from Egypt, and from Pathros, and from Cush, and from Elam, and from Shinar, and from Hamath, and from the islands of the sea. And he will set up an ensign for the nations, and will assemble the outcasts of Israel, and gather together the dispersed of Judah from the four corners of the earth.

The regathering spoken of in this passage is the one in faith in preparation for the millennial kingdom. But this regathering in faith is specifically stated to be a *second* international regathering. The question this raises is: when did the first one occur? It cannot refer to the Babylonian return as that was hardly international as the text demands. Hence, the first international regathering is the one which would be in preparation for judgment. Hence, it is clear that this passage speaks of two international regatherings while emphasizing the second one. The second regathering will be in faith but not the first.

So far passages have been shown that speak of a regathering in unbelief in preparation for judgment as over against other passages that speak of a regathering in faith in preparation for blessing. But these passages have not specifically stated that this regathering in unbelief in preparation for judgment will occur before the tribulation period. However, there are other passages that do pinpoint the regathering in unbelief as occurring before the tribulation period.

One such passage is Zephaniah 2:1-2:

> Gather yourselves together, yea, gather together, O nation that hath no shame; before the decree bring forth, before the day pass as the chaff, before the fierce anger of Jehovah come upon you, before the day of Jehovah's anger come upon you.

In the preceding section of Zephaniah 1:14-18, Zephaniah described some features of a time called "the Day of Jehovah," or as other translations have it, "the Day of the Lord." As will be shown in Chapter VIII, this term *always* describes the Great Tribulation. It is the most common Old Testament name for the tribulation.

Then in 2:1-2, Zephaniah speaks of an event that is to occur before the Day of Jehovah begins. In verse one the nation of Israel is told to gather together. It is clear from this verse that this is a gathering in unbelief.

In verse two the word *before* is used three times in relationship to the preceding passage regarding the tribulation. One of these "befores" includes the "before the day of Jehovah" itself. So while other texts speak of a regathering in unbelief in preparation for judgment, this passage clearly states that this regathering in unbelief will occur before the tribulation actually begins.

Another line of evidence can be mentioned at this point, but will be developed in Chapter IX. It concerns the beginning point of the tribulation period. The tribulation begins with the signing of the seven year covenant (and not with the Rapture). This covenant is made between the Antichrist and the leaders of Israel. Therefore, the signing of such a covenant presupposes a Jewish leadership of a Jewish state. Such a Jewish state has to exist before such a covenant can be signed. The tribulation will not begin until the covenant is signed. This demands the existence of a Jewish state before the tribulation.

Thus, 1948 marked another birth pang of the last days. The restoration of the Jewish state is a fulfillment of those prophecies that spoke of a regathering in unbelief in preparation for judgment. It is another event leading up to the tribulation and so sets the stage for several other pre-tribulational events.

C.   JERUSALEM UNDER JEWISH CONTROL

The third pre-tribulational event involves the Jewish control of Jerusalem. The fact that the Jewish state had to exist before the tribulation does not necessarily require the total Jewish control of Jerusalem. After the end of the Israeli War of Independence in 1948-1949, Israeli forces were in control of West Jerusalem, the newer Jewish section. The Old City of Jerusalem (the biblical city) fell into the hands of the Jordanian Legion and was later annexed into the Hashemite Kingdom of Jordan. So Jerusalem became a divided city and remained that way for the next 19 years.

Nevertheless, prophetically speaking, the Old City of Jerusalem had to fall under Jewish control. This can be deduced from the prophecies dealing with the third Jewish temple, sometimes known as the tribulation temple. There are four passages of Scripture that speak of a specific event in relationship to the tribulation temple that will occur in the middle of the tribulation. They are as follows:

And he shall make a firm covenant with many for one week: and in the midst of the week he shall cause the sacrifice and the oblation to cease; and upon the wing of abominations shall come one that maketh desolate; and even unto the full end, and that determined, shall wrath be poured out upon the desolate. (Daniel 9:27).

When therefore ye see the abomination of desolation, which was spoken of through Daniel the prophet, standing in the holy place (let him that readeth understand). (Matthew 24:15).

Let no man beguile you in any wise: for it will not be, except the falling away come first, and the man of sin be revealed, the son of perdition, he that opposeth and exalteth himself against all that is called God or that is worshipped; so that he sitteth in the temple of God, setting himself forth as God. (II Thessalonians 2:3-4).

And there was given me a reed like unto a rod: and one said, Rise, and measure the temple of God, and the altar, and them that worship therein. And the court which is without the temple leave without, and measure it not; for it hath been given unto the nations: and the holy city shall they tread under foot forty and two months. (Revelation 11:1-2).

All these passages speak of the third Jewish temple, namely the tribulation temple. More will be said concerning the tribulation temple in the next chapter. But for now, suffice it to say that the Jewish temple will be rebuilt and will begin to function again, for these verses view the Jewish temple as having been rebuilt and functioning. All these verses also presuppose Jewish control of the temple compound, and that presupposes Jewish control of the Old City of Jerusalem.

While none of these passages spell out a time factor as to when this was to occur, it was clearly fulfilled in the Six Day War and thus became the third birth pang. While the Six Day War itself was never predicted in the Scriptures, what it accomplished certainly was. The Six Day War brought about the fulfillment of the prophecy regarding the Jewish control of the Old City of Jerusalem. This is the third major pre-tribulational event.

While the first three of these events have already been fulfilled and are now a part of history, the next six pre-tribulational events are all future.

D. THE RUSSIAN INVASION OF ISRAEL — EZEKIEL 38:1-39:16

Ezekiel 38:1-39:16 describes an invasion of Israel from the north and the subsequent destruction of the invading forces once they reach the area of the "mountains of Israel." It will first be necessary to look at the details of this invasion and then deal with the controversial question as to *when* this invasion will take place. The passage will be approached with the questions of who, where, why, what, how, and when. Concerning *who,* in Ezekiel 38:1-6 the prophet named the peoples involved in this invasion:

> And the word of Jehovah came unto me, saying, Son of man, set thy face toward Gog, of the land of Magog, the prince of Rosh, Meshech, and Tubal, and prophesy against him, and say, Thus saith the Lord Jehovah: Behold, I am against thee, O Gog, prince of Rosh, Meshech, and Tubal: and I will turn thee about, and put hooks into thy jaws, and I will bring thee forth, and all thine army, horses and horsemen, all of them clothed in full armor, a great company with buckler and shield, all of them handling swords; Persia, Cush, and Put with them, all of them with shield and helmet; Gomer, and all his hordes; the house of Togarmah in the uttermost parts of the north, and all his hordes; even many peoples with thee.

In verses 1-4 attention is centered on *Gog,* leader of the *land of Magog.* He is the prince of *Rosh, Meshech,* and *Tubal.* Who Gog will be can only be determined at the time of the invasion for "Gog" is not a proper name but a title for the ruler of Magog just as the terms pharoah, kaiser, and czar were titles for rulers and not proper names. Whoever is ruling this alliance at the time of the invasion will be Ezekiel's Gog. The identification of Magog, Rosh, Meshech, and Tubal is to be determined from the fact that these tribes of the ancient world occupied the areas of modern day Russia. Magog, Meshech and Tubal were between the Black and Caspian Seas which today is southern Russia. The tribes of Meshech and Tubal later gave names to cities that today bear the names of Moscow, the capital, and Tobolsk, a major city in the Urals in Siberia. Rosh was in what is now northern Russia. The name *Rosh* is the basis for the modern name *Russia.* These names, then, cover the modern territories of northern and southern Russia in Europe and Siberia to the east in Asia. The modern nation of the Soviet Union encompasses all these areas of Ezekiel.

As if to avoid any further possible doubt, verse six adds that these come from *the uttermost parts of the north.* This is repeated in 38:15 and 39:2. From Israel the uttermost parts of the north is Russia with Moscow being almost a straight line due north from Jerusalem.

Hence, Russia is the leader of the northern confederacy with Gog as the leader of Russia.

But Russia is not alone in the invasion of Israel. She is part of a confederacy and the leader of it. Other nations involved are listed in verses 5-6.

Involved in the confederacy is Persia or present day Iran. Though Iran has generally been pro-western and pro-Israel, this must eventually change.*

Another nation involved is called Cush. There were two places

---

* Written before the Khomeini Islamic revolution. As of now Iran is anti-western and anti-Israel but not as yet within the Russian sphere of influence.

that had that name. One was in Mesopotamia (Genesis 2:13). But all other usages of this word refer to Ethiopia. While current events tempt us to identify it with the Mesopotamian countries of Syria and Iraq, consistency with the usage of the word Cush elsewhere in the Scriptures demands its identification with Ethiopia. Current events must never be the means of interpreting the Scriptures, but, rather, the Scriptures must interpret current events.

Put is mentioned next, and this is not Libya for which the name Lub would be used, but Somaliland or Somalia. Somalia borders Ethiopia.

This is followed by Gomer, located in present-day Germany. The last name is Togarmah, which is present-day Armenia and is totally within Russia. Verse six adds the phrase "even many peoples with thee." This phrase may simply define the numbers of the nations already mentioned, or it may include other nations not mentioned. In all probability, it is the former that is meant. In answer as to *who* is involved in this confederacy, it is the Soviet Union and the allied states of Iran, Ethiopia, Somalia, Germany, and Armenia.* One interesting point is that not a single Arab nation participates in this invasion.

The cup of iniquity of the Soviet Union is almost full. With this invasion it will overflow, and this will precipitate God's judgment on the Soviets. It is God who is in control; it is He that is bringing about the invasion. Thus, while studying this passage, one should note the sovereignty of God in this invasion. This will be the means by which God will punish the Soviets for their sins.

The next section of this passage, 38:7-9, answers the question as to *where* the invasion takes place:

Be thou prepared, yea, prepare thyself, thou, and all thy companies that are assembled unto thee, and be thou a guard unto them. After many days thou shalt be visited: in the latter years thou shalt come into the land that is brought back from the sword, that is gathered out of many peoples, upon the mountains of Israel, which have been a continual waste; but it is brought forth out of the peoples, and they shall dwell securely, all of them. And thou shalt ascend, thou shalt come like a storm, thou shalt be like a cloud to cover the land, thou, and all thy hordes, and many peoples with thee.

---

* While present events concerning these nations appear to be lining them up in such a confederacy, such current events may quickly change. It is too early to say "this is it." It is necessary to wait for exact fulfillment before identifying fulfillment.

This passage continues to address Gog as the leader of this confederacy (verse 7). In verse eight the specific place where the invasion takes place is stated to be the land of Israel, more specifically in the mountains of Israel. Then verse nine describes the massiveness of the invasion picturing it as a storm cloud that covers the entire land.

This is another passage that shows the necessity of the establishment of the Jewish state and also a regathering in unbelief. Israel had to be a state before this invasion could occur. Regardless of one's viewpoint as to when this invasion occurs, each viewpoint does require the pre-existence of the Jewish state. Furthermore, Israel in this passage is regathered in unbelief, for only after the invasion do many in Israel turn to the Lord. So yet another passage demands a restored Jewish state in unbelief. Verse eight describes this Jewish state as being first, a land brought back from the sword; secondly, a land that is gathered out of many peoples; thirdly, a land with mountains that have been a continual waste; and, fourthly, a land that is brought forth out of the peoples. All these statements are true of present-day Israel. This began occurring toward the end of the nineteenth century culminating with statehood in 1948. Since then, the "waste places" have been rebuilt and resettled on a more massive scale.

The next section in 38:10-13 answers the question as to *why* does this invasion take place on the part of Russia:

> Thus saith the Lord Jehovah: It shall come to pass in that day, that things shall come into thy mind, and thou shalt devise an evil device: and thou shalt say, I will go up to the land of unwalled villages; I will go to them that are at rest, that dwell securely, all of them dwelling without walls, and having neither bars nor gates; to take the spoil and to take the prey; to turn thy hand against the waste places that are now inhabited, and against the people that are gathered out of the nations, that have gotten cattle and goods, that dwell in the middle of the earth. Sheba, and Dedan, and the merchants of Tarshish, with all the young lions thereof, shall say unto thee, Art thou come to take the spoil? hast thou assembled thy company to take the prey? to carry away silver and gold, to take away cattle and goods, to take great spoil?

The key reason for the Russian invasion is the matter of "spoil." Exactly what Israel has that Russia would want is not spelled out in the text. The text simply mentions *cattle and goods* and *silver and gold*, but these are general Old Testament references for spoils of war. Much speculation has been involved in what it is that Israel has that Russia would want. One of the more popular reasons given is that of the Dead Sea, which contains 45 billion tons of sodium, chlorine, sulphur, potassium, calcium, magnesium, and bromide. But Russia could also obtain the Dead Sea by invading Jordan.

Another reason centers on the oil crisis with the abundance of oil in the Middle East. The purpose of the invasion might be to gain a solid foothold in the Middle East. A Russian takeover of Israel would give Russia such a foothold without overly upsetting the Arabs, as they would be in favor of the destruction of Israel even if it means a Russian army in the area.

However, the text itself is silent as to the content of the spoils, but for the spoils Russia invades. Whatever Russia's publicly-stated reasons for this invasion may be, the actual reason will be Russia's own self-interest. It is stated in verse 10 that the invasion is premeditated by the Soviets, for they "devise an evil device" and resolve to invade for the purpose of spoils (verses 11-12).

In verse 13, a second group of nations is listed as protesting this invasion, for they recognize it to be an invasion for spoil and for nothing else. Sheba and Dedan are countries in northern Arabia, which shows that at least some of the Arab states will not favor the Russian presence in the Middle East. Another nation named is Tarshish, followed by the phrase "with all the young lions thereof." This phrase is a Hebrew idiom meaning nations that have come out of Tarshish. The Revised Standard Version translates the idiom as *all its villages*, and it is close to the mark. But while the idiom is clear, the real issue is the identity of Tarshish from which the other nations come. Three such places are known as Tarshish in history. One was located on the east coast of Africa, but the exact location is unknown. Nor has that particular area spawned other nations. The second place was in Spain, founded by the city of Tyre. If this is the Tarshish of Ezekiel, the nations spawned would include Central and South America. The third location was in England, and if this is what was meant by Tarshish, it would include the United States of America, Canada, Australia, and other present-day western democracies. It might include the British Commonwealth of Nations. If any conclusion can be reached on Ezekiel's usage elsewhere, the identification would have to be Spain and the Spanish world of the western hemisphere. As Spain was somewhat involved in settling and discovering the North American coastline, it could include the United States. But, historically, Spain cannot really be credited with the United States as can England.

Regardless of the exact identity of Tarshish, it is this group that issues a protest. However, it does not go beyond the protest stage. Russia succeeds in invading, and the invading army is, then, disposed of with no help from the protestors.

In Ezekiel 38:14-16, the invasion is seen as having begun and further answers the question as to *why*, but this time it is seen from God's viewpoint:

> Therefore, son of man, prophesy, and say unto Gog, Thus saith the Lord
> Jehovah: In that day when my people Israel dwelleth securely, shalt thou
> not know it? And thou shalt come from thy place out of the uttermost
> parts of the north, thou, and many peoples with thee, all of them riding
> upon horses, a great company and a mighty army; and thou shalt come
> up against my people Israel, as a cloud to cover the land: it shall come to
> pass in the latter days, that I will bring thee against my land, that the
> nations may know me, when I shall be sanctified in thee, O Gog, before
> their eyes.

In verses 14-16a the invasion begins and the confederate army
covers the land like a storm cloud in massive swarms. Hence, there is
initial success on the part of Russia. In verse 16b God's reason is
given for allowing this invasion to occur, as over against Russia's
reasons given in the preceding verses. God's reason is that He might
be sanctified in the eyes of the nations in light of what is about to
occur.

Having described God's purpose, the answer to the questions of
what and *how* are answered in 38:17-23.

> Thus saith the Lord Jehovah: Art thou he of whom I spake in old time by
> my servants the prophets of Israel, that prophesied in those days for
> many years that I would bring thee against them? And it shall come to
> pass in that day, when Gog shall come against the land of Israel, saith the
> Lord Jehovah, that my wrath shall come up into my nostrils. For in my
> jealousy and in the fire of my wrath have I spoken, Surely in that day
> there shall be a great shaking in the land of Israel; so that the fishes of the
> sea, and the birds of the heavens, and the beasts of the field, and all
> creeping things that creep upon the earth, and all the men that are upon
> the face of the earth, shall shake at my presence, and the mountains shall
> be thrown down, and the steep places shall fall, and every wall shall fall to
> the ground. And I will call for a sword against him unto all my mountains,
> saith the Lord Jehovah: every man's sword shall be against his brother.
> And with pestilence and with blood will I enter into judgment with him;
> and I will rain upon him, and upon his hordes, and upon the many
> peoples that are with him, an overflowing shower, and great hailstones,
> fire, and brimstone. And I will magnify myself, and sanctify myself, and I
> will make myself known in the eyes of many nations; and they shall know
> that I am Jehovah.

As to the question of *what*, with the Russian invasion of Israel,
the cup of iniquity is full, for the apple of God's eye is touched
arousing God's anger so that He moves out in judgment (verses 17-18),
to destroy the invading army. This is followed by the answer to the
question of *how* the invading army is disposed of and destroyed.
Several causes are listed: earthquake (verses 19-20); civil war breaking
out among the invading soldiers themselves (verse 21); pestilence,
blood, flood, hailstones, fire, and brimstone (verse 22). Since these
things totally destroy the invading army without the aid of other

nations, God's purpose is seen as succeeding in its objective. God is indeed sanctified in the eyes of many people (verse 23).

Ezekiel 39:1-16 follows the law of recurrence (see Chapter I) giving further details to the information found in chapter 38. In 39:1-5 there is a further description of the invasion and its subsequent destruction:

> And thou, son of man, prophesy against Gog, and say, Thus saith the Lord Jehovah: Behold, I am against thee, O Gog, prince of Rosh, Meshech, and Tubal: and I will turn thee about, and will lead thee on, and will cause thee to come up from the uttermost parts of the north; and I will bring thee upon the mountains of Israel; and I will smite thy bow out of thy left hand, and will cause thine arrows to fall out of thy right hand. Thou shalt fall upon the mountains of Israel, thou, and all thy hordes, and the peoples that are with thee: I will give thee unto the ravenous birds of every sort, and to the beasts of the field to be devoured. Thou shalt fall upon the open field; for I have spoken it, saith the Lord Jehovah.

The new information added is found in verses two and four where the armies are said to fall specifically on the mountains of Israel. They extend the length of the center of the country beginning at the southern point of the Valley of Jezreel at the town of Jenin in Galilee and continue south until they peter out at a point north of Beersheba in the Negev. These mountains contain the famous cities of Shechem, Samaria, Bethlehem, Hebron, and most important, Jerusalem, which seems to be the goal of this invading army.

Here is another example where the Six Day War has set the stage for the fulfillment of prophecy. Up to the Six Day War in 1967 all of the mountains of Israel, except for a small corridor of West Jerusalem, were entirely in the hands of the Jordanian Arabs. Only since 1967 have the mountains of Israel been in Israel, thus setting the stage for the fulfillment of this prophecy.

Another thing to notice is the mistranslation found in the King James Version of verse two. The King James Version indicates that one-sixth of the invading army is left alive. This is not found in the Hebrew text and has not been translated that way by subsequent translations. It is not true that one-sixth of the invading army will be left alive. The entire invading army will be destroyed when they invade Israel and nothing will remain, not even one-sixth.

In Ezekiel 39:6 another dimension is added to the Russian invasion:

> And I will send a fire on Magog, and on them that dwell securely in the isles; and they shall know that I am Jehovah.

Not only is the Soviet and allied army destroyed in Israel, but the land of Russia itself is devastated by the raining of brimstone causing much destruction in the nation itself. It will cause Russia to cease being a political force in world affairs.

Ezekiel 39:7-8 adds that not only will God's name be sanctified among the Gentile nations, but in Israel as well:

> And my holy name will I make known in the midst of my people Israel; neither will I suffer my holy name to be profaned any more: and the nations shall know that I am Jehovah, the Holy One in Israel. Behold, it cometh, and it shall be done, saith the Lord Jehovah; this is the day whereof I have spoken.

Thus, a revival occurs in Israel causing many Jews to turn to the Lord.

The rest of the section provides the grand finale of the invasion. In 39:9-10 it states that it will take seven years to dismantle all the military equipment left behind:

> And they that dwell in the cities of Israel shall go forth, and shall make fires of the weapons and burn them, both the shields and the bucklers, the bows and the arrows, and the handstaves, and the spears, and they shall make fires of them seven years; so that they shall take no wood out of the field, neither cut down any out of the forests; for they shall make fires of the weapons; and they shall plunder those that plundered them, and rob those that robbed them, saith the Lord Jehovah.

Finally, in 39:11-16 there is a description of the burying of the dead for seven months:

> And it shall come to pass in that day, that I will give unto Gog a place for burial in Israel, the valley of them that pass through on the east of the sea; and it shall stop them that pass through: and there shall they bury Gog and all his multitude; and they shall call it The valley of Hamon-gog. And seven months shall the house of Israel be burying them, that they may cleanse the land. Yea, all the people of the land shall bury them; and it shall be to them a renown in the day that I shall be glorified, saith the Lord Jehovah. And they shall set apart men of continual employment, that shall pass through the land, and, with them that pass through, those that bury them that remain upon the face of the land, to cleanse it: after the end of seven months shall they search. And they that pass through the land shall pass through; and when any seeth a man's bone, then shall he set up a sign by it, till the buriers have buried it in the valley of Hamon-gog. And Hamonah shall also be the name of a city. Thus shall they cleanse the land.

The burial place will be in one of the valleys east of the Mediterranean Sea (verse 11) and will be renamed accordingly. It will take seven months to accomplish the job (verses 12-13). Since the armies are destroyed in the mountains of Israel, many of the bodies will fall in crevices where they will not be easily found. And so special details will be employed by the government for the seven months to search out these bodies for burial in the special valley (verses 14-15). Overlooking the cemetery a new city will be built and named Hamonah (multitude) (verse 16).

These seven months of burying and seven years of burning are crucial in determining *when* this invasion occurs. For any view to be correct it must satisfy the requirements of these seven months and seven years.

The most controversial question is *when*; when in the chronology of prophecy will this event occur? It is obvious from where the event is placed in this work that the author views the Russian invasion as taking place some time *before* the tribulation.

In determining the issue of when, certain clues are to be found in the text. In 38:8, 11-12, and 14, the invasion takes place when, (1) Israel is a state again; (2) the waste places of past centuries are again inhabited; (3) Israel is dwelling in unwalled villages, a good description of present-day kibbutzim; and (4) Israel is dwelling securely. As will be shown later, nowhere in the entire text does it speak of Israel as living in peace. Rather Israel is merely living in security which means "confidence," regardless of whether it is during a state of war or peace.

There is nothing in the various descriptions of Israel given in this passage that is not true of Israel today. So, as far as where Israel stands today, she completely fulfills all the requirements given in the description of Israel in this passage. From this standpoint, the invasion can occur at any time, including some time before the tribulation.

Furthermore, there is the problem of the seven years and the seven months which must be taken into account in resolving the issue of when.

There are four major views as to when this invasion will occur. The opposing views will be looked at first along with their basis followed by the objections against their views. Then, in conclusion, reasons will be given as to why this invasion would best be viewed as occurring before the tribulation period. Objections to this view will be answered.

The *first* view held by some key prophetic Bible teachers puts this invasion in the middle of the tribulation period. There is a two-fold basis for this position. First, the dwelling securely is said to refer to a time of peace resulting from Israel's covenant with the Antichrist in Daniel 9:27. Secondly, this invasion is viewed as being the same as that of "the king of the north" in Daniel 11:40.

However, there are objections to this view. First, "to dwell securely," as will be shown later, does not necessarily have to indicate peace. Secondly, it is hard to see why God would intervene at this point on Israel's behalf and then immediately allow the events of the second half of the tribulation to commence, doing a great amount of damage to Israel. Thirdly, it is agreed with those holding this position that the events described in Daniel 11:40 take place in the middle of the tribulation. But it is wrong to identify *the king of the north* of Daniel 11:40 with Gog of Ezekiel 38:1-39:16. Throughout the book of Daniel references are made to *the king of the south* and *the king of the north*. Consistently, the former is applied to Egypt, including the reference in verse 40. The latter is consistently applied to Syria. Except that when the exponents of this view come to verse 40, they ascribe the reference to Russia and so identify it with Ezekiel 38 and 39. However, context and consistency would demand that the reference apply to Syria. The invasion of Daniel 11:40 is distinct from the Ezekiel 38 and 39 invasion. It is inconsistent and faulty exegesis to make the king of the north throughout the book of Daniel refer to Syria and yet make 11:40 be the one exception in order to connect it with the Russian invasion and put the latter at the middle of the tribulation.

Fourthly, this view fails to solve the problem of the seven months and seven years. This view would require that the seven months of burying take place during the second half of the tribulation, a time when the Jews are in flight and are not able to bury their own dead, let alone those of the Russians. In the chapter dealing with the events of the middle of the tribulation, the Jewish situation will be discussed in greater detail. The state of the Jews in the middle of the tribulation will not permit seven months of burial and building a new city, too. Regarding the seven years of burning, this view would require the Jews to be burning weapons during the second half of the tribulation when Jews are fleeing out of the land. They would also have to continue burning them for 3½ years into the millennium, which is inconsistent with Messiah's cleansing of the land and the renovation which results. The problems the Jews will face during the second half of the tribulation would cause them to try to preserve and salvage these weapons rather than to burn them.

A *second* major view is that this invasion will take place at the end of the tribulation period. The key basis of this position is identifying this invasion along with the Campaign of Armageddon. Since the Campaign of Armageddon does indeed take place at the end of the tribulation and since Ezekiel 38 and 39 are viewed as being part of it by those who hold this view, they have concluded that the Russian invasion will occur at the end of the tribulation.

However, there are a number of problems in this view. The key objection lies in the clear distinction between the Ezekiel 38 and 39 invasion and Armageddon. First, in Ezekiel there are definite allies mentioned and they are limited in number while other nations stand in opposition. In the Campaign of Armageddon all nations are allied together against Jerusalem without exception. Secondly, the Ezekiel invasion comes from the north, but the Armageddon invasion comes from the whole earth. Thirdly, the purpose of the Russian invasion is to take the spoil; the purpose of the Armageddon Campaign is to destroy all the Jews. Fourthly, in the Ezekiel invasion there is a protest against the invasion; in the Armageddon Campaign there is no protest since all the nations are involved. Fifthly, the Ezekiel invasion is destroyed through convulsions of nature; the Armageddon invasion is destroyed by the personal second coming of Jesus Christ. Sixthly, the Ezekiel invasion is destroyed on the mountains of Israel; the Armageddon Campaign is destroyed in the area between Petra and Jerusalem. Seventh, the Russian invasion takes place while Israel is living securely in the land; but the Armageddon Campaign takes place while Israel is in flight and in hiding.

Furthermore, this view fails to solve the problem of the seven months and seven years, since both would have to continue into the millennium to be accomplished. Again, this is inconsistent with other revelation regarding the kingdom.

A *third* major view is to put this invasion in the interlude between the tribulation and the millennium. The basis of this position is the assumption that there is to be a period of time after the second coming of Christ and after Israel is restored but before the actual kingdom is set up.

But there are objections to this view. First, this view is based on the assumption of a period of time between the second coming and the establishment of the millennial kingdom. The fact that there will be an interlude is easily accepted, since there are a number of things which need to be accomplished before the actual institution of the millennium, such as the judgment of the Gentiles, the resurrection of the Old Testament and tribulation saints, etc. There will, indeed, be an interlude. But the problem is that, if this view is to be consistent, it must make this interlude seven years long. However, Daniel 12:12 limits the interlude to just 75 days. Daniel 12:7 states that the latter half of the tribulation will be 1,260 days long which is the same as saying 3½ years. Daniel 12:11 states that there will be a total of 1,290 days during which time the temple will be desecrated. In other words, the temple's desecration will extend 30 days beyond the 3½ year period. However, in Daniel 12:12 those who manage to make it to the 1,335th day are promised a unique blessing which could hardly be anything else but the millennium. That many will not make it to this day is clear from other Scriptures, since they are killed in the interlude. But, the interlude is limited to 75 days only, and this is not enough time for all the events of Ezekiel to transpire.

Secondly, the main problem with this view is that it fails to give a satisfactory answer to the problem of the seven months and seven years. Seven months of burial is a total of 210 days. This would mean that the burial would continue for at least 135 days into the millennium depending on when during the interlude the invasion takes place. This is not consistent with the mass of Scripture describing the millennium and Israel. Added to this are the seven years of the burning of the weapons which makes this view impossible.

A *fourth* major view puts it at the end of the millennium. The key basis of this view is to identify this invasion as the same as that mentioned in Revelation 20:7-9.

But there are two key objections to this view. First, the Ezekiel invasion comes from the north; the Revelation invasion comes from all over the world. Secondly, this view also fails to answer the problem of the seven months and the seven years. This earth is done away with soon after the invasion mentioned in Revelation, not allowing any time (or place!) for seven months of burial or seven years of burning. It would require the burying and burning to continue into the Eternal Order.

The *fifth* major view, which is the view of this author, is that the Russian invasion will occur before the tribulation actually begins. From the text of Ezekiel 38:1-39:16, this view arrives at certain conclusions. First, Israel is established before the tribulation and is dwelling securely. Secondly, the Soviet confederacy invades Israel during this time of security before the tribulation. Thirdly, the confederacy is destroyed in Israel before the tribulation.

There are several points supporting this view. First, the description of Israel found in this passage fits well with the nation as she is now, established before the tribulation. Israel is a land brought back from the sword (38:8). After 1900 years, 46 invasions, the War of Independence, the land is Jewish again and free from foreign domination. This nation is gathered from many nations and peoples (38:8, 12). The Jews in Israel today come from 80-90 different nations. The continual waste places are now inhabited (38:8, 12). The Israelis today are rebuilding the ancient places and turning them into modern towns and cities. They dwell securely (38:11, 14). This has often been misconstrued as meaning a state of peace. But this is not the meaning of the Hebrew root *batach*. The nominal form of this root means "security." This is not the security due to a state of peace, but a security due to confidence in their own strength. This, too, is a good description of Israel today. The Israeli army has fought four wars since its founding and won them swiftly each time. Today Israel is secure, confident that her army can repel any invasion from the Arab states. Hence, Israel is dwelling securely. Israel is dwelling in unwalled villages (38:11). This is very descriptive of the present-day kibbutzim in Israel.

Secondly, Russia today is a first-rate world power before the tribulation. Her rise to this position coincided with the re-establishment of Israel following World War II.

Thirdly, this view best answers the problem of the seven months and seven years. Putting this invasion in the *beginning of the tribulation* presents no real problem with the seven months, but it does have problems with the seven years. This would put it at a time when Israel would be in flight and would not have time to finish the burning of the weapons. *The middle of the tribulation view* has problems with both the seven months and the seven years. The seven months would extend into the second half of the tribulation, a time when Israel has to worry about her own dead, let alone the Russians. The seven years would extend throughout the rest of the tribulation and 3½ years into the millennium, making it inconsistent with the biblical view of the millennium. Furthermore, Israel would need these weapons in the second half of the tribulation. *The end of the tribulation view* has problems with both the seven months and the seven years, since both would extend into the millennium. *The interlude view* or *beginning of the millennium view* has problems with both the seven months and the seven years, since both would extend into the millennium due to the fact that the interlude is only 75 days. *The end of the millennium view* has problems with both the seven months and the seven years. The seven months of burial seem pointless when there is a resurrection after the invasion. The seven years would have to extend into the Eternal Order, an impossibility since there is a whole new earth created. Therefore, the *before the tribulation view* is the only one which has no problems with either the seven months or the seven years. The Jews continue to dwell in the land after this invasion and remain there until the middle of the tribulation. Hence, the seven months of burial is no problem. The seven years also create no problem since they would begin before the tribulation and can extend as far as the middle of the tribulation if at all necessary. According to this view, this invasion must take place at least 3½ years or more before the tribulation starts.

These are the strengths of this particular view. However, there are objections raised to this particular view, and these will now have to be answered.

One objection states that the Ezekiel 38 and 39 passage is in the restoration section of Ezekiel. The answer is that this is true, but which restoration? the partial in unbelief? or the final in faith? It would seem to be the partial one in unbelief. Faith begins in Israel only after this invasion. The chronology of the book of Ezekiel would hardly be a problem for this view. The restoration in faith is covered by Ezekiel 40-48.

A *second* objection, and the one most commonly used, is that the "dwelling safely" or "securely" as used in the Old Testament always refers to millennial peace and security—something that Israel will not receive before the tribulation. However, this is an overstatement. While it is true that the term "dwell securely" is used of life in the millennium, this is only true of the minority of cases and not at all true of the majority. A list of references where this is not true includes: Leviticus 25:18, 19, 26:5; Deuteronomy 12:10; I Samuel 12:11; I Kings 4:25; Psalm 4:8, 16:9; Proverbs 1:33, 3:23, 29; Isaiah 47:8; Jeremiah 49:31 and Zephaniah 2:15. The Jeremiah reference is particularly significant since it uses the very same phrases that are found in Ezekiel 38:11. This phrase is used more in non-millennial contexts than in millennial ones.

A *third* objection states that this destroys the doctrine of imminency. This objection is strictly a straw-man argument. Stating that something must precede the tribulation is *not* the same as stating that it must precede the Rapture unless it is further stated that the Rapture begins the tribulation. However, the act that begins the tribulation is not the Rapture but the signing of the seven year covenant and nothing else. The pre-tribulation view asserts that the invasion will occur before the signing of the seven year covenant. This does not destroy any argument of imminency, because the Rapture may still come even before this. This view does not state that this invasion will occur before the Rapture, it only asserts that this invasion will occur before the tribulation. The Rapture is both imminent and pre-tribulational. All this means is that the Rapture can occur at any time between now and the signing of the seven year covenant. It does not mean that the Rapture begins the tribulation. So then, to say that the invasion takes place before the tribulation does not destroy imminency since it is not the Rapture which begins the tribulation. Another way of showing this is to use these questions: Could the Rapture have come before 1948? The answer is yes, because the Rapture is imminent. However, could the tribulation have come before 1948? The answer is no, because there was no Jewish state and government to sign the covenant which would begin the tribulation. Believing that Israel had to be established before the tribulation was never an argument against imminency. Neither is the belief that the invasion comes before the tribulation an argument against imminency. The author of this book holds to a pre-tribulation Rapture and believes that the Rapture is imminent. Believing that the Russian invasion also occurs before the tribulation in no way destroys the argument of imminency for it is *not* the Rapture which begins the tribulation.

A *fourth* objection states: How could Israel apostatize so soon again after the nation has had a revival? But the real problem is why this should even be a problem. This was often true in Old Testament history. There was speedy apostasy of Israel following the various miracles of the Exodus and the recognition of God at Sinai. There was a speedy apostasy at Ninevah after the city repented under Jonah. This has happened before, and there is no problem with it happening again.

A *fifth* objection states that this event happens in the latter days and years. But these terms simply apply to the whole period of the end times when prophecy is again being fulfilled, and so it can very easily apply to the closing days of the Church Age as well. However, this objection is really based on the faulty assumption that this view holds to a pre-Rapture position, which is not true. This is a position of a pre-tribulation invasion, but not a pre-Rapture invasion.

A *sixth* and final objection states that Israel will not gain any title to the land nor have the right to return till she signs the covenant with the Antichrist. Building on this statement, those who hold this opinion go on to state that this view would have to say that the covenant is signed before the Rapture. The latter is still based on the confusion as to what this view actually states. It has already been shown that this view does *not* state that the invasion comes before the Rapture. Actually this objection is a little ridiculous. In what possible way could the covenant with the Antichrist give the Jews the right to return that the United Nations did not? Israel already possesses the title of the land and has possessed it since God made His covenant with Abraham. Furthermore, the United Nations recognized Israel in 1948, and Jews have had the right to return since then. And Jews are returning. Israel's right to return will not be based on her covenant with the Antichrist any more than it is based on the full recognition by the United Nations. Israel's title to the land is based on the Abrahamic Covenant. The Scriptures predict a regathering before the tribulation in unbelief in preparation for judgment. It is God who is doing the moving, and it is God who is bringing the Jews back into the land, and this is enough for Israel's right to the land. A covenant with the Antichrist will hardly give Israel the right to return. Israel is back in the land before the tribulation, and hence, this invasion could take place before the tribulation.

So from all these facts, this author concludes that the pre-tribulational view is by far the best view. The Russian invasion is another birth pang that will occur before the tribulation begins.

E. THE ONE WORLD GOVERNMENT

The next three events leading up to the tribulation are to be picked up from the previous study of the Times of the Gentiles. These events are all to be found in Daniel 7:23-24:

> Thus he said, The fourth beast shall be a fourth kingdom upon earth, which shall be diverse from all the kingdoms, and shall devour the whole

earth, and shall tread it down, and break it in pieces. And as for the ten horns, out of this kingdom shall ten kings arise: and another shall arise after them; and he shall be diverse from the former, and he shall put down three kings.

The fifth birth pang leading up to the tribulation is the development of a one world government (verse 23). The fourth Gentile empire was to continue until it eventually devours the whole world. The Roman Empire is hardly a fulfillment of this prophecy, nor can refuge be sought in stating that Rome conquered all of the then *known* world, for this, too, is untrue. Reasons for this were given in Chapter II.

Reviewing from the study on the times of the Gentiles, the fourth Gentile Empire of Imperialism, after the first stage of the Roman Empire, eventually split into an east-west division. The east-west axis is a balance of power. The eastern balance of power is now centered in Russia and the communist block of nations while the western balance of power is with the democracies.

But some day this east-west division will give way to a one world government. In light of Ezekiel 38:1-39:16, the eastern balance of power will collapse with the fall of the Russian forces in Israel and the destruction of Russia itself. With the eastern power destroyed, this will open the way for a one world government.

As to the exact nature of this government, nothing is stated. It will be a form of imperialism of course, but whether this will be in the form of the United Nations or the form of a select leadership is unknown. But that this one world government will occur and *devour the whole world* is clear. This will be the fifth birth pang.

F. THE TEN KINGDOMS

This one world government will eventually split up into ten kingdoms according to Daniel 7:24a.

And as for the ten horns, out of this kingdom shall ten kings arise . . .

In recent years much speculation has centered on the European Common Market. According to the usual scenario portrayed, there is to be a revival of the old Roman Empire composed of a confederacy of ten European states.

Eschatology based on "newspaper exegesis" attempts to prove itself from current events. But the Scriptures do not speak of this in this fashion. Textually, after the world falls under the one world government, then and only then does the one world government split up into ten kingdoms. But these ten kingdoms cover the whole world, and not Europe alone. The sixth birth pang will be this division of the one world empire into ten kingdoms with ten kings who will rule the world. At best, the Common Market might become one of the ten, but could hardly become all ten.

Beginning before the tribulation, this ten kingdom stage will continue into the middle of the tribulation, and it will be the sixth birth pang.

G.   THE RISE OF THE ANTICHRIST

Following the division of the world into ten kingdoms, the Antichrist will begin his rise to power in Daniel 7:24b:

> . . . and another shall arise after them; and he shall be diverse from the former, and he shall put down three kings.

That there was to be a revelation of the identity of the Antichrist before the tribulation is clear from II Thessalonians 2:1-3:

> Now we beseech you, brethren, touching the coming of our Lord Jesus Christ, and our gathering together unto him; to the end that ye be not quickly shaken from your mind, nor yet be troubled, either by spirit, or by word, or by epistle as from us, as that the day of the Lord is just at hand; let no man beguile you in any wise: for it will not be, except the falling away come first, and the man of sin be revealed, the son of perdition.

In this passage, two events are said to occur before *the Day of the Lord*, which always refers to the tribulation. The first is the apostasy which was discussed earlier. The second is *the revelation of the man of sin and the son of perdition*. This revelation as to the identity of the Antichrist will come before the tribulation, and it will come at the time after the world has been divided into ten kingdoms. It will be the seventh birth pang.*

Exactly how the Antichrist will be identified is not stated. Perhaps it will be determined by the numerical value of his name (to be discussed in Chapter XI) or by some other means. But he will be known. The Antichrist's rise to power before the tribulation is a biblical necessity. Since the tribulation begins with the signing of the seven year covenant between Israel and the Antichrist, it is necessary for the Antichrist to be in sufficient political power to sign such a covenant.

H.   THE PERIOD OF PEACE AND FALSE SECURITY

Another event leading up to the tribulation is found in I Thessalonians 5:1-3:

---

*   For more details on II Thessalonians 2:1-12, see Appendix II.

But concerning the times and the seasons, brethren, ye have no need that aught be written unto you. For yourselves know perfectly that the day of the Lord so cometh as a thief in the night. When they are saying, Peace and safety, then sudden destruction cometh upon them, as travail upon a woman with child; and they shall in no wise escape.

Once again, the term the *Day of the Lord* is found which is a reference to the tribulation. At a time when men are saying "Peace and safety," the destruction of the tribulation suddenly hits with devastating force. This will require this period to come just before the act that initiates the tribulation itself. So while all the world is under the ten kingdoms and the Antichrist is rising to power, there will be a period of peace and false security. But this will be shattered by the tribulation. Once again, the travail motif is found in verse 3. This is the eighth birth pang leading up to the tribulation.

I.　THE SEVEN YEAR COVENANT

The ninth event leading up to and beginning the tribulation is the signing of the seven year covenant between Israel and the Antichrist. This will be dealt with in Chapter IX, but at this point it should be emphasized that it is *not* the Rapture that begins the tribulation but the signing of the seven year covenant. Keeping this in mind will prevent many misunderstandings concerning the belief in the imminency of the Rapture. It is not the Rapture but the seven year covenant that will begin the tribulation.

SUMMARY

These are the nine events leading up to the tribulation that can be traced in a sequence of events. There are other events, however, which are also stated to be pre-tribulational but that cannot at this time be placed in any sequence of events. It is these events that are the concern of the next two chapters.

CHAPTER V

OTHER PRE-TRIBULATIONAL EVENTS

While some of the events stated to be pre-tribulational can be placed in a chronological sequence of events, others cannot be so placed until they occur. One of these is the Rapture, which will be discussed in a separate chapter following this one. This chapter will be concerned with other pre-tribulational events that cannot at this time be placed in any sequential order.

A. BLACKOUT I

During the end time period, including the last days of the church age as well as the tribulation, the Scriptures speak of five blackouts that will occur. A blackout means that the light of the sun, moon and stars is suddenly blacked out so that the earth is not receiving any light from these sources and is in total darkness. It will be similar to the blackout of Egypt which took place during one of the ten plagues as described in Exodus 10:21-23:

> And Jehovah said unto Moses, Stretch out thy hand toward heaven, that there may be darkness over the land of Egypt, even darkness which may be felt. And Moses stretched forth his hand toward heaven; and there was a thick darkness in all the land of Egypt three days; they saw not one another, neither rose any one from his place for three days: but all the children of Israel had light in their dwellings.

Another example of such a blackout happened during the crucifixion in Matthew 27:45:

> Now from the sixth hour there was darkness over all the land until the ninth hour.

The first of these five blackouts is clearly prophesied to occur before the tribulation in Joel 2:31:

> The sun shall be turned into darkness, and the moon into blood, before the great and terrible day of Jehovah cometh.

Again, the term *the Day of Jehovah* is used which is always a name for the tribulation. The first blackout is to take place beforehand. So at some point before the tribulation one of these world-wide blackouts will occur.

B. THE RETURN OF ELIJAH

Another event clearly predicted to occur before the tribulation is the return of Elijah in Malachi 4:5-6:

Behold, I will send you Elijah the prophet before the great and terrible day of Jehovah come. And he shall turn the heart of the fathers to the children, and the heart of the children to their fathers; lest I come and smite the earth with a curse.

Verse five pinpoints the return of Elijah as coming before *the Day of Jehovah*, namely before the tribulation. Verse six goes on to describe the nature of Elijah's ministry when he returns, that of a Jewish family reunion program. The Jewish family unit, strong for so many centuries, has in these last days begun to break down and, according to the prophetic word, will continue to break down. The ministry of Elijah is to restore this unity in preparation for the second coming of Christ.

There is a great deal of confusion concerning the relationship of Elijah to John the Baptist. It should be kept in mind that Elijah was never promised before the first coming of Christ. Elijah was only promised to come before the second coming of Christ and before the tribulation itself. However, a forerunner was predicted before the first coming of Christ in Malachi 3:1:

Behold, I send my messenger, and he shall prepare the way before me: and the Lord, whom ye seek, will suddenly come to his temple; and the messenger of the covenant, whom ye desire, behold, he cometh, saith Jehovah of hosts.

The coming of a forerunner before the first coming of Christ was also predicted in Isaiah 40:3-5:

The voice of one that crieth, Prepare ye in the wilderness the way of Jehovah; make level in the desert a highway for our God. Every valley shall be exalted, and every mountain and hill shall be made low; and the uneven shall be made level, and the rough places a plain: and the glory of Jehovah shall be revealed, and all flesh shall see it together; for the mouth of Jehovah hath spoken it.

John the Baptist was clearly the fulfillment of these passages as stated in Matthew 3:1-6:

And in those days cometh John the Baptist, preaching in the wilderness of Judaea, saying, Repent ye; for the kingdom of heaven is at hand. For this is he that was spoken of through Isaiah the prophet, saying, The voice of one crying in the wilderness, Make ye ready the way of the Lord, Make his paths straight. Now John himself had his raiment of camel's hair, and a leathern girdle about his loins; and his food was locusts and wild honey. Then went out unto him Jerusalem, and all Judaea, and all the region around about the Jordan; and they were baptized of him in the river Jordan, confessing their sins.

Matthew 11:7-10 makes the same point:

> And as these went their way, Jesus began to say unto the multitudes concerning John, What went ye out into the wilderness to behold? a reed shaken with the wind? But what went ye out to see? a man clothed in soft raiment? Behold, they that wear soft raiment are in kings' houses. But wherefore went ye out? to see a prophet? Yea, I say unto you, and much more than a prophet. This is he, of whom it is written, Behold, I send my messenger before thy face, Who shall prepare thy way before thee.

The same is true in John 1:23:

> He said, I am the voice of one crying in the wilderness, Make straight the way of the Lord, as said Isaiah the prophet.

But while John the Baptist fulfilled those prophecies concerning the forerunner before the first coming of Christ, he was not Elijah who was promised before the second coming. This becomes clear when all the relevant passages are taken into account.

One important passage bearing on this question is found in John 1:19-23:

> And this is the witness of John, when the Jews sent unto him from Jerusalem priests and Levites to ask him, Who art thou? And he confessed, and denied not; and he confessed, I am not the Christ. And they asked him, What then? Art thou Elijah? And he saith, I am not. Art thou the prophet? And he answered, No. They said therefore unto him, Who art thou? that we may give an answer to them that sent us. What sayest thou of thyself? He said, I am the voice of one crying in the wilderness, Make straight the way of the Lord, as said Isaiah the prophet.

In this passage John the Baptist makes it clear that he is not Elijah. He never claimed to be Elijah, and when asked, he denied it.

The next passage is found in Matthew 17:9-13:

> And as they were coming down from the mountain, Jesus commanded them, saying, Tell the vision to no man, until the Son of man be risen from the dead. And his disciples asked him, saying, Why then say the scribes that Elijah must first come? And he answered and said, Elijah indeed cometh, and shall restore all things: but I say unto you, that Elijah is come already, and they knew him not, but did unto him whatsoever they would. Even so shall the Son of man also suffer of them. Then understood the disciples that he spake unto them of John the Baptist.

In answer to the disciples' question regarding the coming of Elijah, Christ first of all states, in the future tense, that Elijah will indeed come to restore all things, which is a strong allusion to his ministry mentioned in Malachi 4:6. But this was a promise in relationship to the second coming and not the first coming. Hence, Elijah is yet to come to do the ministry of restoration. The disciples' confusion at this stage was due to the fact that they did not yet understand the two-fold coming of Christ and were still expecting Christ to set up the kingdom at that time. The parallel passage in Mark 9:9-13 adds the point that if Elijah had come before the first coming and restored all things, then all the prophecies of the sufferings of the first coming would remain unfulfilled. Elijah will indeed come *first* but first before the second coming, not before the first coming. John the Baptist did not accomplish the ministry of restoration Elijah was to accomplish.

But then Christ adds that in one sense John the Baptist was Elijah. But in what sense? Two other passages answer that. The first is in Matthew 11:11-14:

> Verily I say unto you, Among them that are born of women there hath not arisen a greater than John the Baptist: yea he that is but little in the kingdom of heaven is greater than he. And from the days of John the Baptist until now the kingdom of heaven suffereth violence, and men of violence take it by force. For all the prophets and the law prophesied until John. And if ye are willing to receive it, this is Elijah, that is to come.

To understand what is being said, it should be noted that Christ is preaching the good news of the kingdom (verses 11-12). If Israel would receive *it*, that is, the kingdom, then John the Baptist would have fulfilled the function of Elijah and would have accomplished the ministry of restoration. But the kingdom was rejected, and hence, John the Baptist did not fulfill the function of Elijah, and thus Elijah is yet to come to accomplish the work of restoration.

The second passage answering the question as to what way was John the Baptist Elijah is in Luke 1:13-17:

> But the angel said unto him, Fear not, Zacharias: because thy supplication is heard, and thy wife Elisabeth shall bear thee a son, and thou shalt call his name John. And thou shalt have joy and gladness; and many shall rejoice at his birth. For he shall be great in the sight of the Lord, and he shall drink no wine nor strong drink; and he shall be filled with the Holy Spirit, even from his mother's womb. And many of the children of Israel shall he turn unto the Lord their God. And he shall go before his face in the spirit and power of Elijah, to turn the hearts of the fathers to the children, and the disobedient to walk in the wisdom of the just; to make ready for the Lord a people prepared for him.

In announcing the coming birth of John the Baptist, the angel declares that he will come in the spirit and power of Elijah.

Consolidating what these verses are saying, some time before the tribulation Elijah the prophet will return to do his work of restoration. Thus, Elijah will serve as a forerunner of Christ's second coming in the same way as John the Baptist was the forerunner of Christ's first coming. John was a type of Elijah in that he came in the spirit and power of Elijah. If Israel had accepted the message, then John the Baptist would have accomplished the function of Elijah which was the work of restoration. However, John the Baptist and Christ were both rejected, and so Elijah is yet to come to perform the work of restoration before the tribulation.

As with the first blackout, we are unable to pinpoint at this time exactly when Elijah will come before the tribulation. Therefore, it is impossible to place it in any sequence of events.

C.   THE THIRD TEMPLE?

This is presented with a question mark because the biblical data is not sufficient to date the rebuilding of the Jewish temple as before the tribulation with any certainty. The tribulation temple is mentioned in four passages of Scripture. The first is found in Daniel 9:27:

> And he shall make a firm covenant with many for one week: and in the midst of the week he shall cause the sacrifice and the oblation to cease; and upon the wing of abominations shall come one that maketh desolate; and even unto the full end, and that determined, shall wrath be poured out upon the desolate.

The second passage is Matthew 24:15:

> When therefore ye see the abomination of desolation, which was spoken of through Daniel the prophet, standing in the holy place (let him that readeth understand), . . .

The third passage is found in II Thessalonians 2:3-4:

> Let no man beguile you in any wise: for it will not be, except the falling away come first, and the man of sin be revealed, the son of perdition, he that opposeth and exalteth himself against all that is called God or that is worshipped; so that he sitteth in the temple of God, setting himself forth as God.

The fourth passage is found in Revelation 11:1-2:

> And there was given me a reed like unto a rod: and one said, Rise, and measure the temple of God, and the altar, and them that worship therein. And the court which is without the temple leave without, and measure it not; for it hath been given unto the nations: and the holy city shall they tread under foot forty and two months.

All four passages describe events which occur in relationship to the Jewish temple. In all of them the events described take place in the middle of the tribulation, the details of which will be discussed in Chapter XI. The point to be noted for now is that by the time of the middle of the tribulation period, the tribulation temple is standing and functioning, and it has been functioning for at least a little while before the mid-point of the tribulation. This requires that the temple be rebuilt some time before the middle of the tribulation. This allows for only two options. The temple must be rebuilt either before the tribulation or during the first half of the tribulation. It is impossible with this data to dogmatically state when the temple will be rebuilt any more precisely. Hence, the rebuilding of the temple before the tribulation can only be stated as a possibility, for it is also possible that the temple will be rebuilt during the first half of the tribulation. What these texts do make clear is that the temple is built and functioning by the time of the middle of the tribulation.

Once the temple is rebuilt, the sacrificial system of the Mosaic Law will be reinstituted. However, this temple receives no sanction from God. This is clear from Isaiah 66:1-6:

> Thus saith Jehovah, Heaven is my throne, and the earth is my footstool: what manner of house will ye build unto me? and what place shall be my rest? For all these things hath my hand made, and so all these things came to be, saith Jehovah: but to this man will I look, even to him that is poor and of a contrite spirit, and that trembleth at my word. He that killeth an ox as he that slayeth a man; he that sacrificeth a lamb as he that breaketh a dog's neck; he that offereth an oblation, as he that offereth swine's blood, he that burneth frankincense, as he that blesseth an idol. Yea, they have chosen their own ways, and their soul delighteth in their abominations: I also will choose their delusions, and will bring their fears upon them; because when I called, none did answer; when I spake, they did not hear: but they did that which was evil in mine eyes, and chose that wherein I delighted not. Hear the word of Jehovah, ye that tremble at his word: Your brethren that hate you, that cast you out for my name's sake, have said, Let Jehovah be glorified, that we may see your joy; but it is they that shall be put to shame. A voice of tumult from the city, a voice from the temple, a voice of Jehovah that rendereth recompense to his enemies.

Isaiah speaks of a house or temple being built for God which He does not sanction. It cannot refer to Solomon's temple or the temple built by Zerrubbabel, because God did sanction both of them. Nor can it refer to the millennial temple. That one will be built by Christ, and God will certainly sanction it. Therefore, the only temple that this could refer to is the tribulation temple. So Isaiah the prophet foresees the building of a temple that God will not sanction. What God wants Israel to do at this time is to return to Him in faith, not merely to build Him a house.

This passage begins with a protest from God, Who makes it clear that no temple that Israel builds at this time will be acceptable, for God will not come and reside in this one (verse 1) as He did in the first temple. What God will require at this time is not a new temple but faith (verse 2). He will not accept these reinstituted levitical sacrifices any more than He would accept human sacrifices, swine, or idolatry in the Old Testament (verse 3). The very fact that they will build this temple shows their failure to listen to God's word (verse 4) and come to God by faith in Jesus the Messiah. Then Isaiah has a word of encouragement to those faithful Jews who will not participate in the rebuilding of the temple (verse 5) but are seeking to do God's will. So there will be a faithful remnant who will not participate in the rebuilding of the Jewish temple for the tribulation. Finally Isaiah states that this new temple will only end in judgment (verse 6) and not in forgiveness of sin or acceptable worship.

Two other things should be mentioned in regard to the third temple. First, the Six Day War set the stage for the fulfillment of this prophecy in 1967, for until that time the temple compound was under Arab control. During the Six Day War the temple area fell into Jewish control. At the time of this writing there are no efforts being made to rebuild the temple, in spite of much rumor to the contrary (e.g., the new Great Synagogue in Jerusalem is not the temple. The architecture is not in accordance with temple requirements, and it is not in the temple compound.). The Six Day War has at least made possible the rebuilding of the temple, and this possibility exists for the first time in centuries.

A second thing that should be noted about the third temple concerns the tribe of Levi. The tribe of Levi was the only tribe permitted by Mosaic Law to take care of the temple and conduct the sacrificial system. It is interesting to note that while all the other eleven tribes have lost their tribal identity since the records were destroyed in 70 A.D., the tribe of Levi has not. Unless a Jew is a member of the tribe of Levi, he is unable to know which tribe he is a descendant of. But the tribe of Levi has kept their identity. Jews having names such as Levi, Levy, Levin, Levine, Leventhal, Levinson, Cohen and other comparable names are members of the tribe of Levi. For the purpose of conducting sacrifice, only the tribe of Levi matters. It is not important to know who the members of the other tribes are. But it is very important to know who the Levites are, and the tribe of Levi is known.

So in every way the stage is set for the temple to be rebuilt, and it is possible that it will be rebuilt before the tribulation. If it is not, then it will certainly be rebuilt during the first part of the tribulation. For by the middle of the tribulation the temple must be built and functioning and been in operation for a little while.

In any question dealing with the rebuilding of the temple, the question of the Moslem Dome of the Rock enters the picture. The Dome of the Rock is in the temple area, though not exactly on the spot of the old temple site of the previous two temples. In the opinion of some, the Dome of the Rock will have to be removed at some point. In the opinion of others, there is enough room in the temple compound to permit the rebuilding of the Jewish temple without needing to tear down the Dome of the Rock. A novel new theory that has arisen in recent years is that the Arabs might give up trying to get Jerusalem back and will simply move the Dome of the Rock to a better locality. The point that is missed by those who think this way is that it is not the Dome itself that is holy to Islam, but it is the site itself that is holy. In Moslem tradition the Dome of the Rock is built over the spot where they say Mohammed ascended into heaven. It is not the building itself that is holy to Islam, but it is the rock that is holy and is commemorated by the building. Thus, it is rather foolish to think that the Arabs would consent to move the Dome of the Rock. Still another novel theory of recent vintage is that the temple will be rebuilt completely away from the temple area. This is also based upon a misunderstanding of Jewish law and Jewish thinking. The Jews would not accept a new Jewish state anywhere but in Palestine. Nor will the Jews accept a new Jewish temple anywhere but in the temple compound. So the Dome of the Rock remains a problem, and there is much speculation concerning it.

On this question of the Dome of the Rock, the Bible is silent. That the temple will be rebuilt is a clear teaching of Scripture. As to how and where in the temple area this will come about, only the passing of history will reveal.

This chapter, then, has dealt with two events that will clearly come before the tribulation, and with the possibility of a third one, none of which can be put in a chronological sequence of events. However, there is another event that is stated to be pre-tribulational, but also cannot be placed in a sequence of events. This is the Rapture of the church, and it is the topic of the following chapter.

CHAPTER VI

THE ESCHATOLOGY OF THE INVISIBLE CHURCH

The invisible church is composed of all true believers, whereas the visible church can be composed of both unbelievers and believers. The eschatology of the visible church has already been discussed. The eschatology of the invisible church rightly belongs to the study of pre-tribulational events.

A. DEFINITION

A definition of what actually constitutes the invisible church will help to understand exactly who it is that is involved in the Rapture. Five passages need to be noted in composing such a clear definition.

First, in Colossians 1:18 the church is stated to be the body of Christ.

> And he is the head of the body, the church: who is the beginning, the firstborn from the dead; that in all things he might have the preeminence.

Secondly, the composition of this body, that is, the church, is given in Ephesians 2:11-16:

> Wherefore remember, that once ye, the Gentiles in the flesh, who are called Uncircumcision by that which is called Circumcision, in the flesh, made by hands; that ye were at that time separate from Christ, alienated from the commonwealth of Israel, and strangers from the covenants of the promise, having no hope and without God in the world. But now in Christ Jesus ye that once were far off are made nigh in the blood of Christ. For he is our peace, who made both one, and brake down the middle wall of partition, having abolished in his flesh the enmity, even the law of commandments contained in ordinances; that he might create in himself of the two one new man, so making peace; and might reconcile them both in one body unto God through the cross, having slain the enmity thereby.

The composition of the church, the body of Christ, is a combination of Jews and Gentiles united together by faith in Christ. This passage makes clear that there is no such thing as a Gentile church any more than there is a Jewish one. The Gentiles are grafted into a Jewish olive tree and not vice verse (Romans 11:16-24). The Ephesian passage states that it is the Gentiles who are "brought near" to enjoy the blessings of the Jewish covenants, but the covenants themselves are still the possession of Israel. Thus, the Gentiles are *fellow-heirs, and fellow-members of the body, and fellow-partakers of the promise of Christ Jesus through the gospel* (Ephesians 3:6). The Gentiles are fellow-partakers, but not taker-overs. A major purpose of the Church Age is a calling out from among the Gentiles by the gospel according to Acts 15:14:

> Symeon hath rehearsed how first God visited the Gentiles, to take out of them a people for his name.

According to Romans 11:25-27, this calling out of the Gentiles will continue until the full number of Gentiles that God has ordained for the church has been reached:

> For I would not, brethren, have you ignorant of this mystery, lest ye be wise in your own conceits, that a hardening in part hath befallen Israel, until the fulness of the Gentiles be come in; and so all Israel shall be saved: even as it is written, There shall come out of Zion the Deliverer; He shall turn away ungodliness from Jacob: And this is my covenant unto them, When I shall take away their sins.

So while God is performing a work among the Gentiles, it has a purpose that is not merely Gentile-oriented, but one that is also related to the Jews and not apart from them. In fact, one of the purposes for Gentile salvation is to provoke the Jews to jealousy so that during the Church Age many Jews may also come to faith in the Messiah Jesus (Romans 11:11-15). The Gentile believers are enjoying the spiritual blessings of the Jewish covenants and are grafted into a Jewish olive tree that belongs to Israel, *for salvation is from the Jews* (John 4:22). Hence, there is no such thing as a Gentile church. The church is simply a body composed of Jewish and Gentile members united by faith in Christ.

Thirdly, with the church being the body of Christ and that body being composed of Jewish and Gentile believers, I Corinthians 12:13 explains how one gets into the body:

> For in one Spirit were we all baptized into one body, whether Jews or Greeks, whether bond or free; and were all made to drink of one Spirit.

Entrance into the body is by Spirit baptism. Every believer is a member of the body by virtue of having been baptized by the Holy Spirit, a fact that takes place the moment one believes and is saved. Knowing just how one becomes a member of the body of Christ helps to determine when the church began. This in turn is important in determining who is involved in the Rapture.

Fourthly, by use of the future tense, Acts 1:5 makes clear that Spirit baptism was still future as of Acts chapter one:

> For John indeed baptized with water; but **ye shall be** baptized in the Holy Spirit not many days hence. (emphasis added)

Fifthly, if Spirit baptism was future to Acts 1:5, the question is: when did it begin? It is generally agreed that Spirit baptism began in Acts two, but it is impossible to prove this from Acts two since that chapter says nothing about Spirit baptism. Yet, that Spirit baptism did begin in Acts two is clear from Acts 11:15-16:

> And as I began to speak, the Holy Spirit fell on them, even as on us at the beginning. And I remembered the word of the Lord, how he said, John indeed baptized with water; but ye shall be baptized in the Holy Spirit.

When in verse 15 Peter says, *as on us at the beginning*, he is referring to the experience of the Apostles in Acts two. Then in verse 16 Peter quotes Acts 1:5 and states that the prophecy in 1:5 is what was ful- filled "at the beginning" in Acts two.

So then, the church is the body of Christ composed of Jewish and Gentile believers and entrance is by Spirit baptism only. Since Spirit baptism did not begin until Pentecost in Acts two, then the church could not have existed prior to that time. When Jesus spoke of building his church in Matthew 16:18, He used the future tense show- ing that the church had not yet begun. A major reason was that both the Resurrection (Ephesians 1:19-20) and the Ascension with the sub- sequent giving of spiritual gifts (Ephesians 4:7-12) were necessary pre- requisites for the building of the church. The church is composed of all true believers in Christ from Pentecost in Acts two until the Rapture of the church. The Rapture excludes the Old Testament saints. It also excludes the tribulation saints. The only saints that will be raptured are the church saints. The Rapture passages clearly state that it is only those that are in Christ that partake of the Rapture. Those *in Christ* are there because of Spirit baptism which only began in Acts two.

B. THE RAPTURE OF THE CHURCH

1. THE EVENTS OF THE RAPTURE

Three key passages need to be studied for an understanding of the Rapture. The first is found in John 14:1-3:

> Let not your heart be troubled: believe in God, believe also in me. In my Father's house are many mansions; if it were not so, I would have told you; for I go to prepare a place for you. And if I go and prepare a place for you, I come again, and will receive you unto myself; that where I am, there ye may be also.

This passage does not describe the Rapture but does contain a hint of it. In these verses Christ promised to return for the believers.

Nothing is revealed as to the time or the circumstances; only the fact that there is a coming of Christ for His saints. This coming especially for the saints is the subject of revelation in the two other passages.

The second passage is I Thessalonians 4:13-18 which describes the *program* of the Rapture:

> But we would not have you ignorant, brethren, concerning them that fall asleep; that ye sorrow not, even as the rest, who have no hope. For if we believe that Jesus died and rose again, even so them also that are fallen asleep in Jesus will God bring with him. For this we say unto you by the word of the Lord, that we that are alive, that are left unto the coming of the Lord, shall in no wise precede them that are fallen asleep. For the Lord himself shall descend from heaven, with a shout, with the voice of the archangel, and with the trump of God: and the dead in Christ shall rise first; then we that are alive, that are left, shall together with them be caught up in the clouds, to meet the Lord in the air: and so shall we ever be with the Lord. Wherefore comfort one another with these words.

In verses 13-15 Paul answers a question that has been raised in Thessalonica: Do believers who have died miss out on the benefits of the Rapture? These believers did understand that there was a Rapture to come, but they did not understand how dead saints would be involved in the Rapture. Hence, some were thinking that only living believers would enjoy the benefits of the Rapture and that the dead believers would not. This question arose because some of the believers had recently died. Their loved ones who were still living were distressed not knowing what the future had in store for them. Apparently, while Paul had been with them, he had taught some truths concerning the Rapture as it related to the living but not to the dead. So Paul comforts the bereaved members with the truth that dead believers would not miss out on the benefits of the Rapture; in fact, they will begin to receive the benefits first.

In reference to the death of believers, Paul uses the term "sleep." This term when used as a synonym for death is used of believers only and never of unbelievers. Thus, the Bible views the death of believers as a temporary suspension of physical activity until the believer awakens at the Rapture. Just as physical sleep is temporary, a temporary suspension of physical activity until one awakens, yet there is no suspension of mental activity, so is death. This verse does not teach "soul sleeping," for there is no cessation of spirit-soul activity, only physical activity.

In verses 16-17 the program of the Rapture is spelled out in seven steps. First, *the Lord himself shall descend from heaven*. At some point in the future Christ will come out of the heaven of heavens and descend into the atmospheric heavens.

Secondly, *with a shout*. The Greek word used is that of a command of a military leader. The shout is a command for the resurrection and the translation to occur.

Thirdly, *with the voice of the archangel*. Angels are often used to put God's plan into motion. Michael the archangel will be used in the case of the Rapture. The content of what the voice says is not stated. But if known military procedure can be applied to this situation, then this is simply the repetition by the sub-commander of the order (shout) of the chief commander. Christ gives the shout or command for the program of the Rapture to begin, and it is Michael's task to set it into motion and so he repeats the command of Christ.

The fourth stage is *with the trump of God*. The sound of the trumpet was used as a summons either to battle or to worship. With Michael's repetition of Christ's command, the trumpet sounds, and this triggers the Rapture itself. Thus, this trumpet serves as a summons for the plan to move into motion.

The fifth step is *the dead in Christ shall rise first*. This is the resurrection. This is why the dead believers will not miss out on the benefits of the Rapture. They will actually begin to enjoy the benefits of the Rapture first. The expression *in Christ* limits the resurrection at the time of the Rapture to those who were baptized by the Holy Spirit into the body of Christ, which only began in Acts two. Thus, this resurrection of dead saints is to be limited to church saints only. The Old Testament saints will not be resurrected at this time but at a later point in God's prophetic program.

The sixth step concerns the living believers, *then we that are alive, that are left, shall together with them be caught up in the clouds, to meet the Lord in the air*. The resurrection of the dead saints is followed by the translation of the living saints. Every believer without exception will be removed from the earth and will be united with the Lord Jesus Christ in the heavens. The living believers will be caught up (raptured) with the dead ones to meet Jesus Christ in the air.

The seventh step is *so shall we ever be with the Lord*. The final step is the guarantee that once we have been united with Christ in the air, we will permanently remain with Christ and return with Him into heaven.

The third passage in I Corinthians 15:50-58 deals with the *change in the nature of the bodies*:

> Now this I say, brethren, that flesh and blood cannot inherit the kingdom of God; neither doth corruption inherit incorruption. Behold, I tell you a mystery: We all shall not sleep, but we shall all be changed, in a moment, in the twinkling of an eye, at the last trump: for the trumpet shall sound, and the dead shall be raised incorruptible, and we shall be changed. For this corruptible must put on incorruption, and this mortal must put on immortality. But when this corruptible shall have put on incorruption, and this mortal shall have put on immortality, then shall come to pass the saying that is written, Death is swallowed up in victory. O death, where is thy victory? O death, where is thy sting? The sting of death is sin; and the

power of sin is the law: but thanks be to God, who giveth us the victory through our Lord Jesus Christ. Wherefore, my beloved brethren, be ye stedfast, unmovable, always abounding in the work of the Lord, forasmuch as ye know that your labor is not vain in the Lord.

Verse 50 declares the necessity of the change of the raptured living and dead: *flesh and blood cannot inherit the kingdom of God; neither doth corruption inherit incorruption.* The background to this statement is found in Genesis 2:17:

But of the tree of the knowledge of good and evil, thou shalt not eat of it: for in the day that thou eatest thereof thou shalt surely die.

This is further developed in Genesis 3:17-19:

And unto Adam he said, Because thou hast hearkened unto the voice of thy wife, and hast eaten of the tree, of which I commanded thee, saying, Thou shalt not eat of it: cursed is the ground for thy sake; in toil shalt thou eat of it all the days of thy life; thorns also and thistles shall it bring forth to thee; and thou shalt eat the herb of the field; in the sweat of thy face shalt thou eat bread, till thou return unto the ground; for out of it wast thou taken: for dust thou art, and unto dust shalt thou return.

Because of sin, man has become subject to corruption and mortality. All men are seen to be guilty, by imputation, of participating in Adam's sin, according to Romans 5:12-14:

Therefore, as through one man sin entered into the world, and death through sin; and so death passed unto all men, for that all sinned: for until the law sin was in the world; but sin is not imputed when there is no law. Nevertheless death reigned from Adam until Moses, even over them that had not sinned after the likeness of Adam's transgression, who is a figure of him that was to come.

Mankind is living under the sentence of death where his physical body is subject to corruption and mortality. The sin nature is in it, and results of sin are evident in the death of the body. This kind of body, subject to sin, mortality, death, and corruption, cannot enter heaven. So a change will be necessary (resurrection or translation) before the bodies can enter heaven.

In verses 51-53 the change is described. The emphasis is on the quickness and rapidity of the change. It will be done *in a moment*. The Greek term behind this word is where the modern word "atom" originates. The emphasis is that this will be an "atom" of time. It will be that quick. Furthermore, it will be in the *twinkling of an eye*. This is not a reference to blinking, but rather to a sudden flash of recognition. It is like seeing a person, and then in a sudden flash recognizing who he is. It is this sudden flash of recognition which is meant by the twinkling of an eye. This, too, emphasizes the quickness of the change.

The event is said to happen at the time of *the last trump*. Both mid-tribulationists and post-tribulationists try to identify this with the seventh trumpet of the book of the Revelation. But this can not be what is meant by the last trump; at the time that I Corinthians was written, John had not written Revelation. The Corinthians would not have had any knowledge of seven trumpets. Yet it is evident from the fact that Paul used the definite article *the* last trump that he expected the Corinthians to know what he was talking about. The only knowledge they would have of trumpets are those spoken of in the Old Testament; especially those of the Feast of Trumpets. The last trump refers to the Feast of Trumpets and the Jewish practice of blowing trumpets at this feast each year. During the ceremony there are a series of short trumpet sounds concluding with one long trumpet blast which is called the *tekiah gedolah,* the great trumpet blast. This is what Paul means by *the last trump.* His point is that the Rapture will be the fulfillment of the Feast of Trumpets. As such, it says nothing concerning the time of the Rapture.

This trumpet is the same as the *trump of God* found in I Thessalonians 4:16. For in that passage, at the sound of the trumpet the dead are raised as incorruptible and *we*, the living, will be changed. Thus, in verse 53, the problem which keeps the dead body out of heaven, corruption, will be changed through the resurrection and will become incorruptible. The mortal living will put on immortality through translation.

The nature of this new glorified body is not the subject of much revelation, but there are several things which are said. What is revealed clearly about the resurrection body is found in I Corinthians 15:35-49:

> But some one will say, How are the dead raised? and with what manner of body do they come? Thou foolish one, that which thou thyself sowest is not quickened except it die: and that which thou sowest, thou sowest not the body that shall be, but a bare grain, it may chance of wheat, or of some other kind; but God giveth it a body even as it pleased him, and to each seed a body of its own. All flesh is not the same flesh: but there is one flesh of men, and another flesh of beasts, and another flesh of birds, and another of fishes. There are also celestial bodies, and bodies terrestrial: but the glory of the celestial is one, and the glory of the terrestrial is another. There is one glory of the sun, and another glory of the moon, and another glory of the stars; for one star differeth from another star in glory. So also is the resurrection of the dead. It is sown in corruption; it is raised in incorruption: it is sown in dishonor; it is raised in glory: it is sown in weakness; it is raised in power: it is sown a natural body; it is raised a spiritual body. If there is a natural body, there is also a spiritual body. So also it is written, The first man Adam became a living soul. The last Adam became a life-giving spirit. Howbeit that is not first which is spiritual, but that which is natural; then that which is spiritual.

> The first man is of the earth, earthy: the second man is of heaven. As is the earthy, such are they also that are earthy: and as is the heavenly, such are they also that are heavenly. And as we have borne the image of the earthy, we shall also bear the image of the heavenly.

Six points are made concerning the resurrection body: first, it is a body that is incorruptible (verse 42); secondly, it is a glorified body (verse 43). The same point is made by Philippians 3:21:

> Who shall fashion anew the body of our humiliation, that it may be conformed to the body of his glory, according to the working whereby he is able even to subject all things unto himself.

Thirdly, it is a body of resurrection power (verse 43); fourthly, it is a spiritual body (verses 44-46); fifthly, it is a heavenly body (verses 47-49); and sixthly, it is also an immortal body (verse 53).

Another possible source of information as to the nature of the new body may be gleaned from a study of the nature of the resurrected body of Christ. But here some caution must be used. This source of information has one major drawback. It is not always easy to determine if what was true of the body of Christ was due to His resurrection or due to His deity. Thus, some of the following observations concerning the body of Christ could possibly be true of all resurrected bodies. But they may not all be true, for some may be true only because of Christ's divinity.

We know that Christ's voice was recognized as being the same as the one He had before His death and resurrection (John 20:16). Also, His physical features were recognized though not always immediately (John 20:26-29; 21:7). It was a very real body and not a mere phantom body since it was embraceable (John 20:17, 27). The resurrected Christ was able to suddenly disappear (Luke 24:31) and go through walls (John 20:19). It was a body that was able to eat food (Luke 24:41-43).

A number of these factors may be true of all resurrected bodies, but whether all these things will be true cannot be known until the Rapture.

Finally, in I Corinthians 15:54-58 the change from corruption to incorruption and from mortality to immortality results in the final victory over death.

2.   THE TIMING OF THE RAPTURE

The next question concerning the Rapture is *when* will it take place? That the Scriptures teach that the Rapture will occur *before* the tribulation is clear from several lines of evidence.

First, in no biblical passage which discusses the tribulation is the church mentioned. The fact that saints are found in the tribulation does not prove that the church is there any more than the existence of saints in the Old Testament proves that the church was there. It has already been shown that the church began with Pentecost with the baptizing ministry of the Holy Spirit. Thus, the Old Testament saints are not part of the church. In the same way, the existence of saints in the tribulation does not prove that the church is there either. The church as such is never mentioned in any passage dealing with the tribulation. This is especially evident and significant in the book of the Revelation. The church is clearly found in chapters 1-3 dealing with the events prior to the tribulation. Later the church is found in chapters 19-22 dealing with events after the tribulation. But in chapters 6-18, which deal with the tribulation period itself, the church is not even mentioned once. This is most unusual in light of the prominence of the church in the chapters dealing with events prior to and after the tribulation. Outside the book of Revelation the fact remains that in no passage dealing with the tribulation is the church mentioned. This is only an argument from silence, but within the structure of the book of Revelation it is a powerful case indeed. From the viewpoint of pure exposition, it is impossible for anyone to turn to a tribulation passage and to show that the church is there.

One specific passage teaching pre-tribulation deliverance is in I Thessalonians 1:9-10:

> For they themselves report concerning us what manner of entering in we had unto you; and how ye turned unto God from idols, to serve a living and true God, and to wait for his Son from heaven, whom he raised from the dead, even Jesus, who delivereth us from the wrath to come.

The closing words are crucial. The church at Thessalonica was waiting for the return of Christ who was coming to deliver them from *the wrath to come*. The word "wrath" is used of God's general wrath against sin as in Romans 1:18 and also of the wrath of the Great Tribulation as in Revelation 6:17, 14:10,19, 15:1,7, 16:1, etc. The word is *never* used of either hell or the Lake of Fire. The wrath of God here is future, and, hence, cannot refer to the general wrath of God against sin which is a present reality. This wrath is future.

While hell and the Lake of Fire are also future, they cannot be what this passage is referring to. By virtue of his salvation, the believer is *already* redeemed from hell. Christ is not returning for the purpose of delivering the church from hell or the Lake of Fire, for this has already been done at the cross. Thus, the wrath that the church is being delivered from is the wrath of the Great Tribulation. Christ is coming for the specific purpose of delivering the church from "the wrath to come," namely, the tribulation period. The believer is guaranteed deliverance both from God's general wrath against sin (Romans 5:9) and from the tribulation wrath (I Thessalonians 1:10).

Another passage dealing with the timing of the Rapture is in I Thessalonians 5:1-10:

> But concerning the times and the seasons, brethren, ye have no need that aught be written unto you. For yourselves know perfectly that the day of the Lord so cometh as a thief in the night. When they are saying, Peace and safety, then sudden destruction cometh upon them, as travail upon a woman with child; and they shall in no wise escape. But ye, brethren, are not in darkness, that that day should overtake you as a thief: for ye are all sons of light, and sons of the day: we are not of the night, nor of darkness; so then let us not sleep, as do the rest, but let us watch and be sober. For they that sleep sleep in the night; and they that are drunken are drunken in the night. But let us, since we are of the day, be sober, putting on the breastplate of faith and love; and for a helmet, the hope of salvation. For God appointed us not unto wrath, but unto the obtaining of salvation through our Lord Jesus Christ, who died for us, that, whether we wake or sleep, we should live together with him.

In verse nine Paul tells the church in Thessalonica that they have not been appointed to wrath. The meaning of the word *wrath* is to be found in verse two, which is *the Day of the Lord*, a term that always refers to the tribulation. Thus, concerning the wrath of God, or the Day of the Lord, or the tribulation, to *that day* the church was not appointed. The discussion on the Day of the Lord or the tribulation immediately follows the discussion of the Rapture in 4:14-18. Thus, the comfort in 4:18 involves the fact that these church believers will not need to go through the period of the Day of the Lord. Hence the contrasting *but (peri de)* in 5:1, for as over against the previous comfort, the Day of the Lord is a period of wrath.

Verse nine continues to state that the church, while not having been appointed to wrath, has been appointed to *the obtaining of salvation.* In verse eight it is referred to as the *hope of salvation.* The salvation spoken of here is future, and so cannot be soteriological, which is a present reality. The salvation here is eschatological referring to the redemption of the body which will occur at the Rapture. It is this salvation that the church has been appointed to and not to the wrath of the Day of the Lord.

Another point to consider in this passage is found in verses 4-8 where there is a contrast which is aimed to show why the church, being the children of light, will not need to fear the coming Day of the Lord. The Day of the Lord is referred to as a period of darkness and night (Zephaniah 1:14-20; Joel 2:1-2, 10-11). The Day of the Lord, characterized by darkness, will come upon the sons of darkness, that is, the unbelievers. But because the believer is of the day, the Day of the Lord will not come upon him.

Another key verse dealing with the timing element of the Rapture is in Revelation 3:10:

> Because thou didst keep the word of my patience, I also will keep thee from the hour of trial, that hour which is to come upon the whole world, to try them that dwell upon the earth.

In this passage the church is promised to be kept from the period of trial that is about to fall upon the whole earth. In the context of the book of Revelation, it is the tribulation found in chapters 6-19 that is this period of trial that is to fall upon the whole earth. It is from this period of trial that the church is to be kept. This verse does not say that the church will be merely kept safe *during* the trial but it will be kept *from the very hour* of the trial, that is, from the very *time* of it. This requires a removal before the tribulation ever occurs. If Revelation 3:10 only means that the church will be kept safe during the tribulation, then something goes terribly wrong. Throughout the tribulation, saints are being killed on a massive scale (Revelation 6:9-11, 11:7, 12:11, 13:7,15, 14:13, 17:6, 18:24). If these saints are church saints, they are not being kept safe and Revelation 3:10 is meaningless. Only if church saints and tribulation saints are kept distinct does the promise of Revelation 3:10 make any sense.

These passages of Scripture all state that the church will be removed before *the wrath, the Day of the Lord,* the tribulation comes. The removal will come by means of the Rapture of the church. There are a number of other evidences for a pre-tribulation Rapture which will be dealt with in another context.

Another question that needs to be discussed is: *when before* the tribulation does the Rapture take place?

The Scriptures teach that the coming of Christ for the believer is imminent, that is, He can come at any time or moment. For instance, in John 21:20-23, it is clear that Christ could have returned in the days of John the Apostle:

> Peter, turning about, seeth the disciple whom Jesus loved following; who also leaned back on his breast at the supper, and said, Lord, who is he that betrayeth thee? Peter therefore seeing him saith to Jesus, Lord, and what shall this man do? Jesus saith unto him, If I will that he tarry till I come, what is that to thee? follow thou me. This saying therefore went forth among the brethren, that that disciple should not die: yet Jesus said not unto him, that he should not die; but, If I will that he tarry till I come, what is that to thee?

In Romans 13:11-12 the redemption of the body is looked upon as being very near:

> And this, knowing the season, that already it is time for you to awake out of sleep: for now is salvation nearer to us than when we first believed. The night is far spent, and the day is at hand: let us therefore cast off the works of darkness, and let us put on the armor of light.

The salvation here must again be viewed as eschatological rather than soteriological, for this salvation is viewed as future. As each day ends, it brings the believer one day closer to the time when the Rapture may occur. Because of this imminency, it is time for the believers to awaken out of sleep and live a life consistent with the position of being sons of light.

In James 5:7-9 Christ's coming is viewed as being at the door:

> Be patient therefore, brethren, until the coming of the Lord. Behold, the husbandman waiteth for the precious fruit of the earth, being patient over it, until it receive the early and latter rain. Be ye also patient; establish your hearts: for the coming of the Lord is at hand. Murmur not, brethren, one against another, that ye be not judged: behold, the judge standeth before the doors.

The coming of the Lord is at hand, and the judge is standing before the doors. Christ's appearance is certainly viewed as imminent.

The closing statements of Christ in Revelation 22:20 also point to imminency:

> He who testifieth these things saith, Yea: I come quickly. Amen: come, Lord Jesus.

While the earlier passages all clearly taught that the Rapture will precede the tribulation, these last four passages teach that the coming of Christ is imminent; He could come at any moment. Only if the Rapture comes before the tribulation can this be true. In mid-tribulationism the Rapture is always at least 3½ years away. In post-tribulationism it is at least seven years away. It is never imminent.

So then, concerning the question of *when* does the Rapture occur, two things should be noted. First, the Rapture does come before the tribulation. Since the tribulation begins with the signing of the seven year covenant, the very latest point at which the Rapture can occur would be at the time of the signing of the seven year covenant. The Rapture will not occur beyond that point.

Second, the Rapture is imminent. It can come at any moment, and it need not wait until the signing of the seven year covenant.

Combining this information, the conclusion is that the Rapture will occur sometime between this very moment and the signing of the seven year covenant. This is referred to as the *Period of the Rapture* on the second chart.* It means that the specific span of time during which the Rapture can occur is any time between right now and the signing of the seven year covenant. Therefore, the church may see some more pre-tribulational events just as it has already seen three. But it may not see any more, depending on exactly at what point the Rapture will occur.

* See page 36.

The relationship of the Rapture to the tribulation must be clearly focused in the mind. The Rapture *precedes* the tribulation, but it *does not begin* the tribulation, a fact confused by many pre-tribulationists. It is not the Rapture, but the seven year covenant which begins the tribulation. The Rapture will merely come some time before this, and may very well precede the tribulation by a good number of years.

C. THE JUDGMENT SEAT OF CHRIST

The second major element in the eschatology of the invisible church involves the Judgment Seat of Christ, a judgment of the believer's works, not his sins. This is a judgment that will take place in heaven after the Rapture of the church. Three passages deal with this particular judgment. In the first passage, Romans 14:10-12, Paul simply points out that such a judgment will take place:

> But thou, why dost thou judge thy brother? or thou again, why dost thou set at nought thy brother? for we shall all stand before the judgment-seat of God. For it is written, As I live, saith the Lord, to me every knee shall bow, and every tongue shall confess to God. So then each one of us shall give account of himself to God.

The second passage in II Corinthians 5:10 provides the *basis* of this judgment:

> For we must all be made manifest before the judgment-seat of Christ; that each one may receive the things done in the body, according to what he hath done, whether it be good or bad.

The basis of this judgment will be the believer's works done in the body since he became a believer. It is not the believer's sins which will be judged since this has been settled forever at the cross, and *there is now no condemnation for them that are in Christ Jesus* (Romans 8:1). This is not a question of the believer's sins, but a matter of reward on the basis of the believer's deeds.

The third and most detailed passage dealing with this judgment is in I Corinthians 3:10-15:

> According to the grace of God which was given unto me, as a wise masterbuilder I laid a foundation; and another buildeth thereon. But let each man take heed how he buildeth thereon. For other foundation can no man lay than that which is laid, which is Jesus Christ. But if any man buildeth on the foundation gold, silver, costly stones, wood, hay, stubble; each man's work shall be made manifest: for the day shall declare it, because it is revealed in fire; and the fire itself shall prove each man's work of what sort it is. If any man's work shall abide which he built thereon, he shall receive a reward. If any man's work shall be burned, he shall suffer loss: but he himself shall be saved; yet so as through fire.

In verses 10-11 Paul again points out that the basis of the judgment is the works of the believer. This is portrayed as building on a foundation that has already been laid; the judgment is based on *how* one has built on this foundation (Jesus Christ).

Furthermore, in verse 12 this judgment of works will not be based upon quantity, but upon quality. It will not be a question as to *how much* gold, silver, costly stones or wood, hay, stubble; but, *was it* gold, silver, or precious stone, or *was it* wood, hay, or stubble. It is a matter of quality and not of quantity. The concern of this judgment is whether the believer followed what God's will was for him or not. If a believer is doing the will of the Lord, obeys His commandments, and fulfills the ministry for which he received his spiritual gifts, then he is building on the foundation with gold, silver, and precious stones. But where he falls short of these things, he is building wood, hay, and stubble.

In verse 13 the means of testing is said to be fire. When fire is applied to wood, hay or stubble, it is burned up and only ashes remain. But if fire is applied to gold, silver, or precious stones, these elements are refined and become more pure. Again, the means of testing shows that it is a matter of quality and not quantity. Regardless of how little or how much wood, hay, or stubble there will be, fire will burn it all up. Regardless of how much gold, silver, or precious stones there may be, fire refines them all. So some believers will find all their works burned up, and others will merely see them refined.

Finally, in verses 14-15 the results of the judgment are given. In verse 14 those who build with gold, silver, and precious stones will find their works still remaining but purified after the fire has been applied. Thus, these will receive a reward. This passage says nothing about the nature of the reward, but other passages do. They speak of these rewards as being crowns.

The Greek language has two words meaning crown. One is the word *diadem* which is a king's crown. It is the crown of a sovereign and of a person who is royal by his nature and by his position — a king. This is the kind of crown that Christ wears. The second Greek word is *stephanos* which is a crown given to an overcomer, a victor, one who has won a race. These are the kinds of crowns available to believers, because they overcame at the Judgment Seat of Christ.

There are five such crowns mentioned in the Scriptures. In I Corinthians 9:24-25 there is the *incorruptible crown*:

Know ye not that they that run in a race run all, but one receiveth the prize? Even so run; that ye may attain. And every man that striveth in the games exerciseth self-control in all things. Now they do it to receive a corruptible crown; but we an incorruptible.

This is a crown given to those who exercise self-control and gain the mastery and victory in the Christian life. It is for those who have gained the victory over the old man, the old sin nature. It is for those who have learned to live a Spirit-controlled life.

In I Thessalonians 2:19 a second crown is called the *crown of rejoicing*:

> For what is our hope, or joy, or crown of glorying? Are not even ye, before our Lord Jesus at his coming?

This is the crown given to those who win souls for Jesus Christ. It is a crown available to all those who do the work of evangelism, and the fruits of their labors are seen in people coming to Christ through them.

II Timothy 4:7-8 speaks of a third crown, the *crown of righteousness*:

> I have fought the good fight, I have finished the course, I have kept the faith: henceforth there is laid up for me the crown of righteousness, which the Lord, the righteous judge, shall give to me at that day; and not to me only, but also to all them that have loved his appearing.

This is a crown for those who have kept the faith both doctrinally and morally in spite of adverse circumstances. It is a crown given to those *who love his appearing*, those who look longingly for the return of Christ. Looking for the return of Christ is the result of sound doctrine and keeping the faith. A life lived in conformity with the New Testament will include the expectation of the soon return of the Lord. For such there is a crown of righteousness.

A fourth crown is called the *crown of life* and is mentioned in two passages. In James 1:12 it is a crown for those who endure trials:

> Blessed is the man that endureth temptation; for when he hath been approved, he shall receive the crown of life, which the Lord promised to them that love him.

In Revelation 2:10 it is given to those who suffer martyrdom for their faith:

> Fear not the things which thou art about to suffer: behold, the devil is about to cast some of you into prison, that ye may be tried; and ye shall have tribulation ten days. Be thou faithful unto death, and I will give thee the crown of life.

A fifth and final crown mentioned in the Scriptures is a *crown of glory* in I Peter 5:2-4:

> Tend the flock of God which is among you, exercising the oversight, not of constraint, but willingly, according to the will of God; nor yet for filthy

lucre, but of a ready mind; neither as lording it over the charge allotted to you, but making yourselves ensamples to the flock. And when the chief Shepherd shall be manifested, ye shall receive the crown of glory that fadeth not away.

This is a crown for faithfully feeding the flock of God. It is available to those pastors, elders and others who feed the sheep with the milk and meat of the Word of God.

There may be other crowns available, but these are the only ones referred to in the Word of God. At least these five are available to those whose works remain, which were built of gold, silver and precious stones.

These rewards of crowns are for the purpose of determining degree of authority in the messianic kingdom and not for the Eternal Order. In eternity all believers will be equal, but not so in the kingdom where believers may have different positions of authority. In parabolic form, this truth is found in Luke 19:11-27.

The result of those who have built with wood, hay, and stubble is given in I Corinthians 3:15. They will all be burned up. Hence, *he shall suffer loss*. But the loss is merely one of rewards and authority, nothing more. He will not be punished for his sins any more than a runner in a race is punished for not coming in first. But he does lose out on this reward. Lest anyone conclude that the person loses his salvation, the text in no uncertain terms states, *but he himself shall be saved*. His works do not determine his salvation. His salvation is assured for he trusted Christ, and salvation is by grace through faith apart from works. But he will spend the kingdom period with nothing to show for his Christian life.

D. THE MARRIAGE OF THE LAMB

The third factor in the eschatology of the invisible church is the Marriage of the Lamb. To fully understand what is involved at the Marriage of the Lamb, one must first understand the background of the Jewish marriage system which was present in that day and which involved four distinct steps.

First, the father of the groom made the arrangements for the marriage and paid the bride-price. The timing of the arrangement varied. Sometimes it occurred when both children were infants, and at other times it was shortly before the marriage itself. Often the bride and groom did not even meet until their wedding day.

The second step, which could have occurred weeks, years, or decades after the first step, was the fetching of the bride. The bridegroom would go to the home of the bride in order to bring her to his home.

This was followed by the third step, the wedding ceremony, to which a few would be invited.

The fourth step, the marriage feast, would follow, and could last for as many as seven days. Many more people would be invited to the feast.

In the Marriage of the Lamb all four of these steps of the Jewish wedding ceremony are evident. First, God the Father made the arrangements for His Son and paid the bride-price, which in this case was the blood of Christ. This is the background for the statement in Ephesians 5:25-27:

> Husbands, love your wives, even as Christ also loved the church, and gave himself up for it; that he might sanctify it, having cleansed it by the washing of water with the word, that he might present the church to himself a glorious church, not having spot or wrinkle or any such thing; but that it should be holy and without blemish.

Just as a long period of time often transpired between the first and the second steps of the Jewish marriage arrangement, this has been the case here. Almost 2,000 years have now passed since the first step occurred. But in I Thessalonians 4:13-18 discussed earlier in this chapter, the second step will occur. The Rapture is the fetching of the bride. Christ will come in the air in order to fetch His bride to His home, which is in heaven.

In heaven, the third step will take place. This is the marriage ceremony given in Revelation 19:6-8:

> And I heard as it were the voice of a great multitude, and as the voice of many waters, and as the voice of mighty thunders, saying, Hallelujah: for the Lord our God, the Almighty, reigneth. Let us rejoice and be exceeding glad, and let us give the glory unto him: for the marriage of the Lamb is come, and his wife hath made herself ready. And it was given unto her that she should array herself in fine linen, bright and pure: for the fine linen is the righteous acts of the saints.

The marriage ceremony takes place in heaven and involves the church. That it must take place after the Judgment Seat of Christ is evident from verse eight for the bride is viewed as being dressed in white linen, which is the righteous works of the saints. This means that all the wood, hay, and stubble has been burned away and all the gold, silver, and precious stones have been purified. Thus, following the Rapture of the church in which the Bridegroom brings the bride with Him to His home, and following the Judgment Seat of Christ which results in the bride having the white linen garments, the wedding ceremony takes place. It takes place before the actual second coming of Christ.

In the context of Revelation 19, verses 1-10 describe events in heaven prior to the second coming while verses 11-21 describe the second coming and subsequent events. The thing that should be carefully noted here is that the church is already in heaven *before* the second coming. Furthermore, the church has been in heaven long enough to undergo the Judgment Seat of Christ. This clearly means that the Rapture and the second coming cannot be the same thing but must be separated by some duration of time. Previously passages have been cited to show that the Rapture must come before the tribulation starts. Revelation 19:6-8 is further evidence for this fact.

The marriage ceremony will take place in heaven after the Rapture and before the second coming, involving only the church saints.

The fourth step, the marriage feast, will take place on earth after the second coming, and with the feast the messianic kingdom will begin. Whereas the marriage ceremony involves only the church, the marriage feast will include the Old Testament saints and the tribulation saints. The details of the fourth step will be discussed in Chapter XV.

This, then, is the eschatology of the invisible church. The Rapture will occur some time before the tribulation. Next, in heaven will come the Judgment Seat of Christ and the Marriage Ceremony of the Lamb prior to the second advent. Yet there are other events which occur in heaven just prior to the tribulation that need to be examined at this point in the next chapter.

CHAPTER VII

EVENTS IN HEAVEN PRIOR TO THE TRIBULATION

Chapters four and five of the Revelation record events transpiring in heaven just before the tribulation. With these chapters the Revelation begins the third and major section of the book dealing with *the things which must come to pass hereafter*, that is, after the seven churches. This section comprises chapters 4-22. Chapter four deals with the throne of God; chapter five speaks of the Lamb and the seven-sealed scroll.

A. THE THRONE OF GOD — REVELATION 4:1-11

Verse one contains an introduction to these two chapters:

> After these things I saw, and behold, a door opened in heaven, and the first voice that I heard, a voice as of a trumpet speaking with me, one saying, Come up hither, and I will show thee the things which must come to pass hereafter.

Many pre-millennialists see the Rapture of the church in this verse, but this requires somewhat of an allegorical interpretation. Following the golden rule of interpretation, this verse merely contains an invitation for John to come to heaven in vision (verse 2) in order that God can show him the *things which must come to pass hereafter*. John has already described *the things which he saw* (the Glorified Son of Man) and *the things which are* (the seven churches). Now the time has come for John to be shown what must follow the period of the seven churches. The word "hereafter" obviously refers back to 1:19 where the outline of the Revelation was first given. Hence, what follows from chapter four onward covers the events following the time of the seven churches. This itself may indicate a pre-tribulation Rapture. The invitation to John is not a symbol of the Rapture, for, as will be shown shortly, the church is viewed as being already in heaven. This is merely a personal invitation to John to come to where he can receive the rest of the prophecy involved in the Revelation.

Throughout the book two key phrases will be found. One is *after these things* and the other is simply *after this*. These phrases are *chronological*. What is described after these phrases follows chronologically the events found in the previous passage. The connecting link then is a chronological one: They introduce events that will chronologically follow those events described in the immediate previous context.

In verse one, with the phrase "after these things," John introduces events which will chronologically follow the previous context, namely the seven churches. The events of Revelation four and five then chronologically follow the events of the seven churches.

In verses 2-3 John describes the throne and the throne-sitter:

> Straight way I was in the Spirit: and behold, there was a throne set in heaven, and one sitting upon the throne; and he that sat was to look upon like a jasper stone and a sardius: and there was a rainbow round about the throne, like an emerald to look upon.

That John was not physically taken into heaven but only saw it in a vision is clear from the phrase "I was in the Spirit." The person sitting on the throne is God the Father.

Verse four describes the throne attendants:

> And round about the throne were four and twenty thrones: and upon the thrones I saw four and twenty elders sitting, arrayed in white garments; and on their heads crowns of gold.

The identity of these twenty-four elders has been much debated. Some take it to refer to celestial beings, while others take it to refer and represent the church. While the text does not clearly state as to what these twenty-four elders refer, there are clues in the text by which their identity can be deduced. First, these elders are clothed with *white garments* which throughout the Revelation are symbols of salvation. Celestial beings before the throne of God do not need salvation for they were not lost to begin with. But these elders were at one time lost and at some point received salvation as is seen by their wearing of the white garments.

The second clue is the fact that they are wearing crowns. These crowns are not *diadem* crowns worn by those who are royal by nature, which would have been the case had these been celestial beings. These crowns are the *stephanos* crowns, the crowns of an overcomer; the type of crown given as rewards to the members of the church at the Judgment Seat of Christ.

A third clue lies in their very title of *elders*. Nowhere else in Scripture is this term used to describe celestial or angelic beings. This term is used of humans in positions of authority either in the synagogue or church.

Hence, from these three clues, the twenty-four elders must represent the church saints. If this is true, then they provide further evidence for a pre-tribulation Rapture. The church is already in heaven in chapter four and five before the tribulation begins in chapter six. It fits well in the chronological sequence provided by the Revelation. Chapters two and three viewed the church on earth with a promise in 3:10 that the church will be kept from the very time of the tribulation. Now in chapter four, the church is in heaven, and so the promise of 3:10 has been kept. The fact that these twenty-four elders are wearing these *stephanos* crowns also shows that the events described in chapters four and five occur *after* the Judgment Seat of Christ but *before* the Marriage of the Lamb.

The figure "twenty-four" is probably taken from I Chronicles 24 where David divided the tribe of Levi into twenty-four courses to represent the whole. Since the church is a kingdom of priests, these twenty-four elders represent the church as a whole.

The third member of the Trinity, the Holy Spirit, is found in verse five:

> And out of the throne proceed lightnings and voices and thunders. And there were seven lamps of fire burning before the throne, which are the seven Spirits of God;

These seven Spirits of God are representative of seven attributes of the Holy Spirit described in Isaiah 11:2.

Verses 6-8 describe the four living creatures:

> And before the throne, as it were a sea of glass like unto crystal; and in the midst of the throne, and round about the throne, four living creatures full of eyes before and behind. And the first creature was like a lion, and the second creature like a calf, and the third creature had a face as of a man, and the fourth creature was like a flying eagle. And the four living creatures, having each one of them six wings, are full of eyes round about and within: and they have no rest day and night, saying, Holy, holy, holy, is the Lord God, the Almighty, who was and who is and who is to come.

The fact that these creatures are described as having six wings and that they cry the triad "Holy, holy, holy," would make them the same as the *seraphim* in Isaiah 6:1-3:

> In the year that king Uzziah died I saw the Lord sitting upon a throne, high and lifted up; and his train filled the temple. Above him stood the seraphim: each one had six wings; with twain he covered his face, and with twain he covered his feet, and with twain he did fly. And one cried unto another, and said, Holy, holy, holy, is Jehovah of hosts: the whole earth is full of his glory.

The chapter closes in verses 9-11 describing the continuous worship before the throne:

> And when the living creatures shall give glory and honor and thanks to him that sitteth on the throne, to him that liveth for ever and ever, the four and twenty elders shall fall down before him that sitteth on the throne, and shall worship him that liveth for ever and ever, and shall cast their crowns before the throne, saying, Worthy art thou, our Lord and

our God, to receive the glory and the honor and the power: for thou didst create all things, and because of thy will they were, and were created.

Following the crying of the triad, the twenty-four elders cast their crowns before the throne. This need not be taken as a once for all action whereby the saints who have received their crowns give them up permanently to Christ. The cry of the chorus is viewed as being continuous. The cry of the triad comes repeatedly, one after the other, and so does the chorus. Verse eight states that the crying of the triad is continuous and, therefore, so is the casting of the crowns. So then, it is not a question of the church saints giving up the crowns forever, but a continuous removal of the crowns from their heads in worship of God the Father.

B. THE LAMB AND THE SEVEN-SEALED SCROLL — REVELATION 5:1-14

Chapter five describes the Lamb and the seven-sealed scroll. It also serves as a prelude to the seven seal judgments. All three series of judgments (seals, trumpets, bowls) will be preceded by a prelude, and the prelude to the seal judgments is to be found in chapter five.
The seven-sealed scroll is introduced in verse one:

And I saw in the right hand of him that sat on the throne a book written within and on the back, close sealed with seven seals.

It is a scroll (the real meaning of the Greek term translated "book") that is written upon both sides and is sealed with seven seals.
Verses 2-4 describe the problem of the scroll:

And I saw a strong angel proclaiming with a great voice, Who is worthy to open the book, and to loose the seals thereof? And no one in the heaven, or on the earth, or under the earth, was able to open the book, or to look thereon. And I wept much, because no one was found worthy to open the book, or to look thereon.

The problem of the seven-sealed scroll was that no one was found worthy to open it. This difficulty, however, is solved in verses 5-7:

And one of the elders saith unto me, Weep not; behold, the Lion that is of the tribe of Judah, the Root of David, hath overcome to open the book and the seven seals thereof. And I saw in the midst of the throne and of the four living creatures, and in the midst of the elders, a Lamb standing, as though it had been slain, having seven horns, and seven eyes, which are the seven Spirits of God, sent forth into all the earth. And he came, and he taketh it out of the right hand of him that sat on the throne.

The second person of the Trinity is the one who is worthy to open the seven-sealed scroll. In verse five He is referred to as the Lion of Judah, but when John looks, he sees the Lion of Judah as a Lamb standing (verse 6). Thus, the two aspects of the two comings of the Messiah is seen. In the first coming, Christ came as a Lamb of God who died for the sins of the world. But in preparation for His second coming, He is represented as a Lion ready to pour judgment on His enemies.

The Lamb is viewed *as though it had been slain*. This phrase is an idiom referring to a resurrected individual. Christ was killed and by all human experience He should have been dead. But nevertheless, He was very much alive because of His resurrection. Hence, the phrase "as though it had been slain" is an idiom for a resurrected individual.

But with both God the Father and the Holy Spirit present in heaven, how is it that only Christ was "worthy" to open the scroll? In this context it would appear that to become "worthy" to open the seven-sealed scroll required one to die for sins and then be resurrected. Only the Son was "worthy" in this respect.

Since the Lion-Lamb is the one found worthy to break the seals, chapter five concludes with a description of the worship of the Lamb in verses 8-14:

> And when he had taken the book, the four living creatures and the four and twenty elders fell down before the Lamb, having each one a harp, and golden bowls full of incense, which are the prayers of the saints. And they sing a new song, saying, Worthy art thou to take the book, and to open the seals thereof: for thou wast slain, and didst purchase unto God with thy blood men of every tribe, and tongue, and people, and nation, and madest them to be unto our God a kingdom and priests; and they reign upon the earth. And I saw, and I heard a voice of many angels round about the throne and the living creatures and the elders; and the number of them was ten thousand times ten thousand, and thousands of thousands; saying with a great voice, Worthy is the Lamb that hath been slain to receive the power, and riches, and wisdom, and might, and honor, and glory, and blessing. And every created thing which is in the heaven, and on the earth, and under the earth, and on the sea, and all things that are in them, heard I saying, Unto him that sitteth on the throne, and unto the Lamb, be the blessing, and the honor, and the glory, and the dominion, for ever and ever. And the four living creatures said, Amen. And the elders fell down and worshipped.

Thus, chapters four and five describe events in heaven preceding the tribulation. With the opening of the seven seals the tribulation judgments begin. It is now time to turn to a study of the Great Tribulation.

PART III

THE GREAT
TRIBULATION

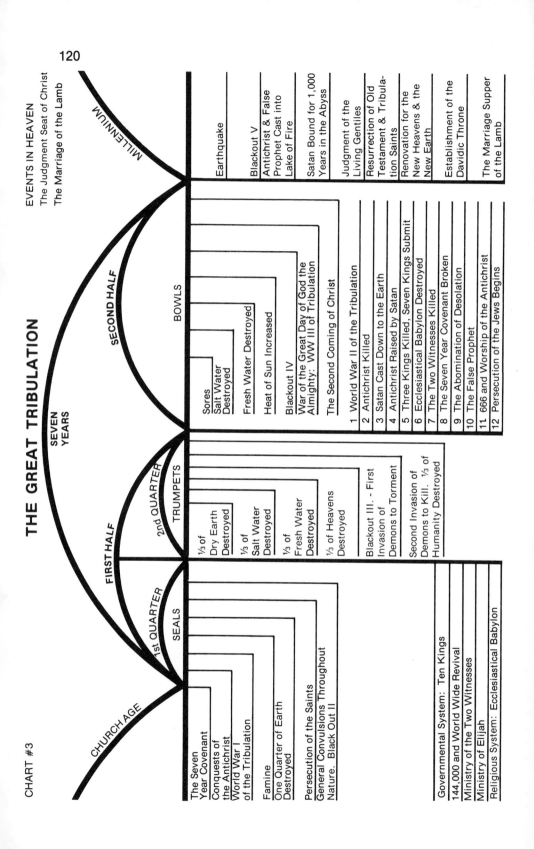

CHART #3

120

THE GREAT TRIBULATION

SEVEN YEARS

FIRST HALF

SECOND HALF

MILLENNIUM

CHURCH AGE

1st QUARTER

2nd QUARTER

SEALS

TRUMPETS

BOWLS

EVENTS IN HEAVEN
The Judgment Seat of Christ
The Marriage of the Lamb

SEALS

The Seven Year Covenant
Conquests of the Antichrist
World War I of the Tribulation

Famine
One Quarter of Earth Destroyed

Persecution of the Saints
General Convulsions Throughout Nature. Black Out II

Governmental System: Ten Kings
144,000 and World Wide Revival
Ministry of the Two Witnesses
Ministry of Elijah
Religious System: Ecclesiastical Babylon

TRUMPETS

⅓ of Dry Earth Destroyed

⅓ of Salt Water Destroyed

⅓ of Fresh Water Destroyed

⅓ of Heavens Destroyed

Blackout III. - First Invasion of Demons to Torment

Second Invasion of Demons to Kill. ⅓ of Humanity Destroyed

BOWLS

Sores
Salt Water Destroyed

Fresh Water Destroyed

Heat of Sun Increased

Blackout IV

War of the Great Day of God the Almighty: WW III of Tribulation

The Second Coming of Christ

1 World War II of the Tribulation
2 Antichrist Killed
3 Satan Cast Down to the Earth
4 Antichrist Raised by Satan
5 Three Kings Killed, Seven Kings Submit
6 Ecclesiastical Babylon Destroyed
7 The Two Witnesses Killed
8 The Seven Year Covenant Broken
9 The Abomination of Desolation
10 The False Prophet
11 666 and Worship of the Antichrist
12 Persecution of the Jews Begins

Earthquake

Blackout V
Antichrist & False Prophet Cast into Lake of Fire

Satan Bound for 1,000 Years in the Abyss

Judgment of the Living Gentiles
Resurrection of Old Testament & Tribulation Saints
Renovation for the New Heavens & the New Earth

Establishment of the Davidic Throne

The Marriage Supper of the Lamb

THE GREAT TRIBULATION:
INTRODUCTION

The second major division of eschatology concerns the seven year period commonly designated as the Great Tribulation. Some simply refer to the period as *the tribulation* and apply the term "Great Tribulation" only to the second half of the seven year period, the last 3½ years. However, in this study the term "Great Tribulation" will be used of the entire seven year period and not just of the latter half. In this introductory chapter three aspects will be discussed: the names of the tribulation, its purposes, and the general descriptions of it given in various parts of Scripture.

A. NAMES

In the Old Testament the most common name for the Great Tribulation is *the Day of Jehovah* or *the Day of the Lord* found in various passages. Every reference will be dealt with at some point in this study. There are some who use the Day of the Lord to include the millennium as well as the tribulation period based upon II Peter 3:10. But as will be shown later in this chapter, this verse is best seen as applying to the tribulation only rather than including the events following it. In *every* passage of the Scriptures that the term the "Day of Jehovah" or the "Day of the Lord" is found, it is always and without exception a reference to the tribulation period. This is the most common name for this period in the Old Testament, and it is also found in various passages of the New Testament.

But there are a number of other names or designations for this time period found in the Old Testament. Following the translation found in the American Standard Version of the 1901 edition, these names include:

The Time of Jacob's Trouble — Jeremiah 30:7
The Seventieth Week of Daniel — Daniel 9:27
Jehovah's Strange Work — Isaiah 28:21
Jehovah's Strange Act — Isaiah 28:21
The Day of Israel's Calamity — Deuteronomy 32:35;
                                        Obadiah 12-14
The Tribulation — Deuteronomy 4:30
The Indignation — Isaiah 26:20; Daniel 11:36
The Overflowing Scourge — Isaiah 28:15, 18
The Day of Vengeance — Isaiah 34:8; 35:4; 61:2
The Year of Recompence — Isaiah 34:8
The Time of Trouble — Daniel 12:1; Zephaniah 1:15

The Day of Wrath — Zephaniah 1:15
The Day of Distress — Zephaniah 1:15
The Day of Wasteness — Zephaniah 1:15
The Day of Desolation — Zephaniah 1:15
The Day of Darkness — Zephaniah 1:15; Amos 5:18, 20;
            Joel 2:2
The Day of Gloominess — Zephaniah 1:15; Joel 2:2
The Day of Clouds — Zephaniah 1:15; Joel 2:2
The Day of Thick Darkness — Zephaniah 1:15; Joel 2:2
The Day of the Trumpet — Zephaniah 1:16
The Day of Alarm — Zephaniah 1:16

The New Testament names and designations include:

The Day of the Lord — I Thessalonians 5:2
The Wrath of God — Revelation 15:1, 7; 14:10, 19; 16:1
The Hour of Trial — Revelation 3:10
The Great Day of the Wrath of the Lamb of God —
                              Revelation 6:16-17
The Wrath to Come — I Thessalonians 1:10
The Wrath — I Thessalonians 5:9; Revelation 11:18
The Great Tribulation — Matthew 24:21; Revelation 2:22; 7:14
The Tribulation — Matthew 24:29
The Hour of Judgment — Revelation 14:7

B. PURPOSES OF THE TRIBULATION

There are three main purposes for the Great Tribulation.

1. TO MAKE AN END OF WICKEDNESS AND WICKED ONES

The first of these purposes is to make an end of wickedness and wicked ones. There are two key passages which express this purpose. The first is found in Isaiah 13:9:

Behold, the day of Jehovah cometh, cruel, with wrath and fierce anger; to make the land a desolation, and to destroy the sinners thereof out of it.

This passage uses the term the "Day of Jehovah" as a reference to the Great Tribulation and gives its goal in the phrase *to destroy the sinners thereof out of it*. The purpose, then, is to destroy *wicked ones* out of the land. This is further described in Isaiah 24:19-20:

The earth is utterly broken, the earth is rent asunder, the earth is shaken violently. The earth shall stagger like a drunken man, and shall sway to and fro like a hammock; and the transgression thereof shall be heavy upon it, and it shall fall, and not rise again.

The closing words of this verse state that the basic reason for the judgments of the tribulation is that the transgression world-wide shall fall and not rise again. Its purpose is to make an end of *wickedness.*

2.   TO BRING ABOUT A WORLD-WIDE REVIVAL

The second purpose of the tribulation is to bring about a world-wide revival. This purpose is given and fulfilled in Revelation 7:1-17. In verses 1-8 John describes the *means* by which God will bring about this world-wide revival while verses 9-17 portray the *results* of the revival. Chapter seven will be examined from a different perspective in Chapter X of this book, but certain things should be mentioned at this time.

Revelation 7:1-4 reads:

After this I saw four angels standing at the four corners of the earth, holding the four winds of the earth, that no wind should blow on the earth, or on the sea, or upon any tree. And I saw another angel ascend from the sunrising, having the seal of the living God: and he cried with a great voice to the four angels to whom it was given to hurt the earth and the sea, saying, Hurt not the earth, neither the sea, nor the trees, till we shall have sealed the servants of our God on their foreheads. And I heard the number of them that were sealed, a hundred and forty and four thousand, sealed out of every tribe of the children of Israel.

Verses 5-8 proceed to state that 12,000 Jews are selected from each of the twelve tribes adding up to a total of 144,000 Jews. It is by means of these Jewish evangelists that God will bring about the world-wide revival and accomplish another goal of the tribulation.

Looking at this from a human viewpoint, there is a decided advantage in using Jews to conduct a world-wide revival in the short time period of 3½ years; for, as will be demonstrated later, this revival will occur during the first half of the tribulation. In the present system of training missionaries for the work of evangelism in a foreign field, the missionary must first study the Scriptures in a Bible school or in a seminary program, either of which takes three to four years. But while the Bible school or seminary graduate may be prepared to teach the Word of God in his own nation, he is still not prepared to minister in a foreign field. The next two years or so must be spent in language study; for he must learn the language of another country in order to communicate the Word there. The modern missionary, then, must spend approximately six years in preparation before he is fully equipped to present the Gospel in a language which is not his own.

However, this revival will be conducted in 3½ years during the first half of the tribulation. So there is not that much time for training. This is where there is a decided advantage in using Jewish people.

First of all, the Jews are scattered all over the world. All of the world's major languages and a great number of the world's minor languages are spoken by some Jews somewhere. Except for American Jewry, most Jews are at least bilingual. The author is bilingual, and the author's parents are multi-lingual, speaking five languages each.

Secondly, with a large segment of American Jewry being the exception, most Jews receive a good and basic understanding of the Old Testament text. They have a greater or lesser degree of knowledge of the Old Testament Scriptures, depending on their background.

Hence, sometime after the Rapture of the church, the Lord will save 144,000 Jews from the twelve tribes and from around the world. These Jews will already speak the languages needed. They will already have a basic knowledge of the Old Testament text. All they will need will be a little time spent in learning the content of the New Testament. So, they could begin to preach the Gospel in a very short period of time.

During the first half of the tribulation, God will evangelize the world by the means of the 144,000 Jews and thus fulfill the prophecy found in Matthew 24:14:

> And this gospel of the kingdom shall be preached in the whole world for a testimony unto all the nations; and then shall the end come.

Following the vision of the 144,000 Jews in the first part of Revelation seven, John saw the results of the ministry of these Jewish evangelists in verses 9-17:

> After these things I saw, and behold, a great multitude, which no man could number, out of every nation and of all tribes and peoples and tongues, standing before the throne and before the Lamb, arrayed in white robes, and palms in their hands; and they cry with a great voice, saying, Salvation unto our God who sitteth on the throne, and unto the Lamb . . . And one of the elders answered, saying unto me, These that are arrayed in the white robes, who are they, and whence came they? And I say unto him, My lord, thou knowest. And he said to me, These are they that come out of the great tribulation, and they washed their robes, and made them white in the blood of the Lamb. (verses 9-10, 13-14).

After the vision of the 144,000 Jews, John saw myriads and myriads of Gentiles as well as other Jews who have come to a saving knowledge of the Saviour during the tribulation. The connecting link *after these things* is chronological and also shows a cause and effect relationship between the first and the second parts of Revelation seven. Thus, by means of the 144,000 Jews, God will accomplish the second purpose of the Great Tribulation, that of bringing about a world-wide revival.

3. TO BREAK THE POWER OF THE HOLY PEOPLE

The third purpose of the tribulation is to break the power or the stubborn will of the Jewish nation. In Daniel 11 and 12, the prophet was given a vision of what conditions will be like for his people (Israel) during the tribulation. Then in Daniel 12:5-7 a question is raised as to how long this period will be allowed to continue:

> Then I, Daniel, looked, and, behold, there stood other two, the one on the brink of the river on this side, and the other on the brink of the river on that side. And one said to the man clothed in linen, who was above the waters of the river, How long shall it be to the end of these wonders? And I heard the man clothed in linen, who was above the waters of the river, when he held up his right hand and his left hand unto heaven, and sware by him that liveth for ever that it shall be for a time, times, and a half; *and when they have made an end of breaking in pieces the power of the holy people, all these things shall be finished.* (italics added.)

This passage provides a third goal of the tribulation. It is to break the power or the stubborn will of the Jewish nation. The tribulation will continue and will not end until this happens. So from this, the third purpose of the tribulation can be deduced: God intends to break the power of the holy people in order to bring about a national regeneration. The means by which God will perform this is given in Ezekiel 20:34-38:

> And I will bring you out from the peoples, and will gather you out of the countries wherein ye are scattered, with a mighty hand, and with an outstretched arm, and with wrath poured out; and I will bring you into the wilderness of the peoples, and there will I enter into judgment with you face to face. Like as I entered into judgment with your fathers in the wilderness of the land of Egypt, so will I enter into judgment with you, saith the Lord Jehovah. And I will cause you to pass under the rod, and I will bring you into the bond of the covenant; and I will purge out from among you the rebels, and them that transgress against me; I will bring them forth out of the land where they sojourn, but they shall not enter into the land of Israel: and ye shall know that I am Jehovah.

In this passage Ezekiel draws a simile with the Exodus which we examined earlier in Chapter IV. What is important to note here is that after God gathers the Jews from around the world, He will enter into a period of judgment (the tribulation) with them. The rebels among the Jewish people will be purged out by this judgment. Only then will the whole new nation, a regenerate nation, be allowed to enter the promised land under King Messiah.

C. GENERAL DESCRIPTIONS

Numerous passages of the Old Testament describe the nature and times of the Great Tribulation, and they can not all be dealt with in the scope of this study. But there are key passages that need to be considered in this introductory material on the tribulation.

1. THE LITTLE APOCALYPSE OF ISAIAH

An important passage pertaining to the tribulation is Isaiah 24:1-27:13. This section has some strong similarities with the Revelation, and so it has been called the Little Apocalypse of Isaiah. Chapter 24:1-13 depicts the earth in utter desolation because of the judgments of the tribulation:

> Behold, Jehovah maketh the earth empty, and maketh it waste, and turneth it upside down, and scattereth abroad the inhabitants thereof. And it shall be, as with the people, so with the priest; as with the servant, so with his master; as with the maid, so with her mistress; as with the buyer, so with the seller; as with the creditor, so with the debtor; as with the taker of interest, so with the giver of interest to him. The earth shall be utterly emptied, and utterly laid waste; for Jehovah hath spoken this word. The earth mourneth and fadeth away, the world languisheth and fadeth away, the lofty people of the earth do languish. The earth also is polluted under the inhabitants thereof; because they have transgressed the laws, violated the statutes, broken the everlasting covenant. Therefore hath the curse devoured the earth, and they that dwell therein are found guilty: therefore the inhabitants of the earth are burned, and few men left. The new wine mourneth, the vine languisheth, all the merryhearted do sigh. The mirth of tabrets ceaseth, the noise of them that rejoice endeth, the joy of the harp ceaseth. They shall not drink wine with a song; strong drink shall be bitter to them that drink it. The waste city is broken down; every house is shut up, that no man may come in. There is a crying in the streets because of the wine; all joy is darkened, the mirth of the land is gone. In the city is left desolation, and the gate is smitten with destruction. For thus shall it be in the midst of the earth among the peoples, as the shaking of an olive-tree, as the gleanings when the vintage is done.

In verses 19-20 the earth is pictured as staggering from the judgments of the tribulation which have fallen upon it because of sin:

> The earth is utterly broken, the earth is rent asunder, the earth is shaken violently. The earth shall stagger like a drunken man, and shall sway to and fro like a hammock; and the transgression thereof shall be heavy upon it, and it shall fall, and not rise again.

Yet the judgments are a necessary corollary to God's righteousness, and this is recognized by the righteous ones living at the time according to Isaiah 26:8-10:

> Yea, in the way of thy judgments, O Jehovah, have we waited for thee; to thy name, even to thy memorial name, is the desire of our soul. With my soul have I desired thee in the night; yea, with my spirit within me will I seek thee earnestly: for when thy judgments are in the earth, the inhabitants of the world learn righteousness. Let favor be showed to the wicked, yet will he not learn righteousness; in the land of uprightness will he deal wrongfully, and will not behold the majesty of Jehovah.

Isaiah 26:20-21 states that the righteous ones are specially protected by God as the judgments are poured out against all unrighteousness:

> Come, my people, enter thou into thy chambers, and shut thy doors about thee: hide thyself for a little moment, until the indignation be overpast. For, behold, Jehovah cometh forth out of his place to punish the inhabitants of the earth for their iniquity: the earth also shall disclose her blood, and shall no more cover her slain.

Indeed, this section of Isaiah is the backdrop filling in and clarifying much that is said in Revelation.

2. THE DAY OF JEHOVAH PASSAGES

The term *the day of Jehovah* is the most common term in the Old Testament for the tribulation. It is a period of time that begins with the signing of the seven-year covenant and ends with the second coming of Christ exactly seven years later. There are some who say the Day of Jehovah starts with the Rapture itself, assuming that it is the Rapture that begins the tribulation. But since there could easily be a period of time between the Rapture and the start of the tribulation, it is better to view the Day of Jehovah as starting with the seven year covenant. Others wish to extend the period of the Day of Jehovah to include the millennium and the aftermath, but a study of the term's uses in every passage will show that it is never used in any context except that of the tribulation. While other expressions such as "that day" or "in that day" are used for both the tribulation and the millennium, the term the Day of Jehovah is never used for anything outside of the Great Tribulation.

Several Day of Jehovah passages refer to Israel during the tribulation, and these will be taken into consideration in Chapter XIII. Right now only those Day of Jehovah passages that deal with the world in general, or relate to a specific Gentile nation will be studied. There are seven such passages that should be noted.

First, Isaiah 2:12-22 emphasizes the terror of Jehovah that will be manifested at that time:

> For there shall be a day of Jehovah of hosts upon all that is proud and haughty, and upon all that is lifted up; and it shall be brought low: and upon all the cedars of Lebanon, that are high and lifted up, and upon all the oaks of Bashan, and upon all the high mountains, and upon all the hills that are lifted up, and upon every lofty tower, and upon every fortified wall, and upon all the ships of Tarshish, and upon all pleasant imagery. And the loftiness of man shall be bowed down, and the haughtiness of men shall be brought low; and Jehovah alone shall be exalted in that day. And the idols shall utterly pass away. And men shall go into the caves of the rocks, and into the holes of the earth, from before the terror of Jehovah, and from the glory of his majesty, when he ariseth to shake mightily the earth. In that day men shall cast away their idols of silver, and their idols of gold, which have been made for them to worship, to the moles and to the bats; to go into the caverns of the rocks, and into the clefts of the ragged rocks, from before the terror of Jehovah, and from the glory of his majesty, when he ariseth to shake mightily the earth. Cease ye from man, whose breath is in his nostrils; for wherein is he to be accounted of?

Secondly, Isaiah 13:6-16 elaborates on the first purpose of the tribulation; to make an end of wickedness and wicked ones:

> Wail ye; for the day of Jehovah is at hand; as destruction from the Almighty shall it come. Therefore shall all hands be feeble, and every heart of man shall melt: and they shall be dismayed; pangs and sorrows shall take hold of them; they shall be in pain as a woman in travail: they shall look in amazement one at another; their faces shall be faces of flame. Behold, the day of Jehovah cometh, cruel, with wrath and fierce anger; to make the land a desolation, and to destroy the sinners thereof out of it. For the stars of heaven and the constellations thereof shall not give their light; the sun shall be darkened in its going forth, and the moon shall not cause its light to shine. And I will punish the world for their evil, and the wicked for their iniquity; and I will cause the arrogancy of the proud to cease, and will lay low the haughtiness of the terrible. I will make a man more rare than fine gold, even a man than the pure gold of Ophir. Therefore I will make the heavens to tremble, and the earth shall be shaken out of its place, in the wrath of Jehovah of hosts, and in the day of his fierce anger. And it shall come to pass, that as the chased roe, and as sheep that no man gathereth, they shall turn every man to his own people, and shall flee every man to his own land. Every one that is found shall be thrust through; and every one that is taken shall fall by the sword. Their infants also shall be dashed in pieces before their eyes; their houses shall be rifled, and their wives ravished.

Thirdly, Ezekiel 30:1-9 describes the effects of the Day of Jehovah on the middle-east nations, particularly on Egypt:

> The word of Jehovah came again unto me, saying, Son of man, prophesy, and say, Thus saith the Lord Jehovah: Wail ye, Alas for the day! For the day

is near, even the day of Jehovah is near; it shall be a day of clouds, a time of the nations. And a sword shall come upon Egypt, and anguish shall be in Ethiopia, when the slain shall fall in Egypt; and they shall take away her multitude, and her foundations shall be broken down. Ethiopia, and Put, and Lud, and all the mingled people, and Cub, and the children of the land that is in league, shall fall with them by the sword. Thus saith Jehovah: They also that uphold Egypt shall fall; and the pride of her power shall come down: from the tower of Seveneh shall they fall in it by the sword, saith the Lord Jehovah. And they shall be desolate in the midst of the countries that are desolate; and her cities shall be in the midst of the cities that are wasted. And they shall know that I am Jehovah, when I have set a fire in Egypt, and all her helpers are destroyed. In that day shall messengers go forth from before me in ships to make the careless Ethiopians afraid; and there shall be anguish upon them, as in the day of Egypt; for, lo, it cometh.

Fourthly, Joel 1:15-20 stresses how the Day of Jehovah will affect the crops of the earth:

Alas for the day! for the day of Jehovah is at hand, and as destruction from the Almighty shall it come. Is not the food cut off before our eyes, yea, joy and gladness from the house of our God? The seeds rot under their clods; the garners are laid desolate, the barns are broken down; for the grain is withered. How do the beasts groan! the herds of cattle are perplexed, because they have no pasture; yea, the flocks of sheep are made desolate. O Jehovah, to thee do I cry; for the fire hath devoured the pastures of the wilderness, and the flame hath burned all the trees of the field. Yea, the beasts of the field pant unto thee; for the water brooks are dried up, and the fire hath devoured the pastures of the wilderness.

Fifthly, Obadiah 10-20 describes the effects on the land of Edom, present day Jordan:

For the violence done to thy brother Jacob, shame shall cover thee, and thou shalt be cut off for ever. In the day that thou stoodest on the other side, in the day that strangers carried away his substance, and foreigners entered into his gates, and cast lots upon Jerusalem, even thou wast as one of them. But look not thou on the day of thy brother in the day of his disaster, and rejoice not over the children of Judah in the day of their destruction; neither speak proudly in the day of distress. Enter not into the gate of my people in the day of their calamity; yea, look not thou on their affliction in the day of their calamity, neither lay ye hands on their substance in the day of their calamity. And stand thou not in the crossway, to cut off those of his that escape; and deliver not up those of his that remain in the day of distress. For the day of Jehovah is near upon all the nations: as thou hast done, it shall be done unto thee; thy dealing shall return upon thine own head. For as ye have drunk upon my holy mountain, so shall all the nations drink continually; yea, they shall drink, and swallow down, and shall be as though they had not been. But in mount Zion there shall be those that escape, and it shall be holy; and the house of Jacob shall possess their possessions. And the house of Jacob shall be a fire, and the house of Joseph a flame, and the house of Esau for

> stubble, and they shall burn among them, and devour them; and there shall not be any remaining to the house of Esau; for Jehovah hath spoken it. And they of the South shall possess the mount of Esau, and they of the lowland the Philistines; and they shall possess the field of Ephraim, and the field of Samaria; and Benjamin shall possess Gilead. And the captives of this host of the children of Israel, that are among the Canaanites, shall possess even unto Zarephath; and the captives of Jerusalem, that are in Sepharad, shall possess the cities of the South.

The Day of Jehovah will be particularly heavy on Edom because of their special mistreatment of Israel. Though other nations are equally guilty, Edom has a unique shame due to its blood relationship to Israel.

Sixthly, Zephaniah 1:14-18 portrays the Day of Jehovah as a time of darkness and distress, and also refers to the first purpose of the tribulation:

> The great day of Jehovah is near, it is near and hasteth greatly, even the voice of the day of Jehovah; the mighty man crieth there bitterly. That day is a day of wrath, a day of trouble and distress, a day of wasteness and desolation, a day of darkness and gloominess, a day of clouds and thick darkness, a day of the trumpet and alarm, against the fortified cities, and against the high battlements. And I will bring distress upon men, that they shall walk like blind men, because they have sinned against Jehovah; and their blood shall be poured out as dust, and their flesh as dung. Neither their silver nor their gold shall be able to deliver them in the day of Jehovah's wrath; but the whole land shall be devoured by the fire of his jealousy: for he will make an end, yea, a terrible end, of all them that dwell in the land.

Seventhly, in II Peter 3:10-12 the Day of Jehovah is described as a time of burning for the earth:

> But the day of the Lord will come as a thief; in the which the heavens shall pass away with a great noise, and the elements shall be dissolved with fervent heat, and the earth and the works that are therein shall be burned up. Seeing that these things are thus all to be dissolved, what manner of persons ought ye to be in all holy living and godliness, looking for and earnestly desiring the coming of the day of God, by reason of which the heavens being on fire shall be dissolved, and the elements shall melt with fervent heat?

The process by which the earth will be burned is by the fiery judgments contained in the seal, trumpet and bowl judgments which will be discussed in Chapters X and XII.

In summary then, the Scriptures give some general descriptions of the Great Tribulation as a time of darkness, torment, anguish, turmoil, confusion, death, and massive destruction, especially by fire.

CHAPTER IX

THE BEGINNING OF THE TRIBULATION

It has been emphasized in several places that it is *not* the Rapture that begins the tribulation, but the signing of the seven-year covenant between the Antichrist and Israel. Two key passages bear this out.

A.   DANIEL 9:24-27

The first passage is Daniel 9:24-27. This is the famous seventy weeks or seventy-sevens of Daniel the prophet. In this passage a 490 year period is decreed over the Jewish people. A careful study of this text will show that the first 483 of the 490 years are now history, having been fulfilled at the time of the first coming of Christ. However, there are seven years left to run in God's prophetic time clock for Israel. These are the same seven years as those of the Great Tribulation. This is also the key passage by which it can be known that the tribulation will last for seven years. The issue now is: What is the one event that begins these last seven years ticking away? Daniel 9:27 answers that question:

And he shall make a firm covenant with many for one week: and in the midst of the week he shall cause the sacrifice and the oblation to cease; and upon the wing of abominations shall come one that maketh desolate; and even unto the full end, and that determined, shall wrath be poured out upon the desolate.

This verse speaks of an individual making a seven year covenant with the Jewish nation. The Hebrew text emphasizes that this will be a firm and strong covenant. The *he* refers back to its nearest antecedent which is the *prince that shall come* in verse 26. This person is better known in Christian circles as the Antichrist. So when the Antichrist signs a seven year covenant with Israel, the last week, or the last seven years of God's prophetic time clock for Israel begins ticking away. This and only this is the starting point of the seven years of the tribulation.

In light of this it should be very evident that it is *not* the Rapture which begins the tribulation. As has already been shown, the Rapture will occur sometime before the tribulation. It may come just before the tribulation, or it may come a number of years before the tribulation. The point is: it is the signing of the seven year covenant between Israel and the Antichrist that begins the tribulation, and not anything else.

Three more things ought to be noted from this passage. First, the covenant is viewed in this verse from man's perspective. Man will perceive it as simply a seven-year covenant between Israel and the

Antichrist which the Antichrist will break half way through.

Secondly, the covenant is made with many but not with all. The Hebrew text has a definite article and so a more correct translation would be *the* many. *The many* who make this covenant will have to include the leaders of Israel empowered to sign covenants of this nature. But there will be a segment of the Jewish people who will refuse to have anything to do with this particular covenant and will not identify themselves with it.

A third thing to notice is that there are three results. *First* the covenant is broken: *in the midst of the week he shall cause the sacrifice and the oblation to cease.* Although the covenant was made for seven years, the Antichrist will break this covenant at the half-way point. The breaking of the covenant is indicated by the forced cessation of the sacrificial system. A *second* result is that, following the breaking of the covenant, desolation falls upon the Jewish people via the one breaking the covenant: *and upon the wing of abominations shall come one that maketh desolate.* The covenant, which originally created a feeling of security, will result in desolation being poured out upon them. The desolation includes an "abomination" which is a term referring to an image or an idol. The desolation includes forced idolatry. The one making the desolation is the "he" of verse 27 and "the prince that shall come" of verse 26: the Antichrist. A *third* result is that following this, the wrath of God will be poured out upon the desolate: *and even unto the full end, and that determined, shall wrath be poured out upon the desolate.* The expression "even unto the full end" means "to finish" or "to complete." The wrath to be poured out will be until the *completion* of the seventy-sevens and to the *finish* of the program God intended for it (verse 24). The tribulation will not go beyond its pre-determined duration and will end to the very day (Matthew 24:26). The last word can be translated either as "desolate" or "desolator." If it is the former, the reference would be to the Jews and their suffering during the second half of the tribulation. If it is the latter, then the reference would be to the Antichrist whose destruction will come on the last day of the seventieth seven.

B.   ISAIAH 28:14-22

While Daniel 9:27 presents the covenant that begins the tribulation from man's perspective, Isaiah 28:14-22 views the covenant from God's perspective. In verse 14 God's viewpoint of *the many* who enter the covenant is given:

> Wherefore hear the word of Jehovah, ye scoffers, that rule this people that is in Jerusalem.

God calls the ones making this covenant *scoffers.* He considers them mockers rather than serious leaders. Verse 15 gives the reason that God considers them thus and provides God's viewpoint of the covenant itself:

> Because ye have said, We have made a covenant with death, and with Sheol are we at agreement; when the overflowing scourge shall pass through, it shall not come unto us; for we have made lies our refuge, and under falsehood have we hid ourselves.

Here in vivid terms, it can be seen why God calls the leaders *scoffers*. It is obvious that the leaders of Israel will go into this covenant in order to obtain some measure of security and to escape the "overflowing scourge." The figure of a flood when used symbolically is always a symbol of a military invasion. Hence, the leaders of Israel will believe that by entering the covenant, they will be free from any further military invasions. However, God declares that this is not a covenant of life, but a covenant of death. It is not a covenant of heaven, but a covenant of hell. Rather than gaining security, they will receive a strong measure of insecurity.

Verse 16 speaks of *the non-many* who refuse to enter into the covenant:

> Therefore thus saith the Lord Jehovah, Behold, I lay in Zion for a foundation a stone, a tried stone, a precious corner-stone of sure foundation: he that believeth shall not be in haste.

This verse makes clear that there will be a segment of Jews, as there were in Daniel 9:27, who will refuse to have anything to do with this covenant. They will not be in haste to enter into it nor to identify themselves with it.

Then in verses 17-22 the same three results are found as in Daniel 9:27. First, in verses 17-18 the covenant is broken followed by the military invasions they hoped to escape:

> And I will make justice the line, and righteousness the plummet; and the hail shall sweep away the refuge of lies, and the waters shall overflow the hiding-place. And your covenant with death shall be annulled, and your agreement with Sheol shall not stand; when the overflowing scourge shall pass through, then ye shall be trodden down by it.

Secondly, in verses 19-20 desolations fall upon the Jewish people:

> As often as it passeth through, it shall take you; for morning by morning shall it pass through, by day and by night: and it shall be nought but terror to understand the message. For the bed is shorter than that a man can stretch himself on it; and the covering narrower than that he can wrap himself in it.

Rather than having security, they will have insecurity. This insecurity is pictured as tremendous discomfiture and is illustrated in two ways. First, it is like a man trying to stretch himself out on a bed that is too short for him. Secondly, it is like a man trying to wrap himself up in a blanket to protect himself from the cold, but the blanket is too small to cover all of his body. In place of comfort, there will be discomfort. In place of security there will be insecurity.

The third result is the wrath of God emphasized in verses 21-22:

> For Jehovah will rise up as in mount Perazim, he will be wroth as in the valley of Gibeon; that he may do his work, his strange work, and bring to pass his act, his strange act. Now therefore be ye not scoffers, lest your bonds be made strong; for a decree of destruction have I heard from the Lord, Jehovah of hosts, upon the whole earth.

Two of the Old Testament names for the tribulation are given in this passage: *Jehovah's strange work* and *Jehovah's strange act*. It is given these two unusual names because of the latter phrase in verse 22, *for a decree of destruction have I heard from the Lord, Jehovah of hosts, upon the whole earth.* This decree is issued in heaven because of the covenant that is signed on earth. It is strange in that it calls for the destruction of the *whole* earth. This decree of destruction is the same as the seven-sealed scroll of Revelation five. As the next chapter will show, with the breaking of the seals, there is massive destruction of the earth. But this decree of destruction will be issued only when the covenant is signed.

So then, the same point made in Daniel 9:27 is made by Isaiah. The tribulation begins with the signing of the seven year covenant between the leaders of Israel and the Antichrist. Once that covenant is signed, the tribulation begins and a decree of destruction is issued by God Himself.

CHAPTER X

THE EVENTS OF THE FIRST HALF
OF THE TRIBULATION

Revelation chapters 6-19 deal with the Great Tribulation period. Chapters 6-9 and 17 are concerned with the events of the first half; chapters 10-14 with the events of the middle; and, chapters 15-16 and 18 with the events of the second half.

Regarding the events of the first half, two things should be noted. *First*, some events occur in chronological sequence with one event following the other in order. The seal judgments of chapter six and the trumpet judgments of chapters 8-9 fall into this category. *Secondly*, other events occur throughout the first half simultaneously with the sequential events. There are five such events occurring throughout the first half. Two of these events actually begin before the tribulation but continue on into and through the first half. One is the ministry of Elijah the prophet. The other is the governmental system of the ten kings and the ten kingdoms. As was stated earlier, after the fall of the one world government before the tribulation, the world is divided into ten kingdoms. This ten-kingdom division continues into and throughout the first half of the tribulation.

The other three events will be discussed later in this chapter. They are the ministry of the 144,000 and the world-wide revival (Revelation 7); the ministry of the Two Witnesses (Revelation 11); and, the rule of the Ecclesiastical Babylon which will control the religious affairs of the world during the first half (Revelation 17).

A. THE SEAL JUDGMENTS

The seal judgments of Revelation six are the first of three series of judgments during the tribulation. These begin as a result of the signing of the seven year covenant and are part of the decree of the destruction upon the whole earth (Isaiah 28:22).

There are seven seal judgments, with the seventh containing the seven trumpet judgments. The seventh trumpet judgment contains the seven bowl judgments. The first four of the seven seal judgments are also known as "the four horsemen of the Apocalypse."

1. THE FIRST SEAL

The first seal is in Revelation 6:1-2:

And I saw when the Lamb opened one of the seven seals, and I heard one of the four living creatures saying as with a voice of thunder, Come. And I saw, and behold, a white horse, and he that sat thereon had a bow; and there was given unto him a crown: and he came forth conquering, and to conquer.

With the first horseman of the Apocalypse, Revelation introduces a man wearing a crown and conquering to conquer. This figure on the white horse will play a major role in the tribulation period. That the figure is not Christ is indicated by the fact that the crown here is a *stephanos* crown, the crown of an overcomer or victor. It is not the *diadem* crown, the crown of sovereignty and royalty, the type of crown Christ will wear. This figure who enters the tribulation conquering to conquer is the Antichrist.

To fully understand the person and the activities of the Antichrist, he needs to be viewed within the framework of the counterfeit trinity. According to Revelation 13, an unholy trinity will be set up in the Great Tribulation. Satan will play the role of the counterfeit father. For just as the true Father gave all His authority to the Son, Satan will give all his authority to the Antichrist. The False Prophet will play the role of the counterfeit holy spirit. The ministry of the Holy Spirit is to call men to worship Christ. The ministry of the False Prophet will be to call all men to worship the Antichrist. In every detail, as will be seen later in this study, the Antichrist will play the part of a counterfeit son. Once the role he is to play is comprehended, many things said of him in the Scriptures will be more easily understood.

a.   THE NAMES OF THE ANTICHRIST

The person who is to have the central role in human affairs during the Great Tribulation is given a number of names throughout the Scriptures. These various names, titles or descriptions simply portray the various facets of his character. Taken together, these names portray him as the epitome of evil in the human realm just as Satan is the epitome of evil in the angelic realm.

The various names are as follows:
   The seed of Satan — Genesis 3:15
   The little horn — Daniel 7:8
   The king of fierce countenance — Daniel 8:23
   The prince that shall come — Daniel 9:26
   The desolator — Daniel 9:27
   The willful king — Daniel 11:36
   The man of sin — II Thessalonians 2:3
   The son of perdition — II Thessalonians 2:3
   The lawless one — II Thessalonians 2:8
   The Antichrist — I John 2:22
   The beast — Revelation 11:7

Of these eleven names, six are found in the Old Testament and five in the New. Of the Old Testament names, all are in the book of Daniel except for one. Of the New Testament names, three are given by Paul, all in one chapter of one book out of his many writings. The other two names are given by the Apostle John in two of his five books.

The vast majority of prophetic scholars have used a single name for this future world dictator: The Antichrist. Although this may not be his most common name in Scripture, it is a well chosen title. It is a title that describes his true intent, which is to be against Christ. All his other names essentially portray the various characteristics which he will use in his opposition to Christ.

However, one should begin to see the counterfeit nature in this multiplicity of names. For just as Jesus has a number of different names, titles and descriptions, so does the Antichrist.

b. THE ORIGIN OF THE ANTICHRIST

The Antichrist, being the counterfeit son, will have both a natural origin and a supernatural origin in imitation of the real Son. The natural origin of the true Son is that He was born of a Jewish woman. The supernatural origin was the miraculous virgin conception by means of the overshadowing of the Holy Spirit. The end product was the God-Man.

(1) HIS NATURAL ORIGIN

As to his natural origin, speculation has centered around his nationality with the question being whether or not the Antichrist will be a Jew.

(a) THE ANTICHRIST WILL NOT BE A JEW

Those who believe that the Antichrist has to be a Jew do so for several reasons. One reason that is given could be classed as the *logical* reason. Stated in a syllogism, this argument goes as follows:

Major Premise: The Jews will accept the Antichrist as the Messiah.
Minor Premise: The Jews will never accept a Gentile as the Messiah.
Conclusion: The Antichrist will be a Jew.

Two assumptions, both of them questionable, are to be found in this argument for the Jewishness of the Antichrist. The first is that the

Jews will accept him as the Messiah. The Scriptures make no such claim. While the Bible teaches that Israel enters into a covenant relationship with the Antichrist, this in no way means that they will accept him as the Messiah. Some have stretched this reasoning to say that the Jews would not even enter into a covenant with a Gentile. But none of this is valid, for Jews have often entered into covenant relationships with non-Jews in the past.*

The second assumption states that the Jews will not accept a Gentile as the Messiah. Even if it is granted (and it is not) that the Jews do accept the Antichrist as the Messiah, this still does not prove that the Antichrist must be a Jew. Jews have been prone to accept Gentile messiahs in previous historic cases, one of which was on August 6, 1806 when large sections of world Jewry declared Napoleon to be the messiah because of his statement that he favored a recreation of the state of Israel in Palestine.

But this logical reason also fails to view the whole issue. It could be asked another way: how would the Gentiles accept him if he is a Jew? So the logical reason could be used either way, and it is not valid in and of itself.

So the argument for his Jewishness based on this kind of logic is not valid. It is an argument based on two assumptions, neither of which is able to stand on its own. Furthermore, the final analysis as to whether something is true cannot be based on logic but on Scripture. The ultimate question is not, "Is it logical?" but "Is it Scriptural?" The assumptions necessary for the logical reason cannot be validated by Scripture.

Another reason people often give for the Jewishness of the Antichrist is based on Revelation 7:1-8. Stated as a syllogism this argument would read as follows:

Major Premise: The tribe from which the Antichrist would come
                  would not be listed among the 144,000.
Minor Premise: Dan is not among the 144,000.
Conclusion: The Antichrist is from the tribe of Dan.

The folly of such reasoning should be clear to anyone holding to a literal interpretation of Scripture. First of all, it is an argument of conjecture. If the interpreter is at all honest, he would have to admit that he really does not know why Dan is left out of the 144,000. The Bible nowhere spells out why Dan is excluded. If the reason is what the pro-

---

* The most recent example is the peace treaty signed between Israel and Egypt. But no one in Israel believed Sadat was the Messiah.

ponents of this view say it is, then it should be explained why an entire tribe is punished because of one man. Furthermore, why is Dan included in the millennial Israel (Ezekiel 48:2) if there is a curse on him? Assuming information where the Bible is silent is a danger to sound hermeneutics.

This argument also involves circular reasoning. To repeat the syllogism:

Major Premise: The tribe from which the Antichrist will come will not be listed among the 144,000.
Minor Premise: Dan is not among the 144,000.
Conclusion: The Antichrist is from the tribe of Dan.

From this syllogism another is developed:

Major Premise: The Antichrist is from the tribe of Dan.
Minor Premise: Dan is a Jewish tribe.
Conclusion: The Antichrist is a Jew.

Or they can be stated another way:

1. The Antichrist is a Jew.
2. The tribe from which the Antichrist would come would not be listed among the 144,000.
3. Dan is not among the 144,000.
4. The Antichrist is from the tribe of Dan.
5. Dan is a Jewish tribe.
6. The Antichrist is therefore a Jew.

No matter how it is put, this is pure circular reasoning, the truth of which is dependent upon the truth of the presupposition. While circular reasoning is consistent within itself, the consistency does not make it scriptural. The presupposition of circular reasoning has no proof on which to base doctrine.

The Scripture text used most often for the Jewishness of the Antichrist is found in Daniel 11:37, which in the King James Version reads as follows:

Neither shall he regard the God of his fathers, nor the desire of women, nor regard any god: for he shall magnify himself above all.

The whole argument rests on the phrase "the God of his fathers" which is taken to be clear-cut evidence that the Antichrist is a Jew. It should be pointed out, however, that the argument for the Jewishness of the Antichrist from this verse is based upon the King James

Version. But even if it is granted (and it is not) that the King James is the correct translation from the original, the phrase "God of his fathers" need not be used exclusively of the Jews. The phrase "God of his fathers" allows for a wider interpretation. For instance, he could be a person who had Christian parents but rejects their God in this sense. It could refer to a Roman Catholic or a pagan just as easily as to a Jewish person. The one phrase where the term "Antichrist" is used in I John 2:18-19 refers to those who apostatize from Christianity and not from Judaism.

Ultimately, Bible doctrine should be based on the Hebrew and Greek texts since they are the closest to the original autographs. To base a doctrine on a translation, especially when that translation is known to contain error, is folly. This is exactly the case with the King James rendering of Daniel 11:37. Any student of Hebrew would see from the original text that the correct translation should be: "the *gods* of his fathers," and not "the *God* of his fathers." In the whole context, Daniel 11:36-39, the term *god* is used a total of eight times. In the Hebrew text, six of these times it is in the singular and twice in the plural, one of which is the phrase in verse 37. The very fact that the plural form of the word "god" is used in a context where the singular is found in the majority of cases makes this a reference to heathen deities and not a reference to the God of Israel.

Moreover, there is much external evidence to show that this is the correct rendering of the text. The earliest known translation of the Old Testament is the Septuagint (LXX) which is a Greek translation of the Old Testament made about 250 B.C. The LXX has translated the word as "gods" which is in keeping with the Hebrew text.

Further evidence that the King James Version is incorrect in its translation here is seen in the fact that almost all other English translations, both from Jewish and non-Jewish sources, have rendered the word for god in the plural. Two major Jewish translations, the Jewish Publication Society of America and the Isaac Leeser translation, have rendered the phrase "the gods of his fathers." In Christian translations the American Standard Version, the Revised Standard Version, the Amplified Old Testament, the New American Standard, the New International Version, among others, have all translated the phrase to read "the gods of his fathers."

Furthermore, the New Scofield Reference Bible, itself based on the King James Version, has done a great service to scholarship by rendering this passage to read in the plural form.

Commentaries based on the Hebrew rather than the English text recognized the correct reading of Daniel 11:37. This is true of the official Orthodox Jewish commentary in the *Soncino Commentary on the Old Testament* as well as the prominent Christian commentary in the *Keil and Delitzsch Commentary*.

All this evidence shows that Daniel 11:37, the chief argument used by proponents that the Antichrist is to be a Jew, gives no validity to this belief. A doctrine of such magnitude must not be based solely on the King James Version as this one is. It has been shown that even if the King James was correct, it would not limit the expression to Jews, but it would be valid for Christians as well. However, the truth is, the text is dealing with heathen deities and not with the Jewish Jehovah. If anything, this passage implies that the Antichrist will be a Gentile rather than a Jew.

(b) THE ANTICHRIST WILL BE A GENTILE

It has been shown that the Bible does not teach that the Antichrist is to be a Jew. This raises the question: do the Scriptures plainly teach that the Antichrist is to be a Gentile? The answer is that they do. This is seen to be true from biblical typology, biblical imagery, and the nature of the times of the Gentiles.

That the Antichrist is to be a Gentile is seen by first looking at *biblical typology*. The only biblical type of the Antichrist is given in the person of Antiochus Epiphanes, a Gentile. Nowhere is a Gentile seen as a type of Christ; and with good reason, for Christ Himself was to be a Jew. So here, the type of the Antichrist is a Gentile, Antiochus Epiphanes. The reason is that the Antichrist himself is to be a Gentile.

Another argument for the Gentile nature of the Antichrist is found in *biblical imagery*. Whenever the word "sea" is used symbolically in the Scriptures, especially in the book of the Revelation, it is a symbol of the Gentile nations. Since the Beast in Revelation 13:1-10 arises out of the sea, and since the sea represents the Gentile nations (Revelation 17:15), this points to the Antichrist as being of Gentile origin.

But the key to his Gentile nationality is to be found in *the nature of the Times of the Gentiles*. It is agreed by most premillennialists that the times of the Gentiles does not end until the second coming of Christ. It is further agreed that the Antichrist is the final ruler of the times of the Gentiles. (Extended information on this was presented in Chapter II). If this is so, how then can a Jew be the last ruler when only the Gentiles can have the pre-eminence? To say that the Antichrist is to be a Jew contradicts the very nature of the times of the Gentiles. A Jew heading up the final world throne of Gentile power is an impossible postulation. So while arguments from typology and imagery are not strong by themselves, when coupled with the clear scriptural teaching of the nature of the times of the Gentiles, they can be powerful evidence that the Antichrist is to be a Gentile.

(c) THE ANTICHRIST WILL BE OF ROMAN ORIGIN

But not only does the Bible reveal the fact that the Antichrist is to be a Gentile, it also reveals the very nationality of the Antichrist. The nationality of the Antichrist can be deduced from Daniel 9:26-27:

> And after the threescore and two weeks shall the anointed one be cut off, and shall have nothing: and the people of the prince that shall come shall destroy the city and the sanctuary; and the end thereof shall be with a flood, and even unto the end shall be war; desolations are determined. And he shall make a firm covenant with many for one week: and in the midst of the week he shall cause the sacrifice and the oblation to cease; and upon the wing of abominations shall come one that maketh desolate; and even unto the full end, and that determined, shall wrath be poured out upon the desolate.

The first order of business is to identify the "he" in verse 27 who makes the seven year covenant with Israel. Does it refer to the Messiah, the prince that shall come, or to a whole new personality? The rules of Hebrew grammar must be used to determine this. The fact that in the Hebrew text the third masculine singular is used means that one must look for an antecedent. The nearest antecedent is *the prince that shall come* in verse 26. So the "he" of verse 27 is the same as "the prince that shall come" of verse 26.

The next order of business is to establish the identity of this prince. It is generally recognized that this prince is the Antichrist himself. Daniel had already spoken of him in chapter seven of his book as "the little horn." So then, "the prince that shall come" is also the "he" who makes the covenant with Israel, and both have reference to the Antichrist. Verse 26 also states that "the prince that shall come" is of the same nationality as *the people* who will destroy the city and the sanctuary. The third step is to establish the nationality of this people, and history has shown that this was accomplished by the Romans in 70 A.D. The obvious conclusion, then, is that the Antichrist is a Gentile of Roman origin.

To summarize the argument of the Gentile Roman origin of the Antichrist, it could be stated as follows:

1. The "he" who makes a covenant and the "prince that shall come" are one and the same person.
2. They both have reference to the Antichrist.
3. The Antichrist is of the same nationality as the people who destroyed Jerusalem and the Temple.
4. The Romans destroyed Jerusalem and the Temple in 70 A.D.
5. The Antichrist, then, will be of Roman origin.

The conclusion is that the Antichrist will not be a Jew. Most people who believe the contrary merely assume it without giving any reason. Those who present a logical reason "how will the Jews accept him if he is not a Jew?" are reminded that the Bible and not logic is the basis for doctrine, including this one. Those who argue from Revelation 7:4-8 are arguing from conjecture and circular reasoning and not from any clear statement from Scripture. Those who argue from Daniel 11:37 are basing doctrine on a faulty translation of the Hebrew text.

Not only has it been concluded negatively that the Antichrist is not a Jew, but it is concluded positively that he is a Gentile as seen from biblical typology and imagery along with the very nature of the times of the Gentiles as presented by the Scriptures. The Bible not only teaches that the Antichrist is a Gentile, but it reveals his exact nationality: a Gentile of Roman origin, as seen by a careful study of Daniel 9:26-27.

(2) HIS SUPERNATURAL ORIGIN

The true Son has both a natural origin and a supernatural origin which became possible by virtue of the virgin birth. Since the Antichrist is to be a counterfeit son, he too will have both a natural and a supernatural origin by means of a counterfeit virgin birth.

His supernatural origin is to be found in Genesis 3:15:

And I will put enmity between thee and the woman, and between thy seed and her seed: he shall bruise thy head, and thou shalt bruise his heel.

This verse not only contains the first prophecy of the coming of the Messiah, it at the same time gives the first prophecy of the Antichrist. It should be noted that this verse speaks of enmity in two pairs. First, there is going to be enmity between Satan and the woman. This Satanic enmity with woman can be seen to play itself out in the account of Genesis six where Satan had some of his demons intermarry with human women for the purpose of perverting womankind in an attempt to nullify the first messianic prophecy. This attempt was stopped by means of the world-wide flood.

But secondly, the verse states that there is going to be enmity between the woman's Seed and Satan's seed. The woman's Seed is Jesus the Messiah. As God, He was eternally existent; as a Man, He was conceived of the Holy Spirit and born of a virgin. So He was truly both God and Man. The very mention of a seed of a woman goes contrary to the biblical norm, for nationality was always reckoned after the seed of the man. That is why in all the geneologies of Scripture, only the male names are given with some very rare exceptions. The reason why the Messiah must be reckoned after the Seed of the woman is explained by Isaiah 7:14: the Messiah will be born of a virgin. Since the Messiah will not have a human father, His national origins will have to be reckoned after the woman, since His humanity comes only from her. So the very expression "her Seed" implied a miraculous conception. In reference to Satan's "seed," this term, being in the same verse, implies the same thing: that of a supernatural and miraculous conception. The enmity against the Seed of the woman comes from the seed of Satan. If the Seed of the woman is Christ, the seed of Satan can only be the Antichrist. From this passage then, it can be deduced that Satan will counterfeit the virgin birth and will someday impregnate a Roman woman who will give birth to Satan's seed who is going to be the Antichrist. The woman herself may not be a virgin, but the conception of Antichrist will be through the miraculous power of Satan. By this means the Antichrist will have a supernatural origin.

Another passage dealing with this is II Thessalonians 2:9:

> Even he, whose coming is according to the working of Satan with all power and signs and lying wonders . . . .

The Greek word translated "working" is the word *energeo* which means *to energize*. His coming, then, will be brought about by the energizing of Satan. In other words, the Antichrist comes into being by some supernatural means, and that supernatural means is by means of a counterfeit virgin birth.

Clearly then, the counterfeit son, in imitation of the true Son, will have both a natural origin and a supernatural origin. As to his supernatural origin, his father will be Satan. As to his natural origin, his mother will be a woman of Roman nationality. A time is coming when the situation of Genesis six will be repeated. A fallen angelic being, this time Satan himself, will impregnate a Gentile woman of Roman origin who will then give birth to Satan's son. The end product will be a counterfeit god-man.

c.   THE CHARACTER AND THE RISE OF THE ANTICHRIST

Because of his supernatural origin as Satan's seed, the Antichrist will always have access to the Satanic and demonic realm. Ultimately, the counterfeit son will accept the offer that the genuine Son rejected. When Satan offered Christ all the kingdoms of the world on the condition that Christ would worship him just once, Christ rejected the temptation by stating that only one person is to be worshipped and that is God Himself. The same offer will be made to the counterfeit son, who will accept Satan's offer of the kingdoms. When this temptation is accepted by the Antichrist, it will mark the beginning of his rise to political and religious domination of the world (Daniel 11:38-39, Revelation 13:2). The rise to power of the Antichrist is described in two passages. The first passage is in Daniel 8:23-25:

And in the latter time of their kingdom, when the transgressors are come to the full, a king of fierce countenance, and understanding dark sentences, shall stand up. And his power shall be mighty, but not by his own power; and he shall destroy wonderfully, and shall prosper and do his pleasure; and he shall destroy the mighty ones and the holy people. And through his policy he shall cause craft to prosper in his hand; and he shall magnify himself in his heart, and in their security shall he destroy many: he shall also stand up against the prince of princes; but he shall be broken without hand.

In this passage it is emphasized that "the king of fierce countenance," or the Antichrist, will have the understanding of "dark sentences." This means that he will have the same supernatural abilities to solve riddles that Daniel had in Daniel 5:12. Daniel's source was God, but the source for the Antichrist will be Satan. The Antichrist will have the power of the occult behind him. This is further spelled out in the following verse where it is clearly stated that his power is going to be mighty, but it will not be his own power. In other words, the Antichrist will have access to a tremendous amount of power, but the power is not his own but originates from another source, that of his father: Satan. He will seek to destroy the holy people of Israel with this supernatural power. Verse 25 states that he is characterized by craftiness and deceit. By these means he will lull rulers into a sense of false security and take advantage of it for the purpose of uprooting them. For a time he will "prosper," that is, be successful in his goals. He shall "magnify himself in his heart" and this will lead to his self declaration of deity (II Thessalonians 2:3-4, Revelation 13:3-9). He will stand against "the prince of princes," the Messiah, and so truly be the ANTI-CHRIST.

A second description of his rise to power is in Daniel 11:36-39:

And the king shall do according to his will; and he shall exalt himself, and magnify himself above every god, and shall speak marvellous things against the God of gods; and he shall prosper till the indignation be accomplished; for that which is determined shall be done. Neither shall he regard the gods of his fathers, nor the desire of women, nor regard any god; for he shall magnify himself above all. But in his place shall he honor the god of fortresses; and a god whom his fathers knew not shall he honor with gold, and silver, and with precious stones, and pleasant things. And he shall deal with the strongest fortresses by the help of a foreign god: whosoever acknowledgeth him he will increase with glory; and he shall cause them to rule over many, and shall divide the land for a price.

In this passage, Daniel describes the Antichrist as a willful king (verse 36a) characterized by self-exaltation above all men, and self-deification by magnifying himself above even God (verses 36b-37). In his self-exaltation he will speak against the God of gods (Daniel 7:25), deifying himself and magnifying himself above all humanity. He will not desire the love of women which is natural to men, and so he will be inhuman in his disregard of women. The enmity of Satan against womanhood continues through Satan's seed. Furthermore, he will be under the total control of Satan (verses 38-39). The passage states that he will honor a god that his ancestors on his mother's side never honored: the god of fortresses, who is Satan. His policy will be that "might makes right." Furthermore, with the help of this foreign god, Satan, he will be able to take over the strongest defenses in the world, and he will appear totally invincible. Those who submit to his authority and deity will be increased and given positions of status and authority in his kingdom. He will divide territory he has conquered among those who will be loyal to him and confess him to be god.

Thus, the Antichrist will be a Satan-controlled and Satan-energized being who will set out in world-wide conquest. The beginning of this conquest is seen in the first seal, though total control does not come until the middle of the tribulation.

This, then, is the first horseman of the Apocalypse representing the key personality during the tribulation period. Later, more will be said concerning him.

2.   THE SECOND SEAL

The second seal is in Revelation 6:3-4:

And when he opened the second seal, I heard the second living creature saying, Come. And another horse came forth, a red horse: and to him that sat thereon it was given to take peace from the earth, and that they should slay one another: and there was given unto him a great sword.

With the second horseman of the Apocalypse peace is removed from the earth. The opposite of peace is war. Thus, the period of peace and false security that existed before the tribulation is now shattered. As the Antichrist comes "conquering and to conquer" in his world-wide conquest, the tribulation begins with a war. There are three major wars during the period of the tribulation, and the second seal is the first of these three wars. The second war will be in the middle of the tribulation and the third, which is the Campaign of Armageddon, towards the end of the tribulation.

3.   THE THIRD SEAL

The third seal is in Revelation 6:5-6:

And when he opened the third seal, I heard the third living creature saying, Come. And I saw, and behold, a black horse; and he that sat thereon had a balance in his hand. And I heard as it were a voice in the midst of the four living creatures saying, A measure of wheat for a shilling, and three measures of barley for a shilling; and the oil and the wine hurt thou not.

The third horseman of the Apocalypse brings a world-wide famine which often comes as a consequence of war. The expression "a measure of wheat for a shilling, and three measures of barley for a shilling," denotes a great scarcity of these food items. The judgment of a world-wide famine, however, is tempered by mercy. For while there is a famine of food, there will be an abundance of medicine, for the oil and wine are not hurt. These items were used for medicinal purposes.

4.   THE FOURTH SEAL

The fourth seal is in Revelation 6:7-8:

And when he opened the fourth seal, I heard the voice of the fourth living creature saying, Come. And I saw, and behold, a pale horse: and he that sat upon him, his name was Death; and Hades followed with him. And there was given unto them authority over the fourth part of the earth, to kill with sword, and with famine, and with death, and by the wild beasts of the earth.

The fourth horseman of the Apocalypse is the deadliest of all, for in this judgment one fourth of the world's population is destroyed. The population is destroyed by four means: the sword, which may mean either massive slaughter or another war; famine, meaning death by starvation; pestilence, meaning death by disease; and, death by wild animals. Once food becomes scarce, wild animals which generally leave man alone will begin to attack man for food.

5.   THE FIFTH SEAL

The fifth seal is in Revelation 6:9-11:

And when he opened the fifth seal, I saw underneath the altar the souls of them that had been slain for the word of God, and for the testimony which they held: and they cried with a great voice, saying, How long, O Master, the holy and true, dost thou not judge and avenge our blood on them that dwell on the earth? And there was given them to each one a white robe; and it was said unto them, that they should rest yet for a little time, until their fellow-servants also and their brethren, who should be killed even as they were, should have fulfilled their course.

The fifth seal deals with the Christian martyrs of the first half of the tribulation. Thus, early in the tribulation there is the persecution of the believers in Christ. This raises two questions. First, with the church already raptured, who are these saints and how is it that they come to believe? Secondly, who is doing the persecuting? As to how these martyrs became believers will be explained in Revelation seven: namely by the preaching of the 144,000 Jews. As to who is persecuting these believers, this will be answered by Revelation 17: namely the Ecclesiastical Babylon.

6.   THE SIXTH SEAL

The sixth seal is in Revelation 6:12-17:

> And I saw when he opened the sixth seal, and there was a great earth-quake; and the sun became black as sackcloth of hair, and the whole moon became as blood; and the stars of the heaven fell unto the earth, as a fig tree casteth her unripe figs when she is shaken of a great wind. And the heaven was removed as a scroll when it is rolled up; and every mountain and island were moved out of their places. And the kings of the earth, and the princes, and the chief captains, and the rich, and the strong, and every bondman and freeman, hid themselves in the caves and in the rocks of the mountains; and they say to the mountains and to the rocks, Fall on us, and hide us from the face of him that sitteth on the throne, and from the wrath of the Lamb: for the great day of their wrath is come; and who is able to stand?

Each series of judgments ends with convulsions of nature, and the sixth seal concludes the first series of judgments with such convulsions. The convulsions begin with an earthquake (verse 12a) followed by a blackout of the sun and moon, followed by a meteor shower (verses 12b-14). As has been stated in Chapter V, the Bible speaks of five blackouts during the end times, and this is the second blackout. Anarchy ensues as men begin to flee from the wrath of God rather than to turn to Him in faith (verses 15-17).

B.   THE 144,000 JEWS AND THE WORLD-WIDE REVIVAL

Revelation seven deals with the second major purpose of the Great Tribulation, that of the world-wide revival. The chapter divides itself into two sections.

1.   THE MEANS OF THE WORLD-WIDE REVIVAL

The means by which God will accomplish the second purpose of the tribulation is found in Revelation 7:1-8:

> After this I saw four angels standing at the four corners of the earth, holding the four winds of the earth, that no wind should blow on the

earth, or on the sea, or upon any tree. And I saw another angel ascend from the sunrising, having the seal of the living God: and he cried with a great voice to the four angels to whom it was given to hurt the earth and the sea, saying, Hurt not the earth, neither the sea, nor the trees, till we shall have sealed the servants of our God on their foreheads. And I heard the number of them that were sealed, a hundred and forty and four thousand, sealed out of every tribe of the children of Israel:
Of the tribe of Judah were sealed twelve thousand;
Of the tribe of Reuben twelve thousand;
Of the tribe of Gad twelve thousand;
Of the tribe of Asher twelve thousand;
Of the tribe of Naphtali twelve thousand;
Of the tribe of Manasseh twelve thousand;
Of the tribe of Simeon twelve thousand;
Of the tribe of Levi twelve thousand;
Of the tribe of Issachar twelve thousand;
Of the tribe of Zebulun twelve thousand;
Of the tribe of Joseph twelve thousand;
Of the tribe of Benjamin were sealed twelve thousand.

This passage describes the third of the five events happening throughout the first half of the tribulation. This vision regarding the 144,000 is something that occurs throughout the entire first half and not merely after the sixth seal judgment. In fact, it is going on during the seal judgments, and it is the means by which the fifth seal saints come to Christ.

In verses 1-3 the four angels which are commissioned to bring judgment on the earth are commanded to hold off their destruction until a specific number of servants are sealed. Sealing was done for two reasons: service and protection. Both reasons apply here. They are sealed for protection so that they cannot be hurt either by the judgments poured out by God or by the persecutions against believers. But they are also sealed for service, for they are the ones who will proclaim the message of the gospel in the tribulation.

In verses 4-8 the identification of those who are sealed is clearly specified as being 144,000 Jews. To make it even more clear, twelve tribes are listed with the statement that 12,000 are chosen from each of the twelve tribes listed. Such careful deliniation definitely indicates that these 144,000 are Jews and will be nothing else, in spite of much speculation to the contrary. The emphasis is on the Jewishness of the 144,000.

Looking at the list of tribal names, some have concluded that the tribe of Ephraim is left out, but this is not the case. In place of the name of Ephraim there is the name of his father Joseph (verse 8), but it is the same tribe.

But one tribe is left out, namely the tribe of Dan. No reason for this is given. A great deal of speculation and guess-work has developed as a result, mainly the idea that the Antichrist will come out of this tribe. But this has already been dealt with earlier. Others claim that the False Prophet will arise out of the tribe of Dan and that is why that tribe is left out. But this too is pure speculation. There is nothing in the context to suggest either of these suppositions. The text itself does not state the reason why the tribe of Dan is left out, so where the text is silent, it is best for the commentator to be silent as well.

This ministry of the 144,000 Jews preaching the gospel fulfills the prophecy of Matthew 24:14.*

2. THE RESULTS

The results of their ministry is seen in Revelation 7:9-17:

> After these things I saw, and behold, a great multitude, which no man could number, out of every nation and of all tribes and peoples and tongues, standing before the throne and before the Lamb, arrayed in white robes, and palms in their hands; and they cry with a great voice, saying, Salvation unto our God who sitteth on the throne, and unto the Lamb. And all the angels were standing round about the throne, and about the elders and the four living creatures; and they fell before the throne on their faces, and worshipped God, saying, Amen: Blessing, and glory, and wisdom, and thanksgiving, and honor, and power, and might, be unto our God for ever and ever. Amen. And one of the elders answered, saying unto me, These that are arrayed in the white robes, who are they, and whence came they? And I say unto him, My lord, thou knowest. And he said to me, These are they that come out of the great tribulation, and they washed their robes, and made them white in the blood of the Lamb. Therefore are they before the throne of God; and they serve him day and night in his temple: and he that sitteth on the throne shall spread his tabernacle over them. They shall hunger no more, neither thirst any more; neither shall the sun strike upon them, nor any heat: for the Lamb that is in the midst of the throne shall be their shepherd, and shall guide them unto fountains of waters of life: and God shall wipe away every tear from their eyes.

In verses 9-10 John sees a multitude of Gentiles from every nationality standing before the throne of God. The expression "after these things" means that the salvation of these myriads of Gentiles follows chronologically the 144,000 Jews and there is a cause and effect relationship.

After describing the worship of the one on the throne (verses 11-12), the text proceeds to identify who these Gentiles are that are found around the throne (verses 13-14). These Gentiles are identified as those who have come out of the Great Tribulation. They are saved Gentiles for they have washed their robes in the blood of the Lamb. Since they follow chronologically the ministry of the 144,000 Jews, the implication is that they are the Gentiles who come to Christ as a result of the preaching of the 144,000 Jews. Included are the fifth seal saints who suffered martyrdom. Because of the massive persecution that

* For more information on the 144,000, see Chapter VIII.

these tribulation saints have undergone, this passage concludes with a description of the comfort they now enjoy in the presence of God (verses 15-17).

From this chapter it should be evident that the Holy Spirit will be still at work in the tribulation, for the work of regeneration is His peculiar ministry. While the work of restraining evil is removed allowing the Antichrist to begin his evil rise to power, the Holy Spirit Himself will still be in the world and will have an active ministry. While He will no longer be baptizing (for that is a special ministry for the church only),* He will be performing some of His other ministries such as regeneration, filling, sealing, etc.

In all this, the second purpose of the tribulation will be accomplished: that of bringing about a world-wide revival.

C. THE TRUMPET JUDGMENTS

1. THE PRELUDE

The second series of judgments in the tribulation, the trumpet judgments, is introduced in Revelation 8:1-6:

> And when he opened the seventh seal, there followed a silence in heaven about the space of half an hour. And I saw the seven angels that stand before God; and there were given unto them seven trumpets. And another angel came and stood over the altar, having a golden censer; and there was given unto him much incense, that he should add it unto the prayers of all the saints upon the golden altar which was before the throne. And the smoke of the incense, with the prayers of the saints, went up before God out of the angel's hand. And the angel taketh the censer; and he filled it with the fire of the altar, and cast it upon the earth: and there followed thunders, and voices, and lightnings, and an earthquake. And the seven angels that had the seven trumpets prepared themselves to sound.

In verses 1-2 the seventh seal is opened and the seventh seal contains the second series of judgments called the trumpet judgments. Verses 3-5 describe events in heaven and earth just preceding the trumpet judgments. The act of adding incense to the prayers of the saints indicates that the trumpet judgments will answer the prayers of the saints, prayers already voiced in the fifth seal judgment. As a warning to the earth that the trumpet judgments are about to start, it is made to tremble with convulsions of nature. Then in verse six the seven angels prepare to sound the seven trumpets.

2. THE FIRST TRUMPET

With the sound of the first trumpet in Revelation 8:7, one-third of

* See Chapter VI.

the earth's dry surface is destroyed.

> And the first sounded, and there followed hail and fire, mingled with blood, and they were cast upon the earth: and the third part of the earth was burnt up, and the third part of the trees was burnt up, and all green grass was burnt up.

3. THE SECOND TRUMPET

The second trumpet in Revelation 8:8-9 destroys one-third of the salt waters including sea life:

> And the second angel sounded, and as it were a great mountain burning with fire was cast into the sea: and the third part of the sea became blood; and there died the third part of the creatures which were in the sea, even they that had life; and the third part of the ships was destroyed.

The great mountain burning with fire may refer to a meteor or a volcano, but the results are supernatural, for they of themselves would not turn the sea into blood. A number of the tribulation judgments are similar to the ten plagues God brought on Egypt, and here is one such similarity.

4. THE THIRD TRUMPET

The third trumpet in Revelation 8:10-11 destroys one-third of the sweet water:

> And the third angel sounded, and there fell from heaven a great star, burning as a torch, and it fell upon the third part of the rivers, and upon the fountains of the waters; and the name of the star is called Wormwood: and the third part of the waters became wormwood; and many men died of the waters, because they were made bitter.

Whenever the word *star* is used symbolically, it is always a symbol of an angel, and this is the case here. The angel's name is Wormwood, showing the angel to be a fallen one. This fallen angel causes one-third of the sweet water to turn bitter which in turn causes the death of many. Fallen angels will be used on several occasions to render judgment on the earth, and this is one such occasion.

5. THE FOURTH TRUMPET

In Revelation 8:12, the fourth trumpet destroys one-third of the earth's light sources:

> And the fourth angel sounded, and the third part of the sun was smitten, and the third part of the moon, and the third part of the stars; that the third part of them should be darkened, and the day should not shine for the third part of it, and the night in like manner.

These verses do not necessarily imply that one-third of the sun, moon, and stars are destroyed, only that their light sources are somehow hindered from reaching the earth. So as a result of this judgment, one-third of the light source for the daytime, and one-third of the light source for the nighttime are completely blocked out.

6.   PRELUDE TO THE WOE JUDGMENTS

With the first four trumpets having sounded, Revelation 8:13 introduces the final three:

> And I saw, and I heard an eagle, flying in mid heaven, saying with a great voice, Woe, woe, woe, for them that dwell on the earth, by reason of the other voices of the trumpet of the three angels, who are yet to sound.

Because the three final trumpet judgments are especially severe for mankind on the earth, they are called woe judgments. As bad as the first four judgments were, the latter three will be far more severe. This severity is so pronounced that there is a warning of their approach sounded with a voice in the atmospheric heavens. The eagle is most likely a seraph (Revelation 4:7) chosen to give this warning to the earth. The first two of these woe judgments are demonic invasions, and the third one contains the bowl judgments.

7.   THE FIFTH TRUMPET — THE FIRST WOE JUDGMENT

The first woe judgment and the fifth trumpet judgment is in Revelation 9:1-11:

> And the fifth angel sounded, and I saw a star from heaven fallen unto the earth: and there was given to him the key of the pit of the abyss. And he opened the pit of the abyss; and there went up a smoke out of the pit, as the smoke of a great furnace; and the sun and the air were darkened by reason of the smoke of the pit. And out of the smoke came forth locusts upon the earth; and power was given them, as the scorpions of the earth have power. And it was said unto them that they should not hurt the grass of the earth, neither any green thing, neither any tree, but only such men as have not the seal of God on their foreheads. And it was given them that they should not kill them, but that they should be tormented five months: and their torment was as the torment of a scorpion, when it striketh a man. And in those days men shall seek death, and shall in no wise find it; and they shall desire to die, and death fleeth from them. And the shapes of the locusts were like unto horses prepared for war; and

upon their heads as it were crowns like unto gold, and their faces were as men's faces. And they had hair as the hair of women, and their teeth were as the teeth of lions. And they had breastplates, as it were breastplates of iron; and the sound of their wings was as the sound of chariots, of many horses rushing to war. And they have tails like unto scorpions, and stings; and in their tails is their power to hurt men five months. They have over them as king the angel of the abyss: his name in Hebrew is Abaddon, and in the Greek tongue he hath the name Apollyon.

The passage begins when a fallen star is given the key to the abyss (verse 1). As always, when used symbolically, the star is a symbol of an angel. Once again it is a fallen angel. The *abyss* is a temporary place of confinement for fallen angels or demons. It is the place that the demons feared to be sent to when they were cast out by Christ (Luke 8:31). It is temporary, for the final abode for fallen angels will be the Lake of Fire. Not all demons are confined there at the present time. Those that are, are waiting there to be released for specific judgments on mankind.

When the abyss is opened by the fallen angel, the third blackout occurs (verse 2), and for the third time there is a total cessation of light from the sun reaching to the earth.

But it is not the blackout that makes the fifth trumpet judgment the first woe judgment. Out of the abyss a great number of demons are released for the first of two demonic invasions (verse 3). These demons are commissioned to carry out the fifth trumpet judgment (verses 4-5). They are commanded to refrain from destroying any vegetation and told to torment only those who do not have the seal of God on their foreheads. So the 144,000 are excluded from any harm in this first demonic invasion (7:3-4). In all likelihood it also includes all believers at that time. Furthermore, these demons are commanded to kill no one, but only to torment men for five months or 150 days. There will be a limit as to how much destruction these demons will be allowed to render. Unsaved mankind will be open to torment but not death.

Not only will the demons be unable to kill, but the tormented men will not be able to kill themselves either (verse 6). Because of the tremendous torment inflicted by these demons, men will seek death. They will attempt suicide, but all suicide attempts will fail. Men will be forced to endure the torment in all its fury.

The description of these "locust-scorpions" given in verses 7-10 clearly shows that they are something other than literal scorpions or locusts. Their origin being the abyss further shows that they are demons. It is not unusual for demons and other angelic beings to have animal-like features.

The description of the first woe ends with the identity of the fallen angel who opened the abyss. His name in Hebrew is *Abaddon* and in Greek *Apollyon*. Both words mean "destruction."

The five months of torment will eventually come to an end. Although mankind may see some relief, it will be short lived as 9:12 makes clear:

The first Woe is past: behold, there come yet two Woes hereafter.

8. THE SIXTH TRUMPET — THE SECOND WOE JUDGMENT

With that, the sixth trumpet judgment is sounded in Revelation 9:13-21:

And the sixth angel sounded, and I heard a voice from the horns of the golden altar which is before God, one saying to the sixth angel that had the trumpet, Loose the four angels that are bound at the great river Euphrates. And the four angels were loosed, that had been prepared for the hour and day and month and year, that they should kill the third part of men. And the number of the armies of the horsemen was twice ten thousand times ten thousand: I heard the number of them. And thus I saw the horses in the vision, and them that sat on them, having breast-plates as of fire and of hyacinth and of brimstone: and the heads of the horses are as the heads of lions; and out of their mouths proceedeth fire and smoke and brimstone. By these three plagues was the third part of men killed, by the fire and the smoke and the brimstone, which pro-ceeded out of their mouths. For the power of the horses is in their mouth, and in their tails: for their tails are like unto serpents, and have heads; and with them they hurt. And the rest of mankind, who were not killed with these plagues, repented not of the works of their hands, that they should not worship demons, and the idols of gold, and of silver, and of brass, and of stone, and of wood; which can neither see, nor hear, nor walk: and they repented not of their murders, nor of their sorceries, nor of their fornication, nor of their thefts.

With the sounding of the sixth trumpet four fallen angels bound at the Euphrates River are released for they are the leaders of the second demonic invasion (verses 13-14). While the first demonic invasion was led by one fallen angel, this one is led by four. While the first demonic invasion was able to torment but not to kill, this one is commissioned to kill one third of the earth's population (verse 15). So the second woe is indeed worse than the first.

The number of demons involved in the second invasion is given as 200 million (verse 16). Sensationalism has had a field day with this figure resulting in some fantastic speculation. In order for this speculation to stand, the 200 million figure must be pulled out of its context. The speculation all rests on current events. Communist China once declared that they can field an army of 200 million. With-out even so much as questioning the truthfulness of this assertion, many have concluded that the 200 million must involve a Chinese invasion of the Middle East. The context just will not allow for this.

In support of a Chinese invasion, the ones who adhere to this theory say that this invasion is led by "the kings of the east" and that the east *must* refer to China. First of all, "the kings of the east" are found in chapter sixteen and are not connected by the text with the 200 million of chapter nine. The kings of the east are part of the bowl judgments, and the 200 million belong to the trumpet judgments. So they are not connected in any way. The events are separated by a period of time.

Furthermore, the consistency of usage demands that we identify the kings of the east as referring to Mesopotamian kings rather than a reference to China. Who the kings of the east are will be explained in Chapter XIV. For now, it is sufficient to point out that the "east" in Scripture is always Mesopotamia and never China.

This army of 200 million are demons and not Chinese. The fact that they are led by four fallen angels shows that they are demons rather than humans. Furthermore, the location of the source of this invasion is the Euphrates River which is not located in China, but in Mesopotamia or ancient Babylonia, a place the Scriptures often connect with demonism.

The announcement of the number in this army is followed by a description of what this army looks like (verses 17-19). A person would be hard pressed to find just one Chinaman who looks like this, let alone 200 million of them. The description given of the army clearly rules them out as being human and requires that they be demonic. Furthermore, the means by which the destruction of one-third of the world's population is accomplished (fire, smoke, brimstone), involves the supernatural rather than the natural.

To summarize why these 200 million are demons and not Chinese, four things should be noted: first, they are led by four fallen angels; secondly, the location of the army is stated to be the Euphrates where Babylon is located (which in the future will be the headquarters of the counterfeit trinity); thirdly, the description given in the text rules this army out as being human; and, fourthly, the kings of the east are not connected with this at all.

Another passage describing these demonic invasions is found in Joel 1:15-2:11:

Alas for the day! for the day of Jehovah is at hand, and as destruction from the Almighty shall it come. Is not the food cut off before our eyes, yea, joy and gladness from the house of our God? The seeds rot under their clods; the garners are laid desolate, the barns are broken down; for the grain is withered. How do the beasts groan! the herds of cattle are perplexed, because they have no pasture; yea, the flocks of sheep are made desolate. O Jehovah, to thee do I cry; for the fire hath devoured the pastures of the wilderness, and the flame hath burned all the trees of the field. Yea, the beasts of the field pant unto thee; for the water brooks are dried up, and the fire hath devoured the pastures of the wilderness.

Blow ye the trumpet in Zion, and sound an alarm in my holy mountain; let all the inhabitants of the land tremble: for the day of Jehovah cometh, for it is nigh at hand; a day of darkness and gloominess, a day of clouds and thick darkness, as the dawn spread upon the mountains; a great people and a strong; there hath not been ever the like, neither shall be any more after them, even to the years of many generations. A fire devoureth before them; and behind them a flame burneth: the land is as the garden of Eden before them, and behind them a desolate wilderness; yea, and none hath escaped them. The appearance of them is as the appearance of horses; and as horsemen, so do they run. Like the noise of chariots on the tops of the mountains do they leap, like the noise of a flame of fire that devoureth the stubble, as a strong people set in battle array. At their presence the peoples are in anguish; all faces are waxed pale. They run like mighty men; they climb the wall like men of war; and they march every one on his ways, and they break not their ranks. Neither doth one thrust another; they march every one in his path; and they burst through the weapons, and break not off their course. They leap upon the city; they run upon the wall; they climb up into the houses; they enter in at the windows like a thief. The earth quaketh before them; the heavens tremble; the sun and the moon are darkened, and the stars withdraw their shining: and Jehovah uttereth his voice before his army; for his camp is very great; for he is strong that executeth his word; for the day of Jehovah is great and very terrible; and who can abide it?

Joel begins to portray this demonic invasion by describing the devastation of the Day of Jehovah, or the tribulation (1:15-20). After announcing its approach (verse 15) he relates the results on the crops (verses 16-17) so that little remains either for the temple (verse 16) or for sustenance (verse 17). This is followed by a description of the devastation of the livestock (verses 18-20).

Joel then proceeds to give an account of the invasion itself (2:1-11). The alarm is sounded (verse 1), announcing the approaching army of demons giving clear evidence that the Day of Jehovah has arrived with vengeance. He then describes the Day of Jehovah (verse 2a) as being composed of darkness, gloominess, clouds and thick darkness. As dawn is sudden and spreads around a mountain, so sudden and widespread is this judgment of the Day of Jehovah.

It is then that Joel points to the invading army (verses 2b-9). He gives their approach (verses 2b-c) which shows their uniqueness (verse 2b) and their devastation (verse 3). What is related here is similar to the Revelation passage which again points to something other than human.

The description of the invading army is presented next (verses 4-9) giving their appearance (verse 4), noise (verse 5), terror (verses 5-6), speed (verse 7), discipline (verse 8) and their attack (verse 9). The similarity with Revelation is striking and again points to these invaders as being demons.

The results (2:10) of this demonic invasion include convulsions of nature and a total blackout, the third one of the end time. The passage concludes with the reason for the invasion (2:11): the judgment of God. The text states that the army is great, for there are 200 million demons and it is enough for God to execute His word: the destruction of one third of humanity. It was pointed out in the introduction that one of the purposes of the Revelation was to give the chronological sequence to many of the Old Testament prophecies. This is just one example.

But even with the sixth trumpet judgment, mankind still refuses to repent (verses 20-21). They continue to worship the same demons which have tormented them for five months and have just destroyed one third of their number.

The trumpet judgments come to an end by the middle of the tribulation period.

D. THE TWO WITNESSES

The fourth event transpiring throughout the first half of the tribulation is the ministry of the Two Witnesses in Revelation 11:3-6:

> And I will give unto my two witnesses, and they shall prophesy a thousand two hundred and threescore days, clothed in sackcloth. These are the two olive trees and the two candlesticks, standing before the Lord of the earth. And if any man desireth to hurt them, fire proceedeth out of their mouth and devoureth their enemies; and if any man shall desire to hurt them, in this manner must he be killed. These have the power to shut the heaven, that it rain not during the days of their prophecy: and they have power over the waters to turn them into blood, and to smite the earth with every plague, as often as they shall desire.

In verse three the *timing* of the ministry is given as 1,260 days which is the equivalent of 3½ years. These 3½ years cover the first half of the tribulation period.

Their *identity* is given in verse four, and they are said to be the fulfillment of Zechariah 4:11-14:

> Then answered I, and said unto him, What are these two olive-trees upon the right side of the candlestick and upon the left side thereof? And I answered the second time, and said unto him, What are these two olive branches, which are beside the two golden spouts, that empty the golden oil out of themselves? And he answered me and said, Knowest thou not what these are? And I said, No, my lord. Then said he, These are the two anointed ones, that stand by the Lord of the whole earth.

These Two Witnesses have been subject to much speculation. Many prophetic teachers try to identify them with two men that have lived in the past. One is always said to be Elijah, while the other is said to be either Moses or Enoch. Those who claim them to be Enoch and Elijah base it on the fact that these two men have never died, and so they will return to die in the tribulation. Often Hebrews 9:27 is used as evidence for "it is appointed unto men once to die." But this is a general principle and not an absolute. For example, take the word "once." Yet some people have died twice, namely, all those who had been resurrected in the Old and New Testaments apart from Christ. Furthermore, what about the living church saints? If indeed Hebrews 9:27 is an absolute rule, it would mean that all living church saints at the Rapture will also have to die some time. Both I Corinthians 15:51 and I Thessalonians 4:15-17 show that Hebrews 9:27 is only a general principle. Also in the light of Hebrews 11:5, it cannot be that Enoch will die in the future:

> By faith Enoch was translated that he should not see death; and he was not found, because God translated him: for he hath had witness borne to him that before his translation he had been well-pleasing unto God.

Enoch is clearly said to have been *translated*, and this involves corruption putting on incorruption and mortality putting on immortality (I Corinthians 15:50-58). Since Elijah has already been taken into heaven, the same is apt to be true of him for no man in his physical state can enter heaven (I Corinthians 15:50). This means that neither Elijah nor Enoch can die for they are now immortal.

Those who wish to make them Elijah and Moses fall back on the fact that these were the two who appeared with Christ at the Transfiguration. But this is very flimsy evidence and hardly shows a cause and effect relationship. Others say it is because these men had unfinished ministries, and they will return to finish it this time. This is a very subjective judgment, and many from the Old Testament could be nominated for the same reason. The fact that the miracles performed by the Two Witnesses are similar to those of Moses and Elijah is hardly sufficient evidence, for God can use others to perform these same miracles.

It is best to take these men to be two Jewish prophets whom God will raise up during the tribulation itself. They are purely future persons and not two men from the past. The Scriptures clearly teach that Elijah is to return before the tribulation and will conduct a ministry during the tribulation. But there is no scriptural warrant to make Elijah one of the Two Witnesses. The Two Witnesses will be simply two Jewish men living in that time whom God will elevate to the office of prophets and will endow them with miraculous powers. Their exact identity then awaits the tribulation.

In verses 5-6 the *character* of their ministry and their authority is described. They have the power to kill men by fire, which will be used against those seeking to kill them before their proper time has come (verse 5). They also have authority to cause drought by withholding rain, to turn water into blood, and to cause other plagues (verse 6), perhaps similar to the ten that fell on Egypt (for the turning of water into blood was one of them).

The center of their ministry will be the city of Jerusalem, whereas that of the 144,000 Jews will be world-wide. More will be said about the Two Witnesses in the next chapter.

E. THE ECCLESIASTICAL BABYLON

The fifth event that occurs throughout the first half of the tribulation is the rule of the Ecclesiastical Babylon in Revelation 17:1-6:

And there came one of the seven angels that had the seven bowls, and spake with me, saying, Come hither, I will show thee the judgment of the great harlot that sitteth upon many waters; with whom the kings of the earth committed fornication, and they that dwell in the earth were made drunken with the wine of her fornication. And he carried me away in the Spirit into a wilderness: and I saw a woman sitting upon a scarlet-colored beast, full of names of blasphemy, having seven heads and ten horns. And the woman was arrayed in purple and scarlet, and decked with gold and precious stone and pearls, having in her hand a golden cup full of abominations, even the unclean things of her fornication, and upon her forehead a name written, MYSTERY, BABYLON THE GREAT, THE MOTHER OF THE HARLOTS AND OF THE ABOMINATIONS OF THE EARTH. And I saw the woman drunken with the blood of the saints, and with the blood of the martyrs of Jesus. And when I saw her, I wondered with a great wonder.

Just as there will be two political systems during the tribulation, one during the first half (the ten kings) and one during the second half (the Antichrist), there will also be two religious systems, one for each half of the tribulation. This passage describes the religious system of the first half of the tribulation. In verses 1-2 John is invited to come and to view the judgment about to fall on the *Great Harlot*. To prostitute something is to take that which has a proper use and to turn it into an improper use. A prostitute takes sex, which has a proper use, and perverts it with an improper use; turning it into something illicit, causing fornication.

In this case the harlot represents "religion," which has a proper use (James 1:26-27) but here has been prostituted for improper use. Rather than serving, it rules. The false use of religion causes spiritual fornication. The word fornication is used both of physical unfaithfulness and also of spiritual unfaithfulness, as in Hosea 1-2; Jeremiah 2:20, 3:1-9; Ezekiel 16:15-41, 22:5-44, etc. It is with this woman that the kings of the earth commit fornication (verse 2) showing this to be a unity of church and state. The woman is sitting upon many waters (verse 1) which is interpreted in verse 15 to refer to the world population:

And he saith unto me, The waters which thou sawest, where the harlot sitteth, are peoples, and multitudes, and nations, and tongues.

In verse three, the harlot is seen to be sitting on the seven-headed and ten-horned beast. This means that this false religious system does have the support of civil government during the first part of the tribulation and is able to rule because of government support.*

The description and identification of this woman is given in verses 4-5. The woman is seen as being very wealthy and influential, and her full name is *Mystery, Babylon the Great, The Mother of the Harlots, and of the Abominations of the Earth.* What is found in these verses is the final form of religious apostasy ending in a one-world super-church. It is the final form of the woman Jezebel cast into the Great Tribulation (Revelation 2:20-22) and united with the apostate Laodicean church. This is the counterfeit bride of Christ presented as a prostitute in contrast with the true Bride of Christ presented as a pure virgin (II Corinthians 11:2, Ephesians 5:25-27, Revelation 19:6-8).

Babylon the Harlot represents the one-world religious system that rules over the religious affairs during the first half of the tribulation. She rules over the nations of the world (the many waters) fully controlling the religious affairs and has the reluctant support of the government. The headquarters of this one world religion will be the rebuilt city of Babylon, the "mother" of idolatry, for it was here that idolatry and false religion began (Genesis 11:1-9).

In verse six the woman is drunk with the blood of those who suffered martyrdom for Christ. This answers the question as to who was killing and hurting the fifth seal saints. It is this false super-church. The myriads of Gentiles who are saved under the ministry of the 144,000 Jews will suffer persecution by the Ecclesiastical Babylon, and many will be martyred.

SUMMARY

These then are the events of the first half of the tribulation. Some are sequential with one following the other in chronological sequence. Included in these are the seal and trumpet judgments.

There are also five events that transpire throughout the first half of the tribulation. They are: 1) The ministry of Elijah; 2) The 144,000 Jews and the world-wide revival; 3) The ministry of the Two Witnesses; 4) The political system of the ten kings; and 5) The religious system of the Ecclesiastical Babylon.

* See Chapter II.

CHAPTER XI

THE EVENTS OF THE MIDDLE OF THE TRIBULATION

The sixth trumpet judgment concludes at the time of the middle of the tribulation and is followed by a temporary cessation of the judgments poured out of heaven. The tribulation enters into the temporary proverbial eye of the hurricane. But it does not mean that the earth will be at peace. The nations will be in turmoil as the Antichrist proceeds to take over the political, economic and religious control of the entire world.

So many things happen at this point that it is difficult to put them in sequential order with any certainty. The following layout is more of a logical order; for the events may not necessarily come in this sequence. That all of the events listed in this chapter occur in the middle of the tribulation is certain. What is uncertain is whether or not they all come in this particular sequence. In the book of Revelation, the events of the middle of the tribulation comprise chapters 10-14 and chapter 17.

A.   THE LITTLE BOOK

The temporary suspension of the judgments from heaven begins after the sixth trumpet judgment in Revelation 10:1-11:

And I saw another strong angel coming down out of heaven, arrayed with a cloud; and the rainbow was upon his head, and his face was as the sun, and his feet as pillars of fire; and he had in his hand a little book open: and he set his right foot upon the sea, and his left upon the earth; and he cried with a great voice, as a lion roareth: and when he cried, the seven thunders uttered their voices. And when the seven thunders uttered their voices, I was about to write: and I heard a voice from heaven saying, Seal up the things which the seven thunders uttered, and write them not. And the angel that I saw standing upon the sea and upon the earth lifted up his right hand to heaven, and sware by him that liveth for ever and ever, who created the heaven and the things that are therein, and the earth and the things that are therein, and the sea and the things that are therein, that there shall be delay no longer: but in the days of the voice of the seventh angel, when he is about to sound, then is finished the mystery of God, according to the good tidings which he declared to his servants the prophets. And the voice which I heard from heaven, I heard it again speaking with me, and saying, Go, take the book which is open in the hand of the angel that standeth upon the sea and upon the earth. And I went unto the angel, saying unto him that he should give me the little book. And he saith unto me, Take it, and eat it up; and it shall make thy belly bitter, but in thy mouth it shall be sweet as honey. And I took the little book out of the angel's hand, and ate it up; and it was in my mouth sweet as honey: and when I had eaten it, my belly was made bitter. And they say unto me, Thou must prophesy again over many peoples and nations and tongues and kings.

Chapter ten is the story of the little book. John saw a strong angel carrying a little book or scroll (verses 1-2). This is the second scroll mentioned in Revelation. The first was the seven sealed book or scroll that contained the seven seal and the seven trumpet judgments which described the events of the first half of the tribulation. Now a second scroll comes into the picture, the content of which will shortly be revealed.

The strong angel cried a great shout after which the seven thunders uttered something that John is forbidden to reveal (verses 3-4).

Up to this point six of the seven trumpets have sounded, so there is yet one more remaining. The results of the seventh trumpet are now announced by the strong angel (verses 5-7). In the days of the seventh angel the judgments of God will be completed. Just as the seventh seal judgment contained the seven trumpet judgments, the seventh trumpet judgment will contain the seven bowl judgments which will finish the judgments of God declared by the prophets. All the prophecies dealing with the tribulation's second half will then be fulfilled. That the seventh trumpet will not be an all-at-once judgment but a process is evident from the statement, *"in the days of* the voice of the seventh angel is the mystery of God finished." The plural number shows that a time period is involved. The bowl judgments all come towards the end of the tribulation and with them the mystery of God is finished. The seventh trumpet that contains the seven bowl judgments is the third woe. For this reason, it is the worst of all.

The little book contains all the information regarding the seventh trumpet with the bowl judgments as found in Revelation 15-16.

Attention is focused on the little book in verses 8-10. John was commanded to eat the book. In his mouth the taste was as sweet as honey but it became bitter in the belly. The clue to the meaning of this symbolic act is found in verse 11 which states what the content of the book is:

> And they say unto me, Thou must prophesy again over many peoples and nations and tongues and kings.

The content of the little book is prophecy, especially the prophecy of the middle and the second half of the tribulation. This gives the clue to the meaning of verses 8-10. To almost all people, prophecy is sweet. Prophetic conferences draw larger audiences than virtually any other kind of conference. The voluminous sale of the more sensational prophecy books is another evidence of how "sweet" Bible prophecy has become to so many people. But if "sweetness" is all there is, then it is worth little. Every student of prophecy should have the second experience that John had: bitterness in the stomach. A knowledge of things to come should give every believer a burden for people. For the way of escape from these things is the Rapture, and the requirement to qualify for the Rapture is acceptance of Christ now. A true student of prophecy will not simply stop with the knowledge of things to come. Rather, this knowledge will create the strong burden to preach the Gospel to others and thereby give them a way of escape.

Thus, Revelation 10 introduces the reader to the events of the middle of the tribulation.

B.   THE SECOND WORLD-WIDE CONFLICT

Whatever kind of peace may have existed between the Antichrist and the ten kings ruling the ten kingdoms of the world is now shattered as the Antichrist begins his move to take political control of the world. Thus, the second world-wide conflict of the tribulation begins with the Antichrist declaring war on the ten kings. This conflict is described in Daniel 11:40-45:

> And at the time of the end shall the king of the south contend with him; and the king of the north shall come against him like a whirlwind, with chariots, and with horsemen, and with many ships; and he shall enter into the countries, and shall overflow and pass through. He shall enter also into the glorious land, and many countries shall be overthrown; but these shall be delivered out of his hand: Edom, and Moab, and the chief of the children of Ammon. He shall stretch forth his hand also upon the countries; and the land of Egypt shall not escape. But he shall have power over the treasures of gold and of silver, and over all the precious things of Egypt; and the Libyans and the Ethiopians shall be at his steps. But tidings out of the east and out of the north shall trouble him; and he shall go forth with great fury to destroy and utterly to sweep away many. And he shall plant the tents of his palace between the sea and the glorious holy mountain; yet he shall come to his end, and none shall help him.

It is war against the ten as the Antichrist moves out in all directions in conquest. He is seen moving against the north (verses 40, 44), the south (verses 40, 42-43), and the east (verse 40). The three kings he will succeed in killing (Daniel 7:8,20,24) will be the king of the north (Syria), the king of the south (Egypt) and the king of the east (Mesopotamia). His conquest of Egypt opens the door for his conquest of Africa (verses 42-43). He will also invade Israel, *the glorious land* (verse 41) (also mentioned in Revelation 11:1-2) setting the stage for the abomination of desolation to be discussed later in this chapter.

Although eventually the Antichrist will gain political control of the whole world, three countries will escape his domination: Edom, Moab, and Ammon (verse 41). All of these three ancient nations are under one government today: the kingdom of Jordan. Why Jordan escapes the domination will be explained in Chapter XIII.

In verse 45 Daniel tells where the Antichrist will plant his head-quarters during this midtribulation war. A more accurate translation of this verse would be:

He shall plant the tents of his palace between the seas at the glorious holy mountain.

The word for "tent" refers to a military tent of a general and the word for "palace" to a royal tent. It is a royal tent of a military general (the Antichrist) that is set up. It is set up *between the seas*, meaning between the Mediterranean Sea and the Dead Sea. Furthermore, it is *at the glorious holy mountain* meaning the temple mount, or Mount Moriah or Mount Zion. This will set the stage for several events to be discussed later in this chapter.

C.   THE ANTICHRIST KILLED

It is apparently during this conflict that the Antichrist is killed. Daniel 11:45b states:

. . . yet he shall come to his end, and none shall help him.

In Revelation 13:3 the death of the Antichrist is stated as:

And I saw one of his heads as though it had been smitten unto death; and his death-stroke was healed: and the whole earth wondered after the beast.

The seventh head which is the Antichrist is smitten unto death. The phrase *as though it had been smitten unto death* does not simply mean apparent death, for it is also used of Christ in Revelation 5:6. This is simply an idiom for a resurrected individual and real death is involved.

So in the course of this conflict between the Antichrist and the other ten kings, the Antichrist is killed.

D.   SATAN CAST DOWN TO THE EARTH

At this point of time Satan is cast down out of his third abode* in the atmospheric heavens to his fourth abode, the earth, according to Revelation 12:7-12:

And there was war in heaven: Michael and his angels going forth to war with the dragon; and the dragon warred and his angels; and they pre-

---

* See Appendix I on the six abodes of Satan.

vailed not, neither was their place found any more in heaven. And the great dragon was cast down, the old serpent, he that is called the Devil and Satan, the deceiver of the whole world; he was cast down to the earth, and his angels were cast down with him. And I heard a great voice in heaven, saying, Now is come the salvation, and the power, and the kingdom of our God, and the authority of his Christ: for the accuser of our brethren is cast down, who accuseth them before our God day and night. And they overcame him because of the blood of the Lamb, and because of the word of their testimony; and they loved not their life even unto death. Therefore rejoice, O heavens, and ye that dwell in them. Woe for the earth and for the sea: because the devil is gone down unto you, having great wrath, knowing that he hath but a short time.

In the middle of the tribulation while war breaks out on earth between the Antichrist and the ten kings, war also breaks out in the atmospheric heavens which is Satan's third abode (verse 7). The conflict is between the Archangel Michael and his forces and the archenemy Satan and his forces. Michael is victorious, and Satan and his cohorts are cast out of the atmospheric heavens and confined to the earth which now becomes Satan's fourth abode (verses 8-9). Five names are given to Satan, all describing his person and his work. In the *great dragon* his fierceness and ferociousness is seen. The *old serpent* points back to the Garden of Eden where, due to his temptation, man fell bringing sin and death into human experience. The Great Tribulation is a judgment of man's sin. In the word *devil*, Satan is viewed as the accuser of all of God's children. *Satan* means adversary, and in this he is seen as the opponent to God's program. As the *deceiver* he is pointed out as the great master counterfeiter by which he attempts to deceive elect and non-elect alike.

Satan's confinement to the earth brings two results: *First*, Satan's access to heaven is removed and he will no longer be able to stand before the Throne of God and be the accuser of the brethren. For this there is rejoicing in heaven (verses 10-12a). *Secondly*, Satan is now full of wrath (verse 12b). His anger is due to the fact that he knows his time is short, namely three and a half years. Because of Satan's wrath, it is *woe for the earth*. This is a very important point to note in the understanding of what is happening during the middle and second half of the tribulation. The full meaning will become apparent later in this study.

E.   THE RESURRECTION OF THE ANTICHRIST

As the rest of Revelation 12 makes clear, Satan then sets out on a course to destroy the Jews. The means by which he will attempt to accomplish this will be the two beasts of Revelation 13. The details of both chapters will be dealt with as this study continues. But he will begin on this course by bringing the Antichrist back to life as seen in Revelation 13:3:

And I saw one of his heads as though it had been smitten unto death; and his death-stroke was healed: and the whole earth wondered after the beast.

Verses 1-2 of chapter 13 have been explained earlier, but it is now clear that it is Satan who will resurrect the Antichrist back to life. Many take the phrase *as though he had been smitten unto death* to mean that the Antichrist appeared to be dead but was not really. However, the same idiom is used of Christ in Revelation 5:6, and there was no question that Christ died. The idiom, then, refers to a resurrected individual. The person was killed and by all human experience should have been dead. But suddenly he is very much alive because of resurrection. This idiom must mean here what it means elsewhere: a reference to a resurrected individual. The text clearly goes on to say that *his death stroke was healed*, that is, by resurrection.

Some wish to interpret this as a reference to the revival of the Roman Empire feeling that this would be enough to cause man to worship it. But a revived Roman Empire would not cause man to worship it to be God anymore than the revival of Poland or Israel did. This kind of thinking is purely imaginary. It is the resurrection of the man Antichrist which creates this worship.

Thus, the Antichrist is the counterfeit son in every respect. There has been a counterfeit multiplicity of names, a counterfeit virgin birth, a counterfeit god-man, and now a counterfeit death and resurrection. A counterfeit second coming to rule the world can be seen as he will move to possess the nations and kingdoms of the world. Satan is playing the part of the counterfeit father in this scenario. For as the true Father gave His authority to the Son, so the counterfeit father will give his authority to the Antichrist.

F.   THREE KINGS KILLED — SEVEN SUBMIT

The attempt of the Antichrist to gain political control will be interrupted by his death. But after his resurrection, the second world war of the tribulation will continue until three of the ten kings are killed. The text dealing with this has already been examined, and it is found in Daniel 7:24:

And as for the ten horns, out of this kingdom shall ten kings arise: and another shall arise after them; and he shall be diverse from the former, and he shall put down three kings.

Once three of the ten are killed, the others submit to his authority. This is stated in Revelation 17:12-13:

And the ten horns that thou sawest are ten kings, who have received no kingdom as yet; but they receive authority as kings, with the beast, for one hour. These have one mind, and they give their power and authority unto the beast.

The ten horns of the beast are the ten kings (verse 12), but they eventually relinquish their power and authority to the Antichrist. The same point is made in verse 17:

For God did put in their hearts to do his mind, and to come to one mind, and to give their kingdom unto the beast, until the words of God should be accomplished.

The other kings will all come to *one mind* which is *to give their kingdom unto the beast*. With this submission, the Antichrist will succeed in taking over the political control of the entire world with the exception of Jordan. The second political system of the tribulation will be initiated at this point. The Antichrist's next goal will be to gain world religious control.

G.   DESTRUCTION OF ECCLESIASTICAL BABYLON

One of the Antichrist's first acts in gaining religious control will be the destruction of the first religious system of the tribulation, the Ecclesiastical Babylon in Revelation 17:16:

And the ten horns which thou sawest, and the beast, these shall hate the harlot, and shall make her desolate and naked, and shall eat her flesh, and shall burn her utterly with fire.

Previously this religious system had the support of the civil government for the first three and a half years. With all civil authority turned over to the hands of the Antichrist who is now in full control, civil government itself will destroy the domination of the Ecclesiastical Babylon.

H.   THE DEATH OF THE TWO WITNESSES

In order to gain further religious allegiance of the world masses, the Antichrist will also move against the Two Witnesses who, because of their supernatural abilities, caused so much havoc for the inhabitants of the earth during the first half of the tribulation. This is recorded in Revelation 11:7-13:

And when they shall have finished their testimony, the beast that cometh up out of the abyss shall make war with them, and overcome them, and kill them. And their dead bodies lie in the street of the great city, which spiritually is called Sodom and Egypt, where also their Lord was crucified. And from among the peoples and tribes and tongues and nations do men look upon their dead bodies three days and a half, and suffer not their dead bodies to be laid in a tomb. And they that dwell on the earth rejoice over them, and make merry; and they shall send gifts one to another; because these two prophets tormented them that dwell on the earth. And after the three days and a half the breath of life from God entered into them, and they stood upon their feet; and great fear fell upon them that beheld them. And they heard a great voice from heaven saying unto them, Come up hither. And they went up into heaven in the cloud; and their enemies beheld them. And in that hour there was a great earthquake, and the tenth part of the city fell; and there were killed in the earthquake seven thousand persons: and the rest were affrighted, and gave glory to the God of heaven.

The Antichrist will war against the Two Witnesses and will succeed in killing them (verse 7). That this incident will happen after his resurrection from the dead is clear from the statement *the beast that cometh up out of the abyss,* and he will come back from the abyss by means of his resurrection by Satan. Along with his resurrection the act of killing the Two Witnesses will provide another reason why mankind will worship him. All previous attempts to kill the Two Witnesses fail because of the miraculous powers of the Two Witnesses which kill those who attempt to murder them. But now their ministry is over, and God allows the Antichrist to have the power over them and to kill them. This power of the Antichrist over the Two Witnesses, when all others failed, will be another reason why mankind will give its allegiance to the Antichrist.

Perhaps in order to display the new power, the Antichrist will not allow the bodies to be buried. They will lie where they die in the streets of Jerusalem for all to see (verses 8-9). The fact that the *whole* world is able to view the bodies indicates that such things would be possible future to John's day. Through modern technology this is no longer impossible to believe and has silenced many a former critic of the Scriptures. The bodies will lie in the streets of Jerusalem unburied for three and a half days.

During the time that the bodies lie in the streets, the inhabitants of the earth will rejoice over the death of the Two Witnesses because of the plagues they suffered via the Two Witnesses (verse 10). The rejoicing extends to the point that they will give gifts to one another in an outward display of joy over the death of the Two Witnesses.

The rejoicing will cease suddenly. After 3½ days the Two Witnesses will be resurrected and taken to heaven in the sight of all (verses 11-12). Suddenly fear will fall on all as they are able to observe the ascension of the Two Witnesses into heaven.

Jerusalem, where the murder will take place and where the bodies will be displayed, will receive sudden judgment (verse 13). Jerusalem will suffer an earthquake that will destroy one-tenth of the city killing 7,000 inhabitants. While the Gentiles will begin to worship the Antichrist, the Jewish inhabitants of Jerusalem will give the glory to the God of heaven. The salvation of the Jews of Jerusalem in the middle of the tribulation will eventually lead to the saving of "all Israel" at the end of the tribulation.

I. THE WORSHIP OF THE ANTICHRIST

The world will see the counterfeit resurrection of the Antichrist from the dead and his power over the Two Witnesses who had tormented the unbelievers for the first 3½ years. Although the Two Witnesses will be resurrected, they will disappear from view and will no longer be heard from. The inhabitants of the earth will begin to worship the Antichrist as the king of the world and as God. Revelation 13:3-10 states:

> And I saw one of his heads as though it had been smitten unto death; and his death-stroke was healed: and the whole earth wondered after the beast; and they worshipped the dragon, because he gave his authority unto the beast; and they worshipped the beast, saying, Who is like unto the beast? and who is able to war with him? and there was given to him a mouth speaking great things and blasphemies; and there was given to him authority to continue forty and two months. And he opened his mouth for blasphemies against God, to blaspheme his name, and his tabernacle, even them that dwell in the heaven. And it was given unto him to make war with the saints, and to overcome them: and there was given to him authority over every tribe and people and tongue and nation. And all that dwell on the earth shall worship him, every one whose name hath not been written from the foundation of the world in the book of life of the Lamb that hath been slain. If any man hath an ear, let him hear. If any man is for captivity, into captivity he goeth: if any man shall kill with the sword, with the sword must he be killed. Here is the patience and the faith of the saints.

As has been shown in Chapter II, the seventh head is the Antichrist stage and this is the head that is smitten unto death, but the deathstroke is healed by means of resurrection (verse 3).

Because he will give his authority to the Antichrist, men will begin worshipping Satan. Thus, Satan will become a counterfeit god the father. As the Father gave His authority to the Son, Satan will give his authority to the Antichrist. Just as the Father is worshipped through the Son, Satan is to be worshipped through the Antichrist (verse 4). And so men will worship him and will give him supreme glory by saying, *who is like unto the beast?* and *who is able to withstand him?*

It should be noted that the worship is coming from the whole earth (verse 3) and not just from Europe.

In verses 5-7 the activities of this pseudo-god are related. He will speak great things and blasphemies (verse 5a); declare himself to be god and call men to begin worshipping him. He will be given authority to continue for 42 months (verse 5b) which is equivalent to 3½ years, and so his control is to extend throughout the second half of the tribulation. He will blaspheme against all that is in heaven, both God and all those who are there (verse 6). He will war against the saints and overcome them (verse 7a) as is evident from his murder of the Two Witnesses, and he will continue to persecute all believers in Christ. He will also hold political authority over the earth for he will be given *authority over every tribe and people and tongue and nation* . This verse also makes it impossible to limit this to Europe alone. What is stated in verses 5-7 is also found in Daniel 7:25.

At this point in time he will not only have political authority over the whole world (verse 7b), but he will also have religious authority over all the earth (verse 8), and *all* unbelievers will worship him that have not had their names written in the *Lamb's Book of Life*.

In light of all this, a warning is given (verses 9-10). The very way that men will treat the saints, God will treat them. If they enslave the saints, they will find themselves enslaved. If they kill the saints, they will be killed. This is a word of patience to the saints. It is a word of comfort to believers living in this period of persecution. They will understand that, whatever suffering they undergo, God will in turn judge those perpetuating the persecution in the same way.

J. THE FALSE PROPHET

In the previous section the rise of the counterfeit father and the counterfeit son was dealt with. To complete the counterfeit trinity, in Revelation 13:11-15 there is a description of the rise of the counterfeit holy spirit in the person of the False Prophet:

> And I saw another beast coming up out of the earth; and he had two horns like unto a lamb, and he spake as a dragon. And he exerciseth all the authority of the first beast in his sight. And he maketh the earth and them that dwell therein to worship the first beast, whose death-stroke was healed. And he doeth great signs, that he should even make fire to come down out of heaven upon the earth in the sight of men. And he deceiveth them that dwell on the earth by reason of the signs which it was given him to do in the sight of the beast; saying to them that dwell on the earth, that they should make an image to the beast who hath the stroke of the sword and lived. And it was given unto him to give breath to it, even to the image of the beast, that the image of the beast should both speak, and cause that as many as should not worship the image of the beast should be killed.

Following the rise of the first beast, the Antichrist, John saw a second beast come out of the earth (as over against heaven). He will appear like a lamb giving the appearance of a true religious character and thus deceive many. But he will speak like a dragon and so will betray his true nature, for he will be an agent of Satan who throughout the book is portrayed as a dragon. This second beast is elsewhere called the False Prophet (16:13, 19:20, 20:10).

His activities as the counterfeit holy spirit are now spelled out (verses 12-15). As the Holy Spirit exercises equal authority with the Son, the False Prophet will exercise equal authority with the Antichrist (verse 12a). Just as the Holy Spirit calls all men to worship the resurrected Son, the False Prophet will call all men to worship the resurrected Antichrist *whose death-stroke was healed* (verse 12b). In order to fully carry out the deception, the False Prophet will have the power of the counterfeit spiritual gifts of miracles and will perform signs for the purpose of deception (verses 13-14a). After convincing the world of the supremacy of the Antichrist, he will command men to make an image of the beast. After the image is made, it will be given life by the False Prophet. This power of giving life will be another factor why men will worship the Antichrist and the image, and those who refuse to do so are put to death (verses 14b-15).

In this manner, the counterfeit trinity will be complete.

K. 666 — THE MARK OF THE BEAST

To counterfeit the seal of God on the foreheads of the saints, the seal of the Holy Spirit, the False Prophet will introduce his own counterfeit mark or seal in Revelation 13:16-18:

> And he causeth all, the small and the great, and the rich and the poor, and the free and the bond, that there be given them a mark on their right hand, or upon their forehead; and that no man should be able to buy or to sell, save he that hath the mark, even the name of the beast or the number of his name. Here is wisdom. He that hath understanding, let him count the number of the beast; for it is the number of a man: and his number is six hundred and sixty and six.

The counterfeit seal is the famous *mark of the beast*. The placing of the mark will be on the forehead or on the right hand (verse 16). It will be given to all who will subject themselves to the authority of the Antichrist and accept him as God. The mark will serve as a passport for business (verse 17a). They will be able to neither buy nor sell anything unless they have the mark. It should be pointed out that this mark has nothing to do with credit as is often taught today. In a credit system, everyone must have a different number. In this case, everyone has the *same* number. The purpose of the mark will be as a sign of identification of those who will own the Antichrist as their god. Only those who have this number will be permitted to work, to buy, to sell, or simply to make a living. The verse does not speak of credit cards, computers, etc.

The interpretation of the mark is given by five clues (verses 17b-18):

> The name of the beast
> The number of his name
> The number of the beast
> The number of a man
> The number is 666

Following through this logical progression, the number of the beast is also the number of a man because the Antichrist will be a man who will be the last ruler of the final form of the fourth Gentile empire. Furthermore, this number is the number of his very own name, and the numerical value of his name is 666. The point is essentially this: whatever the name of the Antichrist will be in Hebrew, the numerical value of that name will be 666. Each letter of the Hebrew alphabet has a numerical value. There are 22 letters in the Hebrew alphabet and in the order of numerical value they are as follows: 1, 2 3, 4, 5, 6, 7, 8, 9, 10, 20, 30, 40, 50, 60, 70, 80, 90, 100, 200, 300, and 400. So everyone's name in Hebrew has a numerical value. The numerical value of the author's name is 966. The name Jesus Christ has the numerical value of 749. In this passage whatever the personal name of the Antichrist will be, if his name is spelled out in Hebrew characters, the numerical value of his name will be 666. So this is the number that will be put on the worshippers of the Antichrist. Since a number of different calculations can equal 666, it is impossible to figure the name out in advance. But when he does appear, whatever his personal name will be, it will equal 666. Those who are wise (verse 18) at that time will be able to point him out in advance.

L. THE SEVEN-YEAR COVENANT BROKEN

Another event occurring at the half-way point of the tribulation is the breaking of the seven year covenant made three and a half years earlier. In the context of the Daniel 11:40-45 passage dealt with earlier, it was stated in verse 41: *He shall enter also into the glorious land.* This involves the Antichrist's invasion of Israel requiring a breaking of the covenant.

In the Isaiah 28:14-22 passage studied in Chapter IX, verse 18 stated that the covenant will be annulled:

And your covenant with death shall be annulled, and your agreement with Sheol shall not stand; when the overflowing scourge shall pass through, then ye shall be trodden down by it.

Other passages dealing with the breaking of the seven year covenant are connected with corollary events to be discussed next.

M.   THE ABOMINATION OF DESOLATION

The first corollary tied in with the breaking of the covenant is the *Abomination of Desolation* in connection with the Jewish temple in Jerusalem. These three elements are all related together in Daniel 9:27:

> And he shall make a firm covenant with many for one week: and in the midst of the week he shall cause the sacrifice and the oblation to cease; and upon the wing of abominations shall come one that maketh desolate; and even unto the full end, and that determined, shall wrath be poured out upon the desolate.

When discussing this key passage in Chapter IX, it was stated that the signing of the seven year covenant will begin the tribulation. This verse reveals just how long the tribulation will last: a total of seven years. But now it goes on to say that *in the midst of the week,* that is, in the middle of the seven-year period, the Antichrist will cause a cessation of the sacrificial system that had been reinstituted. This forced cessation is followed by the statement, *upon the wing of abomination shall come one that maketh desolate.* Thus, the cessation of the sacrifices in conjunction with the breaking of the covenant is followed by an act (or acts) which is labeled as "the abomination of desolation." The exact nature of this act (or acts) is not spelled out at this stage. So exactly what the abomination of desolation consists of is not stated; only that it occurs in the middle of the tribulation. However, the term *wing* refers to the pinnacle of the temple emphasizing the concept of an "overspreading influence." What begins here will spread elsewhere. The term *abomination* refers to an image or an idol.

Another passage, Daniel 12:11, gives the duration of time that the abomination of desolation will last:

> And from the time that the continual burnt-offering shall be taken away, and the abomination that maketh desolate set up, there shall be a thousand two hundred and ninety days.

As in Daniel 9:27, the starting point is the cessation of the sacrificial system. According to this passage, the abomination of desolation will last a total of 1,290 days. This is a full thirty days beyond the end of the tribulation. No reason is given as to why it is permitted to last this extra thirty days. Again, this passage does not reveal exactly what the abomination of desolation will be. But as in Daniel 9:27, the term *abomination* refers to an image or an idol.

This event is also mentioned in Matthew 24:15-16:

> When therefore ye see the abomination of desolation, which was spoken of through Daniel the prophet, standing in the holy place (let him that readeth understand), then let them that are in Judea flee unto the mountains.

This passage is merely a reminder of the Daniel prophecy with no explanation as to what the abomination of desolation is. The only clue given is that it will be something "standing" (like an image or idol) in the holy place. This passage helps to verify the futuristic interpretation of the Daniel passage for it was still considered unfulfilled and future at the time of Christ. The abomination of desolation will serve as a warning to the Jews of Israel to flee the land.

Another text dealing with this is in Revelation 11:1-2:

> And there was given me a reed like unto a rod: and one said, Rise, and measure the temple of God, and the altar, and them that worship therein. And the court which is without the temple leave without, and measure it not; for it hath been given unto the nations: and the holy city shall they tread under foot forty and two months.

This passage also deals with the takeover of the temple as well as the city of Jerusalem (at least the old city) and connects it with the times of the Gentiles. This will be the final Gentile control of Jerusalem, and it will last 42 months or three and a half years. It will be this Gentile takeover of the city and the temple that will cause a cessation of the sacrifices. Although Gentile domination over the city of Jerusalem will last three and a half years, the abomination of desolation will continue an extra month. But there is still no clear explanation as to what the abomination of desolation is.

What, then, is the abomination of desolation? There are probably two elements or stages involved, the first of which is in II Thessalonians 2:3-4:

> Let no man beguile you in any wise: for it will not be, except the falling away come first, and the man of sin be revealed, the son of perdition, he that opposeth and exalteth himself against all that is called God or that is worshipped; so that he sitteth in the temple of God, setting himself forth as God.

In this passage, the Antichrist is described as seating himself in the temple of God declaring to the world that he really is God. In all probability, he will sit in the very holy of holies. Thus, with his initial takeover of Jerusalem in general and the temple in particular, he will seat himself in the very temple of God, will claim to be god, and, by so doing, will set up the second religious system of the tribulation.

His self-declaration of deity will be accompanied with miraculous signs to carry out the work of deception according to II Thessalonians 2:8-12:

> And then shall be revealed the lawless one, whom the Lord Jesus shall slay with the breath of his mouth, and bring to nought by the manifestation of his coming; even he, whose coming is according to the working of Satan with all power and signs and lying wonders, and with all deceit of unrighteousness for them that perish; because they received not the love of the truth, that they might be saved. And for this cause God sendeth them a working of error, that they should believe a lie: that they all might be judged who believed not the truth, but had pleasure in unrighteousness.

His coming is said to be "energized" by Satan for it is by Satan that he will be brought back to life. His post-resurrection rise to power will be with *all power and signs and lying wonders*. The aim of these counterfeit miracles according to verses 10-12 will be to deceive men so that they will worship the Antichrist and accept him as god. These verses have often been interpreted as teaching that if one hears the gospel before the Rapture and rejects it, he will not have an opportunity to be saved after the Rapture. But this is not the teaching of this passage. The point of no return is the acceptance of the "big lie" of the Antichrist's self-proclaimed deity and the submission to the worship of him by means of taking the mark of the beast. It is only then that the point of no return is actually reached. The option of taking the mark of the beast only begins in the middle of the tribulation. Even the context of this passage shows that it speaks of events that occur in the middle of the tribulation. The worshippers of the Antichrist do so because they are deceived by the Antichrist's power of miracles. They are deceived *because they received not the love of the truth.* The rejection of the gospel was not what they may have heard before the Rapture but rather the preaching of the 144,000 Jews and the Two Witnesses.

Though he will declare his deity within the holy of holies of the temple, the Antichrist will not set up his throne there but in Babylon. Yet the abomination of desolation is to last a total of 1,290 days while the Antichrist himself is allowed to continue 1,260 days. Hence, the abomination of desolation must include something more than merely the Antichrist's self-proclamation of deity. Furthermore, the Daniel and Matthew passages implied an image or idol that would be erected in the temple.

The second aspect of the abomination of desolation is in Revelation 13:11-15:

> And I saw another beast coming up out of the earth; and he had two horns like unto a lamb, and he spake as a dragon. And he exerciseth all the

authority of the first beast in his sight. And he maketh the earth and them that dwell therein to worship the first beast, whose death-stroke was healed. And he doeth great signs, that he should even make fire to come down out of heaven upon the earth in the sight of men. And he deceiveth them that dwell on the earth by reason of the signs which it was given him to do in the sight of the beast; saying to them that dwell on the earth, that they should make an image to the beast who hath the stroke of the sword and lived. And it was given unto him to give breath to it, even to the image of the beast, that the image of the beast should both speak, and cause that as many as should not worship the image of the beast should be killed.

In the second stage of the abomination of desolation the False Prophet will be given authority to perform many signs and wonders (verse 13) deceiving mankind in order to cause them to worship the Antichrist (verse 12). These same ideas were evident in II Thessalonians 2:8-12 and both help clarify what the abomination of desolation involves. The great deception is climaxed when the image of the Antichrist becomes alive and men are called upon to worship the image (verses 14-15). So the deification of the Antichrist continues. The image will be set up in the holy of holies to carry on the abomination of desolation. Jerusalem will become the religious capitol of the Antichrist, and the temple will be the center of the worship of the Antichrist where the living image will be standing. So while the Antichrist will be disposed of after 1,260 days, the image will remain in the temple another thirty days beyond that. Then it, too, will be disposed of.

Thus, the two stages of the abomination of desolation lasting a total of 1,290 days will be the declaration of deity by the Antichrist in the holy of holies followed by the setting up of his image in the same place.

N.   THE PERSECUTION OF THE JEWS

A second corollary to the breaking of the seven year covenant is the beginning of a world-wide persecution of the Jews which commences with the abomination of desolation as Matthew 24:15-28 makes clear:

When therefore ye see the abomination of desolation, which was spoken of through Daniel the prophet, standing in the holy place (let him that readeth understand), then let them that are in Judaea flee unto the mountains: let him that is on the housetop not go down to take out the things that are in his house: and let him that is in the field not return back to take his cloak. But woe unto them that are with child and to them that give suck in those days! And pray ye that your flight be not in the winter, neither on a sabbath: for then shall be great tribulation, such as hath not been from the beginning of the world until now, no, nor ever shall be. And except those days had been shortened, no flesh would have been saved: but for the elect's sake those days shall be shortened. Then if any man shall say unto you, Lo, here is the Christ, or, Here; believe it not. For there shall arise false Christs, and false prophets, and shall show great signs and wonders; so as to lead astray, if possible, even the elect. Behold, I have told you beforehand. If therefore they shall say unto you, Behold, he is in the wilderness; go not forth: Behold, he is in the inner chambers; believe it not. For as the lightning cometh forth from the east, and is seen even unto the west; so shall be the coming of the Son of man. Wheresoever the carcase is, there will the eagles be gathered together.

In this passage Christ gave a warning to those Jews living at the time when the covenant is broken and the abomination of desolation occurs (verses 15-19). They are warned that as soon as they hear of that event happening, they are to get out of Israel and to do so quickly. If they happen to be out on the rooftop for some reason, they are not to take the few minutes it takes to come down from the roof and to go into their house to take any possessions. But from the moment their foot touches the ground, they are to get out of Israel. If they happen to be out in the field plowing when they hear about it, they are not to take the time to go into the living quarters to take any possessions. From that field they are to get out of Israel. The emphasis is on a speedy flight.

They are also urged to pray that when this event occurs, that it will not happen during the winter, nor on the sabbath (verse 20).

Why not on the sabbath? In Israel on the sabbath day there is no public transportation. The buses are all locked up and the trains do not run. So unless an Israeli has his own automobile, he will find escape very difficult because of the lack of public transportation. An example of this difficulty was demonstrated in the Yom Kippur War of 1973. The Arabs attacked on a sabbath when public transportation was non-existent. This made it especially difficult for the Israelis to mobilize their forces and get them to the front lines. So prayer is urged that it will not happen on the sabbath.

Prayer is also urged that when this event occurs, it ought not happen during the winter. Why not in the winter? After all, it seldom snows in Israel anyway. The reason for this prayer request is that the Jews will be escaping towards the mountains in the east. Most of the escape routes will force them to use *wadis*, which are dry water beds that only fill up with flash floods when it rains during the winter months. Israel receives no rain between April and October. But from October through the winter months up until April, Israel receives all its rain for the year. When it does rain, many of these wadis become instantly filled and very dangerous to cross. Every year in Israel people are drowned, because they are caught in these dry river beds during a flash flood. So if the abomination of desolation occurs during the winter months, it will make the escape towards the east that much more difficult. So prayer is urged that it will not happen in winter.

The reason for the flight is because at this point, world-wide anti-Semitism breaks out. The world-wide persecution of the Jews begins and will continue for the next three and a half years (verses 21-22).

Verses 23-28 are a special message directed to the believing remnant within Israel, warning them not to heed any rumor that the Messiah has returned and so come out of hiding. For when the Messiah does return, all will be able to see Him and it will be known by all. So while all Jews are persecuted, a special emphasis of deception is aimed against the believing remnant.

A second passage describing the flight of the Jews out of Israel is in Revelation 12:1-17. The passage begins with a historical review and summary in verses 1-5:

> And a great sign was seen in heaven: a woman arrayed with the sun, and the moon under her feet, and upon her head a crown of twelve stars; and she was with child; and she cried out, travailing in birth, and in pain to be delivered. And there was seen another sign in heaven: and behold, a great red dragon, having seven heads and ten horns, and upon his heads seven diadems. And his tail draweth the third part of the stars of heaven, and did cast them to the earth: and the dragon standeth before the woman that is about to be delivered, that when she is delivered he may devour her child. And she was delivered of a son, a man child, who is to rule all the nations with a rod of iron: and her child was caught up unto God, and unto his throne.

These verses summarize the whole life of Christ from just before His birth to His ascension. John saw two signs in the heavens. In the first sign (verses 1-2) Israel is pictured as a woman; a motif taken from the Old Testament concept of Israel as the wife of Jehovah. The sun, moon and twelve stars are all common Old Testament figures relating to Israel. But the Old Testament background for this sign is Joseph's dream in Genesis 37:9-11:

> And he dreamed yet another dream, and told it to his brethren, and said, Behold, I have dreamed yet a dream; and, behold, the sun and the moon and eleven stars made obeisance to me. And he told it to his father, and to his brethren; and his father rebuked him, and said unto him, What is this dream that thou hast dreamed? Shall I and thy mother and thy brethren indeed come to bow down ourselves to thee to the earth? And his brethren envied him; but his father kept the saying in his mind.

From this passage John's vision can easily be interpreted. The sun represents Jacob who was renamed *Israel* and both these names were often used to represent the entire nation (e.g. Isaiah 40:27, 49:5, Jeremiah 30:10 among others). The moon represents Rachel, who in turn became representative of Jewish women, especially Jewish motherhood (Jeremiah 31:15 and Matthew 2:18). The twelve stars represent the twelve sons of Jacob who in turn fathered the twelve tribes of Israel. Clearly then the woman arrayed with the sun, moon and stars is representative of Israel (not the church). In verse two, this woman is seen in the final stages of pregnancy about to give birth to a child. The vision then is of the nation of Israel just before the birth of the Messiah. A good reason why this cannot be the church is that it would be an anachronism with the church giving birth to Christ whereas the opposite is true.

Then John described the second sign. The great red dragon is Satan in all his fierceness (verse 3). The seven heads and ten horns represent the final form of the fourth Gentile world empire (see Chapter II) now shown to be under Satan's control and authority. The seven diadems point to a concept of conquest. Satan wrestled authority over the earth from man, and the Gentile empires wrestled authority from Israel.

In verse four, the two signs come together. Satan brought his entire demonic host out of his third abode*. Using his permission of access to the earth, he brought them down to the earth in an effort to try to slaughter the child about to be born. The demonic host is enumerated as comprising one third of the stars meaning one-third of all the angels that God created. Only from this verse is it possible to learn just how many of the angels fell with Satan in the original revolt during his second abode.* This attempt to destroy the child was the slaughter of the babes of Bethlehem in Matthew 2:16-18. Satan's attempt to destroy the Messiah both before His proper time (Passover) and by the wrong means (stoning in place of crucifixion) continued throughout the course of His ministry. The bringing down of the entire demonic host was evident throughout the life of Christ. There is a tremendous amount of demonic activity in the Gospels in contrast to the minimal demonic activity found in the Old Testament. Following the Gospels, there is a decrease of demonic activity as seen in the book of Acts.

Verse five points out the failure of Satan's attempt to destroy the child. The child, destined to rule the nations with a rod of iron, survived until His proper time for death came. After His resurrection, He ascended into heaven and is presently seated at the right hand of God the Father.

After this historical survey, John's vision moves forward to events that will occur in the middle of the tribulation, one of which is in verse six:

And the woman fled into the wilderness, where she hath a place prepared of God, that there they may nourish her a thousand two hundred and threescore days.

* See Appendix I for the six abodes of Satan.

As in the Matthew passage, the woman pictured here is in flight. In the Matthew passage, the flight was to the mountains, but here it is described as being in the wilderness as well as to one particular place in that wilderness that God had prepared in advance. The exact location will be discussed in Chapter XIII. With Satan's attempt to destroy the child thwarted, Satan will then turn against the nation that produced Him. Satan's perpetual hatred of Israel is based on the fact that it is through Israel that God will fulfill His program of redemption. Furthermore, in this passage, the time of Israel's flight and hiding is given as 1,260 days or three and a half years. This refers to the second half of the tribulation.

The next section of this chapter, verses 7-12 (discussed earlier in a different context) gives the reason or cause of Israel's flight. Satan is cast out of his third abode into his fourth abode* and is confined to the earth for the next three and a half years (verses 7-9). There are two results of this angelic war. *First*, there is rejoicing in heaven because the accuser of the brethren is now cast down (verses 10-12a) and his access to heaven is removed forever. But *secondly*, there is woe for the earth for Satan is now full of wrath and anger knowing his time is short (verse 12b).

Verses 7-12 then are somewhat parenthetical, providing the reason for Israel's flight in verse six.

The next section found in verses 13-17 takes up where verse six left off:

> And when the dragon saw that he was cast down to the earth, he persecuted the woman that brought forth the man child. And there were given to the woman the two wings of the great eagle, that she might fly into the wilderness unto her place, where she is nourished for a time, and times, and half a time, from the face of the serpent. And the serpent cast out of his mouth after the woman water as a river, that he might cause her to be carried away by the stream. And the earth helped the woman, and the earth opened her mouth and swallowed up the river which the dragon cast out of his mouth. And the dragon waxed wroth with the woman, and went away to make war with the rest of her seed, that keep the commandments of God, and hold the testimony of Jesus.

Verse 13 states that once Satan is cast down to the earth he persecutes the woman, Israel. Verse 13 should be connected with verse six as giving a further explanation for Israel's flight into the wilderness. It should also be connected with verse 12, which concluded that there was woe for the earth, for Satan is full of wrath. The reason is that he knows his time is short; namely, three and a half years. So what does he do with this short time left to him? He persecutes Israel in verse 13. A question that needs to be raised is:

* See Appendix I.

What is the logical connection between Satan knowing his time is short and persecuting the woman? Why persecute the Jews just because your time is short? This intriguing question will be answered in Chapter XIII.

In verse 14 Israel flees into the wilderness where she is nourished for a *time, times and a half a time* which is the same as the three and a half years of verse six. The figure of the *wings of an eagle* has provided fertile ground for speculation among "newspaper exegetes." Amazingly, "the wings of the eagle" has been identified as the American Air Force! For after all, the eagle is a symbol of the United States and so, it would appear that the American Air Force will help the Jews escape! But other nations use the eagle as a symbol, and for some reason their air forces are ignored. It has been stated in the very beginning of this book that every symbol in the Revelation is explained either elsewhere in the Revelation itself or somewhere else in the Bible. The figure of flight in connection with the wings of the eagle is to be interpreted by its usage elsewhere. This same figure is found in Exodus 19:4 and Deuteronomy 32:11 in connection with the exodus from Egypt. Obviously, Moses did not have the help of the American Air Force. The figure, then, is to be explained by its usage elsewhere. It describes a successful flight or escape after being pursued. Israel was pursued by the Egyptian army but succeeded in escaping into the wilderness of Sinai. Here again Israel is being pursued but escapes safely into another wilderness. This is all that "the wings of the eagle" represent.

Then in verse 15 the persecution is described in terms of the waters of a river causing a flood so that Israel might be drowned or destroyed by the flood. Whenever the figure of a flood is used symbolically, it is always a symbol of a military invasion. A good example is Daniel 9:26 where the Roman invasion and devastation of Jerusalem fulfilled in 70 A.D. is prophesied or described in terms of a flood. This invasion of Israel sent by Satan was described in Daniel 11:41 as "He shall also enter into the glorious land." This is the same invasion spoken of in Revelation 11:1-2 by which the Antichrist will succeed in taking control of both Jerusalem and the temple and will commit the abomination of desolation.

But this invasion will fail (verse 16) in its attempt to destroy the Jews. For Israel will succeed in fleeing into the wilderness after being pursued by the invading army.

The passage closes (verse 17) describing further the wrath of Satan because of his initial failure to destroy the Jews. In this closing verse, as in the case of the Matthew passage, Satan will then make war specifically against the believing remnant among the Jews, for it states that he now goes to make war with *the rest* of the woman's seed; namely, *those who keep the commandments of God and hold the testimony of Jesus.* These will include all the Hebrew Christians among the Jews at that time as well as the 144,000 Jews.

Revelation twelve is a picture of Satan's persecution of the Jews with all its fierceness during the tribulation. It will begin in the middle after he is cast down to earth. He will set out on a program to destroy all the Jews still living for a reason to be seen in Chapter XIII. But the initial attempt to destroy the Jews in the middle of the tribulation will fail. So now he organizes an all-out world-wide anti-Semitic campaign to try to destroy all the Jews once and for all.

Revelation thirteen describes the two beings whom Satan will use in his program of Jewish destruction: the Antichrist and the False Prophet. Revelation thirteen has already been discussed in previous sections of this chapter but now it is important to see the connection between Revelation twelve and thirteen. In Revelation twelve, John describes Satan's program and desire to destroy all the Jews once and for all. Chapter thirteen then shows the means by which Satan will hope to carry out this program: the two beasts.

To what extent Satan will succeed in his program of Jewish destruction and some other points touching on the Jews in the tribulation will be discussed in Chapter XIII.

O. MID-TRIBULATION ANNOUNCEMENTS

Revelation fourteen serves as a connecting link between the description of the midtribulational events of Revelation 10-13 and the events of the second half of the tribulation in Revelation 15-16. Most of what was found in Revelation 11-13 dealt with the activities of the counterfeit trinity in their attempt to usurp the authority of God and to destroy those who persist in worshipping Him alone. Now in Revelation 14 there are seven proclamations given from the divine side aimed at doing three things: *First*, to predict the failure of the program of the counterfeit trinity; *secondly*, to announce the results of the approaching last seven judgments known as the bowl judgments; and *thirdly*, to give words of assurance, encouragement, and comfort to the saints living in the second half of the tribulation.

The *first proclamation* is in Revelation 14:1-5:

And I saw, and behold, the Lamb standing on the mount Zion, and with him a hundred and forty and four thousand, having his name, and the name of his Father, written on their foreheads. And I heard a voice from heaven, as the voice of many waters, and as the voice of a great thunder: and the voice which I heard was as the voice of harpers harping with their harps: and they sing as it were a new song before the throne, and before the four living creatures and the elders: and no man could learn the song save the hundred and forty and four thousand, even they that had been purchased out of the earth. These are they that were not defiled with women; for they are virgins. These are they that follow the Lamb

whithersoever he goeth. These were purchased from among men, to be
the firstfruits unto God and unto the Lamb. And in their mouth was
found no lie: they are without blemish.

The first verse presents what appears to be a millennial scene
with the 144,000 Jews of Revelation seven now on Mt. Zion with Christ,
the Lamb. They have the name of God the Father on their foreheads
which is the seal that protected them from death (Revelation 7:3-4).
The question is: why bring in a millennial scene at this juncture of the
book of the Revelation? The answer lies in its connection with the
previous two chapters where Satan organized his attempt to destroy
the Jews. The first verse of chapter 14 opens up with the 144,000 Jews
standing on Mt. Zion with the protective seal on their foreheads
prominently displayed. This shows that Satan's attempt at total
Jewish destruction will fail. This is the purpose of the first proclamation, and it will provide comfort to the tribulation saints. Verses
2-3 describe the song of the 144,000, a song that they alone will know.
Four characteristics are described next (verses 4-5): first, they are
male virgins, a necessity in light of their calling to evangelize the
world during the first half of the tribulation, the severity of the
judgments falling on the earth, and the persecution of the saints
initially by the Ecclesiastical Babylon and then by the counterfeit
trinity. Secondly, they follow Christ wherever He may lead. Thirdly,
they are the *firstfruits*, a term that indicates the first of much more to
come. The very fact that the 144,000 are merely the firstfruits of many
more Jewish believers to come further points to the failure of the program of the counterfeit trinity. Where the rest come from is a point
that will be discussed in Chapter XIII. Fourthly, in relationship to their
morality, they are without a lie or blemish. They are not tainted by any
kind of false religious or political system.

The *second proclamation* is in Revelation 14:6-7:

And I saw another angel flying in mid heaven, having eternal good tidings
to proclaim unto them that dwell on the earth, and unto every nation
and tribe and tongue and people; and he saith with a great voice, Fear
God, and give him glory; for the hour of his judgment is come: and worship him that made the heaven and the earth and sea and fountains of
waters.

This proclamation is a final call to the world to accept the Gospel
in light of the Revelation thirteen problem where the Antichrist
declares himself to be god, and the False Prophet is calling all men to
take upon themselves the mark of the beast and thus show their sub-
missive acceptance of the deity of the Antichrist. This proclamation is
a call to the inhabitants of the world to choose between Christ or Antichrist. With the announcement of a final call to heed the Gospel
comes an announcement of the coming final series of judgments

about to be poured out through the bowl judgments. In light of the coming judgments, they are urged to worship Him who made the heavens and the earth.

The *third proclamation* is in 14:8:

And another, a second angel, followed, saying, Fallen, fallen is Babylon the great, that hath made all the nations to drink of the wine of the wrath of her fornication.

This proclamation announces the fall of political Babylon, something that will be detailed in Revelation 18. This point will be discussed further in Chapter XIV. But for now, the announcement is made that the world-wide capital of the Antichrist is due for destruction.

The *fourth proclamation* is in 14:9-12:

And another angel, a third, followed them, saying with a great voice, If any man worshippeth the beast and his image, and receiveth a mark on his forehead, or upon his hand, he also shall drink of the wine of the wrath of God, which is prepared unmixed in the cup of his anger; and he shall be tormented with fire and brimstone in the presence of the holy angels, and in the presence of the Lamb: and the smoke of their torment goeth up for ever and ever; and they have no rest day and night, they that worship the beast and his image, and whoso receiveth the mark of his name. Here is the patience of the saints, they that keep the commandments of God, and the faith of Jesus.

This proclamation concerns those who take upon themselves the mark of the beast. This is the point of no return. The opportunity of salvation will be available to all as long as they are without the mark. But once the mark is taken, signifying the acceptance of the Antichrist as the one true god, they will have forfeited any further opportunity to be saved. Those who take the mark are destined for two things: first, they will *drink of the wine of the wrath of God* which is the bowl judgments of Revelation 15-16; and, secondly, they are doomed to eternal torment in the Lake of Fire. For by taking the mark, they have reached the point of no return.

No one will take the mark out of ignorance for by this time there will have been two world-wide proclamations of the Gospel. First was the 144,000 during the first half of the tribulation and the second was the angel in Revelation 14:6-7 in the middle of the tribulation. Those who accept the mark are those who heard the love of the truth but rejected it (II Thessalonians 2:8-12).

The fourth proclamation concludes in verse 12 declaring that this fact is the patience of the saints. By refusing the mark the saints will undergo heavy persecution and martyrdom. But the encouragement lies in the fact that the persecutors, those with the mark, are doomed to suffer the severe bowl judgments in this life and eternal torment in the next.

The *fifth proclamation* is in 14:13:

> And I heard a voice from heaven saying, Write, Blessed are the dead who die in the Lord from henceforth: yea, saith the Spirit, that they may rest from their labors; for their works follow with them.

As a further word of encouragement and comfort, this proclamation concerns the saints who will die during the second half of the tribulation. A special blessing is promised to them.

The *sixth proclamation* is in 14:14-16:

> And I saw, and behold, a white cloud; and on the cloud I saw one sitting like unto a son of man, having on his head a golden crown, and in his hand a sharp sickle. And another angel came out from the temple, crying with a great voice to him that sat on the cloud, Send forth thy sickle, and reap: for the hour to reap is come; for the harvest of the earth is ripe. And he that sat on the cloud cast his sickle upon the earth; and the earth was reaped.

This proclamation is one of reaping. Reaping is a common symbol for salvation. Thus, this proclamation announces that in spite of the majority accepting the mark, there will be many who during the second half of the tribulation will come to a saving knowledge of Jesus Christ.

The *seventh proclamation* is in 14:17-20:

> And another angel came out from the temple which is in heaven, he also having a sharp sickle. And another angel came out from the altar, he that hath power over fire; and he called with a great voice to him that had the sharp sickle, saying, Send forth thy sharp sickle, and gather the clusters of the vine of the earth; for her grapes are fully ripe. And the angel cast his sickle into the earth, and gathered the vintage of the earth, and cast it into the winepress, the great winepress, of the wrath of God. And the winepress was trodden without the city, and there came out blood from the winepress, even unto the bridles of the horses, as far as a thousand and six hundred furlongs.

This proclamation is one of the treading of the grapes. Whereas reaping is a common symbol of salvation, treading is a common symbol of judgment. The grapes are gathered and then undergo the severity of the wrath of God which is the coming bowl judgments; the treading then is by means of the bowl judgments. This treading takes place *without the city* of Jerusalem where the Valley of Kidron, also known as the Valley of Jehoshaphat is located. The treading in this valley results in blood coming out about 4½ feet high for about 200 miles. With the close of the bowl judgments, there is to be a severe judgment of treading, resulting in massive bloodletting. Since this passage involves the Campaign of Armageddon, it will be discussed further in Chapter XIV.

P.   THE SEVENTH TRUMPET — THE THIRD WOE JUDGMENT

Closing the midtribulation events and announcing the bowl judgments of the second half of the tribulation is the seventh trumpet in Revelation 11:14-19:

> The second Woe is past: behold, the third Woe cometh quickly. And the seventh angel sounded; and there followed great voices in heaven, and they said, The kingdom of the world is become the kingdom of our Lord, and of his Christ: and he shall reign for ever and ever. And the four and twenty elders, who sit before God on their thrones, fell upon their faces and worshipped God, saying, We give thee thanks, O Lord God, the Almighty, who art and who wast; because thou hast taken thy great power, and didst reign. And the nations were wroth, and thy wrath came, and the time of the dead to be judged, and the time to give their reward to thy servants the prophets, and to the saints, and to them that fear thy name, the small and the great; and to destroy them that destroy the earth. And there was opened the temple of God that is in heaven; and there was seen in his temple the ark of his covenant; and there followed lightnings, and voices, and thunders, and an earthquake, and great hail.

The seventh trumpet is also the third woe judgment (verse 14). When the seventh trumpet is blown an announcement is made that with this trumpet Christ will inherit the kingdom of the world (verse 15). It should be noted that the word *kingdom* is singular, and so Christ will inherit the one-world kingdom of the Antichrist. A further announcement is made that the time of the final judgments has also come in order to destroy the ones who are destroying the earth and to avenge the ones who are killing the prophets and the saints (verses 16-18). These announcements are also declaring the results of the bowl judgments, the final series of judgments. Since the results of the seventh trumpet judgment are the same as the results of the bowl judgments it shows that, just as the seventh seal judgment contains the seven trumpet judgments, the seventh trumpet judgment contains the seven bowl judgments. (verse 19).

To summarize Revelation 11-16, Revelation eleven closes with the announcement that the bowl judgments are about to be poured out. Revelation 12-13 then points out the events on earth necessitating the seven bowl judgments contained in the seventh trumpet, namely: the actions of the counterfeit trinity. Revelation fourteen shows how the program of the counterfeit trinity will fail and also announces some of the results of the bowl judgments. The bowl judgments are then described in Revelation 15-16. This is the topic of the next chapter.

This chapter has been primarily concerned with the mid-tribulation events. Now it is necessary to go on to the events of the second half of the tribulation.

CHAPTER XII

THE EVENTS OF THE SECOND HALF
OF THE TRIBULATION

Obviously, the events beginning in the middle of the tribulation discussed in the previous chapter continue into the second half, for it will take some time to accomplish all of the events. Thus, the second half will largely be comprised of events already described. But the latter part of the second half will contain the bowl judgments recorded in Revelation 15-16.

The prelude to the bowl judgments is in Revelation 15:1-16:1:

> And I saw another sign in heaven, great and marvellous, seven angels having seven plagues, which are the last, for in them is finished the wrath of God. And I saw as it were a sea of glass mingled with fire; and them that come off victorious from the beast, and from his image, and from the number of his name, standing by the sea of glass, having harps of God. And they sing the song of Moses the servant of God, and the song of the Lamb, saying, Great and marvellous are thy works, O Lord God, the Almighty; righteous and true are thy ways, thou King of the ages. Who shall not fear, O Lord, and glorify thy name? for thou only art holy; for all the nations shall come and worship before thee; for thy righteous acts have been made manifest. And after these things I saw, and the temple of the tabernacle of the testimony in heaven was opened: and there came out from the temple the seven angels that had the seven plagues, arrayed with precious stone, pure and bright, and girt about their breasts with golden girdles. And one of the four living creatures gave unto the seven angels seven golden bowls full of the wrath of God, who liveth for ever and ever. And the temple was filled with smoke from the glory of God, and from his power; and none was able to enter into the temple, till the seven plagues of the seven angels should be finished. And I heard a great voice out of the temple, saying to the seven angels, Go ye, and pour out the seven bowls of the wrath of God into the earth.

Verse one introduces the prelude with the seven angels who have the seven bowls. These are also the last seven judgments, and they contain and bring to completion the wrath of God. So again, the results spelled out under the seventh trumpet come after the seven bowl judgments are complete.

Then in verses 2-4 there is a view of the martyred saints of the second half of the tribulation. These came off victorious from the pressures to worship the beast and to take the mark of the beast. While they suffered martyrdom, they conquered in the spiritual warfare (verse 2). They are viewed as singing two songs. One is the Song of Moses (verse 3a) which refers to either the song in Exodus 15:1-18, or the one in Deuteronomy 32:1-43. In both cases it is a song of deliverance. The second is the Song of the Lamb (verses 3b-4), the content of which is recorded here.

Then in verses 5-8 the seven bowls are given to the seven angels commissioned to carry out the final series of judgments. As a result of the giving, the temple in heaven is filled with the Shechinah Glory* causing its closure until all the bowl judgments have been poured out.

Finally, in 16:1 the angels are commanded to pour out the seven bowl judgments of the wrath of God. The command comes by a voice out of the temple of God which has just been filled with the Shechinah Glory.

The first bowl judgment is in 16:2:

> And the first went, and poured out his bowl into the earth; and it became a noisome and grievous sore upon the men that had the mark of the beast, and that worshipped his image.

The first bowl is clearly directed at affecting only those who have the mark of the beast in fulfillment of Revelation 14:9-11. It will result in a grievous sore upon the worshippers of the Antichrist. This sore will be some kind of skin ulcers or malignancies on the skin.

The second bowl judgment is in 16:3:

> And the second poured out his bowl into the sea; and it became blood as of a dead man; and every living soul died, even the things that were in the sea.

Whereas under the second trumpet judgment one third of the salt water was affected, in the second bowl judgment the rest of the salt water will be turned into blood, destroying the remainder of sea life.

The third bowl is in 16:4-7:

> And the third poured out his bowl into the rivers and the fountains of the waters; and it became blood. And I heard the angel of the waters saying, Righteous art thou, who art and who wast, thou Holy One, because thou didst thus judge: for they poured out the blood of saints and prophets, and blood hast thou given them to drink: they are worthy. And I heard the altar saying, Yea, O Lord God, the Almighty, true and righteous are thy judgments.

Whereas in the third trumpet judgment one third of the fresh water was destroyed, under the third bowl judgment the remainder of the fresh water in rivers and springs will be destroyed, as it too will become blood (verse 4). Apparently water in wells and cisterns will survive. The act elicits two declarations. First (verses 5-6) the guardian angel assigned to water declares the righteousness of God's judgment in this act. Since men have shed the blood of the prophets and saints, mankind is given blood to drink. The second declaration

* See Appendix IV

(verse 7) comes from the altar further affirming the assessment of God's righteousness being revealed through His judgments.

The fourth bowl is in 16:8-9:

> And the fourth poured out his bowl upon the sun; and it was given unto it to scorch men with fire. And men were scorched with great heat: and they blasphemed the name of God who hath the power over these plagues; and they repented not to give him glory.

Whereas the fourth trumpet judgment affected the sun by destroying one third of the light source, the fourth bowl will also affect the sun, by increasing its temperature to the point that men are totally scorched. Mankind will recognize the source of this judgment as coming from God but instead of turning to Him in faith, they will blaspheme His name.

The fifth bowl judgment is in 16:10-11:

> And the fifth poured out his bowl upon the throne of the beast; and his kingdom was darkened; and they gnawed their tongues for pain, and they blasphemed the God of heaven because of their pains and their sores; and they repented not of their works.

Among the various results of the fifth trumpet judgment was the third blackout. The fifth bowl judgment will result in the fourth blackout of the end times. The entire kingdom of the beast will be darkened which, at this stage, will include the entire world with the exception of the three Tranjordanian nations where light will still exist. Along with the darkness comes a gnawing pain that will cause mankind to blaspheme all the more. This will be a thick darkness that can be felt. The circumstances are not unlike what befell Egypt in Exodus 10:21-23.

The sixth (16:12-16) and seventh (16:17-21) bowl judgments are both concerned with the Campaign of Armageddon which will be discussed in Chapter XIV.

CHAPTER XIII

THE GREAT TRIBULATION:
ADDITIONAL FEATURES AND FACTS

The purpose of this chapter is to fill in some of the gaps concerning the Great Tribulation before dealing with the culminating event of the Campaign of Armageddon. The Old Testament prophets had a great deal to say about the Great Tribulation, and it would be impossible to deal with all of them adequately. So this study will be limited to certain key passages.

A. BABYLON

As has been indicated in several places earlier, Babylon is to be rebuilt and become the Antichrist's world-wide political and economic capital of the world. Passages involving the rebuilding of Babylon will be discussed in connection with the Campaign of Armageddon in the next chapter. All that needs to be noted now is that the prophecies regarding the city of Babylon have never been fulfilled in the past, as any encyclopedia article on Babylon will make quite clear. In order for these prophecies to be fulfilled, it will require the rebuilding of the city of Babylon in the same general area. Ancient Babylon is in present day Iraq. More will be said on this later.

B. ISRAEL AND THE TRIBULATION

Though the whole world will be involved in the Great Tribulation, it will particularly affect Israel as is evident from the massive amount of Old Testament Scripture concerning this time period. Of the three purposes of the tribulation previously presented in Chapter VII, the second and third purposes are directly related to the Jews.* Furthermore, the tribulation will not begin until Israel signs the seven year covenant. This section will deal with some more points relating Israel and the Great Tribulation.

1. ISRAEL IN GENERAL

a. THE TIME OF JACOB'S TROUBLE

The uniqueness of the tribulation's relationship to Israel is especially brought out in Jeremiah 30:4-7:

> And these are the words that Jehovah spake concerning Israel and concerning Judah. For thus saith Jehovah: We have heard a voice of trembling, of fear, and not of peace. Ask ye now, and see whether a man doth travail with child: Wherefore do I see every man with his hands on

---

* See Chapter IX.

his loins, as a woman in travail, and all faces are turned into paleness? Alas! for that day is great, so that none is like it: it is even the time of Jacob's trouble; but he shall be saved out of it.

While the Scriptures have many names for the Great Tribulation, in this passage a name is given that directly relates the tribulation to the Jewish nation: *the time of Jacob's trouble*. For while it is true that all will suffer during that time, Israel will suffer more so. The basic reason for this lies in Israel's relationship to God as God's first born (Exodus 4:22) and therefore receives double both in blessing and cursing. The principle that Israel receives double for all her sins is stated in Isaiah 40:1-2:

Comfort ye, comfort ye my people, saith your God. Speak ye comfortably to Jerusalem; and cry unto her, that her warfare is accomplished, that her iniquity is pardoned, that she hath received of Jehovah's hand double for all her sins.

It is also found in Jeremiah 16:16-18:

Behold, I will send for many fishers, saith Jehovah, and they shall fish them up; and afterward I will send for many hunters, and they shall hunt them from every mountain, and from every hill, and out of the clefts of the rocks. For mine eyes are upon all their ways; they are not hid from my face, neither is their iniquity concealed from mine eyes. And first I will recompense their iniquity and their sin double, because they have polluted my land with the carcasses of their detestable things, and have filled mine inheritance with their abominations.

The principle of Israel receiving double for all her sins is the reason why the tribulation is uniquely the time of Jacob's trouble.

b. GENERAL DESCRIPTIONS

A graphic general description of Israel in the tribulation is found in Isaiah 3:1-4:1:

For, behold, the Lord, Jehovah of hosts, doth take away from Jerusalem and from Judah stay and staff, the whole stay of bread, and the whole stay of water; the mighty man, and the man of war; the judge, and the prophet, and the diviner, and the elder; the captain of fifty, and the honorable man, and the counsellor, and the expert artificer, and the skilful enchanter. And I will give children to be their princes, and babes shall rule over them. And the people shall be oppressed, every one by another, and every one by his neighbor: the child shall behave himself proudly against the old man, and the base against the honorable. When a man shall take hold of his brother in the house of his father, saying, Thou hast clothing, be thou our ruler, and let this ruin be under thy hand; in that day shall he lift up his voice, saying, I will not be a healer; for in my house is neither bread nor clothing: ye shall not make me ruler of the people. For Jerusalem is ruined, and Judah is fallen; because their tongue and their doings are against Jehovah, to provoke the eyes of his glory. The show of their countenance doth witness against them; and they declare their sin as Sodom, they hide it not. Woe unto their soul! for they have done evil unto themselves. Say ye of the righteous, that it shall be well with him; for they shall eat the fruit of their doings. Woe unto the wicked! it shall be ill with him; for what his hands have done shall be done unto him. As for my people, children are their oppressors, and women rule over them. O my people, they that lead thee cause thee to err, and destroy the way of thy paths. Jehovah standeth up to contend, and standeth to judge the peoples. Jehovah will enter into judgment with the elders of his people, and the princes thereof: It is ye that have eaten up the vineyard; the spoil of the poor is in your houses: what mean ye that ye crush my people, and grind the face of the poor? saith the Lord, Jehovah of hosts. Moreover, Jehovah said, Because the daughters of Zion are haughty, and walk with outstretched necks and wanton eyes, walking and mincing as they go, and making a tinkling with their feet; therefore the Lord will smite with a scab the crown of the head of the daughters of Zion, and Jehovah will lay bare their secret parts. In that day the Lord will take away the beauty of their anklets, and the cauls, and the crescents; the pendants, and the bracelets, and the mufflers; the headtires, and the ankle chains, and the sashes, and the perfume boxes, and the amulets; the rings, and the nose jewels; the festival robes, and the mantles, and the shawls, and the satchels; the hand-mirrors, and the fine linen, and the turbans, and the veils. And it shall come to pass, that instead of sweet spices there shall be rottenness; and instead of a girdle, a rope; and instead of well set hair, baldness; and instead of a robe, a girding of sackcloth: branding instead of beauty. Thy men shall fall by the sword, and thy mighty in the war. And her gates shall lament and mourn; and she shall be desolate and sit upon the ground. And seven women shall take hold of one man in that day, saying, We will eat our own bread, and wear our own apparel: only let us be called by thy name; take thou away our reproach.

Verses 1-15 describe the effects of the tribulation on the Jewish leaders for reasons that will be discussed later. This is followed in 3:16-4:1 with a description of the effects on Jewish women. It will involve a removal of their luxury items (3:16-24) and a sharp reduction of the male population until there will be seven Jewish women for each Jewish male (3:25-4:1).

c. THE DAY OF JEHOVAH PASSAGES

There are five *Day of Jehovah* passages that directly relate the Great Tribulation to Israel. *First*, Ezekiel 13:1-7 describes the Day of Jehovah in relationship to the false Jewish prophets in the tribulation:

And the word of Jehovah came unto me, saying, Son of man, prophesy against the prophets of Israel that prophesy, and say thou unto them that prophesy out of their own heart, Hear ye the word of Jehovah: Thus saith the Lord Jehovah, Woe unto the foolish prophets, that follow their own spirit, and have seen nothing! O Israel, thy prophets have been like foxes in the waste places. Ye have not gone up into the gaps, neither built up the wall for the house of Israel, to stand in the battle in the day of Jehovah. They have seen falsehood and lying divination, that say, Jehovah saith; but Jehovah hath not sent them: and they have made men to hope that the word would be confirmed. Have ye not seen a false vision, and have ye not spoken a lying divination, in that ye say, Jehovah saith; albeit I have not spoken?

The multiplication of false prophets among Israel will require a massive cleansing described in Zechariah 13:2-6:

And it shall come to pass in that day, saith Jehovah of hosts, that I will cut off the names of the idols out of the land, and they shall no more be remembered; and also I will cause the prophets and the unclean spirit to pass out of the land. And it shall come to pass that, when any shall yet prophesy, then his father and his mother that begat him shall say unto him, Thou shalt not live; for thou speakest lies in the name of Jehovah; and his father and his mother that begat him shall thrust him through when he prophesieth. And it shall come to pass in that day, that the prophets shall be ashamed every one of his vision, when he prophesieth; neither shall they wear a hairy mantle to deceive: but he shall say, I am no prophet, I am a tiller of the ground; for I have been made a bondman from my youth. And one shall say unto him, What are these wounds between thine arms? Then he shall answer, Those with which I was wounded in the house of my friends.

Secondly, in Joel 2:1-11 the Day of Jehovah is depicted as a time of darkness and invasion:

Blow ye the trumpet in Zion, and sound an alarm in my holy mountain; let all the inhabitants of the land tremble: for the day of Jehovah cometh, for it is nigh at hand; a day of darkness and gloominess, a day of clouds and thick darkness, as the dawn spread upon the mountains; a great people and a strong; there hath not been ever the like, neither shall be any more after them, even to the years of many generations. A fire devoureth before them; and behind them a flame burneth: the land is as the garden of Eden before them, and behind them a desolate wilderness; yea, and none hath escaped them. The appearance of them is as the appearance of horses; and as horsemen, so do they run. Like the noise of chariots on the tops of the mountains do they leap, like the noise of a flame of fire that devoureth the stubble, as a strong people set in battle array. At their presence the peoples are in anguish; all faces are waxed pale. They run like mighty men; they climb the wall like men of war; and they march every one on his ways, and they break not their ranks. Neither doth one thrust another; they march every one in his path; and they burst through the weapons, and break not off their course. They leap upon the city; they run upon the wall; they climb up into the houses; they enter in at the windows like a thief. The earth quaketh before them; the heavens tremble; the sun and the moon are darkened, and the stars withdraw their shining: and Jehovah uttereth his voice before his army; for his camp is very great; for he is strong that executeth his word; for the day of Jehovah is great and very terrible; and who can abide it?

Later, in the *third* passage, Joel 3:14-17, the Day of Jehovah is described as the time of refuge for Israel:

Multitudes, multitudes in the valley of decision! for the day of Jehovah is near in the valley of decision. The sun and the moon are darkened, and the stars withdraw their shining. And Jehovah will roar from Zion, and utter his voice from Jerusalem; and the heavens and the earth shall shake: but Jehovah will be a refuge unto his people, and a stronghold to the children of Israel. So shall ye know that I am Jehovah your God, dwelling in Zion my holy mountain: then shall Jerusalem be holy, and there shall no strangers pass through her any more.

The exact nature of this refuge will be discussed later in this chapter.

Fourthly, in Amos 5:18-20 the Day of Jehovah is again depicted as the time of darkness:

Woe unto you that desire the day of Jehovah! Wherefore would ye have the day of Jehovah? It is darkness, and not light. As if a man did flee from a lion, and a bear met him; or went into the house and leaned his hand on the wall, and a serpent bit him. Shall not the day of Jehovah be darkness, and not light? even very dark, and no brightness in it?

Fifthly, in Zephaniah 1:7-13 the Day of Jehovah is portrayed as being especially heavy against Jerusalem:

Hold thy peace at the presence of the Lord Jehovah; for the day of Jehovah is at hand: for Jehovah hath prepared a sacrifice, he hath consecrated his guests. And it shall come to pass in the day of Jehovah's sacrifice, that I will punish the princes, and the king's sons, and all such as are clothed with foreign apparel. And in that day I will punish all those that leap over the threshold, that fill their master's house with violence and deceit. And in that day, saith Jehovah, there shall be the noise of a cry from the fish gate, and a wailing from the second quarter, and a great crashing from the hills. Wail, ye inhabitants of Maktesh; for all the people of Canaan are undone; all they that were laden with silver are cut off. And it shall come to pass at that time, that I will search Jerusalem with lamps; and I will punish the men that are settled on their lees, that say in their heart, Jehovah will not do good, neither will he do evil. And their wealth shall become a spoil, and their houses a desolation: yea, they shall build houses, but shall not inhabit them; and they shall plant vineyards, but shall not drink the wine thereof.

d. WORLD-WIDE ANTI-SEMITISM

The key passage describing the Great Tribulation as a period of world-wide anti-Semitism is found in Matthew 24:9-28. Since this passage has already been dealt with in detail in the previous sections*

* See Chapters X and XI.

of this book, only a summary is needed here.* Matthew 24:9-14 describes the events of the first half of the tribulation. Verses 9-12 give some general descriptions, and verse 13 promises that those Jews who endure to the end of the tribulation shall be saved, a fact to be discussed in the next chapter. Then in verse 14 there is a description of the preaching of the 144,000 Jews.

Verses 15-28 describe the second half of the tribulation. Verse 15 announces the abomination of desolation followed by a description of the Jews in flight in verses 16-20. The Great Tribulation is described in verses 21-22 as a time of anti-Semitism and in verses 23-26 as a time of false religion and false prophets. The whole thing concludes with the second coming in verses 27-28.

e. ISRAEL AND SATAN

Revelation 12:1-17 is the central passage describing Satan's relationship to Israel during the tribulation. At that time there will be an all-out satanically organized campaign to wipe out the Jews once and for all. Since this, too, has been examined previously in Chapter XI, an outline will suffice here.

Verses 1-5 lay out a historical summary from the birth to the ascension of Christ. Verse six pictures Israel in flight just as Matthew 24:16-20 did. The picture of Jews on the run is followed by the reason why in verses 7-12. Satan will be cast down to the earth, and he will set out to destroy the Jews. Verses 13-14 further explain verse six where Israel is in flight. Finally in verses 15-17 the passage concludes by describing Satan's persecution of the Jews, especially the believing remnant.

f. THE FINAL RESULT

To what extent will Satan succeed in destroying the Jews? Zechariah 13:8-9 provides the answer:

> And it shall come to pass, that in all the land, saith Jehovah, two parts therein shall be cut off and die; but the third shall be left therein. And I will bring the third part into the fire, and will refine them as silver is refined, and will try them as gold is tried: they shall call on my name, and I will hear them: I will say, it is my people; and they shall say, Jehovah is my God.

In the Holocaust under Hitler one third of the world Jewish population died. Under the fierce persecution of the Antichrist, controlled and energized by Satan, two thirds of the Jewish population

---

* See Appendix V for a full exposition of the Olivet Discourse.

will die. This will be the largest and most intense persecution of the Jews ever known in Jewish history.

g. ISRAEL AND MICHAEL

Michael, besides being the archangel, is also the chief prince and protective angel assigned to Israel. It is Michael who will cast Satan out of his third abode in Revelation 12:7-12*. But the key passage pointing out Michael's relationship to Israel in the tribulation is in Daniel 12:1:

> And at that time shall Michael stand up, the great prince who standeth for the children of thy people; and there shall be a time of trouble, such as never was since there was a nation even to that same time: and at that time thy people shall be delivered, every one that shall be found written in the book.

The fact that Israel will survive at all is due to the ministry of the archangel and chief prince Michael.

h. THE FOUR GROUPS OF JEWS

During the Great Tribulation period there will be four distinct groups of Jews, three of whom have been mentioned previously. The first group can be entitled the apostate Jews. These are "the many" of Daniel 9:27 who will enter the seven year covenant that will begin the tribulation. They will comprise about two thirds of the nation, and will die in the world-wide persecution in the tribulation.

The second group is known as the 144,000 Jews. They are part of the one third that will survive the tribulation. These are the Jews who will be saved and sealed sometime after the Rapture of the church. They will be evangelists during the first half of the tribulation conducting a world-wide revival.

The third group can be entitled as other Hebrew Christians. These are Jews who will receive Christ via the preaching of the 144,000 but are not part of that number. The "every" of Revelation 7:9 must also include Israel. Since the context of Revelation 7:9-17 follows the 144,000 in verses 1-8, the Jews in the latter section will not be part of the 144,000. Since some of these other Hebrew Christians will be martyred, some will be part of the two thirds category while others of the one third category will survive.

The fourth group is called the faithful remnant. Since they are the key group involved in the second half of the tribulation, they will be dealt with separately in the following section.

---

* See Appendix I for the six abodes of Satan.

2. THE FAITHFUL REMNANT

Who are the faithful remnant? Based upon all the passages involved, this group will comprise the majority of the one third of the nation that will survive the tribulation. Throughout the tribulation they will be unbelievers as far as the Messiahship of Jesus is concerned and also unbelievers as far as the Antichrist is concerned. These are the "non-many" of Daniel 9:27 who will refuse to have anything to do with the covenant. They are the ones who "shall not be in haste" of Isaiah 28:16.

a. THE FACT OF THE REMNANT

The fact that the remnant will survive is found in Isaiah 10:20-23:

> And it shall come to pass in that day, that the remnant of Israel, and they that are escaped of the house of Jacob, shall no more again lean upon him that smote them, but shall lean upon Jehovah, the Holy One of Israel, in truth. A remnant shall return, even the remnant of Jacob, unto the mighty God. For though thy people, Israel, be as the sand of the sea, only a remnant of them shall return: a destruction is determined, overflowing with righteousness. For a full end, and that determined, will the Lord, Jehovah of hosts, make in the midst of all the earth.

Verse 20 states that unlike the rest of Israel, they will no longer lean on the one who smote them (that is, the Antichrist), but on the Holy One of Israel. While these Jews will be trusting God from the beginning, it will not necessarily be faith in Jesus the Messiah. Then in verse 21 Isaiah declares that ultimately they will return to the God of Israel, a return that can only be accomplished by faith in the Messiah Jesus. Verse 22a points out that in spite of the numerical strength of the Jews, only the remnant will return to God. Verses 22b-23 talk about a decree of destruction that has been determined upon the whole earth which the remnant will survive. The words used here are much the same as those found in Isaiah 28:22 where the decree of destruction is issued with the signing of the seven year covenant beginning the tribulation. Synthesizing these two Isaiah passages together, it is clear that the remnant will survive the persecution of the Jews and the massive destruction of the earth during the tribulation. Hence they are referred to as the *escaped* of Israel here and in Isaiah 4:2, 37:31-32, Joel 2:32 and Obadiah 17.

b. THE PROTECTION OF THE REMNANT

Another section of Isaiah records the protection of the remnant by God's presence with the remnant in 41:8-16:

> But thou, Israel, my servant, Jacob whom I have chosen, the seed of Abraham my friend, thou whom I have taken hold of from the ends of

the earth, and called from the corners thereof, and said unto thee, Thou art my servant, I have chosen thee and not cast thee away; fear thou not, for I am with thee; be not dismayed, for I am thy God; I will strengthen thee; yea, I will help thee; yea, I will uphold thee with the right hand of my righteousness. Behold, all they that are incensed against thee shall be put to shame and confounded: they that strive with thee shall be as nothing, and shall perish. Thou shalt seek them, and shalt not find them, even them that contend with thee: they that war against thee shall be as nothing, and as a thing of nought. For I Jehovah thy God will hold thy right hand, saying unto thee, Fear not; I will help thee. Fear not, thou worm Jacob, and ye men of Israel; I will help thee, saith Jehovah, and thy Redeemer is the Holy One of Israel. Behold, I have made thee to be a new sharp threshing instrument having teeth; thou shalt thresh the mountains, and beat them small, and shalt make the hills as chaff. Thou shalt winnow them, and the wind shall carry them away, and the whirl-wind shall scatter them; and thou shalt rejoice in Jehovah, thou shalt glory in the Holy One of Israel.

This is a promise to preserve the remnant in the midst of tremendous persecution during Satan's campaign to destroy the Jews.

c. THE PROVISION FOR THE REMNANT

Since it is forbidden for anyone to buy or sell without the mark of the beast, how will God preserve and provide for the remnant? Isaiah has much to say regarding this point. Using the combined words "poor and needy," a common designation for the faithful remnant, Isaiah states in 41:17-20:

The poor and needy seek water, and there is none, and their tongue faileth for thirst; I Jehovah will answer them, I the God of Israel will not forsake them. I will open rivers on the bare heights, and fountains in the midst of the valleys; I will make the wilderness a pool of water, and the dry land springs of water. I will put in the wilderness the cedar, the acacia, and the myrtle, and the oil-tree; I will set in the desert the fir-tree, the pine, and the box-tree together: that they may see, and know, and consider, and understand together, that the hand of Jehovah hath done this, and the Holy One of Israel hath created it.

In the wilderness of Sinai God miraculously provided food and water for Israel. He will do so again in the tribulation when the Jews flee to the wilderness. These miraculous provisions will cause them to reconsider their relationship with God.

In another passage, Isaiah shows how on one hand God will supply for the faithful remnant, whereas He will withhold provision from the apostate Jews. This is in Isaiah 65:8-16:

Thus saith Jehovah, As the new wine is found in the cluster, and one saith, Destroy it not, for a blessing is in it: so will I do for my servants' sakes, that I may not destroy them all. And I will bring forth a seed out of Jacob, and out of Judah an inheritor of my mountains; and my chosen shall inherit it, and my servants shall dwell there. And Sharon shall be a fold of flocks, and the valley of Achor a place for herds to lie down in, for my people that have sought me. But ye that forsake Jehovah, that forget my holy mountain, that prepare a table for Fortune, and that fill up mingled wine unto Destiny; I will destine you to the sword, and ye shall all bow down to the slaughter; because when I called, ye did not answer; when I spake, ye did not hear; but ye did that which was evil in mine eyes, and chose that wherein I delighted not. Therefore thus saith the Lord Jehovah, Behold, my servants shall eat, but ye shall be hungry; behold, my servants shall drink, but ye shall be thirsty; behold, my servants shall rejoice, but ye shall be put to shame; behold, my servants shall sing for joy of heart, but ye shall cry for sorrow of heart, and shall wail for vexation of spirit. And ye shall leave your name for a curse unto my chosen; and the Lord Jehovah will slay thee; and he will call his servants by another name: so that he who blesseth himself in the earth shall bless himself in the God of truth; and he that sweareth in the earth shall swear by the God of truth; because the former troubles are forgotten, and because they are hid from mine eyes.

This passage makes clear that, while the apostates will be allowed to suffer and die, the faithful remnant will be divinely protected and provided with food and water. By this means the faithful remnant will be able to survive the persecutions and devastations of the Great Tribulation.

3.   THE CITY OF REFUGE

Several times, in previous sections that have dealt with the Jews and the Great Tribulation, mention was made of the Jews in flight, particularly the faithful remnant. Thus far no particular spot has been pinpointed. Is it possible to locate the exact place where the Jews will be hiding?

Up to now, three clues have been provided. One clue was in Matthew 24:16:

Then let them that are in Judaea flee unto the mountains.

According to this text, the place of flight and refuge is to be the mountains.

The second and third clues were given in Revelation 12:6 and 14:

And the woman fled into the wilderness, where she hath a place prepared of God, that there they may nourish her a thousand two hundred and threescore days.

And there were given to the woman the two wings of the great eagle, that she might fly into the wilderness unto her place, where she is nourished for a time, and times, and half a time, from the face of the serpent.

Not only must the place of refuge fulfill the requirement of being in the mountains, it must also fulfill this second requirement of being in the wilderness. Thirdly, the place in the wilderness was prepared by God in advance and therefore indicates a very adequate place of refuge.

These are the three clues found in passages examined earlier.

Although inconclusive, another passage which may have a bearing on the question of "where?" is found in Isaiah 33:13-16:

> Hear, ye that are far off, what I have done; and, ye that are near, acknowledge my might. The sinners in Zion are afraid; trembling hath seized the godless ones: Who among us can dwell with the devouring fire? who among us can dwell with everlasting burnings? He that walketh righteously, and speaketh uprightly; he that despiseth the gain of oppressions, that shaketh his hands from taking a bribe, that stoppeth his ears from hearing of blood, and shutteth his eyes from looking upon evil: he shall dwell on high; his place of defence shall be the munitions of rocks; his bread shall be given him; his waters shall be sure.

Since the context is dealing with end time events, this passage also points out a distinction between the apostates and the faithful remnant as far as their protection and preservation is concerned. The means by which protection for the remnant will be accomplished is given in verse 16:

> He shall dwell on high
> His place of defence shall be the
> 　munitions of rocks
> His bread shall be given him
> His waters shall be sure

Besides reaffirming the promise mentioned in Isaiah 41:17-20 and 65:8-16 that food and water would be provided, this passage gives some insight as to the nature of the hiding place itself. First it is stated that it will be "on high"; that is, in the mountains, thus reaffirming the Matthew passage. Then it adds that the place of defence will be "the munitions of rocks"; that is, the very nature of the place will make it easy to defend.

This brings the total to four clues. The refuge will be:

1. In the mountains
2. In the wilderness
3. A place prepared in advance
4. Very defensible

Another passage, Micah 2:12, pin-points the place exactly:

I will surely assemble, O Jacob, all of thee; I will surely gather the remnant of Israel; I will put them together as the sheep of Bozrah, as a flock in the midst of their pasture; they shall make great noise by reason of the multitude of men.

The remnant is gathered together as the sheep of Bozrah. Since the sheep of Bozrah are not any different than other sheep, this gathering together as the sheep of Bozrah simply means that they are to be gathered in Bozrah.

The ancient city of Bozrah was located in the region of Mount Seir. Mount Seir is a very rocky range of mountains, and its name means the "hairy mountains." This fulfills the requirement of the Matthew passage. It is located in the wilderness section of ancient Edom and so fulfills the requirement of the Revelation passage. The very nature of the chain of mountains of Mount Seir makes it quite defensible fulfilling the requirements of the Isaiah passage.

Mount Seir is located in the western side of ancient Edom, extending from southeast of the Dead Sea down to the city of Akaba. It towers over the Arabah, part of the rift valley from the south shore of the Dead Sea to the Gulf of Eilat. Today the area is in southern Jordan.

Other passages connecting the remnant to Bozrah will be discussed in the next chapter which deals with the Campaign of Armageddon.

A real fascinating issue is the exact location of Bozrah in the mountain range of Mount Seir. Two places have been suggested. One is the present Arab village of Buseira, which seems to retain the name of Bozrah. This is the main argument in favor of it. Another suggestion is the city now known as Petra.

While both cities meet all the above requirements, this author prefers the identification with Petra.

Petra is located in a basin within Mount Seir, and is totally surrounded by mountains and cliffs. The only way in and out of the city is through a narrow passageway that extends for about a mile and can only be negotiated by foot or by horseback. This makes the city easy to defend, and its surrounding high cliffs give added meaning and confirmation to Isaiah 33:16. Only two or three abreast can enter through this passage at any one time giving this city an even greater defensibility. The name "Bozrah" means *sheepfold*. An ancient sheepfold had a narrow entrance so that the shepherd could count his sheep. Once inside the fold, the sheep had more room to move around. Petra is shaped like a giant sheepfold with its narrow passageway opening up to a spacious circle surrounded by cliffs.

Regardless of which of the two cities is to be taken as Old Testament Bozrah, the general area of Mount Seir remains the same. But is there any other reason that this area is chosen besides its natural defensibility? There is an indication of such in the context of Daniel 11:40-45 which was discussed in Chapter XI. It was noted then that this passage concerns the conquests of the Antichrist in the middle of the tribulation as he begins his world political takeover. The key verse which bears upon the discussion here is in verse 41:

> He shall enter also into the glorious land, and many countries shall be overthrown; but these shall be delivered out of his hand: Edom, and Moab, and the chief of the children of Ammon.

The passage states that while the Antichrist will conquer the whole world, three nations will escape his domination: Edom, Moab and Ammon. All three of these ancient nations currently comprise the single modern state of Jordan. The city of Bozrah in Mount Seir is located in ancient Edom or southern Jordan. Since this area will escape the domination of the Antichrist, it is logical for the Jews to flee to this place. Thus, God will provide a city of refuge outside the Antichrist's domain for the fleeing remnant. It will be a very defensible city located in Mount Seir (regardless of which of the two sites one might pick). Furthermore, as they flee and while they are living there, food and water will be miraculously provided.

4. THE BASIS OF THE SECOND COMING OF CHRIST

The Rapture of the church has no preconditions and can come at any moment. But the second coming of Christ does have a major precondition. There is a condition that must be met before Christ will return to establish the kingdom. But before one can fully understand what the basis of His coming will be, one must first comprehend what the issues were at the time of the rejection of the Messiahship of Jesus.

a. THE REJECTION OF THE MESSIAHSHIP OF CHRIST

(1) MATTHEW 12:22-45

In the layout of the Gospel of Matthew, Christ began His ministry in chapter four. From chapter four until chapter twelve, Jesus went around Israel proclaiming His Messiahship and preaching the gospel of the kingdom. He performed many miracles, and the purpose of all His miracles between chapters four and twelve was to authenticate His person (that He is the Messiah) and His message (the gospel of the kingdom). These miracles were to serve as signs to the nation of Israel to force them to come to a decision about Him. But the purpose of His miracles and His whole ministry underwent a radical change in chapter twelve. The rejection of His Messiahship occurred in Matthew 12:22-37:

> Then was brought unto him one possessed with a demon, blind and

dumb: and he healed him, insomuch that the dumb man spake and saw. And all the multitudes were amazed, and said, Can this be the son of David? But when the Pharisees heard it, they said, This man doth not cast out demons, but by Beelzebub the prince of the demons. And knowing their thoughts he said unto them, Every kingdom divided against itself is brought to desolation; and every city or house divided against itself shall not stand: and if Satan casteth out Satan, he is divided against himself; how then shall his kingdom stand? And if I by Beelzebub cast out demons, by whom do your sons cast them out? therefore shall they be your judges. But if I by the Spirit of God cast out demons, then is the kingdom of God come upon you. Or how can one enter into the house of the strong man, and spoil his goods, except he first bind the strong man? and then he will spoil his house. He that is not with me is against me; and he that gathereth not with me scattereth. Therefore I say unto you, Every sin and blasphemy shall be forgiven unto men; but the blasphemy against the Spirit shall not be forgiven. And whosoever shall speak a word against the Son of man, it shall be forgiven him; but whosoever shall speak against the Holy Spirit, it shall not be forgiven him, neither in this world, nor in that which is to come. Either make the tree good, and its fruit good; or make the tree corrupt, and its fruit corrupt: for the tree is known by its fruit. Ye offspring of vipers, how can ye, being evil, speak good things? for out of the abundance of the heart the mouth speaketh. The good man out of his good treasure bringeth forth good things: and the evil man out of his evil treasure bringeth forth evil things. And I say unto you, that every idle word that men shall speak, they shall give account thereof in the day of judgment. For by thy words thou shalt be justified, and by thy words thou shalt be condemned.

Among the many miracles that Jesus performed was the casting out of demons. Judaism also had exorcists who would cast out demons (verse 27). But in Jewish exorcism, one first had to establish communication with the demon in order to find out his name. Then, using the demon's name, the exorcist could cast him out. On other occasions Jesus did use the Jewish method as in Luke 8:30. When demons speak they use the vocal chords of the person under their control. However, in the case of a dumb demon, Jewish exorcism was to no avail, for communication with that kind of a demon was impossible. But Jewish theology taught that the Messiah, when He came, would even be able to cast out that kind of demon. The Jewish observation that dumb demons were different was validated by Christ in Mark 9:17, 25 and 29.

In verse 22 of Matthew 12, Christ was able to exorcise a dumb demon. In verse 23 this caused the people to begin asking the question, "Can Jesus really be the Messiah?" This was one of the key purposes of this miracle, to get them to see that He indeed was the Son of David.

However, the people were not willing to come to a decision by themselves but were looking to their religious leaders, the Pharisees, to reach a verdict for them. They were waiting for the Pharisees to conclude either that He was the Messiah or that He was not the Messiah.

These were the only two options the Pharisees had. But if they were to conclude that He was not the Messiah, the Pharisees would also have to be able to explain how Jesus was able to perform His many miracles, especially the miracles that were supposed to be unique to the Messiah only.

In verse 24 the Pharisees made their choice. They refused to accept Jesus as the Messiah because He did not fit the Pharisaic mold of what Messiah was supposed to say and do (Luke 7:30-35). Their alternative explanation as to how He was able to perform His miracles was to declare that Jesus Himself was demon possessed, not by a common demon but by the prince of demons, Beelzebub. This name is a combination of two Hebrew words which mean "the lord of the flies." This then became the *basis* of the rejection of the Messiahship of Jesus. This was the leaven of the Pharisees that Jesus would warn His disciples against. They were to beware of the leaven of the Pharisees: the teaching that He was not the Messiah and that He was demon possessed. On these grounds the Pharisees rejected the Messiahship of Jesus.

In verses 25-29 Christ responded and told them that this could not be true because it would mean a division in Satan's kingdom.

Then in verses 30-37 He pronounced a judgment on the Jewish generation of that day. That generation had committed the unpardonable sin: the blasphemy of the Holy Spirit. One should clearly comprehend exactly what the blasphemy of the Holy Spirit is. The unpardonable sin was not an individual sin but a national sin. It was committed by that generation of Israel in Jesus' day and cannot be applied to subsequent Jewish generations. The *content* of the unpardonable sin was the national rejection of the Messiahship of Jesus while He was physically present on the grounds that He was demon possessed. This sin was unpardonable, and judgment was set. The judgment came in the year 70 A.D. with the destruction of Jerusalem and the temple and the world-wide dispersion of the Jewish people. It is not a sin that can be committed by individuals today. It was a national sin committed by the generation of Jesus' day, and for that generation the sin was unpardonable. From this point on a special emphasis is placed on *this generation* in the gospels, for it was guilty of a very unique sin.

There was no way of alleviating the judgment appointed for that generation because there would be no forgiveness for this sin. This judgment was to be fulfilled forty years later in the year 70 A.D.

In verses 38-40, Christ announced His new policy regarding miracles:

Then certain of the scribes and Pharisees answered him, saying, Teacher, we would see a sign from thee. But he answered and said unto them, An evil and adulterous *generation* seeketh after a sign; and *there shall no sign be given to it but the sign of Jonah the prophet:* for as Jonah was three days and three nights in the belly of the whale; so shall the Son of man be three days and three nights in the heart of the earth. (emphasis added)

The Pharisees were stunned by the pronouncement of judgment. They tried to retake the offensive by demanding a sign (verse 38) — as though Jesus had done nothing so far to substantiate His Messiahship! But in verse 39 there is a change of policy regarding His signs. From now on there would be no more signs for the nation except one. While Jesus continued to perform miracles after this event, the purpose of His miracles changed. No longer were they for the purpose of authenticating His person and His message to the nation in order to get the nation to come to a decision. That decision had now been made. Rather, His miracles would be for the purpose of training the twelve disciples for the new kind of ministry they would need to conduct as a result of the rejection of His Messiahship. It is the ministry the apostles performed in the book of Acts. But for that generation there would be no sign but one: the sign of Jonah which is the sign of resurrection. It is a sign that would come for Israel on three occasions: first, at the resurrection of Lazarus; secondly, at Christ's own resurrection; and, thirdly, at the resurrection of the Two Witnesses in the tribulation. The first two were rejected. The third will be accepted for the resurrection of the Two Witnesses will lead to the salvation of the Jews of Jerusalem.*

Then in verses 41-45 Christ concluded with more words of judgment for that generation. It should be noted how often the phrase *this generation* appears:

The men of Ninevah shall stand up in the judgment with *this generation,* and shall condemn it: for they repented at the preaching of Jonah; and behold, a greater than Jonah is here. The queen of the south shall rise up in the judgment with *this generation,* and shall condemn it: for she came from the ends of the earth to hear the wisdom of Solomon; and behold, a greater than Solomon is here. But the unclean spirit, when he is gone out of the man, passeth through waterless places, seeking rest, and findeth it not. Then he saith, I will return into my house whence I came out; and when he is come, he findeth it empty, swept, and garnished. Then goeth he, and taketh with himself seven other spirits more evil than himself, and they enter in and dwell there: and the last state of that man becometh worse than the first. *Even so shall it be also unto this evil generation.*   (emphasis added)

In verse 41 He compared them with Ninevah and explained why Ninevah will stand in judgment of that generation. The same is true with the Queen of Sheba (verse 42). The people in both these verses were Gentiles. With much less revelation than Israel had, they responded even without miracles. But that generation did not.

Then in verses 43-45 the words of judgment conclude with a story about a demon to illustrate what the final outcome of that generation would be.

* See Chapter XI

Jesus related the account of a demon who left on his own volition a man that he had possessed. But when he was unable to find a new body to indwell and control, he returned to his original abode. Although he found it swept and garnished, he also found it still empty. The individual never took the opportunity to fill his life with the Holy Spirit. Nor had another demon entered him. So the demon re-entered the man he originally possessed and then invited seven other demons to join him. The outcome was that the last state of that man had become worse than the first. Originally he was possessed by only one demon. He had the opportunity after the demon left to fill his life with the Spirit of God and failed to do so. Now the last state of that man was worse because now he was possessed by eight demons.

The point of this story is often missed. Christ closed the story with the point that what was true of the man was also true of that particular evil generation. When that generation began, it began with the preaching of John the Baptist. John's ministry was essentially a clean-up ministry, for he was to prepare the people for the reception of the Messiah. By means of the preaching of John, that generation was swept and garnished. But now that Messiah had come, they rejected Him on the basis of demon possession. The nation that was swept and garnished now remained empty on account of the rejection of the Messiahship of Jesus. And because it remained empty, the last state of that generation was to be worse than the first.

When that generation began, it was under Roman domination. Nevertheless, it had a national entity. It had a form of government in the Sanhedrin. Jerusalem stood in all its Herodian glory, and the religious worship system in the temple remained intact. But later as a result of the rejection and the judgment in the year 70 A.D., the national entity of Israel ceased to exist. In the place of bondage they were dispersed by the Roman armies. The temple, the center of Judaism, was completely destroyed so that not one stone stood upon another. Eventually the Jews were dispersed all over the world. So indeed the last state of that generation became worse than the first. They went from bondage to world-wide dispersion.

(2)   JOHN 11:1-57

Even after the events of Matthew chapter 12, the Pharisees approached Christ demanding a sign to authenticate His person and His message (Matthew 16:1-4). But again Christ refused to give them any more signs and promised them only *the sign of Jonah*, which is the sign of resurrection.

The resurrection of Lazarus recorded in John 11:1-44 is the presentation of the first sign of Jonah. Christ raised others from the dead, yet all of the other resurrections are covered in just a few verses.

But here John uses forty-four verses to give great detail about the resurrection of Lazarus. Why? This is the sign of Jonah that Jesus had promised. In verse 42, Jesus made it very clear for whom Lazarus was raised, namely the Jewish multitudes:

> And I knew that thou hearest me always: but because of the multitude that standeth around I said it, that they may believe that thou didst send me.

Then in verses 45-46 there is the response of the Jews:

> Many therefore of the Jews, who came to Mary and beheld that which he did, believed on him. But some of them went away to the Pharisees, and told them the things which Jesus had done.

Some Jews responded correctly to this first sign of Jonah and believed that Jesus was who He claimed to be. But the others still wanted some kind of word or judgment from their leaders, and so they reported to the Pharisees what Jesus had done. Since this was the sign Christ had promised them, they responded to the challenge in verses 47-50 and 53:

> The chief priests therefore and the Pharisees gathered a council, and said, What do we? for this man doeth many signs. If we let him thus alone, all men will believe on him: and the Romans will come and take away both our place and our nation. But a certain one of them, Caiaphas, being high priest that year, said unto them, Ye know nothing at all, nor do ye take account that it is expedient for you that one man should die for the people, and that the whole nation perish not . . . . So from that day forth they took counsel that they might put him to death.

The Pharisees responded in keeping with their original verdict of Matthew twelve. The Sanhedrin gathered together to make a decision as to how to respond to the sign of Jonah given in the resurrection of Lazarus. They issued a decree of rejection and sought an opportunity to put Jesus to death. The rejection of the Messiahship of Jesus was now complete. Going beyond the rejection of His Messiahship, they now condemned Him to death.

Verses 54-57 give the results of the Sanhedrin verdict. *First,* Christ went into hiding for a short period of time because the hour of His death was not yet come (verse 54). *Secondly,* the people still raised questions concerning His person, a logical thing for them to have done in light of the resurrection of Lazarus (verses 55-56). And *thirdly,* the Sanhedrin's verdict filtered down to the masses in verse 57:

> Now the chief priests and the Pharisees had given commandment, that, if any man knew where he was, he should show it, that they might take him.

They sought an opportunity to put Him to death. The rejection of the Messiahship of Jesus that occurred in Matthew twelve culminated in John eleven with a decree of death hanging over the person of Christ. The first sign of Jonah, the resurrection of Lazarus, was rejected.

(3)   LUKE 19:41-44

Further light is shed on the nature of the unpardonable sin in the rejection of the Messiahship of Jesus in Luke 19:41-44. This passage is in the context of the triumphal entry of Jesus into Jerusalem. Thousands of Jews cried, *Hosanna, blessed is He that cometh in the name of the Lord*, which in its Jewish frame of reference is an official messianic greeting, based upon the messianic context of Psalm 118:26. The Jewish masses proclaimed His Messiahship as He approached Jerusalem. But the Jewish leaders had already committed the unpardonable sin. Judgment had already been set upon that generation. Since the sin was unforgivable, there was no way of alleviating that judgment. So in spite of the masses proclaiming Him to be the Messiah, Jesus pronounced words of judgment upon the City of Jerusalem:

> And when he drew nigh, he saw the city and wept over it, saying, if thou hadst known in this day, even thou, the things which belong unto peace! but now they are hid from thine eyes. For the days shall come upon thee, when thine enemies shall cast up a bank about thee and compass thee round, and keep thee in on every side, and shall dash thee to the ground, and thy children within thee; and they shall not leave in thee one stone upon another; because thou knewest not the time of thy visitation.

(4)   MATTHEW 23:1-36

Another passage of Scripture dealing with the judgment of that generation is Matthew 23:1-36. The entire chapter is devoted to a denunciation and condemnation of the Scribes and Pharisees, the leadership of Israel, for various sins. In verses 1-12 they are condemned for their hypocrisy; in verses 13-14 for leading the nation in rejection of the Messiah; in verse 15 for corrupting the proselytes; in verses 16-22 for making the Mosaic Law ineffectual through Pharisaic traditions; in verses 23-24 for majoring on the minors; in verses 25-28 for being concerned with externals only; and in verses 29-36 for rejecting the prophets.

There are two key sections in this condemnation. The first is verse 13:

> But woe unto you, scribes and Pharisees, hypocrites! because ye shut the kingdom of heaven against men: for ye enter not in yourselves, neither suffer ye them that are entering in to enter.

The Pharisees are held accountable not only for their rejection of the Messiahship of Jesus but also for leading the entire nation to the rejection of the Messiahship of Jesus as well. This is an important factor to note for later understanding of what the basis of the second coming of Jesus will be.

The second key passage is verses 29-36:

> Woe unto you, scribes and Pharisees, hypocrites! for ye build the sepulchres of the prophets, and garnish the tombs of the righteous, and say, If we had been in the days of our fathers, we should not have been partakers with them in the blood of the prophets. Wherefore ye witness to yourselves, that ye are sons of them that slew the prophets. Fill ye up then the measure of your fathers. Ye serpents, ye offspring of vipers, how shall ye escape the judgment of hell? Therefore, behold, I send unto you prophets, and wise men, and scribes: some of them shall ye kill and crucify; and some of them shall ye scourge in your synagogues, and persecute from city to city: that upon you may come all the righteous blood shed on the earth, from the blood of Abel the righteous unto the blood of Zachariah son of Barachiah, whom ye slew between the sanctuary and the altar. Verily I say unto you, All these things shall come upon this generation.

These verses emphasize the severity of the judgment on that generation. The judgment is primarily upon the leaders but also upon the nation whom the leaders led in the rejection of His Messiahship. Christ stated that they were not only to be held accountable for the rejection of His Messiahship. They were also to be held accountable for the blood of all the prophets of the Old Testament. In the Jewish order of the books of the Old Testament*, which is what Jesus used, the first book of the Bible is Genesis where Abel is mentioned. The last book is II Chronicles where Zechariah is mentioned. Jesus declared that they were guilty of all the blood from Genesis to II Chronicles; much as people today would say from Genesis to Revelation.

So that generation was guilty of the blood of all the prophets. The reason was that everything God intended to say concerning the Messiah had already been said by the Jewish prophets. That generation possessed in their hands the entire Old Testament canon. Furthermore, they had the preaching of John the Baptist announcing the soon coming of the Lord. Finally, they had the physical manifestation and presence of Jesus the Messiah who came with all the authenticating signs. Nevertheless, they rejected His Messiahship following the example of their leaders. For this reason they would be held accountable for the blood of all the prophets who spoke about the Messiah. This is something unique for that generation as declared in verse 36. *Verily I say unto you, all these things shall come upon this*

---

* The number of books is the same, only the order is different.

generation. It is the judgment for the unpardonable sin.

The point made so far is this: The Messiahship of Jesus was rejected by the Jewish leadership *and* the Jewish leadership led the nation to the rejection of that Messiahship.

A few days after the above words were spoken, the second sign of Jonah was given in the resurrection of Christ. This second sign of Jonah was rejected in the first seven chapters of the book of Acts. The stoning of Stephen in Acts seven by the Sanhedrin marked the official rejection of the second sign of Jonah. That is why only in chapter eight does the gospel for the first time go out to the non-Jewish world.

The book of Hebrews was written to a group of Jewish Christians who, because of persecution, were contemplating a return to Judaism. The writer of the book of Hebrews warned them that they must completely separate themselves from Judaism. If they failed to do so, they would be caught up in the judgment of 70 A.D. and suffer physical death. Only if they separated themselves from Judaism completely would they have the opportunity of escaping the judgment upon that generation. Of course, from Hebrews it is not known what the results were. But it is known from Josephus and Eusebius quoting Hegisippius, a Jewish Christian historian of the second century. These men recorded how the Hebrew Christians, in obedience to the book of Hebrews, separated themselves from Judaism. So when the revolt against Rome began in the year 66 A.D., the entire Jewish Christian community left the country and waited the war out in the town of Pella on the east bank of the Jordan. Although 1,100,000 Jews died in this Jewish revolt against Rome, not one Hebrew Christian was killed. Had they not obeyed the writer of the book of Hebrews, they would have suffered physical death. But since they did obey, they escaped with their lives, and they were freed of the judgment upon that generation.

b. THE PRE-REQUISITE TO THE SECOND COMING

Having said all this, what then is the basis of the second coming of Christ? To discover this it will be necessary to look at five more passages of Scripture.

The first passage is Leviticus 26:40-42:

> And they shall confess their iniquity, and the iniquity of their fathers, in their trespass which they trespassed against me, and also that, because they walked contrary unto me, I also walked contrary unto them, and brought them into the land of their enemies: If then their uncircumcised heart be humbled, and they then accept of the punishment of their iniquity; then will I remember my covenant with Jacob; and also my covenant with Isaac, and also my covenant with Abraham will I remember; and I will remember the land.

In Leviticus 26 Moses predicted how, because of disobedience to God's revealed will, the Jews would be scattered all over the world. According to the New Testament, this came as a direct result of the rejection of the Messiahship of Jesus. By verse 39 the world-wide dispersion is a fact. Up to this point Leviticus 26 has been fulfilled. Then in verse 42, Moses states that God has every intent to give Israel all the blessings and promises of the Abrahamic Covenant, especially as the covenant pertains to the promised land. But before they can begin to enjoy these blessings of the Abrahamic Covenant during the messianic age, it is first necessary for them to fulfill the condition of verse 40: *they must confess their iniquity* and *the iniquity of their fathers.* A thing to notice is that the word "iniquity" is in the singular and that it is specific. There is one specific iniquity which Israel must confess before she can begin to enjoy all of the benefits of the Abrahamic Covenant.

The second passage is Jeremiah 3:11-18:

> And Jehovah said unto me, Backsliding Israel hath showed herself more righteous than treacherous Judah. Go, and proclaim these words toward the north, and say, Return, thou backsliding Israel, saith Jehovah; I will not look in anger upon you; for I am merciful, saith Jehovah, I will not keep anger for ever. Only acknowledge thine iniquity, that thou hast transgressed against Jehovah thy God, and hast scattered thy ways to the strangers under every green tree, and ye have not obeyed my voice, saith Jehovah. Return, O backsliding children, saith Jehovah; for I am a husband unto you: and I will take you one of a city, and two of a family, and I will bring you to Zion: and I will give you shepherds according to my heart, who shall feed you with knowledge and understanding. And it shall come to pass, when ye are multiplied and increased in the land, in those days, saith Jehovah, they shall say no more, The ark of the covenant of Jehovah; neither shall it come to mind; neither shall they remember it; neither shall they miss it; neither shall it be made any more. At that time they shall call Jerusalem the throne of Jehovah; and all the nations shall be gathered unto it, to the name of Jehovah, to Jerusalem: neither shall they walk any more after the stubbornness of their evil heart. In those days the house of Judah shall walk with the house of Israel, and they shall come together out of the land of the north to the land that I gave for an inheritance unto your fathers.

In verses 14-18, Jeremiah begins to describe the blessings which God has in store for Israel in the messianic kingdom. It will be a time of tremendous blessing and restoration for the Jewish people when the kingdom is established by their Messiah. But all these blessings are conditioned by verse 13 where they must acknowledge or confess one specific iniquity which they committed against Jehovah their God.

The third passage is in the book of Zechariah. Zechariah chapters 12, 13 and 14 are a unit of thought and develop one theme. Chapter 13 speaks of the national cleansing of Israel from their sin. Chapter 14 describes the second coming of Christ and the establishment of the kingdom. But the cleansing of Israel followed by the second coming of Christ and the messianic kingdom are all conditioned on Zechariah 12:10:

> And I will pour upon the house of David, and upon the inhabitants of Jerusalem, the spirit of grace and of supplication; and they shall look unto me whom they have pierced; and they shall mourn for him, as one mourneth for his only son, and shall be in bitterness for him, as one that is in bitterness for his first-born.

Before Israel will receive the cleansing of her sin and before Christ will return to establish His kingdom, Israel must first look *unto* (not *upon* as in the KJV) the One whom they have pierced and to plead for His return. Once they do this, then, and only then, will they receive their cleansing and begin to enjoy the blessings of the messianic age.

The fourth passage is in Hosea five. The one who is doing the speaking throughout chapter five of Hosea is God Himself, and God is still speaking in verse 15:

> I will go and return to my place, till they acknowledge their offence, and seek my face: in their affliction they will seek me earnestly.

There are certain presuppositions behind the understanding of this verse. Before anyone can go back to a place he must first leave it. In this passage God states that He is going to go back to His place. God's place is heaven. Before God can go back to heaven, He must first leave it. The question is, when did God ever leave heaven? God left heaven at the incarnation in the person of Jesus of Nazareth. Then, because of one specific offense committed against Him, He returned to heaven at the ascension from the Mount of Olives. This verse further states that He will not come back to the earth until that offense that caused Him to return to heaven is acknowledged or confessed. What is that Jewish national offense committed against the person of Christ? It is not, as so many people think, in killing Him. The actual killing of Christ was done by Gentile, not Jewish, hands. He was condemned and sentenced by a Gentile judge. He was crucified by Gentile soldiers. But all this is ultimately irrelevant for, regardless of Jewish acceptance or Jewish rejection, Jesus would have had to die anyway to become the sacrifice for sin. The national offense of Israel was in the rejection of His Messiahship. According to this verse, only when this offense is acknowledged or confessed will Christ return to the earth.

The fifth passage is in Matthew 23. As was shown earlier, this passage contains Christ's denunciation of the Scribes and Pharisees, the Jewish leadership of that day, for leading the nation in the rejection of His Messiahship. He was still speaking to them in verses 37-39:

> O Jerusalem, Jerusalem, that killeth the prophets, and stoneth them that are sent unto her! how often would I have gathered thy children together, even as a hen gathereth her chickens under her wings, and ye would not! Behold, your house is left unto you desolate. For I say unto you, Ye shall not see me henceforth, till ye shall say, Blessed is he that cometh in the name of the Lord.

Speaking to the Jewish leadership Christ reiterates His original desire to gather them if they would only accept Him (verse 37). Because of their rejection of His Messiahship, in place of being gathered they are going to be scattered. Their house, the Jewish temple, will be left desolate and will be destroyed with nothing remaining (verse 38). But then He declares that they will not see Him again until they say, *Blessed is He that cometh in the name of the Lord.* This is a messianic greeting. It will mean their acceptance of the Messiahship of Jesus.

So Jesus will not come back to the earth until the Jews and the Jewish leaders ask Him to come back. For just as the Jewish leaders lead the nation to the rejection of the Messiahship of Jesus, they must some day lead the nation to the acceptance of the Messiahship of Jesus.

This, then, is the twofold basis of the second coming of Christ: Israel must confess her national sin and then plead for Messiah to return, to *mourn for Him as one mourns for an only son.*

CHAPTER XIV

THE CAMPAIGN OF ARMAGEDDON
AND
THE SECOND COMING OF JESUS CHRIST

The two climactic events of the Great Tribulation are the Campaign of Armageddon and the second coming of Jesus Christ. A considerable amount of data is given about this time period in the Scriptures. One of the greatest difficulties in the study of eschatology is placing these events in chronological sequence in order to see what exactly will happen in the Campaign of Armageddon. This chapter is an attempt to do just that.

The Campaign of Armageddon can be divided into eight stages, and this in turn will facilitate an understanding of the sequence of events.*

THE FIRST STAGE: THE ASSEMBLING OF THE
ALLIES OF THE ANTICHRIST

The Campaign of Armageddon will begin with the sixth bowl judgment recorded in Revelation 16:12-16:

> And the sixth poured out his bowl upon the great river, the river Euphrates; and the water thereof was dried up, that the way might be made ready for the kings that come from the sunrising. And I saw coming out of the mouth of the dragon, and out of the mouth of the beast, and out of the mouth of the false prophet, three unclean spirits, as it were frogs: for they are spirits of demons, working signs; which go forth unto the kings of the whole world, to gather them together unto the war of the great day of God, the Almighty. (Behold, I come as a thief. Blessed is he that watcheth, and keepeth his garments, lest he walk naked, and they see his shame.) And they gathered them together into the place which is called in Hebrew Har-Magedon.

With the outpouring of the sixth bowl judgment, the Euphrates River will be dried up (verse 12). This drying up process will be for the purpose of making it easier for the Antichrist to assemble his forces for the Armageddon Campaign. Although it has become common to identify *the kings of the east* with the Chinese and to combine them with the army of the 200 million of Revelation nine, neither consistency of exegesis nor the structure of the book of Revelation will allow for this.

Relative to the structure of Revelation, the "200 million" and the "kings of the east" belong to two different judgments which must be

---

* See the last page of this chapter for a map of the Campaign of Armageddon.

kept distinct and can not be combined. The "200 million" are in a trumpet judgment whereas "the kings of the east" are in a bowl judgment. Furthermore, within the discussion of Revelation nine, it was shown that the 200 million are demons and not men: Chinese or otherwise. Thus the structure of the book militates against making these two judgments into one.

In regard to consistency of interpretation, it also rules out the "kings of the east" as a reference to the Chinese. Everywhere else in the Scriptures the *east* always refers to Mesopotamia (Assyria and Babylonia). Consistency would demand that this too would be a reference to Mesopotamia and not to China (e.g., Matthew 2:1). The fact that the Antichrist's capital city of Babylon will sit on the banks of the Euphrates River further attests to the fact that the kings that come from the east will be Mesopotamian kings. Thus, consistency of interpretation also militates against matching this reference to China. Consistency of interpretation and not current events must be the basis of determining the meaning of any given text.*

The sixth bowl judgment will dry up the Euphrates River to make it easier for the Antichrist's Babylonian forces to maneuver. A decree will be issued from the capital city of Babylon ordering the allies of the Antichrist to gather their armies together (verses 13-14). The gathering for this final campaign against the Jews is clearly the work of the counterfeit trinity. All three members of the counterfeit trinity are involved: the dragon, or Satan who is the counterfeit father; the beast, or the Antichrist who is the counterfeit son; and the False Prophet who is the counterfeit holy spirit. The summons will be reenforced by demonic activity to make sure that the nations will indeed cooperate in assembling their armies together. These demonic messengers will be empowered to perform signs in order to assure compliance and defeat any reluctance to fall into line on the part of the other kings. These kings are the seven kings that have been under the authority of the Antichrist since the middle of the tribulation.**

While the term "Battle of Armageddon" has been commonly used, it is really a misnomer, for no battle will be taking place in Armageddon. For this reason many prophetic teachers have stopped employing that term and are using the term "Campaign of Armageddon," as in this chapter. But this too is a misnomer to some extent. There will be no fighting in Armageddon itself, for all of the fighting will take place elsewhere. A more biblical name for this final conflict is found in the closing words of verse 14: *the war of the great day of God, the Almighty*. This is a more accurate description of the nature and extent of this final conflict.

The train of thought is now interrupted by the parenthesis of verse 15. This parenthesis contains a message of comfort and hope to

 * See Chapter X for further discussion on this question.
** See Chapters II and XI.

the believers living at this point in the Great Tribulation. They are encouraged to continue in the faith. For when they see the gathering of the armies together, then they can know that the second coming of Jesus Christ is just around the corner. A message of comfort is given at this point to all believers so as to give them hope.

The train of thought is picked up again in verse 16 which names the place where the allies of the Antichrist will be gathered: Har-Mageddon. As the ASV text shows, the word is a combination of two Hebrew words which mean "the mountain of Megiddo." Megiddo was a strategic city located at the western end of the Valley of Jezreel guarding the famous Megiddo Pass into Israel's largest valley. One could see the entire Valley of Jezreel from the mount upon which the city of Megiddo stood. So what is known as the Valley of Armageddon in Christian circles is actually the biblical Valley of Jezreel. The term "Armageddon" is never applied to the valley itself, but only to the mount at the western end. Here, in this large valley of Lower Galilee, the armies of the world will gather for the purpose of destroying all the Jews still living.

It should be noted that the passage says nothing of a battle in this valley for no fighting will take place here. The Valley of Jezreel, guarded by the mountain of Megiddo, will merely serve as the gathering ground for the armies of the Antichrist. Armageddon will play the same role that England played in the closing conflicts of World War II. The allied forces gathered their armies together in England but that is not where the final battle took place. The final battle began on the beaches of Normandy, France, on "D" Day. Armageddon will also serve as a gathering place with the battle beginning elsewhere.

This passage describing the gathering of the armies of the nations is more or less viewed from man's perspective. From man's standpoint, it is merely a military gathering called together by the Antichrist. But two other passages which also speak of this event show God's perspective. The first is in Joel 3:9-11:

> Proclaim ye this among the nations; prepare war; stir up the mighty men; let all the men of war draw near, let them come up. Beat your plowshares into swords, and your pruning-hooks into spears: let the weak say, I am strong. Haste ye, and come, all ye nations round about, and gather yourselves together: thither cause thy mighty ones to come down, O Jehovah.

God's viewpoint is one of mockery. The nations are mockingly encouraged to go ahead and take their farming equipment and turn it into weapons of war. As for those who are weak, let them persuade themselves and pretend that they are strong. Because while Satan and the Antichrist gather the nations for their purpose of destroying the Jews, God has His own very different purpose for permitting this gathering to take place.

This taunting of the gathering of the nations is also portrayed in

Psalm 2:1-6:

> Why do the nations rage, and the peoples meditate a vain thing? The kings of the earth set themselves, and the rulers take counsel together, against Jehovah, and against his anointed, saying, Let us break their bonds asunder, and cast away their cords from us, He that sitteth in the heavens will laugh: the Lord will have them in derision. Then will he speak unto them in his wrath, and vex them in his sore displeasure: yet I have set my king upon my holy hill of Zion.

The gathering of the nations is presented as a gathering against God the Father and His anointed, that is, the Messiah Jesus. By seeking to destroy the Jews, Satan is also seeking to break the cords of God's control of the world. How foolish! Then God is portrayed as sitting in the heavens and laughing, because He will soon have these nations in confusion. It is God who will set up His own king upon Zion, and Satan and the Antichrist will not be able to prevent it.

Although the nations will assemble to carry out the program of the counterfeit trinity, they will actually accomplish the purpose of the triune God.

This gathering of the armies of the nations in the Valley of Jezreel will be the first stage of the Campaign of Armageddon.

THE SECOND STAGE: THE DESTRUCTION OF BABYLON

The fact that the city of Babylon is to be rebuilt and become the world capital of the Antichrist has been mentioned in the previous chapter. But not only is Babylon to become the world political capital, it is also to become the world economic capital. This fact is portrayed in the vision of Zechariah 5:5-11:

> Then the angel that talked with me went forth, and said unto me, Lift up now thine eyes, and see what is this that goeth forth. And I said, What is it? And he said, This is the ephah that goeth forth. He said moreover, This is their appearance in all the land; (and, behold, there was lifted up a talent of lead;) and this is a woman sitting in the midst of the ephah. And he said, This is Wickedness: and he cast her down into the midst of the ephah; and he cast the weight of lead upon the mouth thereof. Then lifted I up mine eyes, and saw, and, behold, there came forth two women, and the wind was in their wings; now they had wings like the wings of a stork; and they lifted up the ephah between earth and heaven. Then said I to the angel that talked with me, Whither do these bear the ephah? And he said unto me, To build her a house in the land of Shinar: and when it is prepared, she shall be set there in her own place.

The ephah was a measure of weight and became the symbol of economy. This symbol of economy, in this case a corrupted one, was to be placed in the land of Shinar which is the same as Babylonia.

Hence, the future center of world economy will be found in Babylon. Indeed, the center of world economy is already shifting into the Middle East, and in the future it will be centralized in the rebuilt city of Babylon. Throughout the second half of the tribulation Babylon will be both the center of world economy and the world political center.

But later, in the second stage of the Campaign of Armageddon, Babylon will suffer a sudden devastation. Several passages are concerned with the future destruction of this city, but this study will be limited to certain key passages. In Isaiah 13:1-14:23 the prophet had much to say about this event.

The means by which this destruction will occur is explained in Isaiah 13:1-5:

> The burden of Babylon, which Isaiah the son of Amoz did see. Set ye up an ensign upon the bare mountain, lift up the voice unto them, wave the hand, that they may go into the gates of the nobles. I have commanded my consecrated ones, yea, I have called my mighty men for mine anger, even my proudly exulting ones. The noise of a multitude in the mountains, as of a great people! the noise of a tumult of the kingdoms of the nations gathered together! Jehovah of hosts is mustering the host for the battle. They come from a far country, from the uttermost part of heaven, even Jehovah, and the weapons of his indignation, to destroy the whole land.

The burden of Babylon that Isaiah saw was another gathering of many peoples. Whereas the gathering in the first stage will be the pro-Babylon or pro-Antichrist forces, these will be anti-Babylon or anti-Antichrist forces. Their purpose will be to destroy Babylon. The details of this destruction are given in Isaiah 13:6-14:23. It should be noted that this prophecy of Babylon's destruction has never been fulfilled in the manner required by the text.

For example, the context of Isaiah 13:6-22 clearly puts the destruction of Babylon announced in verses 1-5 within the scope and time of the Day of Jehovah, a reference to the Great Tribulation. Because this passage was dealt with in Chapter VII, it will not be treated in detail here.

Furthermore, Babylon's destruction is connected with the final redemption of Israel in Isaiah 14:1-2:

> For Jehovah will have compassion on Jacob, and will yet choose Israel, and set them in their own land: and the sojourner shall join himself with them, and they shall cleave to the house of Jacob. And the peoples shall take them, and bring them to their place; and the house of Israel shall possess them in the land of Jehovah for servants and for handmaids: and they shall take them captive whose captives they were; and they shall rule over their oppressors.

In this final destruction, Babylon will become similar to Sodom and Gomorrah in that it will be fit for habitation by only the wild animals of the desert and be uninhabitable for any man. This is the thrust of Isaiah 13:19-22:

> And Babylon, the glory of kingdoms, the beauty of the Chaldeans' pride, shall be as when God overthrew Sodom and Gomorrah. It shall never be inhabited, neither shall it be dwelt in from generation to generation: neither shall the Arabian pitch tent there; neither shall shepherds make their flocks to lie down there. But wild beasts of the desert shall lie there; and their houses shall be full of doleful creatures; and ostriches shall dwell there, and wild goats shall dance there. And wolves shall cry in their castles, and jackals in the pleasant palaces: and her time is near to come, and her days shall not be prolonged.

Isaiah's prophecy concerning Babylon concludes in Isaiah 14:22-23 clearly stating that unlike other nations, Babylon will not even have a surviving remnant:

> And I will rise up against them, saith Jehovah of hosts, and cut off from Babylon name and remnant, and son and son's son, saith Jehovah. I will also make it a possession for the porcupine, and pools of water: and I will sweep it with the besom of destruction, saith Jehovah of hosts.

Another prophet detailing the destruction of Babylon by a number of peoples is Jeremiah with two long chapters (50-51) devoted to it. Because of the length of these chapters, it will be necessary to limit the study of these passages to key verses which portray the destruction of Babylon.

The fact that this prophecy concerns Babylon is clearly stated in Jeremiah 50:1:

> The word that Jehovah spake concerning Babylon, concerning the land of the Chaldeans, by Jeremiah the prophet.

As in Isaiah, Jeremiah 50:9-10 tells of a gathering of many peoples against the city of Babylon:

> For, lo, I will stir up and cause to come up against Babylon a company of great nations from the north country; and they shall set themselves in array against her; from thence she shall be taken: their arrows shall be as of an expert mighty man; none shall return in vain. And Chaldea shall be a prey: all that prey upon her shall be satisfied, saith Jehovah.

The extent of this destruction and the warfare is described in Jeremiah 50:11-16:

> Because ye are glad, because ye rejoice, O ye that plunder my heritage, because ye are wanton as a heifer that treadeth out the grain, and neigh

as strong horses; your mother shall be utterly put to shame; she that bare you shall be confounded: behold, she shall be the hindermost of the nations, a wilderness, a dry land, and a desert. Because of the wrath of Jehovah she shall not be inhabited, but she shall be wholly desolate: every one that goeth by Babylon shall be astonished, and hiss at all her plagues. Set yourselves in array against Babylon round about, all ye that bend the bow; shoot at her, spare no arrows: for she hath sinned against Jehovah. Shout against her round about: she hath submitted herself; her bulwarks are fallen, her walls are thrown down; for it is the vengeance of Jehovah: take vengeance upon her; as she hath done, do unto her. Cut off the sower from Babylon, and him that handleth the sickle in the time of harvest: for fear of the oppressing sword they shall turn every one to his people, and they shall flee every one to his own land.

Later, in Jeremiah 50:21-27, there is a more graphic description of the fall of Babylon:

Go up against the land of Merathaim, even against it, and against the inhabitants of Pekod: slay and utterly destroy after them, saith Jehovah, and do according to all that I have commanded thee. A sound of battle is in the land, and of great destruction. How is the hammer of the whole earth cut asunder and broken! how is Babylon become a desolation among the nations! I have laid a snare for thee, and thou art also taken, O Babylon, and thou wast not aware: thou art found, and also caught, because thou hast striven against Jehovah. Jehovah hath opened his armory, and hath brought forth the weapons of his indignation; for the Lord, Jehovah of hosts, hath a work to do in the land of the Chaldeans. Come against her from the utmost border; open her storehouses; cast her up as heaps, and destroy her utterly; let nothing of her be left. Slay all her bullocks; let them go down to the slaughter: woe unto them! for their day is come, the time of their visitation.

This destruction is to be so total and so final, Babylon will never be inhabited by man again. It will be as total as the destruction of Sodom and Gomorrah according to Jeremiah 50:39-40:

Therefore the wild beasts of the desert with the wolves shall dwell there, and the ostriches shall dwell therein: and it shall be no more inhabited for ever; neither shall it be dwelt in from generation to generation. As when God overthrew Sodom and Gomorrah and the neighbor cities thereof, saith Jehovah, so shall no man dwell there, neither shall any son of man sojourn therein.

Once again Jeremiah speaks of a gathering of many peoples against Babylon in 50:41-42:

Behold, a people cometh from the north; and a great nation and many kings shall be stirred up from the uttermost parts of the earth. They lay hold on bow and spear; they are cruel, and have no mercy; their voice roareth like the sea; and they ride upon horses, every one set in array, as a man to the battle, against thee, O daughter of Babylon.

Jeremiah chapter 50 concludes with a statement of God's decree against Babylon and the anguish of the nations over the destruction of their world capital in verses 45-46:

> Therefore hear ye the counsel of Jehovah, that he hath taken against Babylon; and his purposes, that he hath purposed against the land of the Chaldeans: Surely they shall drag them away, even the little ones of the flock; surely he shall make their habitation desolate over them. At the noise of the taking of Babylon the earth trembleth, and the cry is heard among the nations.

The graphic description of the fall of Babylon in Jeremiah 50 is followed by a more detailed description in Jeremiah 51. It will be Babylon's influence on other nations that will cause God's judgment to fall on her according to Jeremiah 51:7-9:

> Babylon hath been a golden cup in Jehovah's hand, that made all the earth drunken: the nations have drunk of her wine; therefore the nations are mad. Babylon is suddenly fallen and destroyed: wail for her; take balm for her pain, if so be she may be healed. We would have healed Babylon, but she is not healed: Forsake her, and let us go every one into his own country; for her judgment reacheth unto heaven, and is lifted up even to the skies.

According to Jeremiah 51:24, the judgment will be especially severe due to Babylon's evil deeds against the people of Israel:

> And I will render unto Babylon and to all the inhabitants of Chaldea all their evil that they have done in Zion in your sight, saith Jehovah.

Because Babylon has ruled the entire world ruinously, God will now destroy her that had destroyed so many, for Jeremiah 51:25-26 states:

> Behold, I am against thee, O destroying mountain, saith Jehovah, which destroyest all the earth; and I will stretch out my hand upon thee, and roll thee down from the rocks, and will make thee a burnt mountain. And they shall not take of thee a stone for a corner, nor a stone for foundations; but thou shalt be desolate for ever, saith Jehovah.

Indeed, says Jeremiah 51:29, God has purposed a total and complete destruction of the city of Babylon:

> And the land trembleth and is in pain; for the purposes of Jehovah against Babylon do stand, to make the land of Babylon a desolation, without inhabitant.

Once more Jeremiah points out in verses 35-36 that the necessity of this judgment will be due to Babylon's treatment of the Jews:

> The violence done to me and to my flesh be upon Babylon, shall the inhabitant of Zion say; and, My blood be upon the inhabitants of Chaldea, shall Jerusalem say. Therefore thus saith Jehovah: Behold, I will plead thy cause, and take vengeance for thee; and I will dry up her sea, and make her fountain dry.

The destruction of Babylon will bring about great rejoicing among the faithful, and it is viewed as God's vengeance against Babylon for mistreatment of the Jews in Jeremiah 51:48-49:

> Then the heavens and the earth, and all that is therein, shall sing for joy over Babylon; for the destroyers shall come unto her from the north, saith Jehovah. As Babylon hath caused the slain of Israel to fall, so at Babylon shall fall the slain of all the land.

The prophecy of Babylon's destruction closes with a description of the results of Babylon's fall in Jeremiah 51:54-58:

> The sound of a cry from Babylon, and of great destruction from the land of the Chaldeans! For Jehovah layeth Babylon waste, and destroyeth out of her the great voice; and their waves roar like many waters; the noise of their voice is uttered: for the destroyer is come upon her, even upon Babylon, and her mighty men are taken, their bows are broken in pieces; for Jehovah is a God of recompenses, he will surely requite. And I will make drunk her princes and her wise men, her governors and her deputies, and her mighty men; and they shall sleep a perpetual sleep, and not wake, saith the King, whose name is Jehovah of hosts. Thus saith Jehovah of hosts: The broad walls of Babylon shall be utterly overthrown, and her high gates shall be burned with fire; and the peoples shall labor for vanity, and the nations for the fire; and they shall be weary.

To seal the prophecies, Jeremiah the prophet performed a physical act that had a symbolic significance. This act is described in 51:59-64:

> The word which Jeremiah the prophet commanded Seraiah the son of Neriah, the son of Mahseiah, when he went with Zedekiah the king of Judah to Babylon in the fourth year of his reign. Now Seraiah was chief chamberlain. And Jeremiah wrote in a book all the evil that should come upon Babylon, even all these words that are written concerning Babylon. And Jeremiah said to Seraiah, When thou comest to Babylon, then see that thou read all these words, and say, O Jehovah, thou hast spoken concerning this place, to cut it off, that none shall dwell therein, neither man nor beast, but that it shall be desolate for ever. And it shall be, when thou hast made an end of reading this book, that thou shalt bind a stone to it, and cast it into the midst of the Euphrates: and thou shalt say, Thus shall Babylon sink, and shall not rise again because of the evil that I will bring upon her; and they shall be weary. Thus far are the words of Jeremiah.

A copy of Jeremiah 50:1-52:58 was written on a scroll and tied to a rock. After having been read before the Jewish exiles in Babylon, it was cast into the Euphrates River. Just as the scroll sank, so Babylon will sink.

There are two indications in the text of this prophecy that the king of Babylon, the Antichrist, will not be present in the city when his capital city is destroyed. The first is in Jeremiah 50:43:

> The king of Babylon hath heard the tidings of them, and his hands wax feeble: anguish hath taken hold of him, and pangs as of a woman in travail.

The second is in Jeremiah 51:31-32:

> One post shall run to meet another, and one messenger to meet another, to show the king of Babylon that his city is taken on every quarter: and the passages are seized, and the reeds they have burned with fire, and the men of war are affrighted.

The very fact that the king of Babylon will have to be told that his city is destroyed is a clear-cut indication that he will not be there when it happens. Otherwise, there would be no need to tell him. So where is he? By comparing the Scriptures of the first stage with those of the second stage, it would appear that while the Antichrist is meeting his forces in the Valley of Jezreel, his enemies take the opportunity to gather and destroy his capital city.

Prior to the sudden massive destruction of Babylon, a warning will be given to the Jews who are still in Babylon telling them to flee out of the city before it is too late. This warning comes several times in the prophecy of Jeremiah. The first is in 50:6-8:

> My people have been lost sheep: their shepherds have caused them to go astray; they have turned them away on the mountains; they have gone from mountain to hill; they have forgotten their resting-place. All that found them have devoured them; and their adversaries said, We are not guilty, because they have sinned against Jehovah, the habitation of righteousness, even Jehovah, the hope of their fathers. Flee out of the midst of Babylon, and go forth out of the land of the Chaldeans, and be as the he-goats before the flocks.

Later, a second warning is referred to in 50:28:

> The voice of them that flee and escape out of the land of Babylon, to declare in Zion the vengeance of Jehovah our God, the vengeance of his temple.

Those who escape from Babylon will flee to Jerusalem to announce Babylon's destruction to the Jews there. This is God's vengeance on Babylon because of Babylon's mistreatment of the Jews and His vengeance for His temple because of the sinful act of the abomination of desolation.

A third admonition is found in 51:5-6:

For Israel is not forsaken, nor Judah, of his God, of Jehovah of hosts; though their land is full of guilt against the Holy One of Israel. Flee out of the midst of Babylon, and save every man his life; be not cut off in her iniquity: for it is the time of Jehovah's vengeance; he will render unto her a recompense.

God's vengeance is about to be poured out against Babylon. Therefore, the Jews are encouraged to flee lest they also fall prey to this vengeance. As in 50:28, those escaping will go to Jerusalem to declare what God has done according to Jeremiah 51:10:

Jehovah hath brought forth our righteousness: come, and let us declare in Zion the work of Jehovah our God.

This is followed by a fourth warning in 51:45:

My people, go ye out of the midst of her, and save yourselves every man from the fierce anger of Jehovah.

The fifth and final warning is in 51:50:

Ye that have escaped the sword, go ye, stand not still; remember Jehovah from afar, and let Jerusalem come into your mind.

In this final admonition to flee Babylon before her destruction, they are also instructed to make their way to Jerusalem to inform the Jews there.

Thus, prior to the sudden and great destruction of Babylon, the Jews will be given a warning to leave Babylon. They will succeed in their escape and will make their way to Jerusalem.

Reiterating a previous notation: these prophecies of the destruction of Babylon have never been fulfilled in the manner required by the statements of Scripture. The Babylon of past history slowly died out and became a ghost town. Furthermore, this destruction of Babylon is clearly associated with the final regeneration and restoration of Israel. Such events never did happen in connection with ancient Babylon.

Pertinent to the *regeneration* of Israel Jeremiah 50:4-5 states:

In those days, and in that time, saith Jehovah, the children of Israel shall come, they and the children of Judah together; they shall go on their way weeping, and shall seek Jehovah their God. They shall inquire concerning Zion with their faces thitherward, saying, Come ye, and join yourselves to Jehovah in an everlasting covenant that shall not be forgotten.

In these verses the destruction of Babylon will come at the same time that Israel is seeking Jehovah their God and entering into an everlasting covenant with God, the same as the new covenant in Jeremiah 31:31-34.

The destruction of Babylon is associated with the *restoration* of Israel in Jeremiah 50:19-20:

> And I will bring Israel again to his pasture, and he shall feed on Carmel and Bashan, and his soul shall be satisfied upon the hills of Ephraim and in Gilead. In those days, and in that time, saith Jehovah, the iniquity of Israel shall be sought for, and there shall be none; and the sins of Judah, and they shall not be found: For I will pardon them whom I leave as a remnant.

Israel is viewed as restored in her land with all her sins forgiven so that no one will even be able to find her sins anymore. This restoration is to be a result of the destruction of Babylon and can hardly be true of ancient Babylon.

All these things point to the fact that the city of Babylon is to suffer a destruction at the time of Israel's regeneration. This requires Babylon's destruction to come during the Campaign of Armageddon. This in turn requires the city of Babylon to be rebuilt.

Another extensive passage dealing with the destruction of Babylon is Revelation 18:1-24. This chapter of Revelation deals specifically with the political and economic Babylon that will rule the world for three and a half years. The passage begins with a declaration of the fall of Babylon in 18:1-3:

> After these things I saw another angel coming down out of heaven, having great authority; and the earth was lightened with his glory. And he cried with a mighty voice, saying, Fallen, fallen is Babylon the great, and is become a habitation of demons, and a hold of every unclean spirit, and a hold of every unclean and hateful bird. For by the wine of the wrath of her fornication all the nations are fallen; and the kings of the earth committed fornication with her, and the merchants of the earth waxed rich by the power of her wantonness.

With its destruction, Babylon is to become a habitation of demons. This will be the place of demonic abode and confinement during the messianic age (verses 1-2). This is hardly true of Babylon today. The reason for this severe judgment of Babylon will be the global political (kings of the earth) and economic (merchants of the earth) corruption originating in this city because of the Antichrist's rule (verse 3).

As in the Jeremiah prophecies, Revelation 18:4-5 reveals that there will be a call to the Jews to flee the city prior to Babylon's destruction:

> And I heard another voice from heaven, saying, Come forth, my people, out of her, that ye have no fellowship with her sins, and that ye receive not of her plagues: for her sins have reached even unto heaven, and God hath remembered her iniquities.

The cup of Babylon's iniquity will then be full. Lest the Jews become subject to Babylon's judgment, they are urged to flee, and this they will do.

The indictment against Babylon is given next in Revelation 18:6-8:

> Render unto her even as she rendered, and double unto her the double according to her works: in the cup which she mingled, mingle unto her double. How much soever she glorified herself, and waxed wanton, so much give her of torment and mourning: for she saith in her heart, I sit a queen, and am no widow, and shall in no wise see mourning. Therefore in one day shall her plagues come, death, and mourning, and famine; and she shall be utterly burned with fire; for strong is the Lord God who judged her.

Babylon is condemned to receive double the punishment she inflicted on others (verse 6). Because this city through the counterfeit trinity will vaunt itself against the God of heaven (verse 7), it will suffer a swift and sudden destruction by fire (verse 8).

After Babylon's destruction there will be intense lamenting by those who invested heavily in her, became rich by her, but will now be bankrupt by her destruction. Three classes of people will mourn over Babylon, and their lamentations are recorded in Revelation 18:9-19. First is the lamentation of the kings, the political rulers of the world in 18:9-10:

> And the kings of the earth, who committed fornication and lived wantonly with her, shall weep and wail over her, when they look upon the smoke of her burning, standing afar off for the fear of her torment, saying, Woe, woe, the great city, Babylon, the strong city! for in one hour is thy judgment come.

These are the seven kings who have co-reigned with the Antichrist and submitted their authority to the Antichrist, the king of Babylon. Whatever power of authority they held, was held by the grace of Babylon. Seeing their authority waning with Babylon's destruction, they will lament the swiftness of the judgment. They will be able to see the smoke of Babylon "afar off" for they will see it from the Valley of Jezreel in Israel.

The second group of mourners are the merchants in 18:11-17a:

> And the merchants of the earth weep and mourn over her, for no man buyeth their merchandise any more; merchandise of gold, and silver, and precious stone, and pearls, and fine linen, and purple, and silk, and scarlet; and all thyine wood, and every vessel of ivory, and every vessel made of most precious wood, and of brass, and iron, and marble; and cinnamon, and spice, and incense, and ointment, and frankincense, and wine, and oil, and fine flour, and wheat, and cattle, and sheep; and merchandise of horses and chariots and slaves; and souls of men. And the fruits which thy soul lusted after are gone from thee, and all things that were dainty and sumptuous are perished from thee, and men shall find them no more at all. The merchants of these things, who were made rich by her, shall stand afar off for the fear of her torment, weeping and mourning; saying, Woe, woe, the great city, she that was arrayed in fine linen and purple and scarlet, and decked with gold and precious stone and pearl! for in one hour so great riches is made desolate.

Babylon will become the economic center of the world, the center of business and world trade, a city characterized by the luxury items listed in this passage. But it will suddenly all go up in smoke, and the wealth of the merchants will be no more. Swiftly becoming paupers, the merchants will be heard lamenting indeed.

The transporters of goods are the third group who benefited from their association with Babylon. But they too will lament in 18:17b-19:

> And every shipmaster, and every one that saileth any whither, and mariners, and as many as gain their living by sea, stood afar off, and cried out as they looked upon the smoke of her burning, saying, What city is like the great city? And they cast dust on their heads, and cried, weeping and mourning, saying, Woe, woe, the great city, wherein all that had their ships in the sea were made rich by reason of her costliness! for in one hour is she made desolate.

Since the merchants will no longer have goods to market, the transporters will no longer have merchandise to transport by which they have become rich. Hence, they too will lament greatly the sudden destruction.

However, while three groups are in mourning, there will be three other groups rejoicing in 18:20:

> Rejoice over her, thou heaven, and ye saints, and ye apostles, and ye prophets; for God hath judged your judgment on her.

There will be lamenting on the earth by kings, merchants and transporters. But in heaven there will be three groups rejoicing: saints, apostles and prophets. The destruction of Babylon will mark the soon return of Jesus Christ.

The passage ends with a picture of the totality of Babylon's destruction in 18:21-24:

And a strong angel took up a stone as it were a great millstone and cast it into the sea, saying, Thus with a mighty fall shall Babylon, the great city, be cast down, and shall be found no more at all. And the voice of harpers and minstrels and fluteplayers and trumpeters shall be heard no more at all in thee; and no craftsman, of whatsoever craft, shall be found any more at all in thee; and the voice of a mill shall be heard no more at all in thee; and the light of a lamp shall shine no more at all in thee; and the voice of the bridegroom and of the bride shall be heard no more at all in thee: for thy merchants were the princes of the earth; for with thy sorcery were all the nations deceived. And in her was found the blood of prophets and of saints, and of all that have been slain upon the earth.

Jeremiah commanded a scroll-wrapped stone to be thrown into the Euphrates River to symbolize the sinking of the city of Babylon. Now another person, an angel, also casts a stone, the size of a millstone, into the sea to depict how totally Babylon will disappear so as not to be found anymore (verse 21). Babylon will cease to be the world center and capital (verses 22-23), because she was guilty of the blood of the prophets (e.g. the Two Witnesses) and the slaughter of the tribulation saints (verse 24).

To summarize the study of the second stage of the Campaign of Armageddon, while the Antichrist will move his forces into the Valley of Jezreel, his enemies will take the opportunity to destroy the city of Babylon quickly and suddenly. Just prior to this, however, the Jews will be warned to flee out of Babylon. This they will do, and will make their way to Jerusalem to report to the Jews who are there. This sudden destruction of the world political and economic capital will cause great consternation on the earth but not in heaven. For when Babylon's destruction comes, it will signal that the second coming will occur soon and along with it the regeneration and restoration of Israel.

THE THIRD STAGE: THE FALL OF JERUSALEM

Although the Antichrist will have all his allied forces with him when he receives the news that his capital city has been destroyed, he does not move eastward to destroy his enemies. It is Satan who will be in control and it is Satan's program, that of Jewish destruction, that will be uppermost in his mind. So instead of moving east, the Antichrist will move south against Jerusalem.

It is Zechariah who described this third stage in two places. The first is Zechariah 12:1-3:

The burden of the word of Jehovah concerning Israel. Thus saith Jehovah, who stretcheth forth the heavens, and layeth the foundation of the earth, and formeth the spirit of man within him: Behold, I will make Jerusalem a cup of reeling unto all the peoples round about, and upon Judah also shall it be in the siege against Jerusalem. And it shall come to pass in that day, that I will make Jerusalem a burdensome stone for all the peoples; all that burden themselves with it shall be sore wounded; and all the nations of the earth shall be gathered together against it.

The second is in Zechariah 14:1-2:

Behold, a day of Jehovah cometh, when thy spoil shall be divided in the midst of thee. For I will gather all nations against Jerusalem to battle; and the city shall be taken, and the houses rifled, and the women ravished; and half of the city shall go forth into captivity, and the residue of the people shall not be cut off from the city.

From the Valley of Jezreel the armies of the Antichrist will move south, and all the armies of all the nations will gather against Jerusalem. Once again, Jerusalem will fall into Gentile hands, and half of the Jewish population will be taken into slavery while the other half will be allowed to remain in the city to await a later fate.

The capture of Jerusalem by the forces of the Antichrist will not come easy. God will greatly energize the Jews to withstand the attack to a great degree causing heavy losses to the armies of the Antichrist. Zechariah 12:3 stated that all these nations that burden themselves with Jerusalem will be sorely wounded, and Jerusalem will become truly burdensome to them. The temporary empowerment of the Jewish forces is described in Zechariah 12:4-9:

In that day, saith Jehovah, I will smite every horse with terror, and his rider with madness; and I will open mine eyes upon the house of Judah, and will smite every horse of the peoples with blindness. And the chieftains of Judah shall say in their heart, The inhabitants of Jerusalem are my strength in Jehovah of hosts their God. In that day will I make the chieftains of Judah like a pan of fire among wood, and like a flaming torch among sheaves; and they shall devour all the peoples round about, on the right hand and on the left; and they of Jerusalem shall yet again dwell in their own place, even in Jerusalem. Jehovah also shall save the tents of Judah first, that the glory of the house of David and the glory of the inhabitants of Jerusalem be not magnified above Judah. In that day shall Jehovah defend the inhabitants of Jerusalem; and he that is feeble among them at that day shall be as David; and the house of David shall be as God, as the angel of Jehovah before them. And it shall come to pass in that day, that I will seek to destroy all the nations that come against Jerusalem.

These verses describe God's providential dealings at this stage of the Campaign of Armageddon prior to the actual intervention by the personal return of Jesus the Messiah. In the battle for Jerusalem, the Jewish military leaders will be so energized that they appear to strike down the enemy as quickly as a torch begins to burn up wood that is very dry. The feeble among the Jews take on the strength of David and the Davids among them take on the strength of the Angel of Jehovah.

What is meant by God's saving the "tents of Judah first," that is, before Jerusalem, will be discussed later in this chapter. Nevertheless, this is one of the ways that God will begin destroying the nations that have come against Jerusalem (verse 9).

This energizing of the Jewish forces in the battle for Jerusalem is further described in Micah 4:11-5:1:

> And now many nations are assembled against thee, that say, Let her be defiled, and let our eye see our desire upon Zion. But they know not the thoughts of Jehovah, neither understand they his counsel; for he hath gathered them as the sheaves to the threshing-floor. Arise and thresh, O daughter of Zion; for I will make thy horn iron, and I will make thy hoofs brass; and thou shalt beat in pieces many peoples: and I will devote their gain unto Jehovah, and their substance unto the Lord of the whole earth. Now shalt thou gather thyself in troops, O daughter of troops: he hath laid siege against us; they shall smite the judge of Israel with a rod upon the cheek.

The nations will be assembled against Jerusalem (verse 11) for the purpose of destroying it. But in the course of doing so these nations will become like sheaves on the threshing-floor (verse 12), and the Jewish forces will be able to thresh them well. However, the battle will be lost, and the Gentiles will capture Jerusalem and symbolize it by smiting Jerusalem's leader on the cheek (verse 1). After such heavy fighting and great losses, the soldiers of the Antichrist will plunder the Jewish homes of Jerusalem, and Jewish women will be subjected to massive rapes (Zechariah 14:2). With this, the third stage will come to an end.

THE FOURTH STAGE: THE ARMIES OF THE ANTICHRIST AT BOZRAH

It has already been shown in the previous chapter that the main concentration of Jews and Jewish leaders will no longer be in Jerusalem or in Israel but in Bozrah, in the land of Edom or present day southern Jordan. Since the main purpose of the Campaign of Armageddon is the annihilation of the Jews, the armies of the world will move southward from Jerusalem to Bozrah as Jeremiah 49:13-14 makes clear:

> For I have sworn by myself, saith Jehovah, that Bozrah shall become an astonishment, a reproach, a waste, and a curse; and all the cities thereof shall be perpetual wastes. I have heard tidings from Jehovah, and an ambassador is sent among the nations, saying, Gather yourselves together, and come against her, and rise up to the battle.

The next place where the nations of the earth will gather is at Bozrah in order to destroy the remnant of Israel that will be gathered there (Micah 2:12). With the completion of the fourth stage, the last three days of the Campaign of Armageddon and the tribulation begin.

THE FIFTH STAGE: THE NATIONAL REGENERATION OF ISRAEL

It has been pointed out in the previous chapter when speaking of the basis of the second coming of Christ that there are two facets to this basis. First, there must be the confession of Israel's national sin (Leviticus 26:40-42, Jeremiah 3:11-18, Hosea 5:15), and secondly a pleading for the Messiah to return (Zechariah 12:10, Matthew 23:37-39). With the armies of the Antichrist at the city of Bozrah, the Campaign of Armageddon will begin its last three days according to Hosea 6:1-3:

> Come, and let us return unto Jehovah; for he hath torn, and he will heal us; he hath smitten, and he will bind us up. After two days will he revive us: on the third day he will raise us up, and we shall live before him. And let us know, let us follow on to know Jehovah: his going forth is sure as the morning; and he will come unto us as the rain, as the latter rain that watereth the earth.

This passage is actually a continuation of Hosea five. The chapter division is unfortunate, because it breaks the train of thought. This passage contains the acknowledgment of the sin demanded in 5:15. Verses 1-3 are in the form of a call issued by the Jewish leaders exhorting the nation to repent and confess their national sin (verses 1-2). Only then will the physical blessings Israel once enjoyed be restored to her (verse 3). The leaders of Israel will finally recognize the reason why the tribulation has fallen on them. Whether this will be done by the study of the Scriptures, or by the preaching of the 144,000, or via the Two Witnesses (the third sign of Jonah to which the Jews of Jerusalem had already responded), or by the ministry of Elijah, is not clearly stated. Most likely there will be a combination of these things. But the leaders will come to a realization of the national sin in some way. Just as the Jewish leaders once led the nation to the rejection of the Messiahship of Jesus, they will then lead the nation to the acceptance of His Messiahship by issuing the call of Hosea 6:1-3. The confession of Israel's national sin will last for two days as the entire nation becomes regenerated and saved.

The national confession of Israel is given with its actual words in Isaiah 53:1-9:

> Who hath believed our message? and to whom hath the arm of Jehovah been revealed? For he grew up before him as a tender plant, and as a root out of a dry ground: he hath no form nor comeliness; and when we see him, there is no beauty that we should desire him. He was despised, and rejected of men; a man of sorrows, and acquainted with grief: and as

one from whom men hide their face he was despised; and we esteemed
him not. Surely he hath borne our griefs, and carried our sorrows; yet we
did esteem him stricken, smitten of God, and afflicted. But he was
wounded for our transgressions, he was bruised for our iniquities; the
chastisement of our peace was upon him; and with his stripes we are
healed. All we like sheep have gone astray; we have turned every one to
his own way; and Jehovah hath laid on him the iniquity of us all. He was
oppressed, yet when he was afflicted he opened not his mouth; as a lamb
that is led to the slaughter, and as a sheep that before its shearers is
dumb, so he opened not his mouth. By oppression and judgment he was
taken away; and as for his generation, who among them considered that
he was cut off out of the land of the living for the transgression of my
people to whom the stroke was due? And they made his grave with the
wicked, and with a rich man in his death; although he had done no
violence, neither was any deceit in his mouth.

In this confession, they admit that the nation had looked upon
Jesus as nothing more than another man, a criminal who had died for
his own sins. However, on this occasion they recognize that He was
no ordinary man, but the perfect Lamb of God, the Messiah Himself.
Furthermore, it was not for His own sins that Messiah died, but for
theirs, so that they need not be stricken for their sin.

Thus, the national regeneration will come by means of the
national confession of Isaiah 53:1-9. The nation as a nation will be
saved, fulfilling the prophecy of Romans 11:25-27:

For I would not, brethren, have you ignorant of this mystery, lest ye be
wise in your own conceits, that a hardening in part hath befallen Israel,
until the fulness of the Gentiles be come in; and so all Israel shall be saved:
even as it is written, There shall come out of Zion the Deliverer; He shall
turn away ungodliness from Jacob: And this is my covenant unto them,
When I shall take away their sins.

The "all Israel" means just that—every Jew living at that point of
time, meaning the third that are left from the original number of Jews
living at the start of the tribulation (Zechariah 13:8-9). Israel's national
confession and regeneration will be accomplished within two days
after the issuance of the call.

The second facet leading to the second coming is the pleading of
Israel for the Messiah to return and save them from their predicament
of having the world armies intent on their destruction gathered outside of Bozrah.

The pleading of the Jews for the Messiah to come and save them
is the subject of much revelation. It is described in Zechariah
12:10-13:1:

And I will pour upon the house of David, and upon the inhabitants of
Jerusalem, the spirit of grace and of supplication; and they shall look
unto me whom they have pierced; and they shall mourn for him, as one

mourneth for his only son, and shall be in bitterness for him, as one that is in bitterness for his first-born. In that day shall there be a great mourning in Jerusalem, as the mourning of Hadadrimmon in the valley of Megiddon. And the land shall mourn, every family apart; the family of the house of David apart, and their wives apart; the family of the house of Nathan apart, and their wives apart; the family of the house of Levi apart, and their wives apart; the family of the Shimeites apart, and their wives apart; all the families that remain, every family apart, and their wives apart. In that day there shall be a fountain opened to the house of David and to the inhabitants of Jerusalem, for sin and for uncleanness.

The pleading of Israel for the Messiah to return will not be confined to the Jews of Bozrah but will include the Jews still in Jerusalem. It will begin with the confession of the national sin, and then they will plead for His return to save them from the troubles described in the preceding context. They plead for the one whom they have pierced. This will be the result of the outpouring of the Holy Spirit.

Another prophecy of this event is in Joel 2:28-32:

And it shall come to pass afterward, that I will pour out my Spirit upon all flesh; and your sons and your daughters shall prophesy, your old men shall dream dreams, your young men shall see visions: and also upon the servants and upon the handmaids in those days will I pour out my Spirit. And I will show wonders in the heavens and in the earth: blood, and fire, and pillars of smoke. The sun shall be turned into darkness, and the moon into blood, before the great and terrible day of Jehovah cometh. And it shall come to pass, that whosoever shall call on the name of Jehovah shall be delivered; for in mount Zion and in Jerusalem there shall be those that escape, as Jehovah hath said, and among the remnant those whom Jehovah doth call.

Regeneration is the work of the Holy Spirit, and here the nation of Israel will be regenerated because of the outpouring of the Holy Spirit on them creating some dramatic manifestations in their midst (verses 28-29). This will be accompanied by wonders in the heavens as well (verses 30-31). The result of all this is that the Jews of Jerusalem will be delivered and escape as well as the remnant of Bozrah (vs. 32).

In the process of Israel's regeneration and new prophetic manifestations, the false prophets who have led Israel astray during the course of the tribulation will be executed as recorded in Zechariah 13:2-6:

And it shall come to pass in that day, saith Jehovah of hosts, that I will cut off the names of the idols out of the land, and they shall no more be remembered; and also I will cause the prophets and the unclean spirit to pass out of the land. And it shall come to pass that, when any shall yet prophesy, then his father and his mother that begat him shall say unto him, Thou shalt not live; for thou speakest lies in the name of Jehovah;

and his father and his mother that begat him shall thrust him through when he prophesieth. And it shall come to pass in that day, that the prophets shall be ashamed every one of his vision, when he prophesieth; neither shall they wear a hairy mantle to deceive: but he shall say, I am no prophet, I am a tiller of the ground; for I have been made a bondman from my youth. And one shall say unto him, What are these wounds between thine arms? Then he shall answer, Those with which I was wounded in the house of my friends.

At the time of Israel's national cleansing from sin (verse 2) the false prophets will be sought out and executed. Often the parents of the false prophets will themselves be the ones to carry out the execution (verses 2-3). Though many of these false prophets will attempt to hide the fact that they were formerly prophets, the scars on their body, a symbol of their prophetic office, will betray them for what they were. Their denials will not be able to save them (verses 4-6).

That the remnant comes to a saving knowledge of Jesus the Messiah by way of the fires of the tribulation is summarized in Zechariah 13:7-9:

Awake, O sword, against my shepherd, and against the man that is my fellow, saith Jehovah of hosts; smite the shepherd, and the sheep shall be scattered; and I will turn my hand upon the little ones. And it shall come to pass, that in all the land, saith Jehovah, two parts therein shall be cut off and die; but the third shall be left therein. And I will bring the third part into the fire, and will refine them as silver is refined, and will try them as gold is tried: they shall call on my name, and I will hear them: I will say, It is my people; and they shall say, Jehovah is my God.

Verse 7 gives the basic reason why the events of the tribulation will fall on Israel. God's shepherd, the Messiah, was smitten and so His sheep, Israel, were scattered throughout the world. Toward the latter end of the dispersion will come the Great Tribulation through which two thirds of the Jewish population will be killed (verse 8). But the remaining third part will be refined. By means of the national confession of their sin, they will be purified (verse 9). God will then answer their pleading for Him to come and save them. They will once again be His people, and He will be their God.

Isaiah 64:1-12 also describes the pleading for the second coming of Christ:

Oh that thou wouldest rend the heavens, that thou wouldest come down, that the mountains might quake at thy presence, as when fire kindleth the brushwood, and the fire causeth the waters to boil; to make thy name known to thine adversaries, that the nations may tremble at thy presence! When thou didst terrible things which we looked not for, thou camest down; the mountains quaked at thy presence. For from of old men have not heard, nor perceived by the ear, neither hath the eye seen a God besides thee, who worketh for him that waiteth for him. Thou meetest him that rejoiceth and worketh righteousness, those that remember thee in thy ways: behold, thou wast wroth, and we sinned: in them have we been of long time; and shall we be saved? For we are all become as one that is unclean, and all our righteousnesses are as a polluted garment: and we all do fade as a leaf; and our iniquities, like the wind, take us away. And there is none that calleth upon thy name, that stirreth up himself to take hold of thee; for thou hast hid thy face from us, and hast consumed us by means of our iniquities. But now, O Jehovah, thou art our Father; we are the clay, and thou our potter; and we all are the work of thy hand. Be not wroth very sore, O Jehovah, neither remember iniquity for ever: behold, look, we beseech thee, we are all thy people. Thy holy cities are become a wilderness, Zion is become a wilderness, Jerusalem a desolation. Our holy and our beautiful house, where our fathers praised thee, is burned with fire; and all our pleasant places are laid waste. Wilt thou refrain thyself for these things, O Jehovah? wilt thou hold thy peace, and afflict us very sore?

The passage begins with the pleading for the Lord to "come down" and let the nations realize His presence (verses 1-2). The remnant of Israel will remember the mighty works of God in the past (verses 3-7) and seek those mighty works of God again (verse 8). They will ask for the forgiveness of their sins (verse 9). Their disastrous plight is shown by the fact that Jerusalem had been made a desolation by the nations (verses 9-10) and the temple was still defiled (verse 11). The passage ends with a plea for God to intervene lest they, too, become ruined (verse 12).

Several of the Psalms are merely poetic versions of the pleading of the remnant for God to come and save them from the invading armies. One such passage is Psalm 79:1-13:

O God, the nations are come into thine inheritance; thy holy temple have they defiled; they have laid Jerusalem in heaps. The dead bodies of thy servants have they given to be food unto the birds of the heavens, the flesh of thy saints unto the beasts of the earth. Their blood have they shed like water round about Jerusalem; and there was none to bury them. We are become a reproach to our neighbors, a scoffing and derision to them that are round about us. How long, O Jehovah? wilt thou be angry for ever? Shalt thy jealousy burn like fire? Pour out thy wrath upon the nations that know thee not, and upon the kingdoms that call not upon thy name. For they have devoured Jacob, and laid waste his habitation. Remember not against us the iniquities of our forefathers: let thy tender mercies speedily meet us; for we are brought very low. Help us, O God of our salvation, for the glory of thy name; and deliver us, and forgive our sins, for thy name's sake. Wherefore should the nations say, Where is their God? Let the avenging of the blood of thy servants which is shed be known among the nations in our sight. Let the sighing of the prisoner come before thee: according to the greatness of thy power preserve thou those that are appointed to death; and render unto our neighbors sevenfold into their bosom their reproach, wherewith they have reproached thee, O Lord. So we thy people and sheep of thy pasture will give thee thanks for ever: we will show forth thy praise to all generations.

This Psalm is impossible to understand except in the context of the Faithful Remnant pleading for the Messiah to return and save them from the invading Gentile armies. After recalling the events of the fall of Jerusalem (the third stage) with the city in ruins, the abomination of desolation of the temple, and the death of so many Jews (verses 1-4), they will plead for God to come down, to rescue them and to pour His wrath out on the Gentile nations (verses 5-7). They will plead for the forgiveness of the sins of their forefathers (as demanded by Leviticus 26:40) who led the nation to the rejection of the Messiahship of Jesus as well as for the forgiveness of their own sins (verses 8-9). On the basis of what these Gentile nations have done to Israel, they will ask God to avenge them as He had promised and to save them from their enemies (verses 10-12). Then they will give thanks and sing the praise of God forever (verse 13).

Another Psalm that describes the pleading of the remnant is Psalm 80:1-19:

> Give ear, O Shepherd of Israel, thou that leadest Joseph like a flock; thou that sittest above the cherubim, shine forth. Before Ephraim and Benjamin and Manasseh, stir up thy might, and come to save us. Turn us again, O God; and cause thy face to shine, and we shall be saved. O Jehovah God of hosts, how long wilt thou be angry against the prayer of thy people? Thou hast fed them with the bread of tears, and given them tears to drink in large measure. Thou makest us a strife unto our neighbors; and our enemies laugh among themselves. Turn us again, O God of hosts; and cause thy face to shine, and we shall be saved. Thou broughtest a vine out of Egypt: thou didst drive out the nations, and plantedst it. Thou preparedst room before it, and it took deep root, and filled the land. The mountains were covered with the shadow of it, and the boughs thereof were like cedars of God. It sent out its branches unto the sea, and its shoots unto the River. Why hast thou broken down its walls, so that all they that pass by the way do pluck it? The boar out of the wood doth ravage it, and the wild beasts of the field feed on it. Turn again, we beseech thee, O God of hosts: look down from heaven, and behold, and visit this vine, and the stock, which thy right hand planted, and the branch that thou madest strong for thyself. It is burned with fire, it is cut down: they perish at the rebuke of thy countenance. Let thy hand be upon the man of thy right hand, upon the son of man whom thou madest strong for thyself. So shall we not go back from thee: quicken thou us, and we will call upon thy name. Turn us again, O Jehovah God of hosts; cause thy face to shine, and we shall be saved.

This Psalm opens with a pleading for the Shepherd of Israel to come and save them (verses 1-2). Not only will they plead for their physical deliverance, but also for their spiritual salvation (verse 3). The phrase *turn us again* points to the repentance and conversion by which "we shall be saved." After describing the bitter state they find themselves in, having become the laughing stock of the nations, they will plead once again for God to come and save them (verses 4-7).

Recalling God's past dealings with Israel from the Exodus to the kingdom of David and Solomon (verses 8-11), they will mourn over their present state of having been slowly brought down by the Gentile nations (verses 12-13). Therefore, they will appeal to God to turn to them and defend the cause of Israel which had been so badly bruised (verses 14-16). The specific person they are pleading for is the one on God's right hand (verse 17) referred to as *the son of man*. This is none other than Jesus the Messiah who has been sitting at the right hand of God the Father ever since the ascension from the Mount of Olives after He was rejected by Israel. Only by faith in the Son of Man can Israel be regenerated. Only by calling upon the name of the Lord can Israel be saved spiritually (verses 18-19). Only by the return of the Son of Man can Israel be saved physically.

In conclusion, during the fifth stage Israel as a nation will be regenerated and saved after two days of national confession of sin. On the third day they will plead for the second coming of Christ.

THE SIXTH STAGE: THE SECOND COMING OF JESUS CHRIST

In the sixth stage Jesus will return at the Jewish request for Him to do so. The initial place of His return will not be the Mount of Olives as is commonly taught, but the place known as Bozrah. Since this fact is relatively new to most people, it would be best to deal with the *place* of the second coming of Christ before discussing the *manner* of His return.

Four key passages pinpoint the *place* of the second coming as Bozrah. A fifth one has a possible reference to it. The first passage is Isaiah 34:1-7:

> Come near, ye nations, to hear; and hearken, ye peoples: let the earth hear, and the fulness thereof; the world, and all things that come forth from it. For Jehovah hath indignation against all the nations, and wrath against all their host: he hath utterly destroyed them, he hath delivered them to the slaughter. Their slain also shall be cast out, and the stench of their dead bodies shall come up; and the mountains shall be melted with their blood. And all the host of heaven shall be dissolved, and the heavens shall be rolled together as a scroll; and all their host shall fade away, as the leaf fadeth from off the vine, and as a fading leaf from the fig-tree. For my sword hath drunk its fill in heaven: behold, it shall come down upon Edom, and upon the people of my curse, to judgment. The sword of Jehovah is filled with blood, it is made fat with fatness, with the blood of lambs and goats, with the fat of the kidneys of rams; for Jehovah hath a sacrifice in Bozrah, and a great slaughter in the land of Edom. And the wild-oxen shall come down with them, and the bullocks with the bulls; and their land shall be drunken with blood, and their dust made fat with fatness.

Isaiah begins with a call to all the nations declaring that God has indignation against all these nations and against their armies in particular. They are destined to be slaughtered with the sword of the Lord (verses 1-3). Not only will there be convulsions in the earth at this time, but there will be a shaking in the heavens as well (verse 4). But when the sword of God strikes all the armies of all the nations, In what *place* will it strike? The name of the country where all the nations will be smitten is identified as the land of Edom (verse 5). Becoming even more specific, it will occur at the city of Bozrah in the land of Edom (verses 6-7). According to this passage, the exact geographic spot where God will strike all the armies of all the nations will be the city of Bozrah in the land of Edom (southern Jordan).

A far more graphic description is given in Isaiah 63:1-6. While in a prophetic vision, Isaiah the prophet was standing on some high point or mountain in Israel looking eastward towards the land of Edom when suddenly he saw a magnificent but blood-stained figure approaching him in glory and splendor. At that point a question and answer session ensues between Isaiah the prophet and this marching figure. Isaiah initiated the conversation with the first question in 63:1a:

> Who is this that cometh from Edom, with dyed garments from Bozrah? this that is glorious in his apparel, marching in the greatness of his strength?

The figure approaching him is coming from the land of Edom and from the city of Bozrah. His features are reflecting His glory, and there is greatness in His strength. There can be little doubt that this figure arrayed with the Shechinah Glory* is the Jewish Messiah Himself. The answer to Isaiah's question comes in 63:1b:

> I that speak in righteousness, mighty to save.

If there was doubt as to the identify of the person before, it should be very clear now. Only one man can answer, *I that speak in righteousness*. Only one man has the power that is *mighty to save*. It is the person of Jesus the Messiah marching toward Israel from the land of Edom and the city of Bozrah.

Isaiah responds to this answer with a second question in 63:2:

> Wherefore art thou red in thine apparel, and thy garments like him that treadeth in the winevat?

Isaiah noticed that the clothing of this individual, though glorified with the Shechinah Glory, is nevertheless stained with blood. So Isaiah inquires as to how His garments became stained. This question is answered in 63:3-6:

* See Appendix IV.

I have trodden the winepress alone; and of the peoples there was no man with me: yea, I trod them in mine anger, and trampled them in my wrath; and their lifeblood is sprinkled upon my garments, and I have stained all my raiment. For the day of vengeance was in my heart, and the year of my redeemed is come. And I looked, and there was none to help; and I wondered that there was none to uphold: therefore mine own arm brought salvation unto me; and my wrath, it upheld me. And I trod down the peoples in mine anger, and made them drunk in my wrath, and I poured out their lifeblood on the earth.

The staining with blood was caused by a battle fought in the land of Edom and the city of Bozrah. He fought against the nations alone. In the course of trampling the nations, their lifeblood sprinkled on His garments, staining them red (verse 3). The fight was necessary in order for Him to save His redeemed people, Israel (verse 4). He fought all alone and there were none to help Him (verses 5-6).

The main point to learn from this passage is that the battle is initiated in the land of Edom and at the city of Bozrah. By the time Messiah reaches Israel, His garments are already stained with blood from the slaughter of the enemy.

The third scripture that places His initial return in this area is Habakkuk 3:3:

God came from Teman, and the Holy One from mount Paran. His glory covered the heavens, and the earth was full of his praise.

Teman and Mount Paran are both in the vicinity of Bozrah and are located in the same mountain range of Mount Seir. The context is obviously speaking of the second coming of Christ and that event is said to be in the same area.

All these passages clearly pinpoint the *place* of the second coming as being in the land of Edom and at the city of Bozrah. This correlates with where the remnant of Israel will be located in the last days. The remnant of Israel gathered in Bozrah and the second coming are linked together in the fourth passage in Micah 2:12-13:

I will surely assemble, O Jacob, all of thee; I will surely gather the remnant of Israel; I will put them together as the sheep of Bozrah, as a flock in the midst of their pasture; they shall make great noise by reason of the multitude of men. The breaker is gone up before them: they have broken forth and passed on to the gate, and are gone out thereat: and their king is passed on before them, and Jehovah at the head of them.

The remnant of Israel will be gathered in Bozrah (verse 12) where they will be beseiged by the forces of the Antichrist. They are finally able to break the seige, because Jehovah the King is leading them (verse 13). The *breaker*, the *king*, and *Jehovah* are all the same person in this verse. At the second coming the Messiah will enter into battle with the forces of the Antichrist which have gathered at this city.

A fifth passage that may refer to this same event is in Judges 5:4-5:

> Jehovah, when thou wentest forth out of Seir, when thou marchedst out of the field of Edom, the earth trembled, the heavens also dropped, yea, the clouds dropped water. The mountains quaked at the presence of Jehovah, even yon Sinai at the presence of Jehovah the God of Israel.

It is not really certain that these verses are speaking of the second coming of Christ, but if so (and the author leans toward this position with caution), God is seen as coming from Mount Seir and from the land of Edom. Mount Seir is the mountain range of southern Jordan in which the city of Bozrah is located.

Having identified the place of the second coming of Christ, it is now necessary to look at the Scriptures dealing with the *manner* of the second coming and the final battle between Christ and Antichrist. It has already been learned from Isaiah 63:2-6 that when He fights, Messiah will fight alone and no others will participate in the battle.

The manner of the second coming is described in Matthew 24:30 as being with the clouds of heaven:

> . . . and then shall appear the sign of the Son of man in heaven: and then shall all the tribes of the earth mourn, and they shall see the Son of man coming on the clouds of heaven with power and great glory.

Throughout the Old Testament, clouds and the Shechinah Glory are interrelated. In this New Testament passage, the interrelation can be seen again.

According to Acts 1:9-11, Christ will return in the same manner as He left:

> And when he had said these things, as they were looking, he was taken up; and a cloud received him out of their sight. And while they were looking stedfastly into heaven as he went, behold, two men stood by them in white apparel; who also said, Ye men of Galilee, why stand ye looking into heaven? this Jesus, who was received up from you into heaven, shall so come in like manner as ye beheld him going into heaven.

It must be noted that the angels did not prophesy that Jesus would return to the same *place* but rather in the same *manner* in which He had left. Jesus left in the clouds of heaven, and according to Matthew 24:30 He will return in the clouds of heaven.

An extended passage on the second coming is in Revelation 19:1-18. Prior to dealing with the manner of the second coming itself, this chapter has a prelude composed of three elements in 19:1-10. The first element in 19:1-8 is the four-fold hallelujah. The first hallelujah is for the fall of the Ecclesiastical Babylon in 19:1-2:

> After these things I heard as it were a great voice of a great multitude in heaven, saying, Hallelujah; Salvation, and glory, and power, belong to our God: for true and righteous are his judgments; for he hath judged the great harlot, her that corrupted the earth with her fornication, and he hath avenged the blood of his servants at her hand.

The second hallelujah in 19:3 is for the destruction of the city of Babylon, the economic and political capital of the world:

> And a second time they say, Hallelujah. And her smoke goeth up for ever and ever.

The third hallelujah is a worshipful praise to God from those around the throne, namely the twenty-four elders and the four seraphs in 19:4-5:

> And the four and twenty elders and the four living creatures fell down and worshipped God that sitteth on the throne, saying, Amen; Hallelujah. And a voice came forth from the throne, saying, Give praise to our God, all ye his servants, ye that fear him, the small and the great.

The fourth hallelujah in 19:6-8 is for the marriage of the Lamb which was discussed in Chapter VI:

> And I heard as it were the voice of a great multitude, and as the voice of many waters, and as the voice of mighty thunders, saying, Hallelujah: for the Lord our God, the Almighty, reigneth. Let us rejoice and be exceeding glad, and let us give the glory unto him: for the marriage of the Lamb is come, and his wife hath made herself ready. And it was given unto her that she should array herself in fine linen, bright and pure: for the fine linen is the righteous acts of the saints.

The second element of the prelude is an invitation to the marriage supper of the Lamb in 19:9:

> And he saith unto me, Write, Blessed are they that are bidden to the marriage supper of the Lamb. And he saith unto me, These are true words of God.

It is with the marriage supper that the millennium will begin, but the invitations are sent out just prior to the second coming of Christ. They go out to all the redeemed who are not members of the church: i.e., the Old Testament and tribulation saints soon to be resurrected.

Finally, the third element of the prelude comes in the declaration of the spirit of prophecy in 19:10:

> And I fell down before his feet to worship him. And he saith unto me, See thou do it not: I am a fellow-servant with thee and with thy brethren that hold the testimony of Jesus: worship God: for the testimony of Jesus is the spirit of prophecy.

The spirit of prophecy Is the testimony of Jesus. He is the source of all prophecy, and all prophecy moves towards a fulfillment by Christ with a view towards His own glory.

With that prelude completed, the apostle then describes the second coming of Christ in 19:11-16:

> And I saw the heaven opened; and behold, a white horse, and he that sat thereon called Faithful and True; and in righteousness he doth judge and make war. And his eyes are a flame of fire, and upon his head are many diadems; and he hath a name written no one knoweth but he himself. And he is arrayed in a garment sprinkled with blood: and his name is called The Word of God. And the armies which are in heaven followed him upon white horses, clothed in fine linen, white and pure. And out of his mouth proceedeth a sharp sword, that with it he should smite the nations: and he shall rule them with a rod of iron: and he treadeth the winepress of the fierceness of the wrath of God, the Almighty. And he hath on his garment and on his thigh a name written, KING OF KINGS, AND LORD OF LORDS.

This account of the second coming begins by describing Christ as the Judge (verses 11-13) which has many similarities with the descriptions found in the first chapter of Revelation. The war He engages in against the nations is a result of judgment by Him Who is faithful and true. He wears on His head the diadem crowns indicating His natural royalty. His garments are stained with blood just as in Isaiah 63:1-6, for reasons discussed earlier. This is the second coming of the Judge and the incarnate Word of God; Jesus returning in righteousness to judge the nations.

When He returns, Messiah will be followed by armies (verse 14). The word is in the plural number meaning that at least two separate armies will return with Him. One army is known as *hosts of the Lord*, or the angelic army. Matthew 16:27 states:

> For the Son of man shall come in the glory of his Father with his angels; and then shall he render unto every man according to his deeds.

Another army that will return with Jesus is the army of the church saints who had been raptured previously before the tribulation. Jude 14-15 describes the events as follows:

> And to these also Enoch, the seventh from Adam, prophesied, saying, Behold, the Lord came with ten thousands of his holy ones, to execute judgment upon all, and to convict all the ungodly of all their works of

ungodliness which they have ungodly wrought, and of all the hard things which ungodly sinners have spoken against him.

However, Isaiah 63:1-6 made it clear that although the armies of saints and angels will return with Christ, they will not participate in the fighting. Messiah will fight this battle by Himself.

After describing Jesus in His role as a Judge and the armies that return with Him, John next describes Jesus in His office of King (verses 15-16). For after judging the nations as a righteous Judge, He is to rule as a King with a rod of iron. These nations will gather and attempt to destroy the Jews in order to abolish God's rule over them (Psalm 2:1-6). However, they will partake of the wrath of God at the second coming of Jesus Christ, and He will rule over them. Hence, Jesus will indeed be the King of Kings and Lord of Lords.

Because of the massive slaughter of all the armies of the nations, another invitation is issued. This one invites the birds of the heavens to the great supper of God in Revelation 19:17-18:

And I saw an angel standing in the sun; and he cried with a loud voice, saying to all the birds that fly in mid heaven, Come and be gathered together unto the great supper of God; that ye may eat the flesh of kings, and the flesh of captains, and the flesh of mighty men, and the flesh of horses and of them that sit thereon, and the flesh of all men, both free and bond, and small and great.

The birds will eat the unburied carcasses of many who participated in the Campaign of Armageddon. In this way the birds will be filled and satisfied according to Revelation 19:21:

. . . and the rest were killed with the sword of him that sat upon the horse, even the sword which came forth out of his mouth: and all the birds were filled with their flesh.

This feast for the birds is also described in Ezekiel 39:17-20 extending the invitation to the animals of the field:

And thou, son of man, thus saith the Lord Jehovah: Speak unto the birds of every sort, and to every beast of the field, Assemble yourselves, and come; gather yourselves on every side to my sacrifice that I do sacrifice for you, even a great sacrifice upon the mountains of Israel, that ye may eat flesh and drink blood. Ye shall eat the flesh of the mighty, and drink the blood of the princes of the earth, of rams, of lambs, and of goats, of bullocks, all of them fatlings of Bashan, And ye shall eat fat till ye be full, and drink blood till ye be drunken, of my sacrifice which I have sacrificed for you. And ye shall be filled at my table with horses and chariots, with mighty men, and with all men of war, saith the Lord Jehovah.

Ezekiel closely connects these events with the final redemption of Israel in 39:21-29:

And I will set my glory among the nations; and all the nations shall see my judgment that I have executed, and my hand that I have laid upon them. So the house of Israel shall know that I am Jehovah their God, from that day and forward. And the nations shall know that the house of Israel went into captivity for their iniquity; because they trespassed against me, and I hid my face from them: so I gave them into the hand of their adversaries, and they fell all of them by the sword. According to their uncleanness and according to their transgressions did I unto them; and I hid my face from them. Therefore thus saith the Lord Jehovah: Now will I bring back the captivity of Jacob, and have mercy upon the whole house of Israel; and I will be jealous for my holy name. And they shall bear their shame, and all their trespasses whereby they have trespassed aginst me, when they shall dwell securely in their land, and none shall make them afraid; when I have brought them back from the peoples, and gathered them out of their enemies' lands, and am sanctified in them in the sight of many nations. And they shall know that I am Jehovah their God, in that I caused them to go into captivity among the nations, and have gathered them unto their own land; and I will leave none of them any more there; neither will I hide my face any more from them; for I have poured out my Spirit upon the house of Israel, saith the Lord Jehovah.

Only then will the Gentile nations realize that God did not cast off His people forever. Israel's judgment and dispersion was due to sin, primarily the sin of the rejection of the Messiahship of Jesus. So for a time God hid His face and allowed the nations to come and cause havoc and destruction. But later Israel will confess her national sin and seek His face in their affliction (Hosea 5:15). They will seek rescue from the nations that have so sorely afflicted them. The nations will recognize at the second coming of Christ that God is still Israel's God and He will avenge their affliction of Israel. For in gathering all the armies of the world against Israel, they will actually be gathering against Israel's Messiah as Revelation 19:19 clearly states:

And I saw the beast, and the kings of the earth, and their armies, gathered together to make war against him that sat upon the horse, and against his army.

Another passage giving a description of the second coming of Christ is in Habakkuk 3:1-19:

A prayer of Habakkuk the prophet, set to Shigionoth. O Jehovah, I have heard the report of thee, and am afraid: O Jehovah, revive thy work in the midst of the years; in the midst of the years make it known; in wrath remember mercy. God came from Teman, and the Holy One from mount Paran. His glory covered the heavens, and the earth was full of his praise. And his brightness was as the light; he had rays coming forth from his hand; and there was the hiding of his power. Before him went the pestilence, and fiery bolts went forth at his feet. He stood, and measured the earth; he beheld, and drove asunder the nations; and the eternal mountains were scattered; the everlasting hills did bow; his goings were as of old. I saw the tents of Cushan in affliction; the curtains of the land of

Midian did tremble. Was Jehovah displeased with the rivers? Was thine anger against the rivers, or thy wrath against the sea, that thou didst ride upon thy horses, upon thy chariots of salvation? Thy bow was made quite bare; the oaths to the tribes were a sure word. Thou didst cleave the earth with rivers. The mountains saw thee, and were afraid; the tempest of waters passed by; the deep uttered its voice, and lifted up its hands on high. The sun and moon stood still in their habitation, at the light of thine arrows as they went, at the shining of thy glittering spear. Thou didst march through the land in indignation; thou didst thresh the nations in anger. Thou wentest forth for the salvation of thy people, for the salvation of thine anointed; thou woundedst the head out of the house of the wicked man, laying bare the foundation even unto the neck. Thou didst pierce with his own staves the head of his warriers: they came as a whirlwind to scatter me; their rejoicing was as to devour the poor secretly. Thou didst tread the sea with thy horses, the heap of mighty waters. I heard, and my body trembled, my lips quivered at the voice; rottenness entereth into my bones, and I tremble in my place; because I must wait quietly for the day of trouble, for the coming up of the people that invadeth us. For though the fig-tree shall not flourish, neither shall fruit be in the vines; the labor of the olive shall fail, and the fields shall yield no food; the flock shall be cut off from the fold, and there shall be no herd in the stalls: yet I will rejoice in Jehovah, I will joy in the God of my salvation. Jehovah, the Lord, is my strength; and he maketh my feet like hinds' feet, and will make me to walk upon my high places.

This prayer of Habakkuk (verse 1) is a prophetic one for it records in vision what can only be the second coming of Christ. The prayer opens with the pleading of the remnant (verse 2) to save them physically (revive thy works) and spiritually (in wrath remember mercy). In answer to the remnant's request, God is viewed as coming from Edom with all His shining glory (verses 3-4). At His coming, He will begin to render judgment against the gathered nations by various means (verses 5-7). Nature will also be greatly affected by the second coming (verses 8-10) as will the terrestial heavenly sphere (verse 11). The Messiah is next viewed as marching in indignation and threshing the nations (verse 12) on behalf of the people of Israel (verse 13a). The head of the armies, the Antichrist, will be smitten (verse 13b) as well as the soldiers of his armies (verses 14-15), who have come to scatter the Jews afresh. Having seen this vision of the marching armies and the second coming, Habakkuk trembles with the knowledge of what must yet befall his people Israel where so many will be slaughtered (verses 16-17). But he takes comfort in the fact that his personal salvation rests in the Lord who at the second coming will make all things rights (verses 18-19).

The book of Psalms contains many poetical references to the second coming of Christ. A graphic one is found in Psalm 18:8-16:

There went up a smoke out of his nostrils, and fire out of his mouth devoured: coals were kindled by it. He bowed the heavens also, and came down; and thick darkness was under his feet. And he rode upon a cherub, and did fly; yea, he soared upon the wings of the wind. He made darkness his hiding-place, his pavilion round about him, darkness of waters, thick clouds of the skies. At the brightness before him his thick clouds passed, hailstones and coals of fire. Jehovah also thundered in the heavens, and the Most High uttered his voice, hailstones and coals of fire. And he sent out his arrows, and scattered them; yea, lightnings manifold, and discomfited them. Then the channels of waters appeared, and the foundations of the world were laid bare, at thy rebuke, O Jehovah, at the blast of the breath of thy nostrils. He sent from on high, he took me; he drew me out of many waters.

At His second coming, Christ will come with the wrath of God (verses 8-9) riding upon a cherub (verse 10), which will have horse-like features according to Revelation 19:11. There will be convulsions throughout nature at the second coming (verses 11-15) as the entire world is illuminated by the brightness of His glorious return.

So at the sixth stage of the Campaign of Armageddon, Christ will return at the request of Israel and enter into battle with the Antichrist and his armies. With His return to the remnant of Israel in Bozrah, He will indeed *save the tents of Judah first* before saving the Jews of Jerusalem, as Zechariah 12:7 predicted:

Jehovah also shall save the tents of Judah first, that the glory of the house of David and the glory of the inhabitants of Jerusalem be not magnified above Judah.

The term *tents* points to temporary abodes rather than permanent dwellings. The fact that Judah is living in "tents" shows that Judah is not home *in* Judah but is temporarily elsewhere. That elsewhere is Bozrah. Since the Messiah will save the tents of Judah first, this too shows that the initial place of His return will be Bozrah and not the Mount of Olives.

THE SEVENTH STAGE: THE BATTLE FROM BOZRAH TO THE VALLEY OF JEHOSHAPHAT

While the battle between Christ and the Antichrist will begin at Bozrah, it will apparently continue all the way back to the eastern walls of Jerusalem which overlook the Kidron Valley, also known as the Valley of Jehoshaphat.

Among the very first casualties will be the Antichrist himself. Having ruled the world with great power and spoken against the true Son of God, the counterfeit son will be powerless before Christ. Habakkuk 3:13b described it as follows:

Thou woundedst the head out of the house of the wicked man, laying bare the foundation even unto the neck.

The simplicity with which Christ will slay the Antichrist is described by Paul in II Thessalonians 2:8:

> And then shall be revealed the lawless one, whom the Lord Jesus shall slay with the breath of his mouth, and bring to nought by the manifestation of his coming.

The one who has claimed to be god, the one who has been able to perform all kinds of miracles, signs and wonders, the one who exercised all the authority of Satan as he ruled the world, will be quickly dispensed with by the word of the Lord Jesus Christ. For the second time the Antichrist will die.

The arrival of the Antichrist into hell is described in Isaiah 14:3-11:

> And it shall come to pass in the day that Jehovah shall give thee rest from thy sorrow, and from thy trouble, and from the hard service wherein thou wast made to serve, that thou shalt take up this parable against the king of Babylon, and say, How hath the oppressor ceased! the golden city ceased! Jehovah hath broken the staff of the wicked, the sceptre of the rulers; that smote the peoples in wrath with a continual stroke, that ruled the nations in anger, with a persecution that none restrained. The whole earth is at rest, and is quiet: they break forth into singing. Yea, the fir-trees rejoice at thee, and the cedars of Lebanon, saying, Since thou art laid low, no hewer is come up against us. Sheol from beneath is moved for thee to meet thee at thy coming; it stirreth up the dead for thee, even all the chief ones of the earth; it hath raised up from their thrones all the kings of the nations. All they shall answer and say unto thee, Art thou also become weak as we? art thou become like unto us? Thy pomp is brought down to Sheol, and the noise of thy viols: the worm is spread under thee, and worms cover thee.

At the time of the redemption of Israel, the Jews whom the King of Babylon sought to destroy will taunt him with a new parable (verses 3-4) commemorating the greater strength of the power of God (verse 5). The Antichrist ruled the nations of the world (verse 6), but then the whole world will rejoice over his demise (verses 7-8). As the spirit of the Antichrist enters into the gates of hell, the previous great ones of the earth already there will suddenly rise up off their thrones (verse 9) in utter shock that he, too, has entered the abode of hell (verse 10). Yet it will be so, and all the pomp of his world-wide reign will suffer the demise of hell (verse 11).

Having described the spirit of the Antichrist in hell, Isaiah later describes the fate of his dead body on earth in 14:16-21:

> They that see thee shall gaze at thee, they shall consider thee, saying, Is this the man that made the earth to tremble, that did shake kingdoms; that made the world as a wilderness, and overthrew the cities thereof; that let not loose his prisoners to their home? All the kings of the nations, all of them, sleep in glory, every one in his own house. But thou art cast

forth away from thy sepulchre like an abominable branch, clothed with the slain, that are thrust through with the sword, that go down to the stones of the pit; as a dead body trodden under foot. Thou shalt not be joined with them in burial, because thou hast destroyed thy land, thou hast slain thy people; the seed of evildoers shall not be named for ever. Prepare ye slaughter for his children for the iniquity of their fathers, that they rise not up, and possess the earth, and fill the face of the world with cities.

Many will be able to view the body of the Antichrist and will stare in utter disbelief that he died so suddenly and easily considering he had shaken the kingdoms of the world and the earth trembled in his presence (verses 16-17). While lesser kings are buried in pompous sepulchres (verse 18), not so the Antichrist whose body will be trampled by the fleeing feet of his own armies (verse 19). In fact, his body will never be buried at all (verse 20) for reasons to be discussed in the next chapter. His entire family will be destroyed so that they can not try to follow in their father's footsteps and attempt to rule the world (verse 21).

After the death of the Antichrist, the slaughter of his army will continue. Several passages have been cited already which pictured the Messiah as marching through the land in indignation and treading the nations with His feet causing blood to be sprinkled on His garments. Zechariah 14:12-15 describes the manner in which these massive hordes of Antichrist's armies will be destroyed:

And this shall be the plague wherewith Jehovah will smite all the peoples that have warred against Jerusalem: their flesh shall consume away while they stand upon their feet, and their eyes shall consume away in their sockets, and their tongue shall consume away in their mouth. And it shall come to pass in that day, that a great tumult from Jehovah shall be among them; and they shall lay hold every one on the hand of his neighbor, and his hand shall rise up against the hand of his neighbor. And Judah also shall fight at Jerusalem; and the wealth of all the nations round about shall be gathered together, gold, and silver, and apparel, in great abundance. And so shall be the plague of the horse, of the mule, of the camel, and of the ass, and of all the beasts that shall be in those camps, as that plague.

In this manner the fight continues all the way back to Jerusalem, coming to an end in the Valley of Jehoshaphat as Joel 3:12-13 states:

Let the nations bestir themselves, and come up to the valley of Jehoshaphat; for there will I sit to judge all the nations round about. Put ye in the sickle; for the harvest is ripe: come, tread ye; for the winepress is full, the vats overflow; for their wickedness is great.

The nations that have gathered against the Jews (3:9-11) will now find themselves being treaded by the King of the Jews. It is of this treading in the Valley of Jehoshaphat that Revelation 14:19-20 speaks:

And the angel cast his sickle into the earth, and gathered the vintage of the earth, and cast it into the winepress, the great winepress, of the wrath of God. And the winepress was trodden without the city, and there came out blood from the winepress, even unto the bridles of the horses, as far as a thousand and six hundred furlongs.

The city spoken of in these verses is Jerusalem, and the winepress is just outside the city meaning it is in the Valley of Jehoshaphat. From here the armies of the Antichrist will leave for Bozrah, and they will return here as the conflict comes to an end. The blood stretches for 1,600 furlongs which is approximately 200 miles. The 200 miles may refer to the entire area from the Valley of Armageddon to Bozrah which is about 200 miles. Another possible explanation is that it refers to the round trip distance between Jerusalem and Bozrah. The fighting will begin at Jerusalem and move to Bozrah (100 miles), and with the second coming of Christ, will return back from Bozrah to the Valley of Jehoshaphat (another 100 miles). But the best explanation is based on Jeremiah 49:20-22:

Therefore hear ye the counsel of Jehovah, that he hath taken against Edom; and his purposes, that he hath purposed against the inhabitants of Teman: surely they shall drag them away, even the little ones of the flock; surely he shall make their habitation desolate over them. The earth trembleth at the noise of their fall; there is a cry, the noise whereof is heard in the Red Sea. Behold, he shall come up and fly as the eagle, and spread out his wings against Bozrah: and the heart of the mighty men of Edom at that day shall be as the heart of a woman in her pangs.

In the context (see verses 13-14), this passage is dealing with the Campaign of Armageddon. The massive blood-letting that begins at Bozrah begins moving south down the Arabah until it empties in the Red Sea at the present day cities of Eilat and Akaba. The distance from there to Jerusalem is about 200 miles. The level of blood is to be about four feet high. Exactly how this will be fulfilled remains to be seen. It may not be totally human blood but also things turned into blood by divine judgment.

Regardless of what all the blood means, the battle will come to an end in the Valley of Jehoshaphat ending the seventh stage of the Campaign of Armageddon.

THE EIGHTH STAGE: THE VICTORY ASCENT UP UPON THE MOUNT OF OLIVES

After the actual fighting is completed, there will be a victory ascent up the Mount of Olives which is described in Zechariah 14:3-4a:

Then shall Jehovah go forth, and fight against those nations, as when he fought in the day of battle. And his feet shall stand in that day upon the mount of Olives, which is before Jerusalem on the east.

Since this passage is often used as evidence that Christ will initially return to the Mount of Olives, it needs to be studied more carefully especially in light of the other passages.

Earlier in the context, Zechariah 12:7 stated that Christ will *save the tents of Judah* prior to saving the Jews in Jerusalem. The meaning of this was detailed at the end of the sixth stage of this campaign. Other passages also showing His initial return to Bozrah with the fighting commencing in that place have been previously cited. In Zechariah 14, Jehovah is first seen as going forth to fight against the nations that had gathered against the Jews (verse 3). It is only *after* the fighting of verse three that his feet will stand upon the Mount of Olives (verse 4).

Along with this victory ascent upon the Mount of Olives, a number of cataclysmic events will occur as the Great Tribulation comes to an end. These cataclysmic events will be a result of the seventh bowl judgment described in Revelation 16:17-21:

And the seventh poured out his bowl upon the air; and there came forth a great voice out of the temple, from the throne, saying, It is done: and there were lightnings, and voices, and thunders; and there was a great earthquake, such as was not since there were men upon the earth, so great an earthquake, so mighty. And the great city was divided into three parts, and the cities of the nations fell: and Babylon the great was remembered in the sight of God, to give unto her the cup of the wine of the fierceness of his wrath. And every island fled away, and the mountains were not found. And great hail, every stone about the weight of a talent, cometh down out of heaven upon men: and men blasphemed God because of the plague of the hail; for the plague thereof is exceeding great.

With the seventh bowl, a voice cries out, *It is finished*, because the seventh bowl brings the tribulation to a definite end (verse 17). This declaration will be followed by convulsions of nature including the greatest earthquake ever to occur in the history of the earth (verse 18). This will cause the city of Jerusalem to split into three divisions, while the city of Babylon will suffer the full wrath of God (verse 19). Many geographical changes will take place (verse 20) and hail will fall weighing 120 pounds (verse 21).

This earthquake that will shake Jerusalem is further described in Zechariah 14:4b-5:

And the mount of Olives shall be cleft in the midst thereof toward the east and toward the west, and there shall be a very great valley; and half of the mountain shall remove toward the north, and half of it toward the south. And ye shall flee by the valley of my mountains; for the valley of the mountains shall reach unto Azel; yea, ye shall flee, like as ye fled from before the earthquake in the days of Uzziah king of Judah; and Jehovah my God shall come, and all the holy ones with thee.

Not only will Jerusalem be split into three divisions, but the Mount of Olives will be split into two parts creating a valley running east and west. This newly formed valley will provide a way of escape for the Jewish inhabitants of Jerusalem from the earthquake that will destroy the city. In this way the inhabitants of Jerusalem will be rescued following the deliverance of the other Jews in Bozrah.

Another cataclysmic event that will take place at this time is the fifth blackout described in Matthew 24:29:

But immediately after the tribulation of those days the sun shall be darkened, and the moon shall not give her light, and the stars shall fall from heaven, and the powers of the heavens shall be shaken.

The earthquake and the blackout of this time are also described in Joel 3:14-17:

Multitudes, multitudes in the valley of decision! for the day of Jehovah is near in the valley of decision. The sun and the moon are darkened, and the stars withdraw their shining. And Jehovah will roar from Zion, and utter his voice from Jerusalem; and the heavens and the earth shall shake: but Jehovah will be a refuge unto his people, and a stronghold to the children of Israel. So shall ye know that I am Jehovah your God, dwelling in Zion my holy mountain: then shall Jerusalem be holy, and there shall no strangers pass through her any more.

With the multitudes defeated in the closing Day of Jehovah in the Valley of Jehoshaphat (verse 14), the fifth blackout will occur (verse 15) as well as the great earthquake (verse 16a). But a refuge will be provided for the Jews from these cataclysmic events (verses 16b-17) by means of the valley cutting through the Mount of Olives spoken of by Zechariah.

The Great Tribulation will come to an end with these cataclysmic events.

THE CAMPAIGN OF ARMAGEDDON

BABYLON

VALLEY OF MEGIDDO
(ARMAGEDDON)

MOUNT OF OLIVES

VALLEY OF JEHOSHAPHAT

JERUSALEM

BOZRAH OR PETRA

THE EIGHT STAGES –

1 Gathering of the Armies of the Antichrist

2 Destruction of Babylon

3 The Fall of Jerusalem

4 The Armies of the Antichrist at Bozrah

5 The National Regeneration of Israel

6 The Second Coming of Christ

7 End of the Fighting at Valley of Jehoshaphat

8 Victory Ascent Upon the Mount of Olives

PART IV

THE INTERVAL

CHAPTER XV

THE SEVENTY-FIVE DAY INTERVAL

The millennium will not begin the day immediately following the last day of the Great Tribulation, because there will be a seventy-five day interval. During this time between the Great Tribulation and the start of the Messianic Age, a number of events will occur. The existence of this interval is demonstrated in Daniel 12:11-12:

> And from the time that the continual burnt-offering shall be taken away, and the abomination that maketh desolate set up, there shall be a thousand two hundred and ninety days. Blessed is he that waiteth, and cometh to the thousand three hundred and five and thirty days.

In previous discussions, the figure of 1,260 days has often appeared, which is equivalent to three and a half years. Sometimes it is in reference to the first half of the tribulation from the signing of the seven year covenant to the takeover of the Jewish temple and the commitment of the abomination of desolation. Other times it refers to the second half of the tribulation from the abomination of desolation to the second coming during which time the Antichrist will rule the world. The demise of the Antichrist and the end of the tribulation will come 1,260 days after the midpoint of the tribulation.

In this Daniel passage two other figures are given. The first is 1,290 days, an addition of 30 days during which time the abomination of desolation remains in the temple before its removal. The second figure is 1,335 days, which is 45 days beyond the 1,290 day period and 75 days beyond the 1,260 day period. A special blessing is pronounced on those who will make it to the 1,335th day. The blessing is that those who survive until the 75th day of the interval will enter the messianic kingdom. That this is indeed a blessing will be seen in this chapter. There will be many who will fail and die before the 1,335th day comes although they did survive past the 1,260th day.

A number of events will transpire during the seventy-five day interval, and it is impossible to determine the chronological sequence of these events. So these events will be studied thematically rather than chronologically.

A. THE REMOVAL OF THE ABOMINATION OF DESOLATION

The event that will signal the beginning of the second half of the Great Tribulation will be the Antichrist's takeover of the Jewish temple from which he will declare himself to be the almighty God. He will then have the False Prophet set up his image in the temple and thus commits the abomination of desolation. The Antichrist will retain control for 1,260 days after which he will be killed. But the image which had been made alive will be allowed to continue another thirty days as Daniel 12:11 states:

> And from the time that the continual burnt-offering shall be taken away, and the abomination that maketh desolate set up, there shall be a thousand two hundred and ninety days.

The desecration of the temple is allowed to remain for thirty days beyond the end of the tribulation. Then it will be destroyed, bringing the abomination of desolation to an end.

B.   THE ANTICHRIST

Regarding this member of the counterfeit trinity, Revelation 19:20 states:

> And the beast was taken, and with him the false prophet that wrought the signs in his sight, wherewith he deceived them that had received the mark of the beast and them that worshipped his image: they two were cast alive into the lake of fire that burneth with brimstone.

It is declared that the Antichrist will be cast *alive* into the Lake of Fire. In the previous chapter, passages were cited that state that the Antichrist will be killed as one of the first casualties of the second coming of Christ. Therefore, this verse requires that the Antichrist be resurrected at this time and then be cast alive into the Lake of Fire. It is for this reason that Isaiah 14:20 declared that the body of the Antichrist will never see burial.

There is some irony to be found in this fact. As will be seen later in this chapter, the term *the first resurrection* applies to the resurrection of all the righteous although it comes in stages. The term *the second resurrection* applies to the resurrection of all the damned and this too will come in stages.

Christ was the first fruits of the first resurrection. The irony to be found here is that he who would be the counterfeit son will be allowed to act out the counterfeit role to completion by becoming the first fruits of the second resurrection. But the result of his resurrection will be the Lake of Fire.

C.   THE FALSE PROPHET

Also according to Revelation 19:20, the False Prophet, the counterfeit holy spirit, who will have a counterfeit gift of miracles by which he will do his work of deception, calling men to worship the Antichrist, to take upon themselves the mark of the beast and to worship his image, he, too, will be cast alive into the Lake of Fire.

For the first thousand years that the Lake of Fire will be inhabited, the Antichrist and the False Prophet will be there all by themselves.

D. SATAN'S FIFTH ABODE

As for Satan, the counterfeit father, he will be cast into his fifth abode* as described in Revelation 20:1-3:

> And I saw an angel coming down out of heaven, having the key of the abyss and a great chain in his hand. And he laid hold on the dragon, the old serpent, which is the Devil and Satan, and bound him for a thousand years, and cast him into the abyss, and shut it, and sealed it over him, that he should deceive the nations no more, until the thousand years should be finished: after this he must be loosed for a little time.

This passage records the binding of Satan into his fifth abode. The binder will be a member of the rank of common angels (verse 1), the lowest order of celestial beings, yet he will be able to bind a cherub who was the anointed cherub and sealed up the sum in wisdom and beauty. The duration of Satan's confinement will be one thousand years (verse 2). Verse three spells out the place, purpose and promise regarding the binding of Satan. As to the place, it will be the abyss, the temporary place of confinement for fallen angels. As to the purpose, that he should no longer be free to do his work of deception among the nations. But the binding is done with the promise that he will be released for a short while to test mankind at least one more time.

E. THE JUDGMENT OF THE GENTILES

Though a great many Gentiles will be killed through the course of the tribulation and Gentile armies will suffer slaughter in the Campaign of Armageddon, a number will still be living. All these will now be gathered together for a judgment described in two passages of Scripture. The first passage is in Joel 3:1-3:

> For, behold, in those days, and in that time, when I shall bring back the captivity of Judah and Jerusalem, I will gather all nations, and will bring them down into the valley of Jehoshaphat; and I will execute judgment upon them there for my people and for my heritage Israel, whom they have scattered among the nations: and they have parted my land, and have cast lots for my people, and have given a boy for a harlot, and sold a girl for wine, that they may drink.

* See Appendix I for the six abodes of Satan.

The timing of this judgment is given as being in conjunction with the restoration of Israel (verse 1). All the Gentiles will be gathered in the Valley of Jehoshaphat for the judgment (verse 2a). The very place where the Campaign of Armageddon will end is the same place where the Gentiles will be judged. A judgment of this nature resulting in a destiny of eternal life or eternal hell cannot be taken as a national judgment but is an individual one. The word translated *nations* also means *Gentiles*, and this is the way it should be translated.

The grounds for this judgment will be anti-Semitism or pro-Semitism (verses 2b-3). All these Gentiles will be judged on the basis of their treatment of the Jews during the Great Tribulation. The sins committed against Israel listed in this indictment are: first, scattering the Jews (in the middle of the tribulation); secondly, parting the land (Campaign of Armageddon); and thirdly, selling the Jews into slavery (Zechariah 14:1-2).

Each Gentile living at that time will be judged on the basis of his participation or his refusal to participate in these deeds.

The results of this judgment are given in the second passage in Matthew 25:31-46. The judge, the judgment, and those judged are identified in 25:31-33:

> But when the Son of man shall come in his glory, and all the angels with him, then shall he sit on the throne of his glory: and before him shall be gathered all the nations: and he shall separate them one from another, as the shepherd separateth the sheep from the goats; and he shall set the sheep on his right hand, but the goats on the left.

The judge (verse 31) will be none other than the Lord Jesus Christ who will sit on a throne encompassed by His glory in the Valley of Jehoshaphat. All the Gentiles still living will be gathered before Him for the judgment (verse 32). The Greek word translated *nations* is also the common word for *Gentiles*. The latter is the way it should be taken, for this is an individual judgment on the basis of anti-Semitism or pro-Semitism. In this judgment all the Gentiles will be divided into two camps: the pro-Semitic *sheep* camp or the anti-Semitic *goat* camp (verse 33).

Matthew 25:34-40 concerns the pro-Semitic sheep:

> Then shall the King say unto them on his right hand, Come, ye blessed of my Father, inherit the kingdom prepared for you from the foundation of the world: for I was hungry, and ye gave me to eat; I was thirsty, and ye gave me drink; I was a stranger, and ye took me in; naked, and ye clothed me; I was sick, and ye visited me; I was in prison, and ye came unto me. Then shall the righteous answer him, saying, Lord, when saw we thee hungry, and fed thee? or athirst, and gave thee drink? And when saw we thee a stranger, and took thee in? or naked, and clothed thee? And when saw we thee sick, or in prison, and came unto thee? And the King shall

answer and say unto them, Verily I say unto you, Inasmuch as ye did it
unto one of these my brethren, even these least, ye did it unto me.

The pro-Semites are those who will provide help for Christ's
brethren, the Jews, during the Great Tribulation, at a time when it will
be very dangerous to do so. The Jews who will have to flee into the
wilderness without anything with them will often be provided with
food, clothing and shelter by the sheep Gentiles. They will identify
themselves with the Jews by visiting the Jews in prison and will perform other acts of kindness to the Jews. Because of these acts they
will be allowed to enter the messianic kingdom (verse 34). It is the
sheep Gentiles who will be involved in the destruction of Babylon
(Isaiah 13:1-5). They will attain the 1,335th day and will be the ones
who will populate Gentile nations in the messianic kingdom.

As for the anti-Semitic goat Gentiles, Matthew 25:41-45 states:

Then shall he say also unto them on the left hand, Depart from me, ye
cursed, into the eternal fire which is prepared for the devil and his
angels: for I was hungry, and ye did not give me to eat; I was thirsty, and
ye gave me no drink; I was a stranger, and ye took me not in; naked, and
ye clothed me not; sick, and in prison, and ye visited me not. Then shall
they also answer, saying, Lord, when saw we thee hungry, or athirst, or a
stranger, or naked, or sick, or in prison, and did not minister unto thee?
Then shall he answer them, saying, Verily I say unto you, Inasmuch as ye
did it not unto one of these least, ye did it not unto me.

The anti-Semites who will aid the Antichrist in the program of
Jewish destruction will be killed and sent to hell (verse 41). They are
the ones who will fail to attain the 1,335th day and consequently lose
out on the millennial blessing.

The basis of the judgment will not be salvation or lack of it but
anti-Semitism or pro-Semitism. This fact stirs up a question when
compared with 25:46:

And these shall go away into eternal punishment: but the righteous into
eternal life.

The goats will be sent to hell, whereas the sheep will not only
enter the kingdom (verse 34), but they will also inherit eternal life.
Then, is their salvation based on their works be they anti-Semitic or
pro-Semitic? Not at all. The Scriptures make it quite clear that
salvation is always by grace through faith totally apart from works.
During the tribulation the Jews will become the dividing line for those
who are believers and for those who are not. Only believers will dare to
violate the rules of the Antichrist and aid the Jews. Their pro-Semitic
acts will be the result of their saved state. As James would say it, they
will show their faith by their works. But the unbelievers will demon-

strate their unbelief by their anti-Semitic acts. The judgment of the Gentiles then will determine who among the Gentiles will be allowed to enter the messianic kingdom. Only believing Gentiles will be allowed, and the evidence of their faith will be their pro-Semitic works.*

F. THE RESURRECTION OF THE OLD TESTAMENT SAINTS

The Rapture will include only the church saints and it will occur before the Great Tribulation. Later, during the seventy-five day interval, the Old Testament saints will be resurrected. This is stated by two Old Testament passages, the first being in Isaiah 26:19:

> Thy dead shall live; my dead bodies shall arise. Awake and sing, ye that dwell in the dust; for thy dew is as the dew of herbs, and the earth shall cast forth the dead.

This is a general statement of the fact that a resurrection will someday take place. A clearer picture is found in the second passage in Daniel 12:2:

> And many of them that sleep in the dust of the earth shall awake, some to everlasting life, and some to shame and everlasting contempt.

A more literal rendering of this passage would read as follows: "And (at that time) *many* (of thy people) shall awake (or be separated) *out from among* the sleepers in the earth's dust. These (who awake) shall be unto life everlasting but *those* (the rest of the sleepers who do not awake at this time) shall be unto shame and contempt everlasting."

This passage draws a clear distinction between the resurrection of the righteous and the resurrection of the unrighteous. Only the righteous saints will be resurrected at this time in order to partake of the blessings of the millennial kingdom. These are the *friends of the bridegroom* (John 3:29) who will be invited to the wedding feast with which the millennium will begin.

In the context of Daniel 12:2, Daniel is speaking of events after the tribulation, and therefore, this is the time that the Old Testament saints will be resurrected.

G. THE RESURRECTION OF THE TRIBULATION SAINTS

Not only will there be a resurrection of Old Testament saints but also a resurrection of those saints who will be killed in the course of

---

* For more details see Appendix V on "The Olivet Discourse."

the Great Tribulation according to Revelation 20:4:

> And I saw thrones, and they sat upon them, and judgment was given
> unto them: and I saw the souls of them that had been beheaded for the
> testimony of Jesus, and for the word of God, and such as worshipped not
> the beast, neither his image, and received not the mark upon their fore-
> head and upon their hand; and they lived, and reigned with Christ a
> thousand years.

In this verse John sees two groups of saints co-reigning with
Christ. First are those for whom *judgment was given unto them*. The
judgment spoken of here is the judgment seat of Christ. These saints
then will be the church saints who will be resurrected at the Rapture
of the church and will receive their rewards in the course of the
judgment.

But the second group of saints that John sees are identified as
those who have been beheaded because they did not worship the Antichrist or his image nor were they willing to consent to receive the
mark of the beast. Obviously, then, these cannot be anyone else but
the tribulation saints, and they too will be resurrected at this time.

H.   THE FIRST RESURRECTION

The First Resurrection involves the resurrection of believers only.
It is recorded in Revelation 20:5-6:

> The rest of the dead lived not until the thousand years should be
> finished. This is the first resurrection. Blessed and holy is he that hath
> part in the first resurrection: over these the second death hath no
> power; but they shall be priests of God and of Christ, and shall reign with
> him a thousand years.

According to verse five, the resurrection of the tribulation saints
completes the first resurrection, and it is separated from the completion of the second resurrection by one thousand years. The point of
verse six is that the first resurrection involves believers only, and that
is why it is blessed and holy to be a participant in the first resurrection.

However, the first resurrection is not a general one-time resurrection of righteous ones but comes in stages in an orderly progression according to I Corinthians 15:20-23:

> But now hath Christ been raised from the dead, the firstfruits of them
> that are asleep. For since by man came death, by man came also the
> resurrection of the dead. For as in Adam all die, so also in Christ shall all be
> made alive. But each in his own order: Christ the firstfruits; then they that
> are Christ's, at his coming.

After declaring that a resurrection of the righteous will occur (verses 20-22), Paul states that the righteous will be resurrected *each in his own order* (verse 23). The word translated *order* is a military term used for sequence of troops of soldiers marching in a procession or in battle. There is one troop division first followed by another troop division and so on. The point is that all the righteous will not be resurrected at the same time but rather in a definite sequential order.

The first of these orders was the resurrection of Jesus Christ (verse 23). He is the firstfruits of the first resurrection. The second is the resurrection of the church saints at the Rapture of the church (I Thessalonians 4:16) prior to the Great Tribulation. Then will come the Old Testament saints (Isaiah 26:19, Daniel 12:2) during the seventy-five day interval after the tribulation, and finally the tribulation saints (Revelation 20:4). The resurrection of the tribulation saints completes the first resurrection. There will be no such thing as a resurrection of millennial saints for reasons to be discussed in Chapter XVII.

These are the events of the seventy-five day interval leading up towards that long, special period of history the faithful look forward to—the millennium or the Messianic Age.

PART V

THE MESSIANIC KINGDOM

266

CHART #4

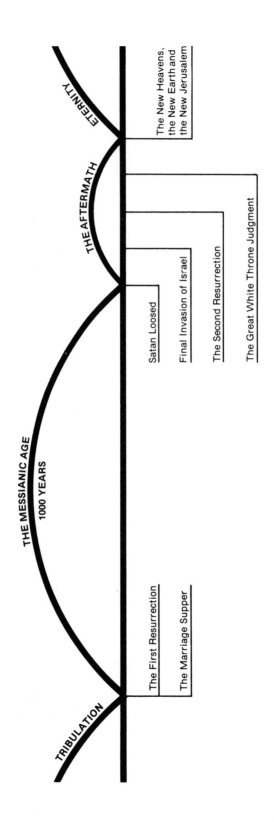

CHAPTER XVI

THE BASIS FOR THE BELIEF
IN THE MESSIANIC KINGDOM

Premillennialists have often been criticized for basing their belief in a millennium entirely on one passage of Scripture, Revelation twenty. Because it is found in a book well noted for its high use of symbols, they say it is foolish to take the "one thousand years" literally. But that is hardly a valid criticism.

To begin with, while it is true that Revelation uses many symbols, it has already been shown that the meaning of all those symbols is explained either by Revelation itself or elsewhere in the Scriptures. Furthermore, never are years used in a symbolic way in this book. If they are symbolic, the symbolism is nowhere explained. The mention of 1,260 days, 42 months, and 3½ years are all literal and not symbolic. Hence, there is no need to take the 1,000 years as anything but literal years. The desire to spiritualize the text always places the burden of proof on the interpreter. Without objective proof it will result in a subjective interpretation.

It is of course true that the figure of *one thousand years* is only found in Revelation twenty. But it is recorded six different times in this one text and if repetition tries to do anything, it certainly endeavors to make a point.

But while it is true that the *millennium* (that is, one thousand years) is found only in Revelation twenty, the belief in the messianic age does not rest on this passage alone. In fact, it hardly rests on it at all. The *basis* for the belief in the messianic age is the numerous prophecies of the Old Testament that speak of the coming of the Messiah who will reign on David's throne and rule over a peaceful kingdom. There is a great amount of material in the Old Testament on the messianic age. The belief in a messianic age rests on the basis of a literal interpretation of this massive material.

The only real contribution that Revelation makes to the knowledge of the kingdom is to disclose just how long the messianic kingdom will last, namely one thousand years, for which the term *millennium* is used. This is the one key truth concerning the kingdom that was not revealed in the Old Testament.

It is in light of this that it is possible to understand why so much of the book is spent on the Great Tribulation and so little on the millennium. While much of the material in Revelation 4-19 is found scattered in the pages of the Old Testament, it is impossible to place these events in chronological sequence using only the Old Testament. The Revelation provides the framework by which this can be done. A great portion of the Revelation was used to accomplish this goal.

On the other hand, all of the various features and facets of the messianic age have already been revealed in the Old Testament. They portray the general characteristics of life in the kingdom, which do not raise the problem of an order of sequence. Hence, there was no reason to spend a great deal of time on the messianic age in Revelation. Most of what was needed to be revealed was already known from the Old Testament.

However, there were two things about the messianic age which were not revealed in the Old Testament. The first was the length of the messianic age. While the Old Testament prophets foresaw a long period of time of a peaceful messianic reign, they did not reveal just how long this would last. To answer this question, the Revelation states that it will be exactly one thousand years.

A second thing that was unknown from the Old Testament prophets was the circumstances by which the kingdom would come to an end and how this would lead into the Eternal Order. This is also revealed by the Revelation.

These two items are all that Revelation twenty added to the knowledge of the messianic age. The belief in a messianic kingdom does not rest on this passage, but is based on the numerous prophecies of the Old Testament prophets.

Another basis for the belief in a coming kingdom rests on the four unconditional, unfulfilled covenants God made with Israel. These covenants are unconditional and so rely solely on God for their fulfillment and not on Israel. They are also unfulfilled and since God is One who keeps His promises, they must be fulfilled in the future. They can only be fulfilled within the framework of a messianic age or a millennial kingdom. More will be said about these covenants in chapter XIX, but the main points will be summarized here.

The first of these is the Abrahamic Covenant that promised an eternal seed developing into a nation that will possess the promised land with some definite borders. While that nation, the Jews, continues to exist, never in Jewish history have they possessed all of the promised land. For this promise to be fulfilled, there must be a future kingdom. Besides, the possession of the land was not merely a promise to Abraham's seed, but to Abraham personally when God said, *To thee will I give it and to thy seed forever.* For God to fulfill His promise to Abraham (as well as to Isaac and Jacob), there must be a future kingdom.

The second covenant is the Palestinian Covenant that spoke of a world-wide regathering of the Jews and repossession of the land following their dispersion. While the dispersion has already occurred and is in effect today, the regathering and repossession of the land still awaits fulfillment in the future. This too requires a future kingdom.

The Davidic Covenant is the third covenant which promised four eternal things: an eternal house (dynasty), an eternal throne, an eternal kingdom, and one eternal person. The dynasty became eternal because it culminated in a Person who is Himself eternal: Jesus the Messiah. For that reason the throne and kingdom will be eternal as well. But Jesus has never yet sat on the throne of David ruling over a kingdom of Israel. The re-establishment of the Davidic throne and Christ's rule over the kingdom still awaits a future fulfillment. It requires a future kingdom.

The last of these covenants is the New Covenant that spoke of the national regeneration and salvation of Israel encompassing each individual Jewish member of that nation. This, too, awaits its final fulfillment and requires a future kingdom.

It is the extensive prophetic writings as well as all of these covenants that provide the basis for the belief in a future messianic kingdom, and not merely one chapter of a highly symbolic book.

CHAPTER XVII

GENERAL CHARACTERISTICS
OF THE MESSIANIC KINGDOM

A great many of the Old Testament prophets directed their attention to the details of the messianic age, providing an overall, comprehensive picture of life during that time. This chapter will be concerned with those passages dealing with the general character-istics of the messianic age that will be true for both Jews and Gentiles alike.

A. PSALM 15:1-5

Jehovah, who shall sojourn in thy tabernacle? Who shall dwell in thy holy hill? He that walketh uprightly, and worketh righteousness, and speaketh truth in his heart; he that slandereth not with his tongue, nor doeth evil to his friend, nor taketh up a reproach against his neighbor; in whose eyes a reprobate is despised, but who honoreth them that fear Jehovah; he that sweareth to his own hurt, and changeth not; he that putteth not out his money to interest, nor taketh reward against the innocent. He that doeth these things shall never be moved.

This passage describes the righteousness that will characterize a citizen in the kingdom. Although not every individual in the kingdom will necessarily be characterized with this kind of righteousness, for reasons to be discussed later in this chapter, most will be.

B. PSALM 24:1-6

The earth is Jehovah's, and the fulness thereof; the world, and they that dwell therein. For he hath founded it upon the seas, and established it upon the floods. Who shall ascend into the hill of Jehovah? And who shall stand in his holy place? He that hath clean hands, and a pure heart; who hath not lifted up his soul unto falsehood, and hath not sworn deceit-fully. He shall receive a blessing from Jehovah, and righteousness from the God of his salvation. This is the generation of them that seek after him, that seek thy face, even Jacob.

This passage describes the establishment of the kingdom and the righteousness that will characterize a man who will be rightly related to God at that time.

C. ISAIAH 2:2-4

And it shall come to pass in the latter days, that the mountain of Jehovah's house shall be established on the top of the mountains, and shall be exalted above the hills; and all nations shall flow unto it. And many peoples shall go and say, Come ye, and let us go up to the mountain of Jehovah, to the house of the God of Jacob; and he will teach us of his ways, and we will walk in his paths: for out of Zion shall go forth the law, and the word of Jehovah from Jerusalem. And he will judge between the nations, and will decide concerning many peoples; and they shall beat their swords into plowshares, and their spears into pruning-hooks; nation shall not lift up sword against nation, neither shall they learn war any more.

In this passage Isaiah describes one of the major characteristics of the messianic kingdom, that of universal peace. While differences between nations will arise, such differences will no longer be settled by military conflicts but only by the Word of the Lord from Jerusalem. Even the art of warfare will be forgotten.

D. ISAIAH 11:6-9

And the wolf shall dwell with the lamb, and the leopard shall lie down with the kid; and the calf and the young lion and the fatling together; and a little child shall lead them. And the cow and the bear shall feed; their young ones shall lie down together; and the lion shall eat straw like the ox. And the sucking child shall play on the hole of the asp, and the weaned child shall put his hand on the adder's den. They shall not hurt nor destroy in all my holy mountain; for the earth shall be full of the knowledge of Jehovah, as the waters cover the sea.

The universal peace described in the earlier passage will extend even to the animal kingdom. All animals will return to the Edenic state and become vegetarians (verses 6-7). The oldest of enemies, man and snake, will be able to live in compatibility in that day (verse 8), for the knowledge of God will permeate throughout the entire world affecting man and animal alike (verse 9).

E. ISAIAH 65:17-25

For, behold, I create new heavens and a new earth; and the former things shall not be remembered, nor come into mind. But be ye glad and rejoice for ever in that which I create; for, behold, I create Jerusalem a rejoicing, and her people a joy. And I will rejoice in Jerusalem, and joy in my people; and there shall be heard in her no more the voice of weeping and the voice of crying. There shall be no more thence an infant of days, nor an old man that hath not filled his days; for the child shall die a hundred years old, and the sinner being a hundred years old shall be accursed. And they shall build houses, and inhabit them; and they shall plant vineyards, and eat the fruit of them. They shall not build, and another inhabit; they shall not plant, and another eat: for as the days of a tree shall be the days of my people, and my chosen shall long enjoy the work of their hands. They shall not labor in vain, nor bring forth for calamity; for they are the seed of the blessed of Jehovah, and their offspring with them. And it shall come to pass that, before they call, I will answer; and while they are yet speaking, I will hear. The wolf and the lamb shall feed together, and the lion shall eat straw like the ox; and dust shall be the serpent's food.

They shall not hurt nor destroy in all my holy mountain, saith Jehovah.

This passage begins with the announcement of the creation of new heavens and a new earth (verse 17). These new heavens and new earth are not to be confused with those of Revelation 21-22. The latter describes the new heavens and new earth of the Eternal Order, while the Isaiah passage describes those of the messianic age which will be a renovation of the present heavens and earth. Those of the Revelation are not a renovation but a brand new order. Hence, for the millennium, there will be a total renovation of the heavens and the earth. The fact that the term *create* is used shows that this renovation will be a miraculous one possible by God alone. The result of this renovation will be a continuation of many things of the old order and a number of new things. A good example of the old and the new is to be seen in what the Scriptures say about the land of Israel. Israel will also undergo the renovation process. Some things of the old order will remain, such as the Mediterranean Sea and the Dead Sea. But a number of things will be brand new, such as the exceeding high mountain (the highest in the world) in the center of the country. Following this announcement of new heavens and a new earth, there is a description of the millennial Jerusalem (verses 18-19). The millennial Jerusalem will be studied in detail in chapter XIX.

Verse 20 is especially significant for it discusses life and death in the kingdom. This verse teaches several things. *First*, there will no longer be any infant mortality in the millennium; everyone who is born in the kingdom will reach a certain age. *Secondly*, the specific age at which one may die is the age of one hundred. So, with infant mortality removed, everyone born in the millennium will live at least until his one hundredth year of life. Because of the prolongation of life in the millennium, those who do die at the age of one hundred will be considered as having died young. *Thirdly*, this verse limits the people dying at the age of one hundred to those who are sinners; namely, unbelievers as only they would be considered *accursed*. So then, death in the kingdom will be for unbelievers only.

Comparing this passage with what is stated about salvation in other passages, the entire concept of life and death in the kingdom can be summarized as follows. When the kingdom begins, all natural men, both Jews and Gentiles, will be believers. The Jews in their entirety will be saved just prior to the second coming of Christ. All unbelieving Gentiles (goats) will be killed during the seventy-five day interval between the tribulation and the millennium and only believing Gentiles (sheep) will be able to enter the kingdom.

However, in the process of time, there will be birth in the kingdom of both Jews and Gentiles. These newly born, natural people will continue to inherit the sin nature from their natural parents and will also be in need of regeneration. Although Satan is confined, thus reducing temptation, the sin nature is quite capable of rebelling against God apart from Satanic activity. In time, there will be unsaved people living in the kingdom in need of regeneration.

As in the past, the means of salvation is by grace through faith and the content of faith will be the death of Christ for sin and His subsequent resurrection. Those born in the kingdom will have up until their one hundredth year to receive Christ. If they do not, they will die in their hundredth year. The unbeliever will not be able to live past his first century of life. However, if they do receive Christ, they will live throughout the millennium and never die. Thus, death in the millennium will be for unbelievers only. This is why the Bible nowhere speaks of a resurrection of millennial saints. This is why the resurrection of the tribulation saints is said to complete the first resurrection (Revelation 20:4-6).

It is also clear from the New Covenant of Jeremiah 31:31-34 that there will be no Jewish unbelievers in the kingdom; all Jews born during the kingdom will accept the Messiah by their one hundredth year. Unbelief will be among the Gentiles only, and therefore, death will exist only among the Gentiles.

Verses 21-24 continue to describe life in the kingdom as a time of personal peace and prosperity. It will be a time of building and planting. He who builds and plants is guaranteed the enjoyment of the labors of his hands, for many of the effects of the curse will be removed (verses 21-22a). Life will be characterized by longevity (verse 22b), absence of calamity and turmoil (verse 23), and instantaneous response from God (verse 24). As in Isaiah 11:6-9, the animal kingdom will be at peace with each other and with man (verse 25).

F. MICAH 4:1-5

But in the latter days it shall come to pass, that the mountain of Jehovah's house shall be established on the top of the mountains, and it shall be exalted above the hills; and peoples shall flow unto it. And many nations shall go and say, Come ye, and let us go up to the mountain of Jehovah, and to the house of the God of Jacob; and he will teach us of his ways, and we will walk in his paths. For out of Zion shall go forth the law, and the word of Jehovah from Jerusalem; and he will judge between many peoples, and will decide concerning strong nations afar off: and they shall beat their swords into plowshares, and their spears into pruning-hooks; nation shall not lift up sword against nation, neither shall they learn war any more. But they shall sit every man under his vine and under his fig-tree; and none shall make them afraid; for the mouth of Jehovah of hosts hath spoken it. For all the peoples walk every one in the name of his god; and we will walk in the name of Jehovah our God for ever and ever.

The first three verses of this passage are the same as those found in Isaiah 2:2-4 which speak of the mountain of Jehovah's house becoming the center of world Gentile attention, the kingdom being characterized as a time of messianic teaching, and the absence of war as universal peace permeates the entire kingdom. But, Micah adds that the kingdom will be a time of personal peace and prosperity (verse 4) with Israel's total allegiance being to God (verse 5).

SUMMARY

To summarize the general characteristics of the messianic kingdom, it will be a time when Satan will be bound, causing a reduction of both sin and death though neither of these two will be eliminated at that time. It will be a time of universal and personal prosperity and peace between man and man, between animal and animal, and between man and animal, with many of the effects (but not all) of the curse removed. It will be a time characterized by truth, holiness and righteousness with justice continually being dispersed from Jerusalem. It will be a time of labor in building and planting with guaranteed results and promised enjoyment of these labors.

CHAPTER XVIII

THE GOVERNMENT OF THE
MESSIANIC KINGDOM

The messianic kingdom will be administered through an absolute monarchy with a definite chain of command and lines of authority. The absolute monarch will be the person of Jesus Christ. The delegated authority will be split into two branches: a Jewish branch of government and a Gentile one, each in turn having a chain of command. It can be charted out as follows:

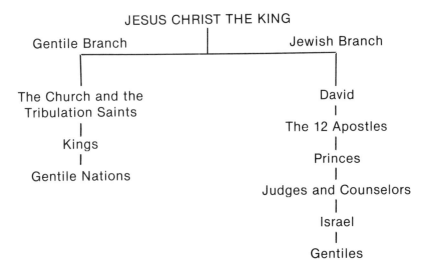

This chapter will be concerned with various Scriptures that speak of the system of government in the kingdom.

A. THE KING — THE LORD JESUS CHRIST

That Christ is to sit upon the throne of David and rule in a kingdom over Israel with a dominion extending over all the Gentiles is the clearcut teaching of the Old and New Testaments. The Davidic Covenant upon which the physical reign of Christ is based will be discussed in the next chapter. In this chapter only those passages that develop the Davidic Covenant and such that speak of Christ as King over a literal kingdom will be dealt with.

1. THE ESTABLISHMENT OF THE THRONE

That it is in the program of God to set up His Son as the King in Jerusalem is the clear teaching of Psalm 2:6-8:

Yet I have set my king **upon my** holy hill of Zion. I will tell of the decree: Jehovah said unto me, Thou art my son; this day have I begotten thee. Ask of me, and I will give thee the nations for thine inheritance, and the uttermost parts of the earth for thy possession.

Although the throne of Christ will be established in Jerusalem, His dominion will not stop at the border of Israel but will extend throughout the entire earth with every Gentile nation falling under His domain.

Christ ruling upon the re-established throne of David and ruling over a kingdom is the theme of Isaiah 9:6-7:

For unto us a child is born, unto us a son is given; and the government shall be upon his shoulder: and his name shall be called Wonderful, Counsellor, Mighty God, Everlasting Father, Prince of Peace. Of the increase of his government and of peace there shall be no end, upon the throne of David, and upon his kingdom, to establish it, and to uphold it with justice and with righteousness from henceforth even for ever. The zeal of Jehovah of hosts will perform this.

A child is born into the Jewish world who is a son of the house of David upon whom the reins of government will rest (verse 6a). Yet, names are given to this child that can only be true of God Himself (verse 6b). The eternity of the Davidic dynasty, throne, and kingdom is assured for it rests in the God-Man. As to His humanity, He is a descendant of David. As to His deity, He is eternal and so is His throne. With these facts clearly established, Isaiah proceeds to describe the establishment of the rule of Christ. The government that will be set up will increase in authority and in peace. Nor will there be any end to the throne of David or of the rule of Christ, for it is the God-Man who will establish it and who will uphold it. It will be characterized by justice and righteousness forever. The guarantee that it will be so established is the burning zeal of God, a zeal that will continue to burn until the kingdom is realized. Since God's zeal intends to perform it, it will surely come about.

To this statement, Isaiah 16:5 adds:

And a throne shall be established in lovingkindness; and one shall sit thereon in truth, in the tent of David, judging, and seeking justice, and swift to do righteousness.

As if to reiterate his previous statement, Isaiah declares again that a throne will surely be established on the basis of God's loyal love. The one sitting on the throne will be a member of the house of David who will be characterized by truth. He will be King and Judge, ensuring that justice is carried out—a justice springing from the righteousness of the King.

Very similar to Isaiah are two prophecies found in Jeremiah. The first is Jeremiah 23:5-6:

> Behold, the days come, saith Jehovah, that I will raise unto David a righteous Branch, and he shall reign as king and deal wisely, and shall execute justice and righteousness in the land. In his days Judah shall be saved, and Israel shall dwell safely; and this is his name whereby he shall be called: Jehovah our righteousness.

Again, there is a descendant of David that will sit on David's throne. Yet this descendant is called *Jehovah our righteousness*. So the One sitting on David's throne is none other than the God-Man. And because it is the God-Man, His reign will be characterized by wisdom, justice and righteousness. It is in Him that the security of Israel will lie.

The second passage, Jeremiah 33:14-17 adds:

> Behold, the days come, saith Jehovah, that I will perform that good word which I have spoken concerning the house of Israel and concerning the house of Judah. In those days, and at that time, will I cause a Branch of righteousness to grow up unto David; and he shall execute justice and righteousness in the land. In those days shall Judah be saved, and Jerusalem shall dwell safely; and this is the name whereby she shall be called: Jehovah our righteousness. For thus saith Jehovah: David shall never want a man to sit upon the throne of the house of Israel.

Beginning with the reaffirmation of God's intention to fulfill His covenant with David (verse 14), Jeremiah restates the basic points of his statements in 23:5-6 (verses 15-16). Under no circumstances will the house of David be allowed to become extinct (verse 17). The rest of Jeremiah 33 continues to reaffirm God's intention to fulfill all the conditions of the Davidic Covenant, and these passages will be dealt with in the next chapter.

Though the throne of Christ is to be established in Jerusalem, the reign of Christ will extend over the entire earth, according to Zechariah 14:9:

> And Jehovah shall be King over all the earth: in that day shall Jehovah be one, and his name one.

In that day, Zechariah points out, the Messiah will be the head of the world and will be considered as the one God by all humanity.

That the re-establishment of the Davidic throne with Christ reigning over the kingdom of Israel is not strictly an Old Testament doctrine is clear from Luke 1:30-33:

> And the angel said unto her, Fear not, Mary: for thou hast found favor

> with God. And behold, thou shalt conceive in thy womb, and bring forth a son, and shalt call his name JESUS. He shall be great, and shall be called the Son of the Most High: and the Lord God shall give unto him the throne of his father David: and he shall reign over the house of Jacob for ever; and of his kingdom there shall be no end.

After declaring to Mary that she is to give birth to a son in spite of her virginity (verses 30-31), Gabriel goes on to explain the future authority of that son. As in the Isaiah and Jeremiah passages, the son will be born into the Jewish world and is to sit on David's throne as the God-Man (verse 32). As to His deity, He is the Son of God, but as to His humanity, He is a descendant of David. The Son will be given the throne of David by divine appointment. He is to reign over Israel, and there is to be no end to His rule (verse 33). This announcement of Gabriel concerning the establishment of Jesus as a King on David's throne is clearly rooted in the prophecies of the Old Testament.

2. THE CHARACTER OF HIS REIGN

A number of passages portray the characteristics of the reign of Christ. One major characteristic, stemming from the absolute monarchy that will exist, is that Christ will rule with a rod of iron. Revelation 12:5 states:

> And she was delivered of a son, a man child, who is to rule all the nations with a rod of iron: and her child was caught up unto God, and unto his throne.

This is reaffirmed by Revelation 19:15:

> And out of his mouth proceedeth a sharp sword, that with it he should smite the nations: and he shall rule them with a rod of iron: and he treadeth the winepress of the fierceness of the wrath of God, the Almighty.

This ironhanded rule by Christ will be a necessity due to the fact that nations will exist and the people populating them will still have their sin nature. It has already been pointed out in the previous chapter that, after the first generation, there will be unbelievers present in the kingdom. The natural outworking of this sin nature will have to be restrained. The kingdom will not be a democracy but an absolute monarchy. The reign of Christ will be a strict one, and the righteous and just laws emanating from Jerusalem will have to be obeyed.

The beginning of the reign of Christ will be marked by a procession of the King into the millennial Jerusalem described in Psalm 24:7-10:

Lift up your heads, O ye gates; and be ye lifted up, ye everlasting doors: and the King of glory will come in. Who is the King of glory? Jehovah strong and mighty, Jehovah mighty in battle. Lift up your heads, O ye gates; yea, lift them up, ye everlasting doors; and the King of glory will come in. Who is this King of glory? Jehovah of hosts, he is the King of glory.

An extended treatment of the character of His reign is in Psalm 72:1-19:

Give the king thy judgments, O God, and thy righteousness unto the king's son. He will judge thy people with righteousness, and thy poor with justice. The mountains shall bring peace to the people, and the hills, in righteousness. He will judge the poor of the people, he will save the children of the needy, and will break in pieces the oppressor. They shall fear thee while the sun endureth, and so long as the moon, throughout all generations. He will come down like rain upon the mown grass, as showers that water the earth. In his days shall the righteous flourish, and abundance of peace, till the moon be no more. He shall have dominion also from sea to sea, and from the River unto the ends of the earth. They that dwell in the wilderness shall bow before him; and his enemies shall lick the dust. The kings of Tarshish and of the isles shall render tribute: the kings of Sheba and Seba shall offer gifts. Yea, all kings shall fall down before him; all nations shall serve him. For he will deliver the needy when he crieth, and the poor, that hath no helper. He will have pity on the poor and needy, and the souls of the needy he will save. He will redeem their soul from oppression and violence; and precious will their blood be in his sight: and they shall live; and to him shall be given of the gold of Sheba: and men shall pray for him continually; they shall bless him all the day long. There shall be abundance of grain in the earth upon the top of the mountains; the fruit thereof shall shake like Lebanon: and they of the city shall flourish like grass of the earth. His name shall endure for ever; his name shall be continued as long as the sun: and men shall be blessed in him; all nations shall call him happy. Blessed be Jehovah God, the God of Israel, who only doeth wondrous things: and blessed be his glorious name for ever; and let the whole earth be filled with his glory. Amen, and Amen.

This entire Psalm describes the reign of the righteous King. His reign will be characterized by justice, holiness and righteousness so that the innocent will receive justice while the guilty will be condemned (verses 1-7). The extent of His domain will clearly be universal and international (verses 8-11). It will extend from *sea to sea*, a reference to the western (Mediterranean Sea) and eastern (Dead Sea) boundaries of the millennial Israel. Furthermore, it will extend from *the River*; that is, the Euphrates which is the prophesied northern boundary of the restored Jewish state. One would expect the next phrase to describe the southern boundary as the "brook of Egypt" but instead the Psalmist writes *unto the ends of the earth*. The point being made is that, although the throne is set up in the land of Israel as seen by the mention of the western, eastern and northern boundaries, the rule will not be confined to Israel alone. It will overflow the boundaries of Israel reaching to the ends of the earth (verse 8). His friends and enemies alike will do obeisance to Him (verse 9), and all other kings among the nations will subject themselves to His authority (verses 10-11). Because He will rule with a rod of iron and in justice, holiness and righteousness, any and all injustices against the righteous will be severely rectified, and the righteous will be exalted (verses 12-15). His reign will be further characterized with an abundance of productivity (verse 16). All will be blessed in the King and they will bless Him, for He is the eternal God-Man (verses 17-19).

Isaiah 11:1-5 provides yet another description of the character of His reign:

> And there shall come forth a shoot out of the stock of Jesse, and a branch out of his roots shall bear fruit: and the Spirit of Jehovah shall rest upon him, the spirit of wisdom and understanding, the spirit of counsel and might, the spirit of knowledge and of the fear of Jehovah; and his delight shall be in the fear of Jehovah; and he shall not judge after the sight of his eyes, neither decide after the hearing of his ears; but with righteousness shall he judge the poor, and decide with equity for the meek of the earth; and he shall smite the earth with the rod of his mouth, and with the breath of his lips shall he slay the wicked. And righteousness shall be the girdle of his waist, and faithfulness the girdle of his loins.

Isaiah begins by describing the origin of the King, namely that of the house of David (verse 1). He is endowed with the fullness of the Holy Spirit depicted by the seven-fold manifestations of the Spirit of God (verse 2). This endowment of the fullness of the Holy Spirit is demonstrated in the five results mentioned in verses 3-4. Finally, the King and His reign are characterized by righteousness and faithfulness (verse 5).

So, the Lord Jesus Christ will be both the King of Israel and the King of the world. Under His absolute authority and monarchy there will be two branches of government established, the Gentile branch and the Jewish branch.

B.   THE GENTILE BRANCH OF GOVERNMENT

1.   THE CHURCH AND THE TRIBULATION SAINTS

The part that the church is to have in the millennial reign of Christ is found in Revelation 20:4-6:

> And I saw thrones, and they sat upon them, and judgment was given unto them: and I saw the souls of them that had been beheaded for the testimony of Jesus, and for the word of God, and such as worshipped not the beast, neither his image, and received not the mark upon their forehead and upon their hand; and they lived, and reigned with Christ a

thousand years. The rest of the dead lived not until the thousand years should be finished. This is the first resurrection. Blessed and holy is he that hath part in the first resurrection: over these the second death hath no power; but they shall be priests of God and of Christ, and shall reign with him a thousand years.

In verse 4, John describes the saints that are to co-reign with Christ. First, there are those to whom judgment has been given. This would be a reference to the church saints who were raptured sometime preceding the Great Tribulation. The judgment spoken of is that of the Judgment Seat of Christ, the judgment of the believer's works. In fact, it is the outcome of this judgment that will determine the position of each church saint in the kingdom.*

A second group of saints who are to co-reign with Christ are those who *had been beheaded for the testimony of Jesus*. These are the believers who will be martyred during the first half of the Great Tribulation and were mentioned under the fifth seal (Revelation 6:9-11).

A third group are those who did not worship the Antichrist or his image, nor received the mark of 666 on their forehead or on their right hand. Since these things were initiated only at the middle of the tribulation. this third group of saints are those of the second half of the Great Tribulation.

So then, both church and tribulation saints will co-reign with Christ for the thousand years. The Old Testament saints will have a different destiny to be discussed in the next chapter.

The facts of verse four mark the conclusion of the first resurrection. The first resurrection is the resurrection of all righteous ones and is separated from the second resurrection by a thousand years. Christ was resurrected three days after His death, and thus He became the first-fruits of the first resurrection (I Corinthians 15:23). The church saints will be resurrected at the Rapture sometime before the tribulation (I Thessalonians 4:16). Finally, the Old Testament saints (Isaiah 26:19, Daniel 12:2) and the tribulation saints (Revelation 20:4) will be resurrected in the seventy-five day interval between the tribulation and the millennium. It has already been shown that death during the kingdom will be for unbelievers only. Therefore, since only unbelievers die during the millennium, no resurrection of millennial saints will be necessary.

As a result, the first resurrection will be totally complete with the resurrection of the tribulation saints. One thousand years will pass before the second resurrection is brought to completion.

The church and tribulation saints will co-reign with Christ over the Gentile nations. They will be the King's representative authority and will carry out His decrees to the nations.

---

* For details see Chapter VI.

2. KINGS

As has been mentioned earlier in Psalm 72, the different Gentile nations will have kings over them. This fact will be seen in some other passages in the next chapter. These kings will have their natural bodies while the saints, who will be over them, will have their spiritual, resurrection bodies. While the individual kings will be the supreme rulers over their own nations, they themselves will be under the authority of the church and tribulation saints.

So then, in the Gentile branch of government, the chain of command will be from Christ to the church and tribulation saints to the kings of the Gentile nations.

C. THE JEWISH BRANCH OF GOVERNMENT

1. DAVID — THE KING AND PRINCE

The absolute monarchy of the Messiah will extend to Israel as well as to the Gentile nations. But directly under Christ, having authority over all Israel, will be the resurrected David, who is given both titles of king and prince. He will be a king because he will rule over Israel, but he will be a prince in that he will be under the authority of Christ. Just as all the Gentile nations will have kings, so will Israel. The difference is that the Gentile kings will all have their natural bodies while David will have his resurrected body.

There are several passages which speak of David as being king over Israel and prince under King Messiah such as Jeremiah 30:9:

> But they shall serve Jehovah their God, and David their king, whom I will raise up unto them.

Not only will Israel in the future serve Jehovah their God, but they will also serve David their king.

Another passage is Ezekiel 34:23-24:

> And I will set up one shepherd over them, and he shall feed them, even my servant David; he shall feed them, and he shall be their shepherd. And I, Jehovah, will be their God, and my servant David prince among them; I, Jehovah, have spoken it.

When the restoration of Israel comes, it will no longer be in the form of two kingdoms with each one having their own king. They will be a reunited nation with only one head, and that head will be the resurrected David who will serve as their prince. So while Jehovah will serve as their God and absolute King, David will serve under Him as God's prince over Israel.

Later, in Ezekiel 37:24-25 the prophet writes:

> And my servant David shall be king over them; and they all shall have one shepherd: they shall also walk in mine ordinances, and observe my statutes, and do them. And they shall dwell in the land that I have given unto Jacob my servant, wherein your fathers dwelt; and they shall dwell therein, they, and their children, and their children's children, for ever: and David my servant shall be their prince for ever.

Ezekiel reiterates the fact that they will have David to function as the king of Israel. He is to be their prince and shepherd. Under his guidance Israel will be able to keep the righteous commandments of God. The land will be restored to them as well as David their king.

One final passage that points to this aspect of the government of the millennium is Hosea 3:5:

> Afterward shall the children of Israel return, and seek Jehovah their God, and David their king, and shall come with fear unto Jehovah and to his goodness in the latter days.

Making the same points as Jeremiah and Ezekiel, Hosea states that in the future restoration, Israel will not only be subservient to Jehovah their God but also to David their king.

While all these passages are often explained as actually referring to David's greater son, Christ, nothing in the text indicates that *David* is to be taken symbolically. In keeping with literal interpretation, it is best to take the text as it reads meaning the literal David who, in his resurrected form, will function as the king over Israel and as a prince in subjection to the King of the world: Christ. It is in this sense that David will serve both as king and prince. From the viewpoint of Israel, David will be their king ruling over them. But from the viewpoint of the Messiah, David will be a prince.

2. THE TWELVE APOSTLES OVER THE TWELVE TRIBES

On two occasions Jesus promised the twelve apostles that in the kingdom they will be in authority over the twelve tribes. The first of these passages is Matthew 19:28:

> And Jesus said unto them, Verily I say unto you, that ye who have followed me, in the regeneration when the Son of man shall sit on the throne of his glory, ye also shall sit upon twelve thrones, judging the twelve tribes of Israel.

The time referred to is that of the regeneration or renovation of the earth when Christ will sit upon the re-established throne of David in His glory. It is then that twelve other thrones will be set up, one over each of the twelve tribes, and the apostles will sit on these.

The second passage is found in Luke 22:28-30:

> But ye are they that have continued with me in my temptations; and I appoint unto you a kingdom, even as my Father appointed unto me, that ye may eat and drink at my table in my kingdom; and ye shall sit on thrones judging the twelve tribes of Israel.

The millennial kingdom that the Father appointed for the Son was extended by Christ to the twelve apostles. The difference is that Christ's domain will be over all the world, David's rule over all Israel, while the apostles' jurisdiction will be over particular tribes. The twelve are promised two privileges with this appointment. The first is that they will be continually with Christ and eating and drinking at His table throughout the kingdom period. The second privilege is to have their own thrones from which they will rule over the tribes of Israel.

Unfortunately, nothing is said as to which apostle is to rule over which tribe. So the answer to that question awaits the fulfillment in the future kingdom.

3. PRINCES

In addition to the already specified positions of government, there is the mention of other rulers simply entitled as *princes*. One such passage is found in Isaiah 32:1:

> Behold, a king shall reign in righteousness, and princes shall rule in justice.

The king reigning in righteousness will be the Lord Jesus Christ. Along with Him there is the mention of *princes* who will be in positions of authority and just in character.

A second passage is Ezekiel 45:8:

> In the land it shall be to him for a possession in Israel: and my princes shall no more oppress my people; but they shall give the land to the house of Israel according to their tribes.

The entire context of this passage (Ezekiel 40-48) will be discussed in the next chapter. But for now, it should be noted that once again there is a mention of *princes* who are in positions of authority in the millennium. Unlike princes in the past, these will not be characterized by oppression. Involved in their authority will be the partitioning of the land of Israel into its twelve tribal divisions.

The resurrected Zerubbabel mentioned in Haggai 2:20-23 will very likely be among these princes:

> And the word of Jehovah came the second time unto Haggai in the four and twentieth day of the month, saying, Speak to Zerubbabel, governor of Judah, saying, I will shake the heavens and the earth; and I will over-

throw the throne of kingdoms; and I will destroy the strength of the kingdoms of the nations; and I will overthrow the chariots, and those that ride in them; and the horses and their riders shall come down, every one by the sword of his brother. In that day, saith Jehovah of hosts, will I take thee, O Zerubbabel, my servant, the son of Shealtiel, saith Jehovah, and will make thee as a signet; for I have chosen thee, saith Jehovah of hosts.

The time of Zerubbabel's exalted position will be after the shaking of the heavens and the earth (verses 20-21) and the destruction of the invading armies (verse 22). Both of these will occur at the second coming of Christ. It is after these events that Zerubbabel is promised an exalted position (verse 23) which will make him as close to God as a signet ring is to a king. Zerubbabel has been chosen for an exalted position in the kingdom and will apparently be among the princes mentioned by the other two prophets. Zerubbabel is also of the house of David.

4. JUDGES AND COUNSELORS

Another group of rulers in the kingdom will be the judges and counselors mentioned in Isaiah 1:26:

And I will restore thy judges as at the first, and thy counsellors as at the beginning: afterward thou shalt be called The city of righteousness, a faithful town.

This position of authority will be particularly related to the city of Jerusalem. These rulers will be responsible for the dispensing of justice in a judicial sense, and there will be no perversion of this justice.

5. ISRAEL OVER THE GENTILES

The final link in this chain of command in the Jewish branch of government is that Israel is to become the head over the Gentiles. More will be said on this in the next chapter, but mention of it must be made here.

The fact that Israel was to become the head of the Gentiles was part of God's promises to Israel in the book of Deuteronomy. One such passage is Deuteronomy 15:6:

For Jehovah thy God will bless thee, as he promised thee: and thou shalt lend unto many nations, but thou shalt not borrow; and thou shalt rule over many nations, but they shall not rule over thee.

The leadership over the Gentiles was to be part of Israel's reward for obedience in Deuteronomy 28:1:

> And it shall come to pass, if thou shalt hearken diligently unto the voice of Jehovah thy God, to observe to do all his commandments which I command thee this day, that Jehovah thy God will set thee on high above all the nations of the earth.

Such obedience and headship awaits Israel's national regeneration. This promise is reiterated in Deuteronomy 28:13:

> And Jehovah will make thee the head, and not the tail; and thou shalt be above only, and thou shalt not be beneath; if thou shalt hearken unto the commandments of Jehovah thy God, which I command thee this day, to observe and to do them.

Besides the statements found in the law of Moses, the prophets also described Israel's future headship over the Gentiles. One such passage is Isaiah 14:1-2:

> For Jehovah will have compassion on Jacob, and will yet choose Israel, and set them in their own land: and the sojourner shall join himself with them, and they shall cleave to the house of Jacob. And the peoples shall take them, and bring them to their place; and the house of Israel shall possess them in the land of Jehovah for servants and for handmaids: and they shall take them captive whose captives they were; and they shall rule over their oppressors.

The Gentiles will not only conduct the Jews back to their land of Israel, but they will be possessed by Israel. They will become servants to Israel. Similar passages are found in Isaiah 49:22-23 and 61:6-7.

The chain of command in the Jewish branch of government is from Christ to David, to the twelve apostles, to the princes, to the judges and counselors, over all Israel which will be serving as the head of the Gentiles.

The rod of iron that will characterize the rule of the government in the kingdom will be implemented through various spheres and positions of authority.

CHAPTER XIX

ISRAEL IN THE MESSIANIC KINGDOM

Israel within the period of the messianic kingdom is a major theme of the Old Testament prophets. Indeed, it was the high point of Old Testament prophecy and every writing prophet with the exception of Jonah, Nahum, Habakkuk and Malachi had something to say about it. To spiritualize and allegorize away such a great amount of Scripture is to confuse the whole science of interpretation. There is no reason to spiritualize any of these prophecies anymore than there is reason to do so to those prophecies dealing with the first coming of Christ such as the virgin birth, the birth in Bethlehem, His death, or His physical resurrection, etc.

Because of the amount of revelation available on Israel in the messianic kingdom, this chapter will be divided into eight major divisions: (1) the four facets of the final restoration of Israel, (2) other characteristics of Israel's final restoration, (3) the millennial mountain of Jehovah's house, (4) the millennial temple, (5) the millennial system of priesthood and sacrifice, (6) the millennial river, (7) the millennial Israel, and (8) the millennial Jerusalem.

A. THE FOUR FACETS OF THE FINAL RESTORATION OF ISRAEL

There are four primary facets to Israel's final restoration with each being based on a specific covenant. Each of these covenants are fully developed in later prophetic revelation. This section will survey each covenant as it relates to Israel's final restoration along with the prophetic development of these covenants.

1. THE REGENERATION OF ISRAEL

a. BASIS: THE NEW COVENANT

The first facet of Israel's final restoration is the national regeneration of Israel. The timing of this regeneration has already been discussed in Chapter XIV. This section is concerned with the development of that motif. The basis of Israel's final regeneration is the New Covenant in Jeremiah 31:31-34:

Behold, the days come, saith Jehovah, that I will make a new covenant with the house of Israel, and with the house of Judah: not according to the covenant that I made with their fathers in the day that I took them by the hand to bring them out of the land of Egypt; which my covenant they brake, although I was a husband unto them, saith Jehovah. But this is the covenant that I will make with the house of Israel after those days, saith Jehovah: I will put my law in their inward parts, and in their heart will I write it; and I will be their God, and they shall be my people: and they shall teach no more every man his neighbor, and every man his brother, saying, Know Jehovah; for they shall all know me, from the least of them unto the greatest of them, saith Jehovah: for I will forgive their iniquity, and their sin will I remember no more.

The announcement of the New Covenant begins with a declaration that it will be a Jewish covenant for it will be made with both houses of Israel (verse 31). It will be in sharp contradistinction with the older Mosaic Covenant (verse 32). Of the five Jewish covenants, the Mosaic was the only conditional one. Although God had been faithful in keeping His terms of the covenant, Israel had not been so faithful, resulting in the Mosaic Covenant being broken. For while the Mosaic Covenant showed the standard of righteousness which the Law demanded, it could never impart to the Jew the power to keep it. But that problem will be rectified in the New Covenant (verse 33) through regeneration which will provide the internal power necessary to meet and to keep the righteous standards of the Law. The result of the New Covenant will be a total national regeneration of Israel (verse 34). Jewish missions and Jewish evangelism will not be needed in the messianic kingdom, because every Jew will know the Lord, from the least to the greatest. The sins of Israel will be forgiven and forgotten. While there will be Gentile unbelievers in the kingdom, there will not be Jewish unbelievers in the kingdom. To a man, all the Jews will believe. There will be no need to tell a Jew to "know the Lord" because they will all know Him.

It is upon this New Covenant that the first facet of Israel's restoration, the regeneration of Israel, is based.

b. PROPHETIC DEVELOPMENT

That Israel was to undergo a national regeneration is not confined to the words of the New Covenant alone. Some passages were already discussed under the Campaign of Armageddon. But there are many others. Isaiah 29:22-24 states:

Therefore thus saith Jehovah, who redeemed Abraham, concerning the house of Jacob: Jacob shall not now be ashamed, neither shall his face now wax pale. But when he seeth his children, the work of my hands, in the midst of him, they shall sanctify my name; yea, they shall sanctify the Holy One of Jacob, and shall stand in awe of the God of Israel. They also that err in spirit shall come to understanding, and they that murmur shall receive instruction.

A promise is made to the patriarch Jacob. Although for most of Jewish history Jacob would have been ashamed of the waywardness of his descendants, when the national regeneration comes, he will have much to be proud of.

Another passage is Isaiah 30:18-22:

> And therefore will Jehovah wait, that he may be gracious unto you; and therefore will he be exalted, that he may have mercy upon you: for Jehovah is a God of Justice; blessed are all they that wait for him. For the people shall dwell in Zion at Jerusalem; thou shalt weep no more; he will surely be gracious unto thee at the voice of thy cry; when he shall hear, he will answer thee. And though the Lord give you the bread of adversity and the water of affliction, yet shall not thy teachers be hidden any more, but thine eyes shall see thy teachers; and thine ears shall hear a word behind thee, saying, This is the way, walk ye in it; when ye turn to the right hand, and when ye turn to the left. And ye shall defile the overlaying of thy graven images of silver, and the plating of thy molten images of gold: thou shalt cast them away as an unclean thing; thou shalt say unto it, Get thee hence.

According to this particular passage, the regeneration will be a result of the judgments of the Great Tribulation which will be God's discipline upon the nation of Israel in order to correct them. It will be by way of the judgments of the tribulation that Israel will come to a saving knowledge of her Messiah.

Later in Isaiah 44:1-5 the prophet wrote:

> Yet now hear, O Jacob my servant; and Israel, whom I have chosen: thus saith Jehovah that made thee, and formed thee from the womb, who will help thee: Fear not, O Jacob my servant; and thou, Jeshurun, whom I have chosen. For I will pour water upon him that is thirsty, and streams upon the dry ground; I will pour my Spirit upon thy seed, and my blessing upon thine offspring: and they shall spring up among the grass, as willows by the watercourses. One shall say, I am Jehovah's; and another shall call himself by the name of Jacob; and another shall subscribe with his hand unto Jehovah, and surname himself by the name of Israel.

It was God who chose Israel from the very beginning (verses 1-2), and Israel has yet to become the chosen vessel for which she was ordained. God will pour out His Spirit upon the entire nation (verse 3) with the result that Israel will begin to bear fruit (verse 4) and will remain ever loyal to her God (verse 5). Later in this chapter, in verses 21-23, Isaiah emphasized the removal of Israel's sins:

> Remember these things, O Jacob, and Israel; for thou art my servant: I have formed thee; thou art my servant: O Israel, thou shalt not be forgotten of me. I have blotted out, as a thick cloud, thy transgressions, and, as a cloud, thy sins: return unto me; for I have redeemed thee. Sing, O ye heavens, for Jehovah hath done it; shout, ye lower parts of the earth; break forth into singing, ye mountains, O forest, and every tree therein: for Jehovah hath redeemed Jacob, and will glorify himself in Israel.

Israel's everlasting salvation and freedom from shame is

emphasized in Isaiah 45:17:

> But Israel shall be saved by Jehovah with an everlasting salvation: ye shall not be put to shame nor confounded world without end.

The two other major prophets also spoke of this final regeneration. Jeremiah 24:7 records:

> And I will give them a heart to know me, that I am Jehovah: and they shall be my people, and I will be their God; for they shall return unto me with their whole heart.

When God regenerates Israel, He will give them a heart to know the Lord. With this regenerated heart, they will be able to return to God with an undivided heart. At the time of Israel's regeneration, her sins will no longer be found, according to Jeremiah 50:19-20:

> And I will bring Israel again to his pasture, and he shall feed on Carmel and Bashan, and his soul shall be satisfied upon the hills of Ephraim and in Gilead. In those days, and in that time, saith Jehovah, the iniquity of Israel shall be sought for, and there shall be none; and the sins of Judah, and they shall not be found: for I will pardon them whom I leave as a remnant.

Ezekiel also emphasized that future regeneration of Israel, and in Ezekiel 11:19-20 he wrote:

> And I will give them one heart, and I will put a new spirit within you; and I will take the stony heart out of their flesh, and will give them a heart of flesh; that they may walk in my statutes, and keep mine ordinances, and do them: and they shall be my people, and I will be their God.

At the time of Israel's regeneration, they will be given a new heart and a new spirit as their human spirit will be reborn (verse 19). The result of this work of God on the heart and spirit of man will be an enablement to walk in and to keep the righteous standards of God.

Later, Ezekiel 36:25-27 states:

> And I will sprinkle clean water upon you, and ye shall be clean: from all your filthiness, and from all your idols, will I cleanse you. A new heart also will I give you, and a new spirit will I put within you; and I will take away the stony heart out of your flesh, and I will give you a heart of flesh. And I will put my Spirit within you, and cause you to walk in my statutes, and ye shall keep mine ordinances, and do them.

Repeating aspects stated earlier and then adding some more information of his own, Ezekiel further describes the coming regeneration. All of Israel's sins will be cleansed (verse 25). A regenerate heart and spirit will be given so that Israel can walk in newness of life (verse

26). Furthermore, the Holy Spirit will indwell the Jews so that they will be empowered to walk in the commandments of the Lord (verse 27).

The regeneration of Israel is also a prominent theme in the minor prophets. Hosea, who spoke a great deal about God's punishment for Israel's sins, did not fail to speak of Israel's regeneration. One such passage is Hosea 1:10-2:1:

> Yet the number of the children of Israel shall be as the sand of the sea, which cannot be measured nor numbered; and it shall come to pass that, in the place where it was said unto them, Ye are not my people, it shall be said unto them, Ye are the sons of the living God. And the children of Judah and the children of Israel shall be gathered together, and they shall appoint themselves one head, and shall go up from the land; for great shall be the day of Jezreel. Say ye unto your brethren, Ammi; and to your sisters, Ruhamah.

Though judgments will decimate the ranks of Israel, nevertheless, the time will come when Israel will increase tremendously in population (verse 10a). Even though for a long period of time they were *Lo Ammi* (not my people), they will once again become *Ammi* (my people), the people of God (verse 10b). When the reunification comes, they will be God's people who have obtained God's mercy (verses 1:11-2:1).

Hosea not only begins his book with Israel's regeneration, but he also ends with it in Hosea 14:4-8:

> I will heal their backsliding, I will love them freely; for mine anger is turned away from him. I will be as the dew unto Israel; he shall blossom as the lily, and cast forth his roots as Lebanon. His branches shall spread, and his beauty shall be as the olive-tree, and his smell as Lebanon. They that dwell under his shadow shall return; they shall revive as the grain, and blossom as the vine: the scent thereof shall be as the wine of Lebanon. Ephraim shall say, What have I to do any more with idols? I have answered, and will regard him: I am like a green fir-tree; from me is thy fruit found.

Israel's backslidings will all be thoroughly healed (verse 4), for only then will Israel receive the manifold blessings of God (verses 5-7). All worship of other gods will cease when the regeneration comes (verse 8).

That this regeneration of Israel will be a result of the outpouring of the Holy Spirit is the point of Joel 2:28-32:

> And it shall come to pass afterward, that I will pour out my Spirit upon all flesh; and your sons and your daughters shall prophesy, your old men shall dream dreams, your young men shall see visions: and also upon the servants and upon the handmaids in those days will I pour out my Spirit. And I will show wonders in the heavens and in the earth: blood, and fire, and pillars of smoke. The sun shall be turned into darkness, and the moon into blood, before the great and terrible day of Jehovah cometh. And it

shall come to pass, that whosoever shall call on the name of Jehovah shall be delivered; for in mount Zion and in Jerusalem there shall be those that escape, as Jehovah hath said, and among the remnant those whom Jehovah doth call.

Once the Holy Spirit is poured out on all Israel, then they will call upon the name of the Lord. God will respond to that call by delivering and saving them.

The national regeneration of Israel will result in the total forgiveness of Israel's sins according to Micah 7:18-20:

Who is a God like unto thee, that pardoneth iniquity, and passeth over the transgression of the remnant of his heritage? he retaineth not his anger for ever, because he delighteth in lovingkindness. He will again have compassion upon us; he will tread our iniquities under foot; and thou wilt cast all their sins into the depths of the sea. Thou wilt perform the truth to Jacob, and the lovingkindness to Abraham, which thou hast sworn unto our fathers from the days of old.

God's loyal love for Israel will cause Him to pardon and to pass over the sins of Israel when He will return to them in all compassion (verses 18-19). And He will do so on the basis of the Abrahamic Covenant (verse 20) especially as it is developed in the salvation aspect by the New Covenant.

Another prophecy that spoke of Israel's regeneration is Zephaniah 3:9-13:

For then will I turn to the peoples a pure language, that they may all call upon the name of Jehovah, to serve him with one consent. From beyond the rivers of Ethiopia my suppliants, even the daughter of my dispersed, shall bring mine offering. In that day shalt thou not be put to shame for all thy doings, wherein thou hast transgressed against me; for then I will take away out of the midst of thee thy proudly exulting ones, and thou shalt no more be haughty in my holy mountain. But I will leave in the midst of thee an afflicted and poor people, and they shall take refuge in the name of Jehovah. The remnant of Israel shall not do iniquity, nor speak lies; neither shall a deceitful tongue be found in their mouth; for they shall feed and lie down, and none shall make them afraid.

Throughout the dispersion the Jews will begin to call upon the name of the Lord. It is important to note that regardless of where the Jews are, they will respond so that the regeneration will indeed be total.

One final passage is Romans 11:25-27:

For I would not, brethren, have you ignorant of this mystery, lest ye be wise in your own conceits, that a hardening in part hath befallen Israel, until the fulness of the Gentiles be come in; and so all Israel shall be saved: even as it is written, There shall come out of Zion the Deliverer; He shall

turn away ungodliness from Jacob: And this is my covenant unto them.
When I shall take away their sins.

As Paul brings to a conclusion his lengthy treatment of the place
of Israel in the program of God, he points out that the present blindness and hardening of Israel is not a permanent one. It is temporary
until the full number of Gentiles preordained for the Body of Christ is
reached (verse 25). It is then that the hardening of Israel will be
removed, and all Israel living at that time will be saved (verses 26-27).

2. THE REGATHERING OF ISRAEL

a. THE BASIS: THE PALESTINIAN COVENANT

The second facet of the final restoration of Israel is the regathering of Israel from all over the world. This is based on the Palestinian
Covenant of Deuteronomy 29:1-30:20. The passage begins with a clear
statement that the Palestinian Covenant is distinct and different from
the Mosaic Covenant (29:1). The former is eternal and unconditional
while the latter is both temporal and conditional. Moses then records
in summary form the forty years of wilderness experience leading up
to the point of being about to enter into the promised land (29:2-9). But
before entrance into the land can occur, another covenant needs to be
made in order to warn them of things to come (29:10-13). They are
warned against turning away from the Lord (29:14-21). Then the
passage proceeds to state that they will do exactly that, resulting in
the dispersion out of the land into the Gentile nations to endure a long
period of many persecutions (29:22-29). But this dispersion out of the
land is not going to be permanent, because eventually there will be a
regathering as described in Deuteronomy 30:1-10:

> And it shall come to pass, when all these things are come upon thee, the
> blessing and the curse, which I have set before thee, and thou shalt call
> them to mind among all the nations, whither Jehovah thy God hath
> driven thee, and shalt return unto Jehovah thy God, and shalt obey his
> voice according to all that I command thee this day, thou and thy
> children, with all thy heart, and with all thy soul; that then Jehovah thy
> God will turn thy captivity, and have compassion upon thee, and will
> return and gather thee from all the peoples, whither Jehovah thy God
> hath scattered thee. If any of thine outcasts be in the uttermost parts of
> heaven, from thence will Jehovah thy God gather thee, and from thence
> will he fetch thee: and Jehovah thy God will bring thee into the land
> which thy fathers possessed, and thou shalt possess it; and he will do thee
> good, and multiply thee above thy fathers. And Jehovah thy God will
> circumcise thy heart, and the heart of thy seed, to love Jehovah thy God
> with all thy heart, and with all thy soul, that thou mayest live. And
> Jehovah thy God will put all these curses upon thine enemies, and on
> them that hate thee, that persecuted thee. And thou shalt return and
> obey the voice of Jehovah, and do all his commandments which I com-

mand thee this day. And Jehovah thy God will make thee plenteous in all the work of thy hand, in the fruit of thy body, and in the fruit of thy cattle, and in the fruit of thy ground, for good: for Jehovah will again rejoice over thee for good, as he rejoiced over thy fathers; if thou shalt obey the voice of Jehovah thy God, to keep his commandments and his statutes which are written in this book of the law; if thou turn unto Jehovah thy God with all thy heart, and with all thy soul.

After the long period of persecution described in chapter 29, there will ultimately be the regeneration of Israel as the people return to the Lord (verses 1-2). Following the regeneration of Israel will be the regathering from all over the world (verse 3) so that even if Jews should be found in the uttermost parts of the heavens, they will nevertheless be returned (verse 4) and brought back into the promised land (verse 5). But this regathering will occur only after the regeneration of Israel (verse 6) at which time the punishments previously applied to Israel will now be applied to the Gentiles (verse 7). Although curses may fall on the Gentiles, there will only be blessings for Israel (verses 8-9) because they will totally return to the Lord (verse 10). The Palestinian Covenant ends with some further admonitions, warnings and promises (30:11-20).

b.   THE PROPHETIC DEVELOPMENT

The regathering of Israel, following the regeneration, is another high point of prophetic revelation to be found in many of the prophets. In Isaiah 11:11-12:6 the final regathering is described as the second of the world-wide regatherings of Israel:

And it shall come to pass in that day, that the Lord will set his hand again the second time to recover the remnant of his people, that shall remain, from Assyria, and from Egypt, and from Pathros, and from Cush, and from Elam, and from Shinar, and from Hamath, and from the islands of the sea. And he will set up an ensign for the nations, and will assemble the outcasts of Israel, and gather together the dispersed of Judah from the four corners of the earth. The envy also of Ephraim shall depart, and they that vex Judah shall be cut off: Ephraim shall not envy Judah, and Judah shall not vex Ephraim. And they shall fly down upon the shoulder of the Philistines on the west; together shall they despoil the children of the east: they shall put forth their hand upon Edom and Moab; and the children of Ammon shall obey them. And Jehovah will utterly destroy the tongue of the Egyptian sea; and with his scorching wind will he wave his hand over the River, and will smite it into seven streams, and cause men to march over dryshod. And there shall be a highway for the remnant of his people, that shall remain, from Assyria; like as there was for Israel in the day that he came up out of the land of Egypt. And in that day thou shalt say, I will give thanks unto thee, O Jehovah; for though thou wast angry with me, thine anger is turned away, and thou comfortest me. Behold, God is my salvation; I will trust, and will not be afraid: for

Jehovah, even Jehovah, is my strength and song; and he is become my salvation. Therefore with joy shall ye draw water out of the wells of salvation. And in that day shall ye say, Give thanks unto Jehovah, call upon his name, declare his doings among the peoples, make mention that his name is exalted. Sing unto Jehovah; for he hath done excellent things: let this be known in all the earth. Cry aloud and shout, thou inhabitant of Zion; for great in the midst of thee is the Holy One of Israel.

Although many commentators identify the first regathering as the return from the Babylonian captivity, that could hardly be described as a world-wide one. The first regathering is the one in unbelief prior to the Great Tribulation, and this has been happening since 1948. The first regathering is in unbelief in preparation for judgment. The regathering described in this passage is the second one (verse 11a) in faith in preparation for the millennial blessings. This regathering is not merely local from the nations of the Middle East (verse 11b) but from all over the world (verse 12). Isaiah then goes on to develop certain characteristics of Israel's final regathering. First of all, the unity between Israel and Judah will be restored (verses 13-14). Ephraim's envy of Judah will cease (verse 13), an envy that developed over the placing of the house of God in Judah (Psalm 78:9-11, 67-68). This unity will enable them to overcome their opponents (verse 14). Secondly, the final regathering will be accompanied by miracles (verses 15-16). *The tongue of the Egyptian Sea*, the Gulf of Suez, will dry up while the Euphrates will be smitten and split up into seven smaller streams so as to make the regathering that much easier. So as a highway was made for Israel at the Exodus, there will likewise be one again in the final regathering. Immediately after the Exodus, Israel sang the song found in Exodus 15:1-18. In the same way, after the final regathering, Israel will sing the song found in Isaiah 12:1-6. The song is in two stanzas. In the first stanza (verses 1-3) Israel gives a thanksgiving to God for turning away anger (verse 1). They now realize that salvation is in Jehovah (verse 2) who has poured out the waters of salvation freely (verse 3). In the second stanza (verses 4-6) they wish to make known God's deeds to all the world, so they give thanks (verse 4), sing (verse 5) and shout out loud of God's goodness (verse 6).

Later in Isaiah 27:12-13 the prophet wrote:

And it shall come to pass in that day, that Jehovah will beat off his fruit from the flood of the River unto the brook of Egypt; and ye shall be gathered one by one, O ye children of Israel. And it shall come to pass in that day, that a great trumpet shall be blown; and they shall come that were ready to perish in the land of Assyria, and they that were outcasts in the land of Egypt; and they shall worship Jehovah in the holy mountain at Jerusalem.

The emphasis in this passage is on the *totality* of the regathering, for every Jew one by one will be brought back into the land of Israel. As in the previous Isaiah passage, the key locality of the regathering will be from the Middle East nations since, as a result of the fall of Israel in the middle of the tribulation, the majority of the Jews will be located in this vicinity and it is here that they will have suffered the most. And so the Jews will be taken one by one out of Egypt and Assyria (modern Iraq). Jews are still to be found in various Arab countries suffering tremendous persecutions. But in the regathering they will be rescued from the land of their enemies. The regathering will be from all over the world, but with a special emphasis on the Middle East nations.

The magnitude of the final regathering of Israel is described in Isaiah 43:5-7:

> Fear not; for I am with thee: I will bring thy seed from the east, and gather thee from the west; I will say to the north, Give up; and to the south, Keep not back; bring my sons from far, and my daughters from the end of the earth; every one that is called by my name, and whom I have created for my glory, whom I have formed, yea, whom I have made.

As far as locality is concerned, the regathering will be world-wide and to emphasize the fact, all four points of the compass are mentioned (verses 5-6). Then the magnitude is illustrated by the usage of three words: created, formed and made (verse 7). These three words are used interchangeably in the creation account of Genesis 1-2. Hence, from God's perspective, the final regathering will be on the magnitude of the original creation.

The comparative magnitude of the final regathering with previous works of God is something Jeremiah also pointed out. In Jeremiah 16:14-15 it is compared with the Exodus:

> Therefore, behold, the days come, saith Jehovah, that it shall no more be said, As Jehovah liveth, that brought up the children of Israel out of the land of Egypt; but, As Jehovah liveth, that brought up the children of Israel from the land of the north, and from all the countries whither he had driven them. And I will bring them again into their land that I gave unto their fathers.

Throughout Jewish history, the Exodus has been considered the high point of Jewish history, but after the final regathering this will change (verse 14). In the future it will be the final regathering of the Jews that will become the high point of Jewish history (verse 15).

Later in Jeremiah 23:3-4 the prophet stated:

> And I will gather the remnant of my flock out of all the countries whither I have driven them, and will bring them again to their folds; and they shall be fruitful and multiply. And I will set up shepherds over them, who

shall feed them; and they shall fear no more, nor be dismayed, neither shall any be lacking, saith Jehovah.

From all over the world the Jews are to be regathered into the land where they will produce much fruit (verse 3). Furthermore, God will provide righteous leaders who will feed the people with righteousness, justice, and understanding (verse 4). Then there is another comparison with the Exodus in Jeremiah 23:7-8:

Therefore, behold, the days come, saith Jehovah, that they shall no more say, As Jehovah liveth, who brought up the children of Israel out of the land of Egypt; but, As Jehovah liveth, who brought up and who led the seed of the house of Israel out of the north country, and from all the countries whither I had driven them. And they shall dwell in their own land.

One other passage in Jeremiah that speaks of the regathering is found in 31:7-10:

For thus saith Jehovah, Sing with gladness for Jacob, and shout for the chief of the nations: publish ye, praise ye, and say, O Jehovah, save thy people, the remnant of Israel. Behold, I will bring them from the north country, and gather them from the uttermost parts of the earth, and with them the blind and the lame, the woman with child and her that travaileth with child together: a great company shall they return hither. They shall come with weeping; and with supplications will I lead them: I will cause them to walk by rivers of waters, in a straight way wherein they shall not stumble; for I am a father to Israel, and Ephraim is my firstborn. Hear the word of Jehovah, O ye nations, and declare it in the isles afar off; and say, He that scattered Israel will gather him, and keep him, as a shepherd doth his flock.

Following the regeneration of Israel (verse 7) all the Jews will be regathered, regardless of their state of health and regardless of their location (verse 8). There will be no hindrances whatsoever to the regathering (verse 9), for the same one who was able to scatter them will also be able to regather them (verse 10).

Ezekiel picked up the same motif in Ezekiel 11:14-18:

And the word of Jehovah came unto me, saying, Son of man, thy brethren, even thy brethren, the men of thy kindred, and all the house of Israel, all of them, are they unto whom the inhabitants of Jerusalem have said, Get you far from Jehovah; unto us is this land given for a possession. Therefore say, Thus saith the Lord Jehovah: Whereas I have removed them far off among the nations, and whereas I have scattered them among the countries, yet will I be to them a sanctuary for a little while in the countries where they are come. Therefore say, Thus saith the Lord Jehovah: I will gather you from the peoples, and assemble you out of the countries where ye have been scattered, and I will give you the land of Israel. And they shall come thither, and they shall take away all the detestable things thereof and all the abominations thereof from thence.

The same God who scattered Israel (verses 14-16) has every intention of regathering them back into their own land (verse 17) so that regenerate Israel can cleanse the land of all pollution (verse 18). Later the prophet restated this doctrine in Ezekiel 36:24:

> For I will take you from among the nations, and gather you out of all the countries, and will bring you into your own land.

The minor prophets were not remiss in speaking of the regathering. One such prophecy is in Amos 9:14-15:

> And I will bring back the captivity of my people Israel, and they shall build the waste cities, and inhabit them; and they shall plant vineyards, and drink the wine thereof; they shall also make gardens, and eat the fruit of them. And I will plant them upon their land, and they shall no more be plucked up out of their land which I have given them, saith Jehovah thy God.

The emphasis of Amos is on *permanency*. Israel is to be regathered in order to rebuild the land (verse 14). In the final regathering, God will plant them in the land so that they will never again be uprooted and dispersed out of the land (verse 15).

The prophet Zephaniah, whose whole theme was one of judgment, closed his book with a promise of the final regathering in Zephaniah 3:18-20:

> I will gather them that sorrow for the solemn assembly, who were of thee; to whom the burden upon her was a reproach. Behold, at that time I will deal with all them that afflict thee; and I will save that which is lame, and gather that which was driven away; and I will make them a praise and a name, whose shame hath been in all the earth. At that time will I bring you in, and at that time will I gather you; for I will make you a name and a praise among all the peoples of the earth, when I bring back your captivity before your eyes, saith Jehovah.

The judgment meted out against Israel is the result of her sins (verses 18-19). These judgments will not have a destructive effect but a corrective one. Once correction takes place, the regathering will indeed occur, and the final regathering will cause Israel to be a name and a praise among the Gentile nations (verse 20).

The final prophet of the Old Testament to speak of the regathering is Zechariah in 10:8-12:

> I will hiss for them, and gather them; for I have redeemed them; and they shall increase as they have increased. And I will sow them among the peoples; and they shall remember me in far countries; and they shall live

with their children, and shall return. I will bring them again also out of the land of Egypt, and gather them out of Assyria; and I will bring them into the land of Gilead and Lebanon; and place shall not be found for them. And he will pass through the sea of affliction, and will smite the waves in the sea, and all the depths of the Nile shall dry up; and the pride of Assyria shall be brought down, and the sceptre of Egypt shall depart. And I will strengthen them in Jehovah; and they shall walk up and down in his name, saith Jehovah.

As Zechariah portrayed the final regathering, he saw it in terms of *hissing* which is the call of a shepherd for his sheep (verse 8a). The regathering will be a result of the redemption and regeneration of Israel (verses 8b-9). While the regathering is to occur from around the world, there will be a special emphasis upon the Middle East nations (verses 10-11). Once all the Jews are regathered, they will never again depart from the Lord (verse 12).

In the New Testament the final regathering revealed by the Old Testament prophets is summarized in Matthew 24:31:

And he shall send forth his angels with a great sound of a trumpet, and they shall gather together his elect from the four winds, from one end of heaven to the other.

In this passage, Jesus stated that the angels will be involved in the final regathering and they will bring the Jews back into the land. As to locality, the emphasis is on the world-wide regathering. The Matthew passage is a rather simple summary of all that the prophets had to say about the second facet of Israel's final restoration. Its purpose was to make clear that the world-wide regathering predicted by the prophets will be fulfilled only after the second coming.

3.   THE POSSESSION OF THE LAND

a.   BASIS: THE ABRAHAMIC COVENANT

The third facet of the final restoration of Israel is the possession of the land encompassing two aspects: its total boundaries and its productivity. The basis for this facet is the Abrahamic Covenant as found in various passages of the book of Genesis. There are too many to cite them all. Therefore, only those passages that deal with the land aspect will be cited. The very beginning of the Abrahamic Covenant is in Genesis 12:1-3:

Now Jehovah said unto Abram, Get thee out of thy country, and from thy kindred, and from thy father's house, unto the land that I will show thee: and I will make of thee a great nation, and I will bless thee, and make thy name great; and be thou a blessing: and I will bless them that bless thee, and him that curseth thee will I curse: and in thee shall all the families of the earth of blessed.

At the time that the covenant was initially made, Abram was simply told to leave for a land that God would show him. When he arrived in the land, God again revealed Himself to Abram in Genesis 12:7:

> And Jehovah appeared unto Abram, and said, Unto thy seed will I give this land: and there builded he an altar unto Jehovah, who appeared unto him.

In this verse, the promise is stated in such a way that it is Abram's seed that is to possess the land. So from this passage alone, it might be concluded that Abram himself was never to possess the land. But that is not the case as another passage on the Abrahamic Covenant makes clear in Genesis 13:14-17:

> And Jehovah said unto Abram, after that Lot was separated from him, Lift up now thine eyes, and look from the place where thou art, northward and southward and eastward and westward: for all the land which thou seest, to thee will I give it, and to thy seed for ever. And I will make thy seed as the dust of the earth: so that if a man can number the dust of the earth, then may thy seed also be numbered. Arise, walk through the land in the length of it and in the breadth of it; for unto thee will I give it.

Although for the time being the area of grazing was divided between Abram and Lot, ultimately all the land that Abram could see is to be possessed by him (verses 14-15). The promise is clearly made that the land is to be possessed by Abram personally as well as by Abram's seed. Yet, Abram died having never possessed any part of the land except for a few wells and a burial cave which he had to purchase with good money. In order for God to fulfill His promise to Abram, two things have to occur. Abram must be resurrected, and the land must be restored to Israel. Since Abram's seed is to possess the land as well, the population of Israel will greatly increase at that time (verse 16). Abram was then directed to walk throughout the land in order to get to know it real well, for someday he will possess it (verse 17).

In the above passage, Abram was told that all the land he could possibly see would be possessed by him, but no exact boundaries were given. Later however, as God confirmed the covenant, the exact boundaries were given in Genesis 15:12-21:

> And when the sun was going down, a deep sleep fell upon Abram; and, lo, a horror of great darkness fell upon him. And he said unto Abram, Know of a surety that thy seed shall be sojourners in a land that is not theirs, and shall serve them; and they shall afflict them four hundred years; and also that nation, whom they shall serve, will I judge: and afterward shall they come out with great substance. But thou shalt go to thy fathers in peace; thou shalt be buried in a good old age. And in the fourth genera-

tion they shall come hither again: for the iniquity of the Amorite is not yet full. And it came to pass, that, when the sun went down, and it was dark, behold, a smoking furnace, and a flaming torch that passed between these pieces. In that day Jehovah made a covenant with Abram, saying, Unto thy seed have I given this land, from the river of Egypt unto the great river, the river Euphrates: the Kenite, and the Kenizzite, and the Kadmonite, and the Hittite, and the Perizzite, and the Rephaim, and the Amorite, and the Canaanite, and the Girgashite, and the Jebusite.

At the time of the signing and the sealing of the Abrahamic Covenant, God spelled out the future history of Abram's seed prior to their initial possession of the land (verses 12-16). Then God signed and sealed the covenant (verse 17) and declared what the boundaries of the land will be (verses 18-20). The borders are to extend from the Euphrates River in the north to the River of Egypt in the south. There is no problem with the identity of the Euphrates in the north, but there has been some confusion over the identity of the River of Egypt. Some have identified the River of Egypt as being the same as the Brook of Egypt mentioned in other passages. Both have at times been identified with the Nile River, making it the southern border. But none of these suppositions are correct.

First of all, the Brook of Egypt and the River of Egypt are not the same. The latter refers to a continuous flowing river, while the former is a *wadi*, a dry river bed that only has water in it periodically during the rainy season. The words for "river" and "brook" are two different Hebrew words, also forcing one to keep the two distinct. The Brook of Egypt is the modern *Wadi-el-Arish* running north and south in the central Sinai Peninsula.

Just as the River of Egypt is not the same as the Brook of Egypt, neither is it the Nile River. Rather, it refers to one of the "fingers" of the Nile River. As the river flows from the south to the north before reaching the Mediterranean Sea, it enters an area known as the Nile Delta where it breaks up into a number of fingers or branches. The most eastern branch or finger was the one known as the River of Egypt. Today, the River of Egypt is along the line of the modern Suez Canal. Hence, according to this passage, Israel's southern boundary is to extend down to about where the Suez Canal is today.

This raises some questions concerning consistency with other passages. In this passage, the southern boundary is given as the River of Egypt; while the passages in the prophets, when dealing with the Jewish settlement of the land in the final restoration, give the southern boundary as the Brook of Egypt. This is not really a contradiction. The difference is simply between the extent of possession and control as over against the extent of actual settlement. In the final restoration of the land, Israel will possess all the way south to the River of Egypt and will control down to that area of the modern Suez

Canal. But as far as where the Jews will be living, the actual boundary of this settlement will only extend as far south as the Brook of Egypt or the modern Wadi-el-Arish.

After Abraham, the covenant is reconfirmed through Isaac in Genesis 26:2-5:

> And Jehovah appeared unto him, and said, Go not down into Egypt; dwell in the land which I shall tell thee of: sojourn in this land, and I will be with thee, and will bless thee; for unto thee, and unto thy seed, I will give all these lands, and I will establish the oath which I sware unto Abraham thy father; and I will multiply thy seed as the stars of heaven, and will give unto thy seed all these lands; and in thy seed shall all the nations of the earth be blessed; because that Abraham obeyed my voice, and kept my charge, my commandments, my statutes, and my laws.

Isaac is commanded to stay in the land and not to leave it (verse 2), for it is to Isaac and to Isaac's seed that the land will be given (verse 3). It should be noted that the promise is not merely to Isaac's descendants but to Isaac himself, requiring Isaac's future resurrection and possession of the land. As for Isaac's seed, it will be greatly increased in population (verse 4). So it is to Isaac and not Ishmael that the Abrahamic Covenant is reconfirmed (verse 5).

After Isaac, the Abrahamic Covenant is reconfirmed to Jacob in Genesis 28:13-15:

> And, behold, Jehovah stood above it, and said, I am Jehovah, the God of Abraham thy father, and the God of Isaac: the land whereon thou liest, to thee will I give it, and to thy seed; and thy seed shall be as the dust of the earth, and thou shalt spread abroad to the west, and to the east, and to the north, and to the south: and in thee and in thy seed shall all the families of the earth be blessed. And, behold, I am with thee, and will keep thee whithersoever thou goest, and will bring thee again into this land; for I will not leave thee, until I have done that which I have spoken to thee of.

It is to Jacob and not to Esau that the covenant is now reconfirmed (verse 13a). The promise is made that the land will be given to both Jacob and to Jacob's seed (verse 13b). So again the possession of the land is not a promise to the seed only, but to the individual Jacob as well. For this reason Jacob must also be resurrected and possess the land. As previously, the seed will be greatly multiplied at that time (verse 14). As for Jacob himself, who was now departing from the land, God will bring him back in his own lifetime (verse 15).

So then, it is on the Abrahamic Covenant, which is reconfirmed through Isaac and Jacob and then to all of Jacob's descendants, that the third facet of Israel's final restoration is based.

b. THE PROPHETIC DEVELOPMENT

This third facet of Israel's final restoration, the possession of the land, was further developed in both the Law and the Prophets. As far as the Law is concerned, it is found in Leviticus 26:40-45:

> And they shall confess their iniquity, and the iniquity of their fathers, in their trespass which they trespassed against me, and also that, because they walked contrary unto me, I also walked contrary unto them, and brought them into the land of their enemies: if then their uncircumcised heart be humbled, and they then accept of the punishment of their iniquity; then will I remember my covenant with Jacob; and also my covenant with Isaac, and also my covenant with Abraham will I remember; and I will remember the land. The land also shall be left by them, and shall enjoy its sabbaths, while it lieth desolate without them: and they shall accept of the punishment of their iniquity; because, even because they rejected mine ordinances, and their soul abhorred my statutes. And yet for all that, when they are in the land of their enemies, I will not reject them, neither will I abhor them, to destroy them utterly, and to break my covenant with them; for I am Jehovah their God; but I will for their sakes remember the covenant of their ancestors, whom I brought forth out of the land of Egypt in the sight of the nations, that I might be their God: I am Jehovah.

Following the regeneration of Israel (verses 40-41) God will fully carry out the promises of the Abrahamic Covenant concerning the land (verse 42). On the basis of the Abrahamic Covenant He will restore to them the land that has lain desolate for so long (verses 43-45).

In another part of the Law, the possession of the land is also part of the Palestinian Covenant in Deuteronomy 30:5:

> And Jehovah thy God will bring thee into the land which thy fathers possessed, and thou shalt possess it; and he will do thee good, and multiply thee above thy fathers.

The prophets of Israel developed this facet even further in both the major and minor prophets. Among the major prophets, Isaiah 27:12 states:

> And it shall come to pass in that day, that Jehovah will beat off his fruit from the flood of the River unto the brook of Egypt; and ye shall be gathered one by one, O ye children of Israel.

In this passage, the first aspect (the borders of the land) is brought out. The northern (Euphrates River) and southern (the Brook of Egypt) boundaries are possessed for the first time in all of Israel's history. Israel will be able to settle in all of the promised land.

In another passage, Isaiah 30:23-26, the second aspect (increased productivity of the land) of the third facet is stressed:

> And he will give the rain for thy seed, wherewith thou shalt sow the ground; and bread of the increase of the ground, and it shall be fat and plenteous: in that day shall thy cattle feed in large pastures. The oxen likewise and the young asses that till the ground shall eat savory provender, which hath been winnowed with the shovel and with the fork. And there shall be upon every lofty mountain, and upon every high hill, brooks and streams of waters, in the day of the great slaughter, when the towers fall. Moreover the light of the moon shall be as the light of the sun, and the light of the sun shall be sevenfold, as the light of seven days, in the day that Jehovah bindeth up the hurt of his people, and healeth the stroke of their wound.

The land will be well watered and will produce abundant food both for men and animals (verses 23-25). Furthermore, there will be a tremendous increase of light with the moon shining as brightly as the sun, while the light of the sun will be increased seven times what it is today.

As for the deserts of Israel, Isaiah 35:1-2 states:

> The wilderness and the dry land shall be glad; and the desert shall rejoice, and blossom as the rose. It shall blossom abundantly, and rejoice even with joy and singing; the glory of Lebanon shall be given unto it, the excellency of Carmel and Sharon: they shall see the glory of Jehovah, the excellency of our God.

Isaiah later brought out the productivity aspect again in 65:21-24:

> And they shall build houses, and inhabit them; and they shall plant vineyards, and eat the fruit of them. They shall not build, and another inhabit; they shall not plant, and another eat: for as the days of a tree shall be the days of my people, and my chosen shall long enjoy the work of their hands. They shall not labor in vain, nor bring forth for calamity; for they are the seed of the blessed of Jehovah, and their offspring with them. And it shall come to pass that, before they call, I will answer; and while they are yet speaking, I will hear.

With the possession of the land of Israel, not only will the Jews be able to build houses and plant vineyards and crops (verse 21) but they will also enjoy the work of their hands, for no enemy will take it from them (verses 22-23). They will enjoy it until a ripe old age.

Another major prophet, Jeremiah, also stressed the greater productivity of the land in the final restoration. In Jeremiah 31:1-6 he wrote:

> At that time, saith Jehovah, will I be the God of all the families of Israel, and they shall be my people. Thus saith Jehovah, The people that were

left of the sword found favor in the wilderness; even Israel, when I went to cause him to rest. Jehovah appeared of old unto me, saying, Yea, I haved loved thee with an everlasting love: therefore with lovingkindness have I drawn thee. Again will I build thee, and thou shalt be built, O virgin of Israel: again shalt thou be adorned with thy tabrets, and shalt go forth in the dances of them that make merry. Again shalt thou plant vineyards upon the mountains of Samaria; the planters shall plant, and shall enjoy the fruit thereof. For there shall be a day, that the watchmen upon the hills of Ephraim shall cry, Arise ye, and let us go up to Zion unto Jehovah our God.

Because of God's everlasting love for His people (verses 1-3), He intends to restore and build them again (verse 4). Once again for Israel there will be a time of plenty (verse 5), and the hills of Ephraim will echo with the call to come and worship God in Jerusalem (verse 6).

Later in the same passage, Jeremiah returned to the theme in 31:11-14:

For Jehovah hath ransomed Jacob, and redeemed him from the hand of him that was stronger than he. And they shall come and sing in the height of Zion, and shall flow unto the goodness of Jehovah, to the grain, and to the new wine, and to the oil, and to the young of the flock and of the herd: and their soul shall be as a watered garden; and they shall not sorrow any more at all. Then shall the virgin rejoice in the dance, and the young men and the old together; for I will turn their mourning into joy, and will comfort them, and make them rejoice from their sorrow. And I will satiate the soul of the priests with fatness, and my people shall be satisfied with my goodness, saith Jehovah.

After the redemption of Israel (verse 11), they will be restored to the land which will produce an abundance (verse 12) giving joy to all the inhabitants of the land (verses 13-14).

After Jeremiah, the next major prophet, Ezekiel, picked up the motif of the possession of the land and stated in Ezekiel 20:42-44:

And ye shall know that I am Jehovah, when I shall bring you into the land of Israel, into the country which I sware to give unto your fathers. And there shall ye remember your ways, and all your doings, wherein ye have polluted yourselves; and ye shall loathe yourselves in your own sight for all your evils that ye have committed. And ye shall know that I am Jehovah, when I have dealt with you for my name's sake, not according to your evil ways, nor according to your corrupt doings, O ye house of Israel, saith the Lord Jehovah.

Israel is to be brought back into their land in accordance with the promises of God to the forefathers in the Abrahamic Covenant (verse 42). Israel will turn away from her sins of the past and will detest them (verse 43) and now serve God alone (verse 44).

Later, Ezekiel 28:25-26 adds:

Thus saith the Lord Jehovah: When I shall have gathered the house of Israel from the peoples among whom they are scattered, and shall be sanctified in them in the sight of the nations, then shall they dwell in their own land which I gave to my servant Jacob. And they shall dwell securely therein; yea, they shall build houses, and plant vineyards, and shall dwell securely, when I have executed judgments upon all those that do them despite round about them; and they shall know that I am Jehovah their God.

Following its regeneration and regathering, Israel will then possess the land in accordance with the Abrahamic Covenant (verse 25). The security in which Israel will live and enjoy the works of her hands is then emphasized (verse 26).

The security aspect along with the element of increased productivity is the theme of Ezekiel 34:25-31:

And I will make with them a covenant of peace, and will cause evil beasts to cease out of the land; and they shall dwell securely in the wilderness, and sleep in the woods. And I will make them and the places round about my hill a blessing; and I will cause the shower to come down in its season; there shall be showers of blessing. And the tree of the field shall yield its fruit, and the earth shall yield its increase, and they shall be secure in their land; and they shall know that I am Jehovah, when I have broken the bars of their yoke, and have delivered them out of the hand of those that made bondmen of them. And they shall no more be a prey to the nations, neither shall the beasts of the earth devour them; but they shall dwell securely, and none shall make them afraid. And I will raise up unto them a plantation for renown, and they shall be no more consumed with famine in the land, neither bear the shame of the nations any more. And they shall know that I, Jehovah, their God am with them, and that they, the house of Israel, are my people, saith the Lord Jehovah. And ye my sheep, the sheep of my pasture, are men, and I am your God, saith the Lord Jehovah.

Since there will no longer be any wild beasts in the land, Israel will be able to enjoy the land in total security (verse 25). The rains will come in their proper time and in proper amounts (verse 26) increasing the productivity (verse 27a). Not only is Israel to be secure from the wild beasts, but also from all her enemies of the past (verses 27b-28). None will come to destroy the crops (verse 29). In every way Israel will be rightly related to God and will be His peculiar possession (verses 30-31).

Nor is this the end of the subject as the prophet continued in Ezekiel 36:8-15:

But ye, O mountains of Israel, ye shall shoot forth your branches, and yield your fruit to my people Israel; for they are at hand to come. For, behold, I am for you, and I will turn unto you, and ye shall be tilled and sown; and I will multiply men upon you, all the house of Israel, even all of it; and the cities shall be inhabited, and the waste places shall be builded;

and I will multiply upon you man and beast; and they shall increase and be fruitful; and I will cause you to be inhabited after your former estate, and will do better unto you than at your beginnings: and ye shall know that I am Jehovah. Yea, I will cause men to walk upon you, even my people Israel; and they shall possess thee, and thou shalt be their inheritance, and thou shalt no more henceforth bereave them of children. Thus saith the Lord Jehovah: Because they say unto you, Thou land art a devourer of men, and hast been a bereaver of thy nation; therefore thou shalt devour men no more, neither bereave thy nation any more, saith the Lord Jehovah; neither will I let thee hear any more the shame of the nations, neither shalt thou bear the reproach of the peoples any more, neither shalt thou cause thy nation to stumble any more, saith the Lord Jehovah.

In spite of years of desolation, the land is to be tilled again (verses 8-9) and populated; that is, the inhabitants of the land will be greatly increased (verses 10-11). Israel will again possess the land (verse 12), and the production of the land will be tremendous (verses 13-15).

Later in this passage, the prophet further elaborated in Ezekiel 36:28-38:

And ye shall dwell in the land that I gave to your fathers; and ye shall be my people, and I will be your God. And I will save you from all your uncleannesses: and I will call for the grain, and will multiply it, and lay no famine upon you. And I will multiply the fruit of the tree, and the increase of the field, that ye may receive no more the reproach of famine among the nations. Then shall ye remember your evil ways, and your doings that were not good; and ye shall loathe yourselves in your own sight for your iniquities and for your abominations. Not for your sake do I this, saith the Lord Jehovah, be it known unto you: be ashamed and confounded for your ways, O house of Israel. Thus saith the Lord Jehovah: In the day that I cleanse you from all your iniquities, I will cause the cities to be inhabited, and the waste places shall be builded. And the land that was desolate shall be tilled, whereas it was a desolation in the sight of all that passed by. And they shall say, This land that was desolate is become like the garden of Eden; and the waste and desolate and ruined cities are fortified and inhabited. Then the nations that are left round about you shall know that I, Jehovah, have builded the ruined places, and planted that which was desolate: I, Jehovah, have spoken it, and I will do it. Thus saith the Lord Jehovah: For this, moreover, will I be inquired of by the house of Israel, to do it for them: I will increase them with men like a flock. As the flock for sacrifice, as the flock of Jerusalem in her appointed feasts, so shall the waste cities be filled with flocks of men; and they shall know that I am Jehovah.

Ezekiel declared that Israel will again possess the land (verse 28) as a result of her regeneration (verse 29). The reproach of Israel will be removed (verse 30), and Israel will detest her past sins (verse 31). It is not for Israel's glory (verse 32) that the regeneration (verse 33), possession (verse 34) and the rebuilding of the land (verse 35) will occur, but it is for God's own glory among the nations (verse 36). As for Israel, the population will increase and the desolate places will be rebuilt (verses 37-38).

The repossession of the land is also promised in the minor prophets such as in Joel 2:18-27:

> Then was Jehovah jealous for his land, and had pity on his people. And Jehovah answered and said unto his people, Behold, I will send you grain, and new wine, and oil, and ye shall be satisfied therewith; and I will no more make you a reproach among the nations; but I will remove far off from you the northern army, and will drive it into a land barren and desolate, its forepart into the eastern sea, and its hinder part into the western sea; and its stench shall come up, and its ill savor shall come up, because it hath done great things. Fear not, O land, be glad and rejoice; for Jehovah hath done great things. Be not afraid, ye beasts of the field; for the pastures of the wilderness do spring, for the tree beareth its fruit, the fig-tree and the vine do yield their strength. Be glad then, ye children of Zion, and rejoice in Jehovah your God; for he giveth you the former rain in just measure, and he causeth to come down for you the rain, the former rain and the latter rain, in the first month. And the floors shall be full of wheat, and the vats shall overflow with new wine and oil. And I will restore to you the years that the locust hath eaten, the canker-worm, and the caterpillar, and the palmer-worm, my great army which I sent among you. And ye shall eat in plenty and be satisfied, and shall praise the name of Jehovah your God, that hath dealt wonderously with you; and my people shall never be put to shame. And ye shall know that I am in the midst of Israel, and that I am Jehovah your God, and there is none else; and my people shall never be put to shame.

God will be jealous for His land (verse 18), and this burning jealousy will bring about a great productivity in the land (verse 19). The land will be secure from any further invasions (verse 20), and it will produce abundantly (verses 21-22). The rains will come at the proper seasons and in proper amounts (verse 23) causing a tremendous amount of surplus in their storages (verse 24) recuperating from all previous losses due to pestilences (verse 25). Israel will never again be shamed (verse 26) but will have a special relationship to God (verse 27).

Later in Joel 3:18 the prophet declared that there will be an abundance of water in the land:

> And it shall come to pass in that day, that the mountains shall drop down sweet wine, and the hills shall flow with milk, and all the brooks of Judah shall flow with waters; and a fountain shall come forth from the house of Jehovah, and shall water the valley of Shittim.

The increased productivity of the land is again pointed out in Amos 9:13:

> Behold, the days come, saith Jehovah, that the plowman shall overtake

the reaper, and the treader of grapes him that soweth seed; and the mountains shall drop sweet wine, and all the hills shall melt.

To summarize, for the first time in Israel's history, she will possess all of the promised land while the land itself will greatly increase in its productivity and be well watered, all on the basis of the Abrahamic Covenant.

4. THE RE-ESTABLISHMENT OF THE DAVIDIC THRONE

a. BASIS: THE DAVIDIC COVENANT

The fourth facet of the final restoration of Israel is the re-establishment of the Davidic throne. This is based upon the Davidic Covenant found in two passages of Scripture. The first is in II Samuel 7:11b-16:

> Moreover Jehovah telleth thee that Jehovah will make thee a house. When thy days are fulfilled, and thou shalt sleep with thy fathers, I will set up thy seed after thee, that shall proceed out of thy bowels, and I will establish his kingdom. He shall build a house for my name, and I will establish the throne of his kingdom for ever. I will be his father, and he shall be my son: if he commit iniquity, I will chasten him with the rod of men, and with the stripes of the children of men; but my lovingkindness shall not depart from him, as I took it from Saul, whom I put away before thee. And thy house and thy kingdom shall be made sure for ever before thee: thy throne shall be established for ever.

In this covenant, David is first of all promised that he will be the head of a dynasty (verse 11b). After David dies, the throne will go to one of his sons (Solomon) and the kingdom will be established in his hand (verse 12). It is Solomon who will build the temple and so God will establish his throne (not Solomon himself) for eternity (verse 13). Solomon will sin and God will have to punish him, but God's loyal love will not be removed from Solomon as it was from Saul (verses 14-15). Nevertheless, the Davidic house or dynasty, the Davidic throne and the Davidic kingdom will be eternal (verse 16).

The emphasis in this first account of the Davidic Covenant has been on Solomon. But a slightly different emphasis is given in the second passage in I Chronicles 17:10b-14:

> Moreover I tell thee that Jehovah will build thee a house. And it shall come to pass, when thy days are fulfilled that thou must go to be with thy fathers, that I will set up thy seed after thee, who shall be of thy sons; and I will establish his kingdom. He shall build me a house, and I will establish his throne for ever. I will be his father, and he shall be my son: and I will not take my lovingkindness away from him, as I took it from him that was before thee; but I will settle him in my house and in my kingdom for ever; and his throne shall be established for ever.

The emphasis in this passage is not on Solomon but on the Messiah. David is promised a dynasty (verse 10b). Sometime after his death, a descendant of one of his sons will be established in the kingdom (verse 11). The Samuel passage spoke of one of David's own sons, Solomon; but Chronicles speaks of a descendant of one of David's sons, namely, Jesus who was a descendant of Nathan, a son of David. This descendant of David, the Messiah, will also build God a temple, the millennial temple, and His throne will be established forever (verse 12). God's mercy will never be removed from this One (verse 13). Since the Samuel passage emphasized Solomon, there was the possibility of sin. But since the Chronicles passage emphasizes the Messiah, there is no possibility of sin, and hence, no mention of sin. Finally it is this person Himself that is established forever and not merely the dynasty, kingdom and throne (verse 14).

In essence then, the Davidic Covenant promised four eternal things: an eternal dynasty, an eternal kingdom, an eternal throne, and an eternal person. The eternalness of the dynasty, kingdom, and throne are guaranteed only because the seed of David culminated in the person who is Himself eternal.

Christ holds three offices: Prophet, Priest and King. However, He does not function in all these offices simultaneously. Rather, the functioning of these three offices is to be carried out in a chronological sequence.

During His ministry on earth at His first coming, Christ functioned in His office of a Prophet. But this ceased at the time of His death. Since His death and resurrection, and until He returns, Christ is functioning in His office of a Priest. This duty will cease at the second coming of Christ. Jesus has never yet functioned in His office of a King. For Him to do so, there must be the re-establishment of the Davidic throne upon which Christ will sit to rule as King over Israel and King of the world. This duty will begin at the second coming.

b. THE PROPHETIC DEVELOPMENT

While this facet of Israel's final restoration has not been as fully developed as the others, it has not been totally ignored. Some of the prophetic developments such as Jeremiah 23:5-6 and Isaiah 9:6-7 have already been discussed in Chapter XVII on the government of the messianic age. But besides these, there are several other passages such as Psalm 89:3-4:

> I have made a covenant with my chosen, I have sworn unto David my servant: thy seed will I establish for ever, and build up thy throne to all generations.

In this passage God states that He has made an eternal covenant with David (verse 3) including the establishment of an eternal dynasty and an eternal throne (verse 4). The eternalness of the dynasty and the throne is restated later in the same Psalm in verse 29:

> His seed also will I make to endure for ever, and his throne as the days of heaven.

Still later, verses 34-37 state:

> My covenant will I not break, nor alter the thing that is gone out of my lips. Once have I sworn by my holiness: I will not lie unto David: his seed shall endure for ever, and his throne as the sun before me. It shall be established for ever as the moon, and as the faithful witness in the sky.

The continuation of the covenant is not dependent upon David or upon his descendants, but upon God's character (verse 34). Since God does not lie, the covenant is sure to stand (verse 35). For that very reason, the eternalness of the dynasty and the throne is assured (verses 36-37).

Another prophetic passage is Jeremiah 33:17-26:

> For thus saith Jehovah: David shall never want a man to sit upon the throne of the house of Israel; neither shall the priests the Levites want a man before me to offer burnt-offerings, and to burn meal-offerings, and to do sacrifice continually. And the word of Jehovah came unto Jeremiah, saying, Thus saith Jehovah: If ye can break my covenant of the day, and my covenant of the night, so that there shall not be day and night in their season; then may also my covenant be broken with David my servant, that he shall not have a son to reign upon his throne; and with the Levites the priests, my ministers. As the host of heaven cannot be numbered, neither the sand of the sea measured; so will I multiply the seed of David my servant, and the Levites that minister unto me. And the word of Jehovah came to Jeremiah, saying, Considerest thou not what this people have spoken, saying, The two families which Jehovah did choose, he hath cast them off? thus do they despise my people, that they should be no more a nation before them. Thus saith Jehovah: If my covenant of day and night stand not, if I have not appointed the ordinances of heaven and earth; then will I also cast away the seed of Jacob, and of David my servant, so that I will not take of his seed to be rulers over the seed of Abraham, Isaac, and Jacob: for I will cause their captivity to return, and will have mercy on them.

The emphasis in this passage is clearly on the eternity of and the impossibility of breaking the Davidic Covenant. Under no circumstances will the house of David ever become extinct (verses 17-18) for the Davidic Covenant is both unconditional and eternal (verses 19-21). Ultimately the seed of David will be greatly multiplied (verse 22). The re-establishment of the Davidic throne will be the antidote to the poisonous teaching that God no longer intends to fulfill His covenants with Israel (verses 23-26). God is not through with Israel (verses 23-24), but will fulfill every promise of the Davidic Covenant (verses 25-26a) and the Abrahamic Covenant (verse 26b).

One other passage in the Old Testament is Amos 9:11-12:

> In that day will I raise up the tabernacle of David that is fallen, and close up the breaches thereof; and I will raise up its ruins, and I will build it as in the days of old; that they may possess the remnant of Edom, and all the nations that are called by my name, saith Jehovah that doeth this.

When the kingdom is established, the ruins of the house of David will be repaired, and the Davidic throne will again exercise all the glory of the days gone by (verse 11). But in addition to all the glory of the past, the authority of the re-established Davidic throne will extend to all the Gentile nations (verse 12).

In the New Testament the re-establishment of the Davidic throne is found in Luke 1:32-33:

> He shall be great, and shall be called the Son of the Most High: and the Lord God shall give unto him the throne of his father David: and he shall reign over the house of Jacob for ever; and of his kingdom there shall be no end.

All four key aspects of the Davidic throne are mentioned here. The Son of Mary is to sit upon the eternal throne over an eternal kingdom, for He was born into the eternal dynasty. The eternalness of the dynasty, throne and kingdom is assured because they all culminate in the Person who is Himself eternal: the Son of God.

The promises that God made to Israel have not been rendered null and void. Israel is yet to enjoy all the promises of the four unfulfilled unconditional covenants, each of which points respectively to the four facets of Israel's final restoration.

B. OTHER CHARACTERISTICS OF ISRAEL'S FINAL RESTORATION

Besides the various features mentioned in the passages dealing with the covenants and their prophetic developments, other passages develop additional characteristics which may or may not necessarily be connected with any specific covenant. Some of these other characteristics which will be true at the time of Israel's final restoration will be dealt with in this section.

1. REUNITED AS A NATION

One of the other major features of the final restoration is that Israel will be reunited as a nation, never to be divided into separate kingdoms again. This is mentioned by Jeremiah 3:18:

> In those days the house of Judah shall walk with the house of Israel, and they shall come together out of the land of the north to the land that I gave for an inheritance unto your fathers.

The key passage for this characteristic is found in the vision of the valley of dry bones of Ezekiel 37:1-23. Ezekiel is first commanded to prophesy over the dry bones scattered all over the valley (verses 1-6). When he does, the bones all come together with sinews and skin, and then the breath of life is given to them so they become alive again (verses 7-10). As God interprets the vision of the valley of dry bones (verses 11-17), these bones are said to represent the whole house of Israel which has become spiritually dead and dispersed (verse 11). Yet God will regather them, and they will again possess the land (verses 12-13). At the time of the regathering and possession of the land, Israel will be regenerated by the Spirit of God so as to have a living and right relationship (verse 14). Then the prophet continues in Ezekiel 37:15-23:

> The word of Jehovah came again unto me, saying, And thou, son of man, take thee one stick, and write upon it, For Judah, and for the children of Israel his companions: then take another stick, and write upon it, For Joseph, the stick of Ephraim, and for all the house of Israel his companions: and join them for thee one to another into one stick, that they may become one in thy hand. And when the children of thy people shall speak unto thee, saying, Wilt thou not show us what thou meanest by these? say unto them, Thus saith the Lord Jehovah: Behold, I will take the stick of Joseph, which is in the hand of Ephraim, and the tribes of Israel his companions; and I will put them with it, even with the stick of Judah, and make them one stick, and they shall be one in my hand. And the sticks whereon thou writest shall be in thy hand before their eyes. And say unto them, Thus saith the Lord Jehovah: Behold, I will take the children of Israel from among the nations, whither they are gone, and will gather them on every side, and bring them into their own land: and I will make them one nation in the land, upon the mountains of Israel; and one king shall be king to them all; and they shall be no more two nations, neither shall they be divided into two kingdoms any more at all; neither shall they defile themselves any more with their idols, nor with their detestable things, nor with any of their transgressions; but I will save them out of all their dwelling-places, wherein they have sinned, and will cleanse them: so shall they be my people, and I will be their God.

Ezekiel is commanded to take two sticks and on one stick he is to write *Judah* and on the other *Joseph*, and then put the two sticks together so they become one stick in his hand (verses 15-17). The interpretation of the miracle is that the two kingdoms will someday be reunited into one nation (verses 18-20). When the regathering of Israel comes (verse 21), they will not be regathered into two nations, but only into one, for they will be under one king in one kingdom (verse 22). At that time they will be thoroughly cleansed of their sins which were the root cause of the original division (verse 23).

2. THE CENTER OF GENTILE ATTENTION

A second major characteristic of Israel's final restoration is that they will become the center of Gentile attention. A number of passages speak of this, such as Isaiah 14:1-2:

> For Jehovah will have compassion on Jacob, and will yet choose Israel, and set them in their own land: and the sojourner shall join himself with them, and they shall cleave to the house of Jacob. And the peoples shall take them, and bring them to their place; and the house of Israel shall possess them in the land of Jehovah for servants and for handmaids: and they shall take them captive whose captives they were; and they shall rule over their oppressors.

After Israel's regeneration and restoration (verse 1a), Gentiles will align themselves with Israel in order to worship the God of Israel (verse 1b). In fact, as Israel is being regathered, not only will this be accomplished with the help of angels, but the Gentiles will be conducting the Jews back into the land (verse 2a). Finally, the Gentiles will be possessed by Israel and will become the servants of Israel (verse 2b).

A similar statement is made in Isaiah 49:22-23:

> Thus saith the Lord Jehovah, Behold, I will lift up my hand to the nations, and set up my ensign to the peoples; and they shall bring thy sons in their bosom, and thy daughters shall be carried upon their shoulders. And kings shall be thy nursing fathers, and their queens thy nursing mothers: they shall bow down to thee with their faces to the earth, and lick the dust of thy feet; and thou shalt know that I am Jehovah; and they that wait for me shall not be put to shame.

Again the regathering of Israel is said to be with the aid of the Gentiles who will conduct the Jews back into the land (verse 22). At that time, the Gentiles of every social strata will become the servants of Israel (verse 23a), and Israel will never again be shamed by them (verse 23b).

According to Isaiah 60:1-3, the reason why Israel will become the center of Gentile attention is due to the fact that the Shechinah Glory will abide over Israel:

Arise, shine; for thy light is come, and the glory of Jehovah is risen upon thee. For, behold, darkness shall cover the earth, and gross darkness the peoples; but Jehovah will arise upon thee, and his glory shall be seen upon thee. And nations shall come to thy light, and kings to the brightness of thy rising.

Isaiah 61:4-9 states:

And they shall build the old wastes, they shall raise up the former desolations, and they shall repair the waste cities, the desolations of many generations. And strangers shall stand and feed your flocks, and foreigners shall be your plowmen and your vinedressers. But ye shall be named the priests of Jehovah; men shall call you the ministers of our God: ye shall eat the wealth of the nations, and in their glory shall ye boast yourselves. Instead of your shame ye shall have double; and instead of dishonor they shall rejoice in their portion: therefore in their land they shall possess double; everlasting joy shall be unto them. For I, Jehovah, love justice, I hate robbery with iniquity; and I will give them their recompense in truth, and I will make an everlasting covenant with them. And their seed shall be known among the nations, and their offspring among the peoples: all that see them shall acknowledge them, that they are the seed which Jehovah hath blessed.

When the regathering takes place, Israel will rebuild all the desolate cities of the land (verse 4). At that time, the Gentiles will become servants to Israel and will feed the flocks and plow the fields (verse 5). As for Israel, they will be the ministers of the Word to the Gentiles (verse 6a) and will receive the wealth of the Gentiles for their enjoyment (verse 6b). Israel will never again be shamed by the Gentiles, but rather they will receive a double portion of all blessings and possessions (verse 7). This will be the result of the New Covenant (verse 8). The Jews will be known among the Gentiles, and all the Gentiles will acknowledge that it is the Jews who have been especially chosen by God for special blessings (verse 9).

Isaiah's contemporary, Micah, also had something to say in this regard in Micah 7:14-17:

Feed thy people with thy rod, the flock of thy heritage, which dwell solitarily, in the forest in the midst of Carmel: let them feed in Bashan and Gilead, as in the days of old. As in the days of thy coming forth out of the land of Egypt will I show unto them marvellous things. The nations shall see and be ashamed of all their might; they shall lay their hand upon their mouth; their ears shall be deaf. They shall lick the dust like a serpent; like crawling things of the earth they shall come trembling out of their close places; they shall come with fear unto Jehovah our God, and shall be afraid because of thee.

Israel is to be regathered in order to possess the land (verse 14), and this regathering will be accompanied by miracles (verse 15). When the Gentiles see this, they will cease reproaching the Jews and will have a reverential fear of the Jews. They will then submit to the God of Israel (verses 16-17).

That Israel's final restoration will cause the Jews to become the center of Gentile attention was also revealed in Zephaniah 3:20:

> At that time will I bring you in, and at that time will I gather you; for I will make you a name and a praise among all the peoples of the earth, when I bring back your captivity before your eyes, saith Jehovah.

Finally, in Zechariah 8:23, the prophet stated:

> Thus saith Jehovah of hosts: In those days it shall come to pass, that ten men shall take hold, out of all the languages of the nations, they shall take hold of the skirt of him that is a Jew, saying, We will go with you, for we have heard that God is with you.

In the past, when ten Gentiles grabbed the clothes of the Jew, it was for other reasons than to say, *Let us go with you, for we have heard God is with you*. At the time of the final restoration, the Jews will no longer be reproached. Instead Jews will be treated with reverential respect for they will be known as the ministers of God.

3. RIGHTEOUSNESS, HOLINESS, PEACE, SECURITY, JOY AND GLADNESS

Another feature of Israel's final restoration combines the various characteristics of righteousness, holiness, peace, security, joy and gladness. Righteousness and peace are the primary characteristics in Isaiah 32:16-20:

> Then justice shall dwell in the wilderness; and righteousness shall abide in the fruitful field. And the work of righteousness shall be peace; and the effect of righteousness, quietness and confidence for ever. And my people shall abide in a peaceable habitation, and in safe dwellings, and in quiet resting-places. But it shall hail in the downfall of the forest; and the city shall be utterly laid low. Blessed are ye that sow beside all waters, that send forth the feet of the ox and the ass.

Holiness, peace, security and joy are emphasized in Isaiah 35:5-10, things that will earmark the time of Israel's regathering:

> Then the eyes of the blind shall be opened, and the ears of the deaf shall be unstopped. Then shall the lame man leap as a hart, and the tongue of the dumb shall sing; for in the wilderness shall waters break out, and streams in the desert. And the glowing sand shall become a pool, and the thirsty ground springs of water: in the habitation of jackals, where they lay, shall be grass with reeds and rushes. And a highway shall be there,

and a way, and it shall be called The way of holiness; the unclean shall not pass over it; but it shall be for the redeemed: the wayfaring men, yea fools, shall not err therein. No lion shall be there, nor shall any ravenous beast go up thereon; they shall not be found there; but the redeemed shall walk there: and the ransomed of Jehovah shall return, and come with singing unto Zion; and everlasting joy shall be upon their heads: they shall obtain gladness and joy, and sorrow and sighing shall flee away.

Joy and gladness are stressed in Isaiah 51:3:

For Jehovah hath comforted Zion; he hath comforted all her waste places, and hath made her wilderness like Eden, and her desert like the garden of Jehovah; joy and gladness shall be found therein, thanksgiving, and the voice of melody.

Joy and peace in nature and man are highlighted in Isaiah 55:12-13:

For ye shall go out with joy, and be led forth with peace: the mountains and the hills shall break forth before you into singing; and all the trees of the field shall clap their hands. Instead of the thorn shall come up the fir-tree; and instead of the brier shall come up the myrtle-tree: and it shall be to Jehovah for a name, for an everlasting sign that shall not be cut off.

In Isaiah 61:10-11 the emphasis is on the righteousness aspect:

I will greatly rejoice in Jehovah, my soul shall be joyful in my God; for he hath clothed me with the garments of salvation, he hath covered me with the robe of righteousness, as a bridegroom decketh himself with a garland, and as a bride adorneth herself with her jewels. For as the earth bringeth forth its bud, and as the garden causeth the things that are sown in it to spring forth; so the Lord Jehovah will cause righteousness and praise to spring forth before all the nations.

C. THE MILLENNIAL MOUNTAIN OF JEHOVAH'S HOUSE

At the time of the second coming of Christ the land will undergo some tremendous geographical and topographical changes. One of the key changes in the land of Israel will be the rise of a very high mountain which will become the highest mountain of the world. On top of this mountain the millennial temple and the millennial Jerusalem will stand.

There are several passages that speak of this millennial mountain of Jehovah's house. One such place is Isaiah 2:2-4:

And it shall come to pass in the latter days, that the mountain of Jehovah's house shall be established on the top of the mountains, and shall be exalted above the hills; and all nations shall flow unto it. And many peoples shall go and say, Come ye, and let us go up to the mountain of Jehovah, to the house of the God of Jacob; and he will teach us of his ways, and we will walk in his paths: for out of Zion shall go forth the law, and the word of Jehovah from Jerusalem. And he will judge between the nations, and will decide concerning many peoples; and they shall beat their swords into plowshares, and their spears into pruning-hooks; nation shall not lift up sword against nation, neither shall they learn war any more.

This clearly states that the mountain upon which Jehovah's house will stand will be the highest of all the mountains, and by far the most exalted (verse 2a). All the nations will move toward it in order to learn the ways of God because the law of the millennial kingdom will emanate from this mountain (verses 2b-3). This will result in world-wide peace because differences among the nations will be settled by the Word of the Lord that will come from the mountain of Jehovah's house (verses 3b-4).

Later, in Isaiah 27:13, the prophet pointed out that this high mountain will become the center of Jewish worship:

And it shall come to pass in that day, that a great trumpet shall be blown; and they shall come that were ready to perish in the land of Assyria, and they that were outcasts in the land of Egypt; and they shall worship Jehovah in the holy mountain at Jerusalem.

But not the Jews only, for Isaiah 56:6-8 points out the fact that this great mountain of Jehovah's house will become a place of prayer for all peoples, Jews and Gentiles alike:

Also the foreigners that join themselves to Jehovah, to minister unto him, and to love the name of Jehovah, to be his servants, every one that keepeth the sabbath from profaning it, and holdeth fast my covenant; even them will I bring to my holy mountain, and make them joyful in my house of prayer: their burnt-offerings and their sacrifices shall be accepted upon mine altar; for my house shall be called a house of prayer for all peoples. The Lord Jehovah, who gathereth the outcasts of Israel, saith, Yet will I gather others to him, besides his own that are gathered.

By means of the Gentile nations the people of Israel will be brought and regathered to the mountain of Jehovah's house according to Isaiah 66:20:

And they shall bring all your brethren out of all the nations for an oblation unto Jehovah, upon horses, and in chariots, and in litters, and upon mules, and upon dromedaries, to my holy mountain Jerusalem, saith Jehovah, as the children of Israel bring their oblation in a clean vessel into the house of Jehovah.

Isaiah's contemporary, the prophet Micah, also spoke of this great mountain in Micah 4:1-2 with words that are similar to Isaiah's:

But in the latter days it shall come to pass, that the mountain of Jehovah's house shall be established on the top of the mountains, and it shall be exalted above the hills; and peoples shall flow unto it. And many nations shall go and say, Come ye, and let us go up to the mountain of Jehovah, and to the house of the God of Jacob; and he will teach us of his ways, and we will walk in his paths. For out of Zion shall go forth the law, and the word of Jehovah from Jerusalem.

The mountain of Jehovah's house will be exalted above every mountain and hill (verse 1), and the law of God will proceed from this mountain (verse 2).

The prophet that received the most revelation regarding the mountain of Jehovah's house was Ezekiel who first introduced it in Ezekiel 17:22-24, which describes *the mountain of the height of Israel* as a place of lush greenery and vegetation:

Thus saith the Lord Jehovah: I will also take of the lofty top of the cedar, and will set it; I will crop off from the topmost of its young twigs a tender one, and I will plant it upon a high and lofty mountain: in the mountain of the height of Israel will I plant it; and it shall bring forth boughs, and bear fruit, and be a goodly cedar: and under it shall dwell all birds of every wing; in the shade of the branches thereof shall they dwell. And all the trees of the field shall know that I, Jehovah, have brought down the high tree, have exalted the low tree, have dried up the green tree, and have made the dry tree to flourish: I, Jehovah, have spoken and have done it.

Later in Ezekiel 20:40-41, the prophet declared that the mountain will serve as the center of Jewish worship in the kingdom. After Israel's regeneration and regathering, she will worship the Lord in this high, lofty and holy mountain:

For in my holy mountain, in the mountain of the height of Israel, saith the Lord Jehovah, there shall all the house of Israel, all of them, serve me in the land: there will I accept them, and there will I require your offerings, and the first-fruits of your oblations, with all your holy things. As a sweet savor will I accept you, when I bring you out from the peoples, and gather you out of the countries wherein ye have been scattered; and I will be sanctified in you in the sight of the nations.

Only in the closing chapters of his book does Ezekiel give the details of what this very high mountain of Jehovah's house will be like in three different places. The first is in Ezekiel 40:1-4:

In the five and twentieth year of our captivity, in the beginning of the year, in the tenth day of the month, in the fourteenth year after that the city was smitten, in the selfsame day, the hand of Jehovah was upon me, and he brought me thither. In the visions of God brought he me into the land of Israel, and set me down upon a very high mountain, whereon was as it were the frame of a city on the south. And he brought me thither; and, behold, there was a man, whose appearance was like the appearance of brass, with a line of flax in his hand, and a measuring reed;

and he stood in the gate. And the man said unto me, Son of man, behold with thine eyes, and hear with thine ears, and set thy heart upon all that I shall show thee; for, to the intent that I may show them unto thee, art thou brought hither: declare all that thou seest to the house of Israel.

In the twenty-fifth year of the seventy years of captivity, Ezekiel was given a final, special revelation of Israel's future in the messianic kingdom (verse 1). As Isaiah and Micah before him, he saw a very high mountain which had the skyline of a city on its southern side (verse 2). As will be seen later, this city is the millennial Jerusalem. Then a message is spoken to the prophet that he is about to be given certain revelations which he is to declare to the house of Israel (verses 3-4).

The second passage, Ezekiel 45:1-8, describes in great detail the mountain of Jehovah's house:

Moreover, when ye shall divide by lot the land for inheritance, ye shall offer an oblation unto Jehovah, a holy portion of the land; the length shall be the length of five and twenty thousand reeds, and the breadth shall be ten thousand: it shall be holy in all the border thereof round about. Of this there shall be for the holy place five hundred in length by five hundred in breadth, square round about; and fifty cubits for the suburbs thereof round about. And of this measure shalt thou measure a length of five and twenty thousand, and a breadth of ten thousand: and in it shall be the sanctuary, which is most holy. It is a holy portion of the land; it shall be for the priests, the ministers of the sanctuary, that come near to minister unto Jehovah; and it shall be a place for their houses, and a holy place for the sanctuary. And five and twenty thousand in length, and ten thousand in breadth, shall be unto the Levites, the ministers of the house, for a possession unto themselves, for twenty chambers. And ye shall appoint the possession of the city five thousand broad, and five and twenty thousand long, side by side with the oblation of the holy portion: it shall be for the whole house of Israel. And whatsoever is for the prince shall be on the one side and on the other side of the holy oblation and of the possession of the city, in front of the holy oblation and in front of the possession of the city, on the west side westward, and on the east side eastward; and in length answerable unto one of the portions, from the west border unto the east border. In the land it shall be to him for a possession in Israel: and my princes shall no more oppress my people; but they shall give the land to the house of Israel according to their tribes.

This holy mountain is referred to as the holy oblation, because somewhere on this mountain the temple is to stand as well as the city of Jerusalem. This very high mountain, the highest in the world, will itself have a fifty-mile square plateau on top (verse 1). This square plateau will be subdivided into three sections. The northern section (verses 2-4) will be twenty miles by fifty miles, having in its center the millennial temple which will be one mile square. The rest of the area of the northern section will be reserved for a certain group of priests to live in.

The central section (verse 5) will also be twenty miles by fifty miles and will be reserved for the members of the tribe of Levi.

The southern section (verses 6-8) will be ten miles by fifty miles. In the center of the southern section will stand the millennial Jerusalem measuring ten miles by ten miles. On either side of the city will be field areas each measuring ten by twenty miles for growing food. These areas will be controlled by the prince, the resurrected David, who will apportion the land according to tribe.

The third place Ezekiel described the details of the mountain of Jehovah's house is in Ezekiel 48:8-20:

> And by the border of Judah, from the east side unto the west side, shall be the oblation which ye shall offer, five and twenty thousand reeds in breadth, and in length as one of the portions, from the east side unto the west side: and the sanctuary shall be in the midst of it. The oblation that ye shall offer unto Jehovah shall be five and twenty thousand reeds in length, and ten thousand in breadth. And for these, even for the priests, shall be the holy oblation; toward the north five and twenty thousand in length, and toward the west ten thousand in breadth, and toward the east ten thousand in breadth, and toward the south five and twenty thousand in length: and the sanctuary of Jehovah shall be in the midst thereof. It shall be for the priests that are sanctified of the sons of Zadok, that have kept my charge, that went not astray when the children of Israel went astray, as the Levites went astray. And it shall be unto them an oblation from the oblation of the land, a thing most holy, by the border of the Levites. And answerable unto the border of the priests, the Levites shall have five and twenty thousand in length, and ten thousand in breadth: all the length shall be five and twenty thousand, and the breadth ten thousand. And they shall sell none of it, nor exchange it, nor shall the first-fruits of the land be alienated; for it is holy unto Jehovah. And the five thousand that are left in the breadth, in front of the five and twenty thousand, shall be for common use, for the city, for dwelling and for suburbs; and the city shall be in the midst thereof. And these shall be the measures thereof: the north side four thousand and five hundred, and the south side four thousand and five hundred, and on the east side four thousand and five hundred, and the west side four thousand and five hundred. And the city shall have suburbs: toward the north two hundred and fifty, and toward the south two hundred and fifty, and toward the east two hundred and fifty, and toward the west two hundred and fifty. And the residue in the length, answerable unto the holy oblation, shall be ten thousand eastward, and ten thousand westward; and it shall be answerable unto the holy oblation; and the increase thereof shall be for food unto them that labor in the city. And they that labor in the city, out of all the tribes of Israel, shall till it. All the oblation shall be five and twenty thousand by five and twenty thousand: ye shall offer the holy oblation four-square, with the possession of the city.

After announcing that the high mountain is to be fifty miles square (verse 8), Ezekiel begins to describe the northern section (verses 9-12). This northern section will be twenty miles by fifty miles (verse 9) and will be inhabited by priests, for in the very center of this section the millennial temple is to stand (verse 10). The priests who are to occupy this area around the temple are the descendants of Zadok, because that segment of the tribe of Levi remained faithful while the rest went astray (verses 11-12).

The central section (verses 13-14) will also measure twenty miles by fifty miles. This area will be reserved for the rest of the tribe of Levi, those Levites who did not belong to the line of Zadok.

The southern section (verses 15-19) is to measure ten miles by fifty miles in the middle of which the millennial Jerusalem is to be built (verses 15-16). Jerusalem will be in the very center of this southern section and will measure ten miles by ten miles (verse 17).

The two remaining portions of the southern section, east and west of Jerusalem, will each measure ten miles by twenty miles and will be for the purpose of growing food for the inhabitants of Jerusalem (verse 18). Jerusalem will not belong to any particular tribe but will be inhabited by members of all the twelve tribes of Israel (verse 19).

Again, Ezekiel states that the total size of this mountain of Jehovah's house is to be fifty miles by fifty miles. It will be the Holy Oblation upon which both the temple and Jerusalem will sit (verse 20).

Putting all these passages together, the mountain of Jehovah's house can be illustrated as follows:

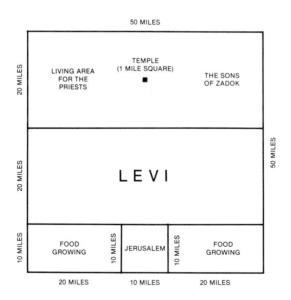

D. THE MILLENNIAL TEMPLE — EZEKIEL 40:5-43:27

In Ezekiel 37:26-28, Ezekiel prophesied that God's sanctuary will be placed in the midst of Israel:

> Moreover I will make a covenant of peace with them; it shall be an ever-lasting covenant with them; and I will place them, and multiply them, and will set my sanctuary in the midst of them for evermore. My tabernacle also shall be with them; and I will be their God, and they shall be my people. And the nations shall know that I am Jehovah that sanctifieth Israel, when my sanctuary shall be in the midst of them for evermore.

There is a great expansion and elaboration of these few verses in Ezekiel 40:5-43:27. The study of this lengthy passage will need to be limited to a survey of the material given by Ezekiel emphasizing only a few important features. There are eight main sections which discuss the various facets of the millennial temple.

The first section in 40:5-27 concerns *the outer court*. After the measure of the outer wall (verse 5), Ezekiel gives a description of the outer court (verses 6-27), mentioning the eastern gate (verses 6-16), the thirty chambers and the pavement around the outer court (verses 17-19), the northern gate (verses 20-23) and the southern gate (verses 24-27).

The second section has a description of *the inner court* in Ezekiel 40:28-47. There are four things which are described. The first item is the gates of the inner court (verses 28-37) composed of the southern gate area (verses 28-31), the eastern gate area (verses 32-34) and the northern gate area (verses 35-37). Secondly, the prophet describes the table for the preparing of the sacrifices (verses 38-43); thirdly, the chambers for the ministering priests (verses 44-46); and fourthly, the altar (verse 47).

The third section describes *the millennial temple* itself in Ezekiel 40:48-41:26. Included in this description are the porch (verses 48-49), the posts (verse 1), the holy place (verse 2), the holy of holies (verses 3-4), the temple wall and chambers (verses 5-11), the separate place (verses 12-14), the interior of the temple (verses 15-20) and the exterior of the temple (verses 21-26). From all these various measurements, it is evident that this particular temple will be the largest of all previous temples, measuring about one mile square. The area of the present temple site is not large enough to hold the temple described by Ezekiel and will require some major geographical changes. That is why the new mountain of Jehovah's house will be necessary.

The fourth section describes *the chambers of the outer court* in Ezekiel 42:1-14.

The fifth section describes *the outer wall* in Ezekiel 42:15-20.

The sixth section records *the return of the Shechinah Glory* in

Ezekiel 43:1-9. Just as the Shechinah Glory authenticated and sanctioned the Solomonic temple, it will also sanction this temple by its return from the same direction that it left (verses 1-5). Once the Shechinah Glory returns it will declare a message in which the promise will be made that the Shechinah Glory will never depart from Israel again but will dwell in the midst of Israel forever (verses 6-9).*

The seventh section, Ezekiel 43:10-12, is *a command to the prophet* to point out the sinfulness of Israel. In light of the coming holy oblation, how much more should Israel be ashamed of their present sinfulness.

The eighth section is a description of *the altar* in Ezekiel 43:13-27. Included in this description is the measure of the altar (verses 13-17) and the consecration of the altar (verses 18-23).

This then is the millennial temple that is to be the center of Jewish and Gentile worship during the millennium.

E. THE MILLENNIAL SYSTEM OF PRIESTHOOD AND SACRIFICE EZEKIEL 44:1-46:24

These three chapters of Ezekiel are concerned with the various laws regulating the millennial system of priesthood and sacrifice. While there are similarities with the commandments of the Law of Moses, there are also some marked differences. For this reason, the millennial system of priesthood and sacrifice must not be viewed as a reinstitution of the Law of Moses which ended permanently and forever with the death of Christ. During the messianic age a whole new system of law will be instituted. There will be no reinstitution of any previous code of law.

This particular passage of Scripture has seven major sections dealing with this theme. The first section in Ezekiel 44:1-3 concerns *the law of the outer eastern gate*. The passage states that in the beginning of the millennium, the outer eastern gate will be shut, never to be reopened again throughout the millennium (verse 1). The reason for the shutting of the outer eastern gate is due to the fact that the Shechinah Glory returned by way of the eastern gate (Ezekiel 43:1-9) never to leave Israel again (verse 2). The closing of the outer eastern gate will symbolize the fact that the Shechinah Glory will never depart from Israel again. Ezekiel then describes the prince and the authority and ministry he will have in relationship to this outer eastern gate (verse 3). The prince, as has already been shown, will be the resurrected David. He will eat before the gate (verse 3a) and entrance will be by means of the porch only (verse 3b). It should be pointed out that this passage of Scripture has nothing to do with the present eastern

---

* For further details see Appendix IV.

gate of Jerusalem, today known as the Golden Gate. This passage, in its context, is not dealing with Jerusalem today but is dealing with the temple gate in the millennium.

The second section (Ezekiel 44:4-8) contains another *message of the Shechinah Glory* which again points out Israel's present sins.

The third section (Ezekiel 44:9-14) describes *the duties of the Levites* who will be the caretakers of the temple.

The fourth section (Ezekiel 44:15-31) concerns *the duties of the sons of Zadok* who will be in charge of the sacrifices of the temple.*

The fifth section (Ezekiel 45:1-8) describes *the holy oblation* or the mountain of Jehovah's house which has already been discussed in this chapter.

The sixth section (Ezekiel 45:9-46:18) describes *the duties of the prince, David.* Three things are stated concerning his duties. First, unlike in Israel's past history, the law of the measurements (45:9-12) will be characterized by true, faithful and just balances. Secondly, the duties will involve the carrying out of the laws of the offerings (45:13-46:16). After listing some general instructions (verses 13-17), Ezekiel describes the law relating to the new year offerings (verses 18-20), the passover offerings (verses 21-24), the offerings for the feast of tabernacles (verse 25), and the Sabbath offerings (verses 1-5), which will take place at the inner eastern gate. The inner eastern gate will be shut for six days, but they will always be opened on the Sabbath throughout the kingdom period. Then, the new moon offerings are described (verses 6-8) along with the special festival offerings (verses 9-12) and the daily sacrifices (verses 13-15). Thirdly, the prince will have some special rights because of his exalted position in relationship to the temple (46:16-18).

The seventh section (Ezekiel 46:19-24) concerns *the laws of the boiling of the sacrifices.*

One of the things present in the Solomonic temple that will be absent in the millennial temple is the ark of the covenant according to Jeremiah 3:16:

> And it shall come to pass, when ye are multiplied and increased in the land, in those days, saith Jehovah, they shall say no more, The ark of the covenant of Jehovah; neither shall it come to mind; neither shall they remember it; neither shall they miss it; neither shall it be made any more.

Since God Himself in the person of the Messiah will be dwelling in and reigning from Jerusalem, there will be no need for any ark of the covenant. Furthermore, the ark of the covenant contained the tablets of stone which were the embodiment of the Law of Moses. The fact that the Law of Moses is no longer in effect is another reason why the

---

* According to Isaiah 66:21, there will also be Gentile priests. See Chapter XX.

ark of the covenant will be missing.

To summarize, there will be a sacrificial system instituted in the millennium that will have some features similar to the Mosaic system along with some brand new laws. For that very reason, the sacrificial system of the millennium must not be viewed as a reinstitution of the Mosaic system, because it is not. It will be a brand new system that will contain some things old and some things new and will be instituted for an entirely different purpose.

A common argument against taking these verses literally is the question as to why such a system would be necessary since the Messiah has already died. If the death of Christ was the final sacrifice for sin, how could these animal sacrifices provide an expiation for sin? Therefore, some say, these chapters of Ezekiel must not be taken literally. But if not, Ezekiel gives a lot of detail that would suddenly become meaningless. Furthermore, if all that detail is intended to be symbolic, the symbols are never explained. So the non-literalist is forced to be subjective in expounding them and must resort to guess work. The literal approach is the safest method to gain understanding of these passages. But what will be the purpose of these sacrifices in light of Christ's death? To begin with, it should be remembered that the sacrificial system of the Mosaic Law did not remove sins either (Hebrews 10:4) but only covered them (the meaning of "atonement" in Hebrew). Its purpose was to serve as a physical and visual picture of what the Messiah would do (Isaiah 53:10-12). The church has been commanded to keep the Lord's supper as a physical and visual picture of what Christ did do on the cross. God intends to provide for Israel in the kingdom a physical and visual picture of what Christ accomplished on the cross. But for Israel, it will be a sacrificial system instead of communion with bread and wine. The purpose of the sacrificial system in the kingdom will be the same as the purpose of communion for the church: *in remembrance of me.*

F.   THE MILLENNIAL RIVER — EZEKIEL 47:1-12

Altogether, there are three passages that speak about the millennial river. One of these is this Ezekiel passage which depicts the river as beginning in the temple area and eventually making its way south to the Dead Sea. The entire Ezekiel passage is summarized in Joel 3:18:

> And it shall come to pass in that day, that the mountains shall drop down sweet wine, and the hills shall flow with milk, and all the brooks of Judah shall flow with waters; and a fountain shall come forth from the house of Jehovah, and shall water the valley of Shittim.

According to Joel, the millennial river will originate in the temple area.

The point of origin is further described in Ezekiel 47:1-2:

> And he brought me back unto the door of the house; and, behold, waters issued out from under the treshold of the house eastward; (for the forefront of the house was toward the east;) and the waters came down from under, from the right side of the house, on the south of the altar. Then he brought me out by the way of the gate northward, and led me round by the way without unto the outer gate, by the way of the gate that looketh toward the east; and, behold, there ran out waters on the right side.

From the front part of the temple, by the threshold of the door and the right side of the altar which will stand in front of the temple, the millennial river will gush out, first heading east until it passes the eastern gate and then heading south toward the Dead Sea. It will not flow directly from the temple to the Dead Sea, but will first flow to Jerusalem as depicted in Zechariah 14:8:

> And it shall come to pass in that day, that living waters shall go out from Jerusalem; half of them toward the eastern sea, and half of them toward the western sea: in summer and in winter shall it be.

While the river will begin in the temple, it is clear from this passage that it will flow southward to the city of Jerusalem where it will be divided in two. The western branch will flow down the mountain and empty into the Mediterranean Sea. The eastern branch will flow into the Dead Sea. The branching out of these waters towards the areas designated for growing food on both sides of Jerusalem will provide the necessary water for the growth of the crops.

Since the eastern branch empties into the Dead Sea, the character of the Dead Sea will change. It will begin swarming with life as prophesied in Ezekiel 47:8-10:

> Then said he unto me, These waters issue forth toward the eastern region, and shall go down into the Arabah; and they shall go toward the sea; into the sea shall the waters go which were made to issue forth; and the waters shall be healed. And it shall come to pass, that every living creature which swarmeth, in every place whither the rivers come, shall live; and there shall be a very great multitude of fish; for these waters are come thither, and the waters of the sea shall be healed, and every thing shall live whithersoever the river cometh. And it shall come to pass, that fishers shall stand by it: from En-gedi even unto Eneglaim shall be a place for the spreading of nets; their fish shall be after their kinds, as the fish of the great sea, exceeding many.

Adding this information to our previous illustration, it can be pictured as follows:

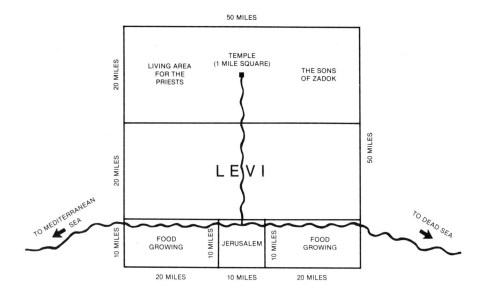

G.   THE MILLENNIAL ISRAEL — EZEKIEL 47:13-48:29

For the first time in Israel's history, the Jews will possess and settle in all of the promised land, and it will again be subdivided into the twelve tribal divisions. But these tribal divisions will be different than those described in the book of Joshua.

This portion of Ezekiel can be subdivided into five sections describing Israel in the messianic kingdom. In the first section (47:13-14) Ezekiel states that the division of all of the promised land will be the final fulfillment of God's covenant promises.

The second section (Ezekiel 47:15-20) deals with the boundaries of the land in the millennium. The northern boundary will extend from the Mediterranean Sea incorporating much of modern day Lebanon and parts of modern Syria over to the Euphrates River (verses 15-17). The eastern bordern will move south from the Euphrates River, incorporating the Golan Heights and portions of Syria almost up to Damascus, and continue south to the Jordan River where it exits from the Sea of Galilee. The border will then run along the river all the way down to the southern end of the Dead Sea (verse 18). The southern border will move from the southern end of the Dead Sea, incorporating the Negev and parts of Sinai all the way along the Brook of Egypt, the modern *Wadi-el-Arish,* to the point that it reaches the Mediterranean Sea (verse 19). The Mediterranean Sea will serve as the western border (verse 20).

The third section (Ezekiel 48:1-7) describes the northern division of the land as subdivided for seven of the twelve tribes. The tribes will be settled running from north to south in the following order: Dan (verse 1), Asher (verse 2), Naphtali (verse 3), Manasseh (verse 4), Ephraim (verse 5), Reuben (verse 6) and Judah (verse 7).

The fourth section (Ezekiel 48:8-22) describes the holy oblation discussed earlier in this chapter. But now Ezekiel notes the exact location of this mountain of Jehovah's house. The mountain of the holy oblation will be situated at the south of Judah's border and will serve as the dividing line between the northern seven tribes and the southern five tribes.

Then the fifth section (Ezekiel 48:23-27) describes the division of the land for the remaining five tribes. Again, running from north to south, the tribes will be settled in the following order: Benjamin (verse 23), Simeon (verse 24), Issachar (verse 25), Zebulun (verse 26) and Gad (verse 27) running along the southern border (verses 28-29).

The millennial Israel along with the holy oblation can be illustrated as follows:

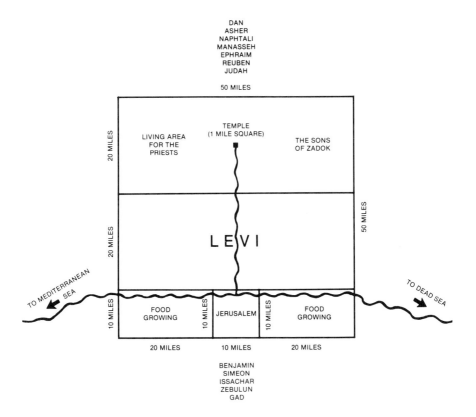

H.   THE MILLENNIAL JERUSALEM — EZEKIEL 48:30-35

Ezekiel closes the final section of his book with a short description of the millennial Jerusalem adding details not found elsewhere in the prophets. All four sides of the city are described along with the gates and their names. The city gates will all be named after the twelve sons of Jacob. The north side (verses 30-31) will measure ten miles (verse 30), and the three gates will be named after Reuben, Judah, and Levi (verse 31). The eastern side (verse 32) will measure ten miles (verse 32a), and its gates will be named after Joseph, Benjamin and Dan (verse 32b). The southern side (verse 33) will measure ten miles (verse 33a) with its three gates named after Simeon, Issachar and Zebulun (verse 33b). Finally, the western side (verse 34) will also measure ten miles (verse 34a) with its gates named after Gad, Asher and Naphtali (verse 34b).

The total measurement of the city will be ten miles square (verse 35a), and Jerusalem's name will be changed to *Jehovah Shammah* which means *Jehovah is there* (verse 35b). Since Christ will personally reign from this particular city, the city will not only fulfill its name of Jerusalem (the city of peace) but also Jehovah Shammah (Jehovah is there). For this same reason the city will also be called *Jehovah Our Righteousness* according to Jeremiah 33:16.

While Ezekiel gives only a short description of the millennial Jerusalem, other characteristics of the millennial Jerusalem are to be found in other parts of Scripture. The Psalms in particular took delight in describing and characterizing the millennial Jerusalem. One such passage is Psalm 48. Verses 1-3 describe it as the residence of the God of Israel:

Great is Jehovah, and greatly to be praised, in the city of our God, in his holy mountain. Beautiful in elevation, the joy of the whole earth, is mount Zion, on the sides of the north, the city of the great King. God hath made himself known in her palaces for a refuge.

In verse 8 it is God who will establish the city:

As we have heard, so have we seen in the city of Jehovah of hosts, in the city of our God: God will establish it for ever.

Because God will dwell in and judge from Jerusalem, the city is to rejoice in verse 11:

Let mount Zion be glad, let the daughters of Judah rejoice, because of thy judgments.

Finally, the inhabitants are encouraged to study the beauty that will characterize the city in that future day in verses 12-13:

> Walk about Zion, and go round about her; number the towers thereof; mark ye well her bulwarks; consider her palaces: that ye may tell it to the generation following.

Because it is God who will establish Jerusalem, Jerusalem will be known as the city of God according to Psalm 87:1-7:

> His foundation is in the holy mountains. Jehovah loveth the gates of Zion more than all the dwellings of Jacob. Glorious things are spoken of thee, O city of God. I will make mention of Rahab and Babylon as among them that know me: behold, Philistia, and Tyre, with Ethiopia: this one was born there. Yea, of Zion it shall be said, This one and that one was born in her; and the Most High himself will establish her. Jehovah will count, when he writeth up the peoples, this one was born there. They that sing as well as they that dance shall say, All my fountains are in thee.

The peace that will characterize the millennial Jerusalem as a result of the re-establishment of the Davidic throne is described in Psalm 122:1-9:

> I was glad when they said unto me, Let us go unto the house of Jehovah. Our feet are standing within thy gates, O Jerusalem, Jerusalem, that art builded as a city that is compact together; whither the tribes go up, even the tribes of Jehovah, for an ordinance for Israel, to give thanks unto the name of Jehovah. For there are set thrones for judgment, the thrones of the house of David. Pray for the peace of Jerusalem: they shall prosper that love thee. Peace be within thy walls, and prosperity within thy palaces. For my brethren and companions' sakes, I will now say, Peace be within thee. For the sake of the house of Jehovah our God I will seek thy good.

The building up of Jerusalem at the time of the regathering of Israel is the point of Psalm 147:2-3:

> Jehovah doth build up Jerusalem; he gathereth together the outcasts of Israel. He healeth the broken in heart, and bindeth up their wounds.

Since it is God who is rebuilding Jerusalem, it will be characterized by strength as well as peace in Psalm 147:12-14:

> Praise Jehovah, O Jerusalem; praise thy God, O Zion. For he hath strengthened the bars of thy gates; he hath blessed thy children within thee. He maketh peace in thy borders; he filleth thee with the finest of the wheat.

It is from this city that the millennial law will emanate according to Psalm 147:15:

> He sendeth out his commandment upon earth; his word runneth very swiftly.

The emanation of the millennial law is also described in Psalm 147:19-20:

> He showeth his word unto Jacob, his statutes and his ordinances unto Israel. He hath not dealt so with any nation: and as for his ordinances, they have not known them. Praise ye Jehovah.

A number of the prophets of Israel also revealed other features and characteristics of the millennial Jerusalem. Among the major prophets is Isaiah who in 1:26-27 described the millennial Jerusalem as being characterized by holiness, justice, and righteousness:

> And I will restore thy judges as at the first, and thy counsellors as at the beginning: afterward thou shalt be called The city of righteousness, a faithful town. Zion shall be redeemed with justice, and her converts with righteousness.

Later in Isaiah 4:3-6, there is the following description:

> And it shall come to pass, that he that is left in Zion, and he that remaineth in Jerusalem, shall be called holy, even every one that is written among the living in Jerusalem; when the Lord shall have washed away the filth of the daughters of Zion, and shall have purged the blood of Jerusalem from the midst thereof, by the spirit of Justice, and by the spirit of burning. And Jehovah will create over the whole habitation of mount Zion, and over her assemblies, a cloud and smoke by day, and the shining of a flaming fire by night; for over all the glory shall be spread a covering. And there shall be a pavilion for a shade in the daytime from the heat, and for a refuge and for a covert from storm and from rain.

Holiness is what is going to characterize the establishment of Jerusalem (verse 3), for all of Jerusalem's previous sins will be purged by God's justice and refining fire (verse 4). Hence, over the entire Mount Zion will be the visible form of the Shechinah Glory (verses 5-6).*

In Isaiah 14:32 Jerusalem will serve as the place of security for the afflicted people:

> What then shall one answer the messengers of the nation? That Jehovah hath founded Zion, and in her shall the afflicted of his people take refuge.

Later, Isaiah 33:20-24 describes the millennial Jerusalem as follows:

> Look upon Zion, the city of our solemnities: thine eyes shall see Jerusalem a quiet habitation, a tent that shall not be removed, the stakes whereof shall never be plucked up, neither shall any of the cords thereof be broken. But there Jehovah will be with us in majesty, a place of broad

---

* For more details see Appendix IV.

rivers and streams, wherein shall go no galley with oars, neither shall gallant ship pass thereby. For Jehovah is our judge, Jehovah is our law-giver, Jehovah is our king; he will save us. Thy tacklings are loosed; they could not strengthen the foot of their mast, they could not spread the sail: then was the prey of a great spoil divided; the lame took the prey. And the inhabitant shall not say, I am sick: the people that dwell therein shall be forgiven their iniquity.

Quietness and security will characterize Jerusalem in that day (verse 20), for Jehovah in the person of the Messiah will dwell in this city (verse 21a). It will be a city of many streams and waters but without any ships of war ever sailing in them (verse 21b). The Messiah in the midst of the city will serve as the Judge, Lawgiver, King and Saviour (verse 22) and so Israel's sins will be totally forgiven (verses 23-24).

The holiness and freedom of Jerusalem is emphasized in Isaiah 52:1-2:

Awake, awake, put on thy strength, O Zion; put on thy beautiful garments, O Jerusalem, the holy city: for henceforth there shall no more come into thee the uncircumcised and the unclean. Shake thyself from the dust; arise, sit on thy throne, O Jerusalem: loose thyself from the bonds of thy neck, O captive daughter of Zion.

Jerusalem in that day will become the holy city and nothing unholy will ever enter into it (verse 1). It will be further characterized by freedom, for the times of the Gentiles will be no more and never again will Jerusalem be subject to bondage (verse 2).

In Isaiah 52:7-10, there is good news that is to be declared to Jerusalem:

How beautiful upon the mountains are the feet of him that bringeth good tidings, that publisheth peace, that bringeth good tidings of good, that publisheth salvation, that saith unto Zion, Thy God reigneth! The voice of thy watchmen! they lift up the voice, together do they sing; for they shall see eye to eye, when Jehovah returneth to Zion. Break forth into joy, sing together, ye waste places of Jerusalem; for Jehovah hath comforted his people, he hath redeemed Jerusalem. Jehovah hath made bare his holy arm in the eyes of all the nations; and all the ends of the earth have seen the salvation of our God.

The good news for Jerusalem is that Messiah will reign in Zion (verse 7), and the Jews will be regathered to Jerusalem (verse 8). Jerusalem will be built all over again, for God will redeem the city (verse 9) and salvation will characterize it (verse 10).

Jerusalem is to become the center of world-wide Gentile atten-tion according to Isaiah 60:10-14:

And foreigners shall build up thy walls, and their kings shall minister unto thee: for in my wrath I smote thee, but in my favor have I had mercy on thee. Thy gates also shall be open continually; they shall not be shut day nor night; that men may bring unto thee the wealth of the nations, and their kings led captive. For that nation and kingdom that will not serve thee shall perish; yea, those nations shall be utterly wasted. The glory of Lebanon shall come unto thee, the fir-tree, the pine, and the box-tree together, to beautify the place of my sanctuary; and I will make the place of my feet glorious. And the sons of them that afflicted thee shall come bending unto thee; and all they that despised thee shall bow themselves down at the soles of thy feet; and they shall call thee The city of Jehovah, The Zion of the Holy One of Israel.

The Gentiles, who will be the servants of Israel, will also be used in building up the millennial Jerusalem (verse 10). The twelve gates named after the twelve sons of Jacob will be continually open, never to be closed throughout the kingdom (verse 11a). The Gentile nations and kings will bring their tribute through these gates (verse 11b), for failure to do so will bring swift judgment (verse 12). The Gentile nations who in the past afflicted the city of Jerusalem will now bow in submission to its authority (verses 13-14).

A rather detailed description is in Isaiah 62:1-12:

For Zion's sake will I not hold my peace, and for Jerusalem's sake I will not rest, until her righteousness go forth as brightness, and her salvation as a lamp that burneth. And the nations shall see thy righteousness, and all kings thy glory; and thou shalt be called by a new name, which the mouth of Jehovah shall name. Thou shalt also be a crown of beauty in the hand of Jehovah, and a royal diadem in the hand of thy God. Thou shalt no more be termed Forsaken; neither shall thy land any more be termed Desolate; but thou shalt be called Hephzi-bah, and thy land Beulah; for Jehovah delighteth in thee, and thy land shall be married. For as a young man marrieth a virgin, so shall thy sons marry thee; and as the bridegroom rejoiceth over the bride, so shall thy God rejoice over thee. I have set watchmen upon thy walls, 0 Jerusalem; they shall never hold their peace day nor night: ye that are Jehovah's remembrancers, take ye no rest, and give him no rest, till he establish, and till he make Jerusalem a praise in the earth. Jehovah hath sworn by his right hand, and by the arm of his strength, Surely I will no more give thy grain to be food for thine enemies; and foreigners shall not drink thy new wine, for which thou hast labored: but they that have garnered it shall eat it, and praise Jehovah; and they that have gathered it shall drink it in the courts of my sanctuary. Go through, go through the gates; prepare ye the way of the people; cast up, cast up the highway; gather out the stones; lift up an ensign for the peoples. Behold, Jehovah hath proclaimed unto the end of the earth, Say ye to the daughter of Zion, Behold, thy salvation cometh; behold, his reward is with him, and his recompense before him. And they shall call them The holy people, The redeemed of Jehovah: and thou shalt be called Sought out, A city not forsaken.

The millennial Jerusalem will be characterized by brightness and righteousness (verse 1). Her righteousness will be recognized by all the nations of the earth (verse 2a). At that time Jerusalem will be given a new name (verse 2b), the one mentioned in Ezekiel 48:35: *Jehovah Shammah*. Jerusalem will be further characterized by beauty (verse 3) never again to be forsaken or desolated by God (verse 4a), for it itself will be God's joy and delight (verses 4b-5).

To make sure that these promises will someday be fulfilled, angelic messengers have been placed upon the walls of Jerusalem whose entire ministry consists of reminding God of His promises to make Jerusalem the joy and praise of the whole earth (verses 6-7). The inhabitants of millennial Jerusalem are promised that they will enjoy the fruits of their labors, for the results of their labor will never again be taken away by their enemies (verses 8-9). The declaration is made that the redemption and salvation of Jerusalem is assured, because God is One who keeps His promises (verses 10-12).

Joy and rejoicing will be prominent characteristics of the millennial Jerusalem in Isaiah 65:18-19:

> But be ye glad and rejoice for ever in that which I create; for, behold, I create Jerusalem a rejoicing, and her people a joy. And I will rejoice in Jerusalem, and joy in my people; and there shall be heard in her no more the voice of weeping and the voice of crying.

Peace and comfort along with joy are features of the city in Isaiah 66:10-14:

> Rejoice ye with Jerusalem, and be glad for her, all ye that love her: rejoice for joy with her, all ye that mourn over her; that ye may suck and be satisfied with the breasts of her consolations; that ye may milk out, and be delighted with the abundance of her glory. For thus saith Jehovah, Behold, I will extend peace to her like a river, and the glory of the nations like an overflowing stream: and ye shall suck thereof; ye shall be borne upon the side, and shall be dandled upon the knees. As one whom his mother comforteth, so will I comfort you; and ye shall be comforted in Jerusalem. And ye shall see it, and your heart shall rejoice, and your bones shall flourish like the tender grass: and the hand of Jehovah shall be known toward his servants; and he will have indignation against his enemies.

Though Isaiah is the primary major prophet describing the millennial Jerusalem, other major prophets spoke of it as well. In Jeremiah 3:17 the re-established Davidic throne will be situated in Jerusalem making it the center of Gentile attention:

> At that time they shall call Jerusalem the throne of Jehovah; and all the nations shall be gathered unto it, to the name of Jehovah, to Jerusalem: neither shall they walk any more after the stubbornness of their evil heart.

It will also be a center of Jewish attraction in Jeremiah 31:6:

> For there shall be a day, that the watchmen upon the hills of Ephraim shall cry, Arise ye, and let us go up to Zion unto Jehovah our God.

The increased size of Jerusalem, its holiness and its indestructibility are the points of Jeremiah 31:38-40:

> Behold, the days come, saith Jehovah, that the city shall be built to Jehovah from the tower of Hananel unto the gate of the corner. And the measuring line shall go out further straight onward unto the hill Gareb, and shall turn about unto Goah. And the whole valley of the dead bodies and of the ashes, and all the fields unto the brook Kidron, unto the corner of the horse gate toward the east, shall be holy unto Jehovah; it shall not be plucked up, nor thrown down any more for ever.

The peace and joy that will return to Jerusalem is described in Jeremiah 33:9-11:

> And this city shall be to me for a name of joy, for a praise and for a glory, before all the nations of the earth, which shall hear all the good that I do unto them, and shall fear and tremble for all the good and for all the peace that I procure unto it. Thus saith Jehovah: Yet again there shall be heard in this place, whereof ye say, It is waste, without man and without beast, even in the cities of Judah, and in the streets of Jerusalem, that are desolate, without man and without inhabitant and without beast, the voice of joy and the voice of gladness, the voice of the bridegroom and the voice of the bride, the voice of them that say, Give thanks to Jehovah of hosts, for Jehovah is good, for his lovingkindness endureth for ever; and of them that bring sacrifices of thanksgiving into the house of Jehovah. For I will cause the captivity of the land to return as at the first, saith Jehovah.

The joy, peace and glory of Jerusalem will attract the Gentile nations from afar (verse 9). All the former desolations of Jerusalem will be forever forgotten (verse 10), for the streets of Jerusalem will bustle with the noise of joy and gladness and with the happy voices of brides and bridegrooms (verse 11).

Scattered among the minor prophets are more references describing the millennial Jerusalem. Jerusalem is to be characterized by holiness and security only because God Himself will dwell in her according to Joel 3:17:

> So shall ye know that I am Jehovah your God, dwelling in Zion my holy mountain: then shall Jerusalem be holy, and there shall no strangers pass through her any more.

It is from Jerusalem that God will reign over the regathered Israel in Micah 4:6-8:

In that day, saith Jehovah, will I assemble that which is lame, and I will gather that which is driven away, and that which I have afflicted; and I will make that which was lame a remnant, and that which was cast far off a strong nation: and Jehovah will reign over them in mount Zion from henceforth even for ever. And thou, O tower of the flock, the hill of the daughter of Zion, unto thee shall it come, yea, the former dominion shall come, the kingdom of the daughter of Jerusalem.

In Zephaniah 3:14-17 the following description is given:

Sing, O daughter of Zion; shout, O Israel; be glad and rejoice with all the heart, O daughter of Jerusalem. Jehovah hath taken away thy judgments, he hath cast out thine enemy: the King of Israel, even Jehovah, is in the midst of thee; thou shalt not fear evil any more. In that day it shall be said to Jerusalem, Fear thou not; O Zion, let not thy hands be slack. Jehovah thy God is in the midst of thee, a mighty one who will save; he will rejoice over thee with joy; he will rest in his love; he will joy over thee with singing.

Jerusalem is to shout for joy and gladness (verse 14), for the city will be redeemed (verse 15a). God Himself will dwell in the city (verses 15b-17) and reign over the inhabitants of the city.

Of all the minor prophets, Zechariah had the most to say concerning the millennial Jerusalem. In the very first chapter of his book, in Zechariah 1:14-17, the prophet reported a promise God made that He has every intention of choosing Jerusalem in spite of desolations afflicted on her by the Gentiles:

So the angel that talked with me said unto me, Cry thou, saying, Thus saith Jehovah of hosts: I am jealous for Jerusalem and for Zion with a great jealousy. And I am very sore displeased with the nations that are at ease; for I was but a little displeased, and they helped forward the affliction. Therefore thus saith Jehovah: I am returned to Jerusalem with mercies; my house shall be built in it, saith Jehovah of hosts, and a line shall be stretched forth over Jerusalem. Cry yet again, saying, Thus saith Jehovah of hosts: My cities shall yet overflow with prosperity; and Jehovah shall yet comfort Zion, and shall yet choose Jerusalem.

Then in Zechariah 2:1-5 he stated:

And I lifted up mine eyes, and saw, and, behold, a man with a measuring line in his hand. Then said I, Whither goest thou? And he said unto me, To measure Jerusalem, to see what is the breadth thereof, and what is the length thereof. And, behold, the angel that talked with me went forth, and another angel went out to meet him, and said unto him, Run, speak to this young man, saying, Jerusalem shall be inhabited as villages without walls, by reason of the multitude of men and cattle therein. For I, saith Jehovah, will be unto her a wall of fire round about, and I will be the glory in the midst of her.

This passage is an elaboration of the promise made in Zechariah 1:14-17 in which God promised that He will choose Jerusalem and rebuild her. Now in Zechariah 2:1-5 the promise is developed. Jerusalem will indeed be rebuilt to a size far greater than ever before (verses 1-2). The rebuilding is portrayed as a city without walls (verses 3-4). It does not state that there will be no walls as if to contradict other passages studied in this chapter. It simply says as without walls. The purpose of walled cities was for protection and security. However, the millennial Jerusalem will not need a wall for the purpose of protection or security since the Messiah Himself will dwell in her midst. The purpose of Jerusalem's wall will not be for protection but for beauty. The reason why the wall will not be needed for security is because on one hand God will dwell in the midst of Jerusalem, while on the other hand the Shechinah Glory* in a form of fire will surround the city (verse 5).

The point is restated in Zechariah 2:10-12:

Sing and rejoice, O daughter of Zion; for, lo, I come, and I will dwell in the midst of thee, saith Jehovah. And many nations shall join themselves to Jehovah in that day, and shall be my people; and I will dwell in the midst of thee, and thou shalt know that Jehovah of hosts hath sent me unto thee. And Jehovah shall inherit Judah as his portion in the holy land, and shall yet choose Jerusalem.

God, in the person of the Messiah, will indeed dwell in Jerusalem (verse 10). For this reason, Jerusalem will be the center of world-wide Gentile attention (verse 11). From His throne in Jerusalem the Messiah will reign over all Israel and the Holy Land (verse 12).

Another graphic description of the millennial Jerusalem is in Zechariah 8:1-8:

And the word of Jehovah of hosts came to me, saying, Thus saith Jehovah of hosts: I am jealous for Zion with great jealousy, and I am jealous for her with great wrath. Thus saith Jehovah: I am returned unto Zion, and will dwell in the midst of Jerusalem: and Jerusalem shall be called The city of truth; and the mountain of Jehovah of hosts, The holy mountain. Thus saith Jehovah of hosts: There shall yet old men and old women dwell in the streets of Jerusalem, every man with his staff in his hand for very age. And the streets of the city shall be full of boys and girls playing in the streets thereof. Thus saith Jehovah of hosts: If it be marvellous in the eyes of the remnant of this people in those days, should it also be marvellous in mine eyes? saith Jehovah of hosts. Thus saith Jehovah of hosts: Behold, I will save my people from the east country, and from the west country; and I will bring them, and they shall dwell in the midst of Jerusalem; and they shall be my people, and I will be their God, in truth and in righteousness.

God's special jealousy for Jerusalem (verses 1-2) will cause Him

---

* See Appendix IV.

to return to Jerusalem to dwell in her midst (verse 3a). At that time Jerusalem will become the city of truth upon the mountain of Jehovah's house (verse 3b). The city will be inhabited by the very young and the very old (verses 4-5). The very young will be those who will be born in the kingdom, while the very old will indeed be very old, for many will be several hundred years of age in the closing centuries of the millennium. The millennial Jerusalem will be a marvelous work that only God can do (verse 6). Once the millennial Jerusalem is established, it will be inhabited by the Jews regathered from all over the world (verses 7-8).

Jerusalem becoming the center of world-wide Gentile attention is the point of Zechariah 8:20-22:

> Thus saith Jehovah of hosts: It shall yet come to pass, that there shall come peoples, and the inhabitants of many cities; and the inhabitants of one city shall go to another, saying, Let us go speedily to entreat the favor of Jehovah, and to seek Jehovah of hosts: I will go also. Yea, many peoples and strong nations shall come to seek Jehovah of hosts in Jerusalem, and to entreat the favor of Jehovah.

The unique situation of Jerusalem in the kingdom is described in Zechariah 14:9-11:

> And Jehovah shall be King over all the earth: in that day shall Jehovah be one, and his name one. All the land shall be made like the Arabah, from Geba to Rimmon south of Jerusalem; and she shall be lifted up, and shall dwell in her place, from Benjamin's gate unto the place of the first gate, unto the corner gate, and from the tower of Hananel unto the king's winepresses. And men shall dwell therein, and there shall be no more curse; but Jerusalem shall dwell safely.

The Messiah will be King in the city (verse 9), and the geography of the land will be greatly altered so that Jerusalem can be enlarged and exalted on the mountain of Jehovah's house (verse 10). Only then will Jerusalem become truly the city of peace and live in total security (verse 11).

Finally, the holiness that will characterize Jerusalem will extend to the very bells upon the horses and to the pots and pans in the kitchens according to Zechariah 14:20-21:

> In that day shall there be upon the bells of the horses, HOLY UNTO JEHOVAH; and the pots in Jehovah's house shall be like the bowls before the altar. Yea, every pot in Jerusalem and in Judah shall be holy unto Jehovah of hosts; and all they that sacrifice shall come and take of them, and boil therein: and in that day there shall be no more a Canaanite in the house of Jehovah of hosts.

The golden age of Jerusalem is yet to come.

CHAPTER XX

THE GENTILES IN THE MESSIANIC KINGDOM

A. GENERAL CHARACTERISTICS

The Gentiles who survive the Judgment of the Gentiles for their treatment of Israel are the ones who will enter and populate the Gentile nations in the millennium. These are the sheep Gentiles who, because of their pro-Semitism, will all be able to participate in and populate the kingdom.

Much has already been said about the place of the Gentiles in the kingdom in the previous chapters relating to the positions of Christ, the church and Israel in the kingdom. This chapter will be concerned with those passages that deal exclusively with the place of the Gentiles in the kingdom as a good number of passages in the major and minor prophets speak to this point.

Of the major prophets, Isaiah is the key. In Isaiah 11:10, the Messiah will be the center of Gentile attraction:

> And it shall come to pass in that day, that the root of Jesse, that standeth for an ensign of the peoples, unto him shall the nations seek; and his resting-place shall be glorious.

According to Isaiah 14:1-2, they will be possessed and be the servants of the people of Israel:

> For Jehovah will have compassion on Jacob, and will yet choose Israel, and set them in their own land: and the sojourner shall join himself with them, and they shall cleave to the house of Jacob. And the peoples shall take them, and bring them to their place; and the house of Israel shall possess them in the land of Jehovah for servants and for handmaids: and they shall take them captive whose captives they were; and they shall rule over their oppressors.

While on one hand the Gentiles will be subject to the King Messiah, they will also receive justice from the King in Isaiah 42:1:

> Behold, my servant, whom I uphold; my chosen, in whom my soul delighteth: I have put my Spirit upon him; he will bring forth justice to the Gentiles.

At that time in a special way, the Messiah will become the light to the Gentiles according to Isaiah 49:5-7:

> And now saith Jehovah that formed me from the womb to be his servant, to bring Jacob again to him, and that Israel be gathered unto him;

(for I am honorable in the eyes of Jehovah, and my God is become my strength;) yea, he saith, It is too light a thing that thou shouldest be my servant to raise up the tribes of Jacob, and to restore the preserved of Israel: I will also give thee for a light to the Gentiles, that thou mayest be my salvation unto the end of the earth. Thus saith Jehovah, the Redeemer of Israel, and his Holy One, to him whom man despiseth, to him whom the nation abhorreth, to a servant of rulers: Kings shall see and arise; princes, and they shall worship; because of Jehovah that is faithful, even the Holy One of Israel, who hath chosen thee.

The calling of the Messiah is not only on behalf of Israel to regather the scattered nation (verse 5a), but also to be the light and the salvation to the Gentiles (verse 6b). So at the time of the final restoration of Israel, Christ will be manifested in the most complete sense as the light to the Gentiles and all the kings of the Gentiles will worship him (verse 7).

A more extensive passage is Isaiah 56:1-8:

Thus saith Jehovah, Keep ye justice, and do righteousness; for my salvation is near to come, and my righteousness to be revealed. Blessed is the man that doeth this, and the son of man that holdeth it fast; that keepeth the sabbath from profaning it, and keepeth his hand from doing any evil. Neither let the foreigner, that hath joined himself to Jehovah, speak, saying, Jehovah will surely separate me from his people; neither let the eunuch say, Behold, I am a dry tree. For thus saith Jehovah of the eunuchs that keep my sabbaths, and choose the things that please me, and hold fast my covenant: Unto them will I give in my house and within my walls a memorial and a name better than of sons and of daughters; I will give them an everlasting name, that shall not be cut off. Also the foreigners that join themselves to Jehovah, to minister unto him, and to love the name of Jehovah, to be his servants, every one that keepeth the sabbath from profaning it, and holdeth fast my covenant; even them will I bring to my holy mountain, and make them joyful in my house of prayer: their burnt-offerings and their sacrifices shall be accepted upon mine altar; for my house shall be called a house of prayer for all peoples. The Lord Jehovah, who gathereth the outcasts of Israel, saith, Yet will I gather others to him, besides his own that are gathered.

At the time of the setting up of the kingdom, there may be some feeling among the sheep Gentiles that, because of the exalted position of Israel, the Gentiles will be excluded from receiving the benefits of the millennial temple worship (verses 1-3). But this will not be the case, for the temple ministry will be open to all Gentiles who are rightly related to the King. Under no circumstances will they be excluded either because they are Gentiles or because they are mutilated (verses 4-5). It is then and only then that the house of God will be called truly a house of prayer for all nations (verses 6-7). And when will that be? At the time of Israel's final regathering (verse 8).

That the Gentiles are to have a place in the millennial temple worship is also taught in Isaiah 66:18-24:

For I know their works and their thoughts: the time cometh, that I will gather all nations and tongues; and they shall come, and shall see my glory. And I will set a sign among them, and I will send such as escape of them unto the nations, to Tarshish, Pul, and Lud, that draw the bow, to Tubal and Javan, to the isles afar off, that have not heard my fame, neither have seen my glory; and they shall declare my glory among the nations. And they shall bring all your brethren out of all the nations for an oblation unto Jehovah, upon horses, and in chariots, and in litters, and upon mules, and upon dromedaries, to my holy mountain Jerusalem, saith Jehovah, as the children of Israel bring their oblation in a clean vessel into the house of Jehovah. And of them also will I take for priests and for Levites, saith Jehovah. For as the new heavens and the new earth, which I will make, shall remain before me, saith Jehovah, so shall your seed and your name remain. And it shall come to pass, that from one new moon to another, and from one sabbath to another, shall all flesh come to worship before me, saith Jehovah. And they shall go forth, and look upon the dead bodies of the men that have transgressed against me: for their worm shall not die, neither shall their fire be quenched; and they shall be an abhorring unto all flesh.

The Shechinah Glory which will be especially manifested in the kingdom will be seen by many of the Gentiles (verse 18), and those who do see it will set off to travel among the Gentiles who have not seen it to tell them of it (verse 19). At the same time, Gentiles will be used to conduct the Jews back into the land of Israel (verse 20a), and they will be brought to the mountain of Jehovah's house in order to worship (verse 20b). Furthermore, from among these Gentiles, God will choose some to serve as priests in the temple (verse 21). Not only is Israel the eternal nation, but the faithful among the Gentiles will also be eternal (verse 22), and they will have a place of worship in the temple for the Sabbath and new moon offerings (verse 23). As for the unfaithful among the Gentiles, their dead bodies and the suffering of their souls will be visible throughout the kingdom (verse 24) illustrating for 1,000 years God's grace to the faithful and His severity to the lost.

Besides these general characteristics there are some specific elements that need to be dealt with.

B. THE OBLIGATION TO OBSERVE THE FEAST OF TABERNACLES

Of the various feasts and celebrations and festival offerings of the millennium mentioned by Ezekiel, there is one feast, the Feast of Tabernacles, that will be obligatory for all Gentile nations. This is declared in Zechariah 14:16-19:

And it shall come to pass, that every one that is left of all the nations that came against Jerusalem shall go up from year to year to worship the King, Jehovah of hosts, and to keep the feast of tabernacles. And it shall be, that whoso of all the families of the earth goeth not up unto Jerusalem to worship the King, Jehovah of hosts, upon them there shall be no rain. And if the family of Egypt go not up, and come not, neither shall it be upon them; there shall be the plague wherewith Jehovah will smite the nations that go not up to keep the feast of tabernacles. This shall be the punishment of Egypt, and the punishment of all the nations that go not up to keep the feast of tabernacles.

All the Gentile nations that will populate the kingdom will be obligated to send a delegation to Jerusalem in order to worship the King at the time of the Feast of Tabernacles (verse 16). It may be at this time that the Gentiles will pay their obligatory tribute to the King (Isaiah 60:11). Though the Gentile observance of the Feast of Tabernacles will be mandatory, not every nation will necessarily be willing to obey. Therefore, if at any time a nation should fail to send a delegation, the rains will be withheld from them for that year (verse 17). As an example of the punishment, Zechariah mentions the case of Egypt (verses 18-19). Should Egypt fail to send a delegation, there will be no rain for Egypt. Using Egypt as an illustration of a reluctant nation to keep the Feast of Tabernacles is especially significant for originally the Feast of Tabernacles was inaugurated as part of a memorial festival of the deliverance of Israel from Egyptian bondage. But regardless of what nation may fail to obey this mandate, the punishment will be the same for all.

C. THE ARAB STATES

Another specific area the Scriptures deal with is the Arab states. The key charge the prophets bring against the various Arab states is their perpetual hatred of Israel. This hatred which was to characterize the descendants of Ishmael and Esau began as early as Numbers 20:14-21 and has continued throughout the biblical period and into modern history. A passage that summarizes this entire attitude is Psalm 83:1-8:

O God, keep not thou silence: hold not thy peace, and be not still, O God. For, lo, thine enemies make a tumult; and they that hate thee have lifted up the head. They take crafty counsel against thy people, and consult together against thy hidden ones. They have said, Come, and let us cut them off from being a nation; that the name of Israel may be no more in remembrance. For they have consulted together with one consent; against thee do they make a covenant: the tents of Edom and the Ishmaelites; Moab, and the Hagarenes; Gebal, and Ammon, and Amalek; Philistia with the inhabitants of Tyre: Assyria also is joined with them; they have helped the children of Lot.

The Psalmist begins by describing a united conspiracy against Israel (verses 1-3). They are a tumultuous and crafty people who unite together against the Jews (verses 1-2). Their aim is the total annihilation of Israel so that the very name *Israel* will no longer be remembered (verse 4). It is no coincidence that Nasser, the former dictator of Egypt, almost repeated this verse word for word just prior to the Six Day War. The various nations consult together into a covenant relationship (verse 5), and they come together to carry out the program of the previous verse: the total destruction and annihilation of Israel. Then in verses 6-8 the various nations are listed. These names are ancient ones, but they cover the territory of the modern Arab states which have different names. The following list shows what area they are comparable to today:

Edom.................................Southern Jordan
Ishmaelites.................Ishmael was one of the fathers
                                        of all the Arabs
Moab.................................Central Jordan
Hagarenes ....Egypt
Gebal...Lebanon
Ammon..........................Northern Jordan
Amalek...........................The Sinai Peninsula
Philistia..............................The Gaza Strip
Tyre ....Lebanon
Assyria.................................Syria and Iraq

While such a conspiracy of the Arab nations has been present since 1948, and was evidenced more so during and after the Six Day War, it is to have its full force in the Great Tribulation, especially during the Campaign of Armageddon.

Two other prophets pointed out the perpetual hatred against Israel, especially by Edom or modern southern Jordan. One prophet is Ezekiel 35:1-5:

Moreover the word of Jehovah came unto me, saying, Son of man, set thy face against mount Seir, and prophesy against it, and say unto it, Thus saith the Lord Jehovah: Behold, I am against thee, O mount Seir, and I will stretch out my hand against thee, and I will make thee a desolation and an astonishment. I will lay thy cities waste, and thou shalt be desolate; and thou shalt know that I am Jehovah. Because thou hast had a perpetual enmity, and hast given over the children of Israel to the power of the sword in the time of their calamity, in the time of the iniquity of the end.

Mount Seir is the long mountain range that overlooks Israel from the land of Edom where the descendants of Esau settled. Now Ezekiel prophesies of a judgment of God that will result in making Edom a desolation (verses 1-4) because of Edom's perpetual hatred against Israel even to the point that they were willing to turn Jewish escapees over to the Babylonians although Edom was also subjugated by

Babylon.

The small book of Obadiah, comprised of only one chapter, also speaks of this hatred against Israel in Obadiah 10-14:

> For the violence done to thy brother Jacob, shame shall cover thee, and thou shalt be cut off for ever. In the day that thou stoodest on the other side, in the day that strangers carried away his substance, and foreigners entered into his gates, and cast lots upon Jerusalem, even thou wast as one of them. But look not thou on the day of thy brother in the day of his disaster, and rejoice not over the children of Judah in the day of their destruction; neither speak proudly in the day of distress. Enter not into the gate of my people in the day of their calamity; yea, look not thou on their affliction in the day of their calamity, neither lay ye hands on their substance in the day of their calamity. And stand thou not in the crossway, to cut off those of his that escape; and deliver not up those of his that remain in the day of distress.

The sins of Edom described in this passage speak of another time preceding the Babylonian destruction when the Edomites committed very similar sins to those they were to commit under Babylon. Once again the reason for Edom's actions is the perpetual enmity towards the Jews.

In determining the place of the Arab states in the kingdom, it should be viewed from the backdrop of the Arabs' perpetual hatred against the Jews with a special greater guilt falling upon Edom or modern southern Jordan.

Ultimately, peace will come between Israel and the various Arab states, but it will come in one of three forms: (1) by means of occupation; (2) by means of destruction; or (3) by means of conversion. It is necessary to deal with the various Arab states individually to get a clearer picture.

1. LEBANON

Peace will come between Israel and Lebanon by means of occupation. This is not so much explicitly stated by Scripture as it is derived from certain facts contained in the Scriptures. As stated in the previous chapter, Ezekiel 47:13-48:29 gives the boundaries of the nation of Israel in the messianic kingdom. The tracing of the northern boundary will show that Israel will encompass all of modern day Lebanon. From this fact, it can be deduced that in the kingdom Israel will occupy and possess all of Lebanon and it will be settled by some of the northern Jewish tribes. So peace will come between Israel and Lebanon by means of occupation.

2. JORDAN

Modern Jordan comprises the ancient countries of Edom, Moab

and Ammon. It is Edom or southern Jordan in particular that the prophets were concerned about. Several passages disclose that peace will come between Israel and southern Jordan by means of destruction. One such passage is Ezekiel 35:6-9:

> Therefore, as I live, saith the Lord Jehovah, I will prepare thee unto blood, and blood shall pursue thee: since thou hast not hated blood, therefore blood shall pursue thee. Thus will I make mount Seir an astonishment and a desolation; and I will cut off from it him that passeth through and him that returneth. And I will fill its mountains with its slain: in thy hills and in thy valleys and in all thy watercourses shall they fall that are slain with the sword. I will make thee a perpetual desolation, and thy cities shall not be inhabited; and ye shall know that I am Jehovah.

The picture is one of massive destruction with blood and dead bodies filling the mountains, hills and valleys (verses 6-8), resulting in Edom becoming a perpetual desolation (verse 9).

Adding to all this, Jeremiah 49:7-13 states:

> Of Edom. Thus saith Jehovah of hosts: Is wisdom no more in Teman? is counsel perished from the prudent? is their wisdom vanished? Flee ye, turn back, dwell in the depths, O inhabitants of Dedan; for I will bring the calamity of Esau upon him, the time that I shall visit him. If grape-gatherers came to thee, would they not leave some gleaning grapes? if thieves by night, would they not destroy till they had enough? But I have made Esau bare, I have uncovered his secret places, and he shall not be able to hide himself: his seed is destroyed, and his brethren, and his neighbors; and he is not. Leave thy fatherless children, I will preserve them alive; and let thy widows trust in me. For thus saith Jehovah: Behold, they to whom it pertained not to drink of the cup shall assuredly drink; and art thou he that shall altogether go unpunished? thou shalt not go unpunished, but thou shalt surely drink. For I have sworn by myself, saith Jehovah, that Bozrah shall become an astonishment, a reproach, a waste, and a curse; and all the cities thereof shall be perpetual wastes.

The emphasis of Jeremiah is on the totality of the destruction of the land of Edom so as to leave nothing remaining of the seed of Esau (verses 7-10). Edom had been given an opportunity to trust in the Lord but failed to respond (verse 11). So now the cup of iniquity is full, and Edom must drink of the cup of God's wrath (verse 12), resulting in the land of Edom becoming nothing but an astonishment, a reproach, a waste, and a curse (verse 13). To all this, Jeremiah later adds in Jeremiah 49:19-20:

> Behold, he shall come up like a lion from the pride of the Jordan against the strong habitation: for I will suddenly make them run away from it; and whoso is chosen, him will I appoint over it: for who is like me? and who will appoint me a time? and who is the shepherd that will stand before me? Therefore hear ye the counsel of Jehovah, that he hath taken

against Edom; and his purposes, that he hath purposed against the inhabitants of Teman: Surely they shall drag them away, even the little ones of the flock; surely he shall make their habitation desolate over them.

Once again there is emphasis on the totality of the destruction with the addition that this final desolation and destruction of Edom will come by means of a war and an armed military conflict.

The smallest book of the Old Testament, Obadiah, centers its entire attention on Edom's destruction. Verses 5-9 read:

If thieves came to thee, if robbers by night, (how art thou cut off!) would they not steal only till they had enough? if grape-gatherers came to thee, would they not leave some gleaning grapes? How are the things of Esau searched! how are his hidden treasures sought out! All the men of thy confederacy have brought thee on thy way, even to the border: the men that were at peace with thee have deceived thee, and prevailed against thee; they that eat thy bread lay a snare under thee: there is no understanding in him. Shall I not in that day, saith Jehovah, destroy the wise men out of Edom, and understanding out of the mount of Esau? And thy mighty men, O Teman, shall be dismayed, to the end that every one may be cut off from the mount of Esau by slaughter.

Obadiah also emphasized the totality of the destruction (verses 5-6) pointing out their failure to be aided either by their friends (verse 7) or by their own wisdom or military might (verses 8-9). Later, in verses 17-21, Obadiah adds:

But in mount Zion there shall be those that escape, and it shall be holy; and the house of Jacob shall possess their possessions. And the house of Jacob shall be a fire, and the house of Joseph a flame, and the house of Esau for stubble, and they shall burn among them, and devour them; and there shall not be any remaining to the house of Esau; for Jehovah hath spoken it. And they of the South shall possess the mount of Esau, and they of the lowland the Philistines; and they shall possess the field of Ephraim, and the field of Samaria; and Benjamin shall possess Gilead. And the captives of this host of the children of Israel, that are among the Canaanites, shall possess even unto Zarephath; and the captives of Jerusalem, that are in Sepharad, shall possess the cities of the South. And saviours shall come up on mount Zion to judge the mount of Esau; and the kingdom shall be Jehovah's.

The time of Israel's final restoration (verse 17) will also be the time of Edom's final destruction. Obadiah states rather clearly that this destruction of Edom will come by means of the children of Israel (verse 18), for the two houses of Israel will be like fire while Edom will be like stubble that quickly catches fire when exposed to the flame. This destruction will be so total that nothing will remain of Esau's descendants, while the descendants of brother Jacob will own and possess the mountains of Edom (verses 19-20). It is out of mount Zion that judgment will fall on Edom (verse 21).

The fact that Israel will be used to bring about the final destruction of Edom is further portrayed in Ezekiel 25:12-14:

> Thus saith the Lord Jehovah: Because that Edom hath dealt against the house of Judah by taking vengeance, and hath greatly offended, and revenged himself upon them; therefore thus saith the Lord Jehovah, I will stretch out my hand upon Edom, and will cut off man and beast from it; and I will make it desolate from Teman; even unto Dedan shall they fall by the sword. And I will lay my vengeance upon Edom by the hand of my people Israel; and they shall do in Edom according to mine anger and according to my wrath; and they shall know my vengeance, saith the Lord Jehovah.

After declaring the sins of Edom, that of taking vengeance against the people of Israel (verse 12), the prophet states that God will now stretch out His hand in judgment against Edom in order to destroy everything in it. So again the totality of the destruction is pointed out (verse 13) which will be by means of the people of Israel in armed military conflict (verse 14).

So Edom, or present day southern Jordan, is to suffer desolation, and the destruction of all descendants of Esau will come by means of the people of Israel. Only via total destruction will peace come between Israel and southern Jordan.

As for Moab, present day central Jordan, it too will suffer destruction (Jeremiah 48:1-46), but it will not be total. A remnant of Moab will return according to Jeremiah 48:47:

> Yet will I bring back the captivity of Moab in the latter days, saith Jehovah. Thus far is the judgment of Moab.

Concerning Ammon, or modern northern Jordan, it will also suffer destruction and become a possession of Israel in Jeremiah 49:1-2:

> Of the children of Ammon. Thus saith Jehovah: Hath Israel no sons? hath he no heir? why then doth Malcam possess Gad, and his people dwell in the cities thereof? Therefore, behold, the days come, saith Jehovah, that I will cause an alarm of war to be heard against Rabbah of the children of Ammon; and it shall become a desolate heap, and her daughters shall be burned with fire: then shall Israel possess them that did possess him, saith Jehovah.

But as with Moab, it will not be a total destruction, for a remnant of Ammon will also be found in the kingdom according to Jeremiah 49:6:

> But afterward I will bring back the captivity of the children of Ammon, saith Jehovah.

To summarize, peace will come between Israel and the three parts of Jordan by means of destruction but not all to the same degree. In the case of Edom or southern Jordan, the destruction will be total, and there will not be a nation of Edom in the kingdom. The Edomites are descendants of Esau, the twin brother of Jacob. In the cases of Moab or central Jordan and Ammon or northern Jordan, the destruction will be partial. There will be a Moab and Ammon in the kingdom, with both subservient to Israel. Both these nations are descendants of Lot, the nephew of Abraham.

3. EGYPT

Peace will come between Israel and Egypt initially by means of destruction and later by means of conversion. A comprehensive story of Egypt's future is given in Isaiah 19:1-22. In verses 1-10 the prophet Isaiah described the punishment of Egypt because of her sins. Egypt will be characterized by civil war, desolation, and famine. In verses 11-15 the prophet stated that the root cause of Egypt's devastation is her leaders who have led Egypt astray. Under the dictatorships of Farouk, Nasser and Sadat, Egypt went to war against Israel on four occasions resulting in heavy losses for Egypt and wrecking its economy. Out of all this, there developed a fear in Egypt of Israel as prophesied in Isaiah 19:16-17:

> In that day shall the Egyptians be like unto women; and they shall tremble and fear because of the shaking of the hand of Jehovah of hosts, which he shaketh over them. And the land of Judah shall become a terror unto Egypt; every one to whom mention is made thereof shall be afraid, because of the purpose of Jehovah of hosts, which he purposeth against it.

Never in ancient history has this been true, and Egyptian forces passed through the land of Israel freely even in the days of Solomon. Only since 1948 and especially since the Six Day War have the Egyptian forces evidenced the fear portrayed in this passage. There has been a fear and dread in Egypt of Israel ever since that time. Egypt having lost four wars against Israel with heavy casualties, the fear is deeply rooted. Prophetically, today is still the period of Isaiah 19:16-17.

But eventually peace will come between Israel and Egypt. Initially the peace is a political one when the Hebrew language will be spoken in Egypt by five cities according to Isaiah 19:18:

> In that day there shall be five cities in the land of Egypt that speak the language of Canaan, and swear to Jehovah of hosts; one shall be called The city of destruction.

In Isaiah's day, the *language of Canaan* was the Hebrew

language. It would appear from this verse that these five cities speaking Hebrew will be Jewish populated cities. Exactly how this prophecy will be fulfilled remains to be seen.*

This in turn will slowly give way to Egypt's conversion in Isaiah 19:19-22:

> In that day shall there be an altar to Jehovah in the midst of the land of Egypt, and a pillar at the border thereof to Jehovah. And it shall be for a sign and for a witness unto Jehovah of hosts in the land of Egypt; for they shall cry unto Jehovah because of oppressors, and he will send them a saviour, and a defender, and he will deliver them. And Jehovah shall be known to Egypt, and the Egyptians shall know Jehovah in that day, yea, they shall worship with sacrifice and oblation, and shall vow a vow unto Jehovah, and shall perform it. And Jehovah will smite Egypt, smiting and healing; and they shall return unto Jehovah, and he will be entreated of them, and will heal them.

An altar to the God of Israel will be built as a sign and a witness of the power of the God of Israel to save the land of Egypt (verses 19-20a). Egypt will be greatly oppressed by the forces of the Antichrist and his cohorts (Daniel 11:42-43), but God will save Egypt from the domination of those oppressors (verse 20b). The Egyptians will realize that Allah the Moslem god cannot save them but only Jehovah the God of Israel. This will lead to a national conversion of Egypt. Egypt shall know the Lord and will worship the God of Israel with oblations, sacrifices and vows (verse 21). The same God who brought about their destruction will also bring about their regeneration and their healing when they turn in faith to Him (verse 22).

In conjunction with the latter days of the tribulation and the Campaign of Armageddon, there will be a national conversion of Egypt. In this manner they will take their place in the ranks of the sheep Gentiles. It should be noted that Egypt will be one of the nations that will move against the Antichrist in Daniel 11:40.

Nevertheless, because of Egypt's longstanding hatred of Israel, in the outworking of the cursing principle of the Abrahamic Covenant, Egypt will suffer a desolation that will be similar to that of Edom according to Joel 3:19:

> Egypt shall be a desolation, and Edom shall be a desolate wilderness, for the violence done to the children of Judah, because they have shed innocent blood in their land.

The sin of Egypt is the same as that of Edom: mistreatment of the Jews, and so punishment will come. With Edom it will be total and per-

---

* Whether the peace treaty of Camp David, signed between Israel and Egypt under Begin and Sadat will have anything to do with this also remains to be seen. Until a full fulfillment comes, all speculation on the relationship of the Camp David peace process must be avoided.

manent (desolation and wilderness). But with Egypt it will be total yet temporary (desolation but not a wilderness). In fact, the desolation of Egypt is to last only for the first forty years of the kingdom as recorded in Ezekiel 29:1-16:

> In the tenth year, in the tenth month, in the twelfth day of the month, the word of Jehovah came unto me, saying, Son of man, set thy face against Pharoah king of Egypt, and prophesy against him, and against all Egypt; speak, and say, Thus saith the Lord Jehovah: Behold, I am against thee, Pharoah king of Egypt, the great monster that lieth in the midst of his rivers, that hath said, My river is mine own, and I have made it for myself. And I will put hooks in thy jaws, and I will cause the fish of thy rivers to stick unto thy scales; and I will bring thee up out of the midst of thy rivers, with all the fish of thy rivers which stick unto thy scales. And I will cast thee forth into the wilderness, thee and all the fish of thy rivers: thou shalt fall upon the open field; thou shalt not be brought together, nor gathered; I have given thee for food to the beasts of the earth and to the birds of the heavens. And all the inhabitants of Egypt shall know that I am Jehovah, because they have been a staff of reed to the house of Israel. When they took hold of thee by thy hand, thou didst break, and didst rend all their shoulders; and when they leaned upon thee, thou brakest, and madest all their loins to be at a stand. Therefore thus saith the Lord Jehovah: Behold, I will bring a sword upon thee, and will cut off from thee man and beast. And the land of Egypt shall be a desolation and a waste; and they shall know that I am Jehovah. Because he hath said, The river is mine, and I have made it; therefore, behold, I am against thee; and against thy rivers, and I will make the land of Egypt an utter waste and desolation, from the tower of Seveneh even unto the border of Ethiopia. No foot of man shall pass through it, nor foot of beast shall pass through it, neither shall it be inhabited forty years. And I will make the land of Egypt a desolation in the midst of the countries that are desolate; and her cities among the cities that are laid waste shall be a desolation forty years; and I will scatter the Egyptians among the nations, and will disperse them through the countries. For thus saith the Lord Jehovah: At the end of forty years will I gather the Egyptians from the peoples whither they were scattered; and I will bring back the captivity of Egypt, and will cause them to return into the land of Pathros, into the land of their birth; and they shall be there a base kingdom. It shall be the basest of the kingdoms; neither shall it any more lift itself up above the nations: and I will diminish them, that they shall no more rule over the nations. And it shall be no more the confidence of the house of Israel, bringing iniquity to remembrance, when they turn to look after them: and they shall know that I am the Lord Jehovah.

Ezekiel is commanded to prophesy against Egypt (verses 1-2) and predict the coming dispersion of the Egyptians from their land (verses 3-5) because of their long history of mistreatment of Israel (verses 6-7). The land of Egypt will suffer a period of total desolation (verses 8-10), which will last for forty years (verses 11-12a), and the Egyptians will be scattered all over the world like Israel was before her (verse 12b). But after the end of the period of forty years, the Egyptians will be regathered (verse 13) and brought back into their land (verse 14).

Though Egypt will become a kingdom again, it will never be a powerful one (verse 15). Nor will Israel ever again be guilty of placing her confidence in Egypt (verse 16), but will trust in the Lord their God. As for the lowly kingdom of Egypt, it will also be required to observe the Feast of Tabernacles (Zechariah 14:16-19).

In summary, peace will come between Israel and Egypt by means of conversion. Only when the Egyptians worship the same God as Israel, through Jesus the Messiah, will peace finally come. For the first forty years of the kingdom, the land of Egypt will be desolate and the Egyptians will be dispersed all over the world. But afterwards the Egyptians will be regathered, becoming a kingdom again.

4. ASSYRIA (IRAQ & SYRIA)

Ancient Assyria is today comprised of modern Iraq and portions of modern Syria, two other implacable Arab enemies of modern Israel. But peace will come between Israel and these two Arab countries by means of conversion according to Isaiah 19:23-25:

> In that day shall there be a highway out of Egypt to Assyria, and the Assyrian shall come into Egypt, and the Egyptian into Assyria; and the Egyptians shall worship with the Assyrians. In that day shall Israel be the third with Egypt and with Assyria, a blessing in the midst of the earth; for that Jehovah of hosts hath blessed them, saying, Blessed be Egypt my people, and Assyria the work of my hands, and Israel mine inheritance.

Verse 23 describes an economic unit that will encompass Egypt, Israel and Assyria. This former highway of the ancient world known as the *via maris* has ceased to function ever since 1948 when Israel became a state. In 1948 Egypt and Syria closed their borders, making the highway inoperable. However, in the kingdom when peace will be restored, all borders will be open, and the highway, a symbol of economy, will be restored between these Middle Eastern states. The means by which this will occur is by means of conversion (verses 24-25). Not only will Egypt undergo a conversion experience but so will the ancient area of Assyria. Assyria will become a blessing in the earth and will receive a blessing from God. The three former enemies will now have a spiritual unity as well as an economic and political one. God declares Egypt will be *my people*, Assyria *the work of my hands*, and Israel *mine inheritance*. The spiritual unity will be the basis for the other unities.

So peace will come between Israel and Assyria (Iraq and Syria) by means of conversion. When this happens, there will be economic, political, and religious unity, because they will all worship the same God.

5. KEDAR AND HAZOR (SAUDI ARABIA)

Peace will come between Israel and Saudi Arabia by means of destruction. This is taught in Jeremiah 49:28-33. The passage describes the total devastation of Saudi Arabia by war until the inhabitants are scattered and dispersed all over the world. As for the land itself, Jeremiah 49:33 states:

And Hazor shall be a dwelling place of jackals, a desolation for ever: no man shall dwell there, neither shall any son of man sojourn therein.

The land of Saudi Arabia will be a perpetual desolation throughout the kingdom, and the residents will be dispersed everywhere. While Egypt's desolation and dispersion will only last for forty years, for Saudi Arabia it will last for all of the one thousand years.

So peace will come between Israel and Saudi Arabia via destruction.

6. ELAM (PERSIA OR IRAN)

Although Persia or Iran (ancient Elam) is not an Arab state but a Persian one, its future will be examined here because they share the same religion (Islam) with the Moslem Arabs.

Peace will come between Israel and Iran by means of destruction according to Jeremiah 49:34-39. In verses 34-38 Jeremiah described the destruction of Elam with the inhabitants being completely dispersed all over the world. But then verse 39 declares:

But it shall come to pass in the latter days, that I will bring back the captivity of Elam, saith Jehovah.

The destruction of Iran will be partial, and the dispersion will be temporary. Eventually the inhabitants will return and resettle Iran. The future of Iran is similar to that of Egypt, but the length of time they will be in dispersion is not revealed.

So peace will come between Israel and Iran via destruction, dispersion, and then a return. There will be a nation of Elam (Persia or Iran) in the kingdom.

D. THE TWO DESOLATE SPOTS OF THE KINGDOM

As has been shown in previous chapters, during the messianic age the entire world will be fruitful and very productive; the whole earth will be characterized by beauty. Nevertheless, there will be two desolate spots throughout the period of the kingdom (Egypt will be desolate for only forty years).

1.   BABYLON

The first of these two desolate spots will be the former world capital of the Antichrist: Babylon. Several passages make this point, one of which is Isaiah 13:20-22:

> It shall never be inhabited, neither shall it be dwelt in from generation to generation: neither shall the Arabian pitch tent there; neither shall shepherds make their flocks to lie down there. But wild beasts of the desert shall lie there; and their houses shall be full of doleful creatures; and ostriches shall dwell there, and wild goats shall dance there. And wolves shall cry in their castles, and jackals in the pleasant palaces: and her time is near to come, and her days shall not be prolonged.

The uninhabitable ruins are described as similar to Sodom and Gomorrah in Jeremiah 50:39-40:

> Therefore the wild beasts of the desert with the wolves shall dwell there, and the ostriches shall dwell therein: and it shall be no more inhabited for ever; neither shall it be dwelt in from generation to generation. As when God overthrew Sodom and Gomorrah and the neighbor cities thereof, saith Jehovah, so shall no man dwell there, neither shall any son of man sojourn therein.

Later Jeremiah emphasized the totality and completeness of Babylon's desolation in Jeremiah 51:41-43:

> How is Sheshach taken! and the praise of the whole earth seized! how is Babylon become a desolation among the nations! The sea is come up upon Babylon; she is covered with the multitude of the waves thereof. Her cities are become a desolation, a dry land, and a desert, a land wherein no man dwelleth, neither doth any son of man pass thereby.

Throughout the kingdom period no man will even so much as pass by the ruins of Babylon; something that is hardly true today.

Not only is Babylon to be a desolate waste throughout the kingdom, it will also be a place of continual burning and smoke throughout the millennium, according to Revelation 19:3:

> And a second time they say, Hallelujah. And her smoke goeth up for ever and ever.

It is obvious that the animal inhabitants, as we know them, mentioned in Isaiah 13:20-22 and Jeremiah 50:39-40, cannot live in a place of continual burning and so cannot be literal animals. What they actually are is explained by Revelation 18:1-2:

After these things I saw another angel coming down out of heaven, having great authority; and the earth was lightened with his glory. And he cried with a mighty voice, saying, Fallen, fallen is Babylon the great, and is become a habitation of demons, and a hold of every unclean spirit, and a hold of every unclean and hateful bird.

This place of continual burning and smoke will be a place of confinement for many demons during the kingdom period. It is clear from Revelation nine and other passages that demons have animal-like features, and this is what the animals of the Isaiah and Jeremiah passages actually represent.

2.   EDOM

The second desolate spot in the kingdom will be Edom. This is also pointed out by several of the prophets, such as Isaiah 34:8-15:

For Jehovah hath a day of vengeance, a year of recompense for the cause of Zion. And the streams of Edom shall be turned into pitch, and the dust thereof into brimstone, and the land thereof shall become burning pitch. It shall not be quenched night nor day; the smoke thereof shall go up for ever; from generation to generation it shall lie waste; none shall pass through it for ever and ever. But the pelican and the porcupine shall possess it; and the owl and the raven shall dwell therein: and he will stretch over it the line of confusion, and the plummet of emptiness. They shall call the nobles thereof to the kingdom, but none shall be there; and all its princes shall be nothing. And thorns shall come up in its palaces, nettles and thistles in the fortresses thereof; and it shall be a habitation of jackals, a court for ostriches. And the wild beasts of the desert shall meet with the wolves, and the wild goat shall cry to his fellow; yea, the night-monster shall settle there, and shall find her a place of rest. There shall the dart-snake make her nest, and lay, and hatch, and gather under her shade; yea, there shall the kites be gathered, every one with her mate.

The reason for Edom becoming a perpetual desolation is their sins against Israel (verse 8). Like Babylon, it is to become a place of continual burning and smoke (verses 9-10) inhabited by various foul birds and animals and characterized by confusion (verse 11). It will be totally uninhabited by men (verse 12) and will be habitable only by the animals mentioned (verses 13-15). Yet these animals as we know them cannot live in a place of burning pitch and burning brimstone. Two clues in this text show that these are not literal birds and animals. The word translated *wild goats* actually means demons in goat form. The word translated *night-monster* means night demons. Like Babylon, Edom will also be an abode of demons.

Another prophecy in Jeremiah 49:17-18 states:

And Edom shall become an astonishment: every one that passeth by it shall be astonished, and shall hiss at all the plagues thereof. As in the over-throw of Sodom and Gomorrah and the neighbor cities thereof, saith Jehovah, no man shall dwell there, neither shall any son of man sojourn therein.

The emphasis is on the totality, for no human will inhabit the land of Edom or even pass through it. Like Babylon, the desolation will be similar to that of Sodom and Gomorrah.

The reason for such massive destruction in Edom is amplified by Ezekiel 35:10-15:

Because thou hast said, These two nations and these two countries shall be mine, and we will possess it; whereas Jehovah was there: therefore, as I live, saith the Lord Jehovah, I will do according to thine anger, and according to thine envy which thou hast showed out of thy hatred against them; and I will make myself known among them, when I shall judge thee. And thou shalt know that I, Jehovah, have heard all thy revilings which thou hast spoken against the mountains of Israel, saying, They are laid desolate, they are given us to devour. And ye have magnified yourselves against me with your mouth, and have multiplied your words against me: I have heard it. Thus saith the Lord Jehovah: When the whole earth rejoiceth, I will make thee desolate. As thou didst rejoice over the inheritance of the house of Israel, because it was desolate, so will I do unto thee: thou shalt be desolate, O mount Seir, and all Edom, even all of it; and they shall know that I am Jehovah.

Because of Edom's glee over the fall of Israel and Judah, the punishment must come (verses 10-13). So while the whole earth is beautified and rejoicing, Edom will be a desolation (verse 14). The calamities, which fell on Israel and over which Edom rejoiced, will now fall on Edom in a more severe way (verse 15).

Finally, Joel 3:19 states:

Egypt shall be a desolation, and Edom shall be a desolate wilderness, for the violence done to the children of Judah, because they have shed innocent blood in their land.

Egypt's desolation will be limited to only forty years. As for Edom, because of her unique violence against Israel, her desolation will be permanent and last throughout the kingdom.

Throughout the millennial kingdom, while the whole earth is beautified and blossoming as the rose, the two areas of Babylon and Edom will be places of continual burning pitch and burning brimstone. The smoke will rise and be visible for the entire one thousand years. While Satan will be confined in the Abyss, his demons will be confined in Babylon and Edom. These two places will be the abode of demons for the entire kingdom period.

PART VI

THE AFTERMATH

CHAPTER XXI

THE AFTERMATH

During the time of the millennium, the most ideal conditions will exist on the earth—the best since the fall. But it will not be a perfect situation. Sin and death, though greatly reduced, will not be eliminated, and a great number of unregenerate men will be alive at the time of the close of the messianic age. It is after one thousand years of ideal conditions and environment that the messianic kingdom ends with one last test for man.

A. THE LOOSING OF SATAN AND THE FINAL INVASION OF ISRAEL

The millennium will end when Satan is released from his fifth abode.* This event is described in Revelation 20:7-10:

> And when the thousand years are finished, Satan shall be loosed out of his prison, and shall come forth to deceive the nations which are in the four corners of the earth, Gog and Magog, to gather them together to the war: the number of whom is as the sand of the sea. And they went up over the breadth of the earth, and compassed the camp of the saints about, and the beloved city: and fire came down out of heaven, and devoured them. And the devil that deceived them was cast into the lake of fire and brimstone, where are also the beast and the false prophet; and they shall be tormented day and night for ever and ever.

When the full one thousand years are completed, Satan will be released out of his confinement in the Abyss (verse 7) and will again do the work of deception among all the nations and Gentiles in the earth (verse 8). By this time, a great number of unbelievers will exist, all of whom will be under one hundred years old. The expression *Gog and Magog* points to the extent of the work of deception reaching the extremities of the earth and hints at a similarity with the invasion described in Ezekiel 38:1-39:16 which will occur prior to the Great Tribulation. The similarity is that this too will be an invasion of Israel. The work of deception will be massive, and a world-wide revolt will begin to form. Eventually a world-wide invasion of the millennial Israel will take place, and the millennial Jerusalem will be surrounded by these deceived Gentile armies. But once these armies arrive at the mountain of Jehovah's house, the invading forces will be quickly dispensed with by fire out of heaven, destroying them quickly and suddenly (verse 9).

At this point, the instigator of this revolt will be placed into his

* See Appendix I.

sixth and final abode: the Lake of Fire (verse 10). This will be both his final and eternal abode—a place of torment for all eternity. He will now join the Antichrist and the False Prophet who entered it one thousand years previously. The career of Satan will then come to an end.

With this final revolt the millennial age will come to an end, and there will be a transfer of authority as described in I Corinthians 15:24-28:

> Then cometh the end, when he shall deliver up the kingdom to God, even the Father; when he shall have abolished all rule and all authority and power. For he must reign, till he hath put all his enemies under his feet. The last enemy that shall be abolished is death. For, He put all things in subjection under his feet. But when he saith, All things are put in subjection, it is evident that he is excepted who did subject all things unto him. And when all things have been subjected unto him, then shall the Son also himself be subjected to him that did subject all things unto him, that God may be all in all.

Ultimately, the power and the authority of the kingdom must be turned over to God the Father. But this can only occur after every enemy of man is abolished and there is no longer any challenge to God's rule, authority and power (verse 24). For this very reason Christ must rule until every single enemy of man has been placed under subjection (verse 25). The last of the enemies of man is not Satan, but death itself (verse 26). It should be remembered that death will still exist in the kingdom. It is only after Satan's final revolt and his confinement in the Lake of Fire that death can be abolished. It is Satan who caused death for man by tempting the first parents. It is only when the originator of death for man is forever confined in his final abode that death can be abolished. And, at this point it will be.

With this, the millennial kingdom will come to an end. All things will now have been placed in total subjection to Christ, and that totality of subjection will now be subjugated to God the Father in order that God may be all in all (verses 27-28).

B. THE GREAT WHITE THRONE JUDGMENT

The Great White Throne Judgment described in Revelation 20:11-12 will come after the end of the millennium and in preparation for the establishment of the Eternal Order:

> And I saw a great white throne, and him that sat upon it, from whose face the earth and the heaven fled away; and there was found no place for them. And I saw the dead, the great and the small, standing before the throne; and books were opened: and another book was opened, which is the book of life: and the dead were judged out of the things which were written in the books, according to their works.

This prophecy begins with a vision of one sitting on the Great White Throne (verse 11a). Although the throne sitter is not named, in all probability, it is the Lord Jesus Christ, for it is to Him that all judgment has been given (John 5:22). A passing away of the old order will occur at the time of the Great White Throne Judgment. The present heavens and earth in existence since Genesis one will be done away with (verse 11b). That which was renovated for the millennium but polluted all over again with man's last revolt will now be done away with forever.

This will leave all things ready for the judgment itself (verse 12). The judgment will be a judgment of all unbelievers of all time. The purpose of this judgment will not be to determine whether a person is saved or not, for that has been settled forever one way or the other at death. The purpose of this judgment will be to determine the degree of punishment. There is a principle in Scripture that does teach degrees of punishment based upon greater or lesser light or knowledge and the response or lack of it to that light. In Matthew 11:20-24 Jesus spoke of things being more tolerable for some than for others in the day of judgment:

> Then began he to upbraid the cities wherein most of his mighty works were done, because they repented not. Woe unto thee, Chorazin! woe unto thee, Bethsaida! for if the mighty works had been done in Tyre and Sidon which were done in you, they would have repented long ago in sackcloth and ashes. But I say unto you, it shall be more tolerable for Tyre and Sidon in the day of judgment, than for you. And thou, Capernaum, shalt thou be exalted unto heaven? thou shalt go down unto Hades: for if the mighty works had been done in Sodom which were done in thee, it would have remained until this day. But I say unto you that it shall be more tolerable for the land of Sodom in the day of judgment, than for thee.

Elsewhere, in Luke 12:47-48, Jesus spoke of few stripes and many stripes:

> And that servant, who knew his lord's will, and made not ready, nor did according to his will, shall be beaten with many stripes; but he that knew not, and did things worthy of stripes, shall be beaten with few stripes. And to whomsoever much is given, of him shall much be required: and to whom they commit much, of him will they ask the more.

In John 19:11 Jesus spoke of greater and lesser sins:

> Jesus answered him, Thou wouldest have no power against me, except it were given thee from above: therefore he that delivered me unto thee hath greater sin.

So one's appearance at this particular judgment will be a direct result of failing to believe on Christ as Saviour. But the degree of punishment will be on the basis of one's works.

In determining the degrees of punishment, "books" are mentioned in addition to the Book of Life. A three-fold distinction should be made between the Book of Life, the Lamb's Book of Life, and the other books mentioned in verse twelve.

The *Book of Life* contains the names of every person who was ever born according to Psalm 139:16:

> Thine eyes did see mine unformed substance; and in thy book they were all written, even the days that were ordained for me, when as yet there was none of them.

Those who believe on Christ have their names retained in the Book of Life according to Revelation 3:5:

> He that overcometh shall thus be arrayed in white garments; and I will in no wise blot his name out of the book of life, and I will confess his name before my Father, and before his angels.

However, in Psalm 69:28, the unsaved have their names blotted out of the Book of Life:

> Let them be blotted out of the book of life, and not be written with the righteous.

So then, at the Great White Throne Judgment, if their names are not found in the Book of Life, it will show them to be unsaved and worthy of partaking in this particular judgment.

It is at that point that the *other books* mentioned in verse twelve are used. These other books contain accounts of one's deeds and responses. It is on the basis of what is written in these books that the degrees of punishment will be determined.

Another book mentioned in the Scriptures that should be kept distinct is the *Lamb's Book of Life*. This book contains the names of every individual who is born again and only those who are born again. Their names were written into this book before the earth was ever created, according to Revelation 13:8:

> And all that dwell on the earth shall worship him, every one whose name hath not been written from the foundation of the world in the book of life of the Lamb that hath been slain.

It is mentioned again in Revelation 17:8b:

> And they that dwell on the earth shall wonder, they whose name hath not been written in the book of life from the foundation of the world, when they behold the beast, how that he was, and is not, and shall come.

In Psalm 69:28 it is known as the Book of the Righteous:

Let them be blotted out of the book of life, and not be written with the righteous.

Based on God's election and foreknowledge, this book contains the names of only those who are born again. And because salvation is eternally sure, it is impossible to be blotted out of this particular book.

C. THE SECOND RESURRECTION

The second resurrection is described in Revelation 20:13:

And the sea gave up the dead that were in it; and death and Hades gave up the dead that were in them: and they were judged every man according to their works.

Following the description of the judgment, there is the account of the second resurrection. Whereas the first resurrection will be composed of believers only, the second resurrection will be composed of unbelievers only. The two resurrections will be separated by one thousand years. Just as the first resurrection is to be in stages (Christ the first-fruits, the church saints, the Old Testament saints, and then the tribulation saints), so the second resurrection will be in stages. The first-fruits of the second resurrection will be the Antichrist, and his death and resurrection have already been described.* One thousand years after the resurrection of the Antichrist there will be the resurrection of all other unbelievers. The dead bodies of all unbelievers will be resurrected in order to be reunited with all the souls relinquished by hell. They will then be judged at the Great White Throne on the basis of their works.

D. THE SECOND DEATH: THE LAKE OF FIRE

Following the sentence of the Great White Throne Judgment will come the execution of it according to Revelation 20:14-15:

And death and Hades were cast into the lake of fire. This is the second death, even the lake of fire. And if any was not found written in the book of life, he was cast into the lake of fire.

The second resurrection will soon give way to the second death in the Lake of Fire, which will be the eternal abode of the lost.

Evangelistic preaching is generally centered around the necessity of accepting Christ in order to avoid spending eternity in hell and in order to spend eternity in heaven. Neither point is biblically true.

* See Chapter XV.

Throughout the pages of the Old Testament, both righteous and unrighteous were said to go to a place called in Hebrew *Sheol* and in Greek *Hades*. While the Old Testament sacrifices covered the sins of the Old Testament saints, it did not remove their sins (Hebrews 10:4). Only the death of the Messiah could do that. So while the sacrificial system was sufficient to keep them from hell, it was not able to get them into heaven. So all who died, both righteous and unrighteous, went to a place known as *Sheol* or *Hades*.

This place contained two compartments, and a description of the two sides of Sheol or Hades is found in Luke 16:19-31:

> Now there was a certain rich man, and he was clothed in purple and fine linen, faring sumptuously every day: and a certain beggar named Lazarus was laid at his gate, full of sores, and desiring to be fed with the crumbs that fell from the rich man's table; yea, even the dogs came and licked his sores. And it came to pass, that the beggar died, and that he was carried away by the angels into Abraham's bosom: and the rich man also died, and was buried. And in Hades he lifted up his eyes, being in torments, and seeth Abraham afar off, and Lazarus in his bosom. And he cried and said, Father Abraham, have mercy on me, and send Lazarus, that he may dip the tip of his finger in water, and cool my tongue; for I am in anguish in this flame. But Abraham said, Son, remember that thou in thy lifetime receivedst thy good things, and Lazarus in like manner evil things: but now here he is comforted, and thou art in anguish. And besides all this, between us and you there is a great gulf fixed, that they that would pass from hence to you may not be able, and that none may cross over from thence to us. And he said, I pray thee therefore, father, that thou wouldest send him to my father's house; for I have five brethren; that he may testify unto them, lest they also come into this place of torment. But Abraham saith, They have Moses and the prophets; let them hear them. And he said, Nay, father Abraham: but if one go to them from the dead, they will repent. And he said unto him, If they hear not Moses and the prophets, neither will they be persuaded, If one rise from the dead.

Sheol or Hades had two compartments. One compartment was for the unrighteous, and it could be called *Hell* in the way we use that term today; it was indeed a place of torment (verses 23-25, 28). The other compartment where the righteous went was known as *Abraham's Bosom* (verse 22); and it was a place of comfort (verse 25) but it was not heaven. Elsewhere the righteous portion of Sheol or Hades is called *Paradise* as in Luke 23:43:

> And he said unto him, Verily I say unto thee, Today shalt thou be with me in Paradise.

While the two sides could see each other and communicate with each other, they were separated by an immense gulf (verse 26) that made it impossible for someone on one side to cross over to the other side.

So, when the Old Testament saint died, his body was buried in the earth while his soul went to Abraham's Bosom or Paradise. On the other hand, when an Old Testament sinner died, his body was also buried in the ground, but his soul went into hell.

When Christ died, He not only paid the price of all future sins, but He also paid the price of all previous sins (Romans 3:25, Hebrews 9:15). Thus, the sins of the Old Testament saints were removed.

What happened next is described in Ephesians 4:8-10:

> Wherefore he saith, When he ascended on high, he led captivity captive, And gave gifts unto men. (Now this, He ascended, what is it but that he also descended into the lower parts of the earth? He that descended is the same also that ascended far above all the heavens, that he might fill all things.)

While the body of Christ remained in the tomb, His soul went down into the Paradise side of Sheol or Hades announcing that the atonement had been made. At the time of His ascension, all the souls of the Old Testament saints were removed out of Abraham's Bosom or Paradise and brought into heaven. In this way the righteous portion of Sheol or Hades was eliminated and is no longer in existence.

Today, when an unbeliever dies, his body is still buried in the ground and his soul still goes into hell. However, when the believer dies, though his body is also buried in the ground, his soul goes immediately into heaven as Paul reveals in II Corinthians 5:8:

> We are of good courage, I say, and are willing rather to be absent from the body, and to be at home with the Lord.

To be in heaven at death is to be with Christ according to Philippians 1:23:

> But I am in a strait betwixt the two, having the desire to depart and be with Christ; for it is very far better.

When the first resurrection occurs, the bodies of the believers will be resurrected and be reunited with their souls. This will occur at the Rapture for the church saints, and for the Old Testament and tribulation saints it will occur after the second coming.

At the time of the second resurrection, the bodies of the unsaved will be resurrected, and the souls of hell will be removed to be reunited with the bodies. At that time, the hell portion of Sheol or Hades will also be eliminated, because hell will not be the eternal abode of the lost. The Lake of Fire will be. Hell is a place of torment for the soul only, but the Lake of Fire will be a place of torment for both soul and body.

On the other hand, heaven will not be the eternal abode of the believer as the last two chapters of the Revelation reveal.

PART VII

THE ETERNAL
ORDER

CHAPTER XXII

THE ETERNAL ORDER

While the messianic age is the high point of Old Testament prophecy, the Eternal Order is the high point of New Testament prophecy. Whereas most of the information in the first twenty chapters of the Revelation can also be found in the Old Testament, the last two chapters of the Revelation contain brand new material not revealed to the prophets of the Old Testament.

The millennium itself is only one thousand years long. However, according to the promises of the Davidic Covenant, there was to be an eternal dynasty, an eternal kingdom and an eternal throne. The eternal existence of the dynasty is assured because it culminates in an eternal person: the Lord Jesus Christ. But the eternal existence of the throne and kingdom must also be assured. The millennial form of the kingdom of God will end after one thousand years. But the kingdom of God in the sense of God's rule will continue into the Eternal Order. Christ will continue His position of authority on the Davidic throne into the Eternal Order.

All that is known about the Eternal Order is to be found in Revelation 21:1-22:5, and that entire passage of Scripture is the concern of this chapter.

A. THE PASSING AWAY OF THE OLD ORDER AND THE CREATION OF THE ETERNAL ORDER — REVELATION 21:1-8

In preparation for the Great White Throne Judgment, the old order of the heavens and the earth will be done away with. Then following the Great White Throne Judgment, there will be a creation of the Eternal Order as recorded in Revelation 21:1-2:

> And I saw a new heaven and a new earth: for the first heaven and the first earth are passed away; and the sea is no more. And I saw the holy city, new Jerusalem, coming down out of heaven from God, made ready as a bride adorned for her husband.

To replace the old order, new heavens and a new earth will be created. A significant element missing on the new earth is the sea. The present earth was originally comprised of a mineral garden completely covered with precious stones and gems, and it served as Satan's second abode (Ezekiel 28:11-16).* But when Satan fell, not only was Satan judged, but also the earth which was under Satan's

* See Appendix I on the "Six Abodes of Satan."

authority. That judgment included the covering of the earth with the oceans (Genesis 1:2). The oceans are part of God's judgment of the first earth, but they will be non-existent in the new earth.

Though the new heavens and the new earth will need to be created, the New Jerusalem will not as it already exists in the present third heaven. When the new earth is created, the New Jerusalem will come down from heaven in order to settle on the new earth and will be adorned with the beauty of a bride prepared for the marriage ceremony. While the greatest details of the New Jerusalem are to be found in these last two chapters of the Revelation, it was mentioned earlier in the pages of the New Testament. Paul described the New Jerusalem as that which is free in Galatians 4:26:

But the Jerusalem that is above is free, which is our mother.

While the Jerusalem on earth was continually under bondage and subjugated by various forces, the New Jerusalem in heaven has been eternally free and will always remain so. It was this particular city that Abraham was seeking according to Hebrews 11:9-10:

By faith he became a sojourner in the land of promise, as in a land not his own, dwelling in tents, with Isaac and Jacob, the heirs with him of the same promise: for he looked for the city which hath the foundations, whose builder and maker is God.

Then in Hebrews 12:22-24 it is described as the eternal abode of all the redeemed:

But ye are come unto mount Zion, and unto the city of the living God, the heavenly Jerusalem, and to innumerable hosts of angels, to the general assembly and church of the firstborn who are enrolled in heaven, and to God the Judge of all, and to the spirits of just men made perfect, and to Jesus the mediator of a new covenant, and to the blood of sprinkling that speaketh better than that of Abel.

This city will serve as the eternal abode of several groups. It will be inhabited by the entire Triune God, the entire angelic host, the church saints and the *spirits of just men made perfect* who are the Old Testament saints. They were *just* in their day because they were justified by their faith, but they were *made perfect* at the death of Christ. Not mentioned but obviously included will be the tribulation saints and the millennial saints.

Following the vision of the creation of the Eternal Order, the first declaration from the One on the throne is given in Revelation 21:3-4:

And I heard a great voice out of the throne saying, Behold, the tabernacle of God is with men, and he shall dwell with them, and they shall be his peoples, and God himself shall be with them, and be their God: and he shall wipe away every tear from their eyes; and death shall be no more; neither shall there be mourning, nor crying, nor pain, any more: the first things are passed away.

Two points are made in this declaration. First, the habitation of God will now be with men. This is a reaffirmation of Hebrews 12:22-24 that the New Jerusalem will be the eternal abode of God, angels and men. The word translated *dwell* literally means *to tabernacle*. It is a reference to the Shechinah Glory* abiding with men as it once did in the tabernacle in the wilderness.

The second point affirms that all the effects of the curse recorded in Genesis 3:16-19 will be removed:

Unto the woman he said, I will greatly multiply thy pain and thy conception; in pain thou shalt bring forth children; and thy desire shall be to thy husband, and he shall rule over thee. And unto Adam he said, Because thou hast hearkened unto the voice of thy wife, and hast eaten of the tree, of which I commanded thee, saying, Thou shalt not eat of it: cursed is the ground for thy sake; in toil shalt thou eat of it all the days of thy life; thorns also and thistles shall it bring forth to thee; and thou shalt eat the herb of the field; in the sweat of thy face shalt thou eat bread, till thou return unto the ground; for out of it wast thou taken: for dust thou art, and unto dust shalt thou return.

When the fall of man came during the beginning of the old order, it caused a great number of side effects in the outworking of the Adamic curse. All these effects of the curse of the old order will be removed with the abolition of the old order. Therefore, in the Eternal Order there will be no tears, death, mourning, crying or pain.

Then the second declaration from the throne is given in Revelation 21:5-8:

And he that sitteth on the throne said, Behold, I make all things new. And he saith, Write: for these words are faithful and true. And he said unto me, They are come to pass. I am the Alpha and the Omega, the beginning and the end. I will give unto him that is athirst of the fountain of the water of life freely. He that overcometh shall inherit these things; and I will be his God, and he shall be my son. But for the fearful, and unbelieving, and abominable, and murderers, and fornicators, and sorcerers, and idolaters, and all liars, their part shall be in the lake that burneth with fire and brimstone; which is the second death.

The second declaration from the throne of God concerns the works of God. First, there is an affirmation that the future creation of the Eternal Order is assured, because the One who makes the promise is both faithful and true (verse 5). Secondly, there is the provision of

---

* See Appendix IV on "The History and Prophecy of the Shechinah Glory."

the fountain of the waters of life (verse 6). Thirdly, the passage refers to the inheritance of the believers (verse 7) which is the new heavens, the new earth, and the New Jerusalem being described in these closing chapters of the Revelation. But fourthly, there is a description of the inheritance of the unbeliever (verse 8) which is the Second Death in the Lake of Fire.

B. THE ETERNAL NEW JERUSALEM — REVELATION 21:9-22:5

The next major section contains a description of the eternal New Jerusalem. Again it should be noted that this is all that can be known from Scriptures about what the Eternal Order is going to be like.

1. THE REVELATION OF THE ESTABLISHMENT OF THE CITY — REVELATION 21:9-10

This section begins in Revelation 21:9-10 with an elaboration of Revelation 21:2 regarding the establishment of the New Jerusalem:

> And there came one of the seven angels who had the seven bowls, who were laden with the seven last plagues; and he spake with me, saying, Come hither, I will show thee the bride, the wife of the Lamb. And he carried me away in the Spirit to a mountain great and high, and showed me the holy city Jerusalem, coming down out of heaven from God.

The announcement to John to *come up hither* again (as in 4:1) is for the purpose that God can show him more things to come. He is told that he is about to be shown more concerning the Bride of Christ (verse 9); namely, the eternal abode of the bride — the New Jerusalem (verse 10) that will come down to the freshly created new earth from heaven where it has eternally been.

2. THE DESCRIPTION OF THE NEW JERUSALEM — REVELATION 21:11-22:5

After the revelation of the establishment of the city, there is a detailed description of the city in Revelation 21:11-22:5. There are eleven things that should be noted.

First, *the glory* of the New Jerusalem is revealed in Revelation 21:11:

> Having the glory of God: her light was like unto a stone most precious, as it were a jasper stone, clear as crystal.

The glory is that of the Shechinah Glory whose final abode will be in the New Jerusalem.

Second, a description of the *city wall* is given in Revelation 21:12-13:

Having a wall great and high; having twelve gates, and at the gates twelve angels; and names written thereon, which are the names of the twelve tribes of the children of Israel: on the east were three gates; and on the north three gates; and on the south three gates; and on the west three gates.

The city wall symbolizes its *protection*. The wall is said to be great and high, but no details about its size or height are given at this point. The city will have a total of twelve gates, and each gate will be given to the authority of an angel. The twelve gates will be named after the twelve tribes of Israel meaning that for all eternity these Jewish names will be remembered. Furthermore, the text states that this great wall will have four sides with three gates on each side. Thus, all the gates will be equally divided.

Third, the *foundations of the wall* are described in Revelation 21:14:

And the wall of the city had twelve foundations, and on them twelve names of the twelve apostles of the Lamb.

The foundations are a symbol of *permanence*, and there will be a total number of twelve foundations named after the twelve apostles of Christ. These names will also be remembered for all eternity.

Fourth, the *measurements of the city* are recorded in Revelation 21:15-17:

And he that spake with me had for a measure a golden reed to measure the city, and the gates thereof, and the wall thereof. And the city lieth foursquare, and the length thereof is as great as the breadth: and he measured the city with the reed, twelve thousand furlongs: the length and the breadth and the height thereof are equal. And he measured the wall thereof, a hundred and forty and four cubits, according to the measure of a man, that is, of an angel.

The measurements of the city symbolize its *spaciousness*. The city will be foursquare and a cube with the height, length and breadth being equal, that is, measuring about 1,500 miles long, wide and high. Obviously, it will be the largest city ever known to man with plenty of room for all the redeemed of all ages to live. As for *the wall* it will measure 216 feet high, so it will indeed be a high wall as stated earlier in verse 12.

Fifth, the *composition of the city* is described in Revelation 21:18-21:

And the building of the wall thereof was jasper: and the city was pure gold, like unto pure glass. The foundations of the wall of the city were adorned with all manner of precious stones. The first foundation was jasper; the second, sapphire; the third, chalcedony; the fourth, emerald; the fifth, sardonyx; the sixth, sardius; the seventh, chrysolite; the eighth, beryl; the ninth, topaz; the tenth, chrysoprase; the eleventh, jacinth; the twelfth, amethyst. And the twelve gates were twelve pearls; each one of the several gates was of one pearl: and the street of the city was pure gold, as it were transparent glass.

The *wall* will be built of jasper, and the entire cubed *city* will be made of transparent gold. As for the twelve *foundations* of the wall, each foundation will be composed of different precious stones with its own dominant color. They can be delineated as follows:

1. Jasper — green
2. Sapphire — blue
3. Chalcedony — greenish
4. Emerald — green
5. Sardonyx — red and white
6. Sardius — fiery red
7. Chrysolite — golden yellow
8. Beryl — aqua green
9. Topaz — greenish yellow
10. Chrysoprase — golden green
11. Jacinth — violet
12. Amethyst — purple

Half of these stones also characterized the first earth before Satan's fall in Ezekiel 28:13. The new earth will enjoy all the perfections of the first earth plus double.

As for the twelve *gates* named after the twelve tribes of Israel, each gate will be made of a single huge pearl. The singular *street* of the city, like the city itself, will be composed of transparent gold.

Sixth, in addition to the absence of oceans in the new earth, several other *omissions* are mentioned in Revelation 21:22-24:

And I saw no temple therein: for the Lord God the Almighty, and the Lamb, are the temple thereof. And the city hath no need of the sun, neither of the moon, to shine upon it: for the glory of God did lighten it, and the lamp thereof is the Lamb. And the nations shall walk amidst the light thereof: and the kings of the earth bring their glory into it.

A second item missing on the new earth is a temple. During historic time, a total of four temples will have existed. But in eternity, there will be no temple, neither will there be any need for one since the entire Triune God will inhabit the city along with all the redeemed of all ages. The third and fourth omissions are the sun and moon. In the original creation of the first earth, there was no sun or moon either, for they were only created on the fourth day of Genesis one. However, there will be a return to that original condition with the absence of the sun and the moon. The source of light in the eternal order will not come from such created things but will be provided by the Creator of light, the Shechinah Glory of the Lamb which will lighten all for the Eternal Order. The Gentiles of the earth will walk by means of this light as well as those who served as kings in the old order. It should be noted that the Jew and Gentile distinction will be maintained for all eternity.

Seventh, there is a description regarding the *entrance* into the city in Revelation 21:25-27:

> And the gates thereof shall in no wise be shut by day (for there shall be no night there): and they shall bring the glory and the honor of the nations into it: and there shall in no wise enter into it anything unclean, or he that maketh an abomination and a lie: but only they that are written in the Lamb's book of life.

Though there will be twelve pearly gates around the city maintained by twelve angels, these gates will never be closed throughout eternity. Then a fifth omission in the Eternal Order is given: the absence of night. The existence of darkness was another result of the curse on the earth at Satan's fall (Genesis 1:2). During the six days of creation there was only a partial removal of the darkness (the sun by day) and the night (the moon and the stars provided limited light) that existed. But in the Eternal Order, since all the effects of sin are to be removed forever, there will be no night. As for the forever-open gates of the New Jerusalem, the righteous of the Gentiles that are found in the Lamb's Book of Life will bring their glory into it. On the other hand, nothing of unrighteousness will ever be allowed to enter into the eternal city. All unrighteousness will now be confined in the Lake of Fire.

Eighth, there is a description of the *river of life* in Revelation 22:1:

> And he showed me a river of water of life, bright as crystal, proceeding out of the throne of God and of the Lamb, in the midst of the street thereof.

Out of the throne of God and the Messiah, a river will begin to flow with the brightness of crystal. It will continue to flow throughout the singular street of the city of the New Jerusalem.

Ninth, the *tree of life* is described in Revelation 22:2:

> ... And on this side of the river and on that was the tree of life, bearing twelve manner of fruits, yielding its fruit every month: and the leaves of the tree were for the healing of the nations.

The tree of life that existed in the Garden of Eden (Genesis 2:9, 3:22, 24) will now return. The trunk of the tree will extend to both sides of the eternal river of life and will be characterized by productivity, bearing fresh fruit each month of the year. It should be noted that the word *month* is used, so some kind of dating system will be present in the Eternal Order. Since there will be no sun, moon, nor night, it will be a radically different dating system than the one in which we presently live. But there will be a dating system of some kind.

The leaves of the tree of life are for *the healing of the nations*. The Greek word translated *healing* is the source of the modern English word *therapeutic*. The purpose of the leaves is not to heal existing sicknesses, for they will not exist in the Eternal Order; rather, it will be health-giving for the nations. There will be no sickness in the Eternal Order because of the leaves of the tree of life.

Tenth, there is a description of the *occupants* of the New Jerusalem in Revelation 22:3-4:

> And there shall be no curse any more: and the throne of God and of the Lamb shall be therein: and his servants shall serve him; and they shall see his face; and his name shall be on their foreheads.

There will be a total absence of the curse in the Eternal Order. The residents of the city will include the Lamb (Christ) and all the redeemed of all ages who will have the name of Jesus on their foreheads.

Eleventh, the presence of the *Shechinah Glory* is reiterated in Revelation 22:5:

> And there shall be night no more; and they need no light of lamp, neither light of sun; for the Lord God shall give them light: and they shall reign for ever and ever.

Once again, the text declares that night will not exist in the Eternal Order, and there will be no need for the light of the sun or the light of a lamp. God Himself will provide all the light that is necessary. As previously stated, this light will be the Shechinah Glory which will provide all the light that is necessary for all eternity.

PART VIII

CONCLUSION

CHAPTER XXIII

CONCLUSION

The conclusion of the book of the Revelation, found in Revelation 22:6-21, contains several important elements.

A. THE AUTHENTICATION OF THE BOOK OF REVELATION — REVELATION 22:6-9

The concluding words begin with the authentication of all that John had written in the book in Revelation 22:6-9. First, there is the authentication by God in Revelation 22:6-7:

> And he said unto me, These words are faithful and true: and the Lord, the God of the spirits of the prophets, sent his angel to show unto his servants the things which must shortly come to pass. And behold, I come quickly. Blessed is he that keepeth the words of the prophecy of this book.

God Himself and Christ in particular authenticate all that John had written. The Spirit of the prophets who inspired all previous writings of the Scripture also inspired this prophecy of the book of the Revelation. The specific means of revelation to John was by means of a holy angel. The book of Revelation ends the same way it begins: with a promise of a blessing to those who keep (in the sense of watching for) the things prophesied in the book.

Secondly, in Revelation 22:8-9, the writing of John is authenticated by the very angel who gave John all the revelation in the first place:

> And I John am he that heard and saw these things. And when I heard and saw, I fell down to worship before the feet of the angel that showed me these things. And he saith unto me, See thou do it not: I am a fellow-servant with thee and with thy brethren the prophets, and with them that keep the words of this book: worship God.

B. DECLARATIONS IN LIGHT OF THE REVELATION — REVELATION 22:10-15

In light of the revelation of things to come in God's program, certain declarations are given in this final chapter of the book in Revelation 22:10-15.

The first declaration concerns the book itself in Revelation 22:10:

> And he saith unto me, Seal not up the words of the prophecy of this book; for the time is at hand.

As Daniel the prophet was closing his book, he was told to seal it in Daniel 12:4a:

But thou, O Daniel, shut up the words, and seal the book, even to the time of the end.

Then again in Daniel 12:8-9:

And I heard, but I understood not: then said I, O my lord, what shall be the issue of these things? And he said, Go thy way, Daniel; for the words are shut up and sealed till the time of the end.

The revelation given to Daniel covered so much territory and expanded over such a long period of time that he was unable to understand much of what he wrote. Daniel was told to seal his book until the time when many of the prophecies would be explained and clarified by later revelation. With the book of Revelation, much of Daniel has been clarified, expanded, detailed, and explained. So John, in contrast to Daniel, was told not to seal up his book. For all prophecy can now be understood, and its fulfillment could begin at any time.

The second declaration is directed at the righteous and the unrighteous in Revelation 22:11:

He that is unrighteous, let him do unrighteousness still: and he that is filthy, let him be made filthy still: and he that is righteous, let him do righteousness still: and he that is holy, let him be made holy still.

Those who are unrighteous are to confirm their unrighteousness by continuing in their unrighteousness, which is something that will naturally occur if God's revelation is rejected. But the righteous are to confirm their righteousness by continuing in their righteousness which will naturally result if God's revelation is accepted. The former will be characterized by filthiness but the latter by holiness.

The third declaration gives the purpose of the coming of Christ in Revelation 22:12:

Behold, I come quickly; and my reward is with me, to render to each man according as his work is.

The purpose of the coming of Christ is to render to each man according to his works. His coming at the Rapture is to reward the saints for the works done in their bodies since salvation. The purpose of the second coming is to render judgment for the works of unrighteousness.

The fourth declaration emphasizes the eternalness of the person of Christ in Revelation 22:13:

I am the Alpha and the Omega, the first and the last, the beginning and the end.

The fifth declaration concerns the inhabitants of the New Jerusalem in Revelation 22:14:

> Blessed are they that wash their robes, that they may have the right to come to the tree of life, and may enter in by the gates into the city.

The inhabitants of the New Jerusalem will be characterized by redemption. It is their redeemed state that will give them the authority to enter the city via the pearly gates and to partake of the tree of life.

The sixth and final declaration in Revelation 22:15 gives the characteristics of the unredeemed who will not have the authority to enter the New Jerusalem:

> Without are the dogs, and the sorcerers, and the fornicators, and the murderers, and the idolaters, and every one that loveth and maketh a lie.

The place "without" will be the Lake of Fire.

C. THE FIRST AFFIRMATION OF CHRIST — REVELATION 22:16

The six declarations are followed by the first affirmation of Christ in Revelation 22:16:

> I Jesus have sent mine angel to testify unto you these things for the churches. I am the root and the offspring of David, the bright, the morning star.

Jesus Himself affirms that it was He who sent the angel to John to reveal all the things found in the book of the Revelation so that John could deliver these things to the churches. It is the same Jesus who, in His humanity, is the root and offspring of David. But as to His deity, He is the Shechinah Glory as seen in the brightness and visibility of the light of the morning star.

D. THE INVITATION OF THE HOLY SPIRIT AND THE CHURCH — REVELATION 22:17

The first affirmation by Christ is followed by an invitation given by the Holy Spirit and the church in Revelation 22:17:

> And the Spirit and the bride say, Come. And he that heareth, let him say, Come. And he that is athirst, let him come: he that will, let him take the water of life freely.

These words contain an invitation to salvation which requires believing in Christ as Saviour. The call to salvation is a divine call by the Holy Spirit and the church. The Holy Spirit does the work of conviction concerning the truth of the gospel, and it is He that does the work of effectual calling and regeneration. It is the church that presents the message which the Holy Spirit uses to convict and to call. Those who respond will have the authority to partake of the waters of life in the New Jerusalem.

E. THE WARNINGS — REVELATION 22:18-19

The call to salvation is followed by two warnings in Revelation 22:18-19:

> I testify unto every man that heareth the words of the prophecy of this book, If any man shall add unto them, God shall add unto him the plagues which are written in this book: and if any man shall take away from the words of the book of this prophecy, God shall take away his part from the tree of life, and out of the holy city, which are written in this book.

The first warning is against any and all additions. Those who do add to what is written will receive the plagues of the book of Revelation, ultimately the Lake of Fire.

The second warning is against any subtractions from this book, for those who do so will not dwell in the New Jerusalem and partake of the tree of life.

Both those who would add and those who would subtract do so as evidence to their unsaved state.

These two warnings against additions and subtractions in their context are concerned specifically with the book of Revelation, and the primary emphasis is not on the Bible as a whole. However, since the book of the Revelation is the final revelation of God's Word, the principle behind the warning can be extended to the Bible as a whole. For the Bible as a whole is complete only with the book of the Revelation.

Examples of those who add are the numerous cults that accept other writings as inspired and authoritative and place them on equal grounds with the Bible; i.e., the Mormons with the *Book of Mormon* and Christian Science with their *Key to the Scriptures*. Examples of those who subtract are those who refuse to accept the entire body of Scripture as God's inspired Word and hold to concepts of partial inspiration or no inspiration.

However, both those who add and those who subtract do so because they are not willing to accept the Scriptures as the final authority. This demonstrates their unsaved state. Hence, they will lose out on dwelling in the New Jerusalem, and the Lake of Fire will be their eternal abode.

F. THE SECOND AFFIRMATION OF CHRIST — REVELATION 22:20

Then, a second affirmation of Christ is given in Revelation 22:20:

> He who testifieth these things saith, Yea: I come quickly. Amen: come, Lord Jesus.

The second affirmation of Christ testifies to the truthfulness of all that John wrote by stating that He soon will be returning to fulfill all the prophecies contained in this book. The term *quickly* applies to the return of Christ at the Rapture from God's perspective. God is not bound to time as we know it, and the past and future are as vivid to Him as the present. For the believer the term emphasizes imminency, meaning He could come at any moment. Although almost two thousand years have passed since this affirmation, nevertheless, the saints are always to be ready and looking for the appearing of the Son of God.

G. THE BENEDICTION — REVELATION 22:21

The book finally ends with the benediction found in Revelation 22:21:

The grace of the Lord Jesus be with the saints. Amen.

Selah.

APPENDIX

APPENDIX I

THE SIX ABODES OF SATAN

That Satan has a career is something that is clearly taught in the Scriptures. However, this career is seldom actually traced from start to finish, and perhaps this can best be done in a book on eschatology. One of the better ways of tracing the career of Satan is by means of his various abodes in which he either has lived in the past, is living in the present, or will live in the future. The first two abodes of Satan, both of which are now past, are to be found in Ezekiel 28:11-15:

> Moreover the word of Jehovah came unto me, saying, Son of man, take up a lamentation over the king of Tyre, and say unto him, Thus saith the Lord Jehovah: Thou sealest up the sum, full of wisdom, and perfect in beauty. Thou wast in Eden, the garden of God; every precious stone was thy covering, the sardius, the topaz, and the diamond, the beryl, the onyx, and the jasper, the sapphire, the emerald, and the carbuncle, and gold: the workmanship of thy tabrets and of thy pipes was in thee; in the day that thou wast created they were prepared. Thou wast the anointed cherub that covereth: and I set thee, so that thou wast upon the holy mountain of God; thou hast walked up and down in the midst of the stones of fire. Thou wast perfect in thy ways from the day that thou wast created, till unrighteousness was found in thee.

The relationship of this passage with the first ten verses of the same chapter should not be ignored. In verses 1-10 Ezekiel is commanded to address a man whom he entitles *the prince of Tyre*. It is quite evident from history that the one addressed as *the prince* was really the king of Tyre, and the rest of the world considered him to be such. Yet when God ordered Ezekiel to prophesy, He gave him a lesser title, that of merely a *prince*, for the real *king* was another personality entirely.

The key problem with this human king whom God called a prince was that of pride. Being king of a major commercial city of the ancient world and in control of much of the sea traffic of the Mediterranean made him an extremely wealthy monarch. One day, while contemplating his wealth and the power and authority that came with it, this king was filled with pride and began to consider himself to be god. For this pride that led to his self declaration of deity he was condemned. The world called him *king*, but God called him *prince*, because the true king of Tyre was a separate personality altogether to whom Ezekiel turned his attention in verse eleven. Satan was the true king of Tyre and controlled the human king. That is why in God's sight the human king was merely a prince. The thing that brought down the human king of Tyre was pride, and that was the very same thing that brought Satan down. Ezekiel was told to address the true king of Tyre in verses 11-19, and in doing so Ezekiel recapitulated Satan's past history providing revelation regarding the first and second abodes of Satan.

THE FIRST ABODE: THE THRONE OF GOD

The first abode of Satan is given in verse fourteen as being over *the holy mountain of God*. Whenever the word *mountain* is used symbolically, it is always the symbol of a king, kingdom, or throne. So Satan's first abode was at the very throne of God where he served as the guardian of God's throne controlling the access to that throne by the other angelic beings.

This passage reveals several things about the nature of this being during the first abode.

First, verse 12b states, *Thou sealest up the sum, full of wisdom, and perfect in beauty*. To *seal up the sum* is to totally fill up a pattern or blueprint. When God set out to do His creative work, He limited His work of creation to a specific pattern and did not choose to go beyond it. When animals were created, they filled up only a portion of the pattern. When man was created, he filled up some more of the pattern. Angels filled even a bit more. But when God created Satan, he filled up the entire pattern in two areas: wisdom and beauty. So of all created beings, Satan was by far the wisest and the most beautiful. This description is in sharp contrast with the usual portraits of Satan painted by centuries of artists which depict Satan as an ugly creature.

Secondly, in verse 14, Satan was *the anointed cherub that covereth*. In the celestial sphere there are three orders or ranks of beings. The lowest rank is the angels over whom is Michael the archangel. Above the angels are the seraphim, noted for having six wings and mentioned in Isaiah six and Revelation four. The highest rank of created beings are the cherubim, and Satan in his original creation was one among many cherubs. He was of the highest order, but one among many equals. However, at some point in eternity past, God took this one cherub and *anointed* or "messiahed" him, which elevated him over the other cherubs in power and authority. With this event then, Satan was the highest of all created beings not only in wisdom and beauty, but also in power and authority.

A third element regarding his nature is given in verse 15a: *Thou wast perfect in thy ways from the day that thou wast created.* When this being was created, he was created in absolute perfection without a single flaw. He was so perfect that he even had the power of contrary choice: i.e., to choose contrary to his nature. This is not a freedom that man has, for fallen man can choose only in accordance with his fallen nature. But Satan was able to choose contrary to his nature. By nature he was a holy and perfect being, yet he had the power to make an unholy and an imperfect choice.

THE SECOND ABODE: THE MINERAL GARDEN OF EDEN

Satan's second abode is described in verse thirteen. Sometime after the creation of angelic beings (Job 38:4-7), God created the heavens and the earth (Genesis 1:1). Different parts of the universe were given over to the authority of different angelic beings. This planet earth was given over to the authority of Satan. The Garden of Eden of Ezekiel 28:13 was not the same as the Garden of Eden of Genesis 2-3. The latter was a vegetable garden, but the former is described as a mineral garden. Ezekiel 28:13 describes how the entire planet earth looked when it was originally created. It had no oceans or seas and was covered with the brightness of the precious stones mentioned in this verse. So this planet, in the form of a total mineral Garden of Eden, served as Satan's second abode for an unknown period of time before any human being was created.

It was during Satan's second abode that the fall described in Ezekiel 28:16-17a took place:

> By the abundance of thy traffic they filled the midst of thee with violence, and thou hast sinned: therefore have I cast thee as profane out of the mountain of God; and I have destroyed thee, O covering cherub, from the midst of the stones of fire. Thy heart was lifted up because of thy beauty; thou hast corrupted thy wisdom by reason of thy brightness.

The problem of the *prince* of Tyre centuries later was the problem of the *king* of Tyre centuries earlier. Looking at his wisdom, beauty, power and authority and meditating upon these things ultimately led to the rise of pride, and thus Satan sinned. That it was pride that led to the fall of Satan is clearly stated in I Timothy 3:6:

> Not a novice, lest being puffed up he fall into the condemnation of the devil.

Paul warned strongly against placing a new believer in a position of authority in the local church. Not having had time to mature spiritually, he may become filled with pride and fall into the same sin that Satan committed. Hence, the sin which was found in Satan was the sin of pride. The content of Satan's pride was his declaration of five *I wills* found in Isaiah 14:12-14:

> How art thou fallen from heaven, O day-star, son of the morning! how art thou cut down to the ground, that didst lay low the nations! And thou saidst in thy heart, I will ascend into heaven, I will exalt my throne above the stars of God; and I will sit upon the mount of congregation, in the uttermost parts of the north; I will ascend above the heights of the clouds; I will make myself like the Most High.

Each *I will* has special significance. By stating, *I will ascend into heaven*, Satan wished to claim a higher estate than he already had and the only higher position was God's own throne. Whenever the word *star* is used symbolically, it is always the symbol of an angel. By stating, *I will exalt my throne above the stars of God*, Satan declared his desire to take over Michael's position as the archangel over all the angels of heaven. The statement *I will sit upon the mount of the con-gregation in the uttermost parts of the north*, uses millennial terms. Knowing it was God's plan for the Messiah to rule over Israel in the kingdom, with this declaration Satan expressed his desire to rule over Israel himself. When the word *cloud* is used symbolically, it is a symbol of the glory of God. By stating, *I will ascend above the heights of the clouds*, Satan was attempting to claim the Shechinah Glory which belongs to God alone. Finally, in stating, *I will make myself like the Most High*, Satan wished to become like God and be the sole possessor of the heavens and earth created in Genesis 1:1 for when-ever God is referred to as the *Most High,* it emphasizes God as the possessor of the heavens and the earth (Genesis 14:18-20).

These five *I wills* resulted from the pride of Satan and caused him to lead a revolt against God in which he was followed by one-third of the angelic host (Revelation 12:3-4). In this way the *Day-Star, Son of the Morning* became Satan the Adversary. At that point judgment came upon him.

When God judged Satan, He judged everything under Satan's authority, which meant judgment on the original earth: the mineral Garden of Eden. So, the conditions of Genesis 1:2 came into being as a result of this judgment.* The earth became waste and void, although it was not originally created that way (Isaiah 45:18). The beautiful mineral garden, that the planet once was, became totally covered by oceans. Sometime after this came the six days of creation recorded in Genesis one. The oceans were partially removed to allow dry land to appear, but the effects of Satan's judgment are still here in that most of the earth is still covered by oceans. The effects of the fall of Satan will not be fully removed until the creation of the new heavens and the new earth which will not have any oceans (Revelation 21:1).

It is evident that this author places the fall of Satan between Genesis 1:1 and 1:2. This position is often referred to as the "gap" theory. But many people who hold to the gap theory do so for "dinosaur space." They attempt to fit the fossil and geological ages into the gap and are forced to make the gap millions of years. This is not the position of the author at all, since scripturally it would be impossible for death to exist before the fall of man (Romans 5:12). Besides, all fossils and mammoth creatures have coexisted with man rather than preceded man. There is a gap between Genesis 1:1 and 1:2 only for the fall of Satan, and this need not be a very long time at all.

* It is agreed by most that Genesis 1:2 describes a chaotic state. The issue boils down to: did God create it in a chaotic state and then bring order to it? or, did some event cause it to become chaotic? The author prefers the second option because of Isaiah 45:18 and because terms used in Genesis 1:2 are used elsewhere in the Hebrew text describing divine judgments. Also, the New Earth in Revelation 21:1-22:5 compares favorably with Ezekiel 28:13 showing that the New Earth will look much like the old earth prior to the covering by seas in Genesis 1:2.

On the sixth day of creation, God created man and gave him the authority over the earth which had been removed from Satan. But when man fell, Satan usurped authority over the earth setting the stage for his activities in his third abode.

THE THIRD ABODE: THE ATMOSPHERIC HEAVENS

The third and present abode of Satan is disclosed in Ephesians:

Wherein ye once walked according to the course of this world, according to the prince of the powers of the air, of the spirit that now worketh in the sons of disobedience. (2:2)

For our wrestling is not against flesh and blood, but against the principalities, against the powers, against the world-rulers of this darkness, against the spiritual hosts of wickedness in the heavenly places. (6:12)

The first passage describes Satan as *the prince of the powers of the air*, while the second describes him as existing *in the heavenly places*. Accordingly, Satan's third abode can be labeled as the atmospheric heavens. He lives in the air or atmosphere.

While Satan lives in the atmosphere, he has permission of access into two places. First, he has access into heaven and often uses it (Job 1:6, 2:1). His purpose for using this permission of access into heaven is to be *the accuser of the brethren*. He functioned that way in the life of Job and continues to do the same in the case of many believers today (Revelation 12:10) and also in the case of the nation of Israel (Zechariah 3:1).

Secondly, Satan has permission of access to the earth and uses it frequently as well. He is still the prince of this world (John 12:31) and the god of this age (II Corinthians 4:4). When Satan comes to the earth, it is in one of two forms. The first form is that of a *roaring lion* (I Peter 5:8). In this form his basic aim is to devour and destroy. This is the way he has often appeared to Israel, and all anti-Semitic campaigns throughout Jewish history have been instigated by Satan as the roaring lion. He has also often appeared to the church in this form, and many of the persecutions against the church throughout church history have been inspired by Satan as the roaring lion.

The second form in which Satan appears when he comes to the earth is *as an angel of light* (II Corinthians 11:14). In this form Satan's basic aim is to deceive. It is the ultimate carrying out of the fifth *I will—I will make myself like the Most High*. Even Satan knew he could not be the Most High, so he decided to become just like the Most High. By instigating a counterfeit program that often looks like the real program, he has been able to implement a work of deception even among the true believers, encouraging them to become very experience orientated and blinding them to their need of a careful study of the Word of God. The program of deception is carried out against both believers (II Corinthians 11:3) and unbelievers (Revelation 20:3). The counterfeit program is spread by counterfeit ministers of Christ (II Corinthians 11:13), preaching a counterfeit Jesus (II Corinthians 11:3) and performing counterfeit signs, miracles and wonders (Matthew 7:22-23).

Also involved as part of Satan's third abode is his work of temptation by which he was able to usurp authority over the earth by causing man to fall. So to this day he is still exercising his authority as the prince (John 12:31) and god (II Corinthians 4:4) of this world. By causing man to fall, Satan succeeded in keeping man from exercising the authority God gave him over the earth at his creation.

The last three abodes of Satan are all future.

THE FOURTH ABODE: THE EARTH

Satan's fourth abode is described in Revelation 12:7-12:

> And there was war in heaven: Michael and his angels going forth to war with the dragon; and the dragon warred and his angels; and they prevailed not, neither was their place found any more in heaven. And the great dragon was cast down, the old serpent, he that is called the Devil and Satan, the deceiver of the whole world; he was cast down to the earth, and his angels were cast down with him. And I heard a great voice in heaven, saying, Now is come the salvation, and the power, and the kingdom of our God, and the authority of his Christ: for the accuser of our brethren is cast down, who accuseth them before our God day and night. And they overcame him because of the blood of the Lamb, and because of the word of their testimony; and they loved not their life even unto death. Therefore rejoice, O heavens, and ye that dwell in them. Woe for the earth and for the sea: because the devil is gone down unto you, having great wrath, knowing that he hath but a short time.

This passage has already been discussed in the main body of this work, and so the details need not be repeated.* In summary, in the middle of the tribulation Satan will be cast out of his present third abode into his fourth abode and so will be confined to this earth for the remainder of the tribulation. He will remain in his fourth abode for a total of three and a half years. His program during his fourth abode will be an attempt to destroy the Jews once and for all (Revelation 12:6, 13-17). He will attempt to do this by means of the two beasts of Revelation 13 (the Antichrist and the False Prophet). The details of his program of Jewish destruction and its outcome were discussed in previous chapters.**

THE FIFTH ABODE: THE ABYSS

Satan's fifth abode is given in Revelation 20:1-3:

---

* See Chapter XI.
** See Chapter XIII.

And I saw an angel coming down out of heaven, having the key of the abyss and a great chain in his hand. And he laid hold on the dragon, the old serpent, which is the Devil and Satan, and bound him for a thousand years, and cast him into the abyss, and shut it, and sealed it over him, that he should deceive the nations no more, until the thousand years should be finished: after this he must be loosed for a little time.

Satan's fifth abode will be the abyss where he will be confined during the one thousand years of the kingdom. As a result of his confinement in the abyss, sin and death in the kingdom will be greatly reduced but not eliminated. Other details of this have already been discussed in Chapters XV and XVII. Here it is important to note it will be during the kingdom that man will achieve his goal, which was to exercise authority over the earth. As a result of Satan's confinement in his fifth abode and through the reign of the God-Man Jesus the Messiah, man will fulfill his calling of exercising authority over the earth. This is clear from Hebrews 2:5-9:

For not unto angels did he subject the world to come, whereof we speak. But one hath somewhere testified, saying, What is man, that thou art mindful of him? or the son of man, that thou visitest him? Thou madest him a little lower than the angels; thou crownedst him with glory and honor, and didst set him over the works of thy hands: thou didst put all things in subjection under his feet. For in that he subjected all things unto him, he left nothing that is not subject to him. But now we see not yet all things subjected to him. But we behold him who hath been made a little lower than the angels, even Jesus, because of the suffering of death crowned with glory and honor, that by the grace of God he should taste of death for every man.

THE SIXTH ABODE: THE LAKE OF FIRE

Satan's sixth abode is described in Revelation 20:7-10:

And when the thousand years are finished, Satan shall be loosed out of his prison, and shall come forth to deceive the nations which are in the four corners of the earth, Gog and Magog, to gather them together to the war: the number of whom is as the sand of the sea. And they went up over the breadth of the earth, and compassed the camp of the saints about, and the beloved city: and fire came down out of heaven, and devoured them. And the devil that deceived them was cast into the lake of fire and brimstone, where are also the beast and the false prophet; and they shall be tormented day and night for ever and ever.

The details of this passage have already been discussed in Chapter XXI. Suffice it to say that the Lake of Fire will serve as Satan's sixth and final abode where he will remain for all eternity along with all other fallen angels and unredeemed men. As a result of Satan's sixth abode, two major effects of Satan's fall will be removed: death (I Corinthians 15:24-26) and the seas (Revelation 21:1).

APPENDIX II

II THESSALONIANS 2:1-12

In any book dealing with eschatology, the well-known passage of II Thessalonians 2:1-12 must be brought into the discussion. There has been much debate as to the exact point or points Paul wished to make, the identity of the restrainer, and exactly what is the relationship between the Antichrist and the restrainer. In dealing with this passage, perhaps it would be best to first summarize the main points made and then proceed to an analysis of the text. The main points appear to be as follows. *First*, to comfort the believers of Thessalonica letting them know that they are not in the tribulation, nor has the tribulation arrived. *Secondly*, to teach that there will be two separate revelations of the Antichrist at different points in time. *Thirdly*, that two things are being restrained: the mystery of lawlessness in general now, and the Antichrist specifically in the future.

With this background, the next step is to take a look at the passage itself, which reads as follows:

> Now we beseech you, brethren, touching the coming of our Lord Jesus Christ, and our gathering together unto him; to the end that ye be not quickly shaken from your mind, nor yet be troubled, either by spirit, or by word, or by epistle as from us, as that the day of the Lord is just at hand; let no man beguile you in any wise: for it will not be, except the falling away come first, and the man of sin be revealed, the son of perdition, he that opposeth and exalteth himself against all that is called God or that is worshipped; so that he sitteth in the temple of God, setting himself forth as God. Remember ye not, that, when I was yet with you, I told you these things? And now ye know that which restraineth, to the end that he may be revealed in his own season. For the mystery of lawlessness doth already work: only there is one that restraineth now, until he be taken out of the way. And then shall be revealed the lawless one, whom the Lord Jesus shall slay with the breath of his mouth, and bring to nought by the manifestation of his coming; even he, whose coming is according to the working of Satan with all power and signs and lying wonders, and with all deceit of unrighteousness for them that perish; because they received not the love of the truth, that they might be saved. And for this cause God sendeth them a working of error, that they should believe a lie: that they all might be judged who believed not the truth, but had pleasure in unrighteousness.

Apparently after Paul left Thessalonica some false teachers came in teaching a post-tribulational doctrine and stated that the believers were now in the tribulation. And so the Thessalonians were troubled that the *day of the Lord*, the most common title for the Great Tribulation, had now arrived (verses 1-2). At this point, Paul stated that the tribulation could not have come yet because two events, both of which must precede the tribulation, had not yet occurred (verse 3). The first is the apostasy of the church, and the second is the revelation of the man of sin and the son of perdition. So there is to be a revelation of the identity of the Antichrist that precedes the tribulation, and it is for the believers living at that time. The Rapture may or may not have occurred by then since the Scriptures do not state just when before the tribulation the Rapture will occur. Therefore the revelation to believers before the tribulation may be to the church if the Rapture has not occurred, or it may be to a new generation of believers who will have accepted the gospel after the Rapture of the church. Whoever the believers may be at that time, they will receive a revelation as to the identity of the Antichrist, and it will occur some-time before the tribulation. This text does not state exactly how this revelation will come, but other Scriptures give indication that this revelation may come because of two things. First, it is clear from Daniel 9:27 that the tribulation will begin with the signing of a seven-year covenant between Israel and the Antichrist. When this forth-coming covenant is announced, believers may become aware of the identity of the Antichrist. But secondly, it is also possible that believers will deduce who he is by the numerical value of the Anti-christ's name, which will be 666.

Then two things are stated concerning this Antichrist (verse 4). First, he will be opposed to God and to all objects of veneration. Secondly, he will take over the Jewish temple and declare himself to be god and will call all men to worship him. This event will occur in the middle of the tribulation in conjunction with the Abomination of Desolation.

Verses 5-7 are somewhat parenthetical as Paul reminds his readers of things he had taught them while he was still with them (verse 5). The key thing he had taught them was the fact that the take-over of the Jewish temple and the self-declaration of deity will be restrained, and until the restrainer is removed, the events of verse four cannot occur (verse 6). It has already been shown in the main body of this book that what will restrain the Antichrist from full political and religious control will be three of the ten kings of the first half of the tribulation and the governments they represent.* It is only when the last of these three kings has been killed leading to complete sub-mission by the other seven kings that the Antichrist will be free to take over full global dictatorship and to carry out the events of verse four. Consequently, the last restrainer of the Antichrist will be the last of the three kings and the government which he represents.

Then Paul reminds his readers that the mystery of lawlessness is already working and is even now being restrained (verse 7). The task of

* See Chapter XI.

restraining evil was given to human government under the Noahic Covenant in Genesis 9:1-17, and this basic doctrinal truth was reiterated by Paul in Romans 13:1-7. So on one hand, human government is even now restraining lawlessness. On the other hand, the government of the last of the three kings will restrain the Antichrist, the lawless one, until the middle of the tribulation.

After the parenthetical reminder of verses 5-7, in verses 8-12 Paul returns to where he left off at verse four. According to verse eight the Abomination of Desolation of verse four will serve as the second revelation of the Antichrist. While the first revelation will be to the believers before the tribulation, the second revelation in the middle of the tribulation will be to Israel. By this very act of the Abomination of Desolation, the Antichrist will be revealed as truly being the lawless one, and then Israel can realize with whom they have made their covenant. The act of the Abomination of Desolation is clearly stated by Jesus to be a sign to Israel in Matthew 24:15-22.

Paul then proceeds to give further facts regarding the Antichrist. He will ultimately be destroyed by the second coming of Christ (verse 8b). He is the one who will be totally energized by Satan and will be able to do miracles (verse 9) for the purpose of world-wide deception, for he will call all men to worship him (verse 10). The ones who will be deceived by him and his counterfeit signs are those who have already rejected the gospel of the Lord Jesus Christ (verses 11-12). These verses have often been taken to mean that those who heard the gospel before the Rapture and did not believe will not have the opportunity to be saved after the Rapture and during the tribulation. However, the passage itself seems to place the rejection of the gospel during the tribulation itself rather than before the tribulation. It should be remembered that during the first half of the tribulation there will be a world-wide preaching of the gospel by the 144,000 Jews (Matthew 24:14, Revelation 7). While myriads will accept the gospel, many more will not. Because these many will refuse to respond to the preaching of the 144,000 during the first half of the tribulation, during the second half they will be deceived by the Antichrist and will begin to worship him. The initial act of worshipping the Antichrist will involve accepting the mark of 666. Once this mark is taken, the individual will have reached the point of no return and will not have the opportunity to be saved from then on (Revelation 14:9-12).

APPENDIX III

THE WIFE OF JEHOVAH AND THE BRIDE OF CHRIST

Many years ago Dr. C. I. Scofield wrote a little booklet entitled, *Rightly Dividing the Word of Truth.* In this booklet he showed how any clear understanding of the Bible required that proper distinctions be maintained. In fact, the mark of a dispensationalist or a non-dispensationalist often revolves around the understanding of key biblical distinctions.

One of these key biblical distinctions is the distinction between Israel and the church. A failure to maintain that distinction will only result in a misinterpretation of what the Scriptures teach.

The Scriptures maintain the distinction between Israel and the church in a number of different ways, one of which is the distinction between the wife and the bride. In the Bible, Israel is represented as *the wife of Jehovah*, whereas the church is represented as *the bride of Christ*.

A. ISRAEL: THE WIFE OF JEHOVAH

The relationship of Israel as the wife of Jehovah is viewed throughout the Scriptures in various ways and facets. This relationship can be divided into six distinct stages through which this relationship develops.

1. STAGE ONE: THE MARRIAGE CONTRACT

To a casual and superficial reader, the book of Deuteronomy seems to be merely a repetition of what Moses had written earlier in the books of Exodus, Leviticus and Numbers. In fact, the very title *Deuteronomy* means *a second law* or *a repetition of the law.* Indeed almost everything found in the book of Deuteronomy can also be found in the three preceding books of the Law of Moses.

However, Deuteronomy is not merely a book of repetitions. The entire format of the book of Deuteronomy is that of both an ancient treaty and an ancient marriage contract. In other words, what Moses did in Deuteronomy was to take all the various facets of the three earlier books and present them in the form of an ancient marriage contract. For in this book we find the marriage contract signed between Israel and God—where Israel became the wife of Jehovah.

It is not feasible in this work to deal with the book of Deuteronomy in its entirety and demonstrate how it fits into the scheme of a marriage contract. However, it is possible to concentrate on certain key passages.

The first passage is Deuteronomy 5:1-3:

> And Moses called unto all Israel, and said unto them, Hear, O Israel, the statutes and the ordinances which I speak in your ears this day, that ye may learn them, and observe to do them. Jehovah our God made a covenant with us in Horeb. Jehovah made not this covenant with our fathers, but with us, even us, who are all of us here alive this day.

This passage declares that God entered into a covenant with His people Israel at Mount Sinai. It will be seen later that the Jewish prophets always viewed this covenant relationship as a marriage contract.

Later, in Deuteronomy 6:10-15, God announced His jealousy over His wife, Israel:

> And it shall be, when Jehovah thy God shall bring thee into the land which he sware unto thy fathers, to Abraham, to Isaac, and to Jacob, to give thee, great and goodly cities, which thou buildest not, and houses full of all good things, which thou filledst not, and cisterns hewn out, which thou hewedst not, vineyards and olive-trees, which thou plantedst not, and thou shalt eat and be full; then beware lest thou forget Jehovah, who brought thee forth out of the land of Egypt, out of the house of bondage. Thou shalt fear Jehovah thy God; and him shalt thou serve, and shalt swear by his name. Ye shall not go after other gods, of the gods of the peoples that are round about you; for Jehovah thy God in the midst of thee is a jealous God; lest the anger of Jehovah thy God be kindled against thee, and he destroy thee from off the face of the earth.

In this passage Israel is warned against adultery. Since Jehovah is Israel's husband, the means by which Israel can be guilty of adultery is by the worship of other gods. God warned Israel not to become an adulteress wife by playing around with other gods. The reason given is God's burning jealousy lest it be kindled against her and eventually cause her expulsion out of the land which God has given her.

In Deuteronomy 7:6-11, Israel is again described as the one chosen by God:

> For thou art a holy people unto Jehovah thy God: Jehovah thy God hath chosen thee to be a people for his own possession, above all peoples that are upon the face of the earth. Jehovah did not set his love upon you, nor choose you, because ye were more in number than any people; for ye were the fewest of all peoples: but because Jehovah loveth you, and because he would keep the oath which he sware unto your fathers, hath Jehovah brought you out with a mighty hand, and redeemed you out of the house of bondage, from the hand of Pharoah king of Egypt. Know therefore that Jehovah thy God, he is God, the faithful God, who keepeth covenant and lovingkindness with them that love him and keep his commandments to a thousand generations, and repayeth them that hate him to their face, to destroy them: he will not be slack to him that hateth him, he will repay him to his face. Thou shalt therefore keep the commandments, and the statutes, and the ordinances, which I command

thee this day, to do them.

In verse six God described the choosing and then in verses 7-8 He gave the reason. God did not choose Israel as His wife due to her size, because Israel was small. He had only one basic reason and that was His love for Israel. Because of His love for Israel, He entered into a covenant relationship with her. This covenant relationship is the marriage contract of Deuteronomy. But now Israel has an obligation, for in verses 9-11 God implored Israel to faithfulness, to be a faithful wife to Jehovah by being obedient and subject to Him.

As was stated earlier, the prophets always looked at this covenant relationship as a marriage contract. One example is found in Ezekiel 16:8:

> Now when I passed by thee, and looked upon thee, behold, thy time was the time of love; and I spread my skirt over thee, and covered thy nakedness: yea, I sware unto thee, and entered into a covenant with thee, saith the Lord Jehovah, and thou becamest mine.

The words used by Ezekiel are words of the wedding night; the covenant at Sinai and the relationship between Israel and Jehovah is described by the prophet in the terms of the wedding night.

Thus, in the first stage of her relationship as the wife of Jehovah, Israel entered into a marriage contract and this marriage contract is the Book of Deuteronomy.

2.   STAGE TWO: THE GREAT ADULTERY

Although Israel was sternly admonished to remain faithful to her husband, rather than being faithful she was guilty of a great adultery, described by several Old Testament prophets. Jeremiah 3:1-5 states:

> They say, If a man put away his wife, and she go from him, and become another man's, will he return unto her again? will not that land be greatly polluted? But thou hast played the harlot with many lovers; yet return again to me, saith Jehovah. Lift up thine eyes unto the bare heights, and see; where hast thou not been lain with? By the ways hast thou sat for them, as an Arabian in the wilderness; and thou hast polluted the land with thy whoredoms and with thy wickedness. Therefore the showers have been withholden, and there hath been no latter rain; yet thou hadst a harlot's forehead, thou refusedst to be ashamed. Wilt thou not from this time cry unto me, My Father, thou art the guide of my youth? Will he retain his anger for ever? will he keep it to the end? Behold, thou hast spoken and hast done evil things, and hast had thy way.

Israel was not merely guilty of a one-time adultery, but she was guilty of playing the harlot with many lovers. Later, in verse 20, Jeremiah wrote:

Surely as a wife treacherously departeth from her husband, so have ye dealt treacherously with me, O house of Israel, saith Jehovah.

In this passage Jeremiah showed that Israel was indeed like a wife who has turned away from her husband. She was a wife guilty of adultery.

Because of this adultery, the original marriage contract was broken according to Jeremiah 31:32:

Not according to the covenant that I made with their fathers in the day that I took them by the hand to bring them out of the land of Egypt; which my covenant they brake, although I was a husband unto them, saith Jehovah.

Adultery meant that the marriage contract was null and void. Jeremiah showed that the problem was not with the husband, for God was a good husband. Rather, the problem was with the wife who insisted on going after other gods and so became guilty of the great adultery.

Another prophet, Ezekiel, described this great adultery in a very extended passage found in 16:15-34:

But thou didst trust in thy beauty, and playedst the harlot because of thy renown, and pouredst out thy whoredoms on every one that passed by; his it was. And thou didst take of thy garments, and madest for thee high places decked with divers colors, and playedst the harlot upon them: the like things shall not come, neither shall it be so. Thou didst also take thy fair jewels of my gold and of my silver, which I had given thee, and madest for thee images of men, and didst play the harlot with them; and thou tookest thy broidered garments, and coveredst them, and didst set mine oil and mine incense before them. My bread also which I gave thee, fine flour, and oil, and honey, wherewith I fed thee, thou didst even set it before them for a sweet savor; and thus it was, saith the Lord Jehovah. Moreover thou hast taken thy sons and thy daughters, whom thou hast borne unto me, and these hast thou sacrificed unto them to be devoured. Were thy whoredoms a small matter, that thou hast slain my children, and delivered them up, in causing them to pass through the fire unto them? And in all thine abominations and thy whoredoms thou hast not remembered the days of thy youth, when thou wast naked and bare, and wast weltering in thy blood. And it is come to pass after all thy wickedness, (woe, woe unto thee! saith the Lord Jehovah,) that thou hast built unto thee a vaulted place, and hast made thee a lofty place in every street. Thou hast built thy lofty place at the head of every way, and hast made thy beauty an abomination, and hast opened thy feet to every one that passed by, and multiplied thy whoredom. Thou hast also committed fornication with the Egyptians, thy neighbors, great of flesh; and hast multiplied thy whoredom, to provoke me to anger. Behold therefore, I have stretched out my hand over thee, and have diminished thine ordinary food, and delivered thee unto the will of them that hate thee, the daughters of the Philistines, that are ashamed of thy lewd way. Thou hast played the harlot also with the Assyrians, because thou wast insatiable; yea, thou hast played the harlot with them, and yet thou wast not satisfied. Thou hast moreover multiplied thy whoredom unto the land of traffic, unto Chaldea; and yet thou wast not satisfied herewith. How weak is thy heart, saith the Lord Jehovah, seeing thou doest all these things, the work of an impudent harlot; in that thou buildest thy vaulted place at the head of every way, and makest thy lofty place in every street, and hast not been as a harlot, in that thou scornest hire. A wife that committeth adultery! that taketh strangers instead of her husband! They give gifts to all harlots; but thou givest thy gifts to all thy lovers, and bribest them, that they may come unto thee on every side for thy whoredoms. And thou art different from other women in thy whoredoms, in that none followeth thee to play the harlot; and whereas thou givest hire, and no hire is given unto thee, therefore thou art different.

Ezekiel declares Israel's guilt in verse 15 by showing her that she had indeed played the part of a prostitute. Although prostitutes generally receive money for their services, Israel was somewhat different because she paid her lovers (verses 16-19), and she paid them with the very things that her true husband, God, had given to her as His wife. Furthermore, Israel's very children were sacrificed to these lovers, the pagan gods (verses 20-21). Israel indeed forgot her love of her youth when God first entered into the covenant relationship with her (verse 22). In verses 23-29 Ezekiel portrayed the lovers that Israel went after. These lovers were the gods of the Egyptians and the Assyrians and the Babylonians. The absurdity of Israel's adultery is clearly spelled out here. The very nations which these foreign gods represented did the most to hurt Israel. Israel suffered terribly from the hands of the Egyptians, Assyrians and Babylonians. Yet rather than turning to her own husband, Jehovah, Israel went after the gods of these nations and committed adultery with those that hurt her the most.

Another prophet, Hosea, also described this adultery in Hosea 2:2-5:

Contend with your mother, contend; for she is not my wife, neither am I her husband; and let her put away her whoredoms from her face, and her adulteries from between her breasts; lest I strip her naked, and set her as in the day that she was born, and make her as a wilderness, and set her like a dry land, and slay her with thirst. Yea, upon her children will I have no mercy; for they are children of whoredom; for their mother hath played the harlot; she that conceived them hath done shamefully; for she said, I will go after my lovers, that give me my bread and my water, my wool and my flax, mine oil and my drink.

Hosea declared the charge God had against Israel: she was guilty of harlotry. She committed adultery (verses 2-3), she produced children of adultery and hence they were illegitimate (verse 4), and she played the part of a prostitute (verse 5).

So in spite of God's manifold blessings to Israel, Israel turned away from God in order to play the part of a prostitute and was guilty of the great adultery.

3.   STAGE THREE: THE SEPARATION

Because of this adultery, in the days of Isaiah a separation took place between God and Israel. This separation is described in Isaiah 50:1:

> Thus saith Jehovah, Where is the bill of your mother's divorcement, wherewith I have put her away? or which of my creditors is it to whom I have sold you? Behold, for your iniquities were ye sold, and for your transgressions was your mother put away.

According to Deuteronomy 24:1, if a husband wished to divorce his wife, he had to write out a decree, or what is better known as a bill of divorcement. After having written it out in longhand he would give it to his wife and then the divorce was final.

By the time Isaiah became a prophet, Israel's adultery was so great that it was necessary for God to withhold His many blessings from her: the blessings described in the book of Deuteronomy, to be received if Israel remained faithful. This removal of the blessings caused many in Israel to say that God had divorced His wife.

Therefore, God spoke to Isaiah the prophet stating that He had not yet divorced His wife. If God had divorced His wife, He would have given to Israel a bill of divorcement; and since no such bill of divorcement was in hand, it meant that a divorce had not taken place.

Rather than a divorce, a separation had taken place. But this separation was caused by their own sins. The sin of Israel in committing adultery created the need for the separation. In the days of Isaiah, God and Israel were not divorced, but they were separated. This separation was due to Israel's adultery and lasted approximately one hundred years.

4.   STAGE FOUR: THE DIVORCE

Even after the one hundred years of separation, during which time the blessings of Deuteronomy continued to be withheld, Israel still failed to return to God her husband. Thus, God was forced to finally issue the bill of divorcement and to divorce His wife, Israel. This bill of divorcement is contained in Jeremiah 3:6-10:

> Moreover Jehovah said unto me in the days of Josiah the king, Hast thou seen that which backsliding Israel hath done? she is gone up upon every high mountain and under every green tree, and there hath played the

harlot. And I said after she had done all these things, She will return unto me; but she returned not: and her treacherous sister Judah saw it. And I saw, when, for this very cause that backsliding Israel had committed adultery, I had put her away and given her a bill of divorcement, yet treacherous Judah her sister feared not; but she also went and played the harlot. And it came to pass through the lightness of her whoredom, that the land was polluted, and she committed adultery with stones and with stocks. And yet for all this her treacherous sister Judah hath not returned unto me with her whole heart, but feignedly, saith Jehovah.

After once again declaring Israel guilty of adultery (verses 6-8), God finally issued His bill of divorcement. To a great extent, almost all of Jeremiah can be declared to be God's bill of divorcement of Israel but especially the passage now under consideration. The reason this bill of divorcement was necessary was due to the adulterous pollution of the land God had given to Israel (verses 9-10).

So in the days of Jeremiah the prophet, Israel was divorced. One hundred years of separation failed to produce repentance in Israel, and finally God had no other choice but to issue the bill of divorcement on the grounds of adultery.

5.   STAGE FIVE: THE PUNISHMENT

The book of Deuteronomy, the original marriage contract, clearly declared that if Israel proved unfaithful as Jehovah's wife it would become necessary for God to punish Israel for her unfaithfulness. And so following the issuing of the bill of divorcement comes a long period of the punishment of Israel for her sins.

Several Old Testament prophecies speak of the punishment of Israel for her unfaithfulness. Ezekiel 16:35-43 states:

Wherefore, O harlot, hear the word of Jehovah: Thus saith the Lord Jehovah, Because thy filthiness was poured out, and thy nakedness uncovered through thy whoredoms with thy lovers; and because of all the idols of thy abominations, and for the blood of thy children, that thou didst give unto them; therefore behold, I will gather all thy lovers, with whom thou hast taken pleasure, and all them that thou hast loved, with all them that thou hast hated; I will even gather them against thee on every side, and will uncover thy nakedness unto them, that they may see all thy nakedness. And I will judge thee, as women that break wedlock and shed blood are judged; and I will bring upon thee the blood of wrath and jealousy. I will also give thee into their hand, and they shall throw down thy vaulted place, and break down thy lofty places; and they shall strip thee of thy clothes, and take thy fair jewels; and they shall leave thee naked and bare. They shall also bring up a company against thee, and they shall stone thee with stones, and thrust thee through with their swords. And they shall burn thy houses with fire, and execute judgments upon thee in the sight of many women; and I will cause thee to cease from playing the harlot, and thou shalt also give no hire any more. So will

I cause my wrath toward thee to rest, and my jealousy shall depart from thee, and I will be quiet, and will be no more angry. Because thou hast not remembered the days of thy youth, but hast raged against me in all these things; therefore, behold, I also will bring thy way upon thy head, saith the Lord Jehovah: and thou shalt not commit this lewdness with all thine abominations.

After stating the cause for the punishment, adultery (verses 35-36), Ezekiel described the punishment itself. Israel will be destroyed by her very own lovers (verses 37-41). Because she worshipped the gods of the Egyptians, the Egyptians will destroy her. Because she worshipped the deities of Assyria, the Assyrians will devastate her. Because she worshipped the idols of Babylon, the Babylonians will make her desolate. The nations who worshipped the very gods Israel committed adultery with will be the ones who will invade and destroy the nation of Israel. Then the jealousy of God will finally be spent (verse 42) for, as the book of Deuteronomy declared, the punishment of Israel would be a result of God's jealousy for His wife. However, all this punishment has a specific aim. The aim of this punishment is not so God can be vengeful and get His revenge upon Israel, but rather to cause her to stop sinning and to stop her adulteries (verse 43).

Later in this chapter, verses 58-59, Ezekiel showed that this punishment was necessary because Israel broke the marriage contract:

Thou hast borne thy lewdness and thine abominations, saith Jehovah. For thus saith the Lord Jehovah: I will also deal with thee as thou hast done, who hast despised the oath in breaking the covenant.

The program of punishment is further described in Hosea 2:6-13:

Therefore, behold, I will hedge up thy way with thorns, and I will build a wall against her, that she shall not find her paths. And she shall follow after her lovers, but she shall not overtake them; and she shall seek them, but shall not find them: then shall she say, I will go and return to my first husband; for then was it better with me than now. For she did not know that I gave her the grain, and the new wine, and the oil, and multiplied unto her silver and gold, which they used for Baal. Therefore will I take back my grain in the time thereof, and my new wine in the season thereof, and will pluck away my wool and my flax which should have covered her nakedness. And now will I uncover her lewdness in the sight of her lovers, and none shall deliver her out of my hand. I will also cause all her mirth to cease, her feasts, her new moons, and her sabbaths, and all her solemn assemblies. And I will lay waste her vines and her fig-trees, whereof she hath said, These are my hire that my lovers have given me; and I will make them a forest, and the beasts of the field shall eat them. And I will visit upon her the days of the Baalim, unto which she burned incense, when she decked herself with her earrings and her jewels, and went after her lovers, and forgat me, saith Jehovah.

The program itself is described in verses 6-7. Israel's searching ways will be blocked by various thorns and walls which speak of God's providential dealings with Israel (verse 6) until her search for her old lovers will prove fruitless (verse 7). The purpose of this program is to show Israel her need for her true husband and not for her false lovers (verse 7b).

Then in verses 8-13, Hosea depicted the punishment itself. It has been shown earlier that the very things God gave to Israel she used in order to pay her lovers. So now these very things she paid her lovers with will be taken away, for they belong to her husband (verses 8-9). She will finally realize her shame only when she sees herself truly spiritually naked, her joy removed, her material blessings gone: all because of the worship of the Canaanite god, Baal (verses 10-13).

Although God has a long program of punishment for Israel's sins, throughout the period of punishment there is a continual call to repentance. This continual call to repentance is presented in Jeremiah 3:11-18:

> And Jehovah said unto me, Backsliding Israel hath showed herself more righteous than treacherous Judah. Go, and proclaim these words toward the north, and say, Return, thou backsliding Israel, saith Jehovah; I will not look in anger upon you; for I am merciful, saith Jehovah, I will not keep anger for ever. Only acknowledge thine iniquity, that thou hast transgressed against Jehovah thy God, and hast scattered thy ways to the strangers under every green tree, and ye have not obeyed my voice, saith Jehovah. Return, O backsliding children, saith Jehovah; for I am a husband unto you: and I will take you one of a city, and two of a family, and I will bring you to Zion: and I will give you shepherds according to my heart, who shall feed you with knowledge and understanding. And it shall come to pass, when ye are multiplied and increased in the land, in those days, saith Jehovah, they shall say no more, The ark of the covenant of Jehovah; neither shall it come to mind; neither shall they remember it; neither shall they miss it; neither shall it be made any more. At that time they shall call Jerusalem the throne of Jehovah; and all the nations shall be gathered unto it, to the name of Jehovah, to Jerusalem: neither shall they walk any more after the stubbornness of their evil heart. In those days the house of Judah shall walk with the house of Israel, and they shall come together out of the land of the north to the land that I gave for an inheritance unto your fathers.

Jeremiah described God's continual call for Israel to repent and come back to Him (verses 11-13). This call is followed by a description of the blessings God has in store for Israel once she does return to Him (verses 14-18). After declaring that Jehovah will again be a husband to her (verse 14), He also promised to restore and to provide for Israel like a husband should (verses 15-18). All these beautiful material blessings are promised to Israel and are awaiting her return to her husband.

To this day Israel is still in the fifth stage of her historical and prophetic relationship with Jehovah, her God. Israel is still in the period of punishment. This is evidenced by the persecutions of the Jews around the world and by the present world-wide dispersion. But there is one stage yet to come.

6. STAGE SIX: THE REMARRIAGE WITH RESTORED BLESSINGS

The Jewish prophets did not leave things hopeless. They spoke of a coming day when Israel will again become the restored wife of Jehovah. Of course, this will require a brand new marriage contract, and this marriage contract is found in Jeremiah 31:31-34:

> Behold, the days come, saith Jehovah, that I will make a new covenant with the house of Israel, and with the house of Judah: not according to the covenant that I made with their fathers in the day that I took them by the hand to bring them out of the land of Egypt; which my covenant they brake, although I was a husband unto them, saith Jehovah. But this is the covenant that I will make with the house of Israel after those days, saith Jehovah: I will put my law in their inward parts, and in their heart will I write it; and I will be their God, and they shall be my people: and they shall teach no more every man his neighbor, and every man his brother, saying, Know Jehovah; for they shall all know me, from the least of them unto the greatest of them, saith Jehovah: for I will forgive their iniquity, and their sin will I remember no more.

What is often known as the new covenant is in many respects a new marriage contract that God will make with the two houses of Israel and Judah. This new covenant of marriage (verse 31) will be necessary because the old marriage covenant was broken (verse 32). Although God was a good husband, Israel strayed away and by means of adultery caused the original marriage contract to be broken. But now with this new marriage contract Israel will again be restored to the place of blessing (verses 33-34).

This remarriage on the basis of a new marriage contract is also described in Ezekiel 16:60-63:

> Nevertheless I will remember my covenant with thee in the days of thy youth, and I will establish unto thee an everlasting covenant. Then shalt thou remember thy ways, and be ashamed, when thou shalt receive thy sisters, thine elder sisters and thy younger; and I will give them unto thee for daughters, but not by thy covenant. And I will establish my covenant with thee; and thou shalt know that I am Jehovah; that thou mayest remember, and be confounded, and never open thy mouth any more, because of thy shame, when I have forgiven thee all that thou hast done, saith the Lord Jehovah.

According to Ezekiel, God will enter into an everlasting covenant with Israel in the future. This everlasting covenant is the same as that of the new covenant in Jeremiah 31:31-34. This new and everlasting covenant is also a new marriage contract upon which the remarriage will be based.

The restoration of Israel as Jehovah's wife is also described in Isaiah 54:1-8:

> Sing, O barren, thou that didst not bear; break forth into singing, and cry aloud, thou that didst not travail with child: for more are the children of the desolate than the children of the married wife, saith Jehovah. Enlarge the place of thy tent, and let them stretch forth the curtains of thy habitations; spare not: lengthen thy cords, and strengthen thy stakes. For thou shalt spread abroad on the right hand and on the left; and thy seed shall possess the nations, and make the desolate cities to be inhabited. Fear not; for thou shalt not be ashamed: neither be thou confounded; for thou shalt not be put to shame: for thou shalt forget the shame of thy youth; and the reproach of thy widowhood shalt thou remember no more. For thy Maker is thy husband; Jehovah of hosts is his name: and the Holy One of Israel is thy Redeemer; the God of the whole earth shall he be called. For Jehovah hath called thee as a wife forsaken and grieved in spirit, even a wife of youth, when she is cast off, saith thy God. For a small moment have I forsaken thee; but with great mercies will I gather thee. In overflowing wrath I hid my face from thee for a moment; but with everlasting lovingkindness will I have mercy on thee, saith Jehovah thy Redeemer.

Isaiah began by declaring that the restored wife will now begin to bear legitimate children (verses 1-3). Israel had produced a lot more children in desolation than she produced when she was previously married to Jehovah (verse 1). In fact, Israel produced many illegitimate children and very few legitimate ones, and the ones who were legitimate were often sacrificed to the foreign gods. But now all this is to change. Isaiah tells Israel to enlarge her house (verses 2-3) in order to accommodate the many legitimate children about to come.

The reason for this new activity and the coming legitimate children is because of the reunion of the marriage (verses 4-8). Israel's former adulteries will all be forgotten (verse 4), and Jehovah will once again be her husband (verse 5). God will again court His wife as He courted her when she was a youth (verse 6), and all past forsakings will now be substituted by renewed blessings (verses 7-8).

This remarriage is further described by Isaiah 62:4-5:

> Thou shalt no more be termed Forsaken; neither shall thy land any more be termed Desolate; but thou shalt be called Hephzi-bah, and thy land Beulah; for Jehovah delighteth in thee, and thy land shall be married. For as a young man marrieth a virgin, so shall thy sons marry thee; and as the bridegroom rejoiceth over the bride, so shall thy God rejoice over thee.

Israel's land that she lost because of her adultery is to be totally restored. Like a new husband rejoices over his virgin bride, in this same way God will rejoice over His restored wife.

Hosea, who had much to say about the adulteries of Israel, also spoke of Israel's reunion with her husband. He wrote in 2:14-23:

> Therefore, behold, I will allure her, and bring her into the wilderness, and speak comfortably unto her. And I will give her her vineyards from thence, and the valley of Achor for a door of hope; and she shall make answer there, as in the days of her youth, and as in the day when she came up out of the land of Egypt. And it shall be at that day, saith Jehovah, that thou shalt call me Ishi, and shalt call me no more Baali. For I will take away the names of the Baalim out of her mouth, and they shall no more be mentioned by their name. And in that day will I make a covenant for them with the beasts of the field, and with the birds of the heavens, and with the creeping things of the ground: and I will break the bow and the sword and the battle out of the land, and will make them to lie down safely. And I will betroth thee unto me for ever; yea, I will betroth thee unto me in righteousness, and in justice, and in loving-kindness, and in mercies. I will even betroth thee unto me in faithfulness; and thou shalt know Jehovah. And it shall come to pass in that day, I will answer, saith Jehovah, I will answer the heavens, and they shall answer the earth; and the earth shall answer the grain, and the new wine, and the oil; and they shall answer Jezreel. And I will sow her unto me in the earth: and I will have mercy upon her that had not obtained mercy; and I will say to them that were not my people, Thou art my people; and they shall say, Thou art my God.

Hosea began by describing the courtship and the wooing in the wilderness (verses 14-15). Israel will again be allured into the wilderness (in the land of Edom and the city of Bozrah) where God will speak to her heart in courtship, and when she responds all her vineyards will be restored.

The results of this restoration are described next (verses 16-23). There will be four results of this reunion.

The first result (verses 16-17) is that Israel will no longer address God as *Baali* but as *Ishi*. There is a very interesting play upon words in the Hebrew text by the usage of these two Hebrew words. Both words, *Baali* and *Ishi*, are good Hebrew words meaning *my husband*. While they both mean "my husband," there is a slight difference of emphasis in their meaning. *Ishi* means "my husband" in the sense of *my man*. *Baali* means "my husband" in the sense of *my master*. Both words are perfectly good Hebrew words for "my husband" and are used interchangeably throughout the Scriptures.

Nevertheless, God said that the title of *Baali* will no longer be used, but only *Ishi*. The reason for this is the fact that the word *Baali* sounds very much like one of the gods with whom Israel committed adultery: the god *Baal*. If Israel was to continue to call God *Baali* in the future, she might begin to remember her former lover, Baal. So in order to avoid even the hint of remembrance of the other lover, Baal, Israel will no longer address God as *Baali* but only as *Ishi*.

The second result (verse 18) is peace and safety. Israel will never again be invaded by the nations whose gods she once worshipped.

The third result (verses 19-20) is the betrothal. The word *betroth* is used three different times, and the three usages describe the three elements of this new betrothal. First, as to *time*, it will be forever. Secondly, as to *content*, it will be in righteousness, justice, loving-kindness and mercy. Thirdly, as to *quality*, it will be in faithfulness.

The fourth result (verses 21-23) is the new meaning to *Jezreel*. This term can mean two things: *God scatters* and *God sows*. During the period of punishment, Israel experienced the first meaning of *God scatters*. But now Israel will experience the second meaning of *God sows*. The Valley of Jezreel, Israel's largest valley and the most productive, had often failed to produce because God removed His blessings. But now with the new remarriage having taken place, all of God's blessings will be restored in the Valley of Jezreel, and it will produce almost as soon as the field is sown.

These, then, are the six stages of Israel's relationship as the wife of Jehovah, a wife whom God married but who committed adultery. Eventually, a separation took place followed by a divorcement, and today Israel is in her period of punishment. However, there will yet come the time when Israel will be remarried at her national regeneration and be reunited to her God with all of her blessings restored.

B. THE CHURCH: THE BRIDE OF CHRIST

There is a totally different picture in the Scriptures regarding the church. What God has to say about the church and her relationship as the bride of Christ is radically different from what has been said regarding Israel as the wife of Jehovah. This demonstrates the necessity of maintaining these distinctions.

The thrust of all New Testament passages regarding this relationship of the church as the bride of Christ is that the church is a betrothed bride that is not yet joined to her husband. There are four key passages of the New Testament that speak of this relationship of the church as the bride of Christ. But again it must always be kept in mind that the church is pictured today as an engaged bride who is not yet joined by marriage to her husband.

1. II CORINTHIANS 11:2 — THE ESPOUSAL

For I am jealous over you with a godly jealousy: for I espoused you to one husband, that I might present you as a pure virgin to Christ.

Speaking to a part of the church, the local church found in the city of Corinth, Paul declared that by means of evangelism they were espoused to one husband for the purpose of eventually being presented as a pure virgin to Christ. The means by which this will be accomplished is by the process of sanctification.

Unlike Israel, who was guilty of adultery, when the union comes between Christ and the church, the church will be presented as a pure virgin.

2. EPHESIANS 5:25-27 — THE PROCESS OF SANCTIFICATION OR MATURING OF THE BRIDE

Husbands, love your wives, even as Christ also loved the church, and gave himself up for it; that he might sanctify it, having cleansed it by the washing of water with the word, that he might present the church to himself a glorious church, not having spot or wrinkle or any such thing; but that it should be holy and without blemish.

Christ loved the church and proved His love by dying for the church. The purpose of the death of Christ in His relationship with the church is that He might sanctify the church, which is necessary in order for the church to be presented as a pure virgin as pictured in II Corinthians 11:2.

This sanctification takes place by a continual washing in the water of the Word. The church is being sanctified by the Word of God. The Holy Spirit is working in the church so that the true church is slowly being conformed to the Word of God by which it will also be cleansed. The *water* in this passage is not water baptism but a description of the Word of God in its cleansing ministry.

The aim of this process of sanctification and cleansing of the church is that the church might be presented a glorious virgin to Christ. When this process is finally complete, the church will be presented without spot (no visible defilement), without wrinkle (no evidence of age or corruption), and holy without blemish (no evidence of sin).

3. REVELATION 19:6-9 — THE MARRIAGE

In order to fully comprehend what is happening in Revelation 19:6-9, it is first necessary to understand the Jewish wedding system which was common in Jesus' day and still used among Jews until the present century. The Jewish marriage system had four distinct stages, all of which are to be found in the relationship of the church as the bride of Christ.

In the first stage, the father of the groom made *the arrangement* for the bride and paid the bride-price. This first stage might happen before the children are born, or when they are very young, or perhaps even a few short weeks prior to the marriage. But a long period of time could transpire between the first and second stage. Often the bride and groom did not see each other until their wedding day. This was true of this author's great grandparents who first met each other on their wedding day.

Eventually came the second stage known as *the fetching of the bride.* In this second stage the groom would come to the home of the bride in order to fetch her and bring her to his home. This was often done in accompaniment with a wedding procession.

Then came the third stage, which was *the marriage ceremony* to which only a few would be invited.

Finally came the fourth stage, *the marriage supper* or *feast* which would last for as long as seven days.

All four stages of the Jewish wedding system are to be found in the relationship of the church and Christ. First, the father of the groom made *the arrangement* for the bride and paid the bride-price. In this case, the bride-price was the blood of Christ. This was described earlier in Ephesians 5:25-27. While the first stage has already been completed, the other three stages are still future.

The second stage was *the fetching of the bride.* Even as a long period of time could transpire between the first and second stages in the Jewish system, so it has been with the church. Almost two thousand years have passed since the first stage was accomplished. But someday the second stage will take place when Christ will come in order to fetch the bride to His home. This fetching of the bride is referred to today as the Rapture of the church and is described in I Thessalonians 4:13-18:

> But we would not have you ignorant, brethren, concerning them that fall asleep; that ye sorrow not, even as the rest, who have no hope. For if we believe that Jesus died and rose again, even so them also that are fallen asleep in Jesus will God bring with him. For this we say unto you by the word of the Lord, that we that are alive, that are left unto the coming of the Lord, shall in no wise precede them that are fallen asleep. For the Lord himself shall descend from heaven, with a shout, with the voice of the archangel, and with the trump of God: and the dead in Christ shall rise first; then we that are alive, that are left, shall together with them be caught up in the clouds, to meet the Lord in the air: and so shall we ever be with the Lord. Wherefore comfort one another with these words.

Thus, with the Rapture of the church some time before the beginning of the tribulation, the second stage will be completed.

The third stage, *the marriage ceremony*, will take place in heaven just prior to the second coming of Christ at the end of the tribulation.

This is described in Revelation 19:6-8:

> And I heard as it were the voice of a great multitude, and as the voice of many waters, and as the voice of mighty thunders, saying, Hallelujah: for the Lord our God, the Almighty, reigneth. Let us rejoice and be exceeding glad, and let us give the glory unto him: for the marriage of the Lamb is come, and his wife hath made herself ready. And it was given unto her that she should array herself in fine linen, bright and pure: for the fine linen is the righteous acts of the saints.

The wedding announcement will be made (verse 6) and the bride will finally be made ready (verse 7). The reason the bride will now be fully ready for the marriage ceremony is because she will have her entire bridal gown on (verse 8). This bridal gown is said to be *the righteous acts of the saints*. This teaches two things. First, it shows that the process of sanctification will indeed be completed, for all that will be showing on the bride are her righteous acts. Secondly, this also shows that the marriage ceremony takes place after the Judgment Seat of Christ when the saints are rewarded for their deeds on earth (I Corinthians 3:10-15). All the wood, hay, and stubble has been burned away and all the gold, silver, and precious stones have been purified. The ones present at the marriage ceremony are the "few," that is, only those in heaven at that time.

After the marriage ceremony will come the fourth stage, *the marriage feast*, described in Revelation 19:9:

> And he saith unto me, Write, Blessed are they that are bidden to the marriage supper of the Lamb. And he saith unto me, These are true words of God.

Since many are bidden and invited to come to the marriage feast, this passage indicates that the marriage supper or feast will be at a different place than the marriage ceremony. We know from the Word of God that the Old Testament saints are resurrected not with the church before the tribulation, but at the end of the tribulation (Daniel 12:2). John the Baptist, who was the last of the Old Testament prophets, called himself a *friend of the bridegroom* and did not consider himself to be a member of the bride of Christ, the church (John 3:27-30). Hence, the "many" who are bidden to attend the marriage supper on earth are all the Old Testament saints and the tribulation saints resurrected after the second coming of Jesus Christ. While the marriage ceremony will take place in heaven just before the second coming of Christ, the marriage feast will take place on earth after the second coming of Christ. In fact, it would seem that the marriage feast is what begins the millennium or messianic age; the church's co-reigning with Christ will start with a tremendous marriage feast.

With the marriage feast, all four stages will be complete.

4. REVELATION 21:9-22:5 — THE ETERNAL ABODE OF THE BRIDE

The final picture that the Scriptures give of the bride of Christ is contained in the closing chapters of the Bible itself. In Revelation 21:9 John states:

> And there came one of the seven angels who had the seven bowls, who were laden with the seven last plagues; and he spake with me, saying, Come hither, I will show thee the bride, the wife of the Lamb.

In this passage, as a result of the four earlier stages, the bride is now the married wife. Then in the following verses (21:10-22:5) there is a graphic description of the glorious eternal wife of Christ in her eternal abode.

CONCLUSION

This concludes our study of what the Bible has to say about the wife of Jehovah and the bride of Christ. While the distinction between Israel and the church is maintained in various ways, this is one of the more picturesque. But this is one area of study that would be impossible to understand without knowing that such a distinction indeed exists. If one makes the wife of Jehovah and the bride of Christ one and the same thing, he is faced with numerous contradictions because of the different descriptions given. Only when one sees two separate entities, Israel as the wife of Jehovah and the church as the bride of Christ, do all such contradictions vanish.

APPENDIX IV

THE SHECHINAH GLORY
IN
HISTORY AND PROPHECY

A. DEFINITIONS

By way of definition, the Shechinah Glory is *the visible manifestation of the presence of God.* It is the majestic presence or manifestation of God in which He descends to *dwell* among men.

The usual title found in the Scriptures for the Shechinah Glory is *the glory of the Lord.* The Hebrew form is *Kvod Adonai*, which means "the glory of the Lord" and describes what the Shechinah Glory *is.* The Greek title, *Doxa Kurion*, is also translated as "the glory of the Lord." However, *doxa* means brightness, brilliance or splendor, and it depicts how the Shechinah Glory *appears.*

Other titles give it the sense of "dwelling" which portrays what the Shechinah Glory *does.* The Hebrew form *Shechinah*, from the root *shachan*, means *dwelling.* The Greek word *Skeinei*, which is derived from the Hebrew Shechinah (Greek has no "sh" sound), means *to tabernacle.*

As has been stated, the Shechinah Glory is the visible manifestation of the presence of God. In the Old Testament most of these visible mainfestations took the form of light, fire, or cloud, or a combination of these. A new form appears in the New Testament. At times it is closely associated with one or more of four elements: (1) the Angel of Jehovah, (2) the Holy Spirit, (3) the cherubim, and (4) the motif of thick darkness.

B. THE SHECHINAH GLORY IN OLD TESTAMENT HISTORY

1. THE GARDEN OF EDEN

It is possible that the first appearance* of the Shechinah Glory is found in Genesis 3:8:

> And they heard the voice of Jehovah God walking in the garden in the cool of the day: and the man and his wife hid themselves from the presence of Jehovah God amongst the trees of the garden.

According to this verse the first parents experienced the personal

---

* It is also possible that the first appearance of the Shechinah Glory was the light of the first day of creation in Genesis 1:3-5. But since this light had to be created, it is not likely that it was.

presence of God. There was a daily manifestation of God's presence fellowshipping with them. No details are given, and whether or not this can indeed be called the first manifestation of the Shechinah Glory is impossible to answer. But the indication is that this was a manifestation of the glory of God. However, if it is not, then Genesis 3:23-24 is where the first appearance of the Shechinah Glory is to be found:

> Therefore Jehovah God sent him forth from the garden of Eden, to till the ground from whence he was taken. So he drove out the man; and he placed at the east of the garden of Eden the Cherubim, and the flame of a sword which turned every way, to keep the way of the tree of life.

The phrase "and he placed" reads in Hebrew *vayashkhein*, which has the same root as "Shechinah," and literally means "and he caused to dwell." This was a visible dwelling of the presence of God, and the visible form it took was the flame of a sword. The definite article makes it specific, "*the* flame" of the sword. Here was a visible manifestation of the glory of God where the Shechinah appeared as fire.

Another point that should be noted here is that the Shechinah is associated with the cherubim, one of four such associations.

2.   THE ABRAHAMIC COVENANT

While the content of the Abrahamic Covenant is found in several parts of Genesis, the sealing and signing of the covenant is in 15:12-18:

> And when the sun was going down, a deep sleep fell upon Abram; and, lo, a horror of great darkness fell upon him. And he said unto Abram, Know of a surety that thy seed shall be sojourners in a land that is not theirs, and shall serve them; and they shall afflict them four hundred years; and also that nation, whom they shall serve, will I judge: and afterward shall they come out with great substance. But thou shalt go to thy fathers in peace; thou shalt be buried in a good old age. And in the fourth generation they shall come hither again: for the iniquity of the Amorite is not yet full. And it came to pass, that, when the sun went down, and it was dark, behold, a smoking furnace, and a flaming torch that passed between these pieces. In that day Jehovah made a covenant with Abram, saying, Unto thy seed have I given this land, from the river of Egypt unto the great river, the river Euphrates.

In verse 12 the motif of an unusual darkness in association with the Shechinah Glory appears for the first time. After summarizing the content of the Abrahamic Covenant (verses 13-16), it was signed (verse 17). God appeared in a visible form: that of a smoking furnace and a flaming torch. Thus, it was by means of the Shechinah Glory that God signed the Abrahamic Covenant, which in turn became the basis of the three other unconditional covenants God made with Israel: the Palestinian, the Davidic, and the New Covenants.

Besides Genesis, the Shechinah Glory is also found in the books of Exodus, Leviticus and Numbers. In the book of *Exodus* the Shechinah Glory took its residence with Israel and authenticated the Law of Moses. In *Leviticus* it authenticated the Aaronic priesthood. In *Numbers* the Shechinah Glory rendered judgment for sin and disobedience.

3.   THE BURNING BUSH

The Shechinah Glory is found next in Exodus 3:1-5:

> Now Moses was keeping the flock of Jethro his father-in-law, the priest of Midian: and he led the flock to the back of the wilderness, and came to the mountain of God, unto Horeb. And the angel of Jehovah appeared unto him in a flame of fire out of the midst of a bush: and he looked, and, behold, the bush burned with fire, and the bush was not consumed. And Moses said, I will turn aside now, and see this great sight, why the bush is not burnt. And when Jehovah saw that he turned aside to see, God called unto him out of the midst of the bush, and said, Moses, Moses. And he said, Here am I. And he said, Draw not nigh hither: put off thy shoes from off thy feet, for the place whereon thou standest is holy ground.

In this passage God manifested Himself to Moses in a visible way. Verses 2-3 state what was visible: a flame of fire and a bush burning with fire. Again, the fire motif is found in relationship to the visibility of the Shechinah Glory. Here the Shechinah Glory is associated with the Angel of Jehovah which, from a study of all related passages, is clearly the Second Person of the Trinity: Messiah Jesus, the Son of God.

That the flame of fire and the bush burning with fire was a manifestation of the Shechinah Glory becomes evident from Deuteronomy 33:16:

> And for the precious things of the earth and the fulness thereof, and the good will of him that dwelt in the bush: Let the blessing come upon the head of Joseph, and upon the crown of the head of him that was separate from his brethren.

In this passage the phrase "of him that dwelt in the bush" reads in Hebrew *shochni sneh*. The first word meaning "dwelling" is from the same root that is found in the word "Shechinah." It is the Shechinah that commissioned Moses to bring Israel from the land of Egypt.

4. THE EXODUS

During the Exodus the Shechinah Glory appeared as the Pillar of Cloud by day and the Pillar of Fire by night. In Exodus 13:21-22 the Shechinah led Israel out of Egypt and into the wilderness:

> And Jehovah went before them by day in a pillar of cloud, to lead them the way, and by night in a pillar of fire, to give them light; that they might go by day and by night: the pillar of cloud by day, and the pillar of fire by night, departed not from before the people.

Exodus 14:19-20 adds a further ministry of the Shechinah Glory:

> And the angel of God, who went before the camp of Israel, removed and went behind them; and the pillar of cloud removed from before them, and stood behind them: and it came between the camp of Egypt and the camp of Israel; and there was the cloud and the darkness, yet gave it light by night: and the one came not near the other all the night.

In this passage the Shechinah Glory protected the Israelite camp from the Egyptians all night, because it separated the Egyptian army from the Israelites. Once again the Shechinah Glory is associated with the Angel of Jehovah. Furthermore, it is associated with thick darkness yet giving light within the thick darkness.

In Exodus 14:24 the Shechinah Glory destroyed the Egyptian host:

> And it came to pass in the morning watch, that Jehovah looked forth upon the host of the Egyptians through the pillar of fire and of cloud, and discomfited the host of the Egyptians.

In Exodus 16:6-12 the Shechinah Glory provided Israel with the quail and the manna:

> And Moses and Aaron said unto all the children of Israel, At even, then ye shall know that Jehovah hath brought you out from the land of Egypt; and in the morning, then ye shall see the glory of Jehovah; for that he heareth your murmurings against Jehovah: and what are we, that ye murmur against us? And Moses said, This shall be, when Jehovah shall give you in the evening flesh to eat, and in the morning bread to the full; for that Jehovah heareth your murmurings which ye murmur against him: and what are we? your murmurings are not against us, but against Jehovah. And Moses said unto Aaron, Say unto all the congregation of the children of Israel, Come near before Jehovah; for he hath heard your murmurings. And it came to pass, as Aaron spake unto the whole congregation of the children of Israel, that they looked toward the wilderness and, behold, the glory of Jehovah appeared in the cloud. And Jehovah spake unto Moses, saying, I have heard the murmurings of the children of Israel: speak unto them, saying, At even ye shall eat flesh, and

in the morning ye shall be filled with bread; and ye shall know that I am Jehovah your God.

In verse seven of this passage the first occurrence of the actual title for the Shechinah Glory appears as it is found in the Scriptures: "the glory of Jehovah." In verse ten the glory appeared and was revealed in the cloud, and this is another form of the visible Shechinah Glory.

5.   MOUNT SINAI

The greatest manifestation of the Shechinah Glory during the time of the Exodus was at Mount Sinai itself. Its initial revelation is in Exodus 19:16-20 at the time of the giving of the Ten Commandments:

And it came to pass on the third day, when it was morning, that there were thunders and lightnings, and a thick cloud upon the mount, and the voice of a trumpet exceeding loud; and all the people that were in the camp trembled. And Moses brought forth the people out of the camp to meet God; and they stood at the nether part of the mount. And mount Sinai, the whole of it, smoked, because Jehovah descended upon it in fire; and the smoke thereof ascended as the smoke of a furnace, and the whole mount quaked greatly. And when the voice of the trumpet waxed louder and louder, Moses spake, and God answered him by a voice. And Jehovah came down upon mount Sinai, to the top of the mount: and Jehovah called Moses to the top of the mount; and Moses went up.

In verse 16 there was the appearance of thunders, lightnings, and a thick cloud. In verse 18 Jehovah descended upon it in fire, and verse 20 shows that this was a visible manifestation of God's presence, for it clearly states that Jehovah came down on Mount Sinai.

But such a manifestation of the presence of God put fear into the people. They saw the glory of Jehovah at Mount Sinai and requested to hear the voice of God no more:

And all the people perceived the thunderings, and the lightnings, and the voice of the trumpet, and the mountain smoking: and when the people saw it, they trembled, and stood afar off. And they said unto Moses, Speak thou with us, and we will hear; but let not God speak with us, lest we die. And Moses said unto the people, Fear not: for God is come to prove you, and that his fear may be before you, that ye sin not. And the people stood afar off, and Moses drew near unto the thick darkness where God was. (Exodus 20:18-21).

This factor is reiterated in Deuteronomy 5:22-27:

These words Jehovah spake unto all your assembly in the mount out of the midst of the fire, of the cloud, and of the thick darkness, with a great voice: and he added no more. And he wrote them upon two tables of stone, and gave them unto me. And it came to pass, when ye heard the voice out of the midst of the darkness, while the mountain was burning with fire, that ye came near unto me, even all the heads of your tribes, and your elders; and ye said, Behold, Jehovah our God hath showed us his glory and his greatness, and we have heard his voice out of the midst of the fire: we have seen this day that God doth speak with man, and he liveth. Now therefore why should we die? for this great fire will consume us: if we hear the voice of Jehovah our God any more, then we shall die. For who is there of all flesh, that hath heard the voice of the living God speaking out of the midst of the fire, as we have, and lived? Go thou near, and hear all that Jehovah our God shall say: and speak thou unto us all that Jehovah our God shall speak unto thee; and we will hear it, and do it.

In Exodus 24:15-18 there is the presence of the Shechinah Glory at the time of the giving of the tablets of the Law:

And Moses went up into the mount, and the cloud covered the mount. And the glory of Jehovah abode upon mount Sinai, and the cloud covered it six days: and the seventh day he called unto Moses out of the midst of the cloud. And the appearance of the glory of Jehovah was like devouring fire on the top of the mount in the eyes of the children of Israel. And Moses entered into the midst of the cloud, and went up into the mount: and Moses was in the mount forty days and forty nights.

In verse 15 a cloud covered Mount Sinai, and verse 16 states that it was the Glory of Jehovah that abode on Mount Sinai. The Hebrew word for "abode" is *vayishkhon*, which contains the root of the word "Shechinah." In verse 17 the appearance of the Glory of Jehovah was like a devouring fire. Here the Shechinah had the forms of cloud, fire, and light.

So in the Mount Sinai appearances of the Shechinah Glory, there are the forms of light, fire, cloud, lightning and the motif of thick darkness; all of which are Old Testament visible manifestations of God's presence.

6. THE SPECIAL MANIFESTATION OF THE SHECHINAH GLORY TO MOSES

Moses received a very special revelation of the Shechinah Glory. In Exodus 33:17-23 Moses made a dramatic request:

And Jehovah said unto Moses, I will do this thing also that thou hast spoken; for thou hast found favor in my sight, and I know thee by name. And he said, Show me, I pray thee, thy glory. And he said, I will make all my goodness pass before thee, and will proclaim the name of Jehovah before thee; and I will be gracious to whom I will be gracious, and will show mercy on whom I will show mercy. And he said, Thou canst not see my face; for man shall not see me and live. And Jehovah said, Behold, there is a place by me, and thou shalt stand upon the rock: and it shall

come to pass, while my glory passeth by, that I will put thee in a cleft of
the rock, and will cover thee with my hand until I have passed by: and I
will take away my hand, and thou shalt see my back; but my face shall not
be seen.

In verse 18 Moses specifically requested to see God's glory. In
verse 23 God stated that Moses will be able to see the back parts but
will not be able to see God's face. Dr. Dwight Pentecost feels that the
word should be translated as "afterglow."[1] In other words, God said
to Moses that he will see His passing brilliance but will not see God
as He really is. While the Hebrew word does not actually mean
"afterglow," the basic idea may be correct. Moses will not see God as
He really is, but he will see a greater visible manifestation of God's
glory than all previous manifestations. This was God's promise to
Moses.

Exodus 34:5-9 records the fulfillment of that promise:

And Jehovah descended in the cloud, and stood with him there, and proclaimed the name of Jehovah. And Jehovah passed by before him, and
proclaimed, Jehovah, Jehovah, a God merciful and gracious, slow to
anger, and abundant in lovingkindness and truth; keeping lovingkindness for thousands, forgiving iniquity and transgression and sin; and
that will by no means clear the guilty, visiting the iniquity of the fathers
upon the children, and upon the children's children, upon the third and
upon the fourth generation. And Moses made haste, and bowed his head
toward the earth, and worshipped. And he said, If now I have found favor
in thy sight, O Lord, let the Lord, I pray thee, go in the midst of us; for it is
a stiffnecked people; and pardon our iniquity and our sin, and take us for
thine inheritance.

In this passage there was another revelation of the Shechinah
Glory of God, and to Moses the very name of the Lord was proclaimed.
Moses saw a new manifestation of God's glory which up to then no
other man had seen. In verse nine, at the conclusion of this manifestation, Moses made a request for the continual dwelling of that
Shechinah Glory in the midst of the people of Israel. It was a request
God would partially answer when He took His abode in the tabernacle,
although Moses' request for the eternal abiding could not be fulfilled
at this time.

This experience of Moses in seeing a new visibility of God's glory
and a greater manifestation of God's presence did not leave Moses
untouched, as Exodus 34:29-35 shows:

And it came to pass, when Moses came down from mount Sinai with the
two tables of the testimony in Moses' hand, when he came down from
the mount, that Moses knew not that the skin of his face shown by reason

[1] J. Dwight Pentecost, *Pattern for Maturity* (Chicago: Moody Press, 1966) pg. 15.

of his speaking with him. And when Aaron and all the children of Israel saw Moses, behold, the skin of his face shone; and they were afraid to come nigh him. And Moses called unto them; and Aaron and all the rulers of the congregation returned unto him: and Moses spake to them. And afterward all the children of Israel came nigh: and he gave them in commandment all that Jehovah had spoken with him in mount Sinai. And when Moses had done speaking with them, he put a veil on his face. But when Moses went in before Jehovah to speak with him, he took the veil off, until he came out; and he came out, and spake unto the children of Israel that which he was commanded. And the children of Israel saw the face of Moses, that the skin of Moses' face shone: and Moses put the veil upon his face again, until he went in to speak with him.

When the face of Moses shone, the Shechinah Glory was visible on Moses' face. It was not the actual glory of the Lord that manifested itself on Moses' face, but rather Moses was *reflecting* the glory he had just seen. The relationship of Moses to the Shechinah was similar to the relationship of the moon to the sun. The light originates from the sun, and the moon simply reflects the light from the sun. In the same way the face of Moses reflected the light that originated with the Shechinah Glory. The shining manifestation of the Glory of God permeated the person of Moses and manifested itself in the shining of his face. After the proclamation of the Law, Moses then veiled his face.

The reason for this veil is not given in Exodus, but it is explained in II Corinthians 3:12-18:

Having therefore such a hope, we use great boldness of speech, and are not as Moses, who put a veil upon his face, that the children of Israel should not look stedfastly on the end of that which was passing away: but their minds were hardened: for until this very day at the reading of the old covenant the same veil remaineth, it is not being revealed to them that it is done away in Christ. But unto this day, whensoever Moses is read, a veil lieth upon their heart. But whensoever it shall turn to the Lord, the veil is taken away. Now the Lord is the Spirit: and where the Spirit of the Lord is, there is liberty. But we all, with unveiled face beholding as in a mirror the glory of the Lord, are transformed into the same image from glory to glory, even as from the Lord the Spirit.

Moses did not veil his face because Israel could not behold this reflected glory. On the contrary, Moses knew that the reflected glory was temporary, and he did not want Israel to see the fading away or the passing away of that reflection. The fact that the reflected glory on Moses' face was temporary was being veiled from Israel.

7.   THE TABERNACLE AND THE ARK OF THE COVENANT

The purpose of the tabernacle is given in Exodus 29:42-46:

It shall be a continual burnt-offering throughout your generations at the door of the tent of meeting before Jehovah, where I will meet with you, to speak there unto thee. And there I will meet with the children of Israel; and the Tent shall be sanctified by my glory. And I will sanctify the tent of meeting, and the altar: Aaron also and his sons will I sanctify, to minister to me in the priest's office. And I will dwell among the children of Israel, and will be their God. And they shall know that I am Jehovah their God, that brought them forth out of the land of Egypt, that I might dwell among them: I am Jehovah their God.

In verse 43 the tabernacle was to be sanctified by the Shechinah Glory. In verse 45 the tabernacle was for the purpose that God could dwell with the children of Israel. The Hebrew for "I will dwell" is *shachanti* which has the same root as the word "Shechinah."

Once the tabernacle was finished, then the Shechinah Glory made its residence within the tabernacle according to Exodus 40:34-38:

Then the cloud covered the tent of meeting, and the glory of Jehovah filled the tabernacle. And Moses was not able to enter into the tent of meeting, because the cloud abode thereon, and the glory of Jehovah filled the tabernacle. And when the cloud was taken up from over the tabernacle, the children of Israel went onward, throughout all their journeys: but if the cloud was not taken up, then they journeyed not till the day that it was taken up. For the cloud of Jehovah was upon the tabernacle by day, and there was fire therein by night, in the sight of all the house of Israel, throughout all their journeys.

Verse 34 describes how the cloud covered the tabernacle, and then "the glory of Jehovah" filled the tabernacle. The Hebrew word for tabernacle is *Hamishkhan,* having the same root as "Shechinah." Thus, the word "tabernacle" can also be translated as "the dwelling place of the Shechinah." In verse 35 the cloud took its abode and dwelling with Israel. The word "abode" is a translation of the Hebrew *shachan* where once again the same root is found. Finally, in verses 36-38 this cloud led Israel through the wilderness wanderings.

On this occasion the Shechinah Glory made its residence with Israel by making its abode in the holy of holies over the ark of the covenant and under the cherubim. After the glory of Moses' face faded, God manifested His glory through the tabernacle. The tabernacle itself had no external beauty in that it was covered with weather-beaten animal skins. But God used the unattractive to reveal and manifest His glory to Israel.

The holy of holies had no window but was absolutely dark and is referred to in other passages as "the thick darkness." It was dark except for the shining of the Shechinah Glory. If one ever wondered how the high priest was able to perform his duties in the holy of holies in pitch blackness, the answer is that he had light as it was manifested through the shining Shechinah Glory.

8.   THE BOOK OF LEVITICUS

While in Exodus the Shechinah Glory authenticated the Law and eventually made its residence in the holy of holies, in the book of Leviticus the Shechinah Glory authenticated those who had to carry out the practice of the Law and the tabernacle, namely the Aaronic priesthood.

The key chapter is Leviticus 9. In verses 6-7 there is the promise of authentication:

> And Moses said, This is the thing which Jehovah commanded that ye should do: and the glory of Jehovah shall appear unto you. And Moses said unto Aaron, Draw near unto the altar, and offer thy sin-offering, and thy burnt-offering, and make atonement for thyself, and for the people; and offer the oblation of the people, and make atonement for them; as Jehovah commanded.

This is followed by the authentication of the priesthood in verses 22-24, and the authentication was by fire:

> And Aaron lifted up his hands toward the people, and blessed them; and he came down from offering the sin-offering, and the burnt-offering, and the peace-offerings. And Moses and Aaron went into the tent of meeting, and came out, and blessed the people: and the glory of Jehovah appeared unto all the people. And there came forth fire from before Jehovah, and consumed upon the altar the burnt-offering and the fat: and when all the people saw it, they shouted, and fell on their faces.

9.   THE BOOK OF NUMBERS

In the book of Numbers the Shechinah Glory rendered judgment for sin and disobedience. This occurred on three occasions.

In Numbers 13:30-14:45 it was the Shechinah Glory that rendered judgment upon Israel at Kadesh Barnea when the people revolted against the rulership of Moses because of the discouraging report by ten of the twelve spies. This judgment sentenced the tribes of Israel to wandering in the wilderness for a period of forty years. In 14:10 the Shechinah Glory protected Moses and Aaron from stoning, and in 14:22 the reason for the severity of the judgment is given: they "saw my glory" and yet they rebelled and would not believe.

The Shechinah Glory is next seen in Numbers 16:1-50 in connection with the rebellion of Korah. In verse 19 the Shechinah authenticated the authority of Moses and rejected Korah. In verse 42 the Shechinah Glory sent out a plague among the people for murmuring over Korah's death.

Finally, in Numbers 20:6-13 the Shechinah Glory appeared in the incident over the waters of Meribah.

10.   THE PERIOD OF JOSHUA AND THE JUDGES

During this long period the Shechinah Glory continued to dwell in the holy of holies of the tabernacle, and apart from that there were no special manifestations of the Shechinah Glory. When the Philistines captured the ark of the covenant from Israel and brought it into Philistia, there was fear among the people that they had lost the visible manifestation of God's presence, according to I Samuel 4:21-22:

> And she named the child Ichabod, saying, The glory is departed from Israel; because the ark of God was taken, and because of her father-in-law and her husband. And she said, The glory is departed from Israel; for the ark of God is taken.

The name *Ichabod* means "the glory has departed." Eli's daughter-in-law was wrong of course for, though the fear of it was certainly there, the Shechinah Glory had not yet departed from Israel at this time.

11.   THE SOLOMONIC TEMPLE

When Solomon built his temple, he also built a brand new holy of holies. At this time the Shechinah Glory was transferred from the tabernacle to the holy of holies in the temple. The key passage is I Kings 8:1-13 (a parallel passage is II Chronicles 5:2-7:3). In verses 1-9 the ark of the covenant was brought into the holy of holies, then in verses 10-13 the transfer of the Shechinah Glory took place:

> And it came to pass, when the priests were come out of the holy place, that the cloud filled the house of Jehovah, so that the priests could not stand to minister by reason of the cloud; for the glory of Jehovah filled the house of Jehovah. Then spake Solomon, Jehovah hath said that he would dwell in the thick darkness. I have surely built thee a house of habitation, a place for thee to dwell in for ever.

In verse 10 the cloud filled the house, and in verse 11 the Glory of Jehovah filled the house. This is similar to what happened at the time that the Shechinah Glory made its abode in the tabernacle. In verse 12 the Shechinah Glory began to "dwell in the thick darkness" of the holy of holies. The phrase "to dwell" is a translation of the Hebrew *lishkhon*, which is from the same root as Shechinah. In verse 13 the point is made that this was a house of habitation, a place for God to dwell in His visible manifestation as the Shechinah Glory. Like Moses before him, Solomon also prayed that the Shechinah Glory would dwell with Israel forever. But again, this was not a prayer God would answer at this time.

12. THE BOOK OF EZEKIEL AND THE DEPARTURE OF THE SHECHINAH GLORY

Historically speaking, the Shechinah Glory next appeared to Ezekiel in order to reveal its coming departure from Israel. That it was the Shechinah Glory that was showing Ezekiel the revelation found in his book is seen in Ezekiel 1:28, 3:12, 23, and 8:3-4. In these passages the Shechinah is always associated with the cherubim, as it was in the Garden of Eden and in the tabernacle and the temple. It is also associated here with the Holy Spirit. The book of Ezekiel relates the departure of the Shechinah Glory. The Shechinah Glory left Israel reluctantly and left in four stages.

The first stage of the departure was from the holy of holies (first position) to the threshold of the door of the temple (second position). This is described in Ezekiel 9:3a:

And the glory of the God of Israel was gone up from the cherub, whereupon it was, to the threshold of the house.

And again in 10:4:

And the glory of Jehovah mounted up from the cherub, and stood over the threshold of the house; and the house was filled with the cloud, and the court was full of the brightness of Jehovah's glory.

The second stage of the departure of the Shechinah Glory occurred with the movement of the Shechinah from the threshold of the door of the temple to the eastern gate (third position), in Ezekiel 10:18-19:

And the glory of Jehovah went forth from over the threshold of the house, and stood over the cherubim. And the cherubim lifted up their wings, and mounted up from the earth in my sight when they went forth, and the wheels beside them: and they stood at the door of the east gate of Jehovah's house; and the glory of the God of Israel was over them above.

In the third stage the Shechinah Glory departed from the eastern gate and moved over to the Mount of Olives (fourth position) in Ezekiel 11:22-23:

Then did the cherubim lift up their wings, and the wheels were beside them; and the glory of the God of Israel was over them above. And the glory of Jehovah went up from the midst of the city, and stood upon the mountain which is on the east side of the city.

Finally, in the fourth stage of departure, the Shechinah Glory left Israel and disappeared from Jewish history. It is only here that we truly see *ichabod*, the glory had departed.

13.   THE SECOND TEMPLE

After the return of the Jews from Babylon, the second temple was built. But the Shechinah Glory was not in the second temple as it was in the first temple according to Haggai 2:3:

Who is left among you that saw this house in its former glory? and how do ye see it now? is it not in your eyes as nothing?

However, Haggai 2:9 contained a promise:

The latter glory of this house shall be greater than the former, saith Jehovah of hosts; and in this place will I give peace, saith Jehovah of hosts.

In this verse Haggai the prophet promised that the glory that had departed would come in some different and greater way to that second temple. Unlike the tabernacle and the first temple, the second temple did not begin with a manifestation of the Shechinah Glory. But the promise was made that the glory that once departed would come in a greater way to that very same second temple. They would again see the manifestation of God's presence in the Shechinah Glory. The fact that this temple was destroyed in 70 A.D. necessitates the fulfillment of Haggai's prophecy to be prior to that time.

C.   THE SHECHINAH GLORY IN NEW TESTAMENT HISTORY

1.   APPEARANCE TO THE SHEPHERDS

The first historical appearance of the Shechinah Glory in the New Testament is in Luke 2:8-9:

And there were shepherds in the same country abiding in the field, and keeping watch by night over their flock. And an angel of the Lord stood by them, and the glory of the Lord shone round about them: and they were sore afraid.

In this passage it was *the glory of the Lord* that appeared and it *shone round about them*. This is clearly the re-appearance of the

Shechinah Glory. It announced the birth of the Messiah to Jewish shepherds.

2.   THE CHRISTMAS STAR

Matthew 2:1-12 contains the record of the visit of the Magi from the east who were led there by a visible star. That this was no ordinary star is evident by the actions that this star took. For one thing, the star led them from the east to the west; secondly, it led them from the north to the south; thirdly, the star stood over the very house where Jesus was; and fourthly, it was "his" star in a sense that is not true of any other star. All this rules out that this star was just an ordinary star. The Greek word for *star* simply means *radiance* or *brilliance*. Coming in the form of a light, this was the re-appearance of the Shechinah Glory, announcing the birth of Christ to Gentiles.

3.   THE COMING OF THE SHECHINAH GLORY IN A NEW FORM

The Shechinah Glory re-appeared in a completely new form in the fulfillment of the Haggai prophecy. This is the point of John 1:1-14. This passage proclaims the coming of the Shechinah light in a new visible manifestation. Verse 14 focuses on the new form of the Shechinah Glory:

> And the Word became flesh, and dwelt among us (and we beheld his glory, glory as of the only begotten from the Father), full of grace and truth.

The word translated *dwelt* is the Greek word *skeinei* which was borrowed from the Hebrew Shechinah and Hellenized (Greek does not have an *sh* sound). But literally the Greek word *skeinei* does not mean "to dwell," for which there is a different Greek word. *Skeinei* means to *tabernacle*. So verse 14 literally reads that "the Word became flesh and *tabernacled* among us." In other words, it was a new visible manifestation of the presence of God dwelling among men. The result of this "tabernacling" was that men were able to behold the glory in the form of a man: the God-Man. This was a fulfillment of Isaiah 9:2 which spoke of the coming of the light:

> The people that walked in darkness have seen a great light: they that dwelt in the land of the shadow of death, upon them hath the light shined.

The many times that Jesus walked in the temple compound during His ministry fulfilled the prophecy of Haggai. His glory was manifested by His cleansing of the temple of the money changers and sellers of sacrifices and His teaching in the temple compound, especially during the feasts of Passover and Tabernacles.

The parallel with the Old Testament should not be missed. In the beginning of its history, the Shechinah Glory appeared and disappeared before making a more permanent abode in the tabernacle and temple. It then departed from the Mount of Olives. In New Testament history, it first appeared and disappeared, and then came in a more permanent form in the person of the Messiah abiding with Israel for an extended period of time. Later, it, too, departed Israel from the Mount of Olives.

4.   THE TRANSFIGURATION

The greatest manifestation of the Shechinah Glory in the person of Christ is found in the transfiguration passages.   The four passages where a description is given are Matthew 17:1-8, Mark 9:2-8, Luke 9:28-36, and II Peter 1:16-18. These passages give different descriptions of what occurred, which, taken singly or all together, picture the brilliance of the Shechinah Glory.

In the Matthew passage, Christ's face shone as the sun, and His garments became white as light. A bright cloud overshadowed Him, and the voice of God spoke out of the cloud authenticating the Messiahship of Jesus. The appearance of the cloud and the voice of God speaking out of the cloud was the very same thing that had occurred at Mount Sinai. This description clearly reflects the Shechinah manifestations of the Old Testament developed further in the New Testament as they are fulfilled in the person of Christ.

The Mark passage states that *his garments became glistering, exceeding white, so as no fuller on earth can whiten them,* and a cloud overshadowed Him.

In the Luke passage, the fashion of His countenance was altered, and His raiment became white and dazzling. They saw His glory while the cloud overshadowed Him.

In the II Peter passage, Peter proclaimed what he saw on the Mount of Transfiguration and claimed to be an *eye witness of His majesty*. The Messiahship of Jesus was authenticated by this majestic glory.

Jesus was the visible manifestation of God's presence in a new form. At the Mount of Transfiguration, the glory that was veiled by the human body shone through, and three of the apostles were able to behold the Shechinah Glory in its brightness and in a form greater than what had appeared in the Old Testament. For besides the repetition of the Old Testament manifestations, there was also the unique Shechinah manifestation of Christ Himself as the God-Man.

Christ as the new manifestation of God's presence is taught in later New Testament writings as well. In II Corinthians 4:5-6 Paul wrote:

> For we preach not ourselves, but Christ Jesus as Lord, and ourselves as your servants for Jesus' sake. Seeing it is God, that said, Light shall shine out of darkness, who shined in our hearts, to give the light of the knowledge of the glory of God in the face of Jesus Christ.

This passage states that through Christ light shines out of darkness, and the light is that of *the knowledge of the glory of God in the face of Jesus Christ*. Clearly then the glory of God was manifested in the person of Jesus, and Jesus was indeed a new manifestation of God's presence.

This is further developed by Hebrews 1:1-3:

> God, having of old time spoken unto the fathers in the prophets by divers portions and in divers manners, hath at the end of these days spoken unto us in his Son, whom he appointed heir of all things, through whom also he made the worlds; who being the effulgence of his glory, and the very image of his substance, and upholding all things by the word of his power, when he had made purification of sins, sat down on the right hand of the Majesty on high.

In verse one it is stated that in the past God had revealed Himself in a number of different ways, but in verse two He has now revealed Himself through the Son. But then verse three describes the Son, and the description is that of the Shechinah Glory. The Son is described as *the brightness of the Father's glory* and the very image of His substance.

Another example is found in the midst of a description of the Glorified Son of Man in Revelation 1:12-16. The latter part of verse 16 reads:

> . . . and his countenance was as the sun shineth in his strength.

The outward appearance of Jesus exuded such brightness that the glory of the shining is comparable to that of the sun. The physical body of Jesus no longer veils the shining brightness of the glory.

5. THE REFLECTION OF THAT GLORY

Just as Moses for a time reflected the glory that he beheld at Sinai when God manifested Himself to Moses in a greater way, believers today can also reflect the glory that is Christ, who was an even greater manifestation of the Shechinah Glory, according to II Corinthians 3:12-18:

Having therefore such a hope, we use great boldness of speech, and are not as Moses, who put a veil upon his face, that the children of Israel should not look stedfastly on the end of that which was passing away: but their minds were hardened: for until this very day at the reading of the old covenant the same veil remaineth, it not being revealed to them that it is done away in Christ. But unto this day, whensoever Moses is read, a veil lieth upon their heart. But whensoever it shall turn to the Lord, the veil is taken away. Now the Lord is the Spirit: and where the Spirit of the Lord is, there is liberty. But we all, with unveiled face beholding as in a mirror the glory of the Lord, are transformed into the same image from glory to glory, even as from the Lord the Spirit.

The imagery is taken from the account of the reflecting of God's glory through Moses' face. It is pointed out that the face of Moses was veiled so that the fading of the glory should not be seen (verses 12-13). This veil still remains for Israel has failed to see the passing away of the Dispensation of the Law (verses 14-15). The veil is removed from Jewish eyes only when they turn from the Law to Jesus the Messiah (verses 16-17). When Moses turned away from the people to the Lord, the veil was removed. In the same way, when the Jew turns away from the Law to the Lord Jesus Christ, that veil is also removed.

Then in verse 18 Paul deals with the reflection of the Shechinah Glory by believers. The believer beholds the glory of the Lord with an unveiled face, and he is transformed into the same image from glory to glory. The glory seen in Christ creates a similar glory in the believer. It is Christ who possesses the Shechinah Glory, but the believer is to reflect the glory of Christ in him. While with Moses the reflection was seen by the shining of his face, in the case of the believer the reflection is to be seen in the transformation of the believer's life into a Christlike character. As it was in the case of the Ezekiel passages, the Shechinah Glory in this passage is connected with the Holy Spirit. For the means of Christlikeness is by means of being filled or controlled by the Holy Spirit.

That believers are to reflect the Shechinah Glory of Christ is also taught in Ephesians chapter one. In verse six the believer is *to the praise of the glory of His grace.* In verse twelve the believer should be *to the praise of His glory.* In verse fourteen the believer is *unto the praise of His glory.* In verse eighteen the believer is *the glory of His inheritance in the saints.* (cf. Romans 8:29; Philippians 3:21; Colossians 3:10).

To summarize, the historical appearance of the Shechinah Glory was primarily manifested in the person of Christ in the New Testament. He was the new visible manifestation of God's presence. However, today it is the obligation of the believer to reflect that glory.

6.   THE BOOK OF ACTS

The Shechinah Glory was seen on two occasions in the book of Acts. Though the first may not be conclusive, there is the possibility that among the things that happened in Acts 2:1-3 was the appearance of the Shechinah Glory:

> And when the day of Pentecost was now come, they were all together in one place. And suddenly there came from heaven a sound as of the rushing of a mighty wind, and it filled all the house where they were sitting. And there appeared unto them tongues parting asunder, like as of fire; and it sat upon each one of them.

The visibility of *tongues parting asunder, like as of fire* may have been the Shechinah Glory. Again, this is not conclusive because the information given is rather scant.

The second occurrence is far more evident: the appearance to Paul on the Damascus Road. It is recorded in three different parts of the book of Acts. First in 9:3-8:

> And as he journeyed, it came to pass that he drew nigh unto Damascus: and suddenly there shone round about him a light out of heaven: and he fell upon the earth, and heard a voice saying unto him, Saul, Saul, why persecutest thou me? And he said, Who art thou, Lord? And he said, I am Jesus whom thou persecutest: but rise, and enter into the city, and it shall be told thee what thou must do. And the men that journeyed with him stood speechless, hearing the voice, but beholding no man. And Saul arose from the earth; and when his eyes were opened, he saw nothing; and they led him by the hand, and brought him into Damascus.

Secondly in 22:6-11:

> And it came to pass, that, as I made my journey, and drew nigh unto Damascus, about noon, suddenly there shone from heaven a great light round about me. And I fell unto the ground, and heard a voice saying unto me, Saul, Saul, why persecutest thou me? And I answered, Who art thou, Lord? And he said unto me, I am Jesus of Nazareth, whom thou persecutest. And they that were with me beheld indeed the light, but they heard not the voice of him that spake to me. And I said, What shall I do, Lord? And the Lord said unto me, Arise, and go into Damascus; and there it shall be told thee of all things which are appointed for thee to do. And when I could not see for the glory of that light, being led by the hand of them that were with me I came into Damascus.

Thirdly in 26:13-18:

> At midday, O king, I saw on the way a light from heaven, above the brightness of the sun, shining round about me and them that journeyed with me. And when we were all fallen to the earth, I heard a voice saying unto me in the Hebrew language, Saul, Saul, why persecutest thou me? it is hard for thee to kick against the goad. And I said, Who art thou, Lord?

And the Lord said, I am Jesus whom thou persecutest. But arise, and stand upon thy feet: for to this end have I appeared unto thee, to appoint thee a minister and a witness both of the things wherein thou hast seen me, and of the things wherein I will appear unto thee; delivering thee from the people, and from the Gentiles, unto whom I send thee, to open their eyes, that they may turn from darkness to light and from the power of Satan unto God, that they may receive remission of sins and an inheritance among them that are sanctified by faith in me.

In 9:3 it is described as a light shining out of heaven. In 22:6 it is further described as being a *great* light out ot heaven, and later in verse 11 Paul testifies that he was blinded because of the *glory* of that light. In 26:13 this light is described as being *above the brightness of the sun*. It is the Shechinah Glory that appeared to Paul to commission him to become the apostle to the Gentiles.

7. THE REVELATION

The last historic appearance of the Shechinah Glory was to the Apostle John in Revelation 1:12-16 discussed earlier. This passage describes how Jesus looks today in the fullness of His glory. His physicai body no longer veils the shining brightness of His glory.

The purpose of this final historic manifestation was to commission John to write the book of Revelation and, by so doing, to bring the Scriptures to a close.

D. THE SHECHINAH GLORY IN PROPHECY

1. THE GREAT TRIBULATION

The only passage that somehow relates the Shechinah Glory with the Great Tribulation is Revelation 15:8:

And the temple was filled with smoke from the glory of God, and from his power; and none was able to enter into the temple, till the seven plagues of the seven angels should be finished.

In this passage the Shechinah Glory is connected with the bowl judgments which will be the final and most severe series of judgments in the tribulation. These judgments will bring to a completion the wrath of God. In the book of Numbers the Shechinah Glory rendered judgment for sin, and it will do so again in the Great Tribulation.

2. THE SECOND COMING OF CHRIST

With the return of Christ there will again be the manifestation of the Shechinah Glory in His visible and physical presence. Matthew 16:27 reads:

For the Son of man shall come in the glory of his Father with his angels; and then shall he render unto every man according to his deeds.

The point of this passage is that the Son of Man will come *in the glory of His Father*. Just as in John 1:14 men were able to behold the glory of the Father at the first coming, it is with the same glory of the Father that Christ will return, and it will be seen by men again.

Another passage relating the Shechinah Glory with the second coming of Christ is Matthew 24:30:

And then shall appear the sign of the Son of man in heaven: and then shall all the tribes of the earth mourn, and they shall see the Son of man coming on the clouds of heaven with power and great glory.

According to this passage, just prior to the second coming of Christ the sign of the Son of Man will appear in the heavens, and that sign will certainly be the Shechinah Glory for *the Son of Man will come in the clouds of heaven with power and great glory*. Parallel passages are Mark 13:26 and Luke 21:27:

3.   THE MILLENNIUM

In prophecy the greatest manifestation of the Shechinah Glory, especially to Israel, will be in the messianic kingdom. Altogether, there will be a total of five manifestations of the Shechinah Glory.

First, there will exist a visible manifestation in the holy of holies of the millennial kingdom. Just as Ezekiel carefully plotted the departure of the Shechinah Glory from Israel, he also prophesied and recorded the future return of the Shechinah Glory in Ezekiel 43:1-7a:

Afterward he brought me to the gate, even the gate that looketh toward the east: and, behold, the glory of the God of Israel came from the way of the east: and his voice was like the sound of many waters; and the earth shined with his glory. And it was according to the appearance of the vision which I saw, even according to the vision that I saw when I came to destroy the city; and the visions were like the vision that I saw by the river Chebar; and I fell upon my face. And the glory of Jehovah came into the house by the way of the gate whose prospect is toward the east. And the Spirit took me up, and brought me into the inner court; and, behold, the glory of Jehovah filled the house. And I heard one speaking unto me out of the house; and a man stood by me. And he said unto me, Son of man, this is the place of my throne, and the place of the soles of my feet, where I will dwell in the midst of the children of Israel for ever.

In verses 1-3 the Shechinah Glory will come from the east, and the earth will shine from its light. To the east is the Mount of Olives from where the Shechinah Glory had departed. In other words, the Shechinah Glory will return from the very same direction it had departed. It will come through the eastern gate (verse 4) and enter the holy of holies of the millennial temple (verse 5). Just as the Shechinah Glory departed through the eastern gate, it will return through the eastern gate as well. Finally, Ezekiel points out that at this point the Shechinah Glory will make its permanent residence with Israel (verses 6-7a). The words "I will dwell" in Hebrew is *eshkhan*, which comes from the same root as Shechinah. At long last the prayers of Moses and Solomon will be answered.

According to Ezekiel 44:1-2, the eastern gate will be shut, never to be re-opened again throughout the millennium as a result of the return of the Shechinah Glory through the eastern gate:

> Then he brought me back by the way of the outer gate of the sanctuary, which looketh toward the east; and it was shut. And Jehovah said unto me, This gate shall be shut; it shall not be opened, neither shall any man enter in by it; for Jehovah, the God of Israel, hath entered in by it; therefore it shall be shut.

It should be pointed out that the gate Ezekiel is speaking of has nothing to do with the present Golden Gate on the present eastern wall of Jerusalem. Many of the more sensational prophecy buffs have tried to relate this passage to the present Golden Gate. But from the context this cannot be, and the present Golden Gate has nothing to do with the Ezekiel passage. The Ezekiel passage is speaking of the millennial temple compound which will have a totally different wall and gate altogether. Furthermore, this gate is shut because the Shechinah Glory will have re-entered Israel through it, and the shutting of the gate symbolizes that the Shechinah Glory will not depart from Israel again. Regarding the present Golden Gate, the Shechinah Glory did not enter through it, nor did Jesus, since the present gate was built centuries after Christ.

Secondly, not only will the Shechinah Glory be in the holy of holies of the millennial temple, it will also cover the entire new Mount Zion according to Isaiah 4:5-6:

> And Jehovah will create over the whole habitation of mount Zion, and over her assemblies, a cloud and smoke by day, and the shining of a flaming fire by night; for over all the glory shall be spread a covering. And there shall be a pavilion for a shade in the daytime from the heat, and for a refuge and for a covert from storm and from rain.

Here the Shechinah Glory is described as a *cloud* and *smoke* by day and the *shining of a flaming fire* by night. Over all the *glory* there is a covering giving protection from the heat, storm and rain. The new Mount Zion, described in various parts of the prophetic word, will be an exceeding high mountain with a fifty-mile square plateau on top with the new city of Jerusalem on the south side and the millennial temple on the north side. But over this mountain will be the visible manifestation of the Shechinah Glory in a cloud and smoke and flaming fire as it was over Mount Sinai in the Old Testament period.

Thirdly, the Shechinah Glory will rest especially over Jerusalem according to Zechariah 2:4-5:

> And said unto him, Run, speak to this young man, saying, Jerusalem shall be inhabited as villages without walls, by reason of the multitude of men and cattle therein. For I, saith Jehovah, will be unto her a wall of fire round about, and I will be the glory in the midst of her.

The prophet states that Jehovah will be a *wall of fire* round about Jerusalem and that He will be the *glory* in the midst of her. These are all manifestations of the Shechinah Glory in relationship to Jerusalem during the millennial age.

Fourthly, other passages show that the Shechinah Glory will be with all Israel and not merely in the temple, or Mount Zion, or the city of Jerusalem. Isaiah 35:1-2 states:

> The wilderness and the dry land shall be glad; and the desert shall rejoice, and blossom as the rose. It shall blossom abundantly, and rejoice even with joy and singing; the glory of Lebanon shall be given unto it, the excellency of Carmel and Sharon: they shall see the glory of Jehovah, the excellency of our God.

The nations will see in Israel *the glory of Jehovah*. This is brought out again in Isaiah 58:8-9a:

> Then shall thy light break forth as the morning, and thy healing shall spring forth speedily; and thy righteousness shall go before thee; the glory of Jehovah shall be thy rearward. Then shalt thou call, and Jehovah will answer; thou shalt cry, and he will say, Here I am.

Concerning Israel, Isaiah says the *light* shall break forth as the morning and *the glory of Jehovah* shall be your rearward.

Also in Isaiah 60:1-3 the prophet writes:

> Arise, shine; for thy light is come, and the glory of Jehovah is risen upon thee. For, behold, darkness shall cover the earth, and gross darkness the peoples; but Jehovah will arise upon thee, and his glory shall be seen upon thee. And nations shall come to thy light, and kings to the brightness of thy rising.

Verse one states that *the glory of Jehovah* is risen over Israel and in verse two His *glory* shall be seen in Israel. In verse three the Gentiles shall come to Israel's *brightness*.

The point of all these passages is that the Shechinah Glory will dwell in a visible manifestation with all Israel, and for the Gentile nations to experience this visible manifestation, they will have to come to the Jews (Zechariah 8:20-23).

Fifthly, the Shechinah Glory will also be seen in the visible reign of Christ. Isaiah 11:10 states:

> And it shall come to pass in that day, that the root of Jesse, that standeth for an ensign of the peoples, unto him shall the nations seek; and his restingplace shall be glorious.

Also in Isaiah 40:5:

> And the glory of Jehovah shall be revealed, and all flesh shall see it together; for the mouth of Jehovah hath spoken it.

Christ will again be a visible manifestation of the Shechinah Glory in the form of the God-Man without the veiling, while other manifestations will be in the forms of cloud, fire and smoke. All of this will be related to Israel, for it is with Israel that the Shechinah Glory will dwell in every one of its manifestations.

4.   THE ETERNAL ORDER

The millennium will only last one thousand years, and then history will enter the period of the Eternal Order. But here, too, the Shechinah Glory will be evident. In Revelation 21:1-3 John writes:

> And I saw a new heaven and a new earth: for the first heaven and the first earth are passed away; and the sea is no more. And I saw the holy city, new Jerusalem, coming down out of heaven from God, made ready as a bride adorned for her husband. And I heard a great voice out of the throne saying, Behold, the tabernacle of God is with men, and he shall dwell with them, and they shall be his peoples, and God himself shall be with them, and be their God.

Verses 1-2 describe the new Jerusalem, but then verse three describes the new presence of God in Jerusalem: the tabernacle of God will be with men and He will dwell with men. The word *dwell* is the Greek word *skeinei* which does not mean "to dwell" but *to tabernacle*. So as it was with the Old Testament, in the Eternal Order the Shechinah Glory will tabernacle with men although there will be no tabernacle or temple per se.

Jerusalem will have the glory of God, because of this tabernacling with men, according to Revelation 21:10-11:

And he carried me away in the Spirit to a mountain great and high, and showed me the holy city Jerusalem, coming down out of heaven from God, having the glory of God: her light was like unto a stone most precious, as it were a jasper stone, clear as crystal.

Since Jerusalem will have the glory of God because of God's dwelling with men, there will be certain results according to Revelation 21:23-24:

And the city hath no need of the sun, neither of the moon, to shine upon it; for the glory of God did lighten it, and the lamp thereof is the Lamb. And the nations shall walk amidst the light thereof: and the kings of the earth bring their glory into it.

Because the Shechinah Glory will be there, there will be no need of the natural light from the sun or the moon nor the artificial light of the lamp. The Shechinah Glory will provide all the light that will be necessary, and all the inhabitants will be able to walk in that light.

So it will be for all eternity.

APPENDIX V

THE OLIVET DISCOURSE

INTRODUCTION

The famous Olivet Discourse of our Lord Jesus Christ came between two significant events. Immediately preceding the Olivet Discourse Christ spoke the final words of His public ministry found in Matthew 23:1-39 which contain a denunciation of the leadership of Israel, especially for their guilt in leading the nation to reject the Messiahship of Jesus. With these words the public ministry of Christ as a prophet came to an end, for during the remainder of His last few days on earth He dealt exclusively with His disciples.

Immediately after the Olivet Discourse came the preparation of the last Passover and the first Lord's Supper. These events came just before His death. Along with the last Passover and the first Lord's Supper, the famous Upper Room Discourse occurred in which there was a transition of Christ's ministry from prophet to priest.

But between these two significant events is the famous Olivet Discourse recorded by three of the Gospel writers: Matthew 24-25, Mark 13 and Luke 21:5-36. The basic purpose of the Olivet Discourse is to answer the question: when and how will Christ's kingdom come into being? Since Israel rejected the kingdom offer of the Messiah, it was impossible to set up the kingdom at that time, and it would have to be set up at a later time. However, in the light of His denunciation of the leadership of Israel in Matthew 23 and in the light of His closing words in verses 37-39, revealing the fact that He will not return until Israel requests His return, when then will the kingdom be set up? The Olivet Discourse answers this question.

To get a complete picture, all three Gospel accounts must be studied. Not one Gospel writer recorded everything Jesus said on that day, and each one recorded only the information most relevant to the theme of his own Gospel account. For that reason it is necessary to study all three accounts, because only then is it possible to get a total picture of what Jesus said during the closing days in His office as prophet. So this study will be in the form of a synthesis with all three Gospel accounts being examined simultaneously.

A. THE HISTORICAL SETTING

The historical setting is recorded in Matthew 24:1-2, Mark 13:1-2 and Luke 21:5-6. The Matthew account reads:

And Jesus went out from the temple, and was going on his way; and his

disciples came to him to show him the buildings of the temple. But he
answered and said unto them, See ye not all these things? verily I say
unto you, There shall not be left here one stone upon another, that shall
not be thrown down.

After His scathing denunciation of the Pharisees, and after
announcing the coming destruction of the temple, Jesus and His
disciples moved out of the temple area for good. But on the way out,
the disciples pointed out the magnificent buildings of the Jewish
temple. Actually, at this time, the temple buildings were not yet completed. The temple compound was begun by Herod the Great in 20
B.C. but it was not finished until 64 A.D., only six years before its
destruction. The words of the Olivet Discourse were spoken in the
year 30 A.D., and so the building of the temple compound had been going on for 50 years. They would continue the building for another 34
years. The stones which so impressed the disciples were indeed
magnificent, and they are to be found to this day. They are called
Herodian stones, being huge stones 10-12 feet in length. Nevertheless, Jesus reiterated the fact that this temple compound was
doomed for destruction and the temple itself would not have one
stone left upon another that would not be thrown down. This prophecy
of Christ's was literally fulfilled in 70 A.D. when the Romans destroyed
the city of Jerusalem. The temple was set on fire, and because there
was so much gold in the building, a great amount of it began to melt
and the liquid gold seeped into the crevices between the stones of the
temple. When the ruins cooled down, the Romans systematically,
stone by stone, removed everything in order to get to the gold that was
now solidified inside the crevices.

However, this prophecy left the disciples perplexed.

B.   THE THREE QUESTIONS

When they arrived at the Mount of Olives, the prophecy of Christ
raised three questions on the part of four of the disciples, and these
are recorded in Matthew 24:3, Mark 13:3-4 and Luke 21:7. The Matthew
account reads as follows:

And as he sat on the mount of Olives, the disciples came unto him
privately, saying, Tell us, when shall these things be? and what shall be
the sign of thy coming, and of the end of the world?

The Luke account reads:

And they asked him, saying, Teacher, when therefore shall these things
be? and what shall be the sign when these things are about to come to
pass?

Altogether, three questions were asked which at the same time included requests for three signs. The first question was: *Tell us, when shall these things be?* "These things" refer to the destruction of the temple that He had prophesied in the previous two verses. In the Luke passage this first question is phrased as *Master, but when shall these things be? and what sign will there be when these things shall come to pass?* The first question then was, "When will the temple be destroyed and what will be the sign that this is about to take place?"

The second question was, *What shall be the sign of thy coming?* This question did not concern the Rapture of the church, because the Rapture is imminent and can happen at any moment having no warning sign preceding it. However, the second coming will be preceded by a sign, and the disciples asked what the sign would be.

The third question was, *What shall be the sign of the end of the world?* The Greek word translated *world* actually means *age*. So they also asked for a third sign, and that was, "What will be the sign that the end of this age has begun?"

Altogether, then, there were three questions in which the disciples asked for three signs to watch for. Christ answered these questions, but not in the same order they were asked. Nor are all three answers found in all three accounts. While Matthew and Mark recorded the answers to the second and third questions, they ignored the answer to the first question. It is Luke who recorded Christ's answer to the first question.

C. THE GENERAL CHARACTERISTICS OF THE CHURCH AGE

Before Christ began to answer any of the three questions, He first provided some general characteristics of the church age in Matthew 24:4-6, Mark 13:6-7 and Luke 21:8-9. The Matthew passage reads as follows:

> And Jesus answered and said unto them, Take heed that no man lead you astray. For many shall come in my name, saying, I am the Christ; and shall lead many astray. And ye shall hear of wars and rumors of wars; see that ye be not troubled: for these things must needs come to pass; but the end is not yet.

Rather than immediately answering all three questions, Jesus decided first to give some general characteristics of the church age, none of which mean that the end has begun. Jesus wanted to make sure that the disciples would not jump to certain conclusions because of various events, and so He chose to tell them of things that would not mean that the end had begun. There were to be two general characteristics of the church age.

The first general characteristic of the church age would be the rise of false messiahs. Historically, Jesus was the first person who claimed to be the Messiah. After Him, many came claiming to be the Messiah. From the time of Jesus until about the middle of the 1850's, a great number of Jewish men arose claiming to be the Messiah, and indeed led many astray. Gentiles have also claimed the Messianic title.* But this was to be a general characteristic of the church age, and the existence of false messiahs in no way meant that the end had begun.

The second general characteristic would be local wars. Jesus stated that when they heard of wars and rumors of wars, these things also would not be signs of the end. The existence of local wars here or local wars there would in no way indicate the end had begun.

Concerning both false messiahs and local wars, Jesus said, *For all these things must come to pass but the end is not yet.* Luke emphasized this point in his passage when he wrote, *For these things must first come to pass; but the end is not immediately* (Luke 21:9). In other words, the rise of false messiahs and long periods of local wars will necessarily come first. But neither of these things would in any shape, way, or form be signs that the end had begun.

D. THE SIGN OF THE END OF THE AGE

Having provided for His disciples certain characteristics that would in no way indicate that the end had begun, Jesus next proceeded to answer the third question which concerned the sign that the end of the age had truly begun. It is recorded in Matthew 24:7-8, Mark 13:8 and Luke 21:10-11. The Matthew account reads:

> For nation shall rise against nation, and kingdom against kingdom; and there shall be famines and earthquakes in divers places. But all these things are the beginning of travail.

According to all three Gospel writers, the sign of the end of the age is said to be *when nation shall rise up against nation, and kingdom against kingdom.* This act will be coupled with famines and earthquakes in various places, and then Jesus clearly stated that this would be *the beginning of travail.* The term *travail* means *birthpang.* It refers to the series of birthpangs that a woman undergoes before giving birth to a baby. The prophets pictured the last days as a series of birthpangs before the birth of the new messianic age. The *beginning* of travail or the *first* birthpang and the sign that the end of the age has begun is when nation rises against nation and kingdom against kingdom.

Jesus had already clearly stated that local wars between a few

---

* The most recent example is Rev. Moon.

nations would not indicate that the end had begun. But then He said when there is "nation against nation, kingdom against kingdom," then that will mean that the end of the age has begun.

To understand what the idiom *nation against nation, kingdom against kingdom* means, it is necessary to return to the Jewish origin of these statements, and this has been discussed in an earlier part of this work.* This expression is a Hebrew idiom for a world war. What Jesus stated here is that when there is a world war, rather than merely a local war, that world war would signal that the end of the age had begun.

World War I of 1914-1918 was the fulfillment of this particular prophecy, for that was the first world war. As virtually all historians agree, World War II was merely a continuation of the first world war. Furthermore, both world wars had a decisive impact on Jewish history. The first world war gave impetus to the growth of the Zionist movement, and the second world war led to the re-establishment of the Jewish state. So since the first world war, history has entered the last days of the church age. However, the last days are an extended period of time.

The sign that the end of the age has begun is the world-wide conflict fulfilled by the first and second world wars.

E.   PERSONAL EXPERIENCES OF THE APOSTLES

Having provided an answer to their third question regarding the sign of the end of the age, Christ then returned back to His own time to spell out some of the personal experiences that the apostles would have to undergo. This is recorded in Mark 13:9-13 and Luke 21:12-19. The Luke account reads:

> But before all these things, they shall lay their hands on you, and shall persecute you, delivering you up to the synagogues and prisons, bringing you before kings and governors for my name's sake. It shall turn out unto you for a testimony. Settle it therefore in your hearts, not to meditate beforehand how to answer: for I will give you a mouth and wisdom, which all your adversaries shall not be able to withstand or to gainsay. But ye shall be delivered up even by parents, and brethren, and kinsfolk, and friends; and some of you shall they cause to be put to death. And ye shall be hated of all men for my name's sake. And not a hair of your head shall perish. In your patience ye shall win your souls.

The Luke account clearly states that what is about to be described is going to occur *before* the sign that the end of the age has begun, as the passage begins with the phrase, *But before all these things . . . .* Jesus then described some personal experiences that the apostles were to go through after He departed from them. Altogether

* See Chapter IV.

He listed nine things. *First*, they will be rejected by the Jews (verse 12a); *second*, they will be rejected by the Gentiles (verse 12b); *third*, they will undergo persecutions, but these persecutions will provide opportunities for testimony (verse 13); *fourth*, they will succeed in proclaiming the Gospel everywhere (Mark 13:10), and this is verified by Romans 10:18 and Colossians 1:6, 23; *fifth*, they need not worry about preparing defenses before their trials because they will be given divine utterance when they are brought before judgment (verses 14-15); *sixth*, they will be rejected by their own family members (verse 16); *seventh*, they will be hated by all men (verse 17); *eighth*, nevertheless, their salvation is assured (verse 18); and *ninth*, they will succeed in winning many souls (verse 19).

That the apostles did indeed experience all of these things is well known both from the book of Acts and from other historical records that trace the activities of the apostles beyond that which is recorded in the book of Acts. So while Christ had already answered their third question concerning the sign of the end of the age before proceeding to answer their other two questions, Christ chose to predict some of the personal experiences that they would have to undergo before the sign of the end of the age would come. They were not to expect the end of the age to come too soon.

F.   THE SIGN OF THE FALL OF JERUSALEM

Only after having spelled out clearly that the apostles would have to undergo a period of suffering as well as having a successful ministry did Jesus go on to answer their first question: the sign of the coming destruction of Jerusalem and the temple. The answer is recorded only by Luke in 21:20-24:

> But when ye see Jerusalem compassed with armies, then know that her desolation is at hand. Then let them that are in Judaea flee unto the mountains; and let them that are in the midst of her depart out; and let not them that are in the country enter therein. For these are days of vengeance, that all things which are written may be fulfilled. Woe unto them that are with child and to them that give suck in those days! for there shall be great distress upon the land, and wrath unto this people. And they shall fall by the edge of the sword, and shall be led captive into all the nations: and Jerusalem shall be trodden down of the Gentiles, until the times of the Gentiles be fulfilled.

In answer to their first question, Christ gave them the sign that would mark the fact that Jerusalem was about to be destroyed. The sign was the surrounding of the city of Jerusalem by armies. The Hebrew Christians were told that when they saw this sign they were to leave Jerusalem and Judea and flee outside the land. This sign would mark the coming desolation of Jerusalem, and Jerusalem from that point on will be continually trodden down of the Gentiles until the times of the Gentiles be fulfilled.

This prophecy was fulfilled in a very marvelous way. In the year 66 A.D., the first Jewish revolt broke out against the Romans. When the revolt first began, the Roman general in the land, Cestus Gallus, came with his armies from Caesarea and surrounded Jerusalem. That surrounding marked the sign that Jesus promised, and the Hebrew Christians knew that Jerusalem would soon be destroyed. Jesus had commanded the Hebrew Christians to desert the city when they saw this. However, it was impossible to do so while the Romans were surrounding the city.

But then Cestus Gallus noticed that his supply lines were not secure and he did not have enough supplies to maintain an extended siege. So he lifted the siege of Jerusalem to go back to Caesarea. On the way, he was attacked by Jewish forces and killed. So temporarily, the city was no longer surrounded by the armies and every single Hebrew Christian was able to leave Jerusalem. They crossed the Jordan River and set up a new Hebrew Christian community in the town of Pella in the Transjordan. There they waited for the prophecy of Jesus to be fulfilled.

In the year 68 A.D. a new Roman general by the name of Vaspasian and his son, Titus, again besieged the city, and in the year 70 A.D. the city and the temple were destroyed. Altogether 1,100,000 Jews were killed in this final onslaught, but not one Hebrew Christian died because of their obedience to the words of their Messiah. Since that time, Jerusalem has indeed been trodden down of the Gentiles and continues so to the present day. Jerusalem will not be free of Gentile nations treading upon her until the Messiah returns.

With these words, Christ answered their first question, the sign of the coming destruction of Jerusalem. That left one more question to be answered.

G.   THE GREAT TRIBULATION

In preparation to answering the second question, Christ turned to the Great Tribulation itself. His words concerning this period are recorded in Matthew 24:9-26 and Mark 13:14-23. In this passage Christ spoke of both the events of the first half and the second half of the tribulation.

1.   THE FIRST HALF OF THE TRIBULATION

The events concerning the first half of the tribulation are recorded in Matthew 24:9-14:

> Then shall they deliver you up unto tribulation, and shall kill you: and ye shall be hated of all the nations for my name's sake. And then shall many stumble, and shall deliver up one another, and shall hate one another. And many false prophets shall arise, and shall lead many astray. And because iniquity shall be multiplied, the love of the many shall wax cold. But he that endureth to the end, the same shall be saved. And this gospel of the kingdom shall be preached in the whole world for a testimony unto all the nations; and then shall the end come.

Although these verses are very similar to those recorded in Mark 13:9-13 and Luke 21:12-19, the differences show that Matthew is not dealing with the same thing. Luke clearly stated that the events he was describing came *before* the sign of the end of the age when nation shall rise up against nation and kingdom against kingdom. However, in the Matthew account, the passage begins with the word *then*, pointing out that what Christ is describing now will come *after* the event of nation rising against nation and kingdom against kingdom. So while the words tend to be similar, these similarities do not prove sameness. For Mark and Luke described events that will happen to the apostles *before* the sign of the first world war, while Matthew dealt with events of the first half of the tribulation that would come *after* the sign of the first world war.

Altogether Christ pointed out five events that will occur during the first half of the tribulation. First, there will be tremendous persecution of the saints (verses 9-10), a fact also given in Revelation 6:9-11. The one-world religious system known as Ecclesiastical Babylon will be doing the persecuting and will be responsible for the death of the saints during the first half of the tribulation (Revelation 17:1-6).

Secondly, the first half of the tribulation will be characterized by the rise of many false prophets (verse 11). This point is also brought out in Zechariah 13:2-6.

Thirdly, there will be a tremendous rise of sin and iniquity (verse 12) because evil will no longer be restrained (II Thessalonians 2:6-7).

Fourthly, those Jews who survive to the end of the tribulation will be saved (verse 13).

The fifth event of the first half of the tribulation will be the worldwide preaching of the Gospel (verse 14) which will be conducted by the 144,000 Jews (Revelation 7:1-8). The results of the ministry of the 144,000 are recorded in Revelation 7:9-17 where it clearly states that a great multitude of Gentiles will come to a saving knowledge of our Lord Jesus Christ.

2. THE SECOND HALF OF THE TRIBULATION

Having given some events of the first half of the tribulation,

Christ next turned to the events of the second half which are recorded in Matthew 24:15-28 and Mark 13:14-23. The Matthew account reads:

When therefore ye see the abomination of desolation, which was spoken of through Daniel the prophet, standing in the holy place (let him that readeth understand), then let them that are in Judaea flee unto the mountains: let him that is on the housetop not go down to take out the things that are in his house: and let him that is in the field not return back to take his cloak. But woe unto them that are with child and to them that give suck in those days! And pray ye that your flight be not in the winter, neither on a sabbath: for then shall be great tribulation, such as hath not been from the beginning of the world until now, no, nor ever shall be. And except those days had been shortened, no flesh would have been saved: but for the elect's sake those days shall be shortened. Then if any man shall say unto you, Lo, here is the Christ, or, Here; believe it not. For there shall arise false Christs, and false prophets, and shall show great signs and wonders; so as to lead astray, if possible, even the elect. Behold, I have told you beforehand. If therefore they shall say unto you, Behold, he is in the wilderness; go not forth: Behold, he is in the inner chambers; believe it not. For as the lightning cometh forth from the east, and is seen even unto the west; so shall be the coming of the Son of man. Wheresoever the carcase is, there will the eagles be gathered together.

More detail is given concerning the events of the second half of the tribulation, and altogether Christ said eight things.

First, Christ dealt with the specific event that will mark the beginning of the second half of the tribulation: *the abomination of desolation standing in the holy place* (verse 15). The abomination of desolation will involve two stages. The first stage will be when the Antichrist will take over the Jewish temple, sit down in the holy of holies, and declare himself to be God (II Thessalonians 2:3-10). The second stage of the abomination of desolation will be when the False Prophet will make an image of the Antichrist and stand it up in the holy of holies (Revelation 13:11-15, Daniel 12:11). This act of the abomination of desolation will signal that the second and worst half of the tribulation has begun.

Second, the abomination of desolation will be the signal for the Jews to flee out of the land (verses 16-20); this flight is also recorded in Revelation 12. This passage reflects a sense of urgency in Israel's flight. In fact, the whole emphasis is on speed and quickness. This emphasis is especially evident in Christ's listing of three difficulties that may be encountered in this flight. The first difficulty is for women who are pregnant or have infant children. In both cases, this makes quick flight difficult as any woman in that condition can certainly verify. The second difficulty is in relation to the sabbath and the third to the winter.

Third, the reason for this flight is because at this time world-wide anti-Semitism will break out in all its fierceness (verse 21).

Fourth, Israel will survive this terrible period though greatly reduced in number (verse 22).

Fifth, the second half of the tribulation will be characterized by a false messiah, as typified in the counterfeit son, the Antichrist (verse 23).

Sixth, the latter half of the tribulation will be characterized by many false signs, miracles and wonders with the purpose of world-wide deception. These false signs will be performed both by the Anti-christ (II Thessalonians 2:8-10) and by the False Prophet (Revelation 13:11-15).

Seventh, Christ warned that there will be people saying that Christ has returned here or that Christ has returned there and that the second coming has secretly occurred (verses 25-27). Christ warned His disciples to believe no such rumor or statement because, unlike the first coming, the second coming will not be in secret. When Christ returns the second time, all men will see it, for it will be like a flash of lightning surrounding the world.

Eighth, Christ gave a hint as to the place of His second coming (verse 28). He said that where the body is, the vultures will be gathered together. The body refers to Israel while the vultures refer to the Gen-tile nations coming against the body of Israel. The place of the second coming of Christ will be in that place where the body of Israel is located, and where the Gentile nations are gathered together. The exact place is known as *Bozrah* in Hebrew, or *Petra* in Greek. That is where the body will be gathered (Micah 2:12-13), that is where the vultures will come against them (Isaiah 34:1-7, 63:1-6), and that will be the place of the second coming (Habakkuk 3:3).

To summarize, in this passage Christ presented the events of the second half of the tribulation, showing it to be an especially difficult period for Israel which will culminate in the second coming of Christ. But He has not as yet answered the second question which concerned the sign that will signal Christ's second coming. Christ turned to this question next.

H.   THE SIGN OF THE SECOND COMING OF CHRIST

The answer to the second question is recorded in Matthew 24:29-30, Mark 13:24-26 and Luke 21:25-27. The Matthew account reads:

> But immediately after the tribulation of those days the sun shall be darkened, and the moon shall not give her light, and the stars shall fall from heaven, and the powers of the heavens shall be shaken: and then shall appear the sign of the Son of man in heaven: and then shall all the tribes of the earth mourn, and they shall see the Son of man coming on the clouds of heaven with power and great glory.

The Luke account states:

> And there shall be signs in sun and moon and stars; and upon the earth distress of nations, in perplexity for the roaring of the sea and the billows; men fainting for fear, and for expectation of the things which are coming on the world: for the powers of the heavens shall be shaken. And then shall they see the Son of man coming in a cloud with power and great glory.

In the Matthew account, Christ stated that just preceding the sign of the second coming of Christ, there will be a total blackout of the earth. No light will penetrate to the earth from the sun, moon or stars (verse 29). Luke adds that there will be a great amount of perplexity on the earth as both physical and non-physical things are shaken in expectation (verses 25-26). At this point Matthew states that the sign of the second coming will appear (verse 30a); and since this sign is coupled with God's glory, it is obviously the Shechinah Glory light that will signal the second coming of Christ. So the answer to the second question, "What will be the sign of the second coming?" is the Shechinah Glory. So *immediately after the tribulation of those days* there will be a total blackout with no light penetrating at all, followed by a sudden, glorious, tremendous light that will penetrate through the blackout. This Shechinah light will be the sign of the second coming of Christ. The light will be followed by the return of Christ Himself (verse 30b).

At this point, Christ had answered all three questions. The sign of the destruction of the Jewish temple was to be the surrounding of Jerusalem by armies. The sign that the end of the age had begun was to be a world-wide war. The sign of the second coming would be the Shechinah breaking through the world-wide blackout. The first sign was given in 66 A.D. The second sign was given in 1914-1918. At the end of the tribulation the third sign will come as well.

Although Jesus had answered all three questions, He still wished to give more information regarding the last days.

I. THE REGATHERING OF ISRAEL

Since the Jewish prophets had predicted in great detail the world-wide regathering of Israel, Jesus did not spend much time with this, but only pointed out that it will occur after His second coming. This regathering is found in Matthew 24:31 and Mark 13:27. The Matthew passage reads:

> And he shall send forth his angels with a great sound of a trumpet, and they shall gather together his elect from the four winds, from one end of heaven to the other.

Following the second coming, Christ will send out His angels all over the world to regather every Jew to bring them back into their land.

J. THE EXHORTATION

Having given an outline of things to come from their own day until the beginning of the kingdom, Christ then presented an exhortation recorded in Luke 21:28:

> But when these things begin to come to pass, look up, and lift up your heads; because your redemption draweth nigh.

The exhortation is that when believers see *these things begin to come to pass*, then they are to *look up*, raise their heads, because it will mark the soon redemption of the believers from this world. In the Luke passage, the expression *these things* refers back to Luke 21:10-11 which was the sign of the world war. Now none of these things described in the Olivet Discourse have been signs of the Rapture but only signs of the coming of the Great Tribulation. However, if these things tell believers that the tribulation is near, it also means that the Rapture of the church is even nearer. Since the Rapture will precede the tribulation by an unknown period of time, the closer time comes to the beginning of the tribulation, the closer it comes to the Rapture. So since the sign of the end of the age, the world-wide conflict, has been fulfilled, and since there have been other signs leading up to the Great Tribulation, believers should be looking up for the completion of their redemption at the Rapture of the church.

K. THE PARABLE OF THE FIG TREE

The Olivet Discourse now comes to a section known as the parable of the fig tree. It is recorded in Matthew 24:32-35, Mark 13:28-32, and Luke 21:29-33. The Matthew account reads:

> Now from the fig tree learn her parable: when her branch is now become tender, and putteth forth its leaves, ye know that the summer is nigh; even so ye also, when ye see all these things, know ye that he is nigh, even at the doors. Verily I say unto you, This generation shall not pass away, till all these things be accomplished. Heaven and earth shall pass away, but my words shall not pass away.

The Luke account states:

> And he spake to them a parable: Behold the fig tree, and all the trees: when they now shoot forth, ye see it and know of your own selves that the summer is now nigh. Even so ye also, when ye see these things com-

ing to pass, know ye that the kingdom of God is nigh. Verily I say unto you,
This generation shall not pass away, till all things be accomplished.
Heaven and earth shall pass away: but my words shall not pass away.

This section has often been misused by those who have
attempted to date the Rapture or the second coming of Christ. The fig
tree is often taken to mean the establishment of the State of Israel in
1948. Then, within a generation, that is forty years of 1948, the second
coming must occur. That would place the event in 1988. Since the
Rapture precedes the second coming by at least seven years, it would
place the Rapture by 1981. This is simple date setting—something the
Scriptures clearly forbade. There are two errors found in this type of
reasoning and its exposition.

First of all, the Bible nowhere limits the period of a generation to
simply 40 years. The one place where the term *generation* is given a
specific time length, it is reckoned to be 100 years (Genesis 15:13-16).
Actually, the term *generation* can mean 20, 40, 70, 80, and 100 years.
Sometimes it means simply *contemporaries*, much as we use the term
today.

A second mistake made in this reasoning is assuming that the fig
tree is a symbol of Israel and that this passage is speaking of the re-
establishment of the Jewish state in 1948. That has been mentioned
nowhere in the entire Olivet Discourse. The re-establishment of Israel
has merely been assumed and presupposed in the passage, but has
never been dealt with specifically in the passage. Furthermore, the
usual symbol of Israel in Scripture is the vine.

However, the real point of this passage is that the fig tree is being
used *literally* as an illustration, not as a *symbol* for Israel. This is
clearly seen from the Luke passage, which reads, *Behold the fig tree
and all the trees* (verse 29). If the fig tree represents Israel, what, then,
do all the other trees represent? If they refer to other nations, and
since a number of nations have risen and keep rising after 1948, then
when does the forty year countdown really begin? Neither the fig tree
nor the other trees are used symbolically to refer to any nation or
nations, but rather they are being used literally as an illustration.

The point of the illustration is this: When the fig tree and all the
other trees begin to blossom, it is a sure sign that summer is on its
way because the blossoming occurs in the spring. Then in application
of the illustration Jesus said, *even so ye also, when you see these
things know that he is nigh, even at the doors*. Just as blossoming of
the fig tree means that summer is on its way, in the same way when
these events that Jesus spoke about occur, then they can know that
His return is near. But what thing is it that signals the soon return of
the Lord? It is not the re-establishment of Israel in 1948, because
Jesus never mentioned that event in this passage. Rather, the event

that He was speaking of was the abomination of desolation. When the abomination of desolation occurs, it will signal the soon return of Christ, namely only three-and-a-half years later. More specific, it will be exactly 1260 days from the abomination of desolation to the second coming.

Then Jesus stated that the generation that sees this event, the abomination of desolation, will still be around when the second coming of Christ occurs three-and-a-half years later. The point of verse 34 is not that the generation that sees the re-establishment of the Jewish state will still be here at the second coming, but rather the Jewish generation that sees the abomination of desolation will still be here at the second coming. Verse 34 is intended to be a word of comfort in light of the world-wide attempt at Jewish destruction. It must be kept in mind that the abomination of desolation signals Satan's and the Antichrist's final attempt to destroy and exterminate the Jews. The fact that the Jewish generation will still be here when the second coming of Christ occurs shows that Satan's attempt towards Jewish destruction will fail, and the Jewish saints of the second half of the tribulation can receive comfort from these words.

The "coming" referred to in this passage is not the Rapture for which no signs are promised but the second coming itself. This is evident from the Luke account, for he states that what the abomination of desolation signals is the coming of the kingdom of God. The kingdom will be a result of the second coming and not of the Rapture.

Again, the point of this section is not that the fig tree represents Israel in 1948, but rather the fig tree is being used literally as an illustration. The point of the illustration is to provide a word of comfort that the world-wide attempt to destroy the Jews is destined for failure; for the Jewish generation that sees the abomination of desolation will still be around when Christ returns.

L.   THE RAPTURE OF THE CHURCH

The time of the second coming of Christ will be clearly known. It will occur exactly seven years after the signing of the seven year covenant and three-and-a-half years (or 42 months, or 1260 days) after the abomination of desolation. But now the passage turns to the issue of the Rapture of the church, the timing of which cannot be known in advance. The discussion concerning the Rapture is in Matthew 24:36-42 and Luke 21:34-36. The Matthew account reads:

> But of that day and hour knoweth no one, not even the angels of heaven, neither the Son, but the Father only. And as were the days of Noah, so shall be the coming of the Son of man. For as in those days which were before the flood they were eating and drinking, marrying and giving in marriage, until the day that Noah entered into the ark, and they knew

not until the flood came, and took them all away; so shall be the coming of the Son of man. Then shall two men be in the field; one is taken, and one is left: two women shall be grinding at the mill; one is taken, and one is left. Watch therefore: for ye know not on what day your Lord cometh.

Concerning the issue of the Rapture, Christ makes three main points: First, as to the question of when, this is known only by one person and that is God the Father (verse 36). It is not known by the angels nor was it known by the Son in His humanity, but only by God the Father. So if the timing of the Rapture has been hidden from both angels and the humanity of Jesus, how much more so is it hidden from mankind in general! For that reason, the only clue given concerning the timing of the Rapture is that it will occur sometime before the tribulation, and it may not necessarily occur just before the tribulation. It might easily occur ten or twenty years before that time. As to the question of *when* will the Rapture occur, the simple answer is: no one knows. This is not true of the second coming which must come seven years after the signing of the seven year covenant or three-and-a-half years after the abomination of desolation.

Secondly, there will not be any signs preceding the Rapture (verses 37-39), as there will be signs preceding the second coming. When the Rapture comes, it will come when there are normal conditions on the earth. The flood also came when there were normal conditions on the earth, when men were eating, drinking, marrying and giving in marriage. Now none of these things are sinful, but are necessary for human survival and propagation. While normal conditions existed on earth, the Noahic flood arrived and swept them all away. In the same way, while there are normal conditions on the earth, the Rapture will suddenly occur sweeping all believers away (verses 40-41). This will not be true of the second coming. When that occurs, conditions on earth will be far from normal as earlier sections of the Olivet Discourse and the book of Revelation clearly show.

Thirdly, there is a supplication to watch (verse 42) for the purpose of escaping the tribulation. Throughout the Olivet Discourse, *to watch* means *to be ready*. Watching is the equivalent of readiness and readiness equivalent to salvation. So the means of escaping the tribulation is by means of salvation. Only those who accept Christ before the Rapture of the church can be ready and watching. Luke 21:36 states it beautifully:

But watch ye at every season, making supplication, that ye may prevail to escape all these things that shall come to pass, and to stand before the Son of man.

Luke gives two reasons for watching. First, so that believers may escape *all these things that shall come to pass* during the tribulation;

and secondly, that the believer might *stand before the Son of man* in heaven. Both these things can only be accomplished by the Rapture, and that is why to watch is to be saved.

M. PARABLES URGING WATCHFULNESS AND READINESS

In order to reinforce His closing point in the previous section, Christ presented five parables, all having as their main point the urging of watchfulness and readiness. These five parables are recorded in Matthew 24:43-25:30 and Mark 13:33-37. In all these parables the distinctions are not between different kinds of believers, but between believers and unbelievers. They express differences in attitudes toward the second coming (not the Rapture) in believers and unbelievers, for the former will be ready while the latter will not.

1. THE PARABLE OF THE PORTER

The first parable is the parable of the porter in Mark 13:33-37:

Take ye heed, watch and pray: for ye know not when the time is. It is as when a man, sojourning in another country, having left his house, and given authority to his servants, to each one his work, commanded also the porter to watch. Watch therefore: for ye know not when the lord of the house cometh, whether at even, or at midnight, or at cockcrowing, or in the morning; lest coming suddenly he find you sleeping. And what I say unto you I say unto all, Watch.

The main point of this parable is the emphasis on the *watching* for the Lord's return. As was noted earlier, watching is always in the sense of readiness and readiness is always in the sense of salvation. For only those who are saved are going to be able to escape these things.

2. THE PARABLE OF THE MASTER OF THE HOUSE

The second parable is the parable of the master of the house in Matthew 24:43-44:

But know this, that if the master of the house had known in what watch the thief was coming, he would have watched, and would not have suffered his house to be broken through. Therefore be ye also ready; for in an hour that ye think not the Son of man cometh.

The emphasis in the second parable is on being *ready*. Again, being ready can only be obtained by means of salvation.

3. THE PARABLE OF THE FAITHFUL
SERVANT AND THE EVIL SERVANT

The third parable concerning the faithful and evil servants is in Matthew 24:45-51:

Who then is the faithful and wise servant, whom his lord hath set over his household, to give them their food in due season? Blessed is that servant, whom his lord when he cometh shall find so doing. Verily I say unto you, that he will set him over all that he hath. But if that evil servant shall say in his heart, My lord tarrieth; and shall begin to beat his fellow-servants, and shall eat and drink with the drunken; the lord of that servant shall come in a day when he expecteth not, and in an hour when he knoweth not, and shall cut him asunder, and appoint his portion with the hypocrites: there shall be the weeping and the gnashing of teeth.

The emphasis in the third parable is on *laboring*. In order to make sure that the believers don't misconstrue the previous emphasis on watching as meaning just to sit there and look at the sky, the third parable emphasizes the necessity of working while one is waiting. So when Christ returns it will be while believers are busy laboring. The believer will be found laboring while the unbeliever will be found not laboring. What this laboring entails will be discussed below.

4. THE PARABLE OF THE TEN VIRGINS

The next two parables provide a more extended treatment of the emphases of the first three parables. The fourth parable concerning the ten virgins is in Matthew 25:1-13:

Then shall the kingdom of heaven be likened unto ten virgins, who took their lamps, and went forth to meet the bridegroom. And five of them were foolish, and five were wise. For the foolish, when they took their lamps, took no oil with them: but the wise took oil in their vessels with their lamps. Now while the bridegroom tarried, they all slumbered and slept. But at midnight there is a cry, Behold, the bridegroom! Come ye forth to meet him. Then all those virgins arose, and trimmed their lamps. And the foolish said unto the wise, Give us of your oil; for our lamps are going out. But the wise answered, saying, Peradventure there will not be enough for us and you: go ye rather to them that sell, and buy for yourselves. And while they went away to buy, the bridegroom came; and they that were ready went in with him to the marriage feast: and the door was shut. Afterward came also the other virgins, saying, Lord, Lord, open to us. But he answered and said, Verily I say unto you, I know you not. Watch therefore, for ye know not the day nor the hour.

The re-emphasis of this parable is on *watching* and *readiness*. The virgins neither represent the church nor Israel in this parable, but simply serve to illustrate a point. In the Jewish wedding system, when the marriage was to be consummated, the bridegroom would go to the home of the bride to fetch her and bring her to his home. As he approached his own home, he would be met by a procession of virgins that would conduct the bride and groom for the marriage ceremony to be followed by the marriage feast. This is the background of this parable. When the Bridegroom returns to the earth with His bride for the marriage feast, the virgins will be responsible for both *watching* for His return, and being *ready* to light the lamps upon His return. The five virgins who were wise will be the ones who will be believers and, hence, will be both ready and watching. They are the ones who have the *oil*, a common symbol of the Holy Spirit. But the five foolish virgins will be the unbelievers and therefore will be neither ready nor watching. They do not have any oil. That is the whole point of this parable and it would be wrong to try to develop too many details from a simple parable. But in this parable there is an extended emphasis on *watching* and *readiness*, both of which are accomplished by faith in Jesus Christ.

5.   THE PARABLE OF THE TALENTS

The fifth parable, concerning the talents, is recorded in Matthew 25:14-30:

> For it is as when a man, going into another country, called his own servants, and delivered unto them his goods. And unto one he gave five talents, to another two, to another one; to each according to his several ability; and he went on his journey. Straightway he that received the five talents went and traded with them, and made other five talents. In like manner he also that received the two gained other two. But he that received the one went away and digged in the earth, and hid his lord's money. Now after a long time the lord of those servants cometh, and maketh a reckoning with them. And he that received the five talents came and brought other five talents, saying, Lord, thou deliveredst unto me five talents; lo, I have gained other five talents. His lord said unto him, Well done, good and faithful servant: thou hast been faithful over a few things, I will set thee over many things; enter thou into the joy of thy lord. And he also that received the two talents came and said, Lord, thou deliveredst unto me two talents: lo, I have gained other two talents. His lord said unto him, Well done, good and faithful servant: thou hast been faithful over a few things, I will set thee over many things; enter thou into the joy of thy lord. And he also that had received the one talent came and said, Lord, I knew thee that thou art a hard man, reaping where thou didst not sow, and gathering where thou didst not scatter; and I was afraid, and went away and hid thy talent in the earth: lo, thou hast thine own. But his lord answered and said unto him, Thou wicked and slothful servant, thou knewest that I reap where I sowed not, and gather where I did not scatter; thou oughtest therefore to have put my money to the bankers, and at my coming I should have received back mine own with interest. Take ye away therefore the talent from him, and give it unto

him that hath the ten talents. For unto every one that hath shall be given, and he shall have abundance: but from him that hath not, even that which he hath shall be taken away. And cast ye out the unprofitable servant into the outer darkness: there shall be the weeping and the gnashing of teeth.

The point of this parable is to re-emphasize in an extended way the necessity to keep on *laboring* while watching and waiting. Again, the distinction is not between different kinds of believers, but between believers and unbelievers. The believers are servants who will keep on laboring while they are watching for the Lord's return. But the unbeliever cannot labor in the work of the Lord and therefore will have nothing to show at the time of the Lord's return.

Altogether then, Christ presented five parables, three short and two extended parables. All emphasized the need for watchfulness, readiness and laboring in the work of the Lord while waiting for His return. The means by which the believers of the Great Tribulation will be watching, ready, and laboring is described in the next section.

N.   THE JUDGMENT OF THE GENTILES

The Olivet Discourse comes to an end with the judgment of the Gentiles in Matthew 25:31-46:

But when the Son of man shall come in his glory, and all the angels with him, then shall he sit on the throne of his glory: and before him shall be gathered all the nations: and he shall separate them one from another, as the shepherd separateth the sheep from the goats; and he shall set the sheep on his right hand, but the goats on the left. Then shall the King say unto them on his right hand, Come, ye blessed of my Father, inherit the kingdom prepared for you from the foundation of the world: for I was hungry, and ye gave me to eat; I was thirsty, and ye gave me drink; I was a stranger, and ye took me in; naked, and ye clothed me; I was sick, and ye visited me; I was in prison, and ye came unto me. Then shall the righteous answer him, saying, Lord, when saw we thee hungry, and fed thee? or athirst, and gave thee drink? And when saw we thee a stranger, and took thee in? or naked, and clothed thee? And when saw we thee sick, or in prison, and came unto thee? And the King shall answer and say unto them, Verily I say unto you, Inasmuch as ye did it unto one of these my brethren, even these least, ye did it unto me. Then shall he say also unto them on the left hand, Depart from me, ye cursed, into the eternal fire which is prepared for the devil and his angels: for I was hungry, and ye did not give me to eat; I was thirsty, and ye gave me no drink; I was a stranger, and ye took me not in; naked, and ye clothed me not; sick, and in prison, and ye visited me not. Then shall they also answer, saying, Lord, when saw we thee hungry, or athirst, or a stranger, or naked, or sick, or in prison, and did not minister unto thee? Then shall he answer them, saying, Verily I say unto you, Inasmuch as ye did it not unto one of these least, ye did it not unto me. And these shall go away into eternal punishment: but the righteous into eternal life.

The *time* of the judgment will be after the second coming of Christ when the throne of David will be set up (verse 31).

The *place* of the judgment is not given in this passage, but it is given in a parallel passage found in Joel 3:1-3. This is a judgment that will take place in the Valley of Jehoshaphat, just outside the city of Jerusalem, which lies between the city and the Mount of Olives.

As to the *subjects* of the judgment, this will be an individual judgment rather than a national one (verses 32-33). The Greek word translated *nations* has the primary meaning of *Gentiles* and is so translated elsewhere in the New Testament. So all the Gentiles who will survive the tribulation and the Campaign of Armageddon will be gathered into the Valley of Jehoshaphat and then be separated by Christ with some brought to His left side and some brought to His right side.

The *basis* of this judgment is going to be anti-Semitism or pro-Semitism. The individual Gentiles will be judged on the basis of their treatment of Christ's *brethren,* namely, the Jewish people during the tribulation (verses 34-40).

The sheep, who are the pro-Semites, are clearly stated to be the righteous ones. Will they be saved then because of their pro-Semitism? This cannot be for that would mean that salvation was purely on the basis of works. This passage is an example of James 2:14-26 of proving one's faith by one's works. Because these Gentiles will be believers in the Lord Jesus Christ, they will refuse to join the policy of the Antichrist in his attempt to destroy the Jews. So while Jews will undergo a great persecution, these believing Gentiles will do what they can to help the Jews under these conditions. Their works toward Christ's brethren will prove their faith. In this manner, they are the ones who will be *watching, ready* and *laboring* in accordance with the admonitions of the five parables. So because they are saved Gentiles, they will be allowed to enter into the messianic kingdom, and they will be the ones who will populate the Gentile nations during the messianic age (verses 34-40).

On the other hand, the goats will be the anti-Semites who, because of their unbelief in Jesus, will join the ranks of the persecutors under the Antichrist's authority. They will show their lack of faith by their works. They are the ones who will *not* be watching, ready or laboring in violation of the five parables. For that reason, they will be killed at this point and be excluded from the messianic kingdom (verses 41-45).

The ultimate and final result after the kingdom is that the believing Gentiles will enter into eternal life while the unbelieving Gentiles will enter into eternal punishment (verse 46).

CONCLUSION

The Olivet Discourse is the most detailed teaching that Christ gave concerning future things. It was His last great discourse as a prophet, because from this point He went into a transitional period from prophet to priest as He both offered a sacrifice, that of His own blood, and then began to function as our High Priest, after the Order of Melchizedek. The Olivet Discourse contains words for believers today (to look up for our redemption draweth nigh), words for unbelievers today (to believe on Christ) and words for both Jews (to flee) and Gentiles (to watch, to be ready, and to labor) who will be living during the Great Tribulation.

APPENDIX VI

OLD TESTAMENT REFERENCES
IN THE BOOK OF REVELATION

As was mentioned in the first chapter of this book, there are over five hundred references to the Old Testament in the book of Revelation. The following is a list of such references, but it makes no claim to being exhaustive or complete.

Some of these references back to the Old Testament do speak of the very same thing as the Revelation does. But in others, the Revelation merely borrows a phrase or motif for the purpose of developing a new area. This distinction should be kept in mind in the study of those Old Testament references.

Revelation 1:1 — Daniel 2:28-29
1:4 — Isaiah 11:2
1:5 — Genesis 49:11; Psalm 89:27
1:6 — Exodus 19:6; Isaiah 61:6
1:7 — Daniel 7:13; Zechariah 12:10-14
1:8 — Isaiah 41:4
1:12 — Exodus 25:37; 37:23
1:13 — Daniel 7:13; 10:5, 16
1:14 — Daniel 7:9; 10:6
1:15 — Ezekiel 1:7, 24; 43:2; Daniel 10:6
1:16 — Judges 5:31; Isaiah 49:2
1:17 — Isaiah 41:4; 44:6; 48:12; Daniel 8:17-18; 10:9, 10, 12, 15, 19
1:18 — Job 3:17; Hosea 13:14
Revelation 2:4 — Jeremiah 2:2
2:7 — Genesis 2:9; 3:22-24; Proverbs 11:30; 13:12; Ezekiel 31:8 (LXX)
2:12 — Isaiah 49:2
2:14 — Numbers 25:1-3
2:17 — Exodus 16:33-34; Isaiah 62:2; 65:15
2:18 — Daniel 10:6
2:20 — I Kings 16:31-32; II Kings 9:7, 22
2:23 — Psalm 7:9; 26:2; 28:4; Jeremiah 11:20; 17:10
2:27 — Psalm 2:7-9; Isaiah 30:14; Jeremiah 19:11
Revelation 3:4 — Ecclesiastes 9:8
3:5 — Exodus 32:32-33
3:7 — Isaiah 22:22
3:9 — Isaiah 43:4; 49:23; 60:14
3:12 — Isaiah 62:2; Ezekiel 48:35
3:14 — Genesis 49:3; Deuteronomy 21:17

```
            3:18  — Isaiah 55:1
            3:19  — Proverbs 3:12
Revelation 4:1  — Ezekiel 1:1
            4:2  — Isaiah 6:1; Ezekiel 1:26-28; Daniel 7:9
            4:3  — Ezekiel 1:26, 28; 10:1
            4:5  — Exodus 19:16; 25:37; Isaiah 11:2; Ezekiel 1:13
            4:6  — Ezekiel 1:5, 18, 22, 26; 10:1, 12
            4:7  — Ezekiel 1:10; 10:14
            4:8  — Isaiah 6:2-3; Ezekiel 1:18; 10:12
            4:9  — Deuteronomy 32:40; Daniel 4:34; 6:26; 12:7
            4:11 — Genesis 1:1
Revelation 5:1  — Ezekiel 2:9-10; Daniel 12:4
            5:5  — Genesis 49:9-10; Isaiah 11:1, 10
            5:6  — Isaiah 11:2; Zechariah 3:8-9; 4:10
            5:8  — Psalm 111:2
            5:9  — Psalm 40:3; 98:1; 144:9; 149:1; Isaiah 42:10;
                   Daniel 5:19
            5:10 — Exodus 19:6; Isaiah 61:6
            5:11 — Daniel 7:10
Revelation 6:2  — Zechariah 1:8; 6:3
            6:4  — Zechariah 1:8; 6:2
            6:5  — Zechariah 6:2
            6:8  — Jeremiah 15:2-3; 24:10; 29:17; Ezekiel 14:21;
                   Hosea 13:14; Zechariah 6:3
            6:12 — Isaiah 50:3; Joel 2:10
            6:13 — Isaiah 34:4
            6:14 — Isaiah 34:4; Nahum 1:5
            6:15 — Psalm 48:4-6; Isaiah 2:10-12, 19
            6:16 — Hosea 10:8
            6:17 — Psalm 76:7; Jeremiah 30:7; Nahum 1:6;
                   Zephaniah 1:14-18; Malachi 3:2
Revelation 7:1  — Isaiah 11:2; Jeremiah 49:36; Ezekiel 7:2; 37:9;
                   Daniel 7:2; Zechariah 6:5
            7:3  — Ezekiel 9:4-6
            7:4  — Genesis 49:1-28
            7:9  — Leviticus 23:40
            7:10 — Psalm 3:8
            7:14 — Genesis 49:11
            7:15 — Leviticus 26:11
            7:16 — Psalm 121:5-6; Isaiah 49:10
            7:17 — Psalm 23:1-2; Ezekiel 34:23
Revelation 8:3  — Psalm 141:2
            8:4  — Psalm 141:2
            8:5  — Ezekiel 10:2
            8:5-6 — Exodus 19:16
```

8:7   — Exodus 9:23-24; Psalm 18:13; Isaiah 28:2
8:8   — Exodus 7:17-19
8:10 — Isaiah 14:12
8:11 — Jeremiah 9:15; 23:15
8:12 — Isaiah 13:10
Revelation 9:1   — Isaiah 14:12-14
9:2   — Genesis 19:28; Exodus 19:8
9:3   — Exodus 10:12-15
9:4   — Ezekiel 9:4
9:6   — Job 3:21
9:8   — Joel 1:6
9:9   — Joel 2:5
9:11 — Job 26:6; 28:22; 31:12; Psalm 88:11; Proverbs 15:11
9:14 — Genesis 15:18; Deuteronomy 1:7; Joshua 1:4
Revelation 10:1 — Ezekiel 1:26-28
10:4 — Daniel 8:26; 12:4-9
10:5 — Deuteronomy 32:40; Daniel 12:7
10:6 — Genesis 1:1; Deuteronomy 32:40; Nehemiah 9:6; Daniel 12:17
10:7 — Amos 3:7
10:9 — Jeremiah 15:16; Ezekiel 2:8-33
10:11 — Ezekiel 37:4, 9
Revelation 11:1 — Ezekiel 40:3-4; Zechariah 2:1-2
11:2 — Ezekiel 40:17-20
11:4 — Zechariah 4:1-3, 11-14
11:5 — Numbers 16:35; II Kings 1:10-12
11:6 — Exodus 7:19-25; I Kings 17:1
11:7 — Daniel 7:3, 7, 8, 21
11:8 — Isaiah 1:9-10; 3:9; Jeremiah 23:14; Ezekiel 16:49; 23:3, 8, 19, 27
11:9 — Psalm 79:2-3
11:11 — Ezekiel 37:9-10
11:15 — Exodus 15:18; Daniel 2:44-45; 7:13-14, 27
11:18 — Psalm 2:1-3; 46:6; 115:13
Revelation 12:1 — Genesis 37:9-11
12:2 — Isaiah 26:17; 66:7; Micah 4:9-10
12:3 — Isaiah 27:1; Daniel 7:7, 20, 24
12:4 — Daniel 8:10
12:5 — Psalm 2:8-9; Isaiah 66:7
12:7 — Daniel 10:13, 21; 12:1
12:9 — Genesis 3:1; Job 1:6; 2:1; Zechariah 3:1
12:10 — Job 1:9-11; 2:4-5; Zechariah 3:1
12:14 — Exodus 19:4; Deuteronomy 32:11; Isaiah 40:31; Daniel 7:25; 12:7; Hosea 2:14-15

                    12:15 — Hosea 15:10
                    12:17 — Genesis 3:15
Revelation 13:1 — Daniel 7:3, 7, 8
                    13:2 — Daniel 7:4-6, 8
                    13:3 — Daniel 7:8
                    13:4 — Daniel 8:24
                    13:5 — Daniel 7:8, 11, 20, 25; 11:36
                    13:7 — Daniel 7:21
                    13:8 — Daniel 12:1
                    13:10 — Jeremiah 15:2; 43:11
                    13:11 — Daniel 8:3
                    13:13 — I Kings 1:9-12
Revelation 14:1 — Psalm 2:6; Ezekiel 9:4
                    14:2 — Ezekiel 1:24; 43:2
                    14:3 — Psalm 144:9
                    14:7 — Exodus 20:11
                    14:8 — Isaiah 21:9; Jeremiah 51:7-8
                    14:10 — Genesis 19:24; Psalm 75:8; Isaiah 51:17
                    14:11 — Isaiah 34:10; 66:24
                    14:14 — Daniel 7:13
                    14:18 — Joel 3:13
                    14:19 — Isaiah 63:1-6
                    14:20 — Joel 3:13
Revelation 15:1 — Leviticus 26:21
                    15:3 — Exodus 15:1-18; Deuteronomy 31:30-32:44;
                             Psalm 92:5; 111:2; 139:14
                    15:4 — Psalm 86:9; Isaiah 66:23; Jeremiah 10:7
                    15:5 — Exodus 38:21
                    15:6 — Leviticus 26:21
                    15:7 — Jeremiah 25:15
                    15:8 — Exodus 40:34-35; Leviticus 26:21; I Kings
                             8:10-11; II Chronicles 5:13-14; Isaiah 6:1-4
Revelation 16:1 — Psalm 79:6; Jeremiah 10:25; Ezekiel 22:31
                    16:2 — Exodus 9:9-11; Deuteronomy 28:35
                    16:3 — Exodus 7:17-25
                    16:4 — Exodus 7:17-21, Psalm 78:44
                    16:5 — Psalm 145:17
                    16:6 — Isaiah 49:26
                    16:7 — Psalm 19:9; 145:17
                    16:10 — Exodus 10:21-23
                    16:12 — Isaiah 11:15-16; 41:2, 25; 46:11; Jeremiah 51:36
                    16:13 — Exodus 8:6
                    16:14 — I Kings 22:21-23
                    16:16 — Judges 5:19; II Kings 23:29-30; II Chronicles
                             35:22; Zechariah 12:11

16:19 — Jeremiah 25:15
16:21 — Exodus 9:18-25
Revelation 17:1 — Jeremiah 51:13; Nahum 3:4
17:2 — Isaiah 23:17
17:3 — Daniel 7:7
17:4 — Jeremiah 51:7; Ezekiel 28:13
17:8 — Exodus 32:32-33; Daniel 12:1
17:12 — Daniel 7:24-25
17:16 — Leviticus 21:9
Revelation 18:1 — Ezekiel 43:2
18:2 — Isaiah 21:9; 34:13-15; Jeremiah 50:30; 51:37
18:3 — Jeremiah 51:7
18:4 — Isaiah 52:11; Jeremiah 50:8; 51:6, 45
18:5 — Jeremiah 41:9
18:6 — Psalm 137:8; Jeremiah 50:15, 29
18:7 — Isaiah 47:7-8; Zephaniah 2:15
18:8 — Isaiah 47:9; Jeremiah 50:31-32
18:9-19 — Ezekiel 26:16-18; 27:26-31
18:9 — Jeremiah 50:46
18:10 — Isaiah 13:1
18:12 — Ezekiel 27:12-25
18:20 — Jeremiah 51:48
18:21 — Jeremiah 51:63-64
18:22 — Isaiah 24:8; Jeremiah 25:10; Ezekiel 26:13
18:23 — Jeremiah 7:34; 16:9; 25:10; Nahum 3:4
Revelation 19:2 — Deuteronomy 32:43; Psalm 119:137; Jeremiah 51:48
19:3 — Isaiah 34:9-10; Jeremiah 51:48
19:5 — Psalm 22:23; 134:1; 135:1
19:6 — Psalm 93:1; 97:1; Ezekiel 1:24; 43:2; Daniel 10:6
19:11 — Psalm 18:10; 45:3-4; Isaiah 11:4-5; Ezekiel 1:1
19:13 — Isaiah 63:3
19:15 — Psalm 2:8-9; Isaiah 11:4; 63:3-6
19:16 — Deuteronomy 10:17
19:17 — Isaiah 34:6-7; Ezekiel 39:17
19:18 — Isaiah 34:6-7; Ezekiel 39:18
19:19 — Psalm 2:2; Joel 3:9-11
19:20 — Isaiah 30:33; Daniel 7:11
19:21 — Ezekiel 39:19-20
Revelation 20:2 — Genesis 3:1, 13-14; Isaiah 24:21-22
20:4 — Daniel 7:9, 22, 27; 12:2
20:5 — Isaiah 26:14
20:6 — Exodus 19:6; Isaiah 26:19
20:8 — Ezekiel 38:2; 39:1, 6

20:9 — Deuteronomy 23:14; II Kings 1:9-12; Ezekiel 38:22; 39:6

20:11 — Daniel 2:35

20:12 — Exodus 32:32-33; Psalm 62:12; 69:28; Daniel 7:10

20:15 — Exodus 32:32-33; Daniel 12:1

Revelation 21:1 — Isaiah 65:17; 66:22

21:3 — Leviticus 26:11-12; Ezekiel 37:27

21:4 — Isaiah 25:8; 35:10; 51:11; 65:19

21:9 — Leviticus 26:21

21:10 — Ezekiel 40:2

21:11 — Isaiah 60:1-2; Ezekiel 43:2

21:12-13 — Ezekiel 48:31-34

21:15 — Ezekiel 40:3, 5

21:19-20 — Exodus 28:17-20; Isaiah 54:11-12

21:23 — Isaiah 60:19-20

21:24 — Isaiah 60:3-5, 16

21:25 — Isaiah 60:11; Zechariah 14:7

21:26 — Isaiah 60:5, 16

21:27 — Isaiah 52:1; Ezekiel 44:9; Zechariah 14:21

Revelation 22:1 — Psalm 46:4; Ezekiel 47:1; Zechariah 14:8

22:2 — Genesis 2:9; 3:22-24; Ezekiel 47:12

22:3 — Genesis 3:17-19; Zechariah 14:11

22:4 — Psalm 17:15; Ezekiel 9:4

22:5 — Isaiah 60:19; Daniel 7:18, 22, 27; Zechariah 14:7

22:10 — Daniel 8:26; 12:4, 9

22:11 — Ezekiel 3:27; Daniel 12:10

22:12 — Psalm 62:12; Isaiah 40:10; 62:11

22:13 — Isaiah 44:6

22:14 — Genesis 2:9; 3:22-24; Proverbs 11:30

22:15 — Deuteronomy 23:18

22:18-19 — Deuteronomy 4:2; 12:32

22:19 — Deuteronomy 29:19-20

SCRIPTURE INDEX

ARIEL MINISTRIES

OUR ROOTS

Ariel Ministries, created to evangelize and disciple our Jewish brethren, has been born from necessity to meet an urgent need.

Ariel means "The Lion of God," representing the Messiah Jesus as the Lion of Judah. It is also an alternate name for Jerusalem (Isa. 29:1) -- the city of peace now waiting for the Prince of Peace to return.

It was in Jerusalem, in 1966, that a burning seed of desire was planted in the heart of Arnold Fruchtenbaum. On December 1, 1977, **Ariel Ministries** was born and the seed began to bloom.

Arnold Fruchtenbaum was graduated from Dallas Theological Seminary in 1971 and received his Ph.D. from New York University in 1989. After graduating from Dallas, he moved to Israel with his wife Mary Ann and established a Bible institute, a school which became so effective in discipleship that after two years certain religious leaders forced Arnold and Mary Ann to return to the United States.

And when they returned they saw a most wonderful thing: the Holy Spirit was doing a tremendous work among Jewish young people, with an explosion of new believers rivaling what is recorded in the Book of Acts.

But along with the joy of seeing hundreds saved came the agony of watching new Jewish Christians falter and ebb in their enthusiasm because of poor discipleship by their older brothers and sisters in the Lord.

The concept of a new and powerful ministry simmered within Arnold's heart during the following years as he worked first with the American Board of Missions to the Jews and then the Christian Jew Foundation in San Antonio, Texas.

Finally, he could resist the call no longer, and **Ariel Ministries** turned from a dream into reality.

OUR REASONS

Today, **Ariel Ministries** has plunged directly into the mainstream of Jewish evangelism by combining two key areas of evangelism and discipleship with a heavy emphasis on Bible theology and doctrine. We seek to develop a balanced program of reaching out to others as we grow in maturity ourselves.

As you read about the goals and organization of **Ariel Ministries**, we pray you will be moved by the Spirit of God to join us in our vision.

Beth Ariel Messianic Centers

We will establish **Beth Ariel** (House of the Lion of God) **Messianic Centers** -- to share Christ and train Jewish believers -- in key Jewish populated areas. **Ariel** will plant fellowships and/or local churches which will have a strong Jewish orientation. Through the years, **Ariel Ministries** has launched fellowships in Baltimore, Maryland; Seattle, Washington; Bergen County, New Jersey; and in Israel. Local churches have been planted in Los Angeles and San Diego, California, as well as in Portland, Oregon. These centers will also be used for the recruitment and training of God-called missionaries.

Missionary, Bible and Prophetic Conferences

These will be held in local churches for the purpose of setting forth God's program for Israel, as well as giving believers an active burden for Jewish missions and a desire to share Jesus with their Jewish friends.

Camping Ministry - Ariel's Camp Shoshanah

This highly successful, three-week camping ministry will continue to bring Jewish believers together in upstate New York to emphasize Bible training and discipleship with a Jewish perspective. This intensive time of study has given numbers of young people a firm rock upon which to build their faith. Many who first came as new believers are now in full-time service. Though these discipleship programs are designed for Jewish believers, Gentile believers are always welcome to attend.

Monthly Magazine

This publication will contain important news of our **Beth Ariel** centers, featuring the progress, actions and plans of our branches. Each issue will also include one or more expositions on Jewish-related Bible studies, as well as serve as a forum for current topics relating to Hebrew Christianity.

Special Short-Term Ministries

Ariel is also engaged in special one-time and short-term ministries, including street evangelism in Israel and evangelizing Soviet Jews in transit camps in Europe. Some unusual and amazing results have come from these campaigns.

FUTURE OBJECTIVES

Schools of Hebrew Christianity

These schools will be established in both the New York area and in Israel for the purpose of teaching Scripture from a Jewish frame of reference. Other Jewish-related subjects and Hebraic studies will also be offered. Topics will include Jewish philosophy, the history of Israel, the life of the Messiah from a Jewish perspective, and classical and modern Hebrew.

Students will be exposed to a whole new viewpoint as they study such Messianic Jewish epistles as Hebrews, James, I and II Peter and Jude. College students will be able to attend an **Ariel** school of Hebrew Christianity for their third year, then return to their own campus to finish their fourth year of study.

The three- or four-year curriculum in Israel will be taught in Hebrew. In the United States, our school need only be supplemental to existing Bible colleges and seminaries, but in Israel it will be necessary to teach the entire counsel of God.

Other Future Objectives

In the future, **Ariel** will publish and distribute literature in English and Hebrew for both believers and unbelievers; issue correspondence Bible courses; make scholarships available for Hebrew Christians in training for the ministry; and provide financial aid for Jewish believers cut off from their families because of faith.

Ariel has already produced literature in tract and book form in English, Hebrew, and Russian and has developed an extensive teaching ministry, available on cassette tapes. A complete list of all tapes and publications is available from our home office. **Ariel** has also provided scholarships and financial aid to Jewish believers as finances allowed.

FINANCIAL POLICY

God's work
Done in God's time
Will never lack God's support

When **Ariel Ministries** has a financial need, we will appeal only to Messiah Jesus, for the Apostle Paul told us, "And my God shall supply all your needs according to His riches in glory in Christ Jesus" (Phil. 4:19). The friends of **Ariel** will receive only 'thank you' letters! No appeal letters will ever be sent.

Ariel missionaries are happy to speak at a church or gathering on the basis of a free-will offering. No minimum honorarium or travel expenses will be asked of local congregations, although these gifts will be gratefully accepted.

Funds designated for a specific **Ariel** ministry will be used only for that ministry.

Ariel will not purchase mailing lists from others, and will keep our own mailing list strictly confidential.

For more information about **Ariel Ministries**, and/or to schedule a missionary speaker or a Bible or prophetic conference, please contact: